THE HISTORY OF THE POLISH LEGIONS IN ITALY

By Leonard Chodzko

Translated by G.F.Nafziger

The History of The Polish Legions in Italy
By Leonard Chodzko
Cover by January Suchodolski

This edition published in 2020

Nafziger Press is an imprint of

Winged Hussar Publishing, LLC
1525 Hulse Rd, Unit 1
Point Pleasant, NJ 08742

ISBN 978-1-950423-12-5 Paperback
ISBN 978-1-950423-45-3 E-book
LCN 2020943115

Bibliographical References and Index
1. History. 2. Napoleonic Wars. 3. Poland

For more information
Visit us at www.wingedhussarpublishing.com

Twitter: WingHusPubLLC
Facebook: Winged Hussar Publishing LLC

ABOUT THE AUTHOR

Leonard Chodźko, (1800 – 1871) was a Polish historian, geographer, cartographer, publisher, archivist, and activist of Poland's post-November-1830-Uprising Great Emigration. He was the son of a politician from Grodno who had taken part in the Kościuszko Uprising. Chodźko was educated at the University of Vilnius under the historian Joachim Lelewel, joining the Philomaths, a secret organization established in 1816 by Vilnius University students including Adam Mickiewicz, Tomasz Zan and Józef Jeżowski.

In 1819, he became secretary to Prince Michał Kleofas Ogiński, where he traveled through Europe before settling in Paris in 1826. He worked at the Sorbonne library, at Sainte-Geneviève, and was the librarian at the Ministry of Public Instruction in Paris.

On 12 February 1830, on the anniversary of the birth of Tadeusz Kościuszko, he organized a major event in the French capital in which Marie Joseph de La Fayette and Victor Hugo participated. At the time of the Three Glorious Revolution in July 1830, he was Captain La Fayette's aide-de-camp

During the November Insurrection in Poland Chodźko supported the uprising and is one of the founding members of the Central Committee for the Poles created in January 1831 by La Fayette. After the defeat of the insurrection in September 1831, he was part of the leadership of the Polish National Committee (Komitet Narodowy Polski) created by Lelewel in November and subsequently played a notable role in the Great Emigration to France.

In 1833, he prepared within the secret society Vengeance du Peuple (Zemsta Ludu) the armed expedition of Colonel Józef Zaliwski to the Kingdom of Poland. Persecuted by the Russian Embassy in Paris, he was forced to leave Paris for Great Britain by French authorities. In 1834, he returned to Paris, and devoted himself to scientific work.

He died in Poitiers in 1871 and was buried in the cemetery of Hôpital-des-Champs Poitiers.

Leonard Chodzko

The History of the Polish Legions was written before the November Insurrection of 1830 and within living memory of the Napoleonic Wars. The author consulted participants as well as primary documents to construct it. While not perfect, it is a great starting point for a history of the Poles in this period.

TABLE OF CONTENTS

THE HISTORY OF THE POLISH LEGIONS IN ITALY

Volume 1

By Leonard Chodzko
Translated by G.F.Nafziger

Originally Published:
Paris
J. Barbezat
1829

Jan Henryk Dąbrowski (1752-1818)

I am Polish!

To retrace the misfortunes of my homeland, to recount its great feats of arms when it fought for liberty, its fight, three times renewed against immense forces, its last efforts in the hour of its agony, finally this resistance which has survived its annihilation, is not for me a matter of self-love, much less an effort in speculation; it is a need of heart, a worship, a duty.

While still young, I owed the knowledge of our disasters only to domestic traditions. When I arrived at the age when impressions passed from memory to heart, twenty years had elapsed since the fatal drama in which Poland carried her last sword. But the wound was still bleeding: the last page of our history, written in blood, was visible to all: if the memories of glory and independence were expressed with reserve within our palaces, they woke up energetically in our thatched cottages. Men, monuments, everything, even the theaters of so many exploits, still throbbed with the interest which attaches to great events; everything recalled the ancient glories of Poland and her present misfortunes.

Seated near the paternal hearth, I eagerly listened to these touching stories in which the story of our setbacks was combined with examples of almost legendary valor. I followed in all their phases the annals of this people, where every man was a soldier, and every soldier a hero. Each one appeared to me in his turn with that halo of glory so fresh and so brilliant, with that marvelous courage that deserved the praise of the first captain of Europe.

Filled with my initial feelings, I wanted, seeking truth, to see if foreign peoples appreciated these virtues; I wanted to seek out the opinion that Europe had formed of those Poles who were so great to me. But what was my surprise! Instead of a living picture, I found only a discolored copy: good faith, impartiality, historical fidelity, everything was missing. In these campaigns, where I expected to see my countrymen appear on the front line, I scarcely saw them in the crowd, and hidden in the shadows! I was indignant, and indignation made me a historian.

However, understanding the task I imposed on myself, I knew how to control this national enthusiasm, which could be like partiality; I understood that to convince others, it was not enough for one to have a deep conviction; I wanted, before starting a story, to give it all the accuracy possible. Placed at the source of the information, having at my disposal some of the Polish archives, the cartons [of documents] of the ambassadors and the unpublished memoirs, I formed a collection of valuable documents, which will serve as the base of the edifice that I propose today; the cornerstone.

In possession of this collection, I added the recollections of exiles and the pieces which are attached to the emigration of the Poles to my material. Traveling through the various countries that had seen their great misfortunes, I looked in St. Petersburg, Berlin, Dresden, and later on the banks of the Po, Arno and Tiber, for the traces of those generous compatriots who made the whole world witnesses of their courage and despair.

Finally, I stopped at Paris, and there, quiet in the heart of a hospitable country, I arranged all my historical treasures, and began to co-ordinate them for the instruction of contemporaries and posterity.

In the midst of so many already published works, I had to place myself on a ground where I could walk alone and without competitors. Modern French writers, de Rulhiere, Garran de Coulon, Malte-Brun, Monnier, de Ferrand; Messrs. from Ségur father Leon Thiessé, of Salvandy, had already, in brilliant works of talent and style, retraced either our complete annals or the last pages of our history. In their turn, Józef Zajączek, in 1797, J. Romarzewski, in 1807, M. Oginski, in 1826, and S. Plater, in 1827, all Poles, writing in French the events of our last revolutions, related the facts as they could see and appreciate them.

However, in selecting the most glorious epochs of our history, none of these authors, except Mr. Oginski[1], had followed the imposing debris of an annihilated people into their exile. None of them, without exception, had sketched this memorable episode of the Polish Legions

[1]Michał Kleofas Ogiński (1765-1833) Polish-Lithuanian statesman, author and composer.

in Italy, commanded by Gen. Dąbrowski[2]. None of these works had depicted these new Trojans fleeing their oppressed country, and who, far from seeking to conquer another people under a foreign sky, never despaired of their destinies. Nobody, finally, had shown us these defeated republicans, asking for iron from a victorious republic, threatened like them by the destroyers of Poland. In the midst of these campaigns, where their blood flowed for an adoptive cause, and when they descended one by one into the grave, nobody at last had represented them, casting a last glance towards their fatherland at the moment of expiring:

et dulces moriens reminiscitur argos.
(as he died, he remembered Argos, the home of his youth. – Virgil)

This painting was therefore unfinished: it was difficult, it is true, because public documents were not enough to complete it. The brilliant actions of these auxiliary bodies, which often decided victory, were forgotten in some impartial reports, and general glories absorbed individual glories.

In spite of all the care I have taken to omit nothing essential, I invite all Poles, worthy of the name, to assist me with their information about our contemporary history. It is unfortunately too true that the history of our country would still be buried in the archives of partitioning powers, if brave hands had not managed to collect some debris which escaped from the flames, wars and political vengeance, and if the private documents had come to supplement the insufficiency of the public documents. Other episodes in Polish history, as interesting as the legions, are still waiting for a writer. I have, no doubt, brought together several important pieces to start them; but, I repeat it again and again, that they send me all that can be obtained. It is essential that we learn the whole truth now; and if Poland is condemned for some time yet to be nothing in the balance of Europe, we must know at least what she has been, and what she can become.

This task I have imposed on myself, I believe I have fulfilled conscientiously: firmness must not exclude prudence, and truth is not

[2]Jan Henryk Dąbrowski (1752-1818) Polish-Lithuanian general who commanded troops in the Saxon, Polish Commonwealth, Polish Legions and Grand Duchy of Warsaw

a power with which one can compromise. It is immutable and, hovering over the passions of this world, it brings everything back to this just balance where kings and past peoples come to sit in turn.

I must now give an account of the sources from which I drew the facts of which this work is composed.

There were authentic memoirs of Gen. Dąbrowski, which the public has never known, and which were in the hands of some close friends of this illustrious warrior. One of them had an exact copy, transcribed on the original manuscript, and that copy was given to me. As the leader and creator of the Polish legions in Italy, Dąbrowski could better account for their efforts and dedication. Placed in the first rank, he could, either in his relations with the French government or in the various battles which he had to support at the head of his legions, furnish to himself alone the material of an authentic and interesting history. I have also used the authentic memoirs of Elie Tremo[3], Aide-de-camp of Gen. Dąbrowski, and those of Kazimirz De la Roche, born at Warsaw, former Secretary of the French Legation in Poland, and subsequently an officer of the Superior General Staff, the same who we will see in this history contributing to the formation of the legions; and finally, several important letters from the most influential members of the Polish association. Bringing all these unpublished materials which are in my possession together, various printed writings which have treated the same subject, I found a new support for the facts which I quote: first in the work on the establishment and overthrow of the constitution of May 3, 1791, published in Polish, in 1793, by Kollontaj, Potocki, Dmochowski; and in the same work reproduced in abridged form and in French, in 1795, by Joseph Wybicki[4] and R. De la Roche, under the title *Mémoires pour servir à l'histoire des Révolutions de Pologne [Memoirs to Serve the History of the Polish Revolutions]*; secondly in the *Histoire de la Révolution de 1794, [History of the Revolution of 1794*], by Zajączek, in 1797; third in the *Règne de Stanislas-Augustus Poniatowski [Reign of Stanislas-Augustus Poniatowski]*, by Joachim Lelewel, in 1818; fourth finally in the *Mémoires de Michel Oginski [Memoirs of Michel Oginski]*, from 1788 to 1815, published in 1826. For everything connected with the military campaigns, I consulted the *Hitoire*

[3]Elie Tremo was a Polish officer and the grandson of King Stanisław Poniatowski's chief.

[4]Józef Wybicki (1747 – 1822) Polish statesman, writer and military officer

des Guerres de la Révolution [History of the Wars of the Revolution] by General Jomini and Battalion Commander J.-B. F. Roch; the collection of the *Victoires et conquêtes des Français [Victoires and Conquests of the French]*, written chiefly by General Beauvais, as well as the *Histoire de la Révolution française [History of the French Revolution]*, by M. A. Thiers. I have to assume that J. Wybicki , confidant of General Dąbrowski, and the soul of the Polish legions, and Amilcar Kosinski[5] , Adjutant Commandant, Chief of the General Staff of the Polish Legion, have their written memoirs concerning the events I have treated; but since the General-in-Chief's manuscript is very detailed, I think the others are simply a repetition of the same facts.

I also know in a positive way that this part of our history was destined to see the day under the auspices of a better-known name than mine, and that it had to coordinate with other equally remarkable episodes. Here is the fact: The Royal Society of Friends of Science of Warsaw, founded in 1801, like the Institute of France, was established either to promote the development for science and art in Poland, or to preserve the language in all its purity. From the outset I wanted to prove by a public act that the glory and the national memories were not foreign to it. To this end, it commissioned various members of its own body to finish the great history of the Polish nation, begun by the illustrious Bishop Naruszewicz[6] , and ending in the year 1386, the time of the glorious union of Lithuania to Poland. This work was shared by reigns and by periods; and if this patriotic task has not yet been fulfilled by some, it has been conscientiously completed by the others. In this partition, the *HISTORY OF THE POLISH LEGIONS* had fallen to Józef Kalasantry Szaniawski[7] ; and, certainly, no one better than he could give life to this brilliant episode of national pomp. An ardent patriot in the War of National Independence in 1794; a refugee in Paris in 1795, and cooperating with his fellow citizens in the reestablishment of Poland, always devoted when it was necessary to stir up patriotic fire, one of the regenerations of the national spirit at the time of the creation of Grand Duchy of Warsaw, distinguished writer and the author of a remarkable eulogium pronounced in honor of the val-

[5]Antoni Amilkar Kosiński (1769 – 1823) Polish general
[6]Adam Naruszewicz (1733 – 1796) historian
[7]Józef Kalasantry Szaniawski (1764-1843) Polish philosopher

iant Godebski [8], what pledges did he not offer to raise an imperishable monument to the glory of dead warriors in a foreign land! Although provided with all the necessary parts to compose my work; I was also busy obtaining new ones in Italy and Paris, on the very spot where the Polish Legions left so many traces of their passage, but I waited for Mr. Szaniawski to publish the work that had been entrusted to him, and I would have done without noise, without pride, sacrificed the materials I possessed, as if this part of our history had been treated in a manner worthy of the subject and the author. But in the several years that I lived abroad; this was confirmed in line came to confirm my expectation. Mr. Szaniawski, on the other hand, seems absorbed in the new charges he accepted, a few years after the reorganization of partition of the Grand Duchy of Warsaw. He became State Councilor, Director General of Public Education AND CENSORSHIP! It is difficult to satisfy this triple occupation!

Well! I, who am not overburdened with so many honors, limit my ambition to pay a solemn tribute to heroes who are no longer citizens. I dare to finish what the coward left incomplete. With less talent, I will have more frankness, and not feeling sufficient titles to aspire to the honor of being part of the illustrious Society of Friends of Science, I will confine myself to deserve the titles of modest patriot and citizen in the eyes of the public.

Now I turn to some observations on the plan and the division of my work.

As it was impossible for me to give an account the Polish Legions without having traced all the misfortunes which gave rise to their formation, in a few chapters I returned to the last events which preceded the annihilation of Poland. I recall this league of the three powers, occult at first, then patent; the memorable works of the Constituent Diet; the plot of the Targowica[9] faction; lastly, that short war of independence, in which Kosciuszko revealed his secret forces in Poland, too late for his salvation, but early enough to cover his chains with a last laurel.

Leaving Poland as a slave to speak of exiled Poland, I turn to the various attempts the refugees made to resurrect their homeland,

[8]Cyprian Godebski (1765-1809) Polish writer and officer
[9]A confederation of nobles in league with the partitioning powers that helped to bring down the 3 May Constitution and the second partition of Poland.

to their efforts in Paris, Venice, Constantinople, Berlin, Milan, Vienna itself, so that the name of a famous people was not destroyed. Finally, after summarily grouping all these facts, I arrive at the formation of the Polish legions; there, taking one by one all those warriors who, not being able to fight for their country, had given their arms to the cause which offered them the most sympathy and the most chances for the future, I will follow them in their work, their victories and their hopes. They are seen as if by magic to appear, reorganized in the shadow of French standards, to unite, with the efforts of the Republican Army, their disinterested efforts, to suffer with courage and to fall without murmuring, convinced that the French nation alone held in its hands their future destinies. And that it must one day divide Europe into constitutional kingdoms, as it did when it cut Italy into republics. Victorious at Rome, Naples, Florence, Mantua, Milan, we accompany them to the peace of Luneville, and there, when all hope will be destroyed for the resurrection of their homeland, some will be forced to follow in Etruria and in Naples the destiny of their new kings, the others, more unhappy, will go under the burning sky of the tropics to fight against a pestilent climate.[10] It is with the first annihilation of the nomadic legions who carried the destinies of Poland with them, that this story will end.

Later they woke up again with one voice taking the measure of Europe; they had their harvest of glory without obtaining anything for their country. It was written, in fact, that the Poles, faithful to their oath, would henceforth serve as an instrument for great ambitions, without profiting by them themselves. This second part of the history of the Polish phalanges will be a favorite work for me later; it will absorb all my attention; not being able to devote my arm to the defense of my country, I have dedicated to it a heart and a plume [pen], which patriotism blazes, and which gold and favor will never buy.

So many truncated and incorrect stories have kept the public uninformed about new publications, that every writer must, in retracing an epoch and the events connected with it, discover all the springs which make his heroes move, and all the sources from which they draw their conviction. I preferred,

[10]Translator: Haiti. Nearly all the Polish legionnaires that were sent there perished from yellow fever.

therefore, to reproduce textually at the end of each volume the official documents and supporting documents on which my book is based. They have so much connection between them, they form a set so compact and so homogeneous that one could, if need be, read and guess my entire story. Some of these pieces may seem too well-known for France; but I have also had to do the part of the Polish readers, who will find together, in two volumes, all that their compatriots have conquered, at that time, of votes and glory by serving the cause of liberty.

I have adopted the French language for my publications because this language has become universal, and that I write not only for the Poles, but for all peoples, whoever they may be, hostile or favorable towards Poland. It must be known, and repeated, that almost forty years ago there existed a warlike nation, great in memory, powerful in bravery; that this nation, conquered by treason as well as by force, has fallen arms in hand; that, subdued and not subject, the subjects of this nation, absent from their country or living in its bosom, have not conceived a wish, uttered a sigh, nor nourished a hope, which did not address the common mother. It is necessary to distinguish between auxiliary warriors offering their selfless help to those who accept the care of their revenge, and mercenary warriors trafficking their services and peddling their courage from one court to another. In fact, when the Polish patriots saw foreign bayonets as mistresses of their capital, inaccessible to favors, inaccessible to the threats of the domineering powers, they preferred exile and revenge to golden chains. France alone was free then: France became their adoptive homeland. They swore allegiance to it, and they were faithful to this oath. Very different from those turncoats who later insulted the fallen colossus, the Poles succumbed in tight ranks around that flag they had sworn to defend. Dresden, Leipzig, Montereau, the summits of Montmartre, Fontainebleau, the Island of Elba, and later the fields of Waterloo, and even the banks of the Loire, witnessed their courageous perseverance; and they too can say with pride: We were there!

Thus, the sacred fire was perpetuated in a people eager for independence: the remnants of that great army under Kosciuszko[11] became a nursery of heroes who had the gaze of Europe fixed on them. When one goes through this story fertile with the strains of heroism, we are proud to be Polish. Too happy if, recalling it to the memory of my compatriots, I revived in their hearts those germs of patriotism which produce great things!

Happier still if high political considerations could flow from my pen, bringing about a rapprochement between the time I have traced and that which we are witnessing. It is not for an isolated author to give the powers lessons in politics; but there is in Heaven a justice that takes care of this, and which reserves for the destroyers of the Polish name an expiatory future. They did not sufficiently foresee that by sacrificing a generous people, they were expecting their own existence; and sooner or later they will reap the fruits of a fatal improvidence. Enough examples, however, have taught the world that everything was to be feared by the sudden onslaughts of those hordes from the North who, weary of their frimats, are overflowing into the southern countries to conquer the sun and riches.

As for myself, if I have been able in an impartial picture to console my compatriots with their misfortunes by linking them with the glory of their warriors, if I could add anything to that interest which the French nation always lavished on our phalanxes, if I have been able to make Prussia feel that sworn faith is not played with impunity, that an usurped territory adds nothing to the strength of Austria, and that violence sooner or later falls upon its authors, to Turkey, Sweden, and England, sometimes repented for being an impassive spectator of iniquity, I will have attained the goal I proposed to myself, I shall have preserved in history its morality and its lessons.

Paris, this 3rd of May, 1829. ***Leonard Chodzko.***

[11]Tadeusz Kosciuszko (1746 – 1817) Polish Patriot and General who fought in the American Revolution and for Polish independence.

Preface

As the history of the Polish legions embraces only one period of General Dąbrowski's life, I believe I will meet the wish of my readers, by letting them know all the titles by which this warrior-citizen presented himself to the admiration of posterity.

Jan-Henryk Dąbrowski was from an old and noble family, son of Jean-Michel Dąbrowski, colonel in the armies of Saxony (under the reign of Augustus III, King of Poland), and Sophie-Marie Lettow, daughter of a Polish general of this name, was born on 29 August 1755, at Pierszowice, a country situated in the Palatinate of Krakow. The young Jean-Henri was raised in the paternal house at Hoyerswerda, and entered as a sub-ensign, into the Uhlan Regiment in 1770, commanded by Prince Albert of Saxony. Promoted successively to the higher ranks, he remained there until he had made the acquaintance of General Bellegarde, a native of Savoy, and general commanding all the Saxon cavalry. Dąbrowski performed the duties of aide-de-camp. This general, a well-educated man, possessed a superb library, especially rich in strategic works. The young Dąbrowski, with his taste for the military art and having enough to satisfy his curiosity, applied himself at an early age to look into books for lessons of strategy, history, geography, and sciences which he had to use later for the service of his homeland.

The new Muscovite power which rose on the remains of the Russia's, either as a vassal or belonging to Poland from time immemorial, and which was already seeking, since the reign of Tsar Peter I, to interfere in the affairs of our republic saw that weakening the armed forces as the surest means of subjugating that country one day, and forced it to reduce its regular army to eighteen thousand men, a number too small for a republic of twelve million to fifteen million inhabitants. The young Poles were therefore obliged to go to their military apprenticeship outside their homeland.

But the time was coming when Poland, recovering all her energy, would think of her regeneration. The work of the Constitutional Diet which increased the national army to one hundred thousand men, soon opened career opportunities for young warriors eager for glory and independence. The Polish Constituent Assembly decided during one of its sessions, towards the end of 1789, the appointment of the various embassies to the foreign courts, charging a mission to the Elector of Saxony, Jean-Népomucène Malachowski[1], nephew of the famous Stanisław Małachowski[2] , Marshal of that diet. This mission consisted of Embassy Secretary François Pieglowski, and Knights of Embassy Ignace Nosarzewski and Ignace Stecki, all distinguished citizens and worthy of representing a reborn nation. Their mission took on a new importance, when the Diet, after having sanctioned the memorable constitution of May 3, 1791, called upon the Elector of Saxony to inherit the Polish Throne, charged Prince Adam-Kazimirz Czartoryski[3] , Starost-General of Podolia, with bringing this news to the Elector and urged him to accept a crown that the national offered him so generously. Prince Czartoryski was accompanied by Joseph Mostowski and Dominique Szymanowski, as well as his secretary Jean Skowronski.

This meeting of so many Poles of distinction reminded Dąbrowski of his old allegiances. At a time when so many new measures opened up new careers, and at the moment when the dictates invited all Poles who were serving abroad to return to their country, the aide-de-camp of General Bellegarde, the young Dąbrowski did not hesitate a moment to go to the call of honor; he left Dresden, came to Poland, entered the service with the rank of major, and campaigned against the Muscovites in 1792, under Prince Joseph Poniatowski.

Men of talent are usually known only in extraordinary events, and it was scarcely until the terrible campaign of 1794, that Dąbrowski gave the measure of his talents and devotion. After the feeble king Stanislas Augustus Poniatowski turned toward the conspiracy of the Targowica faction, and the so-called Diet of Grodno, a scandalous mar-

[1] Jean-Népomucène Malachowski 1759 – 1821, Politician.
[2] Stanisław Małachowski 1736 – 1809, the first Prime Minister and Marshal of the Four-Year Sejm.
[3] Prince Adam-Kazimirz Czartoryski 1734-1823, cousin of King Stanisław Ponitowski, man of letters and father of Adam Jerzy Czartoryski (1770 – 1861).

ket was established, where fortunes were trafficked.

In this general conflagration, it was difficult for the even the most distinguished not to be suspected of treasonous activities. Ambassador Sievers, faithful to the orders of Catherine II, wished to compromise the most distinguished names by slandering them, as well as various distinguished officers including Dąbrowski, to approve the suppression of the national army.

Then with the Prussian declaration, on 16 January 1793, its armies invaded Greater Poland[4], the troops of the Republic, distributed in different small towns of that province, were ordered to retire in front of the Prussians behind the Pilica and Bzura rivers. At this time, Dąbrowski, as vice-brigadier, was on the general staff of Major General Byszewski. He then proposed to his old general that they approach Warsaw, to surprise the Muscovites commanded by General-Minister Igelstrom, to seize the arsenal, and then go to meet the Prussians, commanded by General Möllendorf. But this project failed it when betrayed by Stanislas-Augustus' adjutant-general Gorzynski, through the weakness of Byszewski; and the Proconsul Igelstrom, who was informed by the King himself of this plan, so that the Russian garrison was strengthened, to include a battery of twenty guns at Wola.

Byszewski was ordered move to a different position and set up his headquarters in Konskie, halfway from Warsaw to Krakow.

Having failed in his plan, Dąbrowski did not give up and submitted another plan to General Wodzicki. The latter, who had his headquarters at Krakow, along with two thousand men, was an officer whose bravery equaled his patriotism.

After a lengthy deliberation, he succeeded in having this superior officer adopt a daring project, which aimed at nothing less than a junction with the French army fighting on the banks of the Rhine; but the indecision of General Byszewski, the delays in execution, and especially the surveillance by foreign governments, prevented such grand strategy from being fulfilled. Soon this became impracticable because of the position of the garrisons assigned to the Polish troops, and by the reduction of the army, which was fixed at only fifteen thousand men; but, although this plan failed because of accidental motives, the glory remains none the less to him who had conceived it. Wherever

[4]Wielkopolska – part of the Polish heartland that includes the cities of Poznan and Łódz

Poland called her real children, it was sure to find Dąbrowski there.

Soon after revolt broke out in Little Poland.[5] Scarcely had the banner of independence been raised by Madalinsky, hardly had Kosciuszko founded a new government in Krakow, and the citizens of Warsaw had hardly consumed their regeneration, than Dąbrowski came to this city to support the national cause; there, all of Igelstrom's papers were seized, the crimes of the traitors and the denunciators were brought to light, and the innocence of those who had previously been slandered. Dąbrowski was cleared of the suspicions that had weighed on his head in a meeting of the Provisional Council, dated 30 April 1794. This justification was reproduced in the *Warsaw Gazette,* and 13 May 1794, No. 6, under the title: *Tableau des Opération du Conseil Provisoire.* Moreover, this same information, gave even better proof that Dąbrowski had come out clean of stains, and they entrusted him with some military posts.

However, such was the popular distrust, that without the generous intervention of Mrs. Mokronoska[6], born Princess Marie Sanguszko, we would have, on mere appearances, destroyed the man who would later give his homeland so many pledges of a real devotion.

Since that time, Dąbrowski has always been in the front line of the ranks of Polish officers. Full of talent and bravery, he distinguished himself in the defense of Warsaw against the Prussians, deserving the reward for his zeal, receiving a ring from the hand of Kosciuszko, bearing the inscription; "The homeland to its defender, August 28, 1794." He was sent to Wielkopolska at the time of the insurrection, to join with General Madalinski.[7] Upon his arrival there, a debate of modesty rose between these two warriors about the command. Dąbrowski had announced to the Generalissimo that he would serve under Madalinski's orders. Madalinski, on his side, in the presence of the troops assembled at Kamionna, proclaimed a strong desire to yield, although senior, the command to Dąbrowski. "I have one more rank than you," he said to the latter, "but I know you have more military talents: so order; have everything; I will only obey. Answer by your zeal to my confidence, and

[5] Małopolska – part of the historic heartland of Poland centered around Kraków
[6]Marie Marianna Sanguszko-Kowelska (1770-1827) was a Polish noblewoman and the wife of Stanisław Mokronowski (1761 – 1821) a Polish noble, general and hero of Zieleńce.
[7]Antoni Madaliński (1739 – 1805) general who fought in the Bar Uprising, Defense of the Constitution and the Kosciuszko uprising

usefully serve the country." Noble and sublime subordination, so rare in our day, so worthy of the ancient ages!

As a result of the new services he rendered to the national cause in his operations to Wielkopolska , by the occupation of Labiszyn and Bydgoszcz (Bromberg), Dąbrowski was promoted to the rank of lieutenant-general by Kosciuszko. Then the disasters of Brzesc-Litewski and the decisive battle, fought on 10 October 1794, at Maciejowicé, in which the Generalissimo was taken prisoner, completely changed the face of affairs. Dąbrowski and Madalinski were recalled to Warsaw; but when they arrived at Gora, they learned of the massacres at Praga and the surrender of the capital. General Dąbrowski tried to restore to the army's order with his primitive energy; he propose projects that could save Poland in vain! The hour of enthusiasm was over; the Muscovites and Prussians were victorious on all sides; it was necessary to resign to the facts and to put down arms by signing the Capitulation of Radoszyce, on 18 November 1794. Under Suvorov's terms, Dąbrowski was received with respect and distinction. The enemy general offered him a higher rank in the new army which was being formed under the auspices of the co-invading powers. A generous refusal was the only answer he got.

He retired from all service, but was not free to leave Poland, Dąbrowski lived in Warsaw until February 1796. At that time, the capital was occupied by the Prussians, so he obtained permission to go to Berlin.

From November 1794, Kazimirz de la Boche and Elie Tremo had left Paris with the intention of putting General Dąbrowski at the head of a military representation, which would be organized under the shadow of French flags. After all the necessary steps and a long stay in Dresden and Leipzig, General Dąbrowski finally arrived at Paris Vendemiaire 9, Year V. He solicited and obtained permission from the French government to create a Polish corps in Italy and left for Milan for this purpose. On the Frimaire 12, Year V, he had conferences with General Bonaparte, and soon a convention was signed, under the influence of the latter, between Dąbrowski and the administration of Lombardy.

In order to achieve his plan, a proclamation was written in four languages and signed by Dąbrowski, who departed from the headquarters of Milan on Pluviôse 1, Year V (20 January 1797), warming the hearts of the Poles faithful to his memory.

At this call of honor and independence, a large corps was raised under the command of their fellow countryman and promise Poland an imminent resurrection. It was then that many of the Poles, leaving their oppressed homeland, filled little bags with the earth, which they carried on their breasts and separated from them only after having succumbed on the fields of combat. It is these corps raised out of misfortune, that we will see in this history under the name of the Polish legions. They will be seen, under the orders of Dąbrowski, pacifying Reggio on 15 Messidor (3 July 1797), announcing themselves in the Rome campaign, and occupying the capitol on Floreal 14, Year VI (3 May 1798), to conquer the Kingdom of Naples, and to enter its capital on Pluviôse 4, Year VII (23 January 1799), to undergo all the fatigues of a new war in Lombardy, towards the middle of the Year VII, to support the winter campaign of the Year VIll (1799-I800); finally, under General Bonaparte, after his return from Egypt, conquered Italy for a second time, resulting in the peace of Luneville (26 January 1801), still in activity of service for the French cause and without any positive fruit for their unhappy homeland.

Finally, at that time, and when the general pacification of Europe had deprived these patriotic phalanxes of their last hope, when they absolutely knew that European policy had used their devotion without giving them anything in return, isolated from their illusions, dismembered and disorganized, saw these legions incessantly increasing their enthusiasm for their country and their honor, decimated by the iron of battles, to be revived at a later date, and with their glorious debris form the first cadres of the regiments who have sustained the Poles' military reputation beyond the Pyrenees, the Alps, the Ocean; on the banks of the Danube, the Vistula, the Moscow, the Berezina, and which, rich with so many great memories, are still one of the most beautiful of European armies.

However, at the Peace of Amiens, Dąbrowski passed into the service of the Italian Republic, and later to the Kingdom of Naples, as a général de division, a rank which he had attained in the French army. He contributed through his labors and advice to complete the military organization of this country and judging that sooner or later his talents would be useful to his country, he wished to acquire, in silence, new knowledge to pay it homage on the occasion.

In 1806 the hope of reestablishing Poland seemed to smile again upon the discouraged patriots. The man of destiny (Napoleon) announced loudly that he had the project. General Dąbrowski then reappeared, after fifteen years of absence, in the same palatinates of Greater Poland that he had traveled during the War of Independence of 1794. The proclamation he published jointly with Wybicki, on 3 November 1806, from Posen, produced a magical effect. In less than two months he raised and equipped thirty thousand men from the inhabitants of Greater Poland. The Polish nation, proud to see its flags united to those that victory had so often illuminated, embraced again the cause to which they had so much sympathy.

Three divisions under the orders of Dąbrowski, Poniatowski, and Zajączek, were raised in Poland, initially formed part of the corps of Marshal Mortier; later they were destined to be part of the troops of the Grand Duchy of Baden and those of Saxony to compose the army under the orders of Marshal Lefebvre, who was to besiege Danzig.

After the brilliant action at Graudentz, Dąbrowski took up a position with about seven thousand Poles, in February 1807, at Mewe, on the left bank of the Vistula. Reinforced later by a corps of Baden troops, under the orders of the French General Mesnard, Dąbrowski resolved to repel the enemy from the advantageous position he held at Dirschau[8] ; indeed, he set out on 23 February. The Prussians left Dirschau to march to meet him; but the Polish attack was so impetuous, that the Prussians were obliged to retreat first to the suburb, where they defended themselves long enough under the protection of their artillery, and finally to the town, where Dąbrowski continued the attack. The city was taken after an even bloodier fight, as the Polish and the Baden troops, frustrated by the long resistance of their adversaries, refused to give them quarter. The losses suffered on this occasion by the garrison of Danzig obliged the governor of that city to recall his troops under the cannon of the fortress. Dąbrowski continued to be employed at the siege of Danzig until it surrendered.

At the battle of Friedland, the Poles continued to fight under the command of General Dąbrowski. The Emperor Napoleon was so

[8]Tczew

satisfied with them, that after the battle he sent for the principal officers and told them several times how much he was pleased with them. General Dąbrowski received a glorious wound in this fight.

After the Treaty of Tilsit (9 June 1807) and the formation of the Grand Duchy of Warsaw, the command of the Polish Army as well as the senior rank was entrusted to Prince Joseph Poniatowski. Generals Dąbrowski and Zajączek, who for so long and on every occasion maintained the glory of the Polish name on the fields of Italy, Egypt, and finally so newly at Friedland, Graudentz, and Danzig, were greatly affected by the preference given to Prince Joseph and did not conceal their discontent. The whole Polish Army soon knew of the disagreements of the generals under whom it served, and looked with difficulty at the enmity of those whom their virtues brought together, divided by personal ambitions; but the moment quickly came when these disagreements vanished at the call of the fatherland, when it called its children to recover its rights and its liberty, in the memorable campaign of 1809.

Immediately after the Treaty of Tilsit, General Dąbrowski remained in Poland at the head of his army corps, establishing his headquarters at Posen. Having recovered from his wounds, and still engaged in the care of his division, the long-time widower married a second time on 5 November 1807, to Mademoiselle Barbe Chlapowska, a wife worthy of such a distinguished warrior. For two whole years they enjoyed a happy time together; but scarcely once the country came in danger, he returned to the battlefield.

Proud of its immense preparations, Austria declared war on France, and while numerous armies advanced into Bavaria, Archduke Ferdinand d'Este invaded the Grand Duchy of Warsaw. The battle of Raszyn, fought on 19 April 1809, showed the Austrians that the Poles could fight with an enemy four times their size. However, Prince Joseph Poniatowski, wishing to preserve the capital, evacuated it and occupied the positions of the left bank of the Vistula. There, in a council of war, Dąbrowski advocated on the necessity of marching into Galicia, and reaching out to the patriots who would join with their brethren. At the moment when Prince Poniatowski was turning the Austrian army, General Dąbrowski moved to Greater Poland, in order to encourage its brave inhabitants by his presence. Arriving at Posen, he organized several corps in the rear of the enemy. He managed to assemble as many as ten thousand men who joined Prince Poniatowski when he pursued the Austrians on their retreat towards Krakow. From there Dąbrowski went to Bzura and Piliça.

The results of this glorious campaign were the enlargement of the Duchy of Warsaw, and the living proof of what the Poles could do when they had only one of their neighboring powers to fight!

At the opening of the 1812 campaign, all the citizens thought they had seen the end of their sentences, and, uniting their forces for a last combat, they had no doubt that the hour was about to come when their country would be re-established in all its glory and integrity. Preoccupied with ideals of old honor and independence Dąbrowski forwarded his ideas to Prince Joseph Poniatowski. Prince Poniatowski, who acted as the combined the supreme command of the Polish army and the functions of Minister of War of the Grand Duchy was asked to increase the regiment's depots to more acceptable proportions, and create frontier garrisons, so that so that the Polish refugees from Austria, Prussia, and Russia might find an asylum among their compatriots. If such a step had been taken, it would have been adopted as far as the borders of the Dvina, Dnieper, Ukraine, and Podolia, he said, so that if the French army, after so many battles, must retrace its steps after such an extraordinary campaign, however unlikely, it would be desirable that the Poles alone should be able to defend their soil, to dispute their independence, and cover the French phalanxes. At the first alarm, one could count on raising of twenty thousand men, and most likely within a few months this number would be considerably increased. Events later justified Dąbrowski's project; but then it was too late. For the moment, Prince Poniatowski confined himself to praising the intentions of General Dąbrowski; but whether he feared displeasing Napoleon, or that he did not believe that the expedition, begun under such happy auspices, would have such an unhappy end, he would not agree to it.

In the course of this memorable campaign, Dąbrowski, had one of the three divisions of the 5th Polish Corps under his command, part of the Grand Armée, but remained in ancient Poland in Belrus. After receiving some reinforcements of Lithuanian troops, he occupied Mohilow on the Dnieper. Immediately after Prince Poniatowski's departure, he became active, pushing his scouts out in all directions with great vigor, and established an uninterrupted line of communication with the corps of Reynier and the Austrian General-Minister Schwarzemberg. His detachments were at Hlusk, Sluck, Pinsk, and in the other towns between it and the French and Austrian divisions, whose lines extended as far as the banks of the Bug near Olesko and Kowel. He settled the bulk of his division in the vicinity of Swislocz on the Berezina, in order to observe the fortress of Bobruysk. Russian General Hertel attacked him without success in the month of September with twelve thousand infantrymen and two thousand horse; but his attempts on Pinsk and Hlusk had only insignificant successes, and soon after Hertel returned to take his first position at Mozyr.

As the French army evacuated Moscow, Dąbrowski was charged to maintain the communications between Minsk and Vilna, and to take the measures to preserve the Fortresses of Minsk and Barysaw. He went to Minsk on 15 November; but the Governor of Minsk, Nicolas Bronikowski, lost his head, evacuated the fortress, and retired to Barysaw with about three thousand men, leaving five thousand patients in the hospitals, and immense stores formed by the patriotism of the inhabitants of the government of Minsk.

When he arrived at Barysaw with his division reduced to about four thousand men and twenty cannon, General Dąbrowski hoped to find the corps of Marshal Oudinot, Duke of Reggio on the Berezina, and to his disappointment he found no sight of him. In the meanwhile, the Russian Admiral Tschitschagoff, commanding the Army of Wolhynia, marched on 19 November, to the Berezina, which the perfidious Austrians had abandoned.

On the 21st, at daybreak, the Russians were about to attack the bridgehead before that city. A battalion of the 95th Line Regiment was surprised and pushed in disorder into the city. Dąbrowski's division was also attacked, just as it was preparing to support the movement of a Württemberg battalion. The commander of Barysaw having committed the mistake of not reuniting his troops, to co-ordinate their movement with Dąbrowski's division, the latter had to deal with very superior forces, and was then in a very difficult position. Nevertheless, he knew how to channel the energy of his resources necessary to get away with it, so by maintaining good order and his maneuvers to retreat, always fighting, to the Neman's banks, where he took up position, and where he was joined by the Duke of Reggio's corps. He succeeded in his maneuvers and yielded ground only when the Russian Generals Lambert and Langeron, reinforced with eighteen thousand men, launched a general charge.

The indefatigable Dąbrowski, with the debris of Poniatowski's corps, again contributed to covering the bridges of the Berezina until the last moment; on 26 November, he was seriously wounded, and did not return to Warsaw until December 1812.

In 1813, the wreckage of the Polish army, united in Warsaw, was forced by the Russian's movements to leave the city in February. Some of these troops went from Czestochowa to Krakow, where Prince Poniatowski took command of them; the other part, led by General Lonczynski[9] , marched from Kalisz to Leipzig. General Dąbrowski, wounded, being in the latter city, put himself at the head of this second corps; and, marching from there on Mainz to meet Napoleon, where he formed, by his authorization, the Polish troops under his command, into one of the most beautiful divisions of the army. It consisted of two regiments of infantry, two of cavalry, and a battery of horse artillery. Marshal Mortier was sent by the Emperor to Wetzlar to preside over the organization of this division, with the necessary funds for clothing and equipment. In less than six weeks it was on its feet and setting out for the army. It arrived at Leipzig on the eve of the armistice. Later, and throughout the rest of the campaign, it was completely isolated from the Poles together, and operated separately. Although specifically intended to cover the fortified town of Wittemberg, it had the opportunity to distinguish itself in the actions at Teltof, Insterbourg, and Mattrin. One of the finest feats of arms of this division, and little known perhaps, is the intrepid defense of the suburb of Halle at the battle of Leipzig. In fact, it was Dąbrowski's division which, by its vigorous resistance, prevented the storming of the city; the entrance of the enemy at this point would have had more fatal results than those which took place the next day.

During the armistice, Napoleon came to Leipzig and passed the division in review, testified to General Dąbrowski his satisfaction on its beautiful outfit. He read out promotions and distributed decorations

[9]Jozéf Benedykt Lonczynski (1779 – 1820) officer of the Legions and later the Duchy of Warsaw

to those who had distinguished themselves in the Moscow campaign. This division was then composed as follows:

Commander-in-Chief, Major General DĄBROWSKI.
Chief of Staff, Colonel Ignace MYCIELSKI.

Brigade: Général de brigade Eduward Zoltowski
2nd Infantry Regiment – Colonel Joseph Szymanowski
14th Infantry Regiment – Colonel Malinowski

Brigade: Général de brigade Jean Krukowiecki
2nd Uhlan Regiment – Colonel Rzodkiewicz
4th Uhlan Regiment – Colonel Kostanecki
Artillery: Chef d'escadron Jean Schwerin

Beyond this, there were a large number of officers without troops who had been assigned to this division but were directed to Mainz and placed at the disposition of the Minister of War.

After the unfortunate death of Prince Poniatowski, General Dąbrowski pushed the debris of the Polish Army beyond the Rhine and this was the last feat of arms in the career of General Dąbrowski.

Arriving at Warsaw on 7 June 1815, General Dąbrowski sent officers to all the departments of the Grand Duchy of Warsaw to assemble the Polish servicemen of all arms who were there. In the proclamation which he published on this subject, the following passage was remarked: "The magnanimous Emperor Alexander has left his arms to the remains of our army and has enabled me to return with them to our country. His Majesty was not satisfied with this, he recognized the necessity of increasing the national force, and he ordered that all the Poles who fought in the last war and even those who were made prisoners should receive this benefit."

But in August of the same year, the various rumors that arose in Warsaw about the fate determined by the Allied Powers for the Poles, the fear of seeing Poland reduced to hopelessness again, produced a painful sensation throughout the country, and raised some anxiety among the people and the military. It was these alarming rumors that General-in-Chief Dąbrowski had ordered to assemble the military of all ranks which caused the officers to write the general a letter in which they begged him to frankly explain the purpose of their organization. This letter ended with these words: "Ask the conqueror what he demands of us. We are in his power, but our homeland alone can ask for our blood. As soon as he was assured its independence, we will take up arms for our generous protector. Duty and recognition will then double our courage and national energy; but without this assurance we will not move, we declare it; and we are ready to submit to the harshest of extremes and to be treated as prisoners of war, rather than to be guilty of conduct unworthy of ourselves and of you...... Such are our feelings, to which we are determined to remain faithful."

The Committee on the Military Organization of the Polish troops was formed later, those generals who did not adhere to the points discussed, such as Kniaziewicz, Stanislas Woyczynski, and Francois Paszkowski, resigned; as for General Dąbrowski, after the proclamation in 1815 of the new kingdom of Poland, although he was not in active service, the Emperor appointed him general of cavalry, then senator-palatine, and decorated him with the Order of the White Eagle. He was already a commander of the Polish Military Cross, called Virtuti Militari, commander of the Iron and Royal Crown of the Legion d'Honneur.

Finally, overwhelmed by age and infirmity, after a long and stormy career, Dąbrowski retired to the new Grand Duchy of Posen at Winna Gora, where he took care to put his memoirs on the Italian campaigns in order as well as those of Germany and Russia; he dedicated them to the Royal Society of Friends of Science of Warsaw, and bequeathed to the same society his library, and the collection of antiquities which he had collected abroad. This learned and patriotic society, which counted him among its most distinguished members, wishing to honor his memory, designated a private room for the preservation of all his memories so dear and so glorious for Poland. This room currently bears the title of Dąbrowski Hall.

Until his last moments, the same patriotic idea, which had been the soul of Dąbrowski's life was pursued by this patriotic warrior, and he was seen ready to descend into the tomb, to look anxiously at the destinies of Poland. This devotion, and singlemindedness, has been found to bear out over time, which should silence any detractor of the illustrious general. In fact, in the report of the Inquiry Committee instituted in 1826, in order to judge the members of the Polish Patriotic Society, Dąbrowski's efforts for the rebirth of his unfortunate country are positively expressed in the following passage (page 3):

> "Shortly before his death, this officer-general (Dąbrowski), conversing with a soldier formerly under his command, expressed to him bitterly all the regrets he felt at seeing the fate of the noble Polish nation, of that nation whose valor had so many times contributed to the glory of the leaders who had shown themselves at its head, but who for itself had withdrawn from such sad fruits her many sacrifices and heroic efforts. 'Today (1818),' he said, 'the existence and the constitutional form of our government cannot find, in the still unstable position of Europe, a sufficient guarantee of tranquility.'"
>
> "What do we have to hope for, and what should we not fear? Every day should we not tremble at the fate that awaits us tomorrow? None of the links that would make Poland strong unite her children; and, thus divided, who can reassure them about the still uncertain chances of future events? Had Napoleon escaped from the Island of Elba, had he brought back his triumphant eagles to the banks of the Vistula, what would have happened to Poland? More waves of blood, new fights, new victims; but independence, freedom, never! Whoever for whom the Poles have broken their spears, what does defeat, or victory do for them? Weak because they are disunited, what conditions can they expect from the victor? Only those which politics will agree to impose on them. 'What is it possible,' he added, 'to revive one day the fire that burns in the bottom of all hearts, the true friend of the country! How can I not awaken the ancient energy of these Poles, who, to be strong and powerful like their ancestors, only need to believe in their strength, and to claim their fallen power! What does the yoke under which they are now bent matter? Whoever directs them, and the government which governs them, let them gather their opinions, their desires, and their wishes; that the divided nation becomes itself again; that it be united to even serve the sovereign who commands it today; one day perhaps, one day, if the fortune that

gave him for his master strikes it in turn, Poland could finally recover independence and freedom, and no longer recognize a king that it would never have chosen.'"

These ideas of Dąbrowski strongly struck the one that to whom he communicated them. The general had urged him to spread them, and he hastened to follow his advice. In various interviews with Prince Jablonowski and Lieutenants Colonels Krzyzanowski and Prondzynski, or with other individuals, he conveyed to them the wishes of which he was the interpreter and urged them to act on their side to achieve the goal proposed by General Dąbrowski.

This is a talking piece that can be opposed at any time to the slanderers of General Dąbrowski. It is in the destiny of illustrious men to be exposed to the envious features of some Zoillus;[10] but the judgment of posterity, which hovers over this passionate atmosphere, soon reduces to their value these false and abusive imputations. A work bearing the title supposed: *Lettre de Jean Woytynski, Polonaise, au général Dąbrowski, commandant les légions polonaises [Letter from Jean Woytynski, A Pole, to General Dąbrowski, commanding the Polish legions]* Warsaw, March 1, 1798 (printed in small text in-8", all of 15 pages), appeared at the moment when the general, having triumphed over all the obstacles in the formation of the legions, foresaw the moment when they would be useful. Afterwards, another Pole published a four-page notice on Dąbrowski in Paris, signed Neyman, a Polish refugee patriot, a colonel in the insurgent army of Poland, an invective and a pale summary of the above letter. To these calumnious attacks we have to oppose the whole life of General Dąbrowski, the friendship with which the most illustrious Poles of his age honored him, and finally this boundless confidence that he had inspired his companions in arms, and so many times he has been able to justify.

Finally, after a long and brilliant career, this military citizen ended his days on June 26, 1818, in his lands, at Winna Gora. He wanted to be buried with the uniform he wore at the head of the Italian legions, with the two swords of honor he had earned on the battlefield, one sent by Kosciuszko for the taking of Bromberg in 1794 the other conquered in Italy, as well as three bullets that had been removed from his body and kept until his death.

[10]Translator: Zouillus was a critic of Alexander and a detractor of Homer.

His death was followed by universal mourning, and the country saw three of our first contemporary glories descend successively into the tomb: Poniatowski in 1813, Kosciuszko in 1817, and Dąbrowski in 1818!

Surrounded by the tears of his wife, his children, his friends, he expired in an admirable calm. Everyone, even the simple villagers, ran into the churches to pay homage to his military and civic virtues. The Republic of Krakow, whose capital is proud to possess the tombs of Polish kings and heroes, wanted to claimed the mortal remains of Dąbrowski, to deposit them alongside those of John Sobieski, Joseph Poniatowski, and Thadeus Kosciuszko, but a force majeure prevented this national translation.

TRANSLATOR'S NOTES ON THIS EDITION

The original title of this work is *Histoire des Légions Polonaises en Italie* (Paris: J. Barbezat, 1829).

Some of the French used in the various supporting documents was a little rough, so some liberties were taken. The French Revolutionary dates have been restructured so that they were consistent with the English dating system, i.e. "1 Messidor" became "Messidor 1st."

In the second volume various authors of supporting documents and of the main manuscript refer to French infantry in various ways. I have taken a standardizing approach. French regular or line infantry was referred to occasionally as "de ligne" or "de bataille." It was standardized to simply "demi-brigade." The light infantry demi-brigades are always a number, followed by "Légère." The term "demi-brigade" does not follow.

THE HISTORY OF THE POLISH LEGIONS

CHAPTER ONE

Situation in Poland from 1786 to 1790. — Russia Seeks It's Alliance. — Prussian Opposition. — It Offers a Treaty in Turn. — Convocation of the Polish Diet. — Its Works. — The Treaty of Alliance with Prussia is Signed. — Difficulties on the Subject of a Commercial Treaty. — The King of Prussia Demands Thorn and Danzig. — The Diet Refuses. — Double Politics of the Berlin Court. — Constitution of 3 May 1791. — Russian Peace Treaty with the Porte. — Russian Preparations for War Against Poland. — Perfidy of the King of Prussia. — Weakness of Stanislas-Augustus. — Invasion of Poland by the Russian Armies. — Its Consequences.

The last lights of the 18th century, so fertile in revolutions, so rich in events, seemed destined to provide history with the living contrast of the most unheard-of successes and the most astonishing disasters. Motionless for a long time, the universe shook suddenly, as if struck by an electric shock; and while independent states shared the new world, while in our old Europe a republic was as strong, as great as the ancient republics, a whole kingdom disappeared in its turn from the surface of the earth, and ambitious neighbors, by scratching his name from the map, seemed to say to posterity, in an insolent voice; Here was Poland."

And Poland did not deserve such a spell! Beautiful by its climate, fertile by its soil, with its generous citizens, its indomitable warriors, it only needed a firm king, and that king failed it.

Thrown on the throne by foreign influence, Stanislas Augustus Poniatowski occupied it at that time. The first dismemberment of Poland had already given the measure of its talents and his character, and all the true patriots watched with suspicion the march of the government, determined to prevent, at the risk of their lives, the repetition of such a monstrous violence. Until 1786, it was impossible for them to support their projects in an open manner, but from the moment when Tsarina Catherine II, in concert with Joseph II, Emperor of Germany, declared war on the Ottoman Porte, this thirst of independence, was rekindled by a powerful diversion, awoke with more vigor than ever.

As it became essential for Russia to secure its magazines in Ukraine, and to open a passage for its troops on Polish territory, Catherine felt the necessity of entering into a new alliance with this kingdom. She made some entrees for this purpose; but the Berlin cabinet, uneasy with such a proposal, did not disguise its shady dealings, and the Polish Court declare that it would never agree to such a treaty.

To support this step by threatening measures, thirty thousand Prussians marched towards the Polish frontier, and the minister of the Berlin cabinet began to speak in a more positive manner. Intimidating some, encouraging others, he was hostile towards those who leaned towards Russian influence, and promised to all an alliance on the part of his sovereign.

Although experience would have shown the Poles how much they should beware of foreign insinuations, they found themselves in a position to be unable to choose their protectors. France, absorbed in her feudal system, was too much a slave herself to think of making a free people; Russia and Austria were only waiting for a favorable moment to impose their iron yoke on Poland. The King of Prussia remained alone; he alone could protect it and should protect it, while preserving its entire independence. Not to mention the personal affair of Frederick Wilhelm II and the Elector of Saxony, both bordering on the idea that an intermediate kingdom would remain a barrier to the Muscovite power, so Polish citizens necessarily presumed that an alliance with the Berlin Court would offer more guarantees against a violation of its territory, and against an attack on constitutions independent of their motherland. Thus, combining their present chances and their future fears, they saw an alliance with Prussia as a pact of peace and freedom.

It was under such auspices, and on October 6, that the Diet of 1788 opened its doors in Warsaw, a memorable period when Poland thought it saw its destiny seated again on solid ground, while it walked on the lava of a volcano that was to engulf it.[1]

The first Prussian declaration, presented to the Estates assembled on 12 October 1788, proved a clear opposition between Russian and Prussian interests. It was there that when the King of Prussia spoke of the Muscovite influence in the affairs of Poland, he characterized it as foreign oppression; it was there that, to express all the shame attached to the partisans of Russia, he called true patriots and good citizens those whom he invited to join him.

Such a solemn manifestation on the part of Frederick Wilhelm II produced a magical effect. Everything was electrified, everything was given a new impetus, and on the ruins of obsolete constitutions, a new and generous light would be shining for a moment.

The St. Petersburg Cabinet, fearing that the reform diet would give the Polish people an independent charter, and tear it from its guardianship, threw up marks of discord among the people of the uncomfortable Greek Orthodox Religion, while on his side, the King of Prussia, seconding the national efforts against the rebels, exchanged diplomatic notes with Russia.

The acts of the diet were public; but as the obvious conduct of the Berlin Cabinet deserved special consideration, external relations, and especially those with St. Petersburg, were communicated to the Prussian Minister, either by confidential notes, or by lectures at the committee, or by deputation of foreign affairs. These conferences were witnessed, and to some extent as a guarantor, by the English Ambassador residing in Poland. The latter, by his speeches and his assiduous presence, seemed to approve the advice of the Prussian Ambassador. Both were eager to give the committee the necessary information on the course of political affairs in Europe. It was a matter of hearing from them of a powerful and federative league which, embracing the Ottoman Porte, Prussia, England, Holland, and a portion of the Germanic circles, was intended to constantly keep in check the ambition of the

[1]See Letters from an Anonymous (Hugues Kolinntay) addressed to Stanislas Malachoufski, since then Marshal of the Constituent Diet on the work that was to be undertaken in this diet, for the regeneration of the Republic of Poland. These letters were published in four parts in 1788 to 1790 in Warsaw.

two imperial powers.
In this state of things, Frederick William II moved towards the end of the year 1789, on one side that his influence and that of England had encouraged the Porte to continue the war against Russia, convinced of the other that the Polish Diet, by laws on taxation and the increase of its troops, proved the desire for national independence, ardently renewed the proposal of a defensive alliance between the two states.

A small number of suspicious deputies rose up in the assembly, who rejected, with defiance, the proposed alliance; but the offer of the King of Prussia was too advantageous to stop at a few isolated presentiments. On the other hand, this frank coalition of a formidable government, which could restore Poland's ancient independence, was well calculated to seduce loyal and proud souls, and it was decided by acclamation that it was necessary to quickly occupy themselves with a new constitution in harmony with this new order of things.

At the same meeting, the Committee on Foreign Affairs was instructed to enter into negotiations with the Berlin Court concerning the proposed alliance. In the alternative, it was also necessary to lay the foundations for a commercial treaty.

The basic articles of a new constitution were soon drawn up by the commission appointed *ad hoc*; the diet sanctioned them. As for the double treaty, the thing was not so easy. The alliance was very easily understood, but the commercial pact offered a knot that was difficult to resolve. It was nothing less than the cession of Gdansk, which the King of Prussia demanded; and this tardy and unplanned demand began to sow distrust between the contracting parties.

However, as a delay in the negotiations might have lost all the fruit that was hoped for from them, just as Russia could, by means of a truce with the Porte, become a threat to Poland, the Diet resolved to split the two treaties, and simply conclude that of a defensive alliance on 29 March 1790.

As to the commerce pact, as the King of Prussia insisted on obtaining the cession of Gdansk, it was indefinitely postponed. The only fruit which the Berlin Cabinet then withdrew from this step was to arouse suspicion and weaken its popularity. For his part, the Russian Ambassador, Bulgakov[2] seconded by his secret agents, fanned

[2]Yakov Bulgakov (1743 – 1809) Russian Diplomat

this first spark of discord. He called, in public, the requested cession of invasion of territory, and seemed to draw the consequence of a new partition.

Disconcerted by these unfavorable rumors, Frederick William wanted to retrace his steps. Not being able to do so in a direct manner, he at least endeavored to color his intentions, and declared to the diet, that if he had appeared to insist on the cession of Gdansk and Thorn, it was because he hoped to indemnify himself, Poland obtaining for them at the Congress of Reichenbach a portion of Galicia. Everything happened in exchanged notes which remained without results.

From then on, the majority of Poles could no longer be fooled by the Machiavellian policy of the Prussian Cabinet. The initial enthusiasm which had decided the alliance, was succeeded by a vague mistrust, then by an ill-disguised anger: among the many laws which drew attention to the work of the diet, there was one which seemed to serve as an answer to the requirements of Frederick William. It declared there that "the Kingdom of Poland and the Grand Duchy of Lithuania, with all the provinces, palatinates, lands, districts, fiefs, as well as all the cities and ports that belong to it, united forever to the Republic by solemn and respective treaties, belonged to it invariably and without division. No diet, no king, no authority could exchange, much less detach from the body of the Republic, even in part, by exchange or cession, any of these dependencies."

Such a proud decision irritated the King of Prussia; but, clever at concealing his thoughts, he disguised his resentment; for if it had been doubly advantageous to him to be the despoiler of Poland, even greater interests forbade him from betraying his engagements.

Indeed, it was then that the conferences of Reichenbach[3] were held. They seemed destined to bring peace between the Porte and Russia, and this last power, once freed from the struggle, could make Prussia pay dearly for the hostile attitude it had manifested during the recent events.

This fear of the Berlin Cabinet became even more acute when Catherine II, rejecting all mediation and treating with the Porte, obtaining an advantageous peace from it, the principal condition of which was a in *statu quo ante bellum.* Then later, at the Schistove Congress,

[3]The Treaty of Reichenbach, 1790 – was an agreement between Prussia and Austria to reconcile with each other for territorial gains.

the arrogant Czarina, foiling all the secret pursuits of diplomacy, and instead of undergoing foreign laws, dictated to England and Prussia herself.

Preoccupied with the future, and wishing, if need be, to preserve a courageous ally, the King of Prussia sought to reassure the diet of the good faith of his intentions, and every day brought to Poland new proofs of his friendship and kindness.

A muffled rumor had circulated about the beginning of 1791, of a step taken by the Berlin Cabinet towards the Vienna Court. It was a coalition against Poland, the result of which would have delivered to Austria a portion of Galicia, and to Prussia the cities of Thorn and Danzig, objects of his constant lust. But in this moment of crisis, it was important that Frederick William efface, by a solemn denial, the unfortunate impressions that this news was to sow in the hearts of his loyal allies; so he wrote, in March 1791, the following dispatch to his chargé d'affaires von Goltz, who provisionally replaced Lucchesini, with the formal order to communicate it to the diet: "I cannot sufficiently express to you my surprise at the fact that such a falsehood has been spread with so much assurance in Poland, and even more so that we have been able to add the slightest faith to imputations of this nature. My desire is that, without a loss of time, you must disavow and deny this news, declaring everywhere and in all the proper occasions, in the most solemn way, that it has been invented to compromise me with regard to the diet, and to excite against me the distrust of the nation. I can challenge anyone to produce the slightest proof of a coalition between the Vienna Court and me; and far from the dismemberment of Poland, I would be the first to oppose this measure; His Majesty the King and the Serene Republic of Poland can count on it, and I want them to remain convinced that I never wanted to demand any sacrifice from them; on the contrary, when I expressed the desire for an amicable settlement, I have always posited in principle that it would be convenient to both parties, and that my claims would be compensated by just and sufficient concessions. I hope, moreover, that this declaration, by reassuring the spirits, will destroy a rumor that attacks my personal character as well as my feelings towards the illustrious Polish nation. On your side, you will do further research to discover the source of such unfounded news."

This declaration of Frederick William could be sincere as to the secret treaty between Austria and Prussia, but it was less than honorable as to his intentions on Thorn and Gdansk. This question, and he had a foreboding of it, was in his eyes only a question of form.[4] It was necessary to obtain from Poland this double cession, not by an open break, but by little intrigues and diplomatic ruses. So, dreading the first overtures on this subject, he handed the indirect care of it to the ambassadors of England and Holland.

The two ministers had already been mediators at the time when it was a commercial treaty; they had already insinuated to the Foreign Committee the extent to which the commercial relations of Poland would be hindered, so long as the Prussian territory rose as a barrier between the seaports and the interior of the Kingdom; they had already advised to exchange the two isolated places for advantages and more real guarantees. They added that their respective nations were only waiting for this moment to give more extension to their relations with Polish commerce.

The Committee on Foreign Affairs, whose powers were limited, which on the one hand had to refuse to bear all the responsibility for a breakup, on the other hand was in the presence of the last law on the integrity of the territory, the Committee on Foreign Affairs avoided this double stumbling block by reporting to the diet of the course of the negotiations. The diet, after a lively discussion, instructed the com-

[4]The right of possession of the city of Danzig, separated from Poland, since the first dismemberment of the country in 1772, by all retentions of West Prussia, brought only very slight advantages to the Republic of Poland. They consisted of an annual donation of 12,000 Dutch ducats (144,000 francs), which the city gave to the King of Poland for the maintenance of his privileges: these, although extremely prejudicial to the commerce of Poland, because they rendered the merchants of the city of Gdansk, the arbitrators of the price of all the productions of this country, were always respected by the Poles, their good faith preventing them from making the slightest attack. When the Danes had realized that the King of Prussia wished to enter into negotiations with the Foreign Affairs Committee of the Constituent Diet concerning the cession of that city, they sought every means of putting obstacles in his way, persuaded that if the King of Prussia seized their city and their port, their privileges would not be respected, and would turn to the advantage of the Prussian subjects. The Magistrate of Gdansk invoked the protection of Catherine II, to secure him from Prussian domination. This cession did not take place at that time, the diet not having acceded to it; but in 1793 she made a present of the magistrate and the city of Gdansk to Frederick William, to reward him for his constant merit in executing her plans and imperial orders.

mittee, at its meeting of 1 April 1791, to inform the English and Dutch ministers of the decree which had followed this report.

This decree contained, in essence, "that the Estates having decided nothing on the cession of Danzig, they had no new orders to give to the committee; that, moreover, he could continue the negotiations begun, etc., etc."

This answer of the diet, though politely mitigated, was taken for a direct refusal by the foreign ambassadors, and from that moment they gave up their role of mediators. It was then that the Russian policy began to direct all its efforts to sour Frederick William against the Polish Diet. The St. Petersburg Court, which in Warsaw animated the spirits against Prussian greed, suggested to Berlin the elements of this same greed. The King of Denmark, on his side, advised Frederick William to get closer to Russia, and showed him in perspective what part he would have in dismembering Poland. The diet received word of these gloomy pursuits, and a declaration of the Danish prince was communicated to the cabinets of England and Prussia, on 8 March 1791.

At the same time, Polish residents to foreign courts were giving the diet the encouraging information about the storm threatening Poland.

This prospect, far from cutting down the energy of the patriots, seemed to arm them with new courage, and the diet, to answer the challenge of an concealed league, adopted with fanfare the memorable Constitution of 3 May 1791.[5] Not content to consolidate internal independence, it wished, by bringing a new dynasty to the throne, to assure its strength and its liberty abroad. By turns refused or betrayed, the diet finally cast a glance at the Saxon Elector, Frederick-Augustus. This prince, in fact, either by his family ties or by the position of his states, could increase the moral force of Poland; and his appointment to the throne was one of the principal operations of the Constituent Diet.

The King of Prussia, who still seemed to be allied in good faith, made on this occasion a new step to prove to the Estates how much he accepted the merit of their last act. He wrote the following dispatch to his minister, Count von Goltz, delivered to the committee on 17 May

[5]It should be remembered that although the author represented the King as wanting, he was a prime mover behind the May 3 Constitution.

1791: "I received your note dated May 3, with a supplement which informs me of a very important news, and it is that the Polish Diet has proclaimed the Elector of Saxony a successor to the throne, assuring the said succession to his male descendants, and in default of these to the princess his daughter, or to the future husband, who will choose in concert the Elector of Saxony and the Estates. As a result of my very real friendship with the Republic, a friendship which has always led me to consolidate its new constitution, a friendship of which I have not ceased to furnish all the proofs which depended on me, I admire and applaud the important step which the nation has just made, and which I consider essential to its happiness. The news I receive of it is all the more agreeable to me, because bonds of friendship unite me to that virtuous prince, destined to make Poland happy, and that his house has always preserved with mine a good neighborhood and the most intimate union. I am convinced that this choice of the Republic will strengthen forever the harmony and understanding that reigns between it and me. I recommend you to present, in the most solemn way, my congratulations to the King, the marshals of the diet, and all those who have contributed to such an important work."

The decree of the diet, which called the Elector of Saxony to the Polish throne, became for the Czarina a new subject of discontent. Seeing in this step only the design pronounced to escape her influence, she resolved to lose this unfortunate republic, and secretly proposed its partition to the Berlin Cabinet. But the current state of the continent prevented Frederick William from taking part for the moment in this act of iniquity.

Different ambitions then crossed in Europe, and the powers watched each other with anxiety. Jealous England saw with spite the preponderance which Catherine II was acting in the political equilibrium. Turkey took advantage of a truce to think of fresh combats, and Yusuf-Bacha vigorously pushed his preparations for war. France, occupied with its internal constitutions, was the only one who seemed indifferent to the European debates. In the midst of such a conflict, the King of Prussia, was always ready to devote himself to the strongest party, did not know what interests he should embrace. Yet the fear of a sincere alliance between Russia and Poland, an alliance which new institutions could establish on other bases, the fear still of seeing the Tsarina sacrificing for a moment her ambition to the desire of a personal revenge against the Prussian cabinet, all these motives maintained him in benevolent relations with the diet and the House of Saxony, the adoptive sovereign of Poland.

The Treaty of Pilnitz in August, and the secret conferences subsequently held in Vienna to consolidate the existence of the Polish states, can only be regarded as a derisory project and a true hoax.

It was not until the beginning of 1792 that the work of corruption was decided in a more open manner. A final peace treaty settled the differences between the Porte and Russia, to the advantage of this last power. A project of an armed coalition against the French nation was decided between the courts of Vienna and Berlin, and finally Russia, following the course of her dark pursuits, succeeded in detaching Prussia from the Polish alliance.

Once tranquil on this side and freed from the fear of an invasion on its Turkish frontiers, the Czarina proceeded to her destination, and the Muscovite troops were ordered to march on Poland.

On all sides the surest news of this coming invasion came to the diet. So, anticipating the danger calmly, it began to think of defenses. Persuaded that by concentrating all the power in one hand, it gave a more energetic impulse to the military operations with extensive rights, it conferred on the King, by a Decree of 16 April 1792. The weak Stanislas Augustus was entrusted with the direction of the armed force; he was allowed to contract a loan of several millions of florins in Holland to meet the expenses of the war. Before the adoption of this law, which was entitled: "*Preparations for War*", the King and Marshal Malachowski asked the Prussian minister what steps were necessary to take to avert such an imminent danger. The latter, exhausting himself in protest, answered them; "That it was not credible that the Russians would invade the territory of the Republic, but that it was possible that under friendly appearances, and as protectors of the discontented, they would approach its frontiers." He added that it was for the Poles to form their own destiny, and to call to them, by energetic measures, the interest of the other powers; for it seemed probable that the support which would be lent them would be in consequence of their efforts towards courageous resistance.

It was with such subtleties that the Prussian minister evaded the pressing questions of the Polish leaders, when they desired to know the opinion of his court on the Muscovite aggression. Excessively mistrustful, he refused written explanations, and when he gave verbal ones, they were all illusory and evasive.

In order to prevent the preparations for war from being regarded as an anticipated attack on the part of the Poles, it was formally communicated to all the foreign ministers residing at Warsaw, accompanied by the reasons which had decided its adoption. This step took place especially vis-à-vis the Prussian ambassador, by a note dated April 19 to force him to clearly: his response reached the diet on May 4; and on a style and tone very different from that which had dictated the preceding notes, he said; "That the King his master had received this communication as a mark of attention from the King and the Republic of Poland, but at the same time gave him the order to declare that he could not in any way how to take into consideration the plans that the diet were preparing."

On 18 May 1792, Russia published its war manifesto against Poland. According to its content, the only motive for this aggression was the offense that the Tsarina claimed to have received by a new constitution, which wrenched Poland from her protectorate.

At the very moment when this document was known in Warsaw, the Estates sent it by courier to the Berlin Cabinet demanding armed assistance from it, in accordance with the defensive alliance treaty concluded on 29 March 1790. They explained that the Muscovite troops having already violated their territory, the assistance which they had the right to expect from their allies was to be prompt and efficacious.

The Prussian minister, Jerome Lucchesini, replied to this request with a provisional note in which he declared that while awaiting the subsequent orders of his court, with regard to the request which the Estates had addressed to him, he thought he ought to remind them of the contents of his reply of 4 May, as well as the verbal declarations renewed by him to the Chancellor, to the marshals of the Diet and to the members of the Supervisory Board.[6] Then, adding to this verbiage

[6]The verbal declarations that Lucchesini quotes in this place, as proof of the virtue of his master, and which, however, he did not think proper to present in writing, were stated in these terms: "I have orders, on behalf of my court, to

his personal treachery, he ended by saying that all these steps, perfectly in conformity with the official language, which he had held since his return from Schistow to Warsaw, and particularly after the revolution effected on 3 May 1791, were a new proof of the acknowledged probity of the King of Prussia, who did not wish the Polish nation to be unaware of his feelings towards it and its requests, especially in the critical state in which it was."

In this interval, and the very next day after the war manifesto, the Russian troops under the command of Generals Kakhovsky and Krechetnikv[7] crossed the frontier, and were in front of the Polish army, commanded by Prince Joseph Poniatowski. Too confident in the energy of Stanislas Augustus, the diet adjourned on 29 May 1792.[8] For their part, the partisans of the King, weak men, or disloyal traitors, seemed to believe it impossible that Frederick William could break the faith of treaties and seemed to have less faith in their own strength than on the help of a refractory ally.

As a result, Ignacy Potocki was sent to Berlin: it was presumed that, when he reminded the King of Prussia of all the friendly declarations with which he had overwhelmed the diet, the treaty of union which he had signed, all the successive steps which he taken in favor of the Republic, either at the court of Vienna or at that of St. Petersburg, the shame of an odious defection would be stronger in his eyes than the secret advantages that he expected, and he would come back to openly support the threatened states. But these arguments, so powerful, could do nothing to sway Frederick William; the falsehoods, in spite of all the statements to the contrary, were used to justified the conduct of Lucchesini, and Potocki carried away only from Berlin the certainty that the sovereign was no better than the minister.

Amongst those whose name now belongs to history was Krakow's nuncio, Stanislas Soltyk, who pronounced in the last session of the memorable Constituent Diet, one of those prophetic discourses, in

declare that the King, my master, has in no way contributed to the constitution of May 3, and that if the patriotic party wished to defend it by the force of friends, the King would not think himself obliged to help it under the covenant treaty."

[7]Mikhail Kakhovsky (1734-1800) and Mikhail Krechetnikov (1729-1793)

[8]The Polish patriots who trembled over the future fate of their country, and who dreaded the duplicity of Stanislas Augustus, did not disguise their fears from the nation and the King himself.

which each sentence was as much the speaker's, as he debased him whom he addressed, and who had neither the spirit nor the courage to hear and follow him.

While the indecisive and confident Polish government turned its hopes on Prussia, Stanislaus Augustus secretly negotiated with St. Petersburg. In his eyes, it was not a question of the integrity of the territory, nor of the independence of the Republic;[9] his narrow views and his apathetic selfishness did not go that far; he saw only his favorite toy, his crown, and the whole question was reduced to him losing it or preserving it. The nation alone was great and worthy of better leaders. At the first news of Muscovite aggression, everyone that could take up arms arose spontaneously; every day the treasury received patriotic gifts in gold and silver; some provided horses, others war ammunition, some weapons, some fully equipped companies; finally, a war of enthusiasm was about to begin, if the phantom of the King who presided over the destinies of Poland had not opposed this generous impulse to his cold irresolution. Pressed by all the patriots to go in person to the army, he reassured them by saying to them that it was not on Poland that Catherine II was to bring down her vengeance, but on Frederick William, whose name she had sworn to punish; that she would renounce war from the day when she would see the nation disposed to end everything amicably; that besides, it was better to fight with the pen than with the sword. Sometimes, however, in order to deceive the people, he seemed to be busy with the preparations for his departure, and while he was lowering himself to this unworthy comedy, he was dealing St. Petersburg, and gave the Polish troops the order to retreat.

As a result of this cowardly system, the Russians advanced to the gates of Warsaw, the King received a letter from the Tsarina in which she declared loudly that she would not forgive him for having deceived her hopes. He met with the group of faithful Poles who, had sworn at Targowica to annihilate the Constitution of 3 May under his protection."

Stanislas, still possessed with the fear of losing his crown, was ready to undergo all kinds of insults to preserve it, began by turning

---

[9]Time has proved kinder to Stanislaw Augustus, who was a patriot, but weak and viewed the war against Russia as a bloodshed the nation could not afford and though he could negotiate with Catherine to preserve Poland. He was unfortunately proved wrong and lacked the will to stand up to opposition.

against the national liberty of the powers which the diet had attributed to him for a better use. Under the pretext of an armistice, he gave the army, already fatigued, the order to lay down its arms, and the army, thinking to serve the public cause, obeyed without distrust.

The Russians entered Warsaw as friends and allies, and Stanislaus Augustus breathed more freely among the foreign satellites. To make matters worse, he then disavowed the Constitution which he had sworn fidelity, and to affix his royal hand while at the same time ordered the prosecution of the authors of the Pact of 3 May. Once the Russians were masters of the capital, they distributed all civil and military offices to their lackeys; and that portion of generous citizens whom Frederick William had betrayed and whom Stanislaus Augustus had sold or proscribed, had no choice but between prison in Siberia and exile under a foreign sky.

Some, however, hidden in the depths of the provinces, faced by a thousand perils, swore to watch over the regeneration of their country, while the many exiles appealed to all of Europe for the help of an indignantly deceived nation.

Driven by various fortunes, these generous proscribed individuals put themselves under the protection of one of the monarchical governments, the others under that of free governments, and in spite of this marked contrast, Catherine II knew, by the means of her secret agents, how to reach them all. Those who had taken refuge in Germany were accused of being partisans and propagators of the so-called system of the Jacobins in Europe, and those who lived under free governments were soon taxed and convicted of feudal and anti-constitutional principles. Thus, by opposing motives, they sought to ruin in European opinion the martyrs of one and the same cause, and they wished to extol beforehand the name of a people, whom it was later to annihilate.

In such a critical circumstance, a serious fault, committed by the marshals of the Diet Malachowski and Sapieha, can only with difficulty be excused in the eyes of posterity. Respected as they were for their virtue and devotion to their country, the whole of Poland had their eyes on them, and their example would have been followed by the whole nation. From the moment when these marshals realized that Stanislaus Augustus was deserting the Polish cause to meet with the

Targowicans, they had the right and were even obliged to declare the diet permanent. If they had followed this course, if, in concert with the diet, they had put themselves at the head of the army, the safety of the country was not desperate, and Poland would become herself once again. On the one hand, this imposing step, by showing the people their true armed representatives against oppressors, would have made every citizen a hero ready to sacrifice everything for the maintenance of his liberties. On the other side, the Army, containing sixty thousand men, lacked nothing and was neither discouraged nor beaten.

Nothing was easier than to increase its numerical strength, and if the elected representatives of the nation had walked at its head, all the funds would have been found to pay for it and maintain it. No doubt the generals who commanded it were not very experienced, but they were all full of bravery, patriotic devotion, and that military genius so natural to the Poles. Moreover, the superior officers, and even those who were supposed to be most devoted to the King, such as Joseph Poniatowski, Michel Wielhorski and Stanislaw Mokronoski, would not have hesitated to break the will of the monarch to serve the cause. If the marshals of the diet had gone to the Army. But when these remarkable citizens were seen to remain in utter inaction, instead of summoning the diet, it was learned that they had left Poland, later the King acceded to the Targowica plot, and through this weakness, put the country and the army at the disposal of the Russians, what could the military forces do when isolated from all civil support? The treasury, the stores, the arsenal, everything was in the hands of the King! The Army was ordered to cease hostilities, to return to cantonments and to join the shameful Targowica Confederation. Several generals and officers, whose positions were independent, resigned; the others were forced to submit to circumstances, expecting only a favorable opportunity to wash the stain printed in the name of Poland in the eyes of Europe.

CHAPTER TWO

The Immobility of Austria. — New Russian Intrigues with the Berlin Cabinet. — The Partition of Poland is Decided. — March of the Prussian Armies. — Manifesto. — Conduct of Russia. — Protests and the Universals of the So-Called Targowica Confederation. — Its Dissolution. — Convocation of the Grodno Diet. — Its Illegal Operations under the Influence of the Russian Bayonets. — The Cession vis-à-vis Russia are Sanctioned by the Diet. — The Same Demands from the King of Prussia. — Stormy Debates. — It is Ended By Force. — Indignation of the Polish People. — Symptoms of a General Uprising

Calmly in the midst of these events, Austria kept a passive role. Emperor Leopold, successor of his brother Joseph II, having taken the reins of government in stormy circumstances, exhibited both character and principles towards a peaceful system. A friend of the status quo, he had always maintained friendly relations with the Berlin Court, and the special affection he had for Bischofswerder, a favorite of the King of Prussia, while the common friendship of the two princes for the Elector of Saxony, contributed to this good harmony.

It has been seen above that, after the Pilnitz Congress, the object of which was to assemble Prussia and Austria against the French Republic, secret conferences were held at Vienna between the plenipotentiaries of the two powers. It seems certain that it was necessary to stipulate, by an additional article to the congress, that the independence and free constitution of Poland should be frankly recognized. The two courts also undertook not to allow the princes of their blood to enter into a marriage with the Infanta of Poland, daughter of the

Elector of Saxony. A special clause was to be reached later on this marriage, and finally it was promised to make all the necessary steps with Catherine II to obtain her consent to this order of things.

But the untimely death of the Emperor, which occurred in 1 March 1792, completely changed the face of affairs, and this secret treaty, so favorable to Poland, remained without execution, and followed Leopold to his grave.

Influenced by his ministry, the new Emperor Francis II, a novice and still young, forgot his true interests, and allowed himself to be circumvented by the skillful policy of the St. Petersburg Cabinet. From that moment everything conspired against Poland. In Berlin the conciliatory councils of Bischofswerder had given way to the interventionist views of Hertzberg; at Vienna, Leopold's prudent conduct remained without imitators, and Russia, armed with the tacit consent of Prussia, marched towards her plans of conquest. It was in the midst of such circumstances that Catherine II was officially asked to declare whether she acceded to the Treaty of Vienna. The answer was easy to predict. The Tsarina, while offering the two interested parties a special alliance, expressed her regret at not being able to adhere to all the agreements between them, because of the secret article which concerned Poland.

At the same time, agents renewed bribery with the Berlin Cabinet in the same manner that the Danish Court had made there at another time. Frederick William exaggerated the advantages he would derive from the dismemberment of the Republic; under his eyes, a portion of this territory would be pass to him; it even went so far as to require of him only passive immobility until the full completion of this work of iniquity.

Although the Poles already had sufficient grounds to believe that the King of Prussia was guilty of these accusation, especially since his responses to the Muscovite aggression, all suspicions were changed to certainty when Russian troops, which the Czarina garrisoned in the States of the Republic, in the palatinates of Great Poland, as these lands were allocated by her to Frederick William, in fulfillment of her promises.

However, as the war against the French nation, organized at the same time between the allied courts, seemed to promise them a happy and speedy success, they postponed their final plans on Poland until the triumph of this new league would put it in position to dictate laws to Europe. It was, indeed, at this moment when Stanislaus, joined to the Targowica Confederation, which sacrificed the liberties of Poland to the Russians, while numerous armies, united against the French Republic, were advancing rapidly towards the frontiers of Poland.[1]

The whole universe knows the triumphs of Republican France. A moment of setback was avenged by a series of triumphs. Informed of these first failures, the Prussian ministry then wished, by a cruel compensation, to gain territorial compensation, on the side of Poland, for what it lost as men on the side of France.

Thus, now in agreement on the dismemberment of Poland, Prussia and Russia were concerting together to draw in Emperor Francis II. They thus seized, in order to declare their plans to the Vienna Court, the moment when marked reverses, urgent needs, and the necessity of a support to continue the war with France, did not allow Austria to refuse an assent that was formally requested.

In spite of himself and against his own interests, the Emperor of Germany was obliged to bring himself into the ambitious plans of Catherine and Frederick William; thus, he would remain a motionless spectator of this spoliation by violence.

Be that as it may, as the next invasion of Prussian armies into Greater Poland began to be generally known, King Stanislaus and the Targowica traitors went everywhere, denying this news full of a blind enthusiasm for Catherine II. Closed to reality, they could not persuade themselves that she never consented to share with Frederick William that domination which she could retain for herself alone. The Russians themselves, then scattered throughout Poland, were so convinced of the generous sentiments of their august mistress that they did not wish to believe the aggression of the King of Prussia.

The Chancellor of the Polish Crown, Hyacinth Malachowski, as Head of the Department of Foreign Affairs, was ordered to ask the Prussian Minister whether the King's troops, under his command were there to really take part in the dismemberment of Great Poland. The minister's response was completely negative.

[1]The situation is much more complicated than the author indicates. While the army commanders asked him to join them in the Ukraine to fight the Russian invasion, letters indicate he was more worried about bloodshed and thought he could preserve what was left of the nation be acquiescing to the rebels. In reality Russian troops were the immediate concern of the Polish patriots.

In fact, nothing was yet decided in a definitive way: negotiations were underway in St. Petersburg on the extent of the territory to be invaded, and on the portion that would be included in the sharing parties, and it was very essential for Prussia to disguise, until the appointed moment, her last treachery. What was not decided, moreover, was regarding the substance of this question, to which Frederick William was committed. He fully consented to the dismemberment of the Republic, he did not quibble over the mode of partition, nor over the extent of the land to be apportioned, but he wished to conceal this dishonest act by a few high political reasons, and to justify this scandalous spoliation from the eyes of Europe.

The blind submission of Stanislaus Augustus, the Targowica Confederates and their adherents, all slaves of Russia, could not be considered as rebellious subjects. All that remained to be done was to put false suspicions in place of real plots. People sought out enemies everywhere – people were spied on in private societies, the people were spied on, their sadness was interpreted, their regrets were intended, the complaints against the vexations of the Russian armies, the apprehension of the same torments on the part of the Prussian troops, the mutual consolations between the oppressed citizens, their wishes for the triumph of the French troops, everything, even the tears of the Polish nation, provided material for this denunciation. They needed an excuse that could proceed the invading armies, and these pretexts, this excuse, were soon found, so we read in an absurd and diffused manifesto: that the Courts of Berlin and St. Petersburg could not, without danger to their own states, tolerate the present institutions of Poland; they had deep roots in the spirit and principles of French democracy; that the emissaries of the Parisian Jacobins found assistance and protection in this group; that several popular societies has already been formed and infected with these perverse maxims; that finally this doctrine, dangerous under a monarchical regime, had spread more particularly in Greater Poland, and that there was an immense number of zealots and apostles of this false patriotism.

This is the abridgment of the great motives alleged in the declaration that the Prussian Minister made public on 16 January 1793, at the moment when their troops, under the leadership of General Möllendorf, invaded Polish territory to rob it of its most beautiful provinces.

What is still to be remarked in this statement is that, to conceal the reasons for his aggression, the Berlin Court called it a precautionary measure, in order, it was said, "to guarantee its neighboring provinces from the contagion of the French maxims, to silence the ill-intentioned who excited movements and disorders, to restore and maintain public tranquility, and to provide effective protection to well-intentioned subjects."

This Declaration of 16 January was followed by a second, dated 24 February, concerning the invasion of the port and city of Danzig, which the King of Prussia called a center of Jacobinism. The delay in publishing this second manifesto resulted from England's refusal to assent. A striking difference, which exists between these two declarations of 16 January and 24 February, is that, in the first, the King of Prussia speaks only of the tacit consent of the Emperor Francis II, and that in the other, he positively declares that he has agreed upon Danzig with the powers having a common interest.

In the midst of this contest of circumstances which, in the eyes of the Polish nation, characterized the avid efforts of the neighboring powers, the insinuating Sievers[2] , the new Russian ambassador, arrived from St. Petersburg at Grodno. Questioned by the chiefs of the Confederation of Targowica as to the probable result of the entry of the Prussian troops into Poland, and the intentions of the magnanimous Catherine II, he feigned surprise, and only replied that he was ignorant of the views of Frederick William. Consulted since on the measures to be taken to repel this aggression, he replied that, as a result of the confidence that all the confederates of Targowica had put in the greatness of the soul of his august mistress, a confidence which she deserved in every respect. It seemed to him that no hostile step was to be taken without having first consulted it herself. This advice, of course, concealed an ulterior motive: it only seduced the men sold to the Tsarina, and remained without effect on the healthy part of the nation. From this moment discontent became general, and people spoke loudly against the traitors who had trafficked national liberties, and who, as servants of Russia, had become tyrants of Poland. But the removal of the Targowica Confederation was not yet in the plans of the

[2]Jacob Johan Graf von Sievers (1731 – 1808) a Russian diplomat from the German nobility.

Tsarina. To prevent the events which might have hastened his downfall when he was still in need of help, Sievers suggested to his various allies the idea of preparing some defenses, and this idea, while flattering their self-esteem. served them as a sort of safeguard against general indignation.

Accordingly, they published a protest against the Prussian invasion 3 February 1793. This act, signed by the so-called "true Polish republicans", contained a satire of the Constitution of 3 May, a eulogy to Catherine II, the apology for their own rebellion, and finally hymns of praise to the Russian troops in the first part. In the second part, all the remonstrances made to the King of Prussia before his invasion were recounted; the violence committed by his troops at the moment of their invasion was made known, and protesting a boundless confidence in the justice of Frederick William, and in the generosity of Catherine II, were they shouted against any usurpation of Polish territory: finally, it solemnly declared that the Targowica Confederation had in no way participated in the conventions which could lead to the dismemberment of the country, that all those who were part of it were prepared to defend, at the very risk of their lives, the honor, independence and national integrity of Poland

During this period, the most contradictory arguments came in a crowd: beside bitter complaints against violence was the apology of its authors; using the most servile meanness, using the words of liberty and glory.

Not content with publishing and spreading this protest, the Targowicans drafted universals orders to summon the *arrière-ban général*[3] of the nobility (*pospolite ruszenie*) against the attacks of the King of Prussia. In making such a demonstration, they wished not only to give themselves an air of importance, but also to please the secret wishes of Russia, which they always supposed to oppose the designs of Frederick William. But their error on this point did not last long. At the first appearance of the dissention, Sievers formally declared to them that this step was not the intentions of his sovereign. Consequently, the Russian and Prussian troops, were distributed to the various districts of Poland, were ordered to stand ready to march against those who dared to express views hostile to the plans of the two Allied Courts.

[3]Translator: The arrière-ban général was a general summons, normally by the King, of his nobility to arms.

Despite the threatening attitude of the foreign troops, not all the citizens were equally intimidated, and in several districts, they prepared for a resistance. A single spark which sprang up on the side of Prussia could spread the fire to the Muscovite frontiers. This is why Sievers energetically declared to Targowica's chiefs that they had to neutralize the effect of their declarations for the convocation of the arrière-ban of the nobility. Always slaves of Russian influence, they immediately obeyed, and, in an address published on 22 February 1793, they said in essence "that there remained no other hope for the Republic than the magnanimity of the great Catherine, and if the Poles would not listen to her advice, they would themselves cause the ruin of the state. Consequently, they continued, "in the name of the country which is dear to us all, we call up the citizens who live in the provinces not to form premature assemblies, capable of advancing the fall of the Republic. One will always be in time to meet for the common defense, when an express order from the National Confederation will indicate that the favorable moment has finally arrived."[4]

This ignominious address, sent to the districts, opened the eyes of the most blinded, and henceforth every Pole knew in what scale he should weigh friendship and foreign protection.

To be partially insulted against armed satellites, numerous and always on their guard, would have been to march to certain death, and to compromise the success of the general conspiracy which was secretly brewing all over Poland. Besides, the King's party and the Targowican chiefs still had in their hands all the national resources and the direction of political affairs. And yet, in spite of so many obstacles, this sacred love of the country, which a reverse can tame, but which it cannot extinguish, that sacred fire which the Pole has kept pure in the midst of his calamities, all wore the oppressed patriots towards an uprising against their dominators.

The indignation against the Targowica Confederation was at its height. Odious even to their old partisans, the leaders of this line had become the object of public execration, so much so that the Russians thought it their duty to separate their cause from theirs. Thus, the vile slaves who had served as a steppingstone for the enslavement of Poland, were themselves victims of their betrayal, and Russia un-

[4]It was common for regional councils to form local "confederations"

ashamedly broke the instrument which had so completely served her projects. Moreover, to add to this abandonment the bloodiest irony, she recognized them as traitors to the country only because they had wanted or claimed to want to oppose the Prussian aggression.

To achieve this end, more precise orders were sent from St. Petersburg which authorized Sievers to confer with the Prussian minister after the partition of Poland. When they had agreed, the two ambassadors simultaneously presented, to the Confederates of Targowica at Grodno, on 9 April 1793 a declaration that specified the destiny which had been prepared for Poland.

This declaration was so harsh, so outrageous, that it opened the eyes even to the Targowicans.

Unable to give credence to what was happening and believing that the Russian ministers were acting without Catherine's orders, they sent one of them, Stanislas Felix Potocki, to the St. Petersberg Court to ask for clemency from the Tsarina, to remove the calamities of which they were the first cause from their country; but it seemed to him that the time for prayers had passed, and that the presence of a traitor was odious even to those who had profited by his treason.

Reviled in Poland, despised in St. Petersburg, Potocki went to hide his shame in foreign lands.

Francis Xavier Branacki, whose wife was a niece of Potemkin, lost the name of a Polish citizen, was proud of having managed to arrange a Russian alliance, and henceforth limited his ambition to the honor of having married a lady from Catherine's court.

Sévérin Rzewuski emigrated to Galicia, looking for an asylum against the indignation of his compatriots.[5]

Thus, ended the three leaders of the anti-national league. A memorable example of this fatality that pursues perjury, and which sooner or later brings down on its head the same thunder that it had called upon the others. Be that as it may, the dispersion of the Targowicans only hastened the success of Catherine II. Absolute power returned to the hands of her former favorite, Stanislaw Augustus, and

[5]The judgment of contemporaries is the one upon which posterity supports this. Although culpable, the acts of Potocki and Branacki could never be justified by any official or public step, we cannot however refrain from reporting here the protest of Rzewuski, a protest which his conscience wrested from him, which he wrote on 17 April, and which he brought to the acts of Grodno on 22 April 1793.

her choice of subordinate agents, was restored to the sagacity of his minister Sievers. They were the two brothers Joseph and Simon Kossakowski, one the Bishop of Livonia, and the other the so-called Grand General of Lithuania, dressed in a Russian uniform[6], Joseph Ankwicz and Peter of Alkantara Ozarowski, all eager for money, distinctions, and jobs. They squandered their own property by means as shameful as those they had used to acquire them, insatiable and always destitute, they had sold themselves to Russia.

These were the instruments of disgrace that helped the two powers to complete their last infamy; these are the names that history must submit to the indignation of posterity: without them perhaps, the attempt to dismemberment the country could never have been accomplished, for Poland later proved that she knew what to do when she was guided on the road of honor and independence.

The Courts of St. Petersburg and Berlin, desiring, in their declaration of April 9th, to preserve, as far as possible, the appropriate legal forms, expressed the desire to see a diet be summoned which would legitimize their invasion. But this kind of moral violence was more difficult to impose on the nation than the physical violence of which it was the victim; and the Republic, still proud in its misfortune, had not conceived the idea that its oppression could be legalized.

In fact, forming a diet of deputies appointed by the invaded provinces, was tainting its acts which in fact nullified it; for how can one suppose that people whom Russia treated as slaves would declare that they had freely and voluntarily become it subjects? And, on the other hand, would the citizens of the country that Poland still possessed want to arrogate to themselves, by a public act, the right to sold or sell their brothers?

But the Russian and Prussian ministers were not afraid of any such niceties. Unable to make themselves masters to the opposition of the Polish people, they succeeded in evading it. From the moment when the Russian troops were quartered in the districts had stopped the effect of the levee and suppressed the attempts of the patriots, they collected all the people without scruples, filled the dietines (prepara-

[6]The illustrious citizen Michel Kazimirz Orginski, Grand General of Lithuania, under whose persecution so many victims of patriotism fell, had left the ministry a few months before the insolence of Simon Kossakowski dared to claim one of the highest magistracies of the Republic.

tory assemblies), and thus managed to compose a diet, which though illegal, was entirely devoted to them.

However, although the general choice of the members who were part of it was anti-national, it met, despite the precautions of the Russians, with several honorable citizens who protested loudly against all the violence that this assembly sought to sanction. In the weak opposition party that arose within it, Thadeus Skarzynski the Nuncio of Lomza, Denis Mikorski, the Nuncio of Wyszogrod, Jean Krasnodembski, the Nuncio of Liw, Joseph Kimbar, the Nuncio of Upita, Antoine Karski, Nuncio of Plock, Ignace Goslawski, Nuncio of Sandomir, Simon Szydlowski, Nuncio of Ciéchanow, André Ciemniewski, the Nuncio of Rozan, Vincent Galenzowski, the Nuncio of Lublin, Grelawski, the Nuncio of Sandomir, Ignatius Plichta the Nuncio of Sochaezew, Louis Chodzko, the Nuncio of Oszmiana , and others; but their voices were stifled by the vociferations of a bought majority, and the illegal act, under the name of a treaty of cession, was signed at Grodno on 22 July 1793, by a deputation appointed for that purpose.[7]

After declaring that he would not cooperate with the dismemberment of Poland, the king adhered to it, advised in his tearful style to satisfy the wishes of Russia, and to subscribe to the loss of a part to save the rest. The Kossakowski brothers, on their side, circulated in the assembly and in particular societies, that the submission of the dictates to the wishes of Catherine II would entail the rapprochement of her negotiations with the Berlin Cabinet, and that by means of this condescending with Russia, the Republic would be reassured against the fear of a new sacrifice vis-à-vis Prussia.

Other Russian agents were also spreading encouraging noises. They said that the act of approbation asked of the diet would only serve the Tsarina as a pretext for seducing the King of Prussia by an appearance of hostile proceedings against the Polish states, but that the Empress would not only restore that which she was claiming to usurp, but that she was only waiting for this moment to take Frederick William off guard, and to avenge, at last, his participation in the last

[7]The talent of eloquence united with the sublime feelings of civic courage, is the most beautiful glory that a citizen can acquire. The illustrious Kimbar obtained this double triumph. The speech he gave and which was supported by his virtuous colleagues at the meeting of 17 July, is one of the beautiful models that can be offered to present and future generations! Poles, let us never forget those memorable days when brave men made the voice of truth heard!

changes that had occurred in the Republic, during the constitutional diet.

It was sometimes by such conduct, sometimes by open threats, that some were encouraged, and others intimidated; and it was with the aid of a seductive or violent influence that the so-called Treaty of Cession was signed.

This first sacrifice was scarcely in favor of Russia, as the Prussian minister presented the same request to the diet, insisting that the same deputation should be authorized, or that another should be designated with all power to treat with him.

The discussion about this new requirement brought into play the tactics of the allied courts. Even in the midst of this corrupt assembly, a murmur of dread greeted this overwhelming proposition. Nonetheless, the vote was taken to decide whether the deputation demanded by the King of Prussia should be named or not. It was chance that on that day the number of votes for the negative was equal to that in the affirmative. Such an incident sent back to the King the faculty of deciding the question, and it was resolved in favor of Prussia. Thus, fate, in this remarkable circumstance, decided that Stanislas Augustus would be not only an unhappy prince, but also a guilty prince.

However, this new deputation did not find among the diet as obedient and servile as that which had regulated Russian interests. But Sievers and Buchholtz managed to iron out all the difficulties. The first, having surrounded the castle, where the assembly was held, threatened to massacre them all, without exception, if, on the same day (2 September), they did not authorize the deputation to sign definitively. The cession treaty in favor of Frederick William.

In spite of these haughty threats, some members of the diet, protesting against all violence, declared that they would vote only when they could do so freely, but Sievers, outraged by this noble resistance, had them arrested, and left Grodno in the custody of his Cossacks.

It was in such a state of oppression and servitude that the Diet was questioned as to its agreement to the decree authorizing the deputation to conclude the agreement with the King of Prussia. This decree gave it the right to sign, without any restriction, the Treaty of Cession and it is in this terrible moment that this assembly replied by a gloomy silence. Joseph Ankwicz, Nuncio of Krakow, and Stanislas Bielinski,

Marshal of the Diet, interpreting this silence as unanimous consent, signed the decree with the deputies appointed for this purpose.[8]

While the King of Poland and a corrupt diet, delivered the destiny of their country to the foreign powers, the citizens in the provinces cultivated all the hatred that the sight of their oppressors can inspire in the oppressed. Plans of vengeance, unanimous plots, all moved in secret and prepared in the future this great spectacle of an invaded people who shook their chains and used them like a weapon against its jailers.

Unfortunately, the moment of the rising had not yet arrived, and it was feared that a partial movement, by awakening the foreign protectorates, would not afford them the means of stifling in its birth the general movement which was in preparation.

Frank and loyal, the Poles did little to conceal their hatred and plans for revenge. Some threatening remarks, some popular brawls, the fruits of this excitement were acts without thought, which gave the Russians some suspicions about the storm that threatened them. Struck with a secret foreboding, they forced the Diet of Grodno, before closing its doors, to reduce the army of the Republic to between twelve thousand to fifteen thousand men. They alleged that Russia had undertaken to defend, with her own forces, the portion of the territory that remained of Poland, and that this clause had been stipulated in a treaty of alliance concluded separately with the diet, the 14 October 1793.

This so-called treaty of alliance, considered in its details and as a whole, it was only considered a fraudulent pact to which the nation had been forced to consent. The same is true of this gathering of men without a warrant, of people without mandate, pretended nuncios to the Diet of Grodno, who had appropriated for themselves the right of disposing, in favor of Catherine II, an inalienable territory. But as the Allied Powers had unscrupulously profiled their baseness, they also knew how to use all the arms it put in their hands. This treaty of alliance, which we have just quoted, delivered protection of the internal administration to Russia as well as foreign affairs, the right to declare war or grant peace, finally all the powers of an absolute despot, and

[8]Having quoted from Kimbar's energetic speech, we cannot help but mention Goslawski's statement at the meeting of 6 September, in relation to the three main leaders of the Targowica plot.

the Tsarina left none of her rights without execution.

With the reduction of the Army and by the cantonments which were given to it, they sought to isolate it from the nation; by appointing Russian partisans to all the diplomatic and administrative, civil, and military places, the points of support which it could have found at the Court of Stanislas were removed from the general insurrection.

Finally, on 29 November 1793, unhappy overlord was terminated which had so outrageously compromised the inviolability of the laws and the independence of the nation. So many misfortunes had weighed upon Poland, so many successive outrages had struck her, that her oppressors thought they had consumed their entire work; they persuaded themselves that, henceforth, maintained by a tussle, she would resign herself to the role imposed upon her, and suffer, without a word, that her name should be stricken from the European map.

But far from being conquered by misfortune, far from bowing under the yoke of treason, the Poles only breathed revenge and liberty; forgetting all their internal dissensions, and united for the same cause, they now thought only of the honor of their country. The nobles, whom Frederick William had deceived and whom Catherine had enslaved, seeing themselves betrayed by the unworthy Stanislaus Augustus, at last found the source of all their misfortunes. They saw that a mistrust of Poland's own strength had lost the Republic, and that it would still be standing if it had counted on the support of its children rather than on foreign help. Impatient to avenge so much outrage, this time they addressed a more active and more faithful power, it was to the inhabitants of the cities and the countryside. To excite their enthusiasm even more, they renounced the aristocratic arrogance which was another burden for slaves, and, uttering loud cries of an equal liberty for all, they caused the heart of a generous people to vibrate in its most sensitive strings. It was then beautiful, it was great to see this nation, which had believed itself to be crushed forever, to be reborn from its own ashes, to become free and proud again, and to wash in the blood of its oppressors the shame of their first setbacks.

CHAPTER THREE

Vice-Brigadier Dąbrowski. – His Projects. – Symptoms of the Insurrection. – Secret League. – Kosciuszko is Named Generalissimo. – He Enters Krakow. – His Addresses to the Nation. – Memorable Manifesto to the Powers. – Battle of Raclawice. – Revolution at Warsaw. – The Dzislynski Regiment is Covered with Glory. – Establishment of a Provisional government in this Capital. – The Revolution in Lithuania. – Delivery of Vilna. – Iasinski. – Junction of the Army of the Ukraine. – Punishment of Traitors to the Homeland. – Establishment of the Supreme National Council. – Kosciuszko Pursues the Russians. – Battle of Szezekociny. – The Polish Army Withdraws on Warsaw. – Battle of Chelm. – Zajączek. – Capture of Krakow. – Popular Fury. – Siege of Warsaw by the King of Prussia. – Intrepidity of the Garrison. – Insurrection in Great Poland. – The King of Prussia Raises the Siege. – Reverse in Lithuania. – Capture of Vilna. – Battle of Macielowice. – Kosciuszko is Captured. – Assault on Praga. – Capitulation of Warsaw. – Dąbrowski. – Polish Refugees in Paris and Venice. – Their Efforts to Interest the Powers in the Fate of Poland. – Oginski is Sent to Constantinople.

Although Poland, lost her civilian life, they still had an army. At the beginning of the year 1793, before the Prussian declaration announced its intention to militarily occupy Great Poland, the province still had four-thousand men under arms, commanded by General Arnold Byszewski. This general had a written order from King Stanislaus Augustus, which enjoined him to stand on the defensive, and to guard himself from a surprise on the part of the Prussian troops.

Vice-Brigadier Jan-Henryk Dąbrowski, who was then part of General Byszewski's staff, was completely familiar with these details. A complete military genius, and having no other motive than national honor, he saw the fate of what was being prepared for his country with indignation.

At the news of the first invasion, unwilling to procrastinate when it was necessary to act, he proposed moving by forced marches with the whole Polish division towards Warsaw, to make himself master of the arsenal, then to move against the Prussians, and attack them. But this project failed in the face of the betrayal of Gorzynski, Adjutant-General of Stanislas-Augustus, and the weakness of Byszewski. It was delayed, and shortly thereafter the Polish division was ordered to return to the Palatinate of Sandomir, where it was scattered and deprived of communications.

Untiring in his devotion, the Vice-Brigadier Dąbrowski was not put off by this first failure. In concert with General Wodzicki[1], he began a new project, which the most illustrious captain would not have disavowed. It was a plan to gather what remained of the Polish army together, to march with it towards the frontiers of France, and, falling on the rear of the Prussian armies, to make a junction with the Republican troops. During this time, General Kosciuszko and the Marshals of the Constituent Diet Malachowski and Sapieha unexpectedly returned to Poland, and, raising the nation en masse, which they would threaten Prussia on its double frontiers have by a powerful diversion.

This project was practicable; it was even partly initiated, when the troops stationed in the area of Chelm, in the Palatinate of Lublin, and those stationed in the Ukraine were rallied by bold steps to the armies of Generalissimo Kosciuszko; but everyone was then terrified of Dąbrowski's bold plans; they were confronted with cold calculations and timid observations, and events soon took away all possibility of executing them.

After the Diet of Grodno, it was decided that the Polish and Lithuanian Army should be reduced to fifteen and distributed among the remaining Palatinates of the Republic. They also allowed the Muscovite troops to put garrisons in all the fortresses. All that remained

[1]Stansław Wodzicki (1764-1843)

to the national troops was defensive cantonments, and measures were taken to keep them surrounded by enemy detachments, which seemed to watch their slightest movements.

It was in the face of such circumstances, in the midst of this armed surveillance, that the great drama of a short insurrection broke out over Poland; it was then that fate enabled an illustrious people to distinguish their downfall with heroic devotion, and to prove to the whole world that they were worthy to live in their liberty since they knew how to die for it.

The patience of the nation, driven to extremity by the vexations of Russia, was beginning to grow tired of this foreign domination. The Proconsul Igelström[2], General Minister of the Czarina, seemed determined every day to make the Muscovite yoke harder and its chains more intolerable. It was in a moment of exasperation that the bravest citizens of Warsaw met in a patriotic league and sent some of the faithful to probe the disposition of the national army. The army received their messages by messengers, and all the opinions being found uniform, the patriots, in their nocturnal conferences, proclaimed as head of the association the Citizen Thaddeus Kosciuszko. In these conferences, where the most perfect equality knew distinctions only of those of honor and patriotism, the Citizens Jan Kilinski, shoemaker, Joseph Sierakowski, butcher, and Andre Kapostas, banker, deserve special mention.

Kosciuszko, was in Saxony at that time, was secretly invited to come to Poland. He made his way to the frontiers of the Republic, with General Zajączek. The latter even continued on to Warsaw, in order to consult with the conspiratorial patriots. As for Kosciuszko, his presence on the frontiers was rumored, and having awakened the foreign countries, he thought it more prudent to develop his plans, and took the road to Italy. But the despotism of Igelström was increased, and the exasperation of the Polish people was pushed to the extreme, the leader of the conspiracy had suddenly circle around, and so in the early days of March, 1794, Brigadier of Cavalry Antoine Madalinski raised the flag of independence in his cantonment on the Bug, and marched boldly to Krakow, which Kosciuszko entered during the night of 23/24 March.

---

[2]Count Otto Igelström (1737-1823) Russian General and politician.

Proclaimed Generalissimo of the Armies of Poland and Lithuania, this illustrious citizen was given dictatorial and boundless power, by the act of independence, which the inhabitants of Krakow signed on 24 March 1794. That same day the Generalissimo made an address to the Army, to the nation, and issued a proclamation to Polish women, always famous for their patriotism. He sent manifestos to the Courts of Denmark, Sweden, England, to the French government, to that of the United States of America, and even to the Court in Vienna, assuming that, since Austria had not taken any active part in the second dismemberment of Poland, it could be regarded as differently to the intrigues of Russian and Prussian.

This manifesto, which even day is still exciting, offers in its expressions something so noble that it must be preserved as a historical monument.[3]

The state in which unfortunate Poland is at present is too well known to the world: the indignity of the two neighboring powers and the crime of traitors to the country have pushed it into this abyss. Catherine II, who, in collusion with the deceitful pf Frederick William II, who swore to eradicate the Polish name, has just accomplished her unjust designs: there is no kind of falsehood, perfidy, or betrayal, of which these two governments would not do to satisfy their vengeance and greed. The Czarina, by declaring herself impudently guarantor of the integrity and independence of Poland, afflicted it with all sorts of plagues; and when Poland, weary of wearing her shameful yoke, recovered the rights of its sovereignty, she employed traitors against it: she supported their sacrilegious plots with all her armed forces, and, having artificially diverted the defense from the country the King, to whom a legal diet and the nation had entrusted all their forces, she [Catherine] soon betrayed these same traitors shamefully. By such subterfuge, she become the mistress of the destinies of Poland, she invited Frederick William to take part in its remains, in order to reward him for his deceit, for having broken his most solemn treaty with the Republic, under imaginary pretexts, of which falsity and impiety may be suitable only to tyrants, but in fact to satisfy the insatiable cupidity of extending his tyranny by the invasion of bordering nations.

[3]The original is..

These two powers confederated against Poland have seized upon the immemorial and incontestable possessions of the Republic, and for this purpose they have obtained, in a diet called for this purpose, a claimed approbation of their usurpations, by oath and slavery, by imposing on the citizens the most onerous burdens, and these powers, knowing only an arbitrary will, by a new and unknown language in the law of nations, have audaciously assigned to the existence of a republic inferior to all other powers, by showing clearly that the laws, as well as the limits of the sovereigns, depend absolutely on their caprice, and that they regard the north of Europe as a prey destined for the rapacity of their despotism.

The rest of Poland has not yet been able to buy an improvement of its lot with so many cruel calamities. The Czarina, concealing her later designs, could only be pernicious to the powers of Europe, which meanwhile sacrifices Poland to her barbarous and implacable vengeance, she tramples on the most holy rights of liberty, safety, property of property, and citizens. The thought and the inner feeling of the Poles can shelter themselves from their unbridled persecutions, and they try to enchain the language of the citizens: it is only the traitors to the country who find indulgence with it, and they can commit all kinds of crimes with impunity, and so goods and public revenues have become the prey of their cupidity, they have seized the property of the citizens, they have shared among themselves the offices of the Republic, to adorn themselves with its spoils, because the country was subjugated; and by impiously impersonating the name of a national government, slaves to a foreign tyranny, they execute everything at will.

The Permanent Council[4]*, whose establishment was imposed upon them by a violent usurpation, legally suppressed by the will of the nation, and newly re-established by the traitors, surmounted on the orders of a Russian minister the limits of his power, that he had received with baseness from this minister, by restoring, by re-founding, the arbitrarily suppression of the Constitution which had just been created, and those which had been broken. In a word, the claimed government of the nation, the liberty, the safety, and the property of the citizens, remain in*

[4]The Permanent Council was a ruling council imposed on the rump state of Poland by Catherine in place of the Constitution.

the hands of the slaves of a servant of the Czarina, whose troops flood the country, and serve as a bulwark for their wickedness.

Driven by this immense weight of misery, conquered by treason rather than by the force of enemy weapons, deprived of all protection of the national government, after having lost the country and with it the enjoyment of the most sacred rights of freedom, the security of both individual property and national property; deceived, and become the laughing-stock of some governments, and abandoned by others, we, citizens, inhabitants of the Palatinate of Krakow, sacrificing to our country and our lives, as the only property that tyranny has not deigned to wrest from us, we seize these extreme and violent means that civic despair suggests. Having then the firm resolution to perish and bury ourselves under the ruins of our country, or to deliver the land of our fathers from a fierce oppression and a yoke full of opprobrium, we declare, in the face of Heaven and of the whole human race, and especially of all the nations who know how to appreciate freedom above all the goods of the universe, that by using the incontestable right of defense against tyranny, and armed oppression, we unite, in a spirit of patriotism, civility and fraternity, all our forces; and, convinced that the success of our enterprise depends on our close union, we renounce all the prejudices of public opinion that have divided or might divide the citizens of the same homeland, and we promise each other not to spare any sacrifice; but, on the contrary, to use every means that the sacred love of liberty can inspire in men whom despair has raised in its defense.

After having organized the government, Kosciuszko left Krakow at the head of his army, and marched before the enemy, who thought, by uniting his forces, to crush at the first shock all the Republican troops. On 4 April 1794, the two armies met near the village of Racławice, seven miles from Krakow.[5] The fight was terrible. The Polish peasants, fighting on their native soil, showed exemplary valor. Two of them especially, Glowacki and Swilacki, deserved to be distinguished and cited on the battlefield. General officers Zajączek, Manget, and Madalinski received the praise of the Generalissimo, who

[5]A Polish mile is the equivalent of a German mile, two French leagues, and seven Russian versts. Translator's note: Every city, country, and most provinces had their own measurement systems, so one should be very careful with these measurements.

was conspicuous in bravery, and was promoted by him to the rank of general major. The victory was decisive, but it was less favorable still by its material result than by the effects that followed it. Wherever the news arrived, the long-suppressed patriotic energy emerging with new strength, and from that moment the insurrection assumed a threatening character for Russia.

Kosciuszko, however, returned to Krakow, and the Russians retreated to the Palatinate of Sandomirz, to assemble their forces.

As soon as the sound of Racławice's defeat reached the ears of Igelström, this proconsul, irritated, redoubled his rigor, and appeared to envelop all Poland in his vengeance. He demanded that the authors of the new insurrection should be outlawed, and that enemies and traitors to the country should be declared. The weak Stanislaus Augustus, blindly signing all that was presented to him, dared to affix his royal hand to an act dated April 2, 1794, which formally disavowed the proclamation of independence and Generalissimo Kosciuszko.

On 12 April, the inhabitants of Warsaw received news of the victory the Republicans had won at Racławice. Such unexpected success re-awoke patriotism, and the days of 17 and 18 April were witnesses to the insurrection which took place in that capital. Women, children, old men, all ran to arms, all marched towards the common enemy, and the Muscovites, crushed, hunted on all sides, abandoned a town where the day before they reigned as masters. Dzialynski's regiment, the only one there, commanded by Colonel Haumann, took a large part in this action.

Once liberated, after 19 April, a temporary council was formed. Ignace Wyssygota Zakrzewski was elected president, and General Stanislaw Mokronoski was appointed commander of the city. It was declared that the citizens were in fact in possession of all the rights which the Constitution of 3 May 1791 had guaranteed them, and of which the Russian faction had stripped them. It was also provisionally arranged to regulate all civil and military operations, until Kosciuszko could definitively appoint a supreme national council.[6]

---

[6]The members of the Provisional Council were: Ignace Zarzewski, President, Stanislaw Mokronoski, Commander, Xavier Dialynski, Simon Szjdlowski, Joseph Wjbicki, Elias Aloe, Ignace Zaironezek, Andre Ciemniewski, Jean Horain, Stanislas Rafolowicz, Francois Makarowicz, Michel Wulfers, Francois Tykiel, Francois Gautier, Jean Kilinski.

The Generalissimo, in endeavoring to approach General Grochowski, then advanced to Polaniec, following and descending the left bank of the Vistula. The purpose of this skillful march was to join with this Polish chief, whose courageous army was burning to fight for the regeneration of the country. Happy news began to reach the headquarters from all fronts. In Lithuania, Colonel Jacques Iasinski, an excellent engineer, and an intrepid republican, executed the astonishing revolution of that province. On the night of 23 – 24 April, assisted by five hundred Lithuanians, he rescued the city of Vilna, guarded by three thousand Russians. "Soon the whole country was in insurrection, soon the Polish leaders, who had retired to the country, appeared in arms at the head of the citizens, and Franciszek Sapieha, Oginski, Granowski, the Grabowski, etc., appeared in person in this memorable circumstance.

In these first moments the oppressed people woke up to seek revenge. The so-called Grand General of Lithuania, Simon Kossakowski, was first charged and hanged in Vilna, after a judicial sentence. However, in order to prevent the people from instituting expeditious justice, a Provisional Council was legally established. Iasinski, on his side, was tireless and courageous, went to attack the Russians in three consecutive battles, at Nieinenczyn against Lewis, at Polany against Deioff, and finally at Soly against Nicolas Zouboff.

In Samogitia, uprisings followed the first rumors of the insurrection, and the people gathered by acclamation to the act of national independence. In the events which took place on this occasion, the Citizens Chlewinski, Zawisza, Giedroyc, Niesiolowski, and others, were distinguished.

As for the inhabitants of Volhynia, Podolia, and the Ukraine, their position at an enormous distance from the national movement did not allow them to directly support it, but the Polish commanders stationed in these provinces moved their units move towards the theater of the war, and the intrepid Kopec, Wyszkowski, and Lazninski, after braving a thousand dangers, were able to assemble in the army of the Generalissimo.[7]

[7]At the end of the War to Protect the Constitution, during the negotiations of the second partition, an armistice was in place where units involved in the war remained in place – many in the Ukraine and had to move through Russian occupied areas to meet up with the army.

At the same time, the Warsaw Provisional Council was actively pushing its work. After consolidating the internal administration, it occupied itself with the fate of those traitors who, in conjunction with the co-invading powers, had opened Poland to the abyss of misfortune. A portion of their iniquities was brought to light by the seizure of the papers of the Chancery, which had been found in the hotel formerly occupied by General-Minister Igelström. A commission of twenty members was appointed to begin an examination of these papers; it had already met several times for this purpose, when the news of the Vilna Revolution, and the astonishing success of the courageous Iasinski, gave a new degree to the enthusiasm of the citizens. They learned moreover about the prompt justice Simon Kossakowski[8] had received for his betrayal and crimes; and the people, excited by such an example, loudly demanded for the immediate punishment of the guilty persons who had been arrested. The proceedings were heard, the judgments were rendered, and on 9 May 1794, four of them ascended the scaffold.[9]

A calm settled on the military part of the insurrection, as Kosciuszko attended to the organization of a National Supreme Council at his headquarters at Polaniec. Ignacy Potocki and Hugo Kołłątaj, who were close to him, were made deputies on 24 May in Warsaw, and on the 27th of the same month, the Supreme Council replaced the Provisional Council of 19 April.

After joining up with Grochowski, Kosciuszko could not remain inactive long, and began to pursue the Russians. On the way, he was obliged to detach an army corps under the orders of General Zajączek, in order to contain the portion of enemy troops occupying the Palatinate of Lublin. He continued his march towards the retreating Russians and reached them near Szczekociny. The Muscovite army had joined up with the forty-thousand strong Prussian army, commanded by Frederick William himself. On 6 June 1794, a bloody battle was fought in the fields of Szczekociny, or, according to the Prussians - Rawka. In spite of the frightening disproportion of numbers, the Polish

[8]He was hanged by insurgents in the town square of Wilnius on 24 April 1794.

[9]It was Pierre Ozarowski, Grand-General of the Crown Joseph Ankwicz, Marshal of the Permanent Council, Zabiello, Vice-Grand-General of Lithuania, and Joseph Kossakowski, Bishop of Livonia, the most active member of the Targowica plot, and brother of the one who was executed in Vilna.

troops fought with great valor; victory was disputed for a long time, and when, overwhelmed and not beaten, the Republicans were forced to retreat, their attitude was still so menacing that the Prusso-Russians did not dare to pursue them. In this stubborn affair both Generals Grochowski and Wodzicki were bravely killed; Generals Poninski, Kaminski, Eustache Sanguszko, and Colonel Krzycki were distinguished by brilliant actions. The Generalissimo himself, on this occasion, as in all the others, constantly exposed his person, and in the heat of the fray he was always where the danger was most imminent.

As a result of this battle, Kosciuszko felt obliged to fall back on Warsaw, while the Prussians, gathering all their forces, turned to Krakow. Arriving under its walls, they summoned the commander Ignace Winiawski to surrender, and the city was delivered without fight on 15 June.[10] In the same time, and on 8 June, General Zajączek lost the battle at Chełm.

All this bad news reached Warsaw at the same time. The people, always inclined to exaggerate, did not fail to attribute their setbacks to the King's partisans, who had not yet given up their intrigues. The people were agitated, and painful scenes came to stain this glorious regeneration for a moment. On the 25th, a bill was presented to the Supreme Council asking for various reforms. This petition ended by calling for prompt and severe justice on the heads of the perjurers who were then held in public prisons. The Supreme Council replied that they would proceed by legal means to their judgment; but the people, excited by rumors of secret enemies of the Republican cause, raised their voices with impatience against any judicial delay. Groups formed in the city, and speakers excited the people to do justice themselves, and pointed to the victims. A young man, Kazimierz Konopka, whom we shall see honorably appearing in the Polish legions in Italy, harangued the multitude himself, and on 28 June, the mob was pushed to such a point that eight of the principal culprits were led without trial from prison to the scaffold.[11]

[10]The Military Council, by its decree of 3 July 1794 confirmed by Kosciuszko, recognized the betrayal of Winiawski, and censured him in absentia, for he fled abroad immediately after the surrender of Krakow.

[11]These included Prince Anthony Czetwertynski, Castellan of Przemysl, Prince Ignace Massalski, Bishop of Vilna, Private Counselor Boskanip-Lassopolski, a Grabowski, servant of the Crown, Maïewski, Mathieu Raguski, Pientka, the Attorney Michel Wulfers, suspected of having removed from the archives of the palace of Igelstrom documents that indicted the King and other murky characters.

This popular effervescence would have had more fatal consequences, and other victims would still have succumbed, if a violent rain had come to calm down this thoughtless fury, and if President Zakrzewski, who enjoyed general support, did not make use of his authority to appease their spirits.

This event destroyed Kosciuszko's heart; and for Europe to know the difference which existed between the terror of France and the Polish Revolution, he had the disrupters of public order punished in an exemplary manner.

The city of Warsaw was still in seething, when the King of Prussia, after concentrating all his forces, invested the capital with forty thousand Prussians and ten thousand Russians, under the orders of General Fersen.

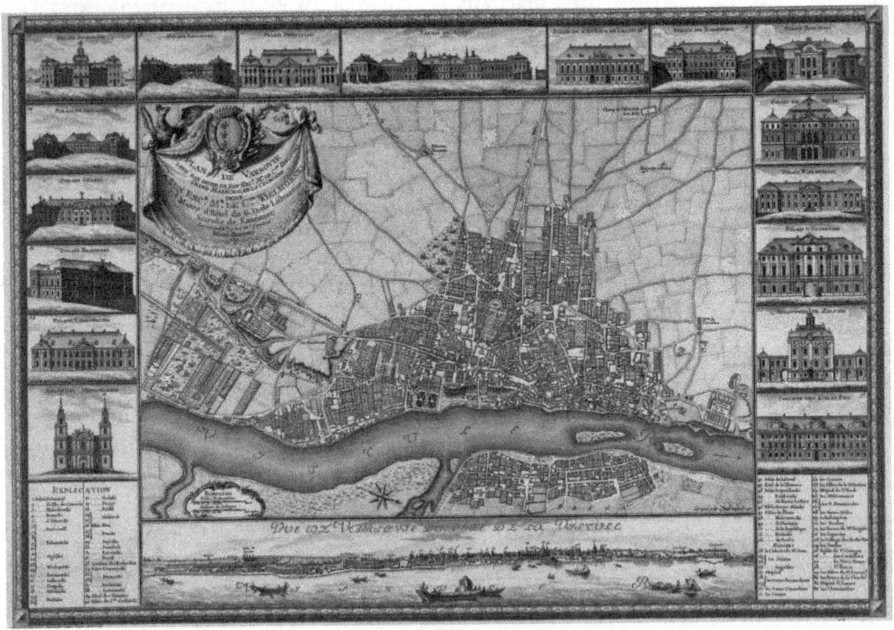

Warsaw 1772

Far from shrinking in fear from this formidable army, the people of Warsaw had their courage redoubled. The members of the Supreme Council, the citizens of all classes, the clergy, the craftsmen, all began to prepare, and worked on the entrenchments. Even women of the first distinction, help in defensive work that their education and delicacy would have seemed to render impossible; standing on the breach, they encouraged the besieged, carried munitions of war to them, and daily gave a thousand proofs of that sublime courage, which Polish women receives and transmits as a noble heritage.

On 21 July 1794, the siege began. On the 27th and the following days the assaults succeeded one another. On 2 August, the King of Prussia, believing that he had intimidated the besieged, summoned them to surrender; but on their refusal the cannonade recommenced more vigorously than ever. From that day until 28 August, there were various partial engagements, and frequent sorties, which showed the determination of the Polish garrison, and finally on 28 August, a deadly attack came to prove to the coalition armies that nothing is impossible for a people fighting for their homes.

In these different engagements Generals Dąbrowski, Poniatowski, Poninski, Zajączek, Kniaziewicz, Brigade Commanders Kopec, Dunikowski, a young Kollontay, and a host of other officers, distinguished themselves by their heroism and bravery. As for the population of Warsaw, fighting for their domestic goods and their freedom, they acted as they had during the memorable days of 17/18 April.

While Generalissimo Kosciuszko, and the beleaguered garrison defended, Warsaw, they resolved to die on the breach before handing over to the conqueror this last asylum of liberty, an unexpected diversion made their task easier and their triumph more complete. For a long time, a mysterious insurrection had been going on in Greater Poland. The inhabitants of the Palatinates of Posnania, Kalisz, Gnesne, Sieradie, etc., were silently preparing their arms against their oppressors. Finally, towards the first days of September, the storm broke, and its consequences were prodigious. Seized with a panic terror, and fearing to pass under the *fourches caudines*[12], the King of Prussia hastily raised the siege of Warsaw, after fifty-three days of opening a trench, and returned incognito to Berlin, where all was ready for his triumph.

To take full advantage of this retreat, and to support the patriots of Great Poland, Kosciuszko sent them, in addition to General Madalinski, an army corps under the command of General Dąbrowski.

[12]Translator: To "pass under the Caudine Forks" (fourches caudines), comes from the battle of the Caudine Forks where the Roman army was forced to pass under the symbolic yoke of the Samnites. The Caudine Forks (Furculae Caudinae in Latin) was the name of a narrow passage between two mountains near Benevento in Italy.

These two chiefs worked together with great vigor, soon seizing the important city of Bydgoszcz (Bromberg), and made Frederick William tremble in his capital.

Unfortunately, they were the last glimmers of a fire that was going to die out, and the Poles, crushed by numbers, surrounded by enemies constantly reborn, were going to pay dearly for these early victories.

The situation in Lithuania, after having offered various hopes, began to become more critical. For a long-time General Lasinski, assisted by Grahowski, Oginski, Kosielski, etc., and opposed to the superior forces of the Russians, commanded by Knorring, Zouhoff, Benningsen, Tzitzianoff, etc., had been able to stymie their attacks and keep them constantly in check. General Wawrzecki, for his efforts raised rebellion in Courland, and General Romuald Giedroyc won a decisive victory at Salaty. But as Iasinski was recalled to Kosciuszko, the command of his army corps was entrusted to General Michel Wielhorski. Stripped of their indefatigable adversary, the Muscovite troops marched on Vilna, and attacked it on 19 July. Repulsed in this assault by a small garrison and the population of the city, the enemy generals awaited new reinforcements. It was then necessary to give way to necessity, and after a courageous resistance, Vilna surrendered on 12 August 1794. The occupation of the capital of Lithuania led to the complete disorganization of the Polish troops of that province, and from that moment the path of the Republican armies began to decline.

On the other hand, General Charles Sierakowski, who was at first opposed by Derfelden's corps, learned that Suvorov was advancing by forced marches towards Volhynia. To stop his progress, Sierakowski advanced towards Kobrin, took position with Krupczyce, and on 16 September, received Suvorov's attack. The battle was terrible, and yet the Poles had only 192 men killed and 67 wounded, while the Russians had three thousand to four thousand hors de combat. In spite of the evident disproportion of this loss, General Sierakowski was obliged to retreat before Suvorov's forces, which were five times his. On the 17th a new battle was fought at Brzesc-Litevsky, and this time the Polish army, crushed by numbers, was annihilated.

Before this disaster, Generalissimo Kosciuszko, informed by Sierakowski of Suvorov's movements, had left Warsaw with a portion of his troops, resolved to meet with Sierakowski, and thus dispute the passage to the Russian general; but the disaster of 17 September destroyed this audacious project. Turning his sights on the other side, Kosciuszko then attempted to make a junction with General Poninski, who countered the passage of the Vistula with General Fersen. He therefore came to the camp to wait for him, but Fersen, with marches and counter-marches, deceived the vigilance of the Polish chief, Kosciuszko saw him unexpectedly appear before him with infinitely superior forces. The battle began: both sides fought with incredible fury. The Republicans, who each had ten enemies to fight, fell at their posts, and were conquered only after all had succumbed. Kosciuszko himself, chief and soldier all at once, covered with blood, riddled with wounds, remained unconscious on the field of battle. Victims of the same fate, Julien-Ursin Niemcewicz, Stanislaw Fiszer, Kniaziewicz, Charles Sierakowski, Kaminski, Joseph Kopec, Joseph Seydlitz, and many other officers, shared his glorious captivity. The brave Colonel Jean Krzycki died as a hero in the middle of the fray.

Thus fell Kosciuszko, that illustrious man who was to raise the ancient republic of Poland, and with him fell its new destinies. The consternation that this event produced is difficult to portray. It seemed that after such a blow, one had only to reach out to receive chains. However, the chiefs who had survived the shipwreck still sought to give impetus to the public mind and wished to remedy the evil as much as the circumstances permitted. General Thomas Wawrzecki was chosen to replace the Generalissimo. All available troops were concentrated in the capital, to defend it against Suvorov, who directed the coalition's combined forces. Arriving at Praga, a suburb of Warsaw, the Russians stormed it on 4 November 1794. The carnage was horrible: fifteen thousand people perished there mercilessly; Muscovite iron respected neither age nor sex. Heroic to the last moment, the Polish patriots buried themselves under the walls that they could not defend and preferred a glorious death to a life of slavery. Thus fell the illustrious Lasinski, Paul Grabowski, Korsak, Kwasniewski, and with them the other victims of the national cause. Then, as all the chances were contrary, Ignacy Potocki, wishing to preserve the capital from the fate of Praga, great as a Roman citizen, and a worthy offspring of a family rich in illustrations, presented himself alone in front of Suvorov, having offered himself as a victim and assuming on his head the vengeance that was to fall on Warsaw. The Russian general, struck by such sublime devotion, was human for the first time, and gave up the course of his sanguinary plans. Talks were held, and on the 9th of the same month Warsaw surrendered to the Russian armies by capitulation.[13] Then all those who had anything to fear from foreign vengeance, far from relying on Suvorov's protests, dispersed and sought refuge against cruel reprisals. Some fragments of the Polish Army, escaping the disaster of Warsaw, met the corps that General Dąbrowski was bringing back from Greater Poland on the Krakow road. There, still busy with the daring plan that he had developed at another time and in other circumstances, Dąbrowski proposed that Wawrzecki execute the same project with more decisive chances. The aim was to unite all Polish troops on the spot, about twenty-thousand men, to take the King and the members of the Supreme Council willingly or by force, and to cross Germany to join the French army, which was fighting on the Rhine. If

[13]The Potocki family has always been one of the most powerful and illustrious families in Poland. Its glorious deeds and his patriotic acts fill the national pomp; military or citizen, its members knew, at the most memorable times, how to cover themselves with a double glory. Hardly, in the long series of distinguished men it has furnished, can we find in its bosom a single isolated individual who has tainted it. And still in the moment even where Stanislas-Felix Potocki, leader of the Targowica faction, dishonored this respected name by delivering his homeland to the Russians, the generous Severin Potocki and his brother Jean Potocki, their cousin Stanislas-Kostka Potocki, taking up arms in the cause of Independence, and later another Stanislaw Potocki, co-operating in the memorable days of the 17th and 18th of April, effaced by a thousand bravura the shame that an unworthy parent impressed on behalf of their family. Later on, a son of the same Stanislaus Felix, so sadly celebrated, a Vladimir Potocki, who had been kidnapped from Poland too soon, washed himself in the blood baptism of the last traces of the paternal task. After following the fortune of the French armies and sharing the works of the glorious campaign of 1809 in the Grand Duchy of Warsaw, he succumbed in 1812 to an inflammatory disease. His ashes lie today in Krakow, in the cathedral church dedicated to St. Stanislaus. His tomb will soon be adorned, thanks to the tender solicitude of his bride, born princess Thècle Sanguszko, with a marble statue, the masterpiece of the sculptor Thorwaldsen, whose chisel embellished Warsaw of the monuments of the great Kopernikus and Prince Joseph Poniatowski.

In recalling these names, so dear to Poland, I may, before making a detailed tribute to other worthy citizens, still quote here the brave Arthur Potocki, who, as aide-de-camp of Prince Poniatowski, during the famous 1809 campaign, later bathed the fields of Moscow with his blood, then fought the allied powers in the campaigns of 1813 and 1814, and who, taking the most active part in the erection of the monument of the immortal Kosciuszko at Krakow paid his sacred debt to the country and the names of its glorious defenders.

this project could have been executed, it would have become one of the most glorious achievements of ancient and modern history. It would have been beautiful, it would have been imposing to see the remains of a nation, its king and its representatives at its head, evacuating, arms in the hand, a country that usurping forces had invaded; and, by a strange contrast, a republic, an enemy of kings, granting an asylum to a dethroned sovereign. But the unfortunate position in which the army was then, the advanced season, and other obstacles, either general or particular, prevented the execution of this heroic project. The mutilated remains of the Army and several officers were forced to capitulate with the Russians. Of this number was General Dąbrowski himself, future leader of the Polish legions in Italy. Disappointed in his plan to retreat, he resigned himself for the moment to the force of events and was taken to Warsaw.[14]

---

[14]We report here the number of 20,000 men, according to the memoirs of Dąbrowski himself, but as the author of the Memoirs sur la Pologne, though an eye-witness of the events in question, is not in accord on this point, although neither of them gives official documents which would have confirmed the strength of the Polish troops and their resources, we therefore believe that we must report here the following passage:

• Dąbrowski was very distressed and dismayed at the news that had reached him from Warsaw; but he did not yet despair of the fate of the country. He communicated to us a plan which he had sent to the Generalissimo (Wawrzecki), and whose favorable response was to be expected, if there was enough courage to execute it.

• According to Dąbrowski's calculation, all our available forces combined could amount to about 40,000 men; we still had 200 cannons, and 10,000,000 Polish florins in the treasury (6,000,000 francs), and proposed to the Generalissimo not to abandon to the enemy these means of continuing the war that still remained in our power, to leave Warsaw with all that could be carried away, and to establish the central government in the midst of our camp.

• He proposed to convince the King of Poland to follow the army, and not to attach the fate of the whole country and nation to the defense of the city of Warsaw.

• Dąbrowski wanted all our forces united to attempt to move closer to the French armies, crossing Prussia; for this purpose, he had drawn up a map which indicated the route to be followed, and that he accompanied a plan of military operations for the different situations in which he might find himself. According to his opinion, the Russians could not pursue us with all their strength; for they needed to leave considerable corps of observation enough to contain the insurgent patriots in the provinces, and especially in the capital, of which the greater mass of the population was still in a state of effervescence. He was persuaded that a Russian army of 20,000 to 30,000 men to be sent for our pursuit would not prevent us from continuing our retreat, and he did not see the possibility that the Prussians might prevent us from getting closer to the French army, which, at the first news of the brave and bold resolution

There, a short time before the unhappy Stanislaus had received orders from Catherine to leave the capital, Dąbrowski was requested by this monarch to come to his home. In the interview that took place Stanislaus asked the general what he intended to do. Dąbrowski replied that, wishing to be useful to his country, he proposed to go to Paris with that intention, but first he wanted to take a trip to Saxony. Thereupon the King told him how much it would please him to be of service to the Elector of Saxony. Furthermore, he gave him a letter of recommendation for this prince, dated 17 December 1794. But General Dąbrowski, did not follow through on this project, so he did not make use of this document. Still busy working for the Polish cause, he quietly waited for a favorable circumstance, which allowed him to work

---

which the leaders of our government would take, would not fail to support our enterprise with all possible aid; for it was in the interest of France to assist us and to make common cause with us. Dąbrowski observed that even if the junction of our troops with those of the French could not take place, in view of the great distance which separated us, it was probable that, to avoid uncertain chances and restore tranquility in Poland, Russia and Prussia would like to deal and negotiate with us; he was convinced that a Polish army of 40,000 men, with the King and the heads of government, was really a national representation, to which only honorable conditions could be proposed; and, consequently, he had no doubt that we could negotiate and obtain an advantageous peace for our country, instead of delivering it ignominiously to the enemy by a shameful capitulation, which had no other purpose than to save momentarily the city of Warsaw.

• We were so enthusiastic about this project, the reading of which and the discussions that followed it occupied us the rest of the night (November 6 to 7, 1794), that I no longer thought of crossing the border in cases where Dąbrowski's proposals would be accepted. But, on the morning of November 7th, a letter from Wawrzecki brought the answer that Dąbrowski's plan had been submitted to the decision of the council of war, which approved and shared his opinion, but that this project was impracticable, because the King would not willingly leave Warsaw; because the people surrounded all the exits of the palace, and threatened with a general uprising if they tried to forcibly remove the King from the capital; and because at last they could no longer count on the energy of the officers and soldiers, who were discouraged by the reverses of the Army, and who no longer had confidence in their leaders. Wawrzecki ended his answer by warning that he was going to leave Warsaw with all the soldiers who would follow him, and he ordered Dąbrowski to join him with his corps at the place he pointed out to him.

• Dąbrowski was appalled by the reply he had just received. However, he assured those around him that he did not despair of the safety of his country; that he did not renounce the duty of serving her; that it was in France that he would seek the means of being useful, and that sooner or later Poland could not fail to be re-established. (*Memoires de Michel Oginski, sur la Pologne et les Polonaise de 1788 à 1815*, Vol. 2, pp. 72-76, Paris, 1826)

even indirectly toward this end; and this circumstance soon presented itself.

The patriots who had not been willing to bear the sight of foreign oppression, or who sought asylum in emigration against personal vengeance, some went to France, where we shall soon see them occupied with the affairs of their country and the others left for Venice. The principal men of this group were Peter Potocki, Starosta of Szczyrzec, former Polish Ambassador to Constantinople, Michael Oginski, former ambassador to Holland, and chief of a regiment raised at his own expense in Lithuania in 1794; Stanislaus Soltyk, Nuncio of Krakow on the Constituent Diet, the two Wyszkowski brothers, the eldest of him, Francis, had distinguished himself in the last war of independence; François Dmochowski and Charles Prozor, the most active members of the revolution; Thadeus Wyssogierd of Lithuania, Gaetan Inagurski of Samogitia, finally Generals Lazninski, Kolysko, and a host of others who set out for Dresden, and thence made their way to Paris. For their part, General Stanislaw Mokronoski, Aloise Sulistrowski, President of the Department of Public Order in the National Supreme Council, and a few others, took the road to Florence.

The refugees in Venice found Lalleinant, the French Minister in this residence, a patron who was welcoming, as he had received orders from his government to treat the Poles on an equal footing with French citizens. It was under his auspices that they established communications with the refugees in Paris. The latter testified on several occasions to what extent they were satisfied with the reception they had received in France. They gave the Poles in Venice the justified hope that the French Republic would take an active part in the reestablishment of Poland, that it would never suffer that this generous nation to disappear from the rank of the European nations, that it would detach the King of Prussia from the coalition with Russia and Austria, and that it would cause Sweden and the Porte to act against the Muscovite Colossus. They added: that France would only demand the Polish refugee's courage and constancy in the face of adversity, and above all a confident patience until they could act in their favor in an efficient manner.

As for the patriots in Venice, who were closer to the frontiers of their country, they maintained communications with the merchants of

Trieste; where they maintained the hope of an imminent regeneration, and sent some consolations to those who, as prisoners, could not deceive the vigilance of their oppressors.

While the Polish refugees obtained, wherever they were, from agents of the French Republic, asylum, assistance, and protection, the same republic signed a peace treaty with the King of Prussia at Basel, on 5 April 1795. The Ministers Plenipotentiary Barthelemy and Hardenberg concluded, on 17 May, an agreement by which France had one less enemy. This treaty, if it was agreed for the benefit of the parties, did not obtain the same consent from interested third parties. On the one hand, England, Russia and Austria, disapproved of the conduct of the King of Prussia, who had sacrificed to the tranquility of his states the interests of the coalition, and on the other hand, the Poles who, basing all their hopes on the French Republic, had created anxieties about this rapprochement, which postponed the day of their deliverance.

Michel Oginski was one of the few refugees who thought that the treaty concluded between France and Prussia, guaranteed by its very nature the respective possessions of the two powers, and it contained no clause relative to the invaded provinces of Poland, the occupation of these provinces, according to the last partition, were ipso facto guaranteed by that same power which the patriots regarded as their only support.

So, from the first news which reached Venice on the negotiations begun between Prussia and France, Oginsky had written to Citizen Francois Barss, an agent of the Poles in Paris, several times since the time of the Constituent Diet. In his letters he urged him to remind the French government that it was presenting itself with a favorable opportunity to act in the interest of the Poles, by imposing on the King of Prussia the conditions of: 1.) disengaging himself from the provinces he had invaded in Poland; and 2.) to co-operate, jointly with the French government, in the re-establishment of a country whose partition had destroyed the European equilibrium. These conditions were to be accepted by the Prussian Cabinet with all the more ease, as the King of Prussia was then in the necessity of asking for peace, and, on the other hand, he must have realized the great preponderance which Russia had acquired by the invasion of most of Poland.

It was to satisfy these just and pressing demands that Citizen Barss submitted to the members of the Republican government the letter from Citizen Michel Oginski, with the support of all his personal influence; but the government replied that the conditions raised could not be put forward in the negotiations begun with the King of Prussia, that it was necessary above all to heal the wounds which anarchy and terror had made to France, to restore the state finance, and interrupt the course of so many victories to grant the troops the rest they needed. It was added that, in the treaty, it would in no way be a question of Poland, and that by the same token it did not guarantee a possession which was so unjustifiably usurped. It was pointed out, moreover, that this peace with the Berlin Cabinet could not be of long duration; that the coalition of the other powers was not dissolved; that these powers would endeavor to drag the King of Prussia back to them; that then the Republicans, deploying all their forces, would take the offensive in their turn, and would be able to wring Poland from its usurpers, if they could not obtain its friendly reinstatement. Barss was induced to send this reply to his countrymen, encouraging them to be patient, and to submit their courage to all the trials which the emancipation of their country would require from them.

Although this answer contained, in evasive terms, vague consolation for the Polish patriots, they had however hoped for better from the French government. But then, repulsed from all sides, they accepted with gratitude this glimmer of hope, and still preserved in all their strength that confidence, which was inspired by a heroic cause.

In addition to the French Republic, Sweden and Turkey provided asylum and relief for the Polish refugees; and some of them conceived the idea of interesting these two powers in the re-establishment of Poland. A favorable circumstance further strengthened them in this idea. Citizen Marie Descorches, French Minister to Warsaw at the time of the Constituent Diet, who was then ambassador at Constantinople, was recalled to Paris, and replaced in his functions by the Citizen Raymond Verninac. The latter, crossing Venice to go to his new post, had brought to the refugees touching proofs of the interest which France took in their lot. By a very special mission of the Committee of Public Safety, he was instructed to announce to the Poles that he would have the opportunity of meeting, that the French government, finally free from the yoke of the anarchists, more dangerous to it than all the foreign forces had a special interest in a nation that defended its liberty so well; that, consequently, he would endeavor to obtain, whether by force or by negotiation, the re-establishment of Poland.

As a result of these formal assurances, Verninac added that the French government thought it useful for the interests of the refugees to have one representative in Constantinople and another in Stockholm. He urged them to defend themselves against the Ottoman Porte, adding that the cause of the Poles, being that of the independence of the people, became inseparable from the cause of France. In finishing, he insisted especially on sending two diplomatic agents to Sweden and Turkey.

To fulfill the wish expressed in the official communication from Verninac, the patriots immediately took care of the choice of their agents. The mission of Turkey was first entrusted to Michel Oginski, who devoted himself to it without hesitation, and the refugees of Paris were promptly advised of this choice. Citizen Barss, on behalf of the latter, wrote, on 20 August 1795, a letter to the patriots gathered at Venice, and another, under the same date, addressed particularly to Oginski. In the past, all the instructions relating to this mission had been presented and read to the Committee of Public Safety on 29 Thermidor, Year III (16 August 1795), and, once approved by the committee, they were dispatched to Lallemant, Ambassador to Venice, and provided by the latter into Oginski's hands.

Once provided with all these documents, Oginski (under the name of Jean Riedel) left Venice on 4 November 1795; but, obstructed by a thousand dangers, beaten by all the persecutions that weighed on the refugees at that time, he succeeded with great difficulty in embarking at Leghorn, on 5 February 1796. Destined for future trials, the Polish representative had still to endure a stormy crossing, and he arrived at Constantinople only in the first days of April.

In this way, from all sides, in Paris, Venice, and Constantinople, the citizens for personal ambition and selfish interest were agitated to revive the name of their country. If their noble project did not receive its fulfillment, it was neither the constancy nor the courage which they lacked, and, unshakable soldiers, we saw them, when all the diplomatic negotiations turned against them, to resuscitate under a foreign sky their national military representation, by creating Polish legions.

CHAPTER 4

Elie Tremo. — He Delivers Xavier Dąbrowski and Goes with Him to Paris. — Their Liaison with Kazimirz De la Roche. — Polish Refugees in Paris. — Their Efforts with the French government. — Reunions at the Hotel Diesbach. — Thibaudeau, Chenier, Talma, etc..Kazimirz De la Roche's Project. — He Hands Over the Care of the Hotel Diesbach to Prozor, Giedroyc, and Mniewski. — Arrival of Wybicki. — De la Roche Leaves with Tremo. — Situation in Europe at this time. — Voyage of de la Roche. — Wybicki's Efforts with Citizen Caillard. — Tremo and De la Roche Arrive at Basel. — Ostensible Mission. — Secret Mission. Hoszkiewicz's Imprudence. — Tremo's Arrival in Warsaw. — His Actions. — Military Situation of the Poles at this Time. — Efforts by Suvorov to Attach General Dąbrowski to the Russian Cause. — Conduct of the Old Prussian Army.

Among the Polish citizens who devoted themselves exclusively to the service of their oppressed homeland was a young officer named Elie Tremo, who lived to avenge her. Coming from a family whose origin was French and employed at the stewardship of the Court of Stanislas-Augustus, this young man, full of enthusiasm and endowed with an independent soul, embraced the military career, at the time of the revolution launched by Kosciuszko. He was seen in the glorious days of 17 and 18 April, when Warsaw pushed the Muscovites from the city; he was seen at the head of the people pursuing the enemy troops within the city, attacking them with admirable courage, and taking an active part in the resulting victory. From then on, an officer in the Mokronoski Regiment, and charged with defending the capital against the Prussians, he gave fresh proof of his valor, and was taken prisoner in a sortie. Held for a long period in Glogau, then in Neisse, it was not until the end of 1794 that he obtained his freedom and permission to return to Posen with his family. There, by chance he came acquainted with Xavier Dąbrowski, one of the insurgent chiefs of Greater Poland, the Palatinate of Kalisz, and the land of Kutno. Dąbrowski, was in Posen, under the supervision of the Prussian police and given a prison sentence of eight years. The unhappy man said only a few words to him. Tremo had barely learned of Dąbrowski position, then calling in all the resources at his disposal as an active and enterprising genius, he did not hesitate to help him. With promises, threats, money, prayers, he made every effort, overcame all obstacles, and these two noble friends, after a thousand dangers, finally managed to emerge from the Prussian states. On entering Saxony, that hospitable land, always open to the unfortunate, Tremo and Dąbrowski threw themselves into each other's arms, and, falling on their knees, thanked Heaven that they could be separated from their oppressors. Soon they were joined by a crowd of their compatriots, whose intention was to go to France.[1]

At that moment, the fourteen armies of this great nation, being constantly triumphant over the enemies of freedom, with protection for the oppressed, the flattering welcome that the people and especially the military lavished on the Poles, told them all that the French Republic was the classic land of independence and the asylum of the persecuted.

These motives, and, moreover, the desire to seek the source of the new lights that then illuminated Europe, drove Tremo and his young companion to this happy country, and in the first days of the year 1795 they both arrived in Paris. Welcomed with cordiality by Francois Barss, the agent accredited to the French government, they saw that this patriot hid, under a cold exterior, was a truly republican soul inside. It was he who gave them advice on how to conduct themselves; it was he who directed them in their relations with the Polish colony, which was then in Paris. Among these refugees were Joseph Wyhicki, Joseph Lipski, Denis Mniewski, Jean Demhowski, Romuald Giedroyc, Adam Bronic, Joseph Wielhorski, Gabriel Taszycki, and a few others. No doubt a single feeling animated all these patriots; but, according to purpose, they were sometimes divided over the choice of means. The disproportion of talents and fortune further contributed to complicate the relations they had between them. At other times, indiscretions of youth came to compromise the whole future of Poland; for in the subaltern crowd that roamed, at that time, the pavement of Paris, there were doubtless spies, bought by the conquering powers, who watched, even in their exile, the remains of an annihilated nation.

In the midst of such opposing elements, it took a great deal of caution and tact not to compromise one's self. A close connection was formed between Xavier Dąbrowski, Romuald Giedroyc, and the generous Tremo. Charles Prozor joined them as well. Forgetting all their own

[1]The romantic circumstances that accompanied the deliverance of Dąbrowski, are detailed in an autograph manuscript of Elie Tremo, which we like to make known to our readers. The dedication of this young patriot, his presence of mind, the dangers that he ran with his companion in escape is of interest not only to the Poles, but also all to sensitive souls. This is a tale that we throw in the middle of a story, but true tale, and the frankness and the strangeness of Eli Tremo's style would be a guarantee for those who would not know the loyalty of his character.

comforts to think only of their unhappy country, they were constantly occupied with it, and ended by treating those who did not share their fiery passion with coldness and indifference. They even included the official agent of the Poles in this group, who, however, was well regarded by the government and by the delegates for Foreign Relations, in consequence of the care taken in this respect by Kazimierz De la Roche.

The latter, born in Warsaw, and son of a former chargé d'affaires of the King of France in Moldavia and Poland, began his career as a volunteer in the battalion of Seine-et-Oise, in 1789 and 1790. Recalled to Poland, he served as the interpreter secretary of the French Legation in Warsaw, he maintained the closest relations with the first families of the Republic, and deserved the thanks of the most active members of the Constituent Diet, including those of Kosciuszko himself; however, De la Roche could never sympathize with Pawlikowski, Meyer, Hoszkiewicz, and many others who represented the purely democratic party. In fact, this party, by its exaggeration and its demands, contributed to maintain false ideas about Poland in the minds of the French, and thus removed the effect of that favorable impression that was attached to such a fine cause.

Kazimierz De la Roche, who moved away from Warsaw in 1792, at the time when the Targowicans seized power, had left diplomacy for a second lieutenant's epaulette, in the legion of the unfortunate Joseph Mionczynski: but he was not active then, and forgot, in this temporary rest, his six or seven months of service at the orders of this general, and those of Dumourier, both friends of his father, both of whom were persecuted and proscribed. Albert Turski, nicknamed the "Sarniate," who profited from De la Roche's departure from Warsaw, to go to Paris with him, had, at that time, solemnly protested at the bar of the National Convention against Muscovite violence, and offered, in the name of the Polish Constitutionalists, to devote their arms to the French cause, if France consented to embrace theirs. He served for some time under Generals Houchard and Custine; but seeing that the intention of avenging his country was a very secondary object for the French government, he sought allies among the Turks, during the embassy of the Marquis de Sainte-Croix, who became Citizen de Descorches at Constantinople.

In fact, at that time (1792) the Committee of Public Safety and the Ministry of Foreign Affairs had given the Polish agents public pronouncements of admiration and friendship, it must be borne in mind that France was at war with all of Europe, that she could form alliances with the Ottoman Porte and Sweden, timid allies, and, moreover, indifferent to the Polish cause; making it impossible for it to organize, at a distance of five hundred leagues, the resistances which it was necessary to multiply on its own frontiers.

Mastered in this way by the force of circumstances, and thwarted in their good intentions, the French appreciated the brave efforts that the Poles had just made, guided by the immortal Kosciuszko. A people, succumbing with arms in hand, was entitled to the interest of contemporaries as much as to the homage of posterity, and although joined under less favorable auspices, the bond which united and unites Poland to France, nevertheless was part of a common source. It is, indeed, in their struggles, their reverses, or their victories against a common enemy, that we must seek the origin of that national sympathy, which binds one people to another. Treaties drawn on the field of battle, cemented by the blood of brave men, have a character far more sacred than treaties of war subsidies for offensive and defensive wars, these sad conventions coldly calculated, dictated by political expediency, where there are tariffs for actions and bonuses for courage. The immortal glory that France has gained by contributing so generously to the independence of North America would have been complete had it been able to reconquer the independence of Poland as well. Everything led one to believe that she would execute under the Republican regime what she had done so gloriously elsewhere under the monarchical regime. This hope, which explains the irresistible sympathy of the Poles for the French nation, was deeply engraved in their minds; and even since that time, whenever a major event has come to threaten the European equilibrium, Poland immediately turns its attention to France as to its North Star.

These were then the unanimous sentiments of the patriots assembled at Paris, and the daily interest which all the classes of the citizens had, only served to strengthen them more. Such was also the result of this rapprochement between the United States and Poland, where the refugees drew consolation for the present, and hope for the future; but more interaction, more representation, more dignity was necessary for them to take advantage of all these favorable chances, and it was necessary to be in agreement, not only on the principles, but also on the actions and on the moves.

Unfortunately, it was on this point that differences broke out. Everyone wanted to see his own opinion triumph, everyone supported themselves with stubborn frankness, and yet, although all of them had the claim, few of them were able to give the negotiations a salutary direction. However, while they finally agreed that individual views, in such delicate circumstances, could be rather harmful than useful: also the most disinterested in this respect, that is to say, the youngest, animated only by that warmth of conviction which sees only the goal, still happy enough to ignore the prestige of ambition, offered themselves as docile instruments to give such pure elements a tendency worthy of them. Still full of memories of their country, of that military glory that had survived its disaster, they gladly devoted themselves to diplomatic troubles, in the hope of advancing the great act of Poland's regeneration. At a respectable distance from the secrecy of the departments, strangers to this political slowness, afraid of passionate individuals, not foreseeing either hindrances or difficulties, ameliorate and glory were their fixed idea; to serve both one and acquire the other, was their only desire.

The young Tremo, who had often heard of the former secretary of the French Legation De la Roche in Poland, was aware of his presence in Paris, and his active co-operation with the proceedings of Barss, hastened along with Dąbrowski to go to his home. Their first interview was quite insignificant, and De la Roche simply sent them back to his colleague. However, after sending them a few questions about the public spirit as well as the military situation, since the unfortunate battle of Maciejowice; he seemed to pay more particular attention when Tremo assured him that no Polish officer was answering the offer to serve in the armies of the invading powers, but that soldiers and non-commissioned officers were being forcibly taken into their ranks, when he returned to the same subject. De la Roche could not restrain himself and said to Tremo warmly: “In doing so, the powers provide these brave men with the means and rations to join us. These prophetic words electrified the fiery Tremo, and from that day these two patriots bound themselves to a closer friendship. However, three or four months later De la Roche opened up to Tremo on his future projects; then he urged him daily to act prudently and discreetly, to restrain himself in his remarks, adding that the only way to carry out a political affair was to treat it calmly, by isolating himself from his own sensations. Tremo realized the accuracy of these observations and endeavored to master the ardor of his character. Sometime later, Joseph Zablocki and Thomas Maruszewski left Paris, and De la Roche, wishing to bring his two new friends closer to him, proposed to Tremo and Ignace Jasinski (brother of General Jasinski, who died on the assault of Praga), to come to the Hotel Diesbach, in the suburb of Saint-Honoré, a lodging which this departure left there for free. In this hotel, which De la Roche had furnished and arranged at his own expense, Polish refugees and prominent men who were interested in their cause met daily. It was here that the military and civil notabilities, the most distinguished writers of the time, and finally all those who, by their political position or their talents, could exert some influence on the future of the Poland. Among the persons who knew how to plead with the greatest eloquence the interests of misfortune and liberty, we find Chénier, Thibaudeau, Fréron, La Harpe, Rousselion, Dalma, and with them the ladies Beauharnais, Tallien, Louvet, La Goree, and finally several intellectuals and artists of the first order.

De la Roche, excelled in politics, and not neglecting any means of achieving his end, made the slight tastes of a nation bow to the accomplishment of the most serious project. Evenings, balls, dinners consisting of twenty, thirty and forty courses, nothing was neglected to put the protectors and the protected in contact. From these daily meetings came intimacy and abandonment, and soon Poles were regarded only as Frenchmen and brothers.

In spite of the patriotic intentions of De la Roche, he had the pain of being faced with slanders from some disgruntled refugees. One could see where people pretended to see in this conduct a secret motive of personal ambition, a suspicion all the more unjust, that this generous patriot saw engulfed in this establishment the remains of a fortune which he never found again. Better still, when his position no longer sufficed for this expense, and after eight months of continual disbursements, still wishing to assure the Poles this much needed meeting point, the house, servants, furniture, silverware, linen and supplies were placed at the disposal of Mniewski, Prozor, and Giedroyc. Auguste Bonneau was asked by the latter to regulate and continue its management.

In spite of all these minor intrigues, and personal discontent, the Polish patriots never ceased to hear one another when the vital question of their independence was agitated, and that idea, which was recurring every day in a new way, by suggesting to individuals of different means, perhaps created alone in the mass these peculiar misunderstandings.

The time in which one lived then, was a period full of events. It seemed as if, tired of its old chains, the whole world was marching towards universal freedom. The national convention was still in full force, and France was throwing a few rays of its luminous influence on all Europe. Pichegru improvised the conquest of Holland. The Peace of Tuscany, the first peace concluded with republican France, made it enter the European system, and Prussia, under the law of necessity, consented, like Tuscany, to a definitive treaty with the Republic. On 13 Vendemiaire (5 October 1795), by serving the fortune of Bonaparte, a new reflection of glory and power was exhibited by this Convention. It seemed that liberty was conquering, and that Europe was going to cover itself with republics. Frightened by this rapid progress, Russia did not know what to do. Austria lacked the strength and energy. Surprised, Prussia silently awaited the outcome of this glorious drama. Fearing in her own breast the explosion of liberal ideas that the universities of Germany had long fomented, fearing the French on one of its frontiers, the Poles on the other, it was so happy then to preserve its neutrality. All was, therefore, favorable; all promised the refugees aid against their tyrants; but it was said, as M. de Norvins observed, that the genius of the Convention should not be seconded by that of Bonaparte, conspiring together for the liberty of the people.[2]

Prior to, and at its meeting on 19 November 1792, the National Convention had, at the proposal of Lepaux, issued a decree that guaranteed relief and fraternity to any people who wished to regain

[2] *L'Histoire de Napoléon*, 4 volumes, 1828.

their independence. The executive power was charged with giving the generals the necessary orders to support these peoples, and to protect the persecuted citizens of the cause of liberty. And on the motion of the Convention Sergeant at Arms, it was furthermore decided that this decree would be translated and printed in all languages.

This decree, from the moment it was issued, was entirely illusory, since France had to defend its own frontiers, the refugees thought it right to invoke it in 1795, as a title to the benevolence of the government. For the rest, it was neither armed assistance nor active protection that they asked for; it was only an asylum, a meeting point where the Poles could evade servitude and ripen their regeneration. It was necessary that this hospitable land should serve as a rendezvous for the generals, who were prisoners of war, and who, fatigued by their chains, were waiting for liberators.

It was no longer the time to execute this bold project, which General Dąbrowski had twice put forward and which he had seen rejected twice. All the efforts of the Polish soldiers had become the object of the most active surveillance, and the slightest attempts would have been suppressed from birth. However, Joseph Wybicki, who was in Paris, was put, in direct contact with the French government by De la Roche and attracted his kind attention to a people worthy of better destinies.

Joseph Wybicki was an ardent and devoted patriot, full of talents and energy, is the same one who, in 1794, was sent with full powers to General Dąbrowski, when he commanded the Army of Great Poland. It is from this period that dates the friendship which united these two generous citizens in friendship that never changed, and which they preserved until the tomb. Even absence did not ordinarily prevent them from giving evidence of sincere affection; but the impossibility of communicating from Paris to Warsaw interrupted their relations for some time. For his part, Dąbrowski, receiving no further news from his friend, and presuming that he had met the faithful group of Polish refugees, made every effort to know the place of their residence; chance soon informed him of their presence in Paris, and their efforts with the Republic. On this news, he immediately sent a trusted man to ascertain the truth; but this man, having arrived on the French frontier, vainly tried to pass it, but was forced to return without being able to fulfill his mission.

Fortunately, in this interval, the citizen Pierre Parendier, who was then in Berlin, informed the refugees of the progress of negotiations between France and the Prussian Cabinet. This Parendier, whom De la Roche had known as a secretary to Ignacy Potocki, in 1791 and 1792, who had since been named, on the recommendation of De la Roche, as an agent for Polish affairs in Germany, had always preserved a tender attachment to the Polish cause, and then endeavored more than ever to give proof of it.[3]

In fact, it was not until after the conclusion of a definitive peace between France and Prussia that the relations between the Polish refugees and those who remained in their native country were renewed. Citizen Caillard, appointed ambassador of the French Republic to the Berlin Court, served them as an intermediary point. This respectable citizen, after having begun his diplomatic career, as secretary of the legation at Parma, then in 1773 at Cassel, followed M. de Verac, in 1774, to Copenhagen, and, in 1780, to St. Petersburg, where, during the absence of the Ambassador, he carried out his duties with prudence and sagacity, which reconciled him with general esteem. Appointed later to the Hague Embassy, he became friends with the Minister Plenipotentiary, Michel Oginski, sent by the Republic of Poland at the time of the Constituent Diet. From this was born the real interest that this diplomat brought to the Polish nation, an interest of which he gave proof by rendering it service whenever circumstances permitted. At the time when these various events were going on, his intervention could exert the greatest influence. Citizen Joseph Wybicki wanted to take advantage of it, and through the Polish Major Forestier, a brave and worthy soldier, he sent to Caillard, in September 1795, the following note concerning the affairs of Poland:

> *By what means can the Polish nation recover its political existence, and how could France cooperate with it?*
>
> *1. If the French Republic allowed a representation of the Polish nation composed of patriotic nuncios of the Diet of May 3, 1791, and if it would then begin negotiations, what would be the goal of the regeneration of the Polish republic?*
>
> *2. Where should the rendezvous of this representation be, or rather of this simply limited diet, which has been the last legal representation of the nation, which is generally recognized for such by all the powers of Europe, with the exception of Russia, and against the annihilation of which Citizen Descorches, the Extraordinary Envoy of the French Republic, to that of Poland, declared.*
>
> *3. Would it be possible, under the authority of this diet and under the auspices of the French Republic, to recruit and raise Polish corps, which would be free to serve, not only in Poland, but wherever circumstances so require? These corps could easily*

[3]On a host of autographed letters that exist in our hands, and which we do not share with our readers, because in the middle of a few sentences concerning Poland, they are almost entirely about details particular to the people who have written them, there are some, however, that we make it a duty to reproduce, addressed at various times by the citizen Parendier to De la Roche, one of which, drawn partly in agreed figures, recalls the state from the Republic to the cruelest moment of invasion, the other is a genuine proof of the efforts this citizen lavished on Berlin for the regeneration of Poland.

train Russian and Austrian deserters; and the officers and soldiers who are still in Poland would hasten to rejoin the flags of their nation, when they would see a legal representation of their nation, under the guarantee of France or her allies.

4. The French nation and its allies could furnish the necessary funds, both for the raising and maintenance of the Polish Army, and for the maintenance of the said diet; which money the Polish nation would certainly not refuse to restore, when a general peace would guarantee its political existence.

5. In the event that political reasons prevent the French government from giving a categorical reply to the above-mentioned articles, would it not be possible to create legions of the Polish Army; and if destiny opposed the regeneration of Poland, its legions could, after having done their duty in the service of France, acquire the rights of citizens?

6. These ideas and the above-mentioned points do not come from a few isolated individuals, but from the greater part of the well-intentioned Poles, and especially from the military side, who have projected them; and if the need so requires, their signatures could be produced despite all the obstacles.

7. In case it is necessary to find in Paris one or more persons enjoying the confidence of the nation to engage them by the foregoing clauses, and to give the clarifications in due course, these persons are all ready to accept the task.

This detailed note, which presented all the questions in their true light, remained for the moment unanswered; for the propitious hour had not yet arrived. We will see later how it was reproduced by Dąbrowski himself, and how successful it was.

The new impetus for opportunities awoke the enthusiasm of Wybicki and De la Roche. They moved more than ever to gather in one and the same center all the debris that had escaped from the great shipwreck, and to organize a new Polish army in the midst of France, with its old leaders and its ancient patriotism. The execution of such a project required special prudence, as it was not wise to confide the secret to the crowd of Polish refugees who were in Paris, it was necessary that the person charged with going to Poland to sound out the public spirit, appear to the eyes of the masses to have a different purpose. There was talk of the need for a raid into Greater Poland to find the necessary funds for Hotel Dirsbach, an essential meeting place for Polish refugees. This measure was discussed, opposed and supported, and as it was finally adopted, Kazimirz De la Roche and Elie Tremo devoted themselves to its fulfillment. The affair was conducted with such skill that the latter only learned of his friends' plan and their true mission on the way.

However, if message was enough on one side to ostensibly disguise the truth from the gullible refugees and prevent their rash actions; on the other hand, it was also essential to take further precautions to deceive the authorities of the countries through which they were to travel. For this purpose, De la Roche and Elie Tremo, being qualified as art dealers, left for Basel with passports of the Minister of External Affairs, and there, 3 December 1795, having exchanged them for other passports at their destination in Berlin, delivered by Minister Hardenberg, they continued on their way to the frontiers of Saxony. In order to conceal their project, many crates of art objects preceded or accompanied them in the direction of Leipzig, and the sales they made served in addition to providing ample expenses for their journey.

Jealous of the sort of mystery with which the triumvirate, who worked so actively for the national cause, was concerned, some of the Paris refugees tried to hinder their efforts, and even to thwart them in reimbursement of their expenses; but they did not know that apart from these scanty resources, De la Roche, in order to give Tremo the facility of penetrating, not only into Southern Prussia, but to Warsaw and as far as Grodno, had given him a second ostensible mission, much more important. They were supposed to claim 21,280 ducats owed by King Stanislas Augustus; 783 ducats by Clement Bernaux, 1,950 ducats from a man named Bresce, a landlord in Warsaw: altogether, 24,013 ducats, or 288,156 francs, to which was added a recovery from the banker Meissner of 166,200 francs, adding to a total of 454,356 francs, in claims on the portion of Poland invaded by Prussia. These claims were the property of French subjects who had handed over the management to De la Roche, and De la Roche had in turn entrusted it to Tremo. But this was only the apparent motive, for their main plan was to find a Polish general in these oppressed lands, who, rescued by their care and encourage by their generosity, would become the head of this national representation which was to rise in the shade of the French flags.

Elie Tremo, who was then coordinating this great idea, felt the importance of his mission: seeing the responsibility levied on him, he resolved to be worthy of the trust that had been given of him.

When they arrived at Leipzig, where they would go in different directions, the two friends summed up their whole plan in a final conference. They had known that General Dąbrowski was urged by Suvorov to accept the rank of lieutenant-general in the service of Russia. Dąbrowski, both through his talents as a soldier and by his personal character, was more than any other capable of fulfilling their patriotic purpose, and they concluded that it was necessary to wrest this illustrious citizen from their enemies, to carry him to the command of the corps of compatriots that were to organize themselves.

Bearing this letter in support of this endeavor, Tremo took care to provide himself with funds and letters of credit in Dresden and Warsaw, which did not lessen the importance of recovering debts as indicated in his ostensible mission and gave a more positive character to his secret mission. His family relations guaranteed him, in any case, unexpected success beyond all others. With such powerful motivational factors, he was eager to reach the goal, and to fulfill his new destiny. At last De la Roche left his friend, and Tremo left for Dresden, where he arrived on 1 January 1796, at the Hotel de Ange d'Or, traveling under the name of Reimont, a merchant from Leipzig.

Through the intermediary of his banker Gregori, Tremo learned that a man named Hoszkiewicz, coming from Paris, had passed there a few days before, making many indiscreet remarks, not only in front of the Poles, but even in front of the foreigners. He inquired to all people and even with concern about the passage of Tremo and De la Roche and seemed very surprised to learn that they had not arrived yet. These reports proved to Tremo how essential it was to hasten his journey to neutralize the effect of this imprudence.

Towards the end of January, he stopped at Posen, at his sister's house, and at Klug; but after having, by all possible precautions, secured his correspondence with De la Roche, he left on the 30th of the same month for Warsaw, where he could, meet with General Dąbrowski under the greatest secrecy.

Once in this capital, while dealing with the confidential interests that were committed to him, Tremo wanted to maintain the cover of his mission. He therefore began to inquire into the manner in which the recovery of claims against King Stanislaus Augustus should take place, when a person arriving from Grodno they informed him that he would arrive at this residence only with a passport sent from the palace itself; that the commission charged with liquidating the debts of the former king was not there, or rather that it did not exist.

This strange news forced Tremo to ask the man from Grodno for more direct information, and to wait for answers to the letters he had sent.

It was his uncle Paul Tremo, who had followed Stanislas Augustus to his new residence, and, on 24 February 1796, satisfied all his requests. He said to him, while recognizing him as validly responsible for these important claims, that all he could do to that end would come to nothing, and that he was referring to it in this way that Chamberlain Duhamel had marked in his last correspondence; that it was necessary to wait until the general affairs were finished, which would probably still take a very long time. He also advised to keep the credentials, to deliver them to the right people when necessary, and submit all claims to Duhamel.

This information, however, was not good for the apparent mission of Tremo, and after some delays while staying in Great Poland, for which he intended to meet the expenses of Hotel Diesbach, he received help from De La Roche, who paid these expenses so he could continue in the principal object of the journey, and saw in it only a plausible means of reaching their true end, prolonging their stay in Poland.

The two envoys had received information from Wybicki, who like them was initiated in the secret plan[4], to be given to the Polish military. They knew that the Russian government attached great importance to being able to incorporate the officer of the old army among its troops. This desire on their part came less from justice rendered to their talents and bravery than from a constant intention of representing the Polish cause as lost, since the major leaders had abandoned it. Tremo and De la Roche, knowing all these details, and agreed to support their cause, showed their compatriots the honor and independence of one side, the shame and servitude of the other. For Poles, the choice was not difficult. Besides, it was well known that the King's nephew, Prince Joseph Poniatowski, and many other superior officers, had rejected the thought of such a defection, and fearing as an outrage to this proposition, kept it discreet.

Placed in the first rank in the military hierarchy, esteemed by the Russians themselves for his personal merit, General Dąbrowski had become the object of General Suvorov's particular aims. Since he was aware that Dąbrowski was without fortune, he was pressed more vigorously than the others; but it is to the honor of this generous citizen to declare that he did not hesitate for a moment to take up the flag of the national cause, when he saw the possibility of securing a more glorious future for his country. Real offers were lavished on him in vain by the opposite party; he tried all sorts of inducements with him; the general, however, remained unshaken and faithful to his oaths.

If there were still some cynical, or some little envious men, who added credence to the vague declamations that were being spread against the Polish patriots, all the official documents that follow will prove that they, on every occasion, sacrificed their own interests to those of their country: real statements against trouble, they teach those who still maintain doubts that either Dąbrowski or any of his companions in arms acted on personal ambition. When the Russians, Prussians, and Austrians, jealous of reputation of such brave warriors, proposed to receive them in their armies at the same rank, they replied with a refusal. Only a few old, disabled officers accepted the four-year salary they were given as an allowance and as a pension. The others would receive nothing from their conquerors, and, free from all engagement, waited in silence for the hour of vengeance to come.

We see how many of these brave soldiers went to the banks of the Rhine and the fields of Italy, when a distant call brought them

[4]The other patriots, such as Barss, Prozor Woyczynski, Kuehanouski, Joseph Wielhorski, etc., who affixed their signatures to the project presented to the French government for the formation of the Polish legions, dated March 1796, which is mentioned in the Mémoires de Oginski, Volume 11, page 183, were not privy to the mission of De la Roche only after his departure to the borders of Poland, at the end of 1795, as we have already said..

back under the banner of the new Polish legions. We see them suffer all privations, and conquer all obstacles, face a thousand deaths to find themselves at the rendezvous of honor. Some, crossing the states of Germany, at the risk of being captured and forced to enlist under the enemy's banner, will make a route of six hundred leagues over land to rejoin their brothers-in-arms; the others, on their way to Constantinople, joined the English or barbarian cruisers, and finally landed in Italy. All, worthy of a better fate, would fight a hundred battles in foreign countries, in the hope of making their way to their homeland, and we shall see them fall as victims, or live as avengers of an imperishable cause.

CHAPTER FIVE

Occupation of Warsaw by the Prussians. — Dąbrowski goes to Berlin. — His Presentation to the King. — Boldness of His Speech. — His Conferences with Bischofswerder and Möllendorf. — His Visit to the Prince Bishop Krasicki. — His Refusal to Serve Prussia. — His Trip to Leipzig. — Rivalry of Generals Dąbrowski and Giedroyc. — Kazimirz De la Roche Intervenes to Stop It. — Momentary Discouragement of Dąbrowski. — Departure of De la Ropche for Berlin. — His Position With the Prince Palatine Radziwill. — Gaffron, Forestier, Caillard. — Change of Politics in the Prussian Court vis-à-vis the Poles. — Sumptuousness of the House of Radziwill. — Alliance Between this Family and the Royal Branch of Ferdinand of Prussia. — Opposition of the Prussian Minister. — Frederick William Consents to this Marriage Despite His Ministers. — Courageous Plea of De la Roche and Favor of the Polish Generals Madalinski, Grabowski, and Gielgrund, Prussian Prisoners. — He Obtains Their Release. — Polish Joy. — Marriage Festival. — Sudden Arrival of General Dąbrowski in Berlin. — His Interview with De la Roche. — Dąbrowski Departs for Leipzig. — His Letter to Minister Caillard. — The Minister's Response. — Dąbrowski Heads for France with Letters for General Jourdan. — His Arrival at the Republican Army. — Refugees from Venice. — Assembly of the Poles on the Turkish Frontiers. — Demarches of Oginski. — Verninac. — Aubert-de-Bayet. — Letter from Orginski to Bonaparte. — Sulkowski. — Verbal Response from Bonaparte. — Xavier Dąbrowski. — His Projects. — Oginski's Return to Paris. — Details on His Trip. — His Arrival.

Upon the occupation of Warsaw by the Prussian troops on 9 January 1796, General Dąbrowski asked and obtained permission to travel to Berlin.[1] He therefore left the old capital of Poland on 19 February, after

[1]The Prussian troops consisted of twelve thousand men, with a large artillery, when they entered Warsaw. The administration was reformed, and the vacant places taken from the Poles were given to the subjects of the King of Prussia. All the affairs were managed, and the justice administered in the German language, which the patricians and the businessmen did not know. The most rigorous measures were taken to prevent and suppress any kind of movement. Two thousand Prussians were constantly on foot and on duty. An order directed all the inhabitants to surrender their arms under certain penalties, and

having, in several conferences with Tremo, combined the most useful measures with the projects of the Parisian confederates.

For his part Dąbrowski assisted in the object of their plan, went to Berlin with the Minister Caillard, Ambassador of the Republic, and with the other Frenchmen attached to the legation. He tried to ascertain if there was any hope left for the future of his country, and having read the note presented by Major Forestier, he presented it again, insisting on an answer.

While Dąbrowski followed his patriotic agenda, Frederick William, who wished to attach himself to it, welcomed him in the most favorable manner. On 17 March 1796, he was presented to the King and Court, in his general's uniform in the service of Poland, and this favor caused a general surprise to foreigners and nationals. The King even wished to grant him a personal audience, but on the general's reply that, having neither grace to ask of him nor any proposal to make him, this favor was useless, Frederick William did not insist further. Taking pleasure in his conversation, however, he questioned him for an entire hour. This conversation turned on the last war of independence, on the siege of Warsaw, which, according to the King, had failed only because of the ill-will of the Russians; finally, Frederick William having asked him what was the public spirit in Poland, Dąbrowski replied that "the Poles would all be his, if, in turn, he wanted to restore their independence, and if, agreeing with the other powers he placed it in the list of nations; that, after such an act of magnanimity on his part, he had no doubt that they would choose a constitutional head in his own person or in that of a prince of his house. The King was silent for some time, and only spoke again to praise the bravery and energy of the Poles. Following this interview, Dąbrowski also had conferences

---

each denouncer who declared to the Prussian regency hidden arms received a reward of fifty ducats, with promises to keep the secret of his name. It was also expressly forbidden to insult Prussian sentinels or patrols with deeds or words; and, on the contrary, they were ordered to show them all the respect that was due to them. However, when it demanded the homage of the city of Warsaw to the minister delegated by the King of Prussia, it declared that after having always been the capital of the Republic of Poland, and the residence of its sovereigns, it could not lend the homage of fidelity to the King himself in person. As a consequence of this, Frederick William recalled Hoym to Berlin, and summoned the Prussian employees destined for the administration of Warsaw. They were replaced by Poles; and Buchholtz also left Poland to go to Breslau in Silesia.

with Bischofswerder, Möllendorf, and was in particular received in the friendliest manner by the Prince Archbishop of Gniezno, Ignacy Krasicki, the famous Polish poet, who lived in Berlin, surrounded by all the honors which are attached to an illustrious writer.

This conduct of the King of Prussia towards Dąbrowski seemed all the more remarkable, since six months prior he was regarded at court as a revolutionary.[2] All was cleared up, however, when the Prussian ministry redoubled its influence with him in order to persuade him to accept service in its armies. The general, always invariable in his principles, replied that he did not wish to be the only one so favored, that his companions in arms were inactive and unhappy; lastly, that he would enter the Prussian service only with thirty thousand men, if Frederick William wished, in concert with the French Republic, to restore his rights to an oppressed people, and to Poland. The King heard this proposition without answering it, but also without giving the slightest sign of disapproval.[3]

Dąbrowski, however, wishing to take advantage of his position, tried new approaches with the Berlin Cabinet, and gave it a memorandum for this purpose, in which he detailed by what means Prussia could restore Poland by covering herself with an immortal glory and working nevertheless in its own interest.

---

[2]It should also be noted that The Prussian King was aligned with Poland and turned its back on the country when Russia attacked in 1792.

[3]The Minister Caillard, whose dispatches addressed to the government provided us with the information that has just been read, besides said in one dated Berlin 12 March 1796, No. 52, and in another of the 13th of the same month, No. 55: "General Dąbrowski has just arrived in Berlin. This soldier, who was the terror of the Prussians, who carried out the insurrection of Greater Poland, who had taken Bromberg, and seized the coffers of the government, is now caressed by Prussia, who, like to Madalinski, made him offers to enter its service, that he did not accept. He is convinced that the fate of Poland is still in the hands of the King of Prussia, and that if that prince sincerely wishes to ally himself with France, and to take with it a determination in accordance with its interests, it is easy for it to wring from Russia and Austria what they have of Poland, and to restore that country to the existence it had at the time of May 3. Dąbrowski will arrange his business in Saxony; he would like to go to Paris, for he feels that it is France which must regulate the destiny of Europe, and that it is by France alone that Poland can preserve some hope. He is for his country a precious instrument; his patriotism, his courage and his enlightenment, deserve the benevolence of the French government. .... Dąbrowski has the confidence of his compatriots and the Polish military; he has talents and means; he is eager for glory; it is necessary to preserve it, especially if the war between Turkey and Austria breaks out.

Persuasive as the arguments of the general might be, and the warmth to which he requested support for a favorable reply, the Prussian ministry only replied in an evasive way, reserving to itself to take the part that circumstances indicated.

Thus, betrayed in his hopes and renouncing any further attempt to convince unbelievers, Dąbrowski left Berlin and went to Saxony. After spending some time in Leipzig, he left for Dresden, where he arrived on 13 June 1796, and where Tremo had already arrived, coming from Warsaw.

It was then more than ever that this young patriot, entering the spirit of his mission, gained the confidence of General Dąbrowski. Recalling to him in all its details the plan that the refugees had conceived in Paris, he saw how much the soul of this warrior was open to good wishes, and from that moment they became inseparable.

Among the Poles who crossed to the capital of Saxony, Dąbrowski met General Romuald Giedroyc at the Palatine of Seeburg, going to join his family in Lithuania, and who was at the same time charged with managing that province.

General Giedroyc was not one of those whom it was thought necessary to share the projected military organization with Paris. Being clear-sighted and ambitious, he had not been deceived about Tremo's and De la Roche's trip. His meeting in Dresden with General Dąbrowski, accompanied by Tremo, the certainty that he later acquired their correspondence with De la Roche, although the latter kept as far as possible from Dresden, put him on the path of their past steps and their future projects. From that moment General Giedroyc could not restrain his spite. He had persuaded himself that no other name than his would be at the head of the new Polish corps. Full of bravery and initiative, he firmly believed that in fact of military notability, no one could fight better than him. Meanwhile, Dąbrowski kept an entire reserve there, protesting that he was coming for service in Saxony, several stormy encounters took place between these two competitors, and caused very unpleasant scenes.

While acknowledging the truth to the noble intentions of General Giedroyc, it must be pointed out here that he was not then in a sufficiently independent position to be able to safely achieve the rank to which he aspired. Without wishing to decide anything about the rights of the two competitors, it was thought that General Giedroyc was careful to keep neutral towards the co-invading powers, either because of his family or because of his fortune. Besides, the French government, which had the upper hand in this project, did not wish to compromise anyone; and if he later deviated from this conduct by calling the Poles to insurrection, it is because the victories of Bonaparte and the soldiers of the reorganized legions were there to support his new decision.

As soon as Kazimierz De la Roche received the first news of the misunderstanding that had broken out between Dąbrowski and Giedroyc, he hurried off from Leipzig, and went to Dresden to stifle these dissensions in their cradle. With his amiable and conciliatory character, he soon persuaded the latter to sacrifice his self-esteem to the national cause. He even had the talent to console himself by saying that if the military organization lost an energetic leader in him, his family would find a father, and Poland a good patriot. Finally, decided by the influence of De la Roche, General Giedroyc left for Lithuania with regrets which praised his heart and character.

This incident, which Dąbrowski beat out his competitor, produced in his soul the opposite effect to that which was to be expected. Far from feeling content with this triumph, far from drawing new strength to justify a glorious choice, his zeal and energy were considerably cooled. From that moment he seemed to be in doubt and seemed to bring caution with every step. He even wrote a letter to The Citizen, in which he seemed undecided as to the course he should follow, and showed a desire to change his means, without, however, changing his purpose. It cannot be positively affirmed here whether this letter is authentic or not, whether or not its content could be detrimental to the Polish cause. All that can be guaranteed is that it exists among the appendices to the memoirs of General Dąbrowski, and that we must therefore quote it. However, it should be noted that the persons mentioned in this document are only identified by their initials, which makes it enigmatic today, while in the crowd of supporting documents that corroborated this story, this case never occurred either in those emanating from Dąbrowski himself, or in those from other sources.

A circumstance, which at this time further cooled Dąbrowski's zeal was the lack of union among the Poles remaining in Paris. Not only did the dissenting portion of the refugees seek to hinder the efforts of those who shared the common interest, but they had not been able to keep the decorum so necessary for their success in the French capital. The Hotel Diesbach, that central point meeting place, which was established at great cost, was destroyed, and the refugees seemed, by their dissensions or carelessness, to declare loudly that they despaired of the future.

De la Roche, tired of so many inconveniences, saw that his presence in Saxony brought no results, believed that, with their comings and goings, the Poles became the object of an active monitoring. He left Tremo with General Dąbrowski and went to Berlin. At the same time, he was recalled to this capital by the Palatine Prince Michel Radziwill, who wanted him to become part of his retinue. This prince, presuming that his presence in Germany was a result of forced emigration, read renewed proposals on this subject made to him some years before, when the French legation had been removed. Instead La Roche prepared to return to France.

This time, instead of rejecting the proposals of the Prince Palatine, De la Roche considered them timely. He reflected that henceforth the capital of Prussia was the most suitable theater for his projects; since he would be in daily contact with Paraudier, Forestier, Gaffron, a former agent of King Frederick II, in Turkey, all his confidants and a supporter of the cause. He thought that he might still be able to watch General Dąbrowski's departure for France, a constant object of his care and solicitude. But having accepted a job with Prince Radziwill, he still wished to maintain his independence, and to put himself at his disposal without accepting special treatment. He needed his freedom for projects he could not communicate.

Arriving at Berlin, De la Roche soon realized that the policy of this court vis-a-vis the Poles had completely changed direction.

In fact, Prussia, which had played the most odious role in the invasion of Poland, seeking to excuse itself in the eyes of Europe from this Machiavellian plot, affecting to redouble respect and benevolence towards those who had been its victims. Following the first days after the dissolution of this unfortunate country, while the dungeons of St. Petersburg and the fortresses of Austria were full of prisoners, Prussia did not exercise the same rigor against three generals, Antoni Madalinski, George Grabowski and Antoni Gielgud. They received, however, the treatment due their rank and character! They were also offered service in the Prussian Army, and they owed their detention only to the most honorable refusal! But the moment had arrived when their noble conduct would find its reward. The King of Prussia, softened to these generous people, was, by giving freedom to these illustrious prisoners, gave Poland a new pledge of her remorse and consequence. Nevertheless, it was necessary to arrive at this course, which was first cause was determined by a romantic incident.

The same Prince Radziwill, Palatine of Vilna, requested De la Roche come to him in the month of January, having just established himself in Prussia, with the intention of settling there. Formerly a declared supporter of Russia, but then very cold towards it, he preferred to console himself of this hatred by putting himself under Prussian protection. He therefore bought one of the most beautiful palaces of Berlin, had it furnished with a very royal magnificence, and confining his ambition to the pleasure of adorning this sumptuous dwelling. He appealed to De la Roche for his assistance, because of his taste in the fine arts. In fact, the old Palatine, if he had not been a prince, would have passed for a true connoisseur in painting, and his children were artists distinguished in music, if they had not had the title of "highness." Soon this dazzling splendor, that luxury which contrasted with the petty economies of the Royal House of Prussia, made Radziwill's palace the center of good tone and magnificence. The honor of being admitted to the brilliant evenings of the Wilhelm Place was coveted; the only thing talked of in Berlin was parties, meals, and concerts which the sumptuous Palatine gave. This was a kind of moral compensation for the physical misfortunes that had weighed on Poland, since, subjugated by the sword, the vanquished came to dominate the arts in the center of the victorious states!

The Ferdinand branch of the Prussian Royal House, which was independent in its position, was the first to approach Radziwill, which, forced to leave the country where its ancestors had played such a large part, and came to ask a neighboring court for asylum and protection. A young princess, born of this branch, brought to the gifts of nature all the charms of talent and education, devoted a particular affection to this family, and soon more intimate relations promised another conclusion.

Indeed, it was not long before they spoke aloud of a marriage project between the young Princess Ferdinande and Prince Antoine Radziwill. At the first news of this alliance, the Prussian Ministry raised a host of obstacles to prevent it. These were sometimes motivation of propriety, sometimes pecuniary motives, and sometimes political motives. As to propriety, Radziwill could fight with advantage. Backed by historical traditions and unquestionable written references, the house had been allied with the Imperial family, and a Princess Radziwill had once brought the principality of Taurogen to the House of Brandenburg. Thus, without compromising his dignity, the Ferdinand branch of Prussia could unite with one of the oldest Polish families. As to the motives of interest, in order to iron out any difficulty, the head of the Radziwill family, feeling the whole price of the new alliance, established in favor of his eldest son a bonus and advantages which, far from derogating, surpassed the endowments of the lateral branches of the royal family. Thus, these first two obstacles having been overcome, there still remained political expediency, and it was there that the ministry leaned on most heavily. The Radziwills presented such decisive arguments to combat them, that the struggle was not long. In fact, to sanction such a marriage, would it not be to prove by a solemn act that henceforth the Poles would be treated by Prussia on the same footing as its natives? Would it not be better to attach them to concessions of a broad and generous policy? Even if some partial obstacles came to oppose this work of reparation, reasons of state alone should have determined it! The King of Prussia understood this: that Russia and Austria, by imposing an iron yoke upon Poland, by watering the nobility with disdain, created in their bosoms only insubordinate subjects or conspiratorial soldiers. By flattering the pride of a people who surpassed their rulers in enlightenment, by bringing them by gentleness to submit to the new order of things, their conquest could be nationalized. Now, this alliance of royal dignity with one of the first houses of Poland, seemed to be both a satisfaction for the present and a pledge for the future. It was not only to bring those portions of Poland that had fallen to Prussia, but to exert unspoken influence over those areas held by the other partitioning powers.

Prince Radziwill quickly addressed all these questions vis-a-vis the King and the royal family, and, placed them on such solid foundations, the union triumphed over the prejudices and pedantry of the Prussian Ministry. Scarcely had this result been known, then public opinion responded with enthusiasm. The two nations seemed for a moment to form only one, and the conduct of the King in this circumstance dampened some grudges and made many forget old misfortunes.

Everyone in Berlin was joyful and there were preparations for a party to which so many hopes rallied, when, a few days before the wedding, Prince Louis Ferdinand, brother of the future groom, went to the house of his future brother-in-law, Palatine Radziwill, to spend the evening and have tea as usual. Kazimierz De la Roche was at the Palatine's that day. It was he who had written a memoir in response to that of the ministry to prove the usefulness of this alliance and was, therefore, well regarded by all parties. Always ready to render service to Poland and the Poles, he brought the general conversation to this subject, and exclaimed warmly, "that the interests of a monarchy ought not to be limited by such a circumstance of simple convenience of the partitioning parties; those ideas of a higher order were connected with it, when it was especially thought that there would enlighten, on one side, Princess Ferdinande and Prince Radziwill, happy at the foot of the altar, and on the other, Generals Madalinski, Grabowski and Gielgud, languishing in their dungeons." These words, pronounced with conviction and feeling, produced an electric effect on the young prince. He rushed to the door, rejoined the King, and left him only after the expedition of the couriers bearing the order to restore the liberty to those victims of the most noble devotion.

This touching episode came to lend a new charm to the festivities that embellished this marriage. Enthusiasm was at a peak in the court, in the public, and even among the Poles, when the last defenders of an expiring country were again proudly offered their tribute of gratitude to the King and the royal family, and especially to the happy couple who had so greatly influenced their destinies. Returned to liberty, these Polish generals returned to their families.

Such favorable news spread like lightning. It came to surprise of General Dąbrowski in Saxony, where he was recovering from a fall, while De la Roche thought he was already in Paris. So, to the astonishment of the latter when he saw Dąbrowski arriving in Berlin with Tremo - his inseparable companion. Not knowing what motives to attribute a journey so diametrically opposed to his hopes, he tried to sound out Dąbrowski, and asking him: "What are you doing here, General, I believed for a long time you were on the road to France?" At first, Dąbrowski appeared embarrassed by this question and replied that it was necessary to come to an understanding with him and with Minister Caillard, before commencing the thorny enterprise for which he had been destined, which was a sufficient motive for doing so; but, returning at once to his usual frankness, he confessed that curiosity was largely the cause of his journey; the desire to see what was happening in Prussia with his own eyes had determined him to undertake it. "You have just given me the best reason," replied De la Roche. "It explains everything; but, as outside the Minister of France, nobody here suspects our plans for the military organization, it should be, General, that you seem animated by the enthusiasm that is now igniting the Poles, an enthusiasm motivated by the change of system adopted in their favor by the Prussian Cabinet. A few words of gratitude in this respect from the mouth of a man like you, of a warrior who has been a terrible adversary to this power, can only produce a very good effect. I am going, General, to announce your arrival to Minister Caillard, and to inform Prince Radziwill of your desire to be presented to the court."

After some slight observations from General Dąbrowski, and many questions on the liberation of Generals Madalinski, Grabowski, and Gielgud: "Admit it, General," continued De la Roche, "that the active part I have taken in this affair contributed not a little to attracting you to Berlin. In making this step, I have only fulfilled a sacred duty for every Pole, and there would have been indifference or weakness on my part, had I neglected the favorable circumstance that presented itself. But you would have been mistaken as to my intentions, if you had supposed that this deliverance was motivated to give you competitors for the command of the Polish corps, which is organizing itself under French pay. This competition will be born of itself with time, but it is advisable for the French government, by providing relief and asylum to the Polish soldiers, to give them, as chief-organizer, a general of a proven reputation, and having administrative knowledge. A nation which fights successfully against a united Europe will gladly see, among the ranks of its defenders, brave men who have also gloriously succumbed for their country. It will be proud again to see a general at their head who has been sought after by the very powers he had fought against. Grasp the opportunity, general, the brilliant role which is reserved for you, and think that it is a question of pursuing the destroyers of the Polish name, wherever they are."

These warm words deeply resonated in General Dąbrowski's soul. Bursting with new energy, he resolved to accomplish the great task devolving upon him. While frequenting the politics in the houses of Radziwill and Ferdinand, he had secret conferences with the Minister of France, or with the agents of the legation, Dodun, Chateaugiron and Caillard's nephew. At last, believing that the favorable hour had arrived, he set out again with Tremo for Saxony, with the intention of continuing his journey towards France.[4]

Arrived at Leipzig, he waited patiently for some time for the instructions that Minister Caillard was to send him; but as this diplomatist opposed Polish enthusiasm with the cold slowness of an expectant politician, Dąbrowski could not conceal his impatience, and wrote him the following letter:

Leipzig, 2 August 1796

> *Citizen Minister, from the moment of my recovery to that of the present, all my attention has been directed solely to finding a favorable mode or occasion, which may draw me from the odious inaction in which I find myself, and to be able to work, in accordance with my principles and my duties, for the good of my country, or to fight for the good cause; that of which I have not ceased, Citizen Minister, to speak to you, even to annoy you with my prayers and my ideas, as I have just done in my last [letter] to citizen Parandier; but the fatality of the fate which pursues us, combined with the onerous circumstances, has constantly hin-*

[4] It is in these circumstances that Prince Louis Ferdinand, bluntly criticizing the awkwardness of the Prussian Ministry, did not seize the opportunity to gain the services the bravest Polish soldiers. De la Roche said to him: "Your Highness all the more reason, that another power will not fail to welcome them." Instead of following the prince's advice, he was exiled to Minden.

dered all my designs, and has left me only the patience and hope of a series of events more suited to our wishes. The moment, so desired, has finally come. Yes, Citizen Minister, the brilliant and repeated victories which have pointed out the intrepid courage of the Republican armies are preparing a most glorious epoch. Everywhere the phalanxes of liberty triumph and we remain idle, while citizens who up to this moment have known freedom only by name, already flatter themselves of the sweet hope of tasting the first fruits of it! And we, victims of tyranny, who carry in all places the feeling of our misfortunes, and those who inspire us with independence and liberty, would we hesitate for a moment to seize it? No, Citizen Minister, it would be to fail in honor, to fail in the duty imposed on us by the misery of a country dear to our children, and we will always be faithful to it until death. Together with that, I must announce that I resolved to leave immediately for Frankfurt, with one of my compatriots, who served as an aide-de-camp in the Polish Patriot Army, named Tremo, and my son. Your virtues, Citizen Minister, your talents and above all the part which you take with every unfortunate individual for the good cause, you have been able to deserve the name of their defender; it is also in this respect, and that of the friendly kindness with which you have honored me during my stay in Berlin, that I dare to flatter myself to succeed in my request to you. It's about, Citizen Minister, a letter of recommendation for General Jourdan, which can put me in a position to show him my high consideration, and the admiration of his military genius, his great military talents, and his reputation he has just been acquired.

I await this great favor, and by the feeling you have inspired in me and by the interest you have in the fate of our unfortunate country, and I assure you that my personal gratitude and the high consideration I have given you will only be extinguished with the existence of your most humble servant and friend.

DĄBROWSKI

In response to this request, Minister Caillard wrote to General Dąbrowski:

Berlin, 26 Thermidor Year IV (13 August 1796.)

General, I think I have quite well understood your character and your feelings in the short time that I had the pleasure of seeing you here, to be persuaded that your repose has excited in you the most greatest impatience, and I would with all my heart be able to open you a way to immediately put your talents and your ardor into action; [but] I do not see any at this moment.

The constitution excludes every foreigner from the service of the Republic; you cannot form any plans to enter the French armies. I do not think it agrees with you to accept the proposals made to you in Prussia; however, I do not claim to give you any advice on this: I only observe that your compatriots, your brothers in arms, might find it odd to see you in the service of this power, when one does not yet know its intentions vis-à-vis the recovery of Poland. However, I only know those two services that might be right for you. All that remains to you now is to wait patiently until the opportunity has arrived to work effectively for the reintegration of your country. By this happy time, you can use time in a very useful way for your country: make every effort to calm the ardor of your fellow citizens; let them know that anything they could do without the help of France and Prussia would be absolutely against [their interests].

It is impossible for the Russians to be the first to excite their courage and their impatience, and to engage them in some brilliant step. But it's a trap, they are careful! One would only want to animate them against Prussia, in order to animate Prussia against them; and in the midst of this reciprocal discontent, give the Empress the means of enslaving under her laws the rest of Poland; it is without doubt what could happen to you would be worse, since it would only remain to bend your head under the yoke of a truly oriental despot. They should keep quiet, endeavor to give no real cause of discontent against them, and if they have legitimate complaints, that they complain, but by regular, peace-

ful and orderly means. Let them persuade themselves that they will never come out of the deep abyss into which they have fallen except through the consent and assistance of Prussia and the Republic; and time alone can bring the necessary circumstances for that. What they could do in the meantime would produce no other effect than to spoil their affairs, and perhaps without remedy. So, no precipitation; the things of this world are of value only by appropriateness. This is, dear general, the doctrine which must be made to taste. Inspire in them also the feelings of union and holy brotherhood. Alas! Is it when we are united by a common misfortune that we must be divided by a particular interest, and work against each other? Is this the time to give the nations that love you a show of personal dissension, instead of meeting all in good faith toward the general goal, except for everyone to assert his claims when this goal is fulfilled? It is to you, General, it is for a wise man, and considered as this you are, to put an end to this kind of scandal; to make your fellow-citizens blush at these unhappy divisions, and to bring them back (in whatever country they live) to sentiments more worthy of them, to sprout in their hearts union, peace, and the desire to mutually avail themselves, waiting for all to be in motion for the service of the fatherland. This is a task I take the liberty to impose on you. This is a noble way of using your time, and of making yourself as useful to your country as the circumstances of the moment permit. Meanwhile, General, on the desire that you join me to meet our brave General Jourdan, and to see the French armies, I send you with much pleasure the letter of recommendation that you made me ask for our hero. You are made for each other, and I do not doubt that you will be very happy to know each other. I only have to recommend myself to your memory and your friendship.

Salute and Brotherhood,
"CAILLARD"

It was thus that Minister Caillard knew how to reconcile, and the precautions which his political position commanded him, and the aid which the French government then granted to the Polish cause.

This letter, if it had been intercepted, could in no way be a shame on the Berlin Cabinet, and the documents it contained, in opening Dąbrowski the way to France, entirely fulfilled its object. In fact, on the one hand, the Minister advised Poles to be patient and resigned and on the other he sent to their general letters of recommendation for French generals who were to assist Dąbrowski's patriotic enterprise.

Equipped with these documents, Dąbrowski was about to present himself before a nation whose armies then subjugated Italy and Germany, of that nation which had never appeared greater than it was at that time; and thinking of the part he was called to play, he felt his heart beat with noble pride. Taking with him his faithful Elie Tremo, he left Saxony, after having written an affectionate letter to Kazimirz De la Roche; and, joining the French army, he presented to General Jourdan the recommendation of Minister Caillard.

Welcomed by Jourdan with such respect as brave men who are honest, he made the acquaintance of Generals Bernadotte and Championnet, who were then in that army so fertile with illustrious men. Attracted to them by a sympathetic movement, he put them in the confidence of his plans, and communicated to them the plan for the organization of the Polish legions. All advised him to go to Paris, and even supported him with urgent letters to the Republican government. General Dąbrowski continued on his way, and arrived in the capital on 9 Vendemiaire, Year V (30 September 1796).

Before following General Dąbrowski to his new residence, before giving an account of his negotiations, let us look back, and see what had happened on the various points where the Poles had found asylum.

The refugees from Venice, combining their efforts with those of the refugees from Paris, had maintained a continual correspondence with the patriots of Moldavia, Wallachia, and Galicia. They preserved in these provinces all the fuel of an insurrection, by spreading the rumor that soon they would attend to the re-establishment of Poland, and that it was necessary to be ready to take up arms at the first signal. Excited by this news, and desirous of seeing their devotion to the common cause, the Polish patriots met at Krakow, in spite of Austrian surveillance, and drew up an act of confederation on 6 January 1796. This act, covered with a crowd of signatures, was delivered in legalized copies, and sent to the refugees of Paris, so that they might present it to the Directory.

General Giedroyc, on the other hand, whom we saw leave Paris to go to Lithuania with the intention of awakening the patriotism of that province, had prepared the people for serious events that were maturing. Citizen Valerian Dzieduszyeki, who had also received from the refugee's word of the patriotic project, had disposed all so that he would not remain an idle spectator of this glorious drama.

On 7 March 1796, the deputation of the Polish patriots, composed of five members, and recognized by the French government, presented to it a note in which it demanded that all Polish prisoners of war, and the deserters of the Austrian Army should be sent to the borders of Turkey to form a nucleus of troops ready to act at the first signal against Russia. The Directory promised to carry out this measure; and Citizen Constantin Stammaty, who at that time was appointed French Consul in Moldavia and Wallachia, was ordered to protect, in particular, the Polish soldiers who would gather there. Even before this official recommendation, Stammaty had friendly relations with the Paris refugees, and one could count on his zeal and good intentions.

Already the officers who had been able to escape the grip of their tyrants, found themselves in arms in these provinces, and had under their orders a few thousand insurgents. At their head were the Citizens Kolysko, Liberadzki, Domeyko and others. On the other hand, Rymkiewicz and Wladislas Yablonowski arrived in Constantinople on 22 May, as delegates of the inhabitants of Galicia. They carried, in this capacity, a letter for Verninac, and the act of confederation of the citizens of their province. The next day, 23 May, Michel Oginski introduced them to Verninac.

Negotiations, at the beginning, appeared to offer favorable chances. The French minister, wishing to win the Sultan over to the Polish cause, requested a conference with Reis-Effendi, and obtained it. The Minister wished to inform him of the new confederation, and in order that he might better understand the whole patriotic project, he submitted to him a letter that Oginski had addressed to him and Verninac, to give him some details, and to claim by his mediation a hearing of the Reis Effendi.

This hearing took place on 13 June 1796, but it was limited to words exchanged without result. Prince Morouzzi, brother of the Hospodar of Wallachia, and First Dragoman of the Porte vis-à-vis the foreign ministers, ended by confirming to the patriots patience and prudence, leaving time and circumstances to realize the hopes of the Poles. A consoling prospect for a people whom misfortune overwhelmed, and who devoured the thirst for vengeance!

While these slow negotiations were following their course, the Polish bodies already organizing themselves in Moldavia were worried at the request of the Russian Consul. Nine soldiers were arrested at Jassy, and they would have even been loaded with irons without the vigorous representations of Emile Gaudin, agent of the French Republic. Oginski, in his turn, not allowing a single opportunity to be useful to his compatriots, wrote a warm letter to Minister Verninac, who seconded his just complaints to the best of his ability.

Always active in his devotion, Oginski had, on the advice of the refugees from Paris, maintained relations with Joseph Sulkowski, his compatriot, who was then the aide-de-camp of General Bonaparte. It was at the time when this young hero was in command in the glorious Italian campaign, which was enough to reveal to the world its future destiny. Oginski urged Sulkowski to interest the general in the Polish cause; but the latter, fearing to displease his chief, at a moment when military operations were absorbing his mind, was always receding, and dared not undertake this thorny mission. Finally, pushed to the limit, he advised Oginski to send a letter to the French general, adding that he was in charge of supporting the effect. Oginski at once put this idea into execution, and wrote a petition to General Bonaparte, dated from Constantinople, which was sent to Napoleon's headquarters on 21 August. This piece was conceived in the following terms:

Constantinople, August 10, 1796.

Citizen General, it is not necessary to illustrate the glory of the French name by some victories and conquests, if it does not act to render you worthy of the title of a defender, well-merited by the homeland, and your ambition, citizen general, is limited to striking down the enemy and making you admired and re-

spected throughout Europe, you can already put an end to your exploits and rest in the shade of your laurels.

Your career, as brilliant as it is dangerous, would deserve, from now on, a distinguished place next to those illustrious men from antiquity whose splendors, whose memories are transmitted to us, and you would find in the bosom of your country and your family a very sweet reward for a hero who fought only to assure peace to Europe, and to consolidate the welfare, the glory and the power of France.

Fifteen million Poles, formerly independent, are today the victims of the force of circumstances, have fixed their eyes on you. They wish to pierce this barrier which separates them from you to share your dangers, to see you crowned with new laurels, and to add to all the titles that you have acquired, that of "Father of the Oppressed."

Do not lose sight, citizen general, this nation whose misfortunes make it interesting and that suffers only for wanting to ensure the freedom and independence of its country. You are one of those whose position can open to the Poles a way to shake off the odious and degrading yoke that they bear with impatience. You will find, as a French citizen, very powerful motives for drawing them from oppression, and your patriotic zeal, seconded by your military talents, will overcome the obstacles which oppose it.

No, it will not be said that the Poles are condemned to carry the chains of slavery as long as France exists ...... If the identity of the feelings that bring the two nations together guaranteed us this consoling certainty, do not our friendship and confidence with the French deserve their fraternal care and powerful support?

Hurry, Citizen General, to make known to the whole world that France gains glory by protecting the weak, and in securing the happiness of the people who claim its protection; hasten to fulfill our wishes and our hopes; restore the equilibrium in Europe, by rendering freedom and independence to the nations which have been deprived of it, and make sure that, from the center of Italy to the sources of the Dnieper, the peoples, returned to their rights, cherish in you the friend of humanity and respect the victorious warrior.

"Michel OGINSKI."

Sulkowski was charged with providing an answer to this letter. He wrote on 15 September 1796, at the headquarters near Legnago, and, announcing the military events of Italy, he added that General Bonaparte, after having read the letter above, had reflected for some time, and, addressing him, said, "Sulkowski, what should I answer? What can I promise? .... Write to your countryman that I love Poles, and that I do so much. That the partition of Poland is an act of iniquity that cannot be sustained .... That after having finished the war in Italy, I will go myself at the head of the French to force the Russians to restore Poland; but tell him also that the Poles must not depend on foreign aid, that they must arm themselves, to worry the Russians, to maintain a communication in the interior of the country. All the beautiful words that will be told to them will come to nothing. I know the diplomatic language and indolence of the Turks. A nation crushed by its neighbors can only get up with arms in hand."

All these promises, however consoling, did not bring any results. On all sides, patience was advised to the Poles, and for the moment it was the only positive aid offered to them; they had a little more hope when Aubert du Bayet, arriving at Constantinople to replace Verninac in his embassy, declared out loud that the principal object of his mission was to reconquer the Crimea from the Muscovites, and to tear from Poland the yoke of its oppressors. He added that the Directory had given him carte blanche to act, and to support him, if need be, by an army of thirty thousand men, who, under his orders and with the alliance of the Porte, would dictate laws to the Czarina.

But soon these caprices were again changed into evasive measures, and the Sultan's indecision on one side and the advanced season on the other rendered the effect of these pompous promises completely null and void. In this interval, insurgents from Moldavia, under the orders of Xavier Dąbrowski, impatient of the slowness of the negotiations, loudly manifested the intention of doing themselves justice, and stated that they numbered two thousand to three thousand men on the frontiers. Of Galicia. Oginski hastened to restrain this movement, while Aubert du Bayet, on the contrary, seemed to testify that he would see this step with pleasure, so that the Turks, compromised by the explosion which would accompany it, would finally leave their lethargy. He had already sent General Carra Saint Cyr, who was then at Bucharest, to the command of the Polish troops, when they were assembled in sufficient number.

In spite of this assurance, Oginski not seeing things from the same point of view, was recalled to Paris by the refugees, and judging his presence at Constantinople useless, he resolved to leave this capital, and entrust the continuation of his mission to General Rymkiewicz. However, to motivate his departure and to see by an authentic document what he had done for Poland and what remained to be done for her, he summed it up in a letter which he addressed to the French Minister so that he could make the proper use of it. This last duty accomplished, he left the banks of the Bosporus, and, passing through Bucharest, he went down with Carra Saint Cyr, and had some meetings with Dąbrowski. This improvised leader of the insurrection had already, by a solemn act, made his title noted, and, without paying any attention to the remonstrances addressed to him, he was preparing to cross the frontiers of Galicia. Combining his military operations as a leader of partisans, he had the design not only of raiding the Austrian customs cash boxes, but also of going to the fairs at Leopol, and of levying a forced tax on the individuals' purses. Better still, he had planned, if his plan was not foiled, to cause the students to rise up, arm the workers and draymen, and finally open the doors of the prisons, if necessary, so that the perpetrators could loot the entire city and to be enriched by the remains of the richest capitalists.

Such a monstrous project would have sufficed to ruin the most beautiful of causes, either in Poland or abroad, and Oginski employed all his authority to prevent it. He summoned Dąbrowski, either in his name or in the name of Auhert du Bayet, Minister of France, to renounce the execution of this hostile movement, and to hand over, so they could be destroyed, all the documents related to it.[5]

[5]This same Xavier Dąbrowski, whom we have seen previously delivered by the generous Tremo, has since been unworthy of the interest shown to him. Seeing himself abandoned in Paris, he wanted in his trip to Moldavia to reconquer by intrigue an influence that his nullity and his character had taken away from him. By creating himself as chief on his own authority, he claimed to form an army to plunder and not for the regeneration of his country. Fortunately, the

Surrounded by a thousand perils, Oginski continued his journey, and remained hidden for some time at Yablonow, at the home of Valerian Dzieduszycki[6], an excellent citizen and devoted friend. It was at his house that a few meetings were held with the faithful patriots who were gathered in this neighborhood, such as Leszczynski, Grzyraala, Racihorowski, Nowowieyski, who were the first authors of the Krakow Confederation Act. But the Austrian police were on the trail of Oginski, so these meetings were short and infrequent. There was fear of compromising this courageous agent of the public cause, at a time when there was a price on his head. All that was left to Oginski was a letter for the refugees from Paris, covered with the signatures of the members of the Confederation of Krakow.

This document, remarkable both in its style and in the spirit that dictated it, indicated in a broad and precise manner the point of view under which the situation of Poland should be considered. Establishing its position both internally and externally, it recalled the conduct to be held vis-à-vis foreign powers, and added that, if by a neglect which could not be calculated, Poland was abandoned, it would have the courage to be self-sufficient, and to trust the resources of the energy of despair.

Equipped with this document, Oginski left Iablonow, after a stay of three weeks, and, with the passport from Dzieduszycki, he continued his perilous journey. Visiting alternately Krakow, Breslau, Dresden, and Berlin, where he had a meeting with Ambassador Caillard, whom he had formerly known at The Hague, he then went

---

prudence and firmness of Oginski succeeded in thwarting this design, and Xavier Dąbrowski, disconcerted, raised the mask, and betraying the cause he had embraced, sold himself to the service of Russia after the accession of Paul. Later, promoted to the command of a regiment under Alexander I, he was guilty of so serious a crime that he was impeached, tried, expelled from the Russian Army and exiled to Siberia. It was he who, changing his name from Dąbrowski to Dombrowsky, published a pamphlet, the exact title of which is as follows: *Recherches politiques et militaires sur la décadence de la Pologne* by His Excellency, Mr. Xavier Dombrowsky, Polish general, and formerly Lieutenant-General-in-Chief of the Uhlans in Russian service, written in Moscow 1804, published in 1809, a miserable rhapsody worthy of a defector, as flat of style as absurd in fact! It must be added, however, to the praise of the refugees, that few such examples emerged from their ranks, and that the religion of liberty and honor barely counts a few renegades.

[6]The virtuous Dziéduszycki, to divert the attention of Austrian spies, accompanied Oginski to Krakow; but he later became a victim of his devotion, suffering a prison sentence of four years.

through Hamburg and Brussels, and arrived at Paris on 2 February 1797. Scarcely had he arrived at the capital when the refugees came in crowds to consult the citizen who had just acquired so many rights of common confidence; they liked to hear him relate his attempts, to learn from his mouth the slightest details of an adventurous mission; and whatever the result of so much effort, there was no despair of a cause, which suggested so much devotion, and provoked so much perseverance.[7]

But while these patriot-citizens, unanimous in the midst of some private dissensions, watched over the great act of regeneration, the military patriots moved in a still more positive manner; and while everything was still doubtful for a civil representation, General Dąbrowski, in his energetic obstinacy, triumphed over all the obstacles, and managed to organize a military representation worthy of the finest days of Polish history.

[7]We borrow all the details about the Citizen Oginski's mission to Constantinople, the work he published in 1826, in which all the efforts for the Polish cause are as sharply described as they are elegantly expressed. And in this regard, let us here make a wish that must be in the soul of all those who are interested in Poland, is to see all the outstanding citizens who took part in the events from this unfortunate republic, to put us in the confidence of the role they played, so that with these materials coordinated together, we can make the definitive history of their courageous efforts and their last setbacks.

CHAPTER SIX

First Acts of General Dąbrowski in Paris. — His Official Correspondence with the Minister of War Petiet. — Report on the Formation of the Polish Legions. — Response of the Minister. — Correspondence of General Dąbrowski with General Kléber. — Departure of the Polish General for Milan. — Situation of the Army of Italy at this Time. — Victories of General Bonaparte. — Defeat of Beaulieu. — Conquest of the Milanese. — Blockade of Mantua. — General Würmser. — Battles at Dezenzano, Salo, Castiglione, and Peschiera. — Their Results. — Formation of the Cispadane and Transpadane Republics. — Alvinzy. — Battle of Arcola. — Formation of the Lombard Legions. Dąbrowski's Arrival at Milan. — He Requests Authorization to Form some Polish Legions. — Convention with the Lombard Administration. — Activity of the Polish General. — He Organizes His Legions. — New Military Events. — Dąbrowski's Proclamation. — Its Results. — The Polish Come from Everywhere. — Manifesto Against the Roman government. — The Church States Submit. — The Enthusiasm that Caused this Event. — Debut of the Military Operations of the Polish Corps. — March on Mantua. — Strzalkowski, Liberadzki, Kosinski, Tremo, Dembowski, Konopka, the Downarowicz Brothers, etc.

Preoccupied with the new opportunities which he could open to his country, on his arrival in the capital General Dąbrowski had only one goal, namely, to co-operate directly or indirectly with the re-establishment of Poland.

Armed with letters of recommendation, which gave him access to the members of the Directory, he, together with Wybicki, organized the training of the Polish legions in the service of France. He then drew up the plan for submission to the authorities. But before submitting this proposal, he thought it useful for his plans to first ask for service as a volunteer in the Republican Army; in fact, he wrote the following letter to the Minister of External Relations, Charles Delacroix, and to the Minister of War, Petiet:

Paris, Vendemiaire 18, Year V (9 October 1796).

From the moment when our misfortunes, combined with the onerous circumstances, reduced us to the sad necessity of yielding to the preponderant force of our enemies, I had at first proposed to myself, Citizen Minister, to come to France to take refuge under the aegis of the loyalty and principles of the French Republican government, and to await the period of the reestablishment of the political existence of Poland, but an accident as unpleasant as it was unexpected disturbed my designs. I had the misfortune of breaking my leg, which forced me to recover until I had completely recovered. As soon as I was healed, I hastened to go to France to serve as a volunteer in the ranks of the Republican armies. I beg you, Citizen Minister, to stir up interest in the Executive Directory for me, so that it may grant me permission to serve the Republic among the Staff of the Army of Sambre-et-Meuse. It is for my instruction, as well as to use honorably, in the defense of a common cause, those talents that I have acquired, which I have the honor to ask by your intercession, Citizen Minister, for this favor from the government of the French Republic.

"The Polish Lieutenant-General
"DĄBROWSKI"

The Minister of War Petiet hastened to answer in the most favorable way:

Paris, Brumaire 3, Year V (24 October 1796).

I have communicated to the Executive Directory, General, the letter by which General Kléber informed me of the motives that determined you to come to Paris. I was persuaded in advance that the honorable title of "Defender of Polish Liberty," which you have so rightly acquired, would make it accept with eagerness the proposal I made to it to receive you among our warriors who are fighting for a cause, which you have so valiantly defended, to inform him that he authorizes you to serve voluntarily with the staff of the Army of Sambre-et-Meuse, commanded by General Kléber.

"This mark of confidence on the part of the French government must be a sure guarantee, General, of the interest which it bears in your person to the true support of Polish liberty.

"PETIET"

Taking advantage of this prompt and favorable decision, General Dąbrowski availed himself of it on the same day with General Kléber[1], and wrote to him;

PARIS, Brumaire 3, Year V (24 October 1796.)

I hasten, General, to announce to you that the Executive Directory gives me the honorable permission to write to you. You will find attached a copy of the letter that the Minister of War wrote to me on this subject. I feel strongly the price of the recommendation which you have deigned to give me, and to which I must exclusively attribute the flattering distinction that the French government has bestowed upon me. Be persuaded, General, that I am deeply imbued with the duties that the goodness of the Directory imposes on me at the same time, and the interest with which you have provoked for an individual, who will use all his efforts to justify them under your orders, to whom I hope to be returned in a few days.

"Polish Lieutenant General,
"DĄBROWSKI"

Not losing sight, however, of the principal aim of his affairs, Dąbrowski addressed his detailed plan to Directory for the formation of the Polish legions: the memorandum he wrote on this subject is a

[1]Jean-Baptiste Klber (1753-1800) Joined the French Royal Army and eventually rose through the ranks during the Revolution and joined Bonaparte during the Egyptian Campaign, eventually commanding the troops in Egypt after Bonaparte fled. He was assassinated in 1800 in Cairo.

historical document, which we copied verbatim:

My aim is not to consider in the political sphere, nor under that of commerce, the fatal result for the whole of Europe resulting from the partition of Poland. As a soldier, it is from this point of view that I would like to direct the attention of the French government to the affairs of this country. It is well-known that the territory of Russia has also been advantageously increased by the annihilation of Poland; that this power has acquired so much military and real power, that it can at any moment surprise Turkey, hold Sweden under its control, threaten Prussia, and be sure of always imposing on Austria, both by impulse of interest and by that of fear. This situation of the North, very disturbing for the powers of the South, must particularly alarm them in many ways. The French government knows, and surely has already weighed it in their wisdom. It would be superfluous to speak of it; I will confine myself to saying that the Poles, who can only expect their political existence from France, can still contribute a great deal to the development of a solid and suitable system in the North. There is no doubt that our last revolution, though hastily conceived and conducted without the support of the powers interested in Polish independence, has made a very useful diversion in favor of the cause of liberty, and has contributed to the sudden change in the face of the constitution. What success could we not promise ourselves of a new plan of insurrection, which would be the result of a combined and deliberate system, the aim of which would be to prepare means for engaging Prussia in taking up arms against Austria and Russia? I will try here to develop these means and then try to answer the objections that may arise against their execution. It would involve the formation of some legions of free Polish corps near the armies of the Republic, those of the Rhine and Italy.

1. The legions would serve as the nucleus and nursery of an army to be formed for Poland.

2. They are composed of some general officers who have served with distinction in the last two Polish campaigns against Russia and her allies.

3. The corps of these legions would be formed from subordi-

nate officers reformed in Poland, who, by national spirit, have almost all refused the service which the government of the co-invading powers has offered them, and Galicians forcibly enlisted in the service of Austria.

4. The legions would serve as volunteers following the armies of the French Republic, would be subordinated to the Republican generals, and would follow any destination that the French government would send them, according to the result of its negotiations.

The execution of this project presents views of major utility for France and Poland.

As for France, the resulting advantages would be:

a. That the Austrian Army would be disorganized as it was the month before in Italy, composed of the Galicians, who would have become Austria's most active enemies if they found, after deserting, a welcome which assured them the means to continue to act according to their first impulse.

b. That the determinations of the allies of the Republic against Russia and Austria could be accelerated.

c. That the Polish officers and soldiers, placed in the wake of the French army, would feed on republican principles, which they would bring back to their country with the feeling of ambition of having been at the school of the French troops, and to have been their companions in arms.

As for the advantages that would result for Poland, here they are:

a. We would honorably employ soldiers who have no means of subsistence and who are capable of fighting for the common cause.

b. These soldiers would continue their education by following the learned operations of the French armies.

c. When the nucleus of this army was formed, and circumstances permit their employment in Poland, it would be easy to increase them by recruits, and to form a respectable army, which would act offensively, according to the plans agreed upon between them with the Republic and its allies.

d. This foundation of the Polish Army, working with the

armies of the Republic, would particularly contribute to maintaining the dispositions of the patriots of the interior of Poland, to rebel against the governments opposed to the system of the French Republic.

e. Once this project is put into execution, it would be attempted, in accordance with the plan of the Republic relative to Turkey, to rally the emigrants of Poland into the provinces of Ottoman domination, and to prepare the nucleus of a particular corps in them. With this body we would gather the Russian malcontents of the Trans-Dnieper provinces who, in our last revolution, declared themselves by secret emissaries willing to make common cause with us. At the same time, they could influence movements in Transylvania and Hungary, thereby rendering the House of Austria unable to continue the present war, as well as diverting it for a long time from attempting to repeat it for other reasons.

We now have to answer some objections to the formation of this army nursery.

FIRST OBJECTION

Would not this formation of the legions bring shame to the Berlin Cabinet? It seems not, for the Berlin Cabinet might be warned that these soldiers cannot, according to the Constitution, serve under the French flag, destined to enter the service of some ally of France, and not being near the French army only for their particular instruction. Besides, the King of Prussia, being now allied with France, all that would result from the French system could not alarm it. In the second place, all the operations which the Polish legions would follow would only tend to weaken the natural enemies of Prussia, namely: Austria and Russia. Moreover, this body, either following the French armies, or in the Polish revolution, which we would organize, being able to act only by the impetus and under the immediate direction of France, could never undertake anything to the contrary to the interests of Prussia, guaranteed by France. Finally, Prussia, by the conviction of its own interest, may not, by approving this project, perhaps agree to co-operate in the restoration of Poland, in which it will find not only a natural ally, but even a nation disposed to see placed at the head of a constitutional government someone from the House of Brandenburg, if that suited the system of general pacification, according to the plans of the French Republic.

SECOND OBJECTION

With regard to the formation of the Polish legions, there is the difficulty of finding funds to organize them; but these difficulties can be removed because:

1. We may count on some assistance from the Polish patriots, who, although generally ruined by the latest events in Poland, will, nonetheless, provide for this object.

2. They should be sought from Dutch private individuals, who are also interested in the existence of Poland, by offering them a mortgage on the national property of Poland. The Dutch would undoubtedly provide something if they saw that the execution of the above project was granted and supported by the French government.

3. There would still be sufficient credit in Turkey, immediately interested in the reestablishment of Poland, if the French Republic wished to interpose on this subject its good offices.

4. Finally, as to the direct assistance of the French Republic, either from the guarantee which the French government would give to the Dutch, or from securities, arms, and munitions of war furnished by France, the repayment of such aid would be one of the first operations of the Polish government.

I will end this paper with the following observations: Without forming a nucleus of an army for Poland, a new explosion in this country is impossible, in spite of the energetic desires of the patriots of the interior of Poland to lend themselves to it. There is no doubt, however, that this is only an insurrectional plan in Poland, which can abort the new plans by the allies of Northern Europe. An explosion in Galicia would awaken the spirit of the malcontents in Hungary, so that Austria, instead of using all her forces against France, would be obliged to divide them to ensure the tranquility of her territory.

"Prussia, the natural ally of France for the sake of her own con-

servation, would adopt an active system as soon as Poland reappeared on the political scene. The Turk would be drawn from his apathy at the moment when he saw the fire of war breaking out in Poland against Austria and Russia. Sweden would abandon a system of caution at the approach of a revolution, which would occupy Russia, and it is then that this last power, threatened on all sides, as much by the neighboring nations as by its own subjects, for the most part dissatisfied and, above all, by the inhabitants of the countries invaded over Poland, would be forced to cease protecting the plots of the French émigres[2] , to light the war against France, and to grow at the expense of Europe. On the contrary, it would have to concentrate all its military and pecuniary resources for its own defense.

"Such would be the necessary results of the project which I have the honor to submit to the attention of the government of the Republic, and as it only confirms the general ideas and is scarcely outlined, I reserve giving details relating to each one of its parts, if the French government deems it appropriate, it flatters me to be able to present it accurately, since the Polish territory, the positions, the frontiers, and the countries of partition, as well as all localities peculiar to armies operations, are well-known to me.

"I feel that the acceptance of this project depends very much on the confidence that the French government shows in the one that represents it.

I flatter myself that by means of the Citizens Descorches, formerly French Minister at Warsaw, Barthelemy and Caillard, I will obtain the votes of the patriotic Poles possessing in all its extent the confidence of the nation.

Paris, Vendémiaire 19, Year V of the Republic (10 October 1796).

"DĄBROWSKI"

[2]Translator: At this time there was an army of emigres fighting France with the Austrians in Germany and with subsidies from Austria and England commanded by the Prince de Condé. There were may plots, including the failed landing at Quiberon Bay in June-July 1795, so the Royalists were a very real concern to the Republican government.

The Minister of War Petiet, replied in advance to this communication with his letter dated Brumaire 5, Year V (26 October 1796), announcing that he would hasten to transmit to the Executive Directory the plan and the projects in question; and General Dąbrowski, in order to inform Minister Caillard of what had just happened, wrote him a confidential letter.

A few days after the provisional note from the Minister of War, the citizen L.M. Reveillère-Lepaux, President of the Directory, wrote to General Bonaparte in terms favorable to the project, and General Dąbrowski received a definitive answer from Citizen Petiet: these two documents were designed as follows:

The Executive Directory to General-in-Chief Bonaparte.

Paris, Brumaire 7, Year V (8 October 1796)

The Polish patriots, anxious of preparing the means of regenerating their country, would like, Citizen General, to stand in the glorious phalanxes of the French Republic. The proposal has just been made by General Dąbrowski to take from the Republic those whom desertion would engage to leave the Imperial troops. Under the terms of the Constitution, the French government cannot take any foreign troops into its pay, so the proposal becomes unenforceable. Nevertheless, as it might not be indifferent to the interest of the Republic to facilitate the Poles, who are now in the service of Austria the means to desert, the Directory urges you to see if it would not be possible to determine the provisional government of the Milanese, the Modenois, etc., to take them in their pay.

L. M. REVEILLÈRE-LEPAUX, President

Letter from Petiet, Minister of War to General Dąbrowski.

Paris, Brumaire 9, year V (30 October 1796)

I communicated to the Directory, as I had told you, General, the report you sent me; it has appeared to him to present ideas which may, indeed, help the Polish patriots by indirect means of working for the regeneration of their country. The Directory, according to the constitution, cannot consent to the formation of the Polish legions assigned to the service of France; but he sees no objection to them being established among the peoples with whom the Republic has a good understanding, and who all use their efforts to recover their liberty. Bologna, Ferrara, the Milanese, have appeared to the Directory to offer the opportunity to carry out the project you have presented to it; and he wrote, accordingly, to General Bonaparte, commander of the Army of Italy.

PETIET

On such a reply, which completely changed the situation of the Poles in France, Dąbrowski hastened to set out for Italy; but, having stopped at Basle, he addressed a letter to General Kleber from that city, informing him of the decision of the French government and its consequent journey. Here are his own expressions:

Basle, 18 November 1796 (Brumaire 28, Year V)

I was on the point of going to see you, General, when I learned that the Directory of the Republic was kind enough to take care of a report, which I presented to it, and which contained some purely military ideas relating to the restoration of Poland, as I have had the honor to communicate to you in time, and which he even deigned to take into consideration; consequently, the Minister of War Petiet, in concert with General Clarke, advised me and represented it as a necessity to go to Italy with General Bonaparte, where a happy coincidence has just gathered a number Polish deserters; which would give me the advantage, not only of implementing the good dispositions of the government of the Republic, but also of making a first attempt by trying to organize the above-mentioned Polish deserters. I therefore thought it my duty to eagerly seize a moment so precious to render service to my country, and to answer the great confidence with which the French government has honored me, and which I must attribute in all to your generous intercession. And as I am leaving at this moment, furnished with letters of recommendation from Minister Petiet and General Clarke, I make it a point to give you new ones, only begging you to keep them at home, because we want to observe the greatest secrecy in this regard. I still have to intercede your good offices in favor of the Polish servicemen who will be able to address you. Deign, general, to be useful to them and to facilitate their means of fighting our common enemies under the flags of liberty. It is, without doubt, obliging you, General, to procure for you the means of giving free rein to sentiments which you have so well displayed towards me.

"Farewell, General, I wish to soon be able to join you, in order to reiterate to you in person my gratitude and the price which I attach to serve under your orders.

"Polish Lieutenant-General,
"DĄBROWSKI"

The answer of General Kleber, who found Dąbrowski in Milan, is one of those characteristic documents in which the frankness of the warrior and the soul of the comrade in arms breathe:

Letter from Major-General Kléber,
Commanding the right wing of the army,
to General Dąbrowski.

Headquarters at Coblentz
Frimaire 12, Year V (2 December 1796)

I expected you, my dear General, with an impatience equal to the pleasure I would have felt if circumstances had brought us closer to one another, when I received your letter from Basle, by which you announced to me your departure for the Army of Italy. I desire, my dear General, that you may derive from this journey all the pleasure, all the fruit you seem to hope for. In any corner of the earth that fate and events may throw you, I will never experience greater pleasure than by learning that you are happy, and that everything is according to your wishes. "Remember, my dear General, that owing to the attachment which you have inspired me to get news of you often, and to keep me informed of all that may interest you individually, as well as your country. If it were to rise up from its fall, and you needed a man who could give a blow, call me close to you, whatever it may be, I'll be proud to return freedom to a people so well made to enjoy it, if only in the most indirect manner.

Be sure, my dear General, that all the Poles who will come to me, or who will fall into my power, will find in your friend a faithful support, which will give them a particular destination that will collect their names, and which will pass to your control; for that you feel the need to educate me exactly of your stay.

I address this to General Bonaparte. I kiss you with all my heart, you and your son. Remind me also of your faithful aide-de-camp, Elie Tremo.

All my military family assure you of its respects. General Bernadotte, who takes the greatest interest in the success of your projects, embraces you most cordially.

Adieu, General, I press you against my heart.
"KLÉBER"

It was under this authority, and with the support of such renowned names, that Dąbrowski marched to his goal; he was proud of having won the esteem of those men who were then the elite of the French nation. In fact while the Republic was divided inside, while the people, tired of all the regimes, burdened by a financial crisis[3], was the

[3]Translator: France had begun funding its war effort by printing assignats, paper currency supported by lands confiscated from the nobles in 1789. Initially this was a good ideal, but as politicians are more interested in spending than in fiscal responsibility, they soon printed millions more francs' worth of assignats than they had property with which to support them. By 1796 the Directory had come close to collapsing the French currency by over printing assignats, which was exacerbated by rampant counterfeiting. As it worked

plaything of some intriguers inside and outside, the feats of arms of Bonaparte, Jourdan, Hoche, and Moreau placed it at the forefront of the military powers.

At that time General Dąbrowski, was finally certain of the success of his project, he went to Milan, at the time when the star of the young Bonaparte threw its first brilliance.

Previously, on 19 Germinal Year IV (9 April 1796), Bonaparte was fighting on the summit of the Alps, and the decisive battle at Montenotte, on 20 Germinal (10 April 1796), opening the gates of Italy to him. The French troops lacked everything, and the little ammunition they got at the point of the sword was barely enough to sustain them. It was necessary to advance and conquer to live; it was necessary to crush superior forces by fighting them. The army did its duty, the genius of its general did the rest, and the battle of Millesimo, on the 21st and 22nd, changed a precarious situation into a threatening situation. While the Austrian army, dazed by its defeat, only thought of rallying and covering the Milanese, the Piedmontese army was in turn knocked down and beaten at Ceva, Vico and Mondovi, from 27 Germinal to 9 Floreal (16-28 April), and this twelve-day campaign delivered the fortresses of Piedmont to the French as a guarantee of the armistice which was the consequence.

It was necessary, however, to march towards the Austrians. Bonaparte descended by forced marches down the right bank of the Po, crossed it at Plaisance and overthrew the enemy lines at Fombio and Codogno, while General Beaulieu was waiting for him on the side of Valenza. In the space of ten days, from the 10th to the 19th Floreal (17 April to 8 May), Bonaparte became master of a large part of the Milanese territory, and entered into an alliance with the Duke of Parma. Helped by the latter, he seized the surrounding country. Frightened by this rapid race, Beaulieu left his positions at Sesia and Tesin, and, moving on the Adda, seeking to oppose the passage of the Republicans. He was forced into the terrible battle of Lodi, which delivered the cities of Cremona, Pizzighetone, Pavia, Italy, and all the places of the Milanese to the French. This new expedition took place in ten days, 20 to 30 Floreal (9 to 19 May.)

out, Napoleon's victories of 1796 and the loot of Northern Italy saved France from bankruptcy.

But an invaded country is not a subjugated one, and Bonaparte's plan embraced a more beautiful task. He wanted to create conditions of liberty and make it the fulcrum of Italy's point d'appui; warrior and legislator at the same time, he wanted to win them over those whom he had forced to submit by force with reason. Supporting this project on the broadest bases, he wanted to march on the capitol; it was by giving back the ancient splendor that it would begin the regeneration of the Italian provinces. In fact, he was soon announcing his vast plan for the whole of Europe by his proclamation of Prairial 1st (20 May).

At the same time he trained his soldiers at this great task; he taught them what conduct ought to be held by men called to so much glory; he soothed and punished uprisings; he made his hidden enemies tremble; he made friends with his admirers; he granted an armistice to the Duke of Modena, by which he exacted the help that he needed; he gathered all the artillery and the troops that could not follow his rapid march, and which he needed to complete his triumph; it is based on Beaulieu, who had rallied or rather hid behind the Mincio; he forced him to Borghetto; he took Peschiera and Verona; finished by annihilating the Austrian army; the remains of it were thrown into the mountains of the Tyrol, and, a fortnight after entering the Milanese, there was no longer an Austrian in Italy, except in the castles at Milan and Mantua, both of which were invested. These were the results of the fifteen days after 16 Prairial to 30 Messidor (4 to 18 June). Continuing the course of his conquests, Bonaparte took Fort Fuentes, north of Lake Como, on the borders of the Grisons, and thus awakened the hopes of their oppressed subjects; he chastised the revolt of the Imperial fiefs near the states of Genoa. He forced Rome and Naples to an armistice and wrested earlier usurpations from the former. Bologna and Ferraro were returned to freedom. He contained Florence; he occupied Livorno [Leghorn], and thereby prepared the evacuation of Corsica, which would complete the expulsion of the English from all the ports of the Mediterranean. He reduced the castle at Milan after twelve days of an open trench; he repressed the uprising of Lugo in the Ferrarois and warned others by the severity. However, a new Austrian general and additional troops arrived in the Tyrol. He found them, contained them, over-ran their entrenchments, continued before their eyes to block

Mantua, and tightened it to the point of finally opening the trench at eighty toises from the walls of the fortress, on Messidor 30th (18 June). At the same time, he was in charge of the fine arts, sciences, and especially political institutions, the greatest of all the means of instruction; and all this in the space of forty-five days of success achieved one after the other.

Beaten so many times, the proud Austrians had formed a new army, so formidable that all Italy regarded the defeat of the French as certain, and this very opinion increased France's danger. The old general Würmser, who saw that Mantua, bombarded for ten days, was at bay, went to its aid on 11 Thermidor (29 July), with two strong columns separated by Lake Garda. That of the right had already surprised and carried the posts of Salo and Brescia. Bonaparte, weakened by his very success, by the vast expanse of country that he was obliged to guard, inferior in numbers, almost overwhelmed, immediately took an extreme course: he raised the siege, gathered all his forces at one point, fell on the Austrian right wing, overthrew it, dispersed it, then cut off the retreat of its remains; and, by a boldness which imposed, because it could not be foreseen, at Lonato, where he had only twelve hundred men, captured four thousand of these Austrian scattered troops, who sought to escape. He returned quickly to the Austrian left wing, pushed it back, and threw it behind the Mincio. The next day he crossed the river in its presence, completely defeated it, and sent it back to the mountains of the Tyrol, leaving twenty-five thousand men wounded, killed, or captured. This is where the fight at Dezenzano, those of Salo, the battles of Lonato and Castiglione, and the fight at Peschiera occurred. They fought ten days in a row, from Thermidor 11th to the 20th (29 July to 7 August).

In truth, the siege of Mantua had been lifted, the works destroyed, the artillery lost; but the blockade was immediately resumed, and as early as 7 Fructidor (24 August), it was fiercely and successfully taken.

On 16 Fructidor (2 September) the pursuit recommenced. Würmser, always beaten and always formidable, was pushed back beyond Trent, marched on the left, and made a last effort to get closer to Mantua. In the midst of his defeats he pierced forward, seized a bridge, which he had forgotten to break, although the order should have been given, took advantage of the error by a guide who misled a French column, and occupied the fortress, under the walls of which he still received a considerable defeat. Thus, after fourteen days of consecutive fighting, during which he lost the battle of Roveredo in Tyrol, that of Bassano in the state of Venice, that of St. George before Mantua, he was in this city with a corps of four thousand or five thousand men, the last remnants of a once powerful army. Such was the course of events from 1 Thermidor to 30 Fructidor (19 July to 16 September).

General Bonaparte had gained a few moments of rest after so many victories. Having no means of besieging Mantua, he confined himself to blockading it, and gave himself up to other cares. He had in front of him a pause in operations from the 1st Complimentary Day[4], Year IV to 11 Brumaire 11, Year V (19 September to 2 November 1796).

In this interval, by the measures which he had taken, the evacuation of Corsica took place, and its reunion with the French Republic; it was at the same time that, taking advantage of the Duke of Modena's infidelities to break all engagements with him, he protected the proclamation of liberty in his states, and favored the joining of Modena and Reggio with Bologna and Ferrara; created the Cispadane Republic, and directed the operations of the Transpadane Republic.

However new enemies had arrived from all parts of Germany having Alvinzy at their head, and always seeking to liberate Mantua. Already several fights, with varied successes had taken place at the entrance of the mountains; the French left, which closed its outlets, had lost its position; and Alvinzy came from behind the Piave, in the State of Venice, to link up with Davidovich. Bonaparte flew to meet him, passed the Adige, wanted to go to Villa Nova to turn the enemy; but on 25 Brumaire Year V (15 November 1796) he was stopped by the village of Arcola, taking up a strong position. It was there that the memorable feats of arms of the Lodi Bridge were renewed; but they had a less rapid success. The General-in-Chief was knocked down, twelve or fifteen officers-general or staff were killed; and it was only two days later that the battle was decided. "This new victory," said the historian Thiers, "caused an extreme joy in Italy and France: on all

[4]Translator : The Revolutionary Calendar used twelve months of thirty days each, with five "Feast Days" or as this author calls them, "Complimentary Days," (six in a leap year). These were used to adjust the calendar to match the three hundred sixty five days in the solar year.

sides this stubborn genius was admired, who with fourteen thousand or fifteen thousand men facing forty thousand men had not thought of retiring; this inventive and profound genius who had discovered on the dikes of Ronco a brand-new field of battle, which annihilated the Austrians, and pierced their flanks. The heroism displayed at the Arcola Bridge was celebrated, and everywhere the young general was represented, with a flag in his hand, in the midst of fire and smoke. The two counsels, declaring, according to custom, that the Army of Italy had still deserved the country's praise, decided, furthermore, that the flags which the two generals, Bonaparte and Augereau, had carried on the bridge of Arcola, would be given to them so that they might be preserved by their families: a beautiful and noble reward, worthy of a heroic age, and much more glorious than the guilty diadem bestowed later by weakness on the almighty genius.[5]

In the midst of his rapid conquests, however, the Republican general did not forget what cause he had come to defend, and in all his proclamations the words "country" and "liberty", those words which sound so well in the ears of the masses, came to rally to his flags the inhabitants of the subjugated countries. The liberation of Italy, once so great in its independence, so petty in its despotism, seemed to be the inevitable consequence of so many victories. The general, moreover, called upon all free and proud souls to contribute to this great work, and seemed to leave to patriotism the care of finishing what courage had begun so well. In order not to tarnish the opinion that had been conceived of them, the Lombards solicited the favor of forming an active legion, and of immediately sending it to join those of their compatriots who had already been admitted to the French army. The administration, by transmitting this petition to the General-in-Chief, gave him the language which General Dąbrowski would soon be using to form the Polish legions. "We have just received," he said, "a writing signed by a large number of patriots, in which these brave citizens demand the formation of a Lombard legion, to unite it with the glorious republican army, and thus defend our liberty and our independence.......

"The administration hopes, Citizen General, that you will wish to second the desire of a people who wants to be free, and that you will not oppose it being armed to defend the country and fight its enemies

---

[5]*Histoire de la Révolution française*, Vol. VIII, p. 510.

who are also yours." Bonaparte welcomed the request of the Milanese. Since then the energy and enthusiasm of these Italians who, together with the Poles, were to be, for several centuries, the emulators of French values, and shared on the whole surface of Europe, and beyond, the glory and the dangers of Republican or Imperial armies.

This was the exact situation of affairs when Dąbrowski arrived in Italy. All the Poles who were there were waiting impatiently for him; pleased to see a young hero crush almost all the Austrian power, they looked forward to the moment when they could share his triumphs. Deprived even of the hope of fighting for their country, they felt some pleasure in thinking that they would at least avenge themselves against a nation, which had been immersed in the heinous act of invading their country.

Arriving at Milan on 12 Frimaire Year V (2 December 1796), General Dąbrowski, on the 14th and 15th (4 and 6 December), presented to the General-in-Chief his ideas concerning the formation of the Polish legions. But Bonaparte, busy with his expeditions and still in the army, could not give an immediate answer either to Dąbrowski or to the administration of Lombardy on the plans of this general. It was only towards mid-Nivôse that the General-in-Chief of the Army of Italy wrote to the Congress of State the following letter:

Bonaparte, General-in-Chief of the Army of Italy at the State Congress.

Milan, this Nivôse 15, Year V (4 January 1797).

General Dąbrowski, a Polish lieutenant-general, a distinguished and interesting officer by the misfortunes of his country, who succumbed under the effort of the same enemy who for so many years tyrannized his fatherland, offers to raise a Polish legion, which would help the Lombard people defend their freedom. This brave nation deserves to be welcomed by a people who aspire to freedom. I urge him to come to an understanding with you, and I will gladly take all the measures you think you ought to take with him."

"BONAPARTE."

On 16 Nivôse (5 January 1797), the general presented his conditions to the Lombard administration, and on the 20th (9th) the following convention was signed by the General-in-Chief, by the administration, and by General Dąbrowski;

CONVENTION

Taken between the General Administration of Lombardy, on behalf of the Lombard people on one side; and Citizen Dąbrowski, a Polish lieutenant-general, on behalf of his compatriots who offer their services for the recovery of the liberty of Lombardy; on the other, supported by the general in Bonaparte, commanding the Army of Italy:

1. The Polish corps which will be formed in Lombardy will retain the title of Polish Auxiliary Legions of Lombardy.

2. The uniforms, the military marks, and the organization of this body will be as close as possible to the uses of the Poles.

3. The Lombard people will be pleased to wear the counter-epaulets in the national colors of Lombardy with the inscription: Gli uomini liberi sono fratelli ("free men are brothers"); besides, both the officers and the soldiers of the Polish corps will wear the French cockade as being that of the protecting nation of free men.

4. The pay, the subsistence, and all that is granted to the national troops, will be common to the Polish corps; that is to say, according to the regulations of the French troops.

5. The general administration of Lombardy will issue the certificates to officers and employees in these bodies, reserving the right to present its reflections to the same individuals, if it deems it necessary. The said patents will also be approved and signed by the commanding general of Lombardy, as directly authorized, ad hoc, by the General-in-Chief of the Army of Italy.

6. The Lombard people declare that they will always look upon the Poles armed for the defense of liberty, as true brethren, and not as foreign troops; as a result of which the general administration formally grants them the rights of genuine Lombard citizens, without this preventing them from being able to go to their own homes if the case so requires, and Lombardy is really recognized as free, and it is not actually at war to support it. This undertaking will be published by a proclamation addressed to the Poles by the administration of Lombardy.

Articles 7, 8 and 9, proposals for details will be executed without delay and with as much activity as possible.

10. All these concerts will be presented to the General-in-Chief of the army

Milan, made at the Palace of the General Administration of Lombardy, this Nivose 20th, Year V (9 January 1797) of the French Republic, and 1st of the Freedom of Lombardy.

The General-in-Chief approves the obligation./

BONAPARTE.

PORCELLI, President. VISCONTI, representative.
CLAVERA, secretary.
Jan DĄBROWSKI, Polish Lieutenant-General.

As soon as all these preliminaries were signed, General Dąbrowski took care of the material formation of the legions. He sent Chef de bataillon Amilcar Kosinski, who had left his country at the time of the Polish Revolution to take service in the French army, and Major Elie Tremo, his aide-de-camp, to Piedmont, a letter from General Berthier. Their mission was to return to France and recruit the Poles, who were among the Austrian prisoners of war. The manner in which these prisoners expressed their joy at serving the national cause in this new engagement is eloquently expressed in a letter that Elie Tremo sent to De la Roche, who had just arrived in Paris.

But in the interval events followed each other with the rapidity of lightning. Generals Massena, Augereau, Victor, Joubert, Leclerc, with their fiery courage, crushed the timid Austrian generals, Alvinzi, Quasdanovich, Vukassovich, Ocksay, etc., while blocking General Provera's attempt to relieve Mantua, where Würmser was still shut up. General Provera, surprised, enveloped on all sides, surrendered with five thousand Austrians. For his part, Bonaparte, made the whole campaign in three days, fought the battle of Rivoli, the engagements at Anghiari and de la Favorite, and by the magical use of his forces destroyed two army corps, made more than twenty thousand prisoners, seized all the enemy's artillery, an immense baggage train, and prevented the Imperial army from conducting the campaign longer. Far from the theater of war, General Dąbrowski was impatient at remaining a stranger to the glorious deeds of triumphant phalanxes. He redoubled his zeal for the recruiting of his legions, and, to initiate the whole universe to the patriotic mission which he had undertaken, he published in four languages and spread on all sides the proclamation that read:

Liberty *Equality*

PROCLAMATION TO THE POLISH PEOPLE

Dąbrowski, Polish Lieutenant General
Authorized to form some Polish Legions in Italy

To His Co-Citizens!

Faithful to my homeland to the last moment, I have fought for its liberty under the immortal Kosciuszko; he has succumbed and there remains to us only the consoling memory of having spilled our blood for the land of our ancestors, and to have seen our triumphant flags at Dubienka, Raclawice, Warsaw, and Vilna.

Poles! Hope shall rally us! France triumphs, it fights for the cause of nations; we try to weaken its enemies; it grants us asylum, we await a better destiny for our land. Let us array ourselves under their flags, they are those of honor and victory. Polish legions are forming in Italy, on this land formerly the sanctuary of liberty; already officers and soldiers, companions of your labors and your courage, are with me, the battalions are already organizing themselves! Come, companions, throw away the arms which you have been forced to carry! Let us fight for the common cause of nations, for freedom under the valiant Bonaparte, conqueror of Italy.

The trophies of the French Republic are our only hope; it is through it, and through its allies that we may be glad to see those cherished homes we have abandoned with tears.

At the headquarters at Milan, the Pluviôse 1, Year V of the French republic one and indivisible (20 January 1797).

Polish Lieutenant-General,
"JEAN Dąbrowski "

For its part, the Lombard administration wanted by a public act to testify with what pleasure it had linked its cause to the Polish cause, also wishing to popularize the legions that were going to rise under its auspices, issued a proclamation dated 15 Pluviôse Year V (15 February, 1797). From that moment everything was organized rapidly: General Dąbrowski himself directed, at Milan, the establishment of the barracks, the depot, the uniforms, and the division into squads and companies. He was perfectly seconded in all this work by his young son Michael, who at the age of twelve had fought two campaigns in Poland, and who promised the general a successor worthy of him.

The two proclamations that assured the soldiers who enlisted in the Polish uniform and the commands in this language, produced a wonderful effect. Then, as if by a stroke of the baton, 1,127 men, all Polish, were under arms on 21 Pluviôse (9 February 1797). They were divided into two battalions, one of grenadiers, and the other of chasseurs, dressed, ordered, and organized according to national customs, but without officers.

Kosinski, appointed commander of the chasseurs, brought a considerable crowd of recruits and officers from Piedmont, who had left their country in 1794, after the War of Independence. In their ranks were Dembowski the Younger, Borowski, Kazimierz Konopka, the two brothers Downarowicz, etc. etc.

In this interval a last triumph had just immortalized the soldiers of the great nation. General Würmser, shut up for six months in Mantua, had finally decided to parley.

The clauses of the capitulation signed on 14 Pluviôse (2 February 1797) guaranteed to the Austrian general the free exit from the place with his staff, two hundred cavalry, five hundred prisoners at his choice, and six pieces of cannon; but the garrison laid down its arms, was taken prisoner, and conducted to Trieste to be exchanged. It still counted from twelve thousand to thirteen thousand men.[6]

The French entered Mantua on 3 February, and took possession of more than five hundred guns, a bridging train of twenty-five pontoons, and sixty flags or standards, which General Augereau, leaving for Paris, was commissioned to present to the Republican Directory in the name of the army.

Master of all the north of Italy, the General-in-Chief, wishing to avenge the perfidies of the Roman Court, pushed, with a new vigor, his victorious march into the heart of the Papal States. It was there that the Poles had to fraternize with the French in the next campaigns with arms in hand; it was there that the exiled soldiers of an annihilated republic were to equal in glory and courage the happy soldiers of the triumphant Republic.

Thundering and prophetic in its manifests, Bonaparte published one on 3 February at the headquarters in Bologna. Recapitulating all the grievances accumulated against the Roman Court, it said that the Pope formally refused to execute articles VIII and IX of the armistice concluded on 20 June, in Bologna, under the mediation of Spain, and solemnly ratified in Rome on 17 June; that since the Roman Court had not ceased to arm and to excite by its manifests the

[6]The old Marshal Würmser could no longer keep one of his officers, Klenau, who was sent to Serrurier to parley. Serrurier returned to the General-in-Chief, who went to the conference. Bonaparte, wrapped in his cloak and not making himself known, listened to the talks between Klenau and Serrurier. The Austrian officer had a great deal of information on the resources which remained to his general and assured him that he had still three months' food. Bonaparte, always enveloped, approached the table near which this conference took place, seized the paper on which Wümser's propositions were written, and began to trace a few lines on the margins, without saying a word, and to the great astonishment of Klenau; "Here," said he, "these are the conditions I grant to your marshal. If he had only a fortnight of food, and spoke of surrender, he would not deserve any honorable capitulation. Since it sends you, it is reduced to the end. I respect his age, his bravery and his misfortunes. Take the conditions I grant him; that he will leave the fortress tomorrow, in a month, or in six, he will have neither better nor worse conditions. He can remain as long as he is suitable for his honor; his position will not be aggravated."

At this language, at this tone, Klenau recognized the illustrious Captain, and ran to Würmser to take the conditions he had left him. The old Marshal was grateful to see the generosity of his young captain towards him, and capitulated. (Thiers, Histoire de la Revolution française, Vol. VIII, p, 565).

people to the crusade against France; that its troops had approached to within ten miles of Bologna and had threatened to invade that city; that it had not feared to begin hostile negotiations against France with the Vienna Court, as was proved by the letters of Cardinal Busca and the mission of Prelate Albani to Vienna; that the Pope confiding the command of his troops to Austrian generals and officers sent by the Court of Vienna, had also refused to respond to the official advances made by Citizen Cacault, Minister of the French Republic, for the opening of a peace negotiation; that, consequently, the treaty of armistice having been violated and broken by the Roman Court, it was broken in fact, and that the parties returned to their former positions.

In other proclamations, which were intended to reassure the lower clergy and the inhabitants of his intentions, Bonaparte said: "This army will penetrate the Pope's territory; it will be faithful to the maxims it professes; it will protect the religion and the people. Woe to those who would attract the vengeance of an army which has, in six months, made one hundred thousand prisoners of the best troops of the Emperor, taken four hundred cannon and destroyed five armies." All the classes of the inhabitants, struck with equal terror, lost their heads. Faenza opened his gates to General Lannes. Ancona did the same, and General Victor entered it on 9 February. Brigadier Marmont seized Lorette. On 18 February, the French were already masters of Romagna, the Duchy of Urbino, the Marchs of Ancona and Umbria, and the districts of Perugia and Camérino. Tremulous Rome was still stupefied by so much success, that when Bonaparte knocked at its gates, and Pope Pius VI declared that he was deferring to French generosity, promising to subscribe in advance to all just and reasonable conditions. In fact, the plenipotentiaries of the Pope, Cardinal Mattei, the prelate Galeppi, the Marquis Massimi and his nephew, the Duke Braschi on the one hand, and General Bonaparte on the other, signed the treaty of peace on the 1 Ventôse 1, Year V (19 February 1797) in Tolentino, headquarters of the Army of Italy.

The effect this magical conquest produced in Europe is beyond any analysis. There existed in all their acts of arms something supernatural, and even the fables of antiquity saw their improbability this time to pale before the truth. In France there was a moment of intoxication and enthusiasm, which was delirious, and this period, so beautiful for the nation, is so warmly traced in the burning pages of a contemporary work, as not to weaken the picture, we must confine ourselves to quoting them. It is therefore to the Histoire de la Revolution française, by M. Thiers, that we take the following lines:

> *The courier who carried the news from Italy arrived at Paris in the evening. The garrison was assembled at once, and his dispatches were read by the light of the torches, to the sound of the fanfares, amid the shouts of all the Frenchmen attached to their country. Days forever famous and forever regrettable for us! At what time was our country more beautiful and greater? The storms of the revolution seemed calmer; the murmurs of the parties sounded like the last noises of the storm. These remains of agitation were regarded as the very life of a free state. Commerce and finance were coming out of a terrible crisis; the whole soil, restored to industrious hands, was to be fertilized. A government composed of middle-class equals governed the Republic in moderation; the best was called to succeed them. All voices were free. France, at the height of power, was mistress of all the soil that extended from the Rhine to the Pyrenees, from the sea to the Alps. Holland and Spain were going to unite their fleets with hers, and to attack maritime despotism in concert. It was resplendent with immortal glory. Admirable armies floated their three colors in the face of kings, who had wished to annihilate it. Twenty heroes, diverse in character and talent, just like age and courage, led France's soldiers to victory. Hoche, Kléber, Desaix, Moreau, Joubert, Masséna, Bonaparte, and a host of others were advancing together. Their various merits were weighed; but no eye yet, so piercing as it could be, saw in this generation of heroes the unfortunate or the guilty; no eye could see the one who was about to be extinguished in the prime of life,[7] suffering from an unknown evil, the one who would die under the Muslim dagger[8] or under enemy fire, the one who would oppress freedom, the one who would betray his homeland[9]: all appeared great, pure, happy, full of future! It was only a moment; but there*

[7]Translator: Hoche
[8]Translator: Kléber
[9]Translator: Moreau

are only moments in the life of peoples, as in that of individuals. We were going to find opulence with rest; as for liberty and glory, we had them!" "It is necessary," said an elder, "that the country be not only happy, but sufficiently glorious. This wish was fulfilled. The French, adds the eloquent historian, who has since seen our stifled freedom, our country invaded, our heroes shot or unfaithful to their glory, let us never forget those immortal days of liberty, grandeur, and hope!

Finally, the fully organized Polish Legion could share the triumphs of the French troops, and on 18 Ventôse (8 March) everyone that was clothed and armed was ordered to march on Mantua. General Dąbrowski, having left Captain Konopka in Milan to watch the depot and activate the recruiting, took the road to that city, and arrived there on the 23rd (13 March) with two Polish battalions, with a strength of two thousand men. These battalions had only five companies, but they numbered two hundred men each because of the small number of officers. The unit was then increased so much at Mantua, either by the prisoners of war or by the deserters who came from all sides, that the 1st Battalion of Fusiliers was created, of which Louis Dembowski was appointed chief. The 2nd Battalion and two artillery companies were organized in Milan.

The officer, Strzalkowski, who had left Poland, a victim of the last revolution, and had since been at the service of Lombardy, requested and obtained his resignation. He was then appointed chief of grenadiers in the legions and was ordered to march, with four hundred men from the depot, against Salo and Brescia, in order to put a check on the disorders that had broken out, and to effectively protect the patriots. To support him in this endeavor, his small troop of fifty men, led by Colonel Liberadzki, who had taken refuge in France in 1795 and newly arrived in the corps, was reinforced. Strzalkowski executed his mission with prudence and courage, and when it was completed, he went to Mantua on the 13th, while Liberadzki remained in the neighborhood of Brescia. Other partial insurrections took place at that time in the mountains of Romagna, and especially at Rimini; but the chief Kosinski having left Mantua, on 13 Germinal (23 March), to contain them, tranquility was soon restored.

Thus, from the beginning, the Polish legions, imbued with the importance of their mission, knew how to unite wisdom with energy, and pacify, as well as submit. The Lombard administration was so pleased with their conduct that it sent them flags, and to Dąbrowski was given a beautifully harnessed horse. It even proposed to this general the formation of a Polish cavalry and an increase in the artillery. The garrisons at the same time asked to be authorized to form a battalion to attach it to the corps subject to his command; but Dąbrowski, lacking officers, was obliged to decline both proposals; however, when his proclamation of the Pluviôse reached Poland, a crowd of former soldiers, officers or soldiers, who had served under Kosciuszko, arrived. For his part, Major Tremo, recruiting among the prisoners of war, sent all the Poles he found in Dijon. At last, on every side, new brothers in arms came to join the ranks of General Dąbrowski, and his legions, so weak at their creation, soon began to become as respectable in number as they were by bravery and patriotism.

Northern Italy in 1796 at the begining of operations

Leonard Chodzko

HISTORY OF THE POLISH LEGIONS IN ITALY

Volume 2

Karol Kniaziewicz, (1762 - 1842) Commanding officer of the 1st Polish Legion 1796

CHAPTER SEVEN

Austria's New Preparations. – Archduke Charles. – Operations of the French Army. – Preliminaries at Leoben. – Dąbrowski's Project. – Discouragement of the Poles. – Dąbrowski's Trip to Gratz. – Movement of the Legions. – Paris Refugees. – Michel Oginski. – His Conferences with De La Croix. – He Decides to Make a Trip to Milan with Mniewski. – Disappointment. – New Operations of the Polish Corps. – Capture of Verona. – Death of Liberadzki. – Bonaparte at Montebello. – Recruitment of the Legions. – New Project of the Paris Refugees. – Plan of an Elite Constituent at Milan. – Bonneau the Second. – His Correspondence with Marshal Malachowski. – Oginski's Opposition. – We Ignore It. – Circular. – Stopping of Convoys. – Regrettable Consequences. – The Refugees are Discouraged. – Wybicki. – He joins General Dąbrowski. – Thriving of the Legions. – Troubles at Reggio. – Dąbrowski's Petition to Bonaparte. – Bonaparte's Response. – Arrival of General Kniaziewicz. – Wielhorski. – Troubles in Venice. – Address to the Polish Officers. – The March of the Legions. – Capture of Fort St.-Leo. – Rapid Conquest of Papal States. – Monsignor Saluzzo. – Capture of Urbino, Citta-di-Castello. – Opinions of the Conquered Cities.

While the Polish legions, inactive in their barracks, only breathed for war and vengeance, events turned to present them with the most favorable events and appeared to open the path to their homeland.

Beaten and crushed so many times, the Austrian armies were reborn from their ashes. The Vienna Cabinet, attributing to the faults of its generals the disgraces it had suffered, they sought to oppose Napoleon with a general worthy of him. The Archduke Prince Charles, who enjoyed a high reputation, was, as a result, recalled from the banks of the Rhine, and the following campaign, prepared under such auspices, promised to be long and murderous.

The General-in-Chief of the Army of Italy, reassured on the side of Rome by the Treaty of Tolentino, and occupied with the organization of the Cispadane and Transpadane Republics, knew that at the same time he had to reinforces his troops with some battalions raised in these new states. As a result, with his accustomed rapidity, he moved into the Venetian possessions to occupy himself with the opening of the campaign.

"As soon as the hostile conduct of Austria was recognized," says the eloquent historian Thiers, "the French government issued the most pressing orders to reinforce the Army of Italy. Bernadotte's division, drawn from the Army of the Sambre-et-Meuse, and Delmas' division from that of the Upper Rhine, were to cross the Alps in the middle of winter. Moreau put the greatest efforts into putting Delmas' division into a state to appropriately represent the Army of the Rhine in Italy. He chose his best troops and exhausted his magazines to equip them. One could not be more moved by such an honorable and delicate sentiment. These two divisions, consisting of over twenty thousand men, passed the Alps in January, at the time when no one doubted their march. They were ready to cross the Alps, when a storm stopped them. The guides advised stopping; but the charge was sounded, and they braved the tempest, drums beating, and flags deployed. These two divisions quickly descended into the Piedmontese plains, which were still unaware of their departure from the Rhine."

Such was the brilliant and almost unbelievable voyage of some republican phalanxes which would repeat this operation four years later at the Saint-Gothard![1]

Despite the mass uprising of the Tyrolians, who threatened to cut the communications of the French armies, despite the hostile enterprises of the Venetians, whose oligarchical government feared the contagion of republican principals, the troops of General Bonaparte reinforced themselves in Frioul and maintained themselves in a threatening position.

At this time Archduke Charles had deployed the bulk of his army in Carniola and covered Trieste. After various insignificant maneuvers, they finally engaged on 26 Ventôse (16 March 1797) near Tagliamento, and the Austrian General met his master. His troops were completely beaten, and he barely had time to escape. On 17 March, the divisions of Guyeux and Bernadotte captured Palma-No-

[1]Translator: This is a reference to Napoleon's crossing the Alps in 1800 as he launched his famous Marengo Campaign, in 1800.

va. Gradisca surrendered to the threats of the intrepid Serrurier. On 2 March, the tricolor flag flew over Pontebba, and at the same time Masséna captured, at Tarvis, four generals, four thousand men, twenty-five cannons, and four hundred baggage wagons. A few days later (28 March), Bonaparte echeloned towards Villach, on the banks of the Drava, the divisions of Masséna, Serrurier, and Guyeux, while a corps of troops under the orders of General Zajączek (newly escaped from the Austrian prisons and he had gone into French service) pushed to Lientz moving up the Drava to establish communications with Joubert's corps acting in the Tyrol. This latter, clearing a path through the Austrian corps, soon rejoined the center of the Army of Italy, and rendered the route completely free. Thus, in the space of twenty days, the Emperor's army was defeated everywhere and found itself reduced by a quarter, fleeing and discouraged. Archduke Charles, who retired behind the Mur River, was not in a state to resist the victorious march of the republican army as it united on the Drava River.

From 29 March, and before the junction of Joubert's corps, the principal army had marched on the road to Klagenfurth, the capital of Carinthia. That same evening Bonaparte established his headquarters there and the next day all his troops were encamped between Saint-Veit and Friesach.

It was there that the French general, seeking to stop the long effusion of blood, took the first steps to bring about an honorable peace and approached Archduke Charles. He wrote him from Klagenfurth, on 31 March; but the Prince's response was negative, it was necessary to give a new impulse to his military operations. Wiped out, pressed on all sides, the Austrians could only move in a rout to another position, and Bonaparte pushed his headquarters to Judenburg. Then the Imperial family, shaken by the prodigious progress of an army that was already pounding on the capital's gates, forced Archduke Charles to begin negotiations. A five-day armistice was signed at Klagenfurth, on 7 April. In the interval, Bonaparte moved in person to the small town of Leoben, and moved Masséna's vanguard on Simmerina, twenty-five leagues from Vienna.

Despite his hostile attitude, Bonaparte desired peace and Generals Bellegarde and Merveldt, plenipotentiaries from the Emperor Francis, regarded him as their only path to salvation. The preliminaries were ordered and signed at Leoben, 29 Germinal Year (18 April 1797).

This peace, which all French historians must call advantageous to France, gave a mortal blow to the hopes of the Poles.

In effect, this brilliant march on Vienna, this rapid conquest of enemy territory had already shown to the refugees their superb oppressor struck in his own states and in his own capital. The Polish Legion, enflamed by this success, awaited the orders to march on Austria. They recalled their accumulated griefs against this lying power, their cooperation in the last partitioning, and they were enflamed on thinking of how this same empire, which had been saved by King Sobieski's bravery, was now defiling the memory of their liberator.[2]

General Dąbrowski, himself, penetrated with the idea that a favorable moment had come, laid out in Mantua a detailed plan by which the Polish Corps would pass by Croatia, Transylvania, and Hungary, would penetrate into Poland and raise the ancient flag of independence. This plan he presented to Bonaparte, and awaiting his response, he took some actions in Paris to push his response.

Even though Bonaparte had at this time thought of the truce that would occur and the peace that would follow it, he was far from rejecting General Dąbrowski's projects, and appeared to act for some time under their influence. On 17 Germinal (16 April), Dąbrowski received orders to march on Palma-Nova, and General Berthier enjoined him to gather all the Polish Corps there.

Dąbrowski, executing this movement with his ordinary activity, directed himself immediately on Palma-Nova with the grenadiers, leaving Chief Dembowski at Mantua, with orders to wait there for the junction of all the detachments, then move to join him. This march was disturbed by a corps of Venetian partisans and by the insurgent peasants that appeared on the road. However, on 28 Germinal (17 April) they arrived at Palma-Nova, where there were soon five thousand Polish soldiers under arms. Burning with patriotic fire, full of ardor and bravery, they only awaited the signal to march on their homes, when suddenly the terrible news came that the preliminaries of a peace had

[2]Translator: King Sobieski broke the Turkish siege of Vienna as the city was about to fall on 12 September 1683. Sobieski crushed the Turkish army, relieved the city, and saved Austria and possibly Germany from Turkish conquest.

been signed at Leoben on 18 April.

Shocked by these events without being knocked down, Dąbrowski wished to return to his source to learn the reason and he quickly went to join Bonaparte. The young heroes were at Gratz and the French army had already evacuated Austria conforming to the concluded treaty. Admitted to the presence of the General-in-Chief, Dąbrowski obtained praise for his devotion and that of the Poles; but when he touched the delicate subject of the delivery of his homeland, Bonaparte could promise him nothing, recommending only patience and perseverance to him. These were foreign virtues to the cult to which the Poles had remained faithful from their first saber blow for the republican cause, to the last days of the Imperial power which fell on the battlefield of Waterloo.

The Polish general returned on his steps and arrived, on 10 Floréal (29 April), at Palma-Nova, where he received orders to march on Treviso. Rejoined by all his detachments and by Kosinski, who, after having forced the passage of the White Canal and the Adige, found himself at Cordogio, Dąbrowski executed the ordered movement, but this troop no longer had the enthusiasm that the previous events had produced.

On their side, the refugees in Paris did not remain idle. The return of Citizen Oginski from his mission to Constantinople gave more activity to the general measures. This patriot, equipped with letters from Aubert-du-Bayet for the Minister of Foreign Affairs, Charles De La Croix, quickly moved to meet with De la Croix and probed the disposition of the French government on the subject of Poland. In the first meeting, De la Croix professed the sharpest interest for the unfortunate land; but when Oginski began to press him and requested what were the intentions of the Directory in its regard, the Minister responded that he could not, for the moment, satisfy his curiosity, because the time had not come to act in an effective manner. He added, nonetheless, that the government was always well disposed, and that he would not let any moment escape to second the operations of the patriots, etc., etc.

On 16 Germinal (5 April), in a second meeting, Minister De la Croix detailed to Oginski all the successive victories that the French had gained in Italy; he observed to him in addition that nothing prevented General Bonaparte from marching on Vienna; but as he supposed that the occupation of this capital by the French would not end the war with Austria, he thought that the most profitable activity for the Poles to do was to rise up in Galicia. He showed him the reports that the government had received on the nature of the spirits in Hungary, in Transylvania, and Dalmatia. The government wished to provoke an insurrection and to organize itself following the example of the Italian republics; but he added that such vast and bold operations could not succeed without much prudence in the formation of a definitive plan, and without much promptitude in its execution. He declared that the Directory could not compromise itself by advising the Poles, the inhabitants of Galicia, to rise up against the government that had taken their country from them; but that it had agreed to tell them that the hour for the regeneration of Poland had arrived, that there was no more suitable moment to act, and that finally it was time for the Poles to do what honor and duty indicated to them.

The Minister of Foreign Affairs proposed then to Oginski that he immediately go to Bonaparte's headquarters to coordinate with him the execution of his projects. He added that it would be easy to write down all the propositions made in the name of the Poles, in order that they might be submitted to the Directory.

But in a note which responded to this last wish of the Minister, Citizen Oginski expressed in such a precise manner his suspicion that the French government looked to use the Polish troops for their purposes and not for those of the Poles, to command an insurrection to profit from it and then abandon the insurgents as a useless instrument, that Charles De la Croix could not conceal his mood, and said angrily; "France does not need the Poles; that if they could not give it their confidence, they could go somewhere else; that moreover they misunderstood the intentions of a government that came to establish the Polish legions, to help them to reclaim their homeland." Finally, he finished saying that the refugees could behave as they might consider appropriate, but that after three days it would be too late to return to the projects in question.

Before risking expressing his distrust, every Polish citizen had to think that his compatriots were in a position of receiving the law and not dictating it; that otherwise the government had given their nation so many public marks of interest that any overt expression of suspicion would be to involuntarily wound it. Finally, one had to reflect if France could do much for the Poles, as the relief of the Poles was a little thing for France.

Upon receiving such an unaccustomed response, the Parisian refugees saw clearly that they had taken a false step. Also wishing to repair relations and prove to the minister that they would accept his councils, they wrote another report, and at the same time, they wrote an address to the inhabitants of Galicia.[3]

This report, composed by Orginski and Wybicki, and signed by Oginski, Mniewski, Wybicki, Prozor, Barss, Taszycki, Jos.-Calass, Szaniawski, Walchnowski, Podoski, Kociell, etc., contained a plan of military movements conforming to that already presented to Bonaparte by Dąbrowski. To support this document, the refugees engaged themselves to send three of them as a deputation to the headquarters of the French Army of Italy. The choice fell on Oginski, Mniewski, and Prozor, but the latter could not accept this mission and the two others alone held themselves ready for it.

After a few days, De la Croix officially informed the refugees that the Directory had approved their project without making any changes to it and had expedited it to General Bonaparte, confiding it to him and recommending its execution.

Citizens Oginski and Mniewski, following their hopes and strong with the support of the Directory, set out for the headquarters of the Army of Italy, when a courier hastily expedited by Bonaparte arrived in Paris with the signed copy of the preliminaries of Leoben!!!!

Let us return now to the Polish legions.

The Venetian government had manifested some hostile views and threatened to disturb the rear of the Republican armies, so Bonaparte, to assure his communications, looked to put a French garrison in the city of Venice. However, the Venetian Senate stubbornly refused to submit to this and took defensive measures. Venice was then blockaded by land and sea. The Polish Legion arrived at Treviso, on 6 May, and marched along the banks of the Adriatic some detachments that

---

[3]The author of *Mémoires sur la Pologone et les Polonais,* in giving all the details of many other official documents contained in his work, only gives a quick summary of the plan in question. I had the good fortune of obtaining a complete copy, drawn from a signed manuscript.

cut off the city from the fresh water that came from the Tagliamento and the Pavia Rivers. But a few days later, when Venice had surrendered, the Polish Corps received orders to march to Bologna, the capital of the newly formed Transpadane Republic.

Colonel Liberadzki, who had been stationed in the vicinity of Brescia and Verona, found himself containing continual insurrections. But when a new riot erupted in Verona and the French garrison assigned to maintain it in obedience was massacred, the city gave itself over to its defense and it became necessary to assault it. Liberadzki, at the head of his detachment, launched an escalade. At the same time republican troops penetrated the city with their bayonets lowered. This brave officer barely enjoyed his first triumph, when a mortal blow struck him, and he died shortly later. He was so regretted by those who truly appreciated his merit, that when they celebrated in Milan, in the Bonaparte Forum, the funerals of the heroes who had died in this campaign, the Lombardy government had engraved on Liberadzki's catafalque the following inscription: *Liberadzkius polon. Cohort. Praefect, in proelio ad Veronam occubuit suis anated monitis aut vivendum aul moriedum pro legel et patria.*

Master of Venice, and having provisionally arranged its fate, Bonaparte transported his headquarters from Milan to Montebello, a beautiful residence three leagues from this capital, and which, placed on a height, dominated the rich plains of Lombardy. There, looking like a crowned prince, he was surrounded by the ministers of Austria, Rome, Naples, Sardinia, Genoa, Venice, Parma, the Swiss Cantons, and several small German states. To assure forever the new destinies of the conquered land, he formed from Lombardy, the Duchies of Modena and Reggio, the legations of Bologna and Ferrara, of Romagne, Bergamo, Brescia, and Mantua, a state that extended to the Adige, which contained three million six hundred thousand inhabitants. This the new Cisalpine Republic, with a French constitution, had its capital at Milan. Bonaparte named five directors and the members of the two councils, then he designated as president of this new Directory, Citizen Jean Galcazzi Serbelloni.

In the middle of such work and of a confused and immense future, the fate of the Polish legions was not forgotten. On 22 Floréal (11 May) they received orders to assemble in Bologna, except for the battalion under the orders of Dembowski, which had four thousand men, and which was destined to form part of the garrison of Mantua. The Polish Corps, obedient to its instructions, arrived in Bologna, 17 May, and it was there that General Dąbrowski received a letter from Lille, dated 23 Germinal (12 April 1797), in which Bialowieyski, a courageous officer, who had distinguished himself under his orders in Poland, announced that, in concert with some other Polish leaders, he had assembled nearly one thousand men, and that they were coming to join him.

It was at this time that Dąbrowski received from General Bonaparte a letter dated from Montebello, on 28 Floréal (17 May) and a second from the General Administration of Milan, dated 18 May, which engaged himself to occupy himself without pause on the definitive organization of the Polish Corps.

It was also around this time that the Paris refugees, recovering from their first discouragement following the Treaty of Leoben, had their hope renewed that they might once against be useful to their homeland, and found in their patriotism new resources.

The example of General Dąbrowski, the military representation that this worthy warrior created with such success, all concurred to stimulate their zeal and to push them down the same path as him. Several of them, among others Barss, Wybickie, and Prozor, reproduced an idea formerly issued, to install a civilian representative at the side of this military representation, and to convoke the old constitutional diet at Milan, the seat of the Cisalpine Republic, which paid and maintained the Polish legions. This project, approved in 1795, by members of the Directory, then submitted by Wybicki to Caillard, French Minister at Berlin, had united, at various times, unanimous suffrage. It was, therefore, natural that one return there with ardor, at a moment where everything promised the most prompt and happy opportunities.

To still further confirm this hope, a new protector arrived, and joining, to the actions of the refugees, his strongest entreaties. This was Citizen Jean-Alexandre Bonneau, formerly Council General from France to Warsaw, who, arrested and thrown into a prison cell by order of Catherine II, after fifteen months of detention, recovered his liberty. As he enjoyed in Paris the confidence of several members of the Directory, he seized with eagerness every occasion to recall to them the affairs of Poland. He did even more and supporting with all his force the idea of a national representation at Milan, he wrote on this subject a letter to Malachowski, Marshal of the Constituent Diet. The response of this illustrious citizen was not long in coming and it was completely in conformance with the high opinion that had been concluded of his character. He indicated to Bonenau that he approved these patriotic projects, and that two members of the Constituent Diet, Woyczynski and Kochanowski, had been sent to Paris on a mission to confer with him.

In effect, he presented himself with a difficulty. The Diet, according to Polish laws, could only be constituted by a reunion of the three estates: the king, the senate, and the equestrian order, that is to say the nonces elected in their respective districts and palatinates. But the old diet had been adjourned and not dissolved, so it still existed with all its powers. It sufficed, as a result, that it moved to reopen its seating at Milan, in protesting against the force majeure which prevented them from continuing their activities in Warsaw. Well, is it not probable that at the first news spreading in Poland of this new project, and of the reasons that caused it to occur, the nonces of the adjourned diet, with its Marshals Malachowski and Sapieha at their head, would come, totally or in part, to take up their seats on the benches where the national cause called them? Was it not probable that they would imitate, as citizens, the example that Dąbrowski's soldiers had given them? As to Stanislas-August, the phantom king, who was finishing his sad career in St. Petersburg, there was no chance that he would come, but with Malachowski representing civil power and Dąbrowski the army, this was sufficient to represent the nation.

Such a large project always encounters opposition. Citizen Oginski, recalled from Constantinople to level all the dissidence between the Poles, appeared to have misunderstood his useful mandate. It should be said to his praise that, on the entreaties of his compatriots, he determined to make another approach to Minister Charles De la Croix on the projected diet. But the Minister, then threatened with his pending dismissal could only naturally qualify this plan as ridiculous and unheard of in the annals of any people.

As he worked towards a positive result, however, it was resolved that Citizen Oginski should address an ostensible letter to Bonneau, by which he could sound out the intention of the members of the Directory, to whom he was admitted, and therefore whose opinion would draw the Polish patriots from their uncertainty.

At this moment, the Directory found itself with divided opinions. Some where laying in wait for the changes that the treaty with the Vienna Court and the return of General Bonaparte would produce in the administration and the army. The ministry was occupied with its renewal, and, in the midst of such flagrant interests, the fate of the Poles was secondary. However, Bonneau insisting on having an answer, he was told that "the refugee project seemed good and useful, but that it depended very much on a competition of events that could not be foreseen."

While awaiting a positive solution on the part of France, the patriots took other steps vis-à-vis Poland. They launched a circular which made public and popular the new resolution of the Paris Committee. It was then that Oginski manifested most firmly his opposition; fighting all the imprudence of such an action, he refuted it with wise and reasonable motives, which were a bit cold for the circumstances. Finally, he took upon himself the writing of this piece, but limited himself to exposing the reasons for which they had thought it necessary to reconstitute the diet at Milan, without approving or disapproving it. Then he affixed his signature next to those of Mniewski, Taszycki, Prozor, Wybicki, Barss, Walchnowski, Ralecki, Kochanowski, Woyczynski, and several others.

The wiser advice than Oginski gave, and which was not listened to either, was to designate no one by name in these circulars, and to abandon to the agent who would bear it the task of handing them over to the persons who would be indicated to him verbally. This idea was opposed by saying that such letters, without superscription, would seem to come from a suspicious source, and the majority insisted on putting direct addresses on them, such as those of Prince Adam Kazimirz Czartoryski, Ignacy Potocki, Stanislas Malachowski, and other influential members of the Constituent Diet.

It was unfortunate that the patriots Narbutt and Kochanowski, who were to perform this delicate mission, were arrested on the frontiers of Poland. All their papers were seized, and new persecutions were the result of this unfortunate attempt. Marshal Malachowski was arrested in Galicia by order of Austria, and, after a year's imprisonment, he was not released until after the payment of sixty thousand francs, advanced by the Court of Vienna for inquiries and costs of justice, which he was sentenced to repay.

While this affair, begun under happy auspices, ended in such a deplorable manner, General Dąbrowski, informed by the Paris refugees, had given their project full consent. Not doubting his success, he had rented the Serbelloni Palace, and had it disposed to receive the members of the Constituent Diet. He found himself strengthened in this idea by the letters he received from Bonneau, who was as enthusiastic as he was, and as he was persuaded of success. But fate, always contrary to the hopes of the Poles, had decided otherwise.

The Paris refugees, on the other hand, distressed by the outcome of their proceedings, and by such disastrous consequences, remained struck by inertia at this news. Wybicki alone did not lose courage; he tried to raise the moral force of his compatriots; he represented to them that fate does not struggle long against perseverance; but the hour of devotion and energy was past. Soon the same dissensions which at different times had neutralized the good intentions of the Poles, broke out with more force. There was even between Bonneau and Parandier a discussion such as was brought to Talleyrand Perigord, then Minister of Foreign Affairs; but as these details are lost in the crowd of secondary interests, they will be found in the supporting documents.

Thus, little by little, by discouragement or disunity, this core of patriots who had given so many marks of their devotion to the national cause, dispersed without hope of return, and carried its new destinies to points where they could be of no use to their country. There were even some who, disregarding their former sentiments, took an oath of fidelity to the governments that had participated in the partition of Poland; we saw some who promised to behave in a wise and loyal manner! Manes des Reytan, Korsak, Fasinski, who were these men with you?

Wybicki, seeing that the national cause was lost in Paris because of its own defenders, left this capital, but he left it to rejoin General Dąbrowski. At least the Poles did not derogate from their dignity, and each day they took on a new consistency. Thus Wybicki, whom the closest friendship bound to the chief of the Legions, now attached himself to his destiny. A skillful diplomat, full of talent and knowledge, he was a powerful contributor to focusing attention on those fellow warriors whose reputation later became European. It was he who wrote the memoirs and projects that General Dąbrowski presented in all forms and on all occasions to demand the reestablishment of Poland. The constant union which reigned between these two distinguished men, so different in character, is the most complete eulogy to warriors and citizens.

As Dąbrowski's manifesto, aided by the public rumor, informed Europe of the formation of the Polish legions, brave men came from all directions to swell their cadres. On his return to Milan General Dąbrowski found General Joseph Wielhorski, Colonel Chamand, Forestier, and Zabrocki together in this capital. Bialowieyski also arrived from Lille with his depot, and every day brought in new recruits, the corps were soon complete. From this moment the organization demanded by the Lombard administration received its execution: two legions of infantry were formed, each composed of three battalions. The battalions were of three companies each, and each company was composed of one hundred twenty-five men.

This organization was accepted and published, then each went to his post. Their service was done in the garrisons according to the French regulations; but all that pertained to clothing, with the exception, however, of corporal punishment, was decided according to Polish custom.

In the meantime, there erupted, on Messidor (30 June 1797), between the patriots and the aristocrats at Reggio disorders which might have had unfortunate consequences. To stifle them from birth, General Dąbrowski received the order on the 15th (3 July) to go there immediately. He arrived at Reggio with one thousand men, commanded by Chief Strzalkowski, and reestablished order to the satisfaction of all the parties.

In reporting to Bonaparte on the success of the mission that had just been confided to him, Dąbrowski, who seized every opportunity of reminding the General-in-Chief of the interests of Poland, sent him a second letter asking him whether would not be possible that, with his protection, the Poles might have a representative at the congress that was going to be held. Here are the terms of this petition:

Lieutenant-General Dąbrowski, in the name of his compatriots, to the General-in-Chief of the Army of Italy, Bonaparte.

At the headquarters at Reggio,
Messidor 22, Year V (10 July 1797).

Allow me, Citizen General, to be with you the organ of the feelings of my compatriots and brothers-in-arms, who have gathered under your auspices in Italy, and suffer that I speak to you for a moment of the interests of an unhappy nation. I do not wish to retrace here the sad picture of our misfortunes; it would be too long and too distressing for a sensible man and friend of humanity; I will only say that, since the moment when it has pleased our enemies to remove us from the list of existing powers, we have not ceased to seek every means of giving ourselves a political existence. He presented himself only once, analogous to the circumstances and capable of fulfilling this purpose. It was to form a nucleus of Polish soldiers.

It was then that, seeing the impossibility of carrying out this project in our country, we unanimously looked upon you, Citizen General, as the only one capable of facilitating our designs, and of protecting us. Honored by the confidence of my compatriots, and approved by your government, I have come to Italy, and I have found in you a support for all my hopes. It was under your own eyes, Citizen General, that our corps was formed and enlarged to the number of six thousand men. Already a flattering future smiled on us, we hoped to gather laurels under your command, to increase our strength more and more, and, following you in the career of your victories, to find a path that would have led us to our country, where already another nucleus of this nature, which was formed in Wallachia by the help of the patriots, awaited only the moment to rally to us under your orders. And all at once the preliminaries of peace have come to destroy all our hopes. But as nothing in the world can make us abandon our plans, and the desire to recover our freedom, we address you, Citizen General, with that confidence that you have so justly inspired in us. The moment has arrived when a general peace must secure the fate of Europe and fix the destiny of the powers that compose it. In such an interesting moment, no one will fall asleep on his own interests, and the enemies of France, even those who have done the most harm to humanity, will seek to secure a certain fate, while the Poles, forgotten, will remain the only victims, and why? For having served the cause of liberty, for having shown to Europe that in the space of five months, separating with three hundred thousand exiled from their country, they have been able to form a corps of six thousand men. That the family of the Bourbons, the Stadtholder[4], and the different princes of Germany and Italy, show us in the course of this war as many armed soldiers in their favor, and yet these rest entirely on propriety, the interests and the ties that bind them to kings and monarchies, while we, far from having a king, or a monarchy for friends, we have all of them as our enemies. We can, therefore, only address the French and Cisalpine Republics, and hope that these will have regard to our situation, and to the goodwill we have shown to them, and that through them we will obtain the incontestable right of having a national representation at the peace convention. This is the intention of the Poles who make up the Legions, that of the patriots scattered throughout France, and the wish of the whole nation.

But we do not wish to make this step, nor any other, without having previously consulted with you, Citizen General, whom all Poles regard as the arbiter of Poland. Tell us what we have to do. Your opinion, your advice will be a compelling law for us. Finally, we will entrust to you our destiny, and we cannot put it in better hands.

"Dąbrowski"

[4]Translator: The Stadtholder was the ruler of Holland.

The response of the General-in-Chief was quickly expedited to the Polish general. Although the flattering praise rendered to the conduct of the Polish troops was very agreeable to them, they would have received it with much more enthusiasm, if the request of General Dąbrowski had been received. This is how Bonaparte spoke in his energetic jacobinism:

Bonaparte, General-in-Chief,
to the Général de division Dąbrowski.

Milan, Messidor 5, Year V (July 13, 1797).

I have seen with pleasure, Citizen General, how quickly you have restored order in the Department of Reggio. One is very satisfied with the keeping and the good conduct of your legions, so that everybody hastens to do all that will be useful for you. If the affairs break, I will return some French and Italian troops to form a line division, and I hope that your legions will appear with honor to the army, for only good information comes to me from all sides on this corps. In the meantime, order that they be exercised everywhere in the handling of weapons and other evolutions.

As for the request you make to me to enter into Congress, you know how difficult it is. The wishes of all the friends of liberty are for the brave Poles, but it belongs only to the time and the destiny to restore them.

"BONAPARTE"

A perfect tranquility reigning in Reggio, we returned to Bologna, and only the 2nd Battalion of the 2nd Legion, under the command of Captain Krolikiewicz, remained in Reggio.

However, the business was not over with the Emperor of Austria, and the French army returned to the field to resume hostilities. The Legion received, accordingly, the order from Bonaparte, on 30 Fructidor (16 September), and General Berthier, on the 1st (17th), orders to go to Mestre, near Venice, to join the army. General Dąbrowski recalled to him the two companies under Krolikiewicz's orders and set out. The 2nd Legion was also ordered to go to Venice, and the Poles at that time flattered themselves that they would soon have to act against Hungary, since they formed the right wing of the French army, and that this was the position assigned to them by General Dąbrowski, in the plan previously submitted to Bonaparte, dated 25 March.

At the moment of his campaign, the General-in-Chief of the Legions had the satisfaction of counting under his banners General Kniaziewicz, who had joined his troops at Reggio, followed by forty Polish officers. These brave warriors had left their homeland, at the very moment when the three occupying powers prohibited, on the penalty of death, any emigration or communication with the Polish legions. But these new inquisitors, in making such a judgment, had not calculated that if, on one side, they frightened some timid minds, they produced the opposite effect on generous souls.

This Kniaziewicz, who in 1792 had fought the Muscovites in four ranged battles (Boruszkowce, Zielence, Wlodzimierz and Dubienka) had been appointed major general by Generalissimo Kosciuszko at the time of the war of independence. Taken prisoner with the generalissimo, in the bloody day of Maciejowice, 10 October 1794, he was transported to Kiev, and remained a prisoner there for a few months. Later, when he returned to liberty, he learned that Polish Corps were forming in Italy, and he braved death to join his brothers-in-arms. Bonaparte, an admirer of such courage, welcomed Kniaziewicz to Campo-Formio, where peace was already being discussed. It was there that this general obtained from the young hero the command of the 1st Legion, while Wielhorski was appointed a brigadier general, and both of them were placed under the orders of Dąbrowski.

But before Kniaziewicz was at the head of the 1st Legion, it arrived, 5 Vendemiaire, Year VI (26 September 1797), at Mestre, and then went on the 17th (8 October) at Molta on Livenza. Wielhorski, at his side, he advanced as far as Lallisana, where the artillery joined him, when General Bonaparte, in signing peace at Campo-Formio, on the 26 Vendemiaire (17 October 1797), stopped all these movements, and rendered these corps stationary.

The Genovese government negotiated with General Dąbrowski for the formation of a Polish demi-brigade. Bonaparte himself wished it; but the general would only consent to it under the same conditions as those stipulated with the Cisalpine government; and, besides, finding it very difficult, in peacetime he entirely renounced the affair, and concluded nothing with Citizen Ruggieri, whom the Genovese government had charged with this commission.

The Legion received, on the 29th (20 October), the order to return to Ferrara; but a battalion immediately occupied Venice, the 2nd was sent there: this city was then in ferment, and the disorders that erupted at every moment obliged this battalion to be almost always under arms, until they were appeased.

The Legion arrived on the 6 Brumaire (27 October) at Ferrara; the artillery and two companies commanded by Captain Krolikiewicz went to Mantua. General Wielhorski took command of the Polish garrison of this place. And soon after the 2nd Battalion came back from Venice. At that time the corps had all necessary officers and was seven thousand one hundred forty-six strong.

The news of Bonaparte's departure for the Rastadt Congress then came to the attention of the Poles. On this occasion several officers of the battalions, who were not in Ferrara, went to this city on the 13 Brumaire (3 November), to testify by this step how much their patriotic intentions persevered. To this end they gave an address to Dąbrowski, with the prayer of renewing some representations to General Bonaparte for the common cause. This address is here:

Ferrara, Brumaire 14, Year VI (4 November 1797)

"Your proclamation, general, inspired by virtue and sentiment, has brought us together on the soil of Italy. It was necessary to have your talents and your indefatigable soul to make the Poles take up arms, at the very moment when their country lost its independence and its liberty. Our legions, guided by you, general, bring hope back to Poland, make the misfortune of their homeland known in Europe, and prepare you for the laurels of good citizenship and gratitude. Peace, so desired by humanity, will end the struggle that bloodies all Europe. We ask you to be our interpreter with Bonaparte, who presides over the destiny of the nations; speak to him with that conviction and the confidence which must inspire you with the salvation, the happiness and

the restoration of our country. "

(Signatures follow.)

In answer to the wishes of his officers, which was only the expression of his own, Dąbrowski, left Ferrara and arrived on the 23rd (13 November) at Milan, where he renewed with Bonaparte the same authorities he had previously made. The moment seemed in fact to favor this new attempt, since the General-in-Chief, after confiding to Alexander Berthier the command of the army, had to leave Milan on 25 Brumaire (15 November) to go to the congress which was about to open.

In the interval of this journey the Polish troops, whose movements are of interest to us, were ordered to occupy Fort San Leo, Poggio's imperial fief, and to drive out the Pope's troops; and on the 25th the various corps set out to reach Rimini, a point designated for the assembly.

The Kniaziewicz Legion left Ferrara, and its 1st Battalion entered Rimini on the 30th (20th), the 2nd arrived at Savignano on 7 Frimaire (27 November), and the 3rd remained in Cesena where it was already on the 29th (19th). For its part the 3rd Battalion of the 2nd Legion, commanded by Zagorski, was directed from Milan to Rimini to join the corps. He arrived there on the 17th (7 December), and took his quarters in Cervia and Cesenatico on the Adriatic.

Chief Wincenty Axamitowski, commanding a Polish artillery company, received the same order; but he was so slow in executing it that he was not able to return to Rimini until the Pluviôse 11th (30 January 1798). Meanwhile, the 1st Battalion of the 2nd Legion left Mantua to go to Milan, where General Wielhorski had transported his quarters, while the 2nd Battalion of the same corps remained stationary in Cuneo.

In the midst of these various movements, General Dąbrowski, always occupied with the fate of his legions, treated with the Cisalpine Directory; and although the convention that he concluded at that time for their definitive organization was not followed by no effect, for lack of the sanction of the legislature, this piece is nevertheless too essential to our history so that we reproduce it with the letter of the Minister of the War Vignolle, which was its consequence.

CONVENTION

Made between the Executive Directory of the Cisalpine Republic, and Lieutenant-General Dąbrowski, Commander-in-Chief of the Polish Auxiliary Legions of the Cisalpine Republic.

1. The Polish legions will bear the title of Polish Auxiliary Legions of the Cisalpine Republic.

2.) The costume, the military distinguishing marks, the color of the uniforms of each battalion, the Military Penal Code, shall be in accordance with Polish military custom and regulations. The code will be printed and published.

3.) The organization, the pay, the subsistence, and all that is granted to the Cisalpine national troops will be common to the Polish Corps.

4.) The Polish artillery will be part of the Polish Corps and will enjoy the same rights as the rest of the Legions. The officers will be presented by General Dąbrowski, who is in charge of maintaining this corps in its entirety. The artillery will immediately be under the command of the commander-in-chief of the artillery of the Cisalpine Republic.

5.) The officers and the soldiers will gratefully carry the national cockade of the Republic, as an ally and friend of the French Republic, from which Poland is awaiting its regeneration.

6.) The Executive Directory of the Cisalpine Republic shall issue the certificates to the officers and employees in the Polish legions, upon the presentation of General Dąbrowski, or the Polish general who shall command the said legions, reserving the right to submit his reflections, even on individuals, if it deems it necessary.

If the Cisalpine Republic wishes to form new Polish battalions in the future, the Poles will see with satisfaction a quarter of the plans of officers occupied by Cisalpine officers.

7.) The Cisalpine Republic declares that it will look upon Poles armed for the defense of freedom as true brothers. In the event that the interest of their homeland orders them to return to Poland, and that the republic is not actively at war for the sup-

port of freedom, the Polish Corps will be allowed to leave Italy. These so-called Polish Corps will be required to surrender the arms and all sorts of equipment that they have received from the Cisalpine Republic unless the government of Poland shall make arrangements for the reimbursement of such effects.
Campaign bonuses awarded to officers shall also be reimbursed.

8.) If in the general pacification the non-existence of Poland is decided, the Cisalpine Republic will grant the right of citizenship to any Polish individual who wishes to settle here, and who has served for two years in the Polish auxiliary legions of the Republic.

9.) As the articles will be binding on both parties only after they have been sanctioned by the Legislature, the Executive Directory undertakes to support this agreement with the Legislature, by testifying of the loyalty with which the Poles have, from the beginning, kept their commitment.

Milan, this 27 Brumaire Year VI (17 November 1797.)
ALESSANDRI, President.

For the Executive-Board,
COSTABILI, director.
Dąbrowski, Lieutenant-General.

General Vignolle, Minister of War,
to Lieutenant General Dąbrowski.

Milan, this Frimaire 7, Year VI (17 November 1797).

The Directory entrusts me, Citizen General, to order you to suspend, in all its points, the execution of the articles agreed upon in the convention that you passed with it on the Brumaire 27th last, until this convention has been ratified by the Legislature. This clause is formally reserved by the last article of this convention, and you no doubt feel that the government must not tolerate its execution, as long as the satisfaction of which it is concerned has not taken place. You will accordingly, at once, revoke all the orders you may have given for the execution of this convention, and in particular to the commander of artillery.

"VIGNOLLE."

Things remained there for the moment, and General Dąbrowski left Milan on 28 Brumaire (18 November), and arrived on the 2 Frimaire (22 November), at Rimini, having taken with the authorities of Bologna and Faenza the arrangements necessary to its expedition. On the 12th (2 December) the 1st Battalion left for Verucchio, and the 3rd for Rimini. Four companies of the 2nd occupied Poggio di Berni without any resistance, and part of the Cisalpine troops was at Longiano, Cattolica and Saloderchio.

On the 13th, the 1st Battalion took position in front of San Leo, and the 3rd at Verucchio. The General having summoned the fort to surrender, the commander of the Papal troops refused, and as we could not seize it by force, since it was built on steep a rock, it was decided to blockade it. The 1st Battalion, therefore, sought to take a position opposite the posts of the fort; but to reach this point, it was necessary to march along the ramparts, and the enemy directed a heavy fire against the besiegers. There was, however, very little loss: Elie Tremo and some soldiers were only slightly wounded. The battalion straddled the road from Urbino to San Leo, and the 3rd Battalion joined the blockade corps on the 14th (4 December). Then strong detachments were sent back to Urbino to fight against the Papal troops who came to San Leon's aid from this place. The enemy numbered one thousand five hundred men, besides one thousand peasants who had joined them; but the Polish Corps, although inferior in number, overthrew them on the 14th and 15th (4th and 5th), left many on the field of battle, and made many prisoners, especially from their cavalry. The peasants, however, did not stop harassing the various corps of troops, the 2nd Battalion was ordered to advance to Verucchio and Pietra-cuta. On his side the Venetian battalion, in the service of the Cisalpine Republic, moved from Longiano to Vardengo, near San Leo.

Finally, the fort, with all its dependencies, surrendered on the 17th (7 December 1797). The garrison came out with arms and baggage and was escorted to Urbino by a detachment of the Venetian battalion.

All the artillery and stores remained in the Republican armies. The battalion commander Moroni, of the 4th Cisalpine Legion, was appointed commander of the place, and the 1st Battalion established its district there. The 3rd Battalion moved towards Macerata and Montefeltro, forcing the Papal troops to retreat to Urbino.[5]

On the 20th (10 December), the headquarters and the 1st Battalion moved to Rimini, the 2nd to Pietracuta, Veruccbio and Poggio, the 3rd to Cesena, and the 3rd of the 2nd Legion to Cervia and Cesenatico, which were under the orders of General Kniaziewicz, and the Cisalpine Corps also took their cantonments near Faenza, Forli, and Ravenna, under the orders of General Lecchi.

However, the troubles were not calmed, and a great fermentation reigned in the Papal States. The corps advanced accordingly and moved towards the frontiers. The 2nd Battalion arrived on the 28th (18th) at Cattolica, and 3rd of the 2nd Legion at Rimini.

On the Nivôse 2nd (22 December), a troop of armed patriots arrested the commander of the Papal troops at Pesaro, who was visiting the advanced posts. Emboldened by this success, they seized the posts themselves, and captured the soldiers who guarded them, as well as those who were at the gates of the city. The governor of the province, Monsignor Saluzzo, seeing himself arrested in his palace, and fearing that he would become the victim of this insurrection, wrote to General Dąbrowski, as a general of a friendly nation, to request his intervention.

Dąbrowski replied that, as an employee in the service of a neutral power, he could not advance his troops, but that if the governor believed his life in danger, he could, under his personal responsibility, offer him humanitarian assistance. General Dąbrowski sent the 2nd Battalion, with one thousand men of Cisalpine infantry and cavalry, followed by two guns, under the command of General Lecchi. The Papal troops were driven from all points. The governor and a few hundred men were made prisoners of war, and two guns, much ammunition, and some magazines fell into the hands of the Italo-Polish troops. The provisional municipality was immediately installed; a civic guard soon

[5]Mr. J. -B. Saignes, in his *Mémoires pour servir à l'Histoire de France*, published in Paris, 1814, Vol. II, p. 53, erroneously said: "10,000 men of Cisalpine troops, commanded by the Polish General Dąbrowski, seized, after three days of siege, Fort Saint-Leon, in the Duchy of Urbino."

appeared under arms, and the pastoral letter of the Bishop of Pesaro recommended that "they devote to the republic today the same obedience which it yesterday devoted to the sovereign pontiff, as temporal prince."

The rest of the Papal army fled to Fano and Urbino. General Lecchi, pursuing it as far as these two cities, found there a population fatigued by the monarchical yoke, and who preferred the exact discipline of the republican troops to the vexations of the troops of the Church, the new government of the conquerors to the pontifical despotism.

On all sides, and principally from the cities of the Duchy of Urbino, Foligno, Città di Castello, and Perugia, came deputations addressed to General Dąbrowski, who asked him, as a special favor, to be occupied by the victorious army. To satisfy their demand, Lecchi, having received some reinforcements from the Cisalpine troops, pushed a reconnaissance through Fano and Fossombrone, and occupied Urbino and Città di Castello, where he was joined by the 2nd Battalion. On the Nivôse 13th (2 January 1798), the Headquarters moved to Pesaro, and the 14th to Fano, on the Adriatic. On the 18th (7th), the 1st Battalion was at Fano and Fossombrone, the 2nd at Gubbio-Casteciaro, the 3rd at Pesaro, and the 3rd of the 2nd Legion at Cagli and Pergola, under the command of General Kniaziewicz, who had its headquarters in the latter place, General Lecchi commanding the right wing, Thullie commanded the center, and Julhien commanded the reserve, stationed at Pesaro and Cattolica.[6]

[6]The inhabitants of the provinces occupied by the Italo-Polish army showed the greatest enthusiasm on all sides. Among the various addresses they sent to both the Polish and French chiefs, that which General Berthier received, before his departure from Milan, from the deputies of the Duchy of Urbino, painted exactly the position in which the States of the Church were then. See Supporting Document No. 40.

CHAPTER EIGHT

Political Shrewdness of the Court of Rome. — Rallying in Villa Medici.— Papal Police. — Conduct of Joseph Bonaparte, Ambassador. — Riot in Front of His Palace. — Duphot is Murdered Under His Eyes. — Joseph Demands His Passports. — He Retires to Florence. — Declaration of War Against Pius VI. — March of the Troops. — General Berthier Enters Rome. — His Discourse at the Capital. — He Proclaims the Independence of the Roman People. — Their Demarche to the Vienna Court. — Masséna. — Brune. — The Polish Legions are Directed on Rome. — Return of Mohammed's Standard to General Dąbrowski. — Souvenirs of Sobieski. — Saber of this Warrior Destined for Kosciuszko. — Arrival of General Rymkiewicz, Colonel Jablonowski, and Godebaki. — New Demarches of Dąbrowski to the Cisalpine government. — Distress of the Polish Troops. — Dąbrowski Gets Them Paid and Dressed. — Insurrection of Cicero. — Passage of the Cosa. — Capture of Frosinone. — Active Cooperation of the Polish Legions. — Macdonald's Letter on this Subject. — The Capture of Terracina. — End of the Insurrection. — Nadolski, Maurice Hauke, Gugemus, Bialowieyski, Podoski, Kwiatkowski, Wistouch, Downarowicz, Laskowski, and Billing. — Their Bravery. — Position of the Legions Before the War with Naples. — Intrigues at Naples. — General Mack and Lord Nelson. — The King of Naples Violates the Treaties. — Declaration of War. — March of the Neapolitan Army. — The French Army, Too Inferior in Number, Retires. — Entrance of the Neapolitans Into Rome. — Battle of Civitta-Castellana and of Calvi. — Kniaziewicz. — Rome Recaptured by the Gallo-Polish. — Chef de bataillon Walter. — March of the French Army on Capua. — Peasant Insurrection. — Capua Surrenders. — Deaths of Eli Tremo, Zelewski, Krause, Ritter, and Vaselle. — Capture of Naples. — General Kniaziewicz is Designated for the Presentation of the Neapolitan Flags to the Directory. — Details of this Ceremony.

While the Italo-Polish Army remained in its positions, ready to act at the first signal, and to go where circumstances would require it, tragic scenes took place in Rome, which brought the attention of the French government back to this point and forced it to resort to rigorous measures against a cunning and perfidious court.

The conduct of General Bonaparte, full of consideration and moderation towards Pius VI, did not agree with the secret instructions of the Executive Directory; however, as the influence of the young chief was then sovereign in France, the government had finally approved of the conduct he had held towards the Christian Pontiff, and Joseph Bonaparte, Napoleon's eldest brother, had been appointed to the Embassy of Rome.

Upon the arrival of the new minister, the most perfect harmony appeared at first to reign between Pius VI and the envoy of the republic; but the members of the Sacred College were not long in renewing their intrigues. They persuaded the Pope that his character as leader of the Christian world was compromised if he did not shake the yoke of an excommunicated nation; they made him see the Queen of Naples, supported by the King of England, embracing the cause of the Holy See, and putting him in a position to shake the French Republic in its turn.

Pius VI, blind and confident, allowed himself to be carried away, and from that moment the Englishman Acton, Minister at Naples, secretly became the soul of Roman politics. At his instigation, the treaty concluded between France and Naples, and that of Tolentino with the Pope, were trampled underfoot. They did not even bother to conceal this; and instead of the marks of confidence, of the attentions which had previously been lavished on Joseph Bonaparte, he was now treated with coldness and suspicion. The Pope even seemed to hesitate for a moment when it came to recognizing the newly constituted Cisalpine Republic; finally, the appointment of the Austrian General Provera, to the chief command of the Papal troops, left no more doubt on the projects of the Court of Rome. General Provera, constantly opposed to the French in the last campaigns, twice taken prisoner by them, was the most hostile choice that could be made in such circumstances.

Joseph Bonaparte, faithful to his conciliatory character, had hitherto shown reserve; but on the arrival of General Provera he broke his silence, and, addressing himself directly to the Sovereign Pontiff, asked him for a frank and positive explanation of such proceedings. He even demanded the dismissal of the Austrian general, and as nothing was yet ripe for an explosion, his request was granted. Meanwhile a fire was burning under the ashes, and the tranquility did not last long. There were so many elements of dissension in Rome that a storm was inevitable. On the one hand, the people, who, in the presence of the regeneration of the North of Italy, were greatly moved by ideas of glory and independence; on the other were the Roman notables, who saw falling with the old order, the cult of their prerogatives, and all these various interests which came to meet in the same enclosure, presaged a near and stormy collision.

In fact, the 6 Nivôse Year VI (26 December 1797), some individuals came to Joseph Bonaparte, to warn him that there should be, in the course of the next night, a revolution against the Papal government. The ambassador pointed out to them that the character with which he was clothed prevented him from entering into such a communication, that all he could do was to report it to the Directory for his opinion, but that he advised them provisionally to renounce all insurrectional attempts. The conspirators left the Embassy Hotel, Corsini Palace, apparently unhappy with the Minister's reception, but promised to abandon their plans.

The next day, Don Nicolas Azzara, the Spanish Ambassador, who exercised a great influence in Rome, and who had constantly given sincere proofs of friendship to Joseph Bonaparte, came to meet him, and told him that an insurrectional movement was being prepared, but that he inspired the Roman government with very little anxiety. Various other information soon convinced the French ambassador that two conspiracies were growing at the same time, and could explode together: one against the French, deftly authorized by some ministers of the Pope; and the other, aiming at the overthrow of the Pontifical government, to establish a republic.

On the 27 December, a rally was held at Villa Medici, with the object of sounding out the dispositions of the people. Most of the men who composed it wore the tricolor cockade. It only took a few soldiers to dispel it; however, a small number of seditious people resisted, and two dragoons perished in this riot.

Informed of this peculiarity, Joseph Bonaparte went to the Cardinal Secretary of State, Joseph Doria-Pamphili, to declare to him that the French government was a stranger to all these movements, and that he would even undertake to search for mutineers. However, a new rally was formed in front of the Hotel de France, shortly after the return of the ambassador, who had left the Secretary of State, apparently full of perfect security. These crowded men uttered the cries of "Long live the Republic! Long live the Roman people!" One of them asked to speak to Joseph Bonaparte and said to him vehemently: "We are free, we ask the support of France." He was enjoined, as well as all those who accompanied him, to leave the jurisdiction of France at once, threatening to repulse them by force. But as the crowd increased, there were several snitches of the Papal police, who vociferated the cries of "Long live the Republic!" Long live the Roman people! This remark indicated at once to the representative of France the only conduct worthy of his character. He dressed himself in his ambassador's uniform and left the hotel to harangue the seditious himself and order them to retire. But at the same time a fight began between the people and the Papal army. The blood began to flow then Joseph Bonaparte, to impose obedience, drew his sword, as did General Duphot, Adjutant-General Scherlock, and two other officers. Throwing themselves in the midst of these madmen, they want, by their presence and authority, to restore order and intelligence. Unfortunately, all their efforts were in vain. The brave Duphot, still a young and distinguished officer of the Army of Italy, rushed on the bayonets, and wished, at the risk of his life, to prevent the shedding of blood. But the soldiers drag him along, and, victim of his courage, he fell pierced with blows. Joseph Bonaparte himself had only time to escape Duphot's assassins, and to return to his hotel. There he resolved to leave at once a perfidious city, and to vow it to French vengeance. Before asking for his passports, he wanted to have at least an explanation with the Cardinal Secretary-State, to ask him about the attacks committed against the legation. He invited her to go to the Embassy Hotel; but Doria brought so much obstinacy and bad faith into the affair, that it was only in the third letter of Joseph Bonaparte, a letter in which he threatened the pontifical government with terrible reprisals from the French Republic, that the latter decided to send Joseph the necessary passports and an order to obtain post horses. The secretary-cardinal added an answer, in which he tried, after twelve hours of absolute silence, to excuse the events of the day, and sought to prevent the departure of the French minister; but he was inflexible; and after having recommended the French who remained in Rome to the Knights Azzara, Spanish Ambassador, and Angiolini, envoy of the Grand Duke of Tuscany, he set out for Tuscany on the 29 December, and went to Florence, to the French Minister, Cacault. Arrived at this residence on the 11 Nivôse, Year VI (31 December 1797), the French ambassador hastened to address to the Minister of Foreign Affairs, Talleyrand-Perigord, the detailed report of all that had just happened at Rome, and which we just read the excerpt. "I would think to insult the Republic," he added in concluding this official note, "if I insisted on the revenge that the Directory must take from this impious government, which, the assassin of Basseville it has become, willingly, from the French First Ambassador who deigned to send him, and, in fact, from a general distinguished by his valor in an army where each soldier was a hero. This government does not at all deny: clever and bold in order to commit the crime, loosing and menacing when it was committed, now the Directory is at Minister Assara's knees in seeking the Minster's return to Florence near me, to then take me with him back to Rome."

An event of such gravity produced in the Cisalpine Republic, and among all the Italian patriots, the greatest indignation against the Papal government. The Army of Italy was clamoring to march on Rome, and although the ministers of His Holiness, fearing the continuation of these events, were doing their utmost to obtain their pardon from the French nation, things had been pushed too far; and whatever the inconveniences of a hostile determination, it was resolved to go to war against the Pope. Consequently, General Alexander Berthier, appointed by Bonaparte to the command of the Army of Italy, received the order from the Directory to march on Rome. He therefore assembled all the available forces, assembled the levies made by the Cisalpine government, and directed them to forced marches. On 10 January 1798, all the troops were united under the walls of Rome, and the vanguard took possession of the Castel Sant-Angelo, which the Pope's troops dared not attempt to defend. General Berthier, however, unwilling to push further, prohibited his soldiers from entering the city, and waited outside the walls for the result of the efforts which the inhabitants were going to attempt to shake off the pontifical yoke. He had informed the main leaders that they could count on the protection of French arms.

Strengthened by such elements, the insurrection did not take long to burst. The Romans, prepared for the entrance of Berthier, awaited him impatiently. Finally, on 27 Pluviôse, Year VI (15 February 1798), the 23rd anniversary of the pontificate of Pius VI, a mass of inhabitants gathered in the Roman Forum. The cries of " Long live the Republic! Down with the Pope!", were heard on all sides; and that an act, which the leaders of the insurrection had written in advance, and, which showed the resumption of the right of sovereignty by the people, was openly communicated to them.

General Berthier, prepared for this event, made his solemn entry into the city of Caesars and the successors of St. Peter. Arrived at the gate known as "Del Popolo", the deputies presented him an olive crown in the name of the Roman people. The General consented to receive it, but declaring that it belonged to General Bonaparte, whose genius and victories had prepared the Roman revolution; that he would receive it for him and send it to him in the name of the Roman people. He then went up to the capitol, bowed, in the name of the French people, to the new Roman Republic, recognized it as free and independent by the will of France, and gave the following speech:

> *Sons of Cato, Pompey, Brutus, Cicero, and Hortensius, receive the homage of the free French, in the capitol, where you have so often defended the rights of the people, and illuminated the Roman Republic.*
>
> *These children of the Gauls, the olive tree of peace in hand, come to this august place to restore the altars of freedom, erected by the first of the Brutus.*
>
> *And you, Roman people, who have just recovered your legitimate rights, remember the blood flowing in your veins; cast your eyes on the monuments of glory that surround you, resume your ancient greatness and the virtues of your fathers."*

Pius VI, obliged to end his temporal reign, asked and obtained from General Berthier permission to retire to Tuscany. On 20 February 1798, the Holy Father left his pontifical residence, and went to seek an asylum in an obscure cell in the Carthusian monastery near Florence. The revolution that occurred in Rome spread rapidly in all the other cities of the Pope's states, and they hastened to send their adhesion to the changes that had just taken place.

In the midst of these serious events, the Polish Corps, following the order given by General Berthier, was to keep its positions until it was relieved by the French troops advancing for that purpose, to retire then to the Cisalpine territory and leave the 3rd Battalion of the 2nd Legion in Pesaro and Fano.

As a result, General Dąbrowski's headquarters was established on the 17th (6 January) in Rimini with the 1st Battalion and the Polish artillery. The 2nd went to San-Arcangelo, and the 3rd to Savignano.

At this time the body commanded by Dąbrowski took the name of “la division au-delà du Pô” [Division beyond the Po].

Always frustrated in their hopes, but always indefatigable in their devotion, the Poles did not miss a single opportunity to think of their patriotic cause. Fighter under the banner which alone, at that time, carried liberty into the universe, they thought they would serve Poland by following it to the fields of glory; they saw the tricolor obliging, by force of its victories, the whole universe to live free, and their active imagination read the future in the present. Full of bravery and ardor, they knew that sooner or later perseverance would triumph over all obstacles, and that independence as well as fortune would not be acquired in repose.

With such a noble purpose, everything, even dreams of delirious enthusiasm, become positive and respectable. It is from this point of view that we must consider the steps taken by the Polish warriors, under the orders of Dąbrowski. After having successively and without fruit solicited Prussian mediation and French intervention, they wished, among singular contrasts, to try to interest Austria in their position. They even wanted to prove to it what the force of events has since shown, that the re-existence of Poland was indispensable to its own preservation. Such a measure requiring a great influence of talent and character on the part of the negotiator, it was reasonable to believe that this double title was united in the person of General Bernadotte, then ambassador of the Republic at Vienna.

Once this measure had been decided, relations between the various patriots resumed some activity, and Citizen Bonneau also expressed the desire to support the new attempt. During this time, and during General Dąbrowski's stay at Rimini, a Pole, distinguished for his talents, his patriotism, and the high office he had exercised in Poland, sent him a precise note on the negotiations that could be initiated, usefully with the Emperor. For his part, General Dąbrowski, having found that the ideas developed in the note communicated were perfectly in agreement with his, signed this document, and had it sent to Vienna and placed in the hands of General Bernadotte, by Captain Joseph Biernacki, a commendable officer, and who could add to the written information many verbal explanations. Bonneau, on his side, wrote to Bernadotte to take care of this affair with all the energy that his character promised, and the influence that was commanded by the rank of which he was clothed. Although this approach, like all the others, was followed by no result, as it is nevertheless connected with the history of the Polish Legions, we refer to the end of the volume for the interesting documents attached to it.

On 13 Ventôse (3 March 1798), the 2nd Battalion relieved the one stationed at Pesaro and Fano, which, on the 14th, entered San Arcangelo; the 3rd went to Cesena on the 23rd (13 March).

General Berthier, having been called to the post of Chief of the General Staff of the Army of England, whose formation was being prepared with a great activity, was replaced, in the command of the Army of Rome, by General Masséna. Consequently, Berthier left this capital on 10 Ventôse (28 February 1798). As a result of this change, the Polish troops, under the orders of General Kniaziewicz, assembled on the 18th (8 March) at Rimini, with the Cisalpine Army, under the orders of General Lecchi at Faenza. It was presumed that Berthier would take this road, but the general made his way through Florence and Bologna.

As it was now necessary to obtain further instructions on the subsequent march of the Legions, General Dąbrowski made the journey to Milan again. When he arrived there, he found General Brune, who, after his expedition to Switzerland, took command of the stationary army in the Cisalpine Republic, while General Schawemburg replaced him in that of the French troops in Helvetia. It was from the mouth of his new chief that General Dąbrowski received, on Germinal 23rd (12 April), the order to go to Rome, with the 1st Legion, the Polish artillery and eight cannon, and sent, at the same time, the 3rd Battalion 2nd Legion to Mantua, under the command of General Wielhorski.

On 29 Germinal (18 April), the corps destined for the Rome expedition gathered at Rimini, and General Dąbrowski, passing through Ancona and Spoleto, entered the capital of the Christian world, at the head of his legions, on 14 Floréal, Year VI (3 May 1798), the anniversary of a very memorable era. General Kniaziewicz, having under his command the 1st Battalion and the artillery, occupied the capitol, where the Polish headquarters were established.

Thus, one saw this handful of brave men, exiled from their country and toys of a contrary fate, come and sit as conquerors on the ruins of Roman splendor.

This rapprochement caused the hearts of the patriots to beat with pride, and they drew from the aspect of the monumental city the love of the fine arts, which consoles misfortunes. Dąbrowski, wished that the stay of Rome be of profit to his companions in arms, seeking to preserve their leisure from a corrupting idleness, advised them, in an agenda, to devote the free moments of military occupation to the culture of languages, history and mathematics. He made them feel that in all positions, and especially in that where they were, the Poles were to draw the attention of Europe to them, not by their number, but by knowledge and virtues that set them above those required of common warriors.

As soon as the Polish troops arrived ion Rome, the General-in-Chief opened their national church and raised the seals which had been put on the effects necessary for the exercise of their worship. The Feast of St. Stanislas, their patron, having arrived at this time, it was celebrated with the usual solemnities. Throughout the Italian campaign the Polish troops scrupulously observed all the ceremonies of their religion, and even their enemies did not fail to spread false information about it. It was claimed that they were left to superstition and fanaticism. They proved nevertheless that they knew how to put the priests in their place, when they deviated from the duties which their religion prescribed for them, and, when instead of words of peace, they uttered cries of discord and civil war.[1]

A century had elapsed since the time when John Sobieski, delivering the capital of Austria of a certain capture, had cut in pieces the Turks encamped under its ramparts, and had captured the flag of Mahomet. The campaign over, Sobieski had sent to Notre-Dame-de-Lorette, with the Ottoman flag, the saber he had used to conquer this trophy. Loretto had accepted these remains, and since then they had remained hanging on the walls of his temple.

The Roman consulate, taking into consideration that regenerated Rome was then inhabited and defended by Polish legions, conceived the idea of placing a glorious restitution in their hands. He informed General Dąbrowski, therefore, that there was a monument in Loretto to the military glory of his country and showed a keen desire to pay him homage.

Dąbrowski was not insensible to this step, and, taking advantage of the good disposition of the Roman consulate, he charged Captain Kozakiewicz, who had remained at Fano and Sinigaglia with a few hundred men, to take the standard of Mohammed, and carry it to Rome. This order was executed. Captain Kozakiewicz, having assembled all the scattered detachments, arrived at Rome on 19 June with the flag, which was deposited, with all the military honors, at the house of General Dąbrowski. The flag, since that day, constantly fol-

---

[1]The Polish National Church in Rome, dedicated to St. Stanislas, is built on Delli-Polacchi Street. It was founded in 1580 by Cardinal Stanislaus Hosius, a Pole and Prince-Bishop of Warmia. He was famous as a scholar, one of the first dignitaries of our country and president of the Council of Trent in 1562. The same Hosius founded a refuge here for Polish pilgrims, and the main facade of this temple bears the following inscription: SS. Salvatoris et Stanislai hospitalium Nationis Polonorum 1580. Queen Anne, wife of Stephen Batory, then Andrew Stanislas Kostka Zaluski, Bishop of Krakow, richly endowed this pious foundation of Hosius. The monuments erected to Queen Anne's honor, and to that of the founding cardinal, are preserved, although his remains are deposited in the Church of St. Mary Transteverine. This last monument was not long ago raised by Eustache Wollowicz, Bishop of the Diocese of Kalisz, as rector of this church. In the midst of the events in question, the management of the funds attached to this foundation passed into private hands; but since the new organization of part of Poland, in 1815, the government has taken care of it.

lowed the headquarters of the Legion; and even when it was dispersed, faithful to the fortune of Dąbrowski, it was, after his death, deposed in 1818, in a hall of the castle of the Royal Society of Friends of Science of Warsaw, where it is preserved religiously.

As for the sword, as it existed at the time of the Roman Consul Angelucci, naked and without diamonds (the Pope's chamber having sold those that had adorned it), General Dąbrowski received it as a present. But, wishing to give this weapon a destination worthy of it, he sent it later, in the name of the Legions, to the immortal defender of Polish liberty, Generalissimo Kosciuszko. He received this pledge of gratitude from Kniaziewicz, when, later on, this superior officer of the Legions traveled to Paris to present the flags taken from the Neapolitans to the Directory.

At this time, the presence of the army having become necessary to Civita-Vecchia, Chef de bataillon Bialowieyski left Rome on 3 Prairial (22 May), with a force of four hundred men to form its garrison.

It was then that the Consulate of Rome, in order to remedy the scarcity of day laborers, which rendered labor very expensive, and made it impossible for the proprietors to harvest, without considerable expense, had decided that part of the Polish troops would help the farmers with their harvest. Thus, the same soldiers who, armies in hand, watched over the safety of the republic, reaped, like the Roman soldiers, the fields that were to feed it.

It was also in the same interval that General Rymkiewicz appeared in Rome, the same who, in concert with Colonel Wladislas Jablonowski, had been commissioned by the patriots of Galicia to solicit the help of the Ottoman Porte and the Ambassador of France Verninac. But, deceived both in their hopes, and seeing the Divan persist in its apathetic system, they left the banks of the Bosporus and found on those of the Tiber more hope and a future. Rymkiewicz was appointed chief of the 2nd Legion, and after a short stay in Rome, he left to rejoin it at Mantua.

Cyprian Godebski, a Polish patriot, arrived in Rome almost at the same time. There he was not long in earning the esteem and confidence of General Rymkiewicz, and he became his aide-de-camp. Hardworking and active, he devoted all his time to work, and when Rymkiewicz left for Mantua, to take command of the 2nd Legion, Dąbrowski charged him to maintain an active correspondence with the two legions, as well as with the other patriots who remained in Poland. Godebski proved, in this important and delicate circumstance, what patriotism can do when supported by talent and activity. It was at Mantua again that General Rymkiewicz, guided by the same principles that General Dąbrowski had issued in his agenda of 3 May 1798, sought to maintain the culture of the national language, that imperishable link which, at every time, on every occasion, and under all regimes, must unite the scattered children of Sarmatia.

As there was no Polish printing house, he had translated and copied excerpts of the best foreign works and read them to the soldiers as a result of the orders of the day. These excerpts, which usually filled two sheets, appeared every ten days, and were entitled "The Legionary Decade." Cyprien Godebski was chiefly engaged in this work, and besides the excerpts he made from the foreign gazettes of the time, whenever he mentioned the Poles, he also added prose and literature, and especially anything that could spur the national spirit. Captain Paszkowski also spent several hours teaching the elements of history, mathematics and languages.

As for the youths who, before leaving Poland, had the facility of training in the highest sciences, they found a protector and a guide in perfecting themselves in the person of the respectable and indefatigable Wybicki, who, having devoted long services to his country, tried to be useful to them by these means.

While these events were taking place, General Wielhorski solicited from the Cisalpine government and its legislature their adhesion to the agreements with General Dąbrowski, 27 Brumaire, Year VI (17 November 1797). The result of these proceedings was that the Grand Council charged the Directory, in the fourth article of its decree, to make with the Legions a particular convention that would be sanctioned by the legislative body. On 6 Prairial (25 May) General Dąbrowski sent Colonel Chamand to Milan, giving him all the necessary powers to act in concert with General Wielhorski, and handing him, in support of his mission, the letter following for the Executive Board.

Lieutenant-General Dąbrowski, Commander of the Polish Legions,to the President of the Executive Directory of the Cisalpine Republic.

Rome, 6 Prairial, Year VI (25 May 1798)

As in the decree emanating from the Grand Council, dated Floréal 2nd, it is said in Art. 4, concerning the auxiliary legions of the Republic, that the Executive Directory is authorized to make a special convention with the auxiliary legions, which it will sanction by the legislative council; therefore I hasten to send to you Colonel Chamand, who is the bearer of the last convention which I had the honor to do with you in the name of the Legions, on the date of 27 Brumaire Year VI (17 November 1797), and who is responsible for knowing whether your intentions are to keep this convention as it is or to make some changes to it. In the latter case, Colonel Chamand, knowing the intentions of our legions, he will be able to communicate them to you and report the result of your decision.

Your loyalty, Citizen Directors, and our conduct, do not leave me doubting for a moment that you will put all the interest in concluding a convention that must cement the ties which exist between our legions and the Cisalpine Republic, and put us in a position to testify to it more and more our attachment and the recognition that we carry to it.

I must also observe that, as our legions form a body of Polish patriots, I cannot take it upon myself to sign this last convention, which must fix the existence of the Polish legions, without at least the leaders of the Legions and artillery to sign it with me in the name of their corps.

Your justice and the love you have for freedom will undoubtedly make you approve of my request.

Dąbrowski.

The answer of the Directory was: "that the discussion of the convention made between the Cisalpine government and the Polish legions should be postponed until their return to the Cisalpine territory".

But all the attempts to return the Legions to this territory were unsuccessful, because the French troops, who guarded the Roman Republic, embarked at Civita-Vecchia for the Egyptian expedition, and a general insurrection brooded under the ashes in Rome and its surroundings. The Polish troops were therefore obliged to suffice for everything. Indeed, Chief Seydlitz was sent on the 7th (26 May) to Angari, with three hundred men, and Major Joseph Chlopieki received, the following day, 8 Thermidor (27 May), the order to follow him with four hundred men.

At this juncture, General Macdonald took command of the Army of Rome, and General Gouvion-Saint-Cyr was recalled to Paris. Polish troops were neither clothed nor paid. More than forty supernumerary officers were with the corps; a great part, by patriotism, served as non-commissioned officers, and the rest replaced the sick or absent leaders. Despite all possible instances, the government gave them nothing, not even rations. Those of them who could do it, ate at their own expense, and as for those who had no means of subsistence, their brothers in arms provided for their needs, leaving them with a tenth of their pay and sharing with them their rations and lodging. The soldier himself was very poorly nourished, and yet he suffered without murmuring. We never heard any complaints and insubordinations, the fruits of misery, in the ranks of the Poles. Confronting death as brave men, they bore heroically other cruel privations, instilled confidence in the future, this hope of glory and liberty, remain dominate in their hearts despite all the present sufferings! It was these same soldiers who were charged with reconciling their differences and maintaining order in the countries where they had their quarters. Wherever they passed, their eulogy was in every mouth, and the French, their companions in glory, were pleased to render public justice to the noble deeds of these auxiliary legions.[2]

[2]Several Italian theaters sang hymns in honor of the Poles, and the addresses of the Italian nation to our soldiers were filled with the most generous sentiments and promises. Here is the beginning of one of these songs performed in a public theater:

"La Italica libertade
Che tanto deve a voi
Bravi Polacchi, volgevi
Lieta gli sguardi suoi, etc. "

As the soldiers' misery became more and more disturbing, General Dąbrowski, who, in spite of his severity, loved his soldiers like a father, tried to find a way of remedying these evils. After having confided to General Kniaziewicz the command of the Legion, he set out for Milan himself, to claim what was due to his troops, and to draw them from the precarious position they found themselves. He arrived on 14 Thermidor (1 August 1798). Having already learned in Rome that Generalissimo Kosciuszko, having returned from America, had stopped at Paris, and he counted through him to obtain some support for the Legions from the French government. But not being able to go to the French capital himself, Dąbrowski sent his aide-de-camp, Major Elie Tremo, to the former chief of national independence, who was there on 22 Thermidor (9 August).

The 2nd Legion and artillery under the orders of General Wielhorski, stationed in the Cisalpine Republic, had the 1st Battalion at the outposts on the Adige, the 2nd at Cremona, the 3rd at Ferrara, and the artillery at Mantua and in Pizzighettone. The depot continued to recruit, and it was stationed in Milan under Kazimierz Konopka.

New insurrections, as we shall see soon, had broken out in the Roman state. Bialowieyski had therefore left Civita-Vecchia to return to Rome. General Macdonald was compelled to strengthen the garrison of this city, and to assemble a larger force. It was around this time that the Circeo revolt broke out. This revolt was so dangerous that it had dismayed the Roman government. General Macdonald proved in this circumstance how well he knew how to combine coolness and military calculations with courage and activity. He placed under the orders of Brigadier-General Girardon a small body composed of Frenchmen and Poles, in order to go with all speed against the rebels. The first shock occurred at Ferentino on 11 Thermidor (29 July); it was terrible. After several hours of fighting, the insurgents were overthrown, and there was a great carnage. However, guided by experienced chiefs, their debris soon rallied behind the La Cosa River; resting on the right to Verdi, on the left to Frosinone, they dared to propose a conditional treaty in this position; but they did not compose with rebels; they marched on them on the 15th, with the familiar audacity of the Gallo-Polish soldiers.

The passage of the La Cosa River offered immense obstacles, and still more vigorous resistance awaited the army at the foot of the rock on which Frosinone was built. Its escarpment, which rendered it impregnable, did not frighten the republicans; they climbed, through a very sharp fire of canister and musketry, as far as the city gate. There it was necessary to mount a gun to break it down; they succeeded, the gate was broken; a priest, saber in hand, commanded the insurgents who guarded it; he and his men were cut down with bayonets. The Gallo-Poles entered the city; but all the houses were crenelated, and they had much more to suffer from the fire that poured from them. They resorted to torches, and whoever wished to escape the flames perished under the steel of our soldiers. The French and Polish blood flowed in this terrible affair; but revenge did not leave their losses unpunished; all that were found in arms in the city were put to the sword.

General Macdonald, in his letter to Citizen Florent, the French commissioner, thus rendered the courage of the Poles justice:

> *I have received the official news that the city of Frosinone has just submitted. The French and Polish troops have done their duty perfectly. Polish Major Nadolski entered the city first.*
>
> *The Bishop of Veroli came in deputation to bring the submission of this city, and to ask pardon for the inhabitants; it will be garrisoned today. The few rebels who escaped returned to their villages or fled to their mountains. A well-ordered police will suffice to purge them.*
>
> *I hope I will soon announce the end of the unfortunate and cruel war at Circeo.*

At the moment when the brave Girardon finished with the rebels of Frosinone, another rebellion erupted in Terracina. The French commander, Citizen Leduc, was murdered; ten chasseurs of the 19th Chasseur à cheval Regiment, who were with him, owed their salvation in the lightness of their horses. In two days their number rose to three thousand.

Scarcely had the General-in-Chief had word of it, than he sent against them, by forced marches, a corps composed of the French and the Poles, under the conduct of his chief of staff, the Adjutant-General

Maurice Mathieu. It was necessary to drive out the rebels everywhere by force, and all the insurgent cities were to be stormed.

The Gallo-Poles arrived at daybreak on 22 Thermidor (9 August), within sight of Terracina. An infinite number of peasants, concealed in the swamps and gardens that adjoin this city, soon brought death to the ranks, discharging at almost close range; the affair then proceeded with great fury. The Gallo-Polish Army had only opened the Appian Way and the old road to Naples, and the rebels swept them with a continual fire from fifteen heavy caliber cannons. Six hours of fighting had done almost nothing; it was necessary, however, to terminate this butchery. There were two choices; first to charge the cannon, and the second to retreat, the consequences of which would have been terrible. The order to attack the cannon was given. The Poles rivaled the French with ardor; the bayonet decided success. Terracina was carried by assault, and the rebels found there, were pitilessly slaughtered. Some, however, managed to gain the Neapolitan territory through the mountains; others escaped on boats, some of which were sunk by the artillery.[3]

The Republican troops, on entering Terracina, found an altar in the middle of the street, on which priests officiated during the fight; they were armed with pistols: the bayonets of the soldiers purged the ground.[4]

General Macdonald then published two severe laws against the seditious who had disturbed the public tranquility. In the first, every individual convicted of having provoked sedition by speeches, by false and alarming news, was to be judged and punished by death. The individuals known by the name of the Society of the Faith of Jesus, organized in the Department of Clitumno, were to be immediately translated before a military commission.

By the second decree, the department of Circeo was declared in a state of siege. Agnani, Alatri, Veroli, Ferentino, Frosinone, Piperno and Terracina, were thus in the power of the Republican troops.

---

[3]In General Dąbrowski's manuscript, he gives the date of the capture of Terracina as 4 Thermidor (22 July 1798).

[4]See Supporting Document No.46, General Macdonald's letter to the French commissioner, in which he praised the bravery that the Poles displayed at Terracina.

Chef de bataillon Bialowieyski, at the head of four hundred men; Major Nadolski with three hundred men, and Lieutenant Maurice Hauke and Gugenmus, with two cannons, went to reinforce the garrison of these conquered places. The Polish Legion, in addition to the losses that it suffered from the feverish exhalations of the Pontine Marshes, lost thirty grenadiers at Terracina, the brave Major Podoski, and Captain Kwiatkowski. Lieutenant Wistouch died from his injury. Captains Downarowicz, leading grenadiers, Laskowski, Billing and Lieutenant Hauké, were badly wounded. Chef de bataillon Bialovrieyski, Major Nadolski and Lieutenant Gugenmus, were particularly distinguished for their intrepidity and their presence of mind above all eulogy.

Finally, all these fights cost the Poles nearly sixty dead and fifty wounded.

The detachments of the 2nd and 3rd Battalions returned to Rome, on 9 Fructidor (26 August), and the 1st Battalion remained in Terracina and the environs.

From the 2nd Legion, the 3rd Battalion arrived on the 17th (3 September) at Mantua, and the 1st at Ferrara, and the 2nd remained at Cremona.

While the Legions distinguished themselves so brilliantly, General Dąbrowski was busy in Milan with the improvement of the lot of his soldiers. On 24 Fructidor (10 September) he presented to General-in-Chief Brune, a nominative list of all the officers, requesting that the sixty-five supernumerary officers be appointed second lieutenants and then be placed. The French general signed the list and gave orders to meet on the spot at the request of General Dąbrowski. He found it much more difficult to obtain the payment of arrears owing to the Polish Corps, the clothing and the certificates for the officers, because of the changes that took place both in the Cisalpine government and among the chief generals and the French ambassadors.

For his part, Major Tremo returned from Paris on the 20th (6 September), where he had gone to Kosciuszko; but, less happy than Dąbrowski, he brought nothing consoling.

On 10 Brumaire (31 October), General Brune was called to Paris; General Joubert took command of the army.

Finally, the Cisalpine government, acceding to the request of General

Dąbrowski, gave orders to pay the Polish Legion the arrears due, and the general sent the funds to Rome by Major Tremo, who arrived on 23 Brumaire (13 November).

The Legions were dressed anew, and Captain Dembowski left with the effects for the 1st Legion, the Frimaire 9th, for Rome, passing through Bologna and Ancena.

The artillery stationed in Rome had orders to go to Mantua, and there arrived on 15 Brumaire (5 November). It was there later augmented by a company.

Strzalkowski was ordered to remain at Milan, to receive the certificates promised to officers by the Directory, and to bring them to the corps.

On 16 Vendemiaire (7 October), the 2nd Battalion, commanded by Forestier, had relieved the 1st Battalion at Terracina, holding its outposts on the borders of Naples. The 1st and 3rd Battalions remained in Rome. This was the position of the Polish Army when the war in Naples opened a new field of glory. It was there that, sharing the perils and the successes of the French troops, that it was able, by fighting for a cause which was not its own, to give the measure of what it would have done if it had fought for its country and its soldier's homes.

The Treaty of Campo-Formio, while pacifying the Continent, had nonetheless singularly modified the situation of Europe. The republican system became dominating, and the political map of old Europe, opposing the sharp colors that drew the Batavian, Swiss, Cisalpine, Ligurian and Roman Republics, from the despotism and feudalism of other states, made the old monarchies tremble before these daughters of the mother republic. Frightened by so much success, the British Cabinet awoke to stoke a new war against France. Austria and Russia contracted an alliance with England; but the first of these powers still hesitated to enter into a struggle with the giant of liberty. The Court of Naples, impatient at any delay, and being relieved of the presence of the terrible Bonaparte, who at that time was planting the tricolor on the summits of the pyramids and the minarets of Cairo, soon violated the sworn faith.

The King of Naples Ferdinand, yielding to his weakness and the fate of the Bourbons, who at that time seemed, by an inconceivable fatality, to be led by their wives, increased the audacity of Minister

Acton and the confidence of Queen Caroline in her means to fight the French. A treaty of alliance was immediately signed between the Cabinets of St. James and Naples, in defiance of that concluded previously in Paris. Admiral Nelson, returning from Aboukir, obtained the honors of triumph in Naples Harbor. The French Ambassador Garat made his protest against such a clear violation of the peace treaty. The explanation was abolished, and the French who were at Naples experienced indirect persecution. In the meanwhile, a fifth of the population had been ordered to remain there; novenas were sung to all the saints, and especially to Saint Janvier.

The French troops at Rome were not sufficient to oppose the sixty thousand Neapolitans whom the English subsidies had equipped. For want of a general capable of commanding this large army, King Ferdinand addressed Austria to obtain one, and General Mack was sent to Naples. The campaign soon opened, and England congratulated itself on having obtained the dissolution of the Congress of Rastadt, and for having conquered the irresolution of Austria.

The Neapolitan Army, therefore, began to advance towards the Roman territory 4 Frimaire (24 November 1798), and three days after it invaded it on five points simultaneously. The generals who commanded these five columns had sufficient strength to execute General Mack's plan. Micheroux commanded ten thousand eight hundred men, with thirty-eight pieces of cannon and forty-five caissons. San Filippo had nine thousand men under his command, with seven cannons; the Count von Saxe nine thousand men, twenty caissons and twenty-four guns; lastly, General Mack commanded a column of fifteen thousand men, with sixty caissons and thirty heavy guns; which made in all, except for the Neapolitan columns, fort-eight thousand eight hundred men, two hundred thirty seven caissons, one hundred six cannons. These army corps were abundantly supplied with food. Several transport ships were to follow alongside the Tronto army, as it made progress.

The right wing went along the Adriatic going towards Porto-di-Fermo. The center descended the Apennines by Aquila and marched on Rieti. A detached body of partisans left Sulmona and advanced towards Terni; finally, the left wing, where King Ferdinand and General-in-Chief Mack were, crossed the Garigliano in three columns, on the side of Isola, Ceprano, and Santa Agata, and marched straight on Rome by the Pontine Marshes, Valmontone and Frascati.

The Gallo-Italo-Polish republican armies presented barely sixteen thousand men scattered over a vast field. All the corps were incomplete, the artillery was badly drawn, the stores empty. The right of this army occupied Terracina, Piperno, Prossedi, Frosinone, Veroli, and Tivoli; the center was in Rieti. Ascoli, Fermo, Macerata and Ancona, were occupied by the troops of the left. But in this mountainous country communications became difficult. And in the meantime, the French General-in-Chief was obliged to detach three thousand men to reinforce the garrison of Corfu.

While General Mack attacked the inferior and disjointed forces of the French without a prior declaration, Championnet, who had distinguished himself on the Rhine, and was appointed General-in-Chief of the Army of Rome, had just arrived in that city.

The 2nd Battalion of the Polish Legion, as well as the French detachments were already posted around Terracina, retreated to Rome crossing the Pontine Marshes. The 1st and 3rd Battalions encamped 4 Frimaire (24 November) under Terra-Nova in the vicinity of Alhano, to cover the retreat of the other troops, and the 5th (25th) these troops, followed by the enemy, arrived at the Terra Nova camp. Then, as everything was fermenting at Rome, the Legion entered on the 6th (26th) and bivouacked at Fortress Navonne; and while the sick and the baggage were directed to Civita-Castellana, the Castel Sant'Angelo fired the alarm, the general[5] was beaten in the city, and Championnet left from the 6th to the 7th (26 to 27 November), at the head of the few French and Polish troops who were there, after having been ordered to cut the bridge of Tivoli on the Teverone; but he placed in the Castel Sant'Angelo a garrison of eight hundred men, formed of a battalion of the 30th Demi-brigade, and a part of the Roman troops, all under the command of the Chef de bataillon Walter, enjoining him to hold on, and promising him to return victorious to Rome after twenty days; and he kept his word.

These precautions taken, the General continued his retreat in good order, and went in three columns to Monte Rosi. The Legion, commanded by General Kniaziewicz, formed part of the right. On Fri-

[5]Translator: The "general" is a drum signal calling the troops to assemble.

maire 8th, the entire right wing, under the orders of General Macdonald, took position in front of Monte Rosi; the Polish Legion was on the left wing. On the 9th, it took a position at Civita-Casteliana with most of the French troops. On 1 December, General Kniaziewicz received orders to cross the Tiber, and to attack the enemy at Magliano, where they had strongly entrenched themselves. The latter, having perceived the movement of the Legion, pretended to wish to fall on its left flank; but Kniaziewicz detached the 2nd Battalion from his legion and two squadrons of French cavalry, under the orders of Colonel Chamand, who held them in respect. Kniaziewicz forced the entrenchments and drove the enemy out of Magliano, with his troops' bayonets at their backs. The enemy abandoned their tents and his luggage. The French troops advanced and took up positions there; the Polish Legion occupied the positions of Borghetto and Ponte-Felice on the Tiber. Thus, the French army, standing against the mountains, observed the road from Rome to Civita-Castellana, and that which leads to Florence. The bulk of the troops took position behind the Civita-Castellana Ravine, while Championnet had the fortified castle occupied. The bridge at Borghetto was entrenched; General Lemoine occupied Rieti, and General Rusca placed himself on the Tronto, where he was reinforced: the headquarters were established at Terni.

While Championnet placed himself thus to receive his enemy, who advanced proudly on all roads, King Ferdinand entered Rome on 9 Frimaire Year VII (29 November 1798), where he was treated as a conqueror and liberator. He went down to the Farnese Palace, of which he was the proprietor. On the following day he received the congratulations of the nobles, prelates, and deputies of the different classes of inhabitants, and of that same people, who had lately appeared to have applauded the establishment of the republican government. The Princes Aldobrandini-Borghese and Gabrielli, the Marquis Camillo-Massimi and Rieci were appointed by Ferdinand, to be members of the Provisional government; and the Chevalier Valentini took the command of the bourgeois guard.

All the memories of the French, the coat of arms of the Roman Republic and those of France were cut down. The persecution against everything that had anything to do with the French was pushed with the utmost rigor. Finally, the King of Naples was so sure of his success, that he even wrote to Pope Pius VI, committing him "to leave his modest retreat, to descend into the Vatican, which was to be purified by his presence."

While these events were going on, Admiral Nelson had landed seven thousand Neapolitan troops in the port of Livorno to insult Tuscany and cut the communications of the French army with the north of Italy.

However painful was the position of General Championnet, his courage, his talents, and his rare activity, however, made up for the inferiority of the troops under his command. He placed scouts at Perugia and waited in his positions for the advancing enemy. General Mack lost valuable time, summoning Castillo St. Angelo, where the brave Chef de bataillon Walter commanded; but he at last resolved to march forward, and, after having assembled his forty-thousand men, he left Rome and soon came to blows with the French.

All the towns and villages of the Roman state having revolted, made common cause with the Neapolitans against the republicans. As a result, General Kniaziewicz was forced to storm the towns of Fabbrica and Fallari, where Captain Brzychwa and thirty men were wounded, Lieutenant Goslawski and twenty soldiers killed, while the French troops did the same on their side and fought with the Neapolitans in the neighborhood of Monte-Rosi.

The Polish Legion remained in position near Falari, on the right wing of the corps commanded by General Macdonald. On 14 Frimaire (4 December), at daybreak, the Neapolitan army, under General Mack, attacked General Macdonald, who was not afraid of the disproportionate superiority of the attackers. The Gallo-Polish Army was not ranged in line, but it crowned the heights of the plain, between Baccano, Nepi and Civita-Castellana, the old Veies. The wings were for this reason refused to the right, and the center was in front. Arrived near Rignano, Mack attacks with his center that of the French, who withdrew slowly towards Civita-Castellana, and the fight then became general. The French were attacked near Nepi; but, commanded by the intrepid Général de brigade Kellermann, they routed the Neapolitans and pursued them; the left wing attacked the Neapolitans and threw them back. General Kniaziewicz arrived with the Polish and Roman Legions, attacked the center of the army, believing that it is its left wing, when suddenly this wing, which was hidden or delayed, emerged from the Falari Wood and threatened to fall on his flank and rear. Immediately he detached the 1st and 3rd Battalions, under the orders of Chief Bialowieyski, and fell with the rest of his brigade upon the enemy, just as he unfurled his columns, and put him in a complete rout. All the pains given by the Count von Saxe, who commanded this wing, to capture the fugitives, were useless, and if Bialowieyski had been able to execute his movement more quickly on the right, no one would have escaped. The Count de Saxe himself was in the hands of the Polish grenadiers; his personal bravery saved him, but he was dangerously wounded. Sixteen guns, three thousand prisoners, several flags and baggage, which Kniaziewicz seized, crowned this brilliant charge of Polish troops.

This battle, was won solely by the Gallo-Poles, is called the Battle of Nepi, or Civita-Castellana. Thus, General Macdonald had the glory of repelling, with six thousand men, forty thousand Neapolitans. In the meantime, a column of Neapolitan troops advanced by Calvi and Otricoli, and cut off the right wing of the army corps. The brigade of General Maurice Mathieu, composed of the 11th Cavalry Regiment, two squadrons and the 16th Dragoon Regiment, then left Otricoli, on the night of 18 Frimaire (8 December), to arrive at daybreak on the 19th, in front of Calvi.

General Kniaziewicz's brigade, composed of the 1st and 2nd Battalions of the 20th Demi-brigade of the Roman Legion, a squadron of the 19th Chasseurs à cheval Regiment and a 3pdr cannon, had received the same order to leave Magliano, where this general had been covered with glory, and at daybreak go to Calvi.

General Mathieu's brigade first captured the heights, while General Kniaziewicz enveloped the town on the ravine side; but, immediately after the arrival of General Mathieu's column before Calvi, the enemy, who had shut himself up in the city, made a sortie with a part of his troops to dispute the heights.

This force was the remainder of the column that General Mathieu had already beaten. He worked so well again that he took all his artillery, and immediately sending the 11th Demi-brigade, which went with incredible speed towards the mountain, he drove the Neapolitans, who returned to the city, where they barricaded themselves, after having made a breach the wall. General Mathieu summoned the Neapolitan generals to surrender, and sent, in the name of General Macdonald, a summons, which required that in five minutes they should lay down their arms. After some negotiations, he granted the generals and officers that they would keep their baggage and that they would all be prisoners of war.

In this city there were four thousand men, three hundred of them cavalry. These troops were commanded by General Moetsch or Metzer and Carillo. Twenty senior officers and another one hundred were also taken prisoner.

General Mathieu had no artillery with him; but by the skillful manner in which he had disposed his troops, the energetic summons he made to the Neapolitans, he determined them to surrender. His column, with that of General Kniaziewicz, formed about three thousand five hundred men. Only two men were killed and very few were wounded.

The 11th Demi-brigade, Chef de bataillon Calvinet[6], with his two colonels, performed prodigies of valor. The adjutant general of the National Guard Barghen, who served as an aide-de-camp to General Mathieu, gave proof of military talents and great bravery. In this he followed the example of Captain Trinqualli, the aide-de-camp of this general.

The Roman Legion, composed of the citizens of the re-established republic, distinguished itself in all these occasions. Proud to repeat their history and reconquer the glory of their fathers after twenty centuries of lethargy, these new Romans dashed with a brilliance worthy of their old name in the career of freedom.

Finally, officers and soldiers all rivaled each other that day with zeal and energy.

General Kniaziewicz surrounded the enemy on the side of the ravine; he could not, therefore, act as he wished, but he sent to General Mathieu a battalion, which was very useful to him.

Thus, four thousand prisoners, two generals, twenty senior officers, another one hundred officers, five thousand muskets, five mountain cannons, military munitions, baggage, seventeen flags or standards, these are the trophies of Calvi.

[6]Translator: This makes no sense in that a "chef de bataillon" should have two colonels under him. It is probable that Calvinet was actually a chef de brigade.

It was about this time that General Dąbrowski, who left Milan on 1 Frimairet, arrived at the camp; but leaving the command of the Legion to General Kniaziewicz, who, following this glorious campaign, was appointed géněral de brigade, followed Macdonald's headquarters. Mack, without stopping, hastily retired to Rome, and was pursued by the whole army. The Polish Legion went, on the 23rd (13 December), to Colle-Vecchio, and encamped on the 24th (14th) near the Correze. The same day, the French entered Rome without finding the enemy. The headquarters of the army went there on the 23rd (13th), and the Legion encamped near the city, at the San Lorenzo Gate, having its front towards Tivoli and Frascali.

Thus, was the promise made by General Championnet to the garrison of Castel Sant'Angelo by evacuating Rome. The French troops returned to the capital of the Christian world on 15 December, after twenty-seven days of absence, during which time they had destroyed more than fifteen thousand Neapolitans, took forty cannon, almost all the baggage with which this army was so abundantly provided, and twenty flags.

The depot at Civita-Castellana was sent to Foligno, and another was established in Rome for the sick, wounded, convalescents and recruits. Many Poles, deserters of the Austrian armies in the course of the Year IV and Year V, who had been forcibly recruited under the Neapolitan flags, put down their arms when they were confronted by their compatriots and left a monarchical cause to defend a republican cause.

At that time, Captain Dembowski, the Elder, was in Ancona with the clothing depot. Although his intention was to continue his journey, the bad roads and the absolute lack of means of transport had prevented him from going further.

The peasants, always ready to rebel when they were not content, began to revolt again when they saw the army moving away from them and entering the Neapolitan territory. Foligno's depot sent some detachments to Canosa and Serra-Valle. Nearly two hundred Poles that had assembled in Rome, being sent with Captain Tomaszewski to reinforce the corps that besieged Civita. All these different detachments and depots were under the orders of Colonel Chamaud.

On the night of 25th/26th (15/16 December), a light fight was fought near the Saint-Jean-de-Latran Gate. Neapolitan troops came to occupy Rome, unaware that this city was already reconquered. The French guards and outposts defeated them completely, and made General Pignatelli, with one thousand men, prisoners of war. General Dąbrowski was in person in this affair, but the Legion took no part in it.

In the meantime, General-in-Chief Championnet, by attending to Rome to restore the republican government, also gave his orders to station troops in the most advantageous positions. General Rey was instructed to go after the enemy, who had abandoned the positions of Frascati and Albano, and not to give the enemy a moment's respite.

The right wing of the army thus left Rome on 28 Frimaire (18 December), and crossed without any obstacle the Marais-Pontins. The Polish Legion arrived on 8 Nivôse (28 December) at Fondi, the first city on the borders of the kingdom of Naples, forming, with a regiment of cavalry and two cannon, the vanguard of the army, under the orders of General Rey. General Dąbrowski never left the Legion since that time. The enemy had strongly entrenched themselves between Itri and Fondi. They had made the mountains almost impenetrable, and a great battery, named the St. Andrew Battery, equipped with eight 12pdrs, defended the road leading to Naples.

General Dąbrowski made arrangements on the 9th (29 December) to attack and turn this post. As a result, Captain Sznayder, with four companies of the 3rd Battalion, was to occupy the Sperlonga post, right on the sea, and show himself, on the 10th, if necessary, in the rear of the battery. Captain Ilinski, with two companies of the 1st Battalion, was ordered to mach in the mountains, on the left, to then fall on the right flank of the enemy; and Captain Laskowski was in charge of pushing ahead, between Itri and Sperlonga. This movement was arranged so that everyone had to be returned to his post in the same minute, then attack together. The enemy, posted on the mountains, perceiving the combined movement of the republican troops, suddenly took flight after a few cannon shots, leaving them masters of the position, the battery, and the cannon. General Rey, who arrived at this moment, ordered that the enemy should be pursued, and on the morning of the 10th, the troops arrived, without striking a blow, in front of Gaeta's gates, while Captain Sznayder advanced from Sperlonga to Gaeta along the shore.

In this position General Kniaziewicz, placed in the vanguard, pushed to Mola-di-Gaeta, with the 2nd and 3rd Battalion, while General Dąbrowski, with the 1st Battalion and the French artillery, invested the fortress of Gaeta. General Rey summoned the commander to surrender, and the latter refused and gave orders to fire the howitzer and some cannon, the only artillery he had at his disposal. The garrison replied very feebly, and towards evening the captain capitulated. The garrison, with a strength of two thousand men, was taken prisoner of war, and more than one hundred guns and much ammunition and provisions were found in the place. The same evening, at 10 o'clock, the 1st Battalion took possession of the place, and at 11 Nivôse (31 December) the garrison was sent to Rome.

General Kniaziewicz, pursuing his success, advanced the same day to the Garigliano River, and occupied Traetta. On 12 Nivôse (1 January 1799), the Poles made a boat bridge over this river, and General Rey passed it with the corps under his command, having only left five fusiliers of the 1st Battalion garrisoned at Gaeta. On the 14th (3 January), he made his junction with General Macdonald near Sparinisi.

When a large number of Neapolitan train horses and artillery fell into the hands of the Poles, as well as the stud farms of the King of Naples around Mondragone, General Dąbrowski obtained permission from the General-in-Chief to form a regiment of Polish cavalry. In a short time, this regiment, numbering three hundred men, composed of officers and soldiers who had formerly served in the cavalry in Poland, was in a position to serve.

General-in-Chief Championnet, who, after having ordered the disarmament of the city of Rome, had left it on 20 December, followed by Generals Macdonald, Kellermann, Thiebault, Maurice Dumas, Duhèsme, Lemoine, Dupresse, Forestier, march directly on Capua, as soon as the Gallo-Polish troops under the orders of General Rey had cleared the road which led to it.

The Polish Legion also moved to Capua to block the city on the north side and was posted near Volturno. Small and insignificant battles succeeded each other until 22 Nivôse (11 January 1799), the day of the conclusion of the armistice.

However, more serious events, which required special attention, took place during this time on the rear of the army. Several inhabitants of the towns, and especially the peasants named Scarpetti, a ferocious people, who live only on contraband, hunting, and brigandage, having united themselves with the Neapolitan soldiers scattered and commanded by officers of that nation, had fallen on the republican detachments, had slaughtered the garrisons, cut off the provisions, and ruined the communication bridge on the Garigliano.

The small detachments sent to halt their progress had already lost many people without succeeding; on the contrary, they had made the rebels much more obstinate and more daring. If the enemy's army had held firm near Capua, and if it had helped the insurgents, the republican troops would have found themselves in the most critical position; but at the moment when General Championnet was going to take the most rigorous measures to remedy this terrible incident, the parliamentarians from Capua proposed an armistice to him, in order, they said, to arrive at the conclusion of a solid and durable peace. They offered to surrender the city and demanded that a military line should be traced so that the two armies could await the decision of their respective governments. However advantageous these proposals might be, Championnet, in order to impose and conceal his position on the parliamentarians, demanded the submission and surrender of Naples. The Neapolitan officers retired and returned the next day to make the same proposals; they were renewed like the day before.

Meantime, the insurrection became general, and the massacres did not discontinue; the army would be at any moment in a most critical position. It even began to despair of its salvation, when the same parliamentarians appeared again at the forefront. Conducted before Championnet, they told him that they were authorized by the viceroy to consent to any request from the head of the French army, except at the surrender of the city of Naples. However strange this new approach of the Neapolitan chiefs appeared to Championnet, however, having received the opinion of the generals assembled in a council of war, he instructed his chief of staff, General Bonnamy, to deal with the two Neapolitan envoys, the Prince of Miliano and the Duke of Gesso, and the convention was signed at the camp near Capua, 10 January

1799 (Nivôse 17, Year VII).

That same night, General Elbe entered Capua; the next day, 11 January, it received a French garrison, and Brigadier Darnaud was appointed commandant of the place. The rest of the troops took position in front of Capua.

Free of the enemy he had in mind by the armistice concluded, Championnet was seriously concerned with the punishment of the insurgent Neapolitans. General Rey set out with his division, and sent strong detachments to restore good order, either by force of arms or amicably. Sezza, Itri, Castiglione, Mola-di-Gaeta, Cascana and Castel-Forte were taken by force. Traetta, a small town situated in the mountains on the right bank of Garigliano, and several others, surrendered unconditionally. On the night of 4/5 Germinal (24/25 March 1799), the column under the orders of General Watrin, composed of the 30th Line, the riflemen of the 15th Légère and a detachment of the 1st Polish Legion, arrived at this city, one of the principal places of refuge of the brigands from the region. As soon as the arrangements were made to surround the city, the signal of the attack was given, and soon, in spite of the vigorous resistance of the rebels, the French bayonets penetrated all the points and made a frightful carnage; more than twelve hundred rebels perished there, the city was burned and the ramparts were razed.

After this expedition, General Watrin, leaving the Poles to Tratta, made his way to Castel-Forte, which he carried away with great force; the city was delivered to the flames and the walls were also destroyed. The Polish Legion lost a lot of people in these different affairs. It had to regret especially the good Chef de bataillon Elie Tremo, massacred with a detachment of thirty to forty men, on 29 Nivôse (9 January 1799), aide-de-camp of General Dąbrowski, finally one of the founders of these legions that perpetuated the traditions of Polish bravery.

The name of Elie Tremo, inseparable from that of Dąbrowski, although placed in the background, will not remain less surrounded by a halo of fresh and pure glory, and history will repeat it to the generations to prove that it has pages for all brave deeds and crowns for all the dedicated.

Lieutenants Zelewski, Krause, Ialbrzykowski of the infantry, Surgeon-Major Ritter and Lieutenant Vaselle of the cavalry, had the fate of the brave Tremo. Vaselle, refusing to go with twenty men to the insurgents at Traeta, was killed, opening a passage in the midst of them, at the head of his detachment. Only six men came back. Captains Kosinski and Kochanski were seriously injured.

General Kniaziewicz took Sezza and Cascano by assault with the 2nd Battalion. General Dąbrowski forced the passage of the Garigliano with the two others, the 15th Légère Demi-brigade, the 7th Chasseurs à cheval Regiment and two cannons. From there he extended to Terracina to restore order to the rear of the army. In this action, Dąbrowski had two horses wounded under him.

The terror that struck the city of Naples saw the emergence of different parties. The Lazzaroni[7] seized all the arms and declared General Mack as a traitor. Reduced to the alternative of perishing as a victim of the populace, or to demanding asylum from General Championnet, he preferred the latter; he was seen arriving at the Caserta headquarters, surrendering himself unconditionally. The French general promised the Austrian general a passport and an escort to accompany him to Milan, where he asked to retire, and where, sometime later, the French Directory shamed itself by arresting him as a prisoner of war.

The Lazzaroni, furious to see the one whom they regarded as the author of all public misfortunes escaped and turned to one of the French outposts. This unforeseen aggression of the Lazzaroni necessarily broke the armistice; it became the signal for an attack on Naples. General Championnet thought himself free from King Ferdinand and did not hesitate to invade his capital. Divisions accordingly received orders to set themselves in motion. On 20 January, the French army went to Naples. The brilliant valor of the Chef de bataillon Thiébault in the attack on the Capuana fortress, which earned him the rank of adjutant-general, as well as the presence of spirit and the intrepidity of Chef de brigade Broussier, to the gorges of the Apennines, known by the celebrated name of the Caudine Forks, and which obtained as a reward the rank of general, opened the gates of the capital of the two Sicilies. The possession of Naples, however, cost a great deal of

[7]Translator: The Lazzaroni (or Lazzari) of Naples were the poorest of the lower class in the city and kingdom of Naples, Italy. Described as "street people under a chief", they were often depicted as "beggars"—which some actually were, while others subsisted partly by service as messengers, porters, etc.

blood on both sides; but the 3 Pluviôse (22 January 1799) the French seized this capital; on the 6th a Te Deum was solemnly sung in all the churches by order of General Championnet, and the liberty of the Neapolitan people was proclaimed. The French army even took the name of the Army of Naples. King Ferdinand having taken refuge at Pagan, the General-in-Chief chose twenty-five citizens to whom he entrusted the task of preparing a new constitution. They were divided into six committees which formed a legislative assembly. The new Paraithean Republic was proclaimed, and the following citizens were nominated for its provisional composition: Abamonti, Albanese, Baffi, Bassal, Bisciglia, Bruno, Cestari, Ciaja, Gennaro, Philippis, Rensis, Doria, Falcigni, Fasulo, Forges, Lauberl, Logoteta, Manthonè, Pagano, Paribelli, Pignatelli-Vaglio, Porta, Riarj, Rotondo.

The former Prince Moliterni was appointed president of the new government.[8]

On 5 Pluviôse (24 January), General Dąbrowski was charged with the command of the division which extended from Capua inclusively to Terracina, and Colonel Chamand was appointed, on the 17th (5 February), in the place of General Kniaziewicz, for chief of the 1st Legion.[9]

[8]By consulting the remarkable work in all respects and entitled: Saggio Storico sulla Rivoluzione di Napoli, seconda edizione, Milano 1806, and made public by an anonymous author. I cannot refrain here from paying a tribute to another anonymous Italian author of the *Histoire militaire d'Italie.* M. César de Laugier, of a family from Lorraine, a superior officer in the guard of the Grand Duke of Tuscany, having obtained his honorable distinctions on the battlefields in Spain, Germany, Poland, Russia, Switzerland and Italy, today devotes his talents to the military glory of his nation. He has already produced an important work of *Gli Italian in Russia, memorie di un Ufiziale italiano, per allire storia della Russia, della Polonia and dell 'Italia, nel 1812.* (Florence, 1826-1827, 4 vols.) It is here that this writer brings to light the infidelity and partiality that several foreign authors have brought to their judgment on the Polish nation, and that he restores the truth in a swift picture of Poland and the Poles. Not content with giving all the details relating to the Russian expedition of August, the honorable author is now engaged, and on the same plan, to include the history of the wars in Italy from 1798 to 1815.

The friendship with which M. de Laugier has been good enough to honor me during my stay in Florence (1813-1826), and the particular interest he takes in the glory of my compatriots, make me presume that the part which the Polish Legions took in these events may give him the opportunity of fulfilling the omissions which I might have made in this history, and that he will by that very thing add a new floret to his literary glory, and a new title to a foreign recognition.

[9]See supporting documents, Nos. 46, 47, 48, 49, 50, and 51, on the glorious share of the Poles in this memorable campaign. In a host of traits of hero-

The Polish troops having been covered with glory in the various actions that had preceded the surrender of Naples, General Championnet was desirous of giving them a public testimony of his satisfaction. At that time, the most distinguished honor that could be accorded to a soldier was to let him present to the Directory the flags captured from the enemy. From the beginning of the campaign, this favor had been granted to Citizen Laraitrie, first aide-de-camp of the General-in-Chief, who had solemnly presented, on 16 Nivôse (5 January 1799), the Neapolitan flags taken at the outbreak of hostilities. General Championnet, wishing then to grant the same favor to the Poles, commissioned, on 16 February, one of his most illustrious warriors, General Kniaziewicz, to go to Paris to present to the Directory the captured flags. Kniaziewicz, accompanied by Captains Drzewiecki, Dąbrowski (son), and Kossecki, who, during this campaign, had served him as an aide-de-camp, left the city of Naples on 17 Pluviôse (5 February), to get to his destination.

On the way, General Kniaziewicz was on the point of becoming the victim of insurgent bands infesting the road from Rome to Florence. Passing through Rome, he learned that the rebels gathered in large numbers were headed by a bishop, who lived in Acquapendente. The two relay posts which preceded this city were most dangerous; but, seeing it shameful to turn back, and trusting in his presence of mind, Kniaziewicz immediately went to the outposts of the insurgents.

---

ism that great upheavals and revolutions bring out, the following is very remarkable. The 5th Ventôse (February 23, 1799), a detachment of Gallo-Polish troops traveling with General Cambrai through some areas rife with fanaticism, and that the wise measures of the general got back into order, arrived in Cingoli, a town and department of Tronto, of the new Roman Republic, from which the rebels, who had been there the day before, had been seized by a republican column. These robbers, on their arrival in this commune, sought, to murder the Citizen Francesco Coufidati, a zealous supporter of the republican government, and, not finding it, seized his two daughters, Adelaide and Helen Confidati, the first aged twenty years, and the second seventeen. After binding their hands behind their backs, they tied them to a tree, erected a pyre around it, and, with the torches in their hands, threatened to set them on fire, if they did not immediately declare the retreat of their father; but these heroines, whom pending death could not intimidate, replied that they wished to die with their secret.

The brigands were stupefied at this unexpected reply; and, while they were undecided, the Gallo-Polish detachment arrived and made them take flight; in an instant they broke the bonds of these two victims, whom a crowd of citizens brought back in triumph, admiring their heroism and their filial piety!

When he arrived there, he claimed to be the ambassador of the King of Spain, who was returning from Naples to Madrid; he formally announced his intention of going to the bishop to give him news of the highest importance and asked for a safeguard to make this route.

Led to Aquapendente, Kniaziewicz informed the bishop of the object of his trip and informed him that Naples was in French hands. The bishop, alarmed at this news, and fearing the vengeance of the victorious troop, threw himself at the knees of the Polish general and asked for his protection. As the General himself at the mercy of this partisan chief, they made mutual concessions, and Kniaziewicz immediately wrote a letter to General Championnet, asking him to grant a general pardon to the insurgent bishop. Thus, escaping a dangerous encounter, General Kniaziewicz continued his way to Paris, charged with his glorious cargo.

The ceremony that accompanied the presentation of the flags to the Directory occurred on 18 Ventôse, Year VII (8 March 1799), at two o'clock in the afternoon, in the Hall of Public Audiences in the Directorial Palace (Palais de Luxembourg).

These flags, draped with gold and silver, which by their magnificence contrasted so greatly against the simplicity of the national flag, slack, as weak as one was tall and strong, these flags were presented in this circumstance by a foreign citizen who paid homage to his adoptive homeland.

All the members of the diplomatic corps attended this august ceremony. A large and select crowd besieged the dictatorial palace: it was a question of celebrating one of the most beautiful conquests that the Republic had made and the waving trophies which spoke so well to the nation of its glory and its triumphs, which were greeted by repeated impulses of enthusiasm. This very circumstance, which had earned a Pole the honor of representing the Republican Army in one of its most brilliant exploits, added to this festival a charm and more interest.

As all the details of this memorable ceremony have a grandeur worthy of the ancient ages, they will undoubtedly be found with pleasure, meticulously traced and as the leaves of the time we transmit them.

The Minister of War, Dubois-Crancé, presenting the thirty-five flags or standards taken from the Neapolitans, opened the session with the following speech:

Citizen Directors, these trophies are a new monument to the success of our arms, the delirium of our enemies and the perfidy of the English government.

History, in retracing political extravagances, will no doubt offer those of the Court of Naples as a frightful lesson for kings; neither the feeling of its weakness nor the experience of our forces has stopped this blind court. The hatred of a woman, the plans of a foreigner, and English gold, that is his motive and his resources.

The French army meets the enemy; less terrible in number than in name and valor, it advances; its march is a series of victories. In vain does the foreigner, to whom Naples has entrusted its destiny, seek a last weapon in fanaticism, and hasten to raise up a lost people; the craftsman of the war is the first victim of his artifice, and finds only in our camp and in French loyalty an asylum against public fury. Naples receives our army, and royal and religious fanaticism yields once more to the ascendancy of liberty.

O sons of Sucy and of our brothers slaughtered! Your blood will sprout in this land of slaves, and you will bring forth avengers.

Thus kings, deceived by England, become the instrument of the crimes which it bribes; they seem to play against their subsidies their armies and their thrones. Thus, this corrupting government clears Europe, and its gold serves to anchor the yoke under which it burns to bend the navy of all the powers, and the commerce of the world.

A host of military prodigies, the Naples war over, a state entirely subject to our arms, this is the work of the army of Naples for a few months; it is under these glorious auspices that this army, after a long rest, has recommenced the war; daughter and rival of the Army of Italy, all its battles were triumphs; surprised, destitute and small, it conquered its weakness of their needs.

Among the warriors who have seconded him, the Gener-

al-in-Chief is fond of counting, and I like to quote to you the brave Poles who fight under our flags; their conduct proves that neither talent nor courage has failed them to preserve their independence, and that they are worthy to find among us a country and liberty. Under these flags which they helped to conquer, you see, Citizen Directors, General Kniaziewicz, one of those foreigners, who are not for us.

The honor of offering you these trophies is the price of his military virtues and services.

This great warrior and his brothers-in-arms were born almost under the same sky, whence, on the faith of England and some traitors, a prince, the oppressor of Poland, and our enemy even to fanaticism, sends his soldiers to search in foreign ranks for contempt, sickness, and death. Thus, we arrive at once, from the north of Europe, enemies and defenders.

May the kings who are still our enemies be enlightened by so many examples! Peace is their salvation. Our armies have conquered only for peace; but if they dare to refuse it, let them tremble to oblige them still to conquer! The first cry of victory rang from the tip of Italy to the summit of the Alps, and to the banks of the Rhine; it may extend to the very depths of Germany; and, I attest to the genius of the Republic, one day we will frighten the Thames.

Hardly had the Minister of War finished speaking than General Kniaziewicz, whose republican and martial attitude corresponded to the praise bestowed upon him by the General-in-Chief of the Army of Naples, expressed himself in these terms:

> Governing Citizens, I have the honor to place in your hands the flags, which the Army of Rome conquered from the Neapolitans.
>
> This army has just annihilated all the power of a perjurious king. The heroes who compose it, by indicating to the new warriors of the Cisalpine and Roman Republics a vast field of glory, have put them in a position to prove to the universe that the man who devotes himself to the cause of holy liberty becomes

an invincible soldier.

It is still consoling for Poles, to whom you allowed, citizen directors, to associate their work with those of the French republicans, to see one of their brothers, authorized by the Army of Rome, bring you the trophies that it has just plucked. You see, citizen directors, in this act of the Army of Rome, a proof of this sublime disinterestedness which does not allow it to enjoy the triumphs that belong to it alone, without involving those whom it has kindly admitted to contribute to it. My compatriots, therefore, grateful, and full of hope in the benevolence of the great nation, have sworn in their souls that the cause of the French Republic will always be sacred to them, for they regard it as common and forever inseparable from theirs: Long live the Republic!

This speech, covered with unanimous applause, was followed by a response by the President of the Directory, Barras:

The Executive Directory receives with great pleasure the many trophies of republican valor, those glorious pledges of the invincible courage of the Army of Naples.

The scepter of Ferdinand is broken; but unfaithful to the sworn faith, the miserable toy of an insolent minister and a corrupt court, a monarch enslaved by the tyrant of the Thames, Ferdinand had for a long time dug the abyss beneath his feet. Innumerable friends of liberty have long called for lightning to strike this guilty head. Nothing equaled the audacity of this blind despot, as the magnanimous patience of the French Republic; but finally, an imprudent violator of the holiest treaties, he is suddenly armed: he attacks the allies of the great nation as a brigand. A gleam of success doubles his temerity; he penetrates into Rome, which is evacuated, and already he thinks himself master of the destinies of the world, but shame follows closely perfidy and disloyalty. Barely a few days have elapsed when Rome is returned to liberty, Piedmont breaks its chains, Naples is submissive, and Italy finds itself freed from the horrible tyrants who oppress it: thus, the news of the cowardly attacks of the coalition against the law of nations had not reached the confines of Europe, than already the thrones of the perfidious aggressors were overthrown.

But it is not enough: the nations listen, and their justice pronounces sentence. Detached, a fugitive, without a diadem, without a homeland, the coward Ferdinand has found the art of withering up his misfortune. It is by massacres, by unheard-of crimes in the history of civilized peoples; it is by the assassination of unfortunate prisoners, strangers even to his disaster, and covered with honorable wounds, that he teaches Italy that he is still breathing.

May at least the example of his fall, by avenging outraged humanity, still instruct all the enemies of the great nation! Peace, that is the wish of the Directory; the happiness of the people, the tranquility of the Earth, the prosperity of all, that is what it meditates and what it desires. What hope is enraptured by the enemy kings of France! Would they count on the success of some agents, to whom they ordered to foment among us intestine dissensions? But let the warlike trumpet ring, and all the French, united in intention and will, answer it by giving the signal of their destruction. Do they not know that the fate of a free people is to conquer? Do they want to exterminate the last of their subjects, and reign only over the dead? But in vain they would make a rampart for heaped corpses, unhappy victims of their fury. The genius of liberty will be able to reach them in their horrible entrenchments: the fate of Ferdinand awaits them.

Return, citizen, to the conquerors of Capua and Naples; look at those brave Poles who preferred exile to slavery: The Republic has adopted them, and France is their homeland. Review the ranks of these republican heroes, companions and witnesses of your exploits; share with them all the esteem of the country and the congratulations of the Directory; tell the Roman and Cisalpine Legions that their courage has shown that they were worthy of liberty; return to the Army of Naples and tell them that if history offers nothing comparable to its triumphs; it must still crown the honorable laurels that the soldier receives from discipline. The object of the admiration of the warriors of all ages, let it still be the model by the severity of its conduct, and add to the honor of being invincible the no less lasting honor of republican habits.

After the presentation of the flags, the Directory and all its procession went in ceremony to the main door of its palace, overlooking Rue de Tournon, to witness the planting of a freedom tree. A platform had been erected on which the Directory placed itself with its ministers.

Then the Conservatory of Music performed the *Hymne aux Libertés*, a song with the words of the Citizen Mahérault and the music of Citizen Grétry.[10]

The tree planted, the Directory advanced near the tree, and Citizen Barras, its president, attached a tricolor flag to it.

Under the roots of the tree were placed two lead boxes, containing a silver medal (for Agriculture); a large bronze medal (to the Inquisitors of tyranny), and several coins of the republican type. Such were the details which accompanied the presentation of the Neapolitan standards; such was the august ceremony devoted to the glory of the Gallo-Polish Army.

---

[10]Translator: The lyrics of this song have been omitted.

CHAPTER NINE

New Hostilities by the Coalition. – Brune, Bernadotte, Joubert, Schérer, Macdonald, and Championnet. – Fights with the Scarpetti. – Lombardy Campaign Under Schérer. – The 2nd Polish Legion Takes Part. – Engagement at Porto-Legnago. – Lipnicki, Straszewski, Regulski, Boguslawski, Brothers Bodebski, Lipczynski, Darewski, Zadera, Malewicz, Kozlowski, and Zielinski. – Letter from the Directory to the Poles. – Retreat of General Schérer. – Checks suffered by the Gallo-Polish Army at Magnano. – Death of General Rymkiewicz. – Zefferyn, Lysakowski, Cyprien Godebski, Louis Dembowski, Krolikiewicz, Wiaskowski, Daszkiewicz, Paciorkowski. – Movements of the Army and the Legions. – The 2nd Polish Legion Receives Orders to Reinforce the Garrison of Mantua. – Invasion of Tuscany by General Gauthier. – His March on Florence. – His Entrance. – Grand Duke Ferdinand III Abandons his Capital. – The Republican Government is Proclaimed in Tuscany. – Demarches of General Dąbrowski. – Complement of the Legions. – Retreat of General Schérer. – His Resignation. – Moreau Takes Command of the Army. – It Retreats Behind the Tessin and from there to Novarre. – New Battles. – Progress of Field Marshal Suvorov. – March of General Macdonald, Commander of the Army of Naples. – The 1st Polish Legion Assembles at Terracina. – Insurrection in Tuscany. – Actions at Arezzo and Castiglione. – Kaminski, Karski, Dembowski, Zoltowski, Pokrzywnicki, Vinert, Rutier, Dziurbas, Notkiewicz, Wonsowicz. – March of the Legion in the Apennines. – Various Actions Given in this Position. – Arrival of General Macdonald at Florence. – The Army's Maneuver. – It's Arrival at Florence. – Temporization of Moreau. – Macdonald's Army Faces Suvorov. – Battle of Trebbia. – Dąbrowski, Chlopicki, etc. – The Army is Forced to Retreat. – The Polish Legion is Charged to Support It. – Personal Courage of General Dąbrowski. – Results of this Campaign for the Poles. – Georges Grabowski. – Jablonowski. – Kazimierz De la Roche, etc.

But while the victories won over the Neapolitans were celebrated in Paris, the horizon of Italy was still covered with dark clouds, and a new storm threatened the numerous republics that the French glory had planted there. A second time the slave satellites thrown up by the

North were about to rush over these barely free countries, and the fields of Lombardy were to witness an even more bloody and deadly struggle.

At that time the situation of France was not great enough to triumph, playing with a new coalition. The Republic, then mistress of all Italy and Holland, had, in order to defend the immense line which extends from the Gulf of Tarento to the Texel, only one hundred sixty thousand to one hundred seventy thousand men, that is to say, to say, ten thousand in Holland and a few thousand men on the Rhine, because the troops, which had been destined for this corps of observation were occupied with the pacification the interior of the Republic and to contain the Vendée. The Army of the Danube had, at most, forty thousand men, that of Switzerland of thirty thousand men, that of Italy of fifty thousand men, and finally that of Naples of thirty thousand men.

The coalition, on its side, had three hundred thousand men, besides two other announced Russian contingents, which were to be combined with the English troops, and which were destined for Holland, and the other to the King of Naples.

In the meanwhile, General Brune was promoted to the command of the Army of Bavaria, and Bernadotte had the Army of the Rhine; the important Army of the Danube was entrusted to General Joubert; Masséna was chief of the Army of Helvetia; General Schérer, who served as Minister of War in Paris, obtained command of the Army of Italy, and General Macdonald replaced Championnet in the Army of Naples.

As to the Neapolitan troops, although entirely dispersed and defeated, and since the greater part of this former kingdom was occupied by the French corps, they were nevertheless continually obliged to march against the insurgent towns. The Neapolitan soldiers scattered here and there and united with the Scarpetti[1], constantly harassed the little detachments, made the roads unsafe, and cut off communications, especially in the mountains, on the Garigliano, Volturno, and Itri.

[1]Translator: *Scarpetti* - Rope–soled shoes used by mountain climbers. [Ital. *scarpetto* a light shoe, diminutive form of scarpa a shoe]. In other words, these are mountain peasants.

The Polish division, reinforced by two French Demi-brigades, was constantly on the move and engaged on all sides. It was also obliged to maintain strong garrisons at Capua and Gaeta. The troops lacked neither food nor money; but they were without clothes, and Captain Dembowski could not send the uniforms from Ancona for lack of means of transport and the various insurrections.

Such, then, was the situation of the Gallo-Polish troops in the south of Italy, when a new campaign against the Austrian army was opened in the north.

To support it with a more imposing force, General Schérer, according to the precise orders of the Directory, was to take his positions on the frontiers of the Cisalpine Republic, and to communicate with General Macdonald, who commanded the Army of Naples who were under the orders of the General-in-Chief.[2]

Although the Austrian army was superior to that of the French, it did not, however, think it proper to begin hostilities before the arrival of the auxiliary corps of Muscovites promised by the Czar Paul I. This circumstance determined General Schérer to take the initiative, attacking the Austrians on the Lower Adige, and maneuvering them so as to reject them on the Brenta. Unfortunately, this general did not have enough youth and had lost popularity during his ministry. On 5 Germinal Year VII (25 March 1799), the Austrian army, commanded by General Baron de Kray, the senior of the Austrian lieutenant-generals, who replaced acting General Baron de Melas, who had fallen sick, was camped on the left bank of the Adige, behind the fortresses of Verona and Legnago. All the other corps were stationed so that the enemy right touched Lake Garda, his left at Adige; his center occupied Verona, San-Massimo and Santa Lucia.

The French General-in-Chief had established his army, which had just been reinforced by conscripts, behind the fortresses of Peschi-

[2]The total forces of the Austrian army on the Adige, on 20 March 1799, were 57,021 men, and those of the French Army of Italy on the Adige, at 30 March 1799, were 46,366, and out of this number the Polish troops forming part of the left division, commanded by General Grenier, having under his command 800 men of the 2nd Polish Legion, commanded by the Général de brigade Wielhorski. In the center division, commanded by General Moreau, General Victorius had under his command the detachment of the same 2nd Polish Legion, with 700 men, while in the right wing, under the command of General Montrichard, there were 780 Poles. Thus, the entire force of the 2nd Polish Legion under the orders of General Rymkiewiez was at that time 2,280 men.

era and Mantua, where the headquarters were. As for the Poles, their artillery remained at Mantua; but the 1st Battalion of the 2nd Legion, under the command of General Rymkiewicz, advanced to the right wing of the army to join Montrichard's division. Adjutant General Amilcar Kosinski was employed with this corps. The 2nd Battalion, under the orders of General Joseph Wielhorski, joined the Delmas division on the left wing of the army, and the 3rd Battalion was sent to the center of Victor's division.

Brescia and Bergamo had only four battalions; but General Schérer thought that his left flank would be sufficiently secured by the division of the Army of Helvetia, commanded by General Dessolles, who occupied the Valtelline, and by the troops of the same army, that General Lecourbe had orders to send him his first requisition.

Deciding to attack the Austrians, Schérer formed the I Corps of the French army, composed of the divisions of Montrichard, Victor and Hatry, under the direction of General Moreau, to make a false attack on Verona and Porto-Legnago, in order to stop and to keep in check the aid, which the enemy could direct from these fortresses on Pastrengo, by the right bank of the Adige; the II Corps, composed of three divisions commanded by the Generals Delmas, Grenier, and Serrurier, under the direction of General Schérer himself, was to attack and turn the positions of the Austrians on Lake Garda.

On 5 Germinal, Year VII (25 March 1799), the entire Gallo-Polish Army was opposite the line of the Adige. The next day, 6 Germinal (26 March), at daybreak, it attacked the enemy at all points, and drove them back everywhere, except on the right, where Montrichard's division was defeated near Legnago. The 1st Polish Battalion did some prodigies of valor on this occasion. This battalion, having the brave General Rymkiewicz at its head, attacked the enemy at Vaganza and Vigo, pursued him as far as the bridge at Legnago, and when the whole division was later obliged to retire, it was it again who had the perilous task of covering it. He divided himself for this purpose into three parts, one of which was commanded by General Rymkiewicz, the other by Adjutant-Commander Kosinski, and the third by Chef de bataillon Louis Dembowski. Each of these commanders, animated by heroic courage, defended his post to the last extremity. Major Lipnicki and Captain Straszewski distinguished themselves especially on that day. Captains

Regulski and Boguslawski were injured. General Rymkiewicz had a wounded horse under him, and Chef de bataillon Dembowski, was one of the slain. Lieutenant N. Godebski and two hundred men, both non-commissioned officers and soldiers, remained on the battlefield. Chance had it that the latter should arrive from Poland at the beginning of the action; and, at the same moment when he was shaking the hand of his brother Cyprien Godebski, a cannonball carried off the newcomer and thus separated him from the brave Cyprian forever.

The 2nd Battalion, under the command of General Wielhorski, who commanded a brigade of French troops in Delmas's division, took part in the victory of this division, and pursued the enemy as far as Verona; but he paid dearly for these advantages; for he lost his brave leader Lipczynski and more than one hundred fifty non-commissioned officers and soldiers, killed or wounded. Among them were Colonel Darewski, a seventy-year-old man who, after fighting the Muscovites in the Bar confederation (1768-1772), later took a glorious share in the War of National Independence (1794) under Kosciuszko; regardless of his age, he had found his youth to fight the enemy, and had fled to Italy as a volunteer under the republican banner. Still young, with zeal and bravery, Darewski was one of the first who rushed with his grenadiers in the midst of the enemy fire. The lieutenants Theodore Zadera and Rozys, and the Sous-lieutenants Michel Zadera and Maïewicz, following the example of Colonel Darewski, distinguished themselves particularly there and were also wounded.

The 3rd Polish Battalion, forming that day the vanguard of Victor's division, defeated and drove back the Austrians. This battalion was constantly engaged with the latter all day, and consequently made a considerable loss, having been compelled to tear by force the ground from the enemy, and to occupy it step-by-step, by pulling it back. Captain Kozlowski and Lieutenant Zielinski found the death of brave men. About four hundred men were killed, wounded or taken prisoner in the war.

For their part the Austrian Generals Minkwitz, Liptay, and Kaim were dangerously wounded, and Dewins was killed. As for the French, they counted Generals Delmas and Dalesme among the wounded.

General-in-Chief Schérer, according to the reports of the generals commanding the divisions, sent to the French Directory a praise so advantageous to the bravery of the 2nd Polish Legion, which he sent, through the commanding general of the Legions in Italy, Dąbrowski, the most flattering letter, addressed particularly to these brave phalanges. This letter follows:

The Executive Directory, to the Polish troops who fought Germinal 6th, in Italy, with the Army of the French Republic.

Paris, this Floréal 9, Year VII (April 28, 1799).

Brave Poles! You have not been able to tear your homeland from servitude, but you have sworn to defend liberty wherever it will carry its banners! It was with a courage worthy of it that you fought on Germinal 6th. The Executive Directory, to which the General-in-Chief of the Army of Italy has reported, testifies its satisfaction. By cementing the republican edifice with your blood, you will leave to your compatriots your memory, your example, and the noble desire to imitate you.

The President of the Executive Power,
BARRAS

By the Executive Directory,

LAGARDE

This first advantage won by General Schérer could not deter him from his plan of retreat, although General Moreau advised him judiciously to preserve his position in front of Verona.

In order to conceal this retrograde movement, the General-in-Chief gave General Serrurier the order to execute a false attack on Verona; the action was brilliant, but the French lost nearly five thousand men. General Schérer established his headquarters at Isola Della Scala, and the Gallo-Polish forces were concentrated between the Adige and the Tartaro. In this position a new fight soon took place.

In fact, on 16 Germinal (5 April), the army attempted a new attack on all points, but this time it was beaten and pursued on all sides; and although the loss was equal in both parties, it was, however, more considerable on the French side, especially in the artillery. In the Austrian army, Field Marshal Lieutenant Mercantin, two generals and seven officers, had been seriously wounded, while the French army had among its wounded Generals Beaumont, Dalesme, Pigeon and the brave General Delmas himself, who had been struck again by a bullet. General Montrichard praised the conduct of the 1st Polish Battalion commanded by General Rymkiewicz, who, twice wounded that day, died a few days later. This loss caused the sharpest regret in the Legions; the memory of this valiant warrior will remain forever indelible in the memory of the Poles. Illustrated by more than a title, this general united to the talents of a warrior all the virtues of a citizen. The last words he uttered before expiring were still for Poland, and he exclaimed, “Why did destiny not permit me to die on the soil of my country?”

Nearly three hundred men of the Legion remained in the square. Lieutenants Zefferyn and Lysakowski, Cyprien Godebski, brother of the one who died on 6 Germinal (26 March), were badly wounded, and the latter obtained the rank of lieutenant on the battlefield. General Moreau, an eyewitness of the bravery of the Polish battalion, also appointed General Rymkiewicz, Général de brigade, in the course of the action, but death did not permit him to enjoy this honor for a long time. Chef de bataillon Louis Dombowski was also appointed Chief of the Legion; Captain Krolikiewicz was promoted to chef de bataillon, and Lieutenants Zefferyn, Reinhold and Modzelewski, obtained the rank of captain.

In the 2nd Polish Battalion Lieutenant Wiaskowski was killed; Captain Kirkor and Lieutenant Berensdorf wounded.

In the 3rd, Captain Daszkiewicz and Lieutenant Paciorkowski expired on the battlefield.

The entire 2nd Polish Legion lost in this unhappy day up to one thousand men killed, wounded or prisoners of war.

This battle under the walls of Verona was called the battle of Magnano, because the French headquarters had been established the day before in this village.

Discouraged by this first failure, the French army revived, and having occupied the line of the Mincio, Mantua was put in a respectable state of defense.

After the battle, the 1st Polish Battalion was ordered to cover the retreat of its division.

Then Adjutant General Kosinski withdrew with the remains of the 2nd and 3rd Battalions to Nogara, where they arrived on the 17th and protected a great artillery train which was directed on Mantua. Arriving at Castellaro, he received orders from General Delmas to cover the Molinella bridge and to favor the retreat of the division. On the 18th, the 2nd Battalion moved to Due-Castelli, and Kosinski with the 3rd Battalion to Roverbella. When the whole army took up position behind the Molinella, on the 19th it received the order to occupy Rotta-Vecchia with this battalion and part of the French troops from Marengo, not far from Mincio, to Castellaro.

On the 22nd (11 April), in the night, the whole army withdrew, and the Polish Legion received the fatal order to remain at Mantua, to be part of the garrison, whose chief command was entrusted to General Foissac-Latour. Shortly after the Austrians invested this fortress and intercepted all communications with the army.[3]

Locked up in Mantua, General Wielhorski was in command of all the works that were outside the Ceres Gate, that is to say Thé Island, Migliaretlo and the entrenched camp, which were defended in large part by Polish infantry. The artillery, of which the 1st and 2nd Companies were a part, was under the command of Chef de bataillon Wincenty Axamitowski. The 3rd Company was employed in the defense of the Pradella hornwork, and the Chef de bataillon Iakubowski commanded the artillery of Fort St. George, where the company was. This superior officer had occasion, during the blockade, to demonstrate his courage and his military knowledge at various times.

But before continuing with the details of the blockade of Mantua, let us look back for a moment, and take a look at the events which at that time agitated Tuscany, and the causes which determined them. Austria was then defiled by an unheard-of attack: three French ministers at Rastadt, Jean Debry, Bonnier, and Roberjot, had been indignantly assassinated on 9 Floréal (28 April). Irritated by such a perfidy,

---

[3] All the wounded after the battle of Magliano were carried to the French hospital at Mantua. According to the order usually observed in the hospitals, the table for dressing the wounded arrived near a French grenadier who was the first in the line; but he exclaimed: “Go and visit, before me, that Pole, for he has been in the enemy’s battery before me.”

and frightened by the declaration of a new war, the chances of which were so unfavorable, the Directory wished to remove and expel from Italy all that was directly or indirectly in the interests of the Court of Vienna. The Grand Duke of Tuscany Ferdinand III was brother of the Emperor of Austria.

To undergo a favorable change, Tuscany did not present itself at this moment in a reassuring point of view for the French cause. In fact, the Army of Italy, under the orders of Schérer, could not then be rescued by the division stationed on the frontiers of the Grand Duchy of Tuscany, and commanded by General Gauthier, who the instructions of the Directory directed to invade Tuscany, or by the Army of Naples under the orders of Macdonald.

Nevertheless, by a series of ill-conceived plans, and to obey the notes received from Paris, the forces of the French armies were scattered at the very moment when they needed concentration.

Tuscany, placed between so many new republics and surrounded by so many republican troops, had hitherto resisted the changes that were taking place around it only by the wise conduct of its virtuous Grand Duke Ferdinand III. And although, as early as March, 1798, a little tree of liberty had been planted in Florence, on the so-called Grand Duke's Square, with this significant inscription: "It will grow in a bit"; although the next day they read on the door of the Ducal Palace (Palazzo Vecchio) these words in large print: "National palace, formerly the Ducal Palace"; and in another place: "The people alone are sovereign"; although Florence had been inundated with pages, patriotic pamphlets, and writings in favor of republican liberty, yet tranquility had been maintained till that moment. But the time had come for Ferdinand III to be obliged to obey necessity.

On 5 Germinal, Year VII (25 March 1799), the French presented themselves at the San Gallo Gate. Commanded by General Gauthier, they advanced into the city without finding any resistance, and, in a moment, the two citadels and all the public establishments were occupied. Two French camps were formed in the Santa Croce and Santa Maria Novella Squares, and pickets took possession of the houses of the ministers of Austria, Portugal, Naples, England, and Russia.

All these arrangements were made in the midst of an immense population, and in the greatest calm.

During the morning of the 7th (27 March), the Grand Duke left the city with his wife and children, escorted a detachment of French troops, leaving his scepter and his palace, and took the road to Vienna.

On the same day, trees of liberty were erected in the public squares, and the new government released Citizen Micheli, who had been imprisoned following a judgment against him, as leader of the revolutionary party in Tuscany.

While Gauthier occupied Florence, General Miollis, with four thousand men, took, on 4 Germinal (24 March), possession of the city and the port of Livorno, where, on 6 Germinal, the Tree of Freedom was also planted on the Grande Place d'Armes.

Citizen Charles Reinhard, who served as commissioner from the French Directory, remained in charge of the civil organization of the Grand Duchy of Tuscany. The French regime was put into effect: each city had its municipality, and the learned Fontana was appointed president of this council, where the citizens were Ombrosi, Bellucci, Ferroni, Sarchiani, Poloni, Gianni, Maritti, Dini and Nenci. Finally, on 20 Germinal (9 April 1799), was celebrated with the greatest pomp a feast on the national square, before Piazza del Palazzo-Vecchio, for the solemn plantation of a large Liberty Tree.[4]

While these events were going on in Upper Italy, and even before the hostilities had begun between the Austrian and French armies, General Wielhorski had written to General Dąbrowski that the war with the Emperor had been decided, and that General Schérer had taken command of the Army of Italy.

General Dąbrowski, still occupied with his principal purpose, and returning to the old project that he had conceived of acting with his troops against a wing of the Austrian army, proposed again to the General-in-Chief his ideas on the coming war. He explained to him by what means the Austrian army, being repulsed on the right wing, the Polish Corps could penetrate into Poland by Hungary.

To this end he sent his aide-de-camp, Major Zawadzki, to General Schérer, to solicit the order for the Legion and for the cavalry regiment to join the Army of Italy. Citizen Joseph Wybicki accompanied him to support this approach with his advice. They left Sezza on 9

[4]Among several other citizens of Tuscany who took an active part in these events, we noticed Beccheroni and Micheli in Florence; Pierre Coruzzi in Livorno, etc.

Ventôse (27 February), and General Dąbrowski, persuaded of the success of this mission, prepared to march with the Polish Cavalry Regiment, of four hundred men, armed with lances, pistols and swords and commanded by General Karwowski, who had already distinguished himself in 1794 in the War of National Independence.

Besides this, General Dąbrowski formed a battalion of three companies of grenadiers from the Legion, of one hundred fifty men each, and gave the command to Major Kazimirz Malachowski. He also formed another, composed of three companies of chasseurs, gave command of it to Major Iasinski, and tried at the same time to concentrate as much as possible the detachments far away from the main body.

To this end, Tomaszewski, after the capture of Civita-Vecchia, received, on his passage through Rome, the order to move with his detachment, four hundred strong, to Isola and Sora, in the Apennines, on the Garigliano where the Scarpetti, hunted by the French troops, had withdrawn, and cut off all communication with Aquino. Captain Ilinski was sent to Ponte Corvo to support him.

Colonel Chamand, commanding the depots at Ancona and Foligno, was also ordered to be ready to march. Dąbrowski, having had all the necessary uniforms prepared, went to Foligno, with the baggage, to await further orders.

Major Zawadzki, returning on 2 Floréal (21 April), brought the order to General Dąbrowski to join, with the corps under his orders, the Army of Italy, dated from the 7 Germinal (27 March). He informed him at the same time of the unfortunate outcome of the battle of Verona, and the death of the brave General Rymkiewicz.

As for Citizen Wybicki, seeing that his services were useless for the moment, he retired to Paris to cultivate the letters, and reappeared on the political scene in 1806, at the first entry of the French armies into Poland.

In the midst of these partial movements, General Schérer, whom we have left on the Mincio, having been outflanked since 8 April 1799 by the Austrian army, remained convinced that this line of the Mincio was no longer tenable, and determined to leave it. This resolution, taken without prior combat, caused great discouragement in the ranks of the French army; and this retrograde movement would still result in the isolation of the Army of Naples, under the orders of Mac-

donald, and the loss of the means of communication with Genoa, the states of Parma, and Upper Tuscany. Mantua was thus confined by the Austrians. However, despite the progress of the Austrian army, General Kray seemed to await the arrival of the Russian army to push the French more vigorously. In fact, Field Marshal Suvorov entered Verona on 14 April, and arrived the next day at the Austrian headquarters at Campagnola, where he took the supreme command of the troops united under the name of the Austro-Russian Army. General Melas also rejoined the Austrian army and took the command under Suvorov.
The forces of the two fighting armies were so disproportionate that the outcome of the campaign could not be doubtful. According to the French historians, the Russian army, composed of elite troops, contained forty thousand men, and this number, added to that of the sixty thousand forming the strength of the army, which the Austrians already had in Italy, presented a total of one hundred thousand soldiers. As for the French troops, which were weakened by the reverses suffered since the opening of the campaign, they had scarcely more than twenty-eight thousand to thirty thousand men, not including the Cisalpine troops.

According to the data of the Russian authors, the Russian corps, commanded by the General of Infantry Rosenberg, was about eighteen thousand strong. The Austrian army, since its entry into the field, had received reinforcements from its rear, as well as from the Tyrol, which had brought it up to forty-four thousand men, in spite of the losses it had already suffered. Thus, the strength of the combined army at that time can be estimated at sixty-two thousand combatants. Another Russian corps of ten thousand men, and four thousand Austrians, were immediately sent to reinforce this army. The French army was reduced to thirty thousand men.[5]

In this position General Schérer, withdrawn behind the Adda, could not resist the storm. He resigned, and, on 26 April, he handed over the provisional command of the army to Moreau. The latter took the measures which he considered most suitable for his retirement. He tried, by all practicable means, to approach the Apennines and the coast of Genoa, in order to facilitate Macdonald's junction with the

[5] See *Victoires et Conquêtes des Français*, Vol. X, p. 172, and *Relation historique et critique de la campagne de 1799 des Austro-Russes en Italie*, by B *** (Boutourlin), Officer of the Chevalier-Gardes, Petersburg, in 1811, p. 29.

Army of Italy. The Cassano bridgehead was completely fortified and lined with artillery. However, the French could not hold out for long, and while on the left of the French line the Austro-Russians carried the village of Pozzo, General Melas had attacked Cassano. After having fought with all the energy of despair, the French were forced into their entrenchments. Moreau retreated as far as the Ticino River, beyond Milan, taking with him the members of the Cisalpine Directory; and, on 29 April, Suvorov took possession of Milan, in the name of the Emperor of Germany. However, as the French garrison of one thousand five hundred men, under the orders of General Bechscher, still held the Milan Citadel, it was immediately blockaded by a corps of four thousand men, commanded by the General Latermann.

Leaving then to General Melas the care of the administrative reorganization of Lombardy, Suvorov continued his victorious march and went with his army to Novara and Pavia. He detached, to the north and on the right, columns to successively occupy the valleys above the lakes, to penetrate the gorges and the passages towards Switzerland, and to join to the left of the army of Archduke Charles, beyond the Gotthard. To the south, and to his left, he sent a division to observe the arrival of Macdonald's army.

After the passage of the Adda and the evacuation of Milan, the retreat of the French army on Lodi had been in good order. It continued thus to Plaisance, Voghera, Vigevano, and Novara, where Moreau had established his headquarters on 2 May. The main forces of the French being in the direction of Genoa, Moreau went to Turin to calm the disorders, and to work on the defense of the citadel, which he entrusted the command of to General Fiorella. On 7 May, he left Turin and took his headquarters to Alessandria. Although his forces were inferior to those of the Austro-Russians, General Moreau nevertheless took up position under the walls of Tortona with the bulk of his troops, resolving to remain there as long as possible. He extended his right towards the Apennines, in order to favor the junction with the Army of Naples.

Suvorov, meanwhile, resolved to act against Moreau with all possible vigor. The plains of Marengo, in the days of 15/16 May, witnessed the valor of the two armies; Moreau, not having sufficient strength to resist, abandoned his lines, retired on 19 May, and moved, by Asti and Cherasco, to Coni, where he arrived on the 22nd. Nevertheless, he had reached his greater goal, that of having given General Macdonald the necessary time to approach the Army of Italy, to complete his retreat by Tuscany, and to attempt his junction in the country of Genoa.

On 21 May, Suvorov occupied Alexandria. On the 27th, he entered Turin. General Moreau, having detached Victor's division from his army, had sent it to meet Macdonald's army. On 7 June, Suvorov appeared before Coni; but Moreau, even more weakened by the detachment that he had just made did not believe a defense was possible, and had already retired on the Col de Tende, leaving a garrison in the fort at Cuneo.

Urged, as we have seen, to join Moreau's army, General Macdonald gave his orders to all the divisions of the Army of Naples to make this important junction. Already, from 5 Floréal (24 April) General Dąbrowski, as soon as the Polish Corps was relieved by the French troops, was sent to Florence. Captain Amira, who had distinguished himself as an engineer officer during the Polish War of Independence in 1791, was at that time the chief-of-staff of the corps.

Accordingly, the whole Polish Corps assembled in Terracina. Ilinski and Tomaszewski were ordered to join the Legion as soon as possible at Rome; Chamand and the depot were to go to Civila-Castellana, where the road to Siena leaves that of Foligno.

The entry of the Polish Legion into Rome took place again this time on 14 Floréal, Year VII (May 3, 1799), an anniversary forever glorious for the Poles, by the constitution of the year 1791! Ilinski and Tomaszewski arrived at the same time.

At this time the news of General Schérer's defeat had already spread everywhere. It was even known that the Army of Naples was beginning to retire; which occasioned the new disturbances in the neighborhoods of Foligno, Spolette, and Perugia. General Belaire, commanding the Rome Division, had no troops, and the consulate had no means to appease them. They accordingly invited General Dąbrowski to take his route on this side, in the hope that in his march he would succeed in reestablishing tranquility, at least until the arrival of the French troops. But what still determined the Polish general to choose this route was that Chamand had sent an officer to assure him that it would be impossible to carry all the effects and baggage to Civita-Castellana at within appointed time. The soldiers lacked shoes, shirts and coats, and they would have lost everything if they did not go through Foligno. Accordingly, the Polish Corps departed from Rome on Floréal 16th (5 May), and arrived, on the 21st (10th), at Perugia where the uniforms and other effects awaited them. All the towns and places through which they passed were in perfect tranquility, and there was no need to engage the rebels.

On the very day of the entry into Perugia, clothes and other effects were distributed, and the depot was divided among the companies. Captain Dembowski had been so successful in making clothing, that the regiment of cavalry received besides saddlebags which had not been expected until Milan.

In the meantime, a general insurrection had broken out in Tuscany, and all those who were in a condition to bear arms, the soldiers in the service of the Grand Duke Ferdinand III, all commanded by Austrian officers, assembled at Arezzo and at Cortona, and threatened Florence, where General Gauthier was without troops. He had in fact been obliged to send the little that remained to him to Lucca and Sarzana, both to quell the insurrection and to stop the Austrians who, having forced the French troops into the Apennines, were already advancing towards La Spezia. It was then that the Polish Legion learned that the Army of Italy had been routed, and that it had taken up a position in the Apennines; that Mantua was blockaded, and that our 2nd Legion, with the artillery, was shut up in the fortress.

Thus, the idea that General Dąbrowski had to act against a wing of the Austrian army, and then to find the means of penetrating Poland, faded for the third time!

Meanwhile, General Dąbrowski received en route letters from General Gauthier, from Florence, and from General Belaire, of Rome, who pressed him, one to suppress the insurrection as much as he could; the other to arrive for the 27th (16 May) in Florence, and to take the cities of Cortona and Arezzo.

On 23 Floréal (12 May) the Polish vanguard set in motion from Perugia, and the corps left on the 24th. Even before reaching Magione on Lake Perugia (formerly Trasimeno, memorable for the battle won by Hannibal), the Polish Legion had already been attacked by the insurgents on all sides: it repulsed them while continuing its journey to Cortona. The vanguard, commanded by the Chef de bataillon Seydlitz, composed of the 3rd Battalion and a cavalry squadron under Major Kaminski's command, met defeated repeated attacks by armed peasants, and overcame all the obstacles that a country could offer; but as soon as the Legion arrived, these obstacles were raised and the enemy chased away. He then retired to the gardens, behind the walls, and to the neighboring houses of Cortona, and his men defended themselves with despair. The city of Cortona, surrounded by good walls, was located on a height that dominates the whole country. General Dąbrowski made the necessary preparations to attack it. The enemy was driven out of the houses and the suburbs, and many people were killed. The sappers forced the gates with axes, in spite of the desperate fire from the houses and the windows. But the rebels had erected walls with embrasures behind these posts, and it was impossible to penetrate further into the city. So, there was nothing left to do but to wait for the night in the position where they were, and then move where the corps could not be disturbed, neither by the sorties from the fortress nor by the insurgents of Arezzo.

The latter were in full march for Florence; but when they learned of the arrival of an enemy corps, they retired to their village.

The Polish Legion lost Lieutenant Wasilkowski, and about twenty men in this combat, and among the wounded were Majors Kaminski, Karski, Captains Dembowski, Zoltowski, Pokrzywnicki, Winert, Rutier; the Lieutenants Dziurbas, Nolkiewicz and Wonsowicz, and about thirty men.

Major Kaminski especially gave evidence of admirable intrepidity and perseverance. Arrived at the bottom of the barricaded door, a ball struck him in the leg; though lame and losing his blood, he was still advancing when another bullet smashed his other leg; still falling, he crawled forward and gave with his last breath a heroic example to the detachment that followed him.

On the 25th (14 May), the corps started at break of day. It was busy throughout the day, relentlessly supporting the detachments protecting its flanks, which were constantly engaged by the rebels.

Castiglione-Fiorentino, a mountain town, surrounded by a good wall, was forced to open its gates, as soon as the insurgents were driven from all the posts in the neighborhood, and as soon as the preparations for the attack on the fortress were made. The Polish Corps crossed it, and it was then learned that the Aretines, with some cannon, had taken up their position in advance of their city, with the object of disputing its passage.

Accordingly, General Dąbrowski gave Colonel Chamand orders to proceed forward on the high road, with the 2nd Battalion and a cavalry squadron, to keep them in check, while he would move to the left with the corps to take a position near Bastardo, setting off by this movement between Florence and Arezzo. The rebels, having perceived this design, delivered several attacks in order to prevent its execution; but all their efforts were useless, and this position was carried before sunset. Colonel Chamand was killed in this skirmish, and the news of the death of this brave and worthy officer, generally loved, having reached the ranks, so much enraged the soldiers, that rushing on these hordes of rebels, they massacred a few hundred of them, cut one of their leaders into pieces, and took off a flag.

General Dąbrowski promoted, on the battlefield Chef de bataillon Forestier to the rank of Chef de Légion; Major Joseph Chlopicki, chef de bataillon, and Captain Ossowski to major of the 2nd Battalion. On the 26th (15 May), the Legion encamped near San Giovanni, hardly troubled by the rebels. They attacked the rearguard, however, but it soon got rid of them. Finally, the Poles entered Florence on 28th (17th) and stayed there on the 29th (18 May 1799).

The same day General Dąbrowski was ordered to occupy the Apennines, and to take command of the troops under the orders of General Merlin, under the name of the "Division of the Passes of the Apennines."

The Austro-Russians were already threatening to seize La Spezia and thereby cut off all communication with the Army of Italy.

In order not to waste time, General Dąbrowski divided the Legion, and ordered the 2nd Battalion, commanded by Chef Chlopicki, to immediately reinforce the San Pellegrino Gate, occupied by the 3rd Demi-brigade, forming the right of the division, to cover, with more force, the Modena Pass. The corps itself went through Lucca to Sarzana, leaving in the first a reserve composed of French troops and Polish cavalry. The enemy had already penetrated as far as Borghetto on the Vara, at Aulla on the Magra, and at Sassalbo on the summits of the Apennines. The 3rd Battalion, reinforcing the Fivizzano Gate, then joined the 55th Demi-brigade under the orders of Chef de brigade Ledru. The 1st Battalion reinforced the position opposite Borghetto, joining the 8th Demi-brigade, commanded by Brigadier Brun.

General Dąbrowski stopped at Sarzana with the grenadiers and chasseurs, and part of the cavalry under the orders of the Chef Forestier, to observe the enemy at Aulla. Its main purpose was to drive out the enemy, who was in force at Pontremoli, and to force him to leave the Apennines.

The 4 Prairial (23 May), he issued his orders. They were executed well, with the exception of the center column where the 3rd Battalion was located, which, instead of turning Pontremoli, leaving this city to its left in the order given, joined the reserve on the 8th (27th) near Scorsetolo, and did not occupy Monte Sungo. If this column had not missed the prescribed route, not one enemy could have escaped from this parade.

The left column under Ledru, of which the 1st Battalion was a part, attacked the enemy on the 6th (25th) near Borghetto, and pushed them back. Before then taking up a position at Cento-Croci, it attacked the enemy there again on the 7th, and compelled them, after a very obstinate fight, to take flight.

Brun went to Borgo-Taro on the 8th, and sent detachments to Bardi, Varzi, and Belforte, along Zeno and Taro, to observe the enemy at Fornovo. The corps of French light troops, with a Genoese battalion under the orders of Chief Graziani, drove out the enemy stationed between the Vara and the Magra, and occupied Cissa on the 8th (27 May).

General Dąbrowski commanded the reserve in person. He attacked the enemy, at Aulla, on all sides and drove them out of their position. The enemy stopped and strengthened themselves in Villafranca; but seeing that the general made arrangements to turn them with the chasseurs and attack them at the same time frontally with grenadiers, they retired to Filatiera, where they were pursued by the Polish troops who forced them to Pontremoli. However, the center column having been wrong, as we have seen, could no longer arrive as it should have done on the morning of the 8th at Monte-Sungo. Dąbrowski entered Pontemoli that day, which the enemy had left with all diligence, and sent back the center column to Monte Sungo, where the enemy, wishing to oppose any resistance, was at once attacked and routed. The column pushes out to San Terenzo, where the enemy rallied. The detachment of this column, destined to dislodge the Imperialists from Sassalbo, immediately attacked them, compelled them to retreat and pursued them to Culagna on the Secchia, and occupied on their left the post of Abatidi-Liveri.

The right-hand column, of which the 2nd Polish Battalion was a part, under the orders of the leader De Partes, went forward on the 6th, and attacked the enemy at Sillano on the Serchio on the 7th, put them to flight, and pursued them to Ospedaletto, where he was joined by the patrol of the center column. The greater part of the column was directed by De Partes to Frasinone, from where the enemy was always threatening to fall on his flank. The Austrians, protected by mountains, and defending the ground step by step, were nevertheless charged so impetuously that they were forced to retire to Paullo and Sassuolo. This column made its junction on its right with Montrichard's division, posted at Pieve-Pelago, which, having made a retrograde movement as far as the Apennines, after the retreat of the Army of Italy under the orders of General Moreau, had taken position.

The Gallo-Polish troops thus became, by this movement, the masters of the Apennines and all the passes which open into the plain. Six cannons were captured at Aulla, along with a large supply of cartridges that came in handy, since they were beginning to run short, large food stores abandoned by the enemy at Pontremoli, and six hundred prisoners, were the fruits of this victory. The Legion lost in these various fights about sixty men and counted as many wounded.

General Dąbrowski had, on the 8 Prairial (27 May), finished this expedition, and occupied the position that General Victor, detached from the Army of Italy, should have taken in the very moment when he was just arriving at the Spezia.

In the meantime, the Army of Naples, after having rapidly crossed the territory of the new Parthenopean Republic, arrived successively at Rome on 27 and 28 Floréal (16/17 May). General Macdonald, anxious to travel to Tuscany, spent a short time in Rome, and, to make his march more rapid, he abandoned the greater part of his heavy baggage, and kept only the artillery and ammunition, which were indispensable to him.

The French Army, left Viterbo on the 20th (18 May), passing through Siena, and arrived in Florence on 8 Prairial (26 May). Generals Gauthier, Miollis, and Vignolles, who were in Tuscany, facilitated General Macdonald's march, so much so that the activity of these distinguished officers controlled all the Apennines' passes.

As soon as he arrived in Florence, Macdonald took steps to improve his position and to communicate with General Moreau. All the detachments scattered in Tuscany and in the Roman Republic were united, and, containing nine thousand to ten thousand men, were placed under the orders of General Montrichard: they thus carried the effective force of the army of Macdonald to about twenty-eight thousand men. Moreover, the expected junction of General Victor's division, detached by Moreau to Tuscany, and the Polish Legion of Dąbrowski, would put Macdonald in a position to remain in the field.

Already General Dąbrowski had received the order, as soon as General Victor had occupied Pontremoli, and General Salm, who was part of the Army of Naples, at Sillano, to concentrate his division at Fivizzano, and to dismiss all demi-brigades and French detachments in their different divisions, with the exception of the 8th and a battalion of the 62nd. On 14th and 15th Prairial (2 - 3 June), the Polish Legion, joined to these last troops, occupied the passes Fosdinovo, Fivizzano and Sassalbo.

On the 16th (4 June), the 1st Battalion of the Legion, commanded by Chef de brigade Forestier, chased the enemy near Busano, and the 2nd Battalion, commanded by Chlopicki, went there to reinforce it.

On 19 Prairial (7 June), there arrived an order, dated 18th (6th), by which the division had to make its junction, on the 25th (13th), with the bulk of the army at Reggio, as a consequence of a resolution as bold and adventurous as General Macdonald had formed, which he had proposed to General Moreau.[6]

It was nothing less than breaking the blockade of Mantua and cutting Suvorov's line of operations in Italy. Seeing that this generalissimo had divided his forces into two great corps, one of which, under his direct command, was in Piedmont, and the other, commanded by General Kray, was in Mantua, Parma, Piacenza, the Modena

[6]See *Victoires et Conquêtes des Français, Vol. X, and l'Histoire des Guerres de la Révolution,* Vol. XII.

and Bologna, General Macdonald thought that by hurling themselves precipitately between these two corps, they might perhaps succeed in successively beating them and thus deliver Italy by a bold maneuver, worthy of the conceptions of Bonaparte. General Macdonald, therefore, invited Moreau to advance, with the Army of Italy, by the Levant River, on Pontremoli, to affect the meeting of the two armies between Parma and Piacenza.

General Moreau first appeared to adopt this plan, the importance of which he understood. He moved his army, but the irresolution of his character disposed him to do otherwise.

Already, on 20 Prairial (8 June), Macdonald had ordered nearly all the dispositions of this plan, concerted with Moreau, and which Moreau seemed disposed to execute in his own interest. On the same day, the Polish division moved to Sassalbo, and the 1st Battalion, under the orders of Chef de bataillon Brun, drove the enemy outposts out of Cervarezza and Campo-Forte.

On the 24th (12 June), the enemy wanted to stop the march of the army near Grassano on the Modolena, at the descent of the mountains. The enemy showed their infantry ranged in line, and their cavalry in the plain. The Gallo-Poles had very little cavalry, and as they were at Sassalbo it was almost impossible to get horses; besides, the enemy had armed peasants on all sides to dispute the passes.

The Polish Chasseur Battalion was divided into two parts on both flanks of the vanguard on the left, leaving the Crostolo on its right. The peasants were immediately dispersed by the chasseurs, and the enemy, on his side, sent detachments to meet ours. The division, however, continued to advance, while the enemy retreated from position to position; and, threatened by various detachments to be flanked, they retired to the Reggio plain. They encamped near Vezzano, pushing the outposts as far as the heights ahead of Rivalta. The Poles took, that day, some prisoners of war from the enemy; they killed some hussars and took their horses which could not cross the hedges and jump the ditches, being hotly pursued by the chasseurs. Many armed peasants were cut down without mercy.

On the morning of 25th (13 June), the division was ready to attack the enemy at Reggio, and set out, when it was learned that they had already left the place. The outposts pursued them, attacked their rear-guard at Castelnovo-di-sotto and then at Santa-Vittoria, and put them to flight. The division passed through Reggio, and took position on the road of Parma, near Quaresimo. Towards noon the Army of Naples, commanded by Macdonald, arrived from Modena and took up position on the rear of the Polish division. This junction took place after an obstinate and bloody battle, which General Macdonald, having under his command Generals Oliver and Forestier, delivered to General Prince Hohenzollern, on 24 Prairial (June 12th). General Forestier was killed, and Macdonald himself was wounded rather seriously.

On the 26th (14th), the Gallo-Polish Army moved to Parma, and on the 27th (15th) to Piacenza. The Legion went to Gaida by way of Montecchio and Monte-Chiaraguala to the camp of Vicoforte, near Parma, and supported its right on Montrichard's division. A battery of light artillery, two squadrons of Polish cavalry, under the orders of Chef d'escadron Biernacki, and a squadron of French cavalry, joined this division.

General Macdonald was very surprised, on his arrival at Piacenza, not to find news from General Moreau, who, fearing to compromise Genoa, remained in the latter town, and contented himself with sending to Bobbio and the Trebbia Valley, a detachment under the orders of General Lapoype.

In the meanwhile, the Austro-Russians, informed of the movements of General Macdonald, rallied their troops by forced marches, and, however painful, Macdonald's position had become, deprived of Moreau's co-operation, he nevertheless took the resolution to fight, by sparing Suvorov the task of anticipating him.[7]

---

[7]The Army of Naples, in its various situations in the north and south of Italy contained, on Prairial 7, Year VII (May 26, 1799), 41,383 men of all arms. Of this number, General Dąbrowski formed the 5th Division and had under his orders:

8th Demi-brigade d'infanterie légère.	555 men
1st Polish Legion	2,800 men
Polish cavalry	200 men
	Total 3,555 men.

As for the forces of the belligerent parties on the Trebbia, the Gallo-PolishArmy had 26,686 men, including the losses suffered at Modena, while the Austro-Russian Army had, on the day of battle, 36,785 men, not including detached corps.

On the 27th (15th), the Polish division passed the Taro; on the 28th (16th), it encamped near Ponte Nura, having its right on the road on which General Rusca leaned his left, and General Victor his right. On the 29th (17th), it crossed Piacenza and surrounded the citadel of this fortress, occupied by the enemy, so that with their cannon could do no harm to the column. The Poles left the Po nearby on their right. Victor's division formed the vanguard. It was followed by Rusca's division, and this by the Polish division. Having passed the Trebbia near San Antonio, the same march continued quietly to the Tidone. At the moment that the advance guard of Victor's division, under the command of General Charpentier, had crossed this river, they began to struggle, and the Polish outposts drove out those of the enemy. Victor's division passed the Tidone; General Rusca's cavalry performed the same movement with part of the infantry and artillery, which preceded Victor's division on the right. The remaining infantry and artillery of Rusca's division was formed in line. The Polish division formed column on the left wing of Rusca's division. The battalion of chasseurs was sent forward and crossed the Tidone to cover the front; but General Dąbrowski, perceiving that the enemy was beginning to turn to the right, gave orders to Chef Brun to go, with part of the French cavalry, and the 1st Polish Battalion, on the left, towards Cantone and Arcello, which prevented the enemy from crossing the river and falling on his left flank. The division deployed in ranks by battalions, refusing its left; the artillery was obliged to remain inactive on the high road; the ground, which was very broken, prevented it from maneuvering.

In this position, the Polish vanguard pushed Suvorov's outposts to Castel San Giovanni, where his army corps was; but being attacked then by superior forces, the vanguard was obliged to fall back. All that had passed the Tidone soon came to blows and was forced to cross the river again. To give time to the troops of Rusca's division, on which the enemy fell en masse, to pass the Trebbia, General Charpentier made a movement on the left with his division, thus he covered his retreat and prevented the enemy from crossing the river on the very back of Rusca's division. The Polish division followed, the movement to the left of General Charpentier, who, observing the enemy, sought every means of falling on their flanks; but some battalion fires and some movements made the enemy give up this project. The night having come, the army was ordered to take up a position behind the Trebbia, occupying its right bank. As a result, the divisions withdrew consecutively; the Polish division formed the rearguard. The Austro-Russians pursued very feebly, considering the great darkness of the night. In this affair many Poles perished, and Major Iasinski, who commanded them, was taken prisoner of war. After passing the Trebbia in the night, the army took position near Gossolengo, on the left wing. But Brun, with his detachment of French troops, and the 1st Polish Battalion, under the command of Konopka, returned by Campremoldo-di-Sopra to the division, and covered the left wing of the army.

At daybreak on the 30th (18 June), it found itself in this position. The 2nd Polish Battalion and the French cavalry, under Chlopicki's command, passed the Trebbia and occupied Casaliggio. It is well to observe here that the Tidone, the Trebbia, and almost all the rivers that flow from the Apennines that throw themselves into the Po, are of considerable breadth, but fordable, in summer, in many places, both for the infantry and for the artillery, with the difference, however, that the artillery can maneuver only with difficulty off of the highways, and the cavalry out of the bed even of these rivers, because of the woods, ditches, canals and vineyards that border the two banks. The same day General Victor took command of the left wing of the army, composed of Victor's divisions, commanded by General Charpentier, and those of Rusca and Dąbrowski.

Towards noon General Dąbrowski received orders to cross the Trebbia with his division and to occupy Casaliggio, Tuna, and Gazzola. He destined the 8th Demi-brigade, the 1st Polish Battalion, and part of the Polish cavalry to occupy Gazzola; the grenadiers, the chasseurs, and the 3rd Battalion, with the rest of the cavalry under the command of Chef de brigade Forestier, who was with General Dąbrowski was to occupy Tuna. The 2nd Battalion, commanded by Chlopicki, with the French cavalry, had already taken a position at Casaliggio. The division was formed in three columns and crossed the Trebbia at the sight of the enemy, at the place where it was most fordable. The enemy outposts were immediately put to flight; but as soon as the Poles arrived at the positions of Tuna and Gazzolo, the whole Austro-Russian army fell on them, and attacked with all their strength the positions the Poles had occupied. Brun, with his demi-brigade and the 1st Polish

Battalion, commanded by Konopka the Younger, tried to reach Tuna; but finding it already occupied, he was obliged to retire to the mountains. General Dąbrowski, wishing to follow him, formed at once an angle composed of a front and a flank to maintain itself in its position; but after having had a cannon dismounted and the commanding officer mortally wounded, incessantly attacked with impetuosity by the enemy, it began to retire towards Casaliggio. The detachment, which had occupied this post, having also been attacked with superior forces, had slowly withdrawn behind the Trebbia and had taken up position there. Seeing that the enemy was still ahead of them, they threw themselves into the Trebbia; the grenadiers and the 3rd Battalion defended themselves with the greatest obstinacy; but surrounded by the enemy, a large part was taken prisoner of war, and the rest retreated to the 2nd Battalion, whose commander Chlopicki had displayed that day a rare military talent. The division commander, Forestier, Chefs de bataillon Zawadzki and Malachowski, and several other officers, after unheard-of efforts, were among the prisoners taken by the enemy. General Dąbrowski himself had been in the hands of the enemy's cavalry, and although wounded, he had cut his way out with his saber. The cavalry officers Biernacki and Potrykowski, as well as his aide-de-camp Stuart, fought as lions against the Austrian dragoons and the Cossacks, in order not to let their general be taken. At last Dąbrowski cut off the lance of a Cossack who was about to pierce him, shouting "rendezvous" at him in Russian, and he had time to push his horse towards the river, and swim across it. The officers of his staff followed him, and Captain Stuart was wounded. The general, having joined the 2nd Battalion, took position on the left wing of the army, which during the affair had quietly remained in the camp. Brun, being obliged to open, with the 1st Battalion, a passage through the enemy, did not reach the corps until the next day at noon.

The next day, the whole enemy army presented itself in front of the French army, on the other side of the Trebbia, the right wing of the one far exceeding the left of the other. General Victor arrived at the moment when the enemy seemed to want to cross the river from Tuna. The whole of the opposite wing turned to the left to overtake the enemy, where they formed, arriving at this point, in battalion columns of companies. On the right of the Polish division followed Rusca's division, and then that of Victor. The enemy was attacked in this manner in columns and was overthrown on all points.

In this situation the 2nd Polish Battalion took two cannons from the Russians, and the French drove the enemy beyond the Trebbia; but the cavalry, though charging the enemy could not pursue them far, because the ground was extremely rough, and it took up a position behind the ditches and impenetrable hedges, reinforced by its second line. This second line was impetuously attacked, but it was routed like the first. There was desperate fighting on both sides, despite the fatigue of everyone. At last the enemy again received reinforcements, and then they managed to force the Gallo-Polish Army back across the river. Chlopicki was consequently obliged to abandon the two cannon he had taken. He reached the old position on the right bank of the Trebbia in front of the enemy, without the enemy daring to pursue him, and nightfall put an end to this terrible combat. The French army had to regret the loss, on that day, of the brave Leblanc leader of the 16th Dragoon Regiment, who, although mortally wounded, exhorted his dragoons to avenge his wound.

Brun having opened a path through the Austro-Russians with his demi-brigade and the Polish battalion, had held them in such respect, that he had neither the time nor the boldness to fall upon the left flank of the army. Major Konopka, commanding the 1st Battalion, was seriously wounded. During the night the division made a movement to its left, to be opposite Rivalta; it was shut up by Calvin's brigade.

On 1 Messidor (19 June), all the Gallo-Polish Army attacked again that of the Austro-Russians. The Polish division crossed the Trebbia near Rivalta. It marched by its right, so that the 2nd Battalion was in the lead: the battalion composed of grenadiers, chasseurs, and the remains of the 3rd Battalion followed; the 2nd and Calvin's Brigade formed the rear. The land on the other side of the river was not conducive to the movement of artillery and cavalry, so they remained in reserve on this side to protect the retreat when needed. Brun, with his demi-brigade and 1st Battalion, covered this movement to the left.

The enemy wanted to dispute the crossing of the Trebbia but was immediately driven from Rivalta.

The division made a half turn to the right, whose pivot was this village, and posted itself forward. However, the interval being too great, General Dąbrowski redirected a French demi-brigade, which had not yet completed its movement, and placed itself there to cover it. By this movement this position became perpendicular to the Trebbia and the army. The attack began in steps; Calvin's brigade first, then the Polish Legion, and then the French demi-brigade. The enemy was dislodged from one position to another. They were chased out of all the houses and gardens they had occupied and they were constantly pursued. The right wing of the division had already passed Tuna and had joined Rusca's division, which had attacked and pushed the enemy to the front, so that the Polish Corps was obliged to move even further to the left. Calvin's Brigade, in turn, fell on the enemy's right flank with astonishing bravery, and routed it, without ever allowing it to resume its position. The enemy again received reinforcements, and the division made a new movement to the left to turn its flanks, take it in the rear, and make room for Rusca's division, so that it could advance further. The enemy artillery was already in full retreat, when suddenly, by an impulse which came at last from the center of the army, and which communicated itself to Rusca's division, this division was forced to retreat; the right wing of the Polish division was already beginning to follow this movement; but General Dąbrowski, who had two wounded horses under him, hastened to it, and brought the Legion back to the enemy, seized Rivalta while Calvin's Brigade took up positions on the heights to the left of that village. This movement prevented the Imperialists from continuing further and did not allow them to push between Rusca's division and the Polish division. The good countenance, especially of the French demi-brigade, which was on their right, made them fail in their enterprise.

The Gallo-Polish Army finally retreated behind the Trebbia, resumed its position on the right bank of this river, and remained there until night. General Dąbrowski was slightly injured. His aide-de-camp Pflugbeile had his wounded horse under him, and could not return until two days later, because he was obliged to march on foot. For the rest, we lost a few people that day; six hundred prisoners of war were taken, and Calvin's Brigade took off a flag.

Thus, ended the terrible days of the Trebbia. Had heroism and bravery been able to triumph over numbers, the Austro-Russian army would have been destroyed. Of all the generals of the Army of Naples, Watrin and Calvin remained alone untouched; the others were all either killed or wounded: among the first were Forest and Cambrai, and among the last Olivier, who had his leg shot off, Rusca, Dąbrowski, Salm, Grandjean, Sarrazin, Liébaud, and Blondeau; in all, twenty-eight to thirty senior officers. Some demi-brigades lost up to forty officers; the rest in proportion. According to these data, we can estimate the loss of the Gallo-Poles at seven thousand, and that of the Allies at five thousand-six hundred men *hors de combat.*

General Rusca, commander of the 2nd Division, in spite of his personal bravery, did not retain all his presence of mind in the days of the Trebbia. General Dąbrowski was obliged to bring back to the enemy the 2nd Division which was beginning to fold. Nevertheless, General Rusca, in his report on the various engagements of that day (1 Messidor), believed, blaming another for the mistakes which he had committed there, to wash himself of the reproach which they laid on him: "It is certain that this day would have been to our advantage and assured forever the liberty of Italy, if the Generals Calvin and Dąbrowski had been able to pierce and support our left. It is still believed that General Charpentier was too slow in his passage; it is true that he was opposed by almost all the artillery of the enemy; but as soon as he saw that its fire was on our flank, in pressing his movement, while we were pressing him in the flank, we would have inevitably been the masters of his artillery, if he had wanted to hold."

The order was given to the whole army, during the night, to begin the retreat. The Polish Legion left for San Giorgio on the Nura, without being pursued by the enemy.

Brigadier Brun then joined with his demi-brigade and the 1st Battalion. General Rusca, having been wounded, was then taken prisoner of war at Piacenza. The left wing of the French army consisted of only two divisions; that of Victor, commanded by General Charpentier, and that of Dąbrowski. The Polish Legion was placed to the left of the division.

On 2 Messidor (20 June), around noon, the outposts began to skirmish and cannon began to fire on both sides. During this time the army corps retreated, although the enemy managed to slip between our division and the army corps itself. General Victor fixed the retrograde march on Cadeo and Firenzuola, with the enemy light troops attacking, and being obliged to pass by very small roads with all the artillery and the train of the army. It was necessary to think seriously of putting it in safety. A French demi-brigade and the 2nd Polish Battalion were immediately ordered to cover them, while the corps itself would protect them frontally and in the flanks. All attempts by the enemy to take it were useless. He charged on all sides several times, and it was only after having valiantly repulsed these attacks, that this corps was able to make his retreat. Once the train was safe, he finally began to march in four columns, formed of two wings of each division; the 1st Battalion accordingly covered the retreat of the left column.

The enemy pursued the Gallo-Polish army, and charged it impetuously into front and flank, but was repulsed with the same bravery. At each step it was necessary to jump the ditches, to cross the hurdles, to endure the most terrible fire, and often to leave detachments behind. The whole train was, however, fortunately saved, and not a wagon fell into the hands of the enemy. General Dąbrowski was again, in this affair, enveloped by the enemy light infantry; it seemed impossible that he could escape them, but the brave grenadiers of the 1st Demi-brigade, commanded by Captain Castel, perceiving him in this danger, rushed to his assistance, dispersed the enemy, and gave him time to cross the ditch and get to safety. His horse was twice wounded in this melee. His suite was so scattered that the two service officers, Captain Chlusowicz and Lieutenant Nieborski, were the only ones to follow him.

In this state of affairs, General Victor was compelled not to retire by Firenzuola, but by Castel-Arquato. The division passed the Larda and was able to camp there. For his part the enemy, seeing that all his attempts to stop it were unsuccessful, ceased to pursue it. We continued marching on the 3rd (21 June) on Borgo-San-Domino. The Taro was passed, and the Polish 1st Legion joined the army corps, and took up position at Ponte-Taro-Rovinato.

The 1st (22nd), Victor's division detached itself from the body of the army, and left to go to the mountains of Pontremoli, always following the Taro. The Gallo-Polish division, which was in the rearguard, arrived at Reggio, on the 5th (22nd), without being pursued by the enemy. It left the French artillery and cavalry, and went to occupy the mountains of Fivizzano, with the 17th and the 55th Line Demi-brigades and 8th Légère. The corps passed through Modena, Bologna, and then to the Apennines.

According to the new organization that had been made in the army by 4 Messidor, Year VII (22 June 1799) agenda, issued on the Enza Bridge, it resulted that General Watrin, commander of the division, composed of the advance guard and its battle corps, had for Généraux de brigade General Calvin and Chef de brigade d'Arnault; for Chief of Staff, Adjutant-General Gautrin.

The advance guard, under the command of General Calvin, was composed of the 15th Légère, the 11th Demi-brigade, and the 1st Hussars.

The 1st Division, composed of the 12th, 30th, 73rd, and 97th Demi-brigades, the 7th and 19th Chasseurs à cheval Regiments, as well as the 26th and a light artillery company.

The 2nd Division, under the command of General Dąbrowski, was composed of his legion, the 8th, 17th, and the 55th Demi-brigades. The 3rd Division, under the command of General Montrichard, remained as it was.

The 4th Division, called the reserve, under the orders of Adjutant-general Pamphile-Lacroix, was composed of 62nd and 78th Demi-brigades, 16th and 19th Dragoons, and half of a light artillery company.

On the 7th (25th), the headquarters and the Legion arrived at Fivizzano. The division sent out its outposts to Castelnuovo-ne-Monti, Cervarezza, Culagna, etc.

In the bloody and terrible battle of the Trebbia, as well as in the other battles in which one fought with unparalleled fury, the Polish Legion suffered enormous losses. At that time the Polish soldier braved death with all the more rage and animosity, as he faced his two sworn enemies, the two oppressors of his unfortunate country; that he saw in front of him the same Suvorov, with the same Muscovites who had soaked their hands in the horrible carnage of the Praga, a suburb of Warsaw. To avenge the death of their brothers on their murderers, to crush the Coalition troops of their tyrants, that was the aim of the Legions, and if fate again betrayed their hopes this time, they proved by falling at their posts, competing for victory with their courage on these fatal days, where if they were always devoted to the French cause, they were still more so when a circumstance of any kind came to bind them to that of oppressed Poland. The Legion had lost one thousand men killed or prisoners, and about five hundred wounded, besides a considerable number of officers wounded and prisoners. It is true that it did a great deal of harm to the enemy, but its losses were none the less irreparable.

If, however, any misfortune brings its compensation, it had at least the advantage that many Polish soldiers who had been made prisoners of war found the means of escaping, and returned to their units; still others, Poles in the Russian and Austrian armies, captured that day, enlisted with joy into the Legion's battalions.

At that time, the cavalry could not survive in the mountains because of the scarcity of forage, so the Polish regiment was sent to Massa and Carrara, where the party that had remained in Lucca, under the orders of General Karwowski, came to join it.[8]

After tracing all these events, we cannot help but say a few words about the formation of the Roman legions by Championnet, while he was commander-in-chief. The French superior officers, so necessary to their own army, could not be employed to command these new troops; the national military was inexperienced; it was therefore necessary to cast a glance at those of the Poles who had no direct command in the Polish legions, and to this end Generals Georges Grabowski and Wladislas Iabionowski were invited to preside over this formation. It was then also that several other Poles such as Joseph Turski, Nielepiec, Szumlanski, Lapinski, Zenowicz, Deschert and others began to gather around these military notabilities. Kasimir de la Roche, whom we had lost sight of since the first chapters of this history, also labored to hasten the march of the Army of Naples after the disasters of Legnago and Verona. He accepted the rank of captain in the new Roman legions and was attached for a time to the staff of General Grabowski. However, in spite of the example and the efforts of these various Polish officers, for

[8]See Supporting Documents Nos. 53 and 54, in which we give the two reports of Generals Victor and Calvin, who maintained a more direct communication with the Polish division, and who consequently furnish more details on the latter than are given by other French reports.

the organization of the Roman Army, the lack of organization, of pecuniary means, and especially the lack of soldiers and NCOs, blocked all these projects. Moreover, in spite of the bravery displayed by some voluntary detachments of the Roman corps under the orders of Championnet, only two distinguished officers remained of this army. These were the Prince de Santa Croce and Palombini, who owed their origin and rank as generals to this formation of the Roman Army.

CHAPTER TEN

March of the Legion. — Wladislas Iablonoski. — Strzalowski, Kasimir Konopka. — Depot at Nice, Pflugbeile, Zagorski, Au, Stuart, and Potrymowski. — Paul Tremo, Dembowski, Ascier, and Smauch Are Attached to the Staff of the Major General. — Downarowicz, Borowski. — Severoli Attacks the Enemy Advance Posts near Monte di Carega. — The Citadels of Turin and Alessandria Capitulate. — Mantua is Heavily Pressed by the Austro-Russian Army. — Position of the Enemy Quarters. — Ost, Lattermann, and Zopf. — Bagration. — Foissac-Latour, Commander of Mantua. — Conduct of the Austrians vis-à-vis the Polish Prisoners. — General Jozef Wielhorski is Charged with the Defense of Migliaretto. — Vigorous Sortie of the Garrison. — The Polish Legion Distinguishes Itself. — Iakubowski Commands the Artillery of the Fort. — Wolinski, Borkowski, Skwarkowski, Strzemecki, and Potocki. — The Besieging Army Redoubles its Vigor. — Axamitowski, Viereck, Francois, Krawczynski, Kohylanski, and Pieckowski. — General Kray Opens the First Parallel. — Anonymous Letter to General Foissac-Latour. — Kosinski Identifies Himself as its Author. — Fort Saint-Georges is Evacuated. — The Commanding General Reports on the Devotion of the Polies that Occupy It. — Advice of the Officers Convoked by General Foissac-Latour. — Parliamentary. — They Decide to Capitulate. — Propositions of the Garrison. — They are Refused by the Besieging Army. — Mantua Capitulates. — Clauses of the Capitulation. — Machiavellian Conduct of the Austrians. — Bad Treatment Towards the Polish Soldiers.

The Polish Legions, weakened by the various engagements, looked to repair their losses.

General Vladislas Jablonowski, nicknamed "The Black," an old classmate of Napoleon at Brienne, the same man we saw arrive at Rome from Constantinople with General Rymkicwicz, and who had initially accepted service in the Roman troops, came to join the Polish Legions, and had been named général de brigade. The Poles occupied themselves equally with completing the cadres of their units and officers were newly dispatched to the various prisoner of war camps to recruit Poles. To more easily achieve this goal, these officers were presented to General-in-Chief Moreau, commander of the Army of Italy, and took orders as a result.

The outposts of two armies were sometimes harassed near Castelnovo-ne'-Monti, but no remarkable engagement had taken place.

The Army of Naples, under the orders of Macdonald, commencing, after the battle of La Trebbià, to retire to Genoa by its right wing, the Legion's turn soon arrived. It left Fivizzano on 1 Thermidor (19 July 1799), and took position, the 2nd, at Fosdinovo, where the whole division was to assemble.

The Polish cavalry came to join it on the 3rd (21st) at Sarzana, and the whole corps continued its march along the coast of the Mediterranean to Genoa.

Colonel Strzalkowski, who was at Milan at the beginning of hostilities under General Schérer, and who had left that capital of the Cisalpine Republic with the French army, had followed the staff of General Moreau; he also arrived at Genoa with his compatriots, and took command of the Legion.

Major Kazimirz Konopka, commander of the depot in Milan, also came there following the army and at the head of five hundred Poles, as well as various officers of the 2nd Legion, sick or wounded in the battles of Magnano and Verona. This little corps repeatedly found the opportunity to distinguish itself during the retreat on Genoa.

A detachment of the Polish artillery, which had been part of Montrichard's division, and which occupied, before the battle of Trebbia, the Apennines, between Florence and Bologna, also arrived at the headquarters, under the leadership of Lieutenant Zielinski.

General Dąbrowski obtained the order to establish a depot in Nice: he gave command of it to his aide-de-camp Pflugbeile, later named Major of the Legion. Chef de bataillon Zagorski's battalion was to assemble and form a depot for the 2nd Legion; Major Au for the 1st, Captain Stuart for the artillery, and Captain Potrykowski for the cavalry.

All the sick, the officers, the wounded soldiers, and the baggage that were not needed, were embarked at Genoa and transported to Nice.

The newly arrived soldiers with Major Konopka were distributed into the Legion, except for those who were part of the 2nd; and the 1st Legion, joined to the regiment of cavalry, was then about two thousand five hundred strong under arms.

General Dąbrowski elevated Major Dembowski to the rank of chef de bataillon, and Major Paul Tremo, brother of Elie Tremo, who died on the battlefield at Traetia, appointed both as his aides-de-camp. Captain Ascier and Lieutenant Artillery Szmauch were added to the general staff. He also replaced the dead officers or those lost as prisoners of war in proportion as the number of soldiers increased. The battalion of grenadiers and that of chasseurs were reorganized: the 1st at the orders of Major Downarowicz, and the last at those of Major Borowski.

On 8 Thermidor (26 July), the division reinforced by the Calvin Brigade occupied the mountains and outlets of Toriglio. General Dąbrowski established his headquarters at Toriglio itself.

At that time, General Macdonald, suffering from his wounds, left the army and went to Paris. The Polish cavalry remained at Genoa, except for a squadron, which went to Cosella, to maintain communication between the Cosella and Toriglio.

The grenadiers and the 1st Battalion were placed at the latter place; the 2nd at Scafera; the 3rd at Caglio, and the chasseurs at Monte-Bruno. The division occupied positions between Cabane and Coreglia, joining the left wing of Watrin's division and the Barba-Gelata post, joining to the right of Miollis' division. This position was important, it is true, but too tiring. The troops got up every three days, so that the Polish Legion also occupied it. The enemy outposts often came to harass the French posts near Monte-di-Carega. General Dąbrowski sent Chef Severoli with a battalion of Cisalpine troops to hunt them, which he did with great bravery and fearlessness. The heights were then occupied, and the enemy dared not show himself.

Such was the state and position of the 1st Polish Legion under the immediate orders of General Dąbrowski, when new setbacks occurred.

They threatened a nation, so long victorious, and brought on the battle of Novi, the results of which were so fatal to French arms. But, before continuing the course of events, let's go back to the Polish

2nd Legion, which we left locked in Mantua, under the orders of General Wielhorski.

The results of the battle of the Trebbia, which had so much affected the fate of Italy, necessarily implied the loss of the strongholds that were in the power of the republican armies. While the Generals Moreau and Macdonald maneuvered to affect the meeting of the troops under their command, the Austro-Russian divisions had vigorously pushed the siege of the various strongholds. Seeing the two generals-in-chief abandon successively the various regions of Italy, the French commanders lost the hope of being rescued.
The citadel of Turin, where General Fiorella commanded, capitulated on 23 June, after a continuous bombardment, led by Kaim.

The citadel of Alessandria, having a garrison under the orders of General Gardanne, bombarded by Field Marshal Suvorov himself, also capitulated on 22 July. Mantua, the famous Mantua, the bone of contention of the warring parties, since the opening of the campaign of 1796, after the events of the Trebbia, saw before its ramparts about forty thousand Austro-Russian troops, and six hundred guns, under the command of General Kray.

The siege army was distributed into three camps, which enveloped most of the outer enclosure of the fortress. Generals Ott, Lattermann and Zopf commanded before the Pradella Gate. The Russians, under the orders of Bagration, camped separately and pressed closely the citadel or Porto Fortress. All the inhabitants of the country around were forced to help the besiegers.

The Général de division Foissac-Latour, named commander of the Mantua Fortress, was there since 9 Germinal, Year VII (29 March 1799), and the following day, by an order of the day, he had given showed his authority. The total strength of Mantua consisted of a garrison of about twelve thousand men. It was therefore in this situation of the two warring parties that the Austrians began the siege.

Although Austria's resentment was great towards the French who had so often crushed its armies, in its pitiful and petty vengeance, it seemed to devote even more hatred to the soldiers of the Polish legions, whom it considered as deserters from the Austrian army. In fact, from the beginning of the siege, whenever Polish officers had the misfortune, in their sorties, to fall into the hands of their oppressors, they were forced to serve in the Austrian army as simple soldiers. Such conduct infuriated General Foissac-Latour, and he did not fail to express it to General Kray, by a letter he addressed to him, on 24 Germinal, inviting him to act from now on with more respect towards the brave allies of France. Much better, as in the midst of the arrangements that the Commander-in-Chief had taken for his garrison, the 2nd Polish Legion was not treated on a par with the other troops, General Wielhorski submitted on this subject some observations to the justice of Foissac Latour, and, by his letter of 28 Germinal (17 April), this general rendered a complete satisfaction to the legitimate demands of General Wielhorski, by ordering that the Polish Legion should be included in the distributions like all the rest of the garrison. By the same letter, General Wielhorski obtained command of the advanced posts of Migliaretto, which the enemy had attacked the same day.

About this mission, General Foissac-Latour, in his *Précis sur le siêge de Mantoue*, page 70, speaking of the Polish general, adds: "General Wielhorski, a general officer full of courage, knowledge, and presence of spirit deserved all the more the confidence I had in assigning him this post, that to all these qualities he joined the republican zeal, which had caused him to abandon his fortune in Poland to meet in the south of Europe, the defenders of liberty, who was always dear to his valiant nation."[1]

Invested in such an important position, General Wielhorski, with his ordinary activity, was engaged in the work of the defense of his assigned post; but his fatigues having caused him great suffering, it was Citizen Girard, chef de bataillon in the 31st Demi-brigade, who was appointed temporary commander of Migliaretto, under the orders of General Wielhorski. The agenda of 4 Floréal (23 April 1799), which had announced it, had decided at the same time that no deserters were to be received in the place, with the exception of the Poles alone, because it was said, "This republican nation can supply good recruits to the Polish Corps who serve it."

---

[1]This work, from which we detail the details of the siege of Mantua, is entitled: *Précis ou Journal historique et raisonné des opérations militaires et administratives qui ont eu lieu dans la place de Mantoue, depuis le 9 germinal jusqu'au 10 thermidore de l'an VIII de la République française, sous le commandement de F.P. Foissac-Latour, général de division; écrit par lui-même,* (Paris : Magimel, 1800).

The besieging army, however, pushed the siege work with remarkable vigor; and the General Commander-in-Chief of the fortress, issued an order of the day, dated 6 Floréal (25 April), calling his superior officers to a council of war, to render all more effective his defense measures. This defense council, which assembled each day at the General-in-Chief's for ten days, was presided over by ten members: 1. General-in-Chief Foissac-Latour, President; 2.) Général de brigade Meyer, commander at Fort Saint-Georges; 3.) Général de brigade Monnet, commander at the citadel; 4.) Général de brigade Wielhorski, commander at Migliaretto; 5.) Chef de brigade Balleydier, commander at Pradella; 6.) Adjutant-General Gastine, Chief of the General Staff; 7.) the Chef de brigade Borthon, commanding the artillery; 8.) Chef de brigade Maubert, commander of the engineers; 9.) Lieutenant Pagès, Commander of the navy; 10.) the War Commissioner Leclèrc, serving as secretary.

Various works of the besiegers being undertaken to press the fortress more closely, the General-in-Chief, by his extraordinary order of the 15 Floreal (4 May), had announced a sortie by all of the fortress' gates. According to the general provisions, this sortie was composed of four principal columns, namely, that which was to leave by the Cérèse Gate, that by the Saint George Gate, that by the Citadel Gate, and that finally by the Pradella Gate.

The day of 19 Floreal (8 May) was indicated for this feat of arms; the Polish Legion, which was to cover itself with glory by competing with its brothers-in-arms on this occasion, had the honor of forming the first main column, left by the Cérèse Gate, and was commanded by the Chef de brigade Louis Dembowski.

The action that followed this general sortie was long and vigorous; it was fought fiercely by both sides. The Polish Legion had six men killed, both non-commissioned officers and soldiers; ten officers and fifty-nine non-commissioned officers and soldiers wounded; nineteen NCOs or soldiers lost as prisoner. General Wielhorski, in his report of 19 Floreal, did justice to the valor of the troops under his command, as well as to a detachment of the French 31st Demi-brigade.

Chef de brigade Dembowski, who commanded the second column that left by the Cérèse Gate, carried away by his personal bravery, forgot himself, in the midst of an action, to the point of striking some soldiers under his command. This circumstance gave rise to a denunciation which was leveled against him. The officers of the Legion addressed their remonstrances to General Foissac-Latour; but the latter, to stifle the germ of misunderstanding at its birth, which could be fatal in the position of the troops, recommended that the issue be forgotten. The results of this conciliation were not at first fruitful, but then calm was restored. All these steps gave rise, however, to detailed explanations that can be found in the supporting documents.

Whatever may be the result of these differences, the soldiers of the 2nd Polish Legion deserved the most honorable mention from the General-in-Chief for the sortie of 19 Floreal. Of the various awards that were given to the bravest, the agenda of the 23 April (May 17, 1799) mentioned Citizen Lakubowski, commander of the fort's artillery, who deserved great praise for the manner in which he directed his service, and which obtained, in the name of the French nation, a reward of one hundred francs. As to the second column at the Cérèse Gate, directed by General Wielhorski, and in which the detachment of the French 31st Demi-brigade acquired a fine reputation, the General-in-Chief awarded a gratuity of twelve hundred livres to be distributed to the men of this column.

However, to alter the joy of the deeds of this memorable day, the Polish Legion also noted the death of several brave officers and the loss was greater than could be replaced by other fellow warriors. Among the dead were Captains Wolinski, Borkowski and Skwarkowski, Lieutenant Strzemecki an Sous-Lieutenant Potocki. More than two hundred men were killed, wounded or made prisoners of war. Chef Krollikiewicz, Captains Sieradzki, Biernacki; Lieutenants Borkowski, Bergonzoni, Litwinski and Lipnski were among the wounded.

Among so many brave men who distinguished themselves in all these deadly combats, it is necessary to cite Lieutenant Kobylanski, of the artillery, who lost his left arm to the attack at the Pradella Gate. A lieutenant of the same corps, Pieckowski, was wounded defending the Ceres Tower. In a word, the Polish artillery attracted the admiration of the whole garrison, during the whole time of the siege, by the accuracy, precision, and indefatigable activity of both the officers and Polish gunners.

Meanwhile the fatal moment was approaching, when all this bravery and the most heroic devotion were to succumb to disease and the progressive weakening of the garrison. On 10 July, General Kray attacked the fortress on the south side, and General Saint-Julien succeeded in capturing the entrenchments at the Cérèse Gate by force, as well as of the bridgehead, which covered the sluice. In the night of 13th to 14th, the first parallel was opened facing the works of the Thé Island. General Foissac-Latour responded vigorously, but the enemy kept on beating front and back the entrenchments of the Thé Island and Migliaretto. With the Pradella front being the weakest, General Kray chose it for his main attack. On 29 Messidor (17 July), the work of the enemy was pushed with amazing activity.[2]

It was in the meantime that among the various projects that were debated in the defense council, to select the most suitable means, that on one day an anonymous letter was received by General Foissac-Latour, containing the critical observations on the provisions given by his orders. Instead of being angry, the Commander-in-Chief, by an order of the day, praised the zeal of the author of the letter in question, and desired to know the anonymous author. Adjutant General Kosinski sent, in a second letter dated 1 Thermidor (19 July), the same observations, and signed it. The next day General Foissac-Latour made him a flattering reply and invited him to his house to talk with him.

From 3 to 6 Thermidor (21 - 24 July), the besiegers' attack became even more deadly. General Wielhorski was then kept in bed by gout, and it was General Fontanier and Chef Girard, who replaced him at such an important moment. Chef de bataillon Axamitowski then depended on the former and received his orders. Général de brigade Meyer, commander of the defense of Migliaretto and Thé Island, replacing General Wielhorski, who was ill, did not cease, on the other hand, to praise the activity of the Commander of Artillery Iakubowski, who was in Fort Saint George, which had to be evacuated as it could no longer be held. The loss of the Saint George garrison was considerable. Général de brigade Meyer, in his report of 8 Thermidor (20 July), to General Foissac-Latour, could not refrain from making a truly touch-

[2]See supporting documents Nos. 65, 66, 67, 68 and 69, where one will find all the details of the feats of arms of the Polish Legion from 18 Messidor to 1 Thermidor (July 6-19, 1799).

ing picture of it. "These brave men," he said, "as commendable by their disinterestedness, their discipline, their delicacy, as by a foolhardy courage, perceived, at the moment when I ordered their retreat, a few small cannons that were on the flank of the bridgehead, and that, for want of sufficient horses, could not be brought into the city, so many of them immediately grabbed the guns and by hand pulled them back into the city.

"Nothing was equal to their pain when they learned of the order to evacuate Fort Saint-Georges; they called it their "favorite colony", because they had seen its birth and the development of it; they had so many times cemented its maintenance by their blood! You remember, general, that the various camps I had established looked like so many separate villages: the men who had gathered there had built, each at his pleasure, large and convenient huts on the ruins of a city once rich and flourishing by its industry and its arts. Each cabin had its shelters against the sun, domestic animals, its garden formed with taste and intelligence, its household established in form. It was there, under a burning and murderous climate, that they kept talking about their dear country, the mourning of their families, the splendor of their ancient exploits; it was there, in the midst of the sweetest harmony, that they had so much faith in all the privations imposed upon them by the present moment, and that they were constantly drawing new strength from the love of their country and in that noble emulation that was established among them."

Finally, the place was no longer tenable, for the dike that joined the of St. Nicholas Bastion to the Migliaretto Bastion No. 2, having been broken, the waters flowed in with a frightening rapidity. The enemy did not pause his fire, and the bombs and shells were falling day and night into the city.[3]

General Foissac-Latour, wishing to fully understand the state of the defense, convoked, at ten a.m., on 9 Thermidor, a general council of all the superior and general officers of the garrison, with an invitation previously made by the Chief of Staff, to each, to go to the front of the Allied attack before going to the meeting, so that they could give an informed opinion. The General-in-Chief was himself ready to go

[3]See supporting documents Nos. 71, 72, 73, 74, 75, and 76, containing the particulars of the feats of arms of the Legion.

there, to reason with them, when the enemy's batteries ceased firing and a French officer announced the arrival of a parliamentarian. He was in a boat and had a white flag displayed, asking to be admitted on the part of the besieging general; he proposed to stop fire against the fortress and that those of the Austrians was already suspended.

General Foissac-Latour acceded to this request, and only an hour afterwards Count Orlandini, Lieutenant-Colonel to the corps of the Imperial Engineers arrived; he was accompanied by a lieutenant of hussars and an aide-de-camp of General Kray. Orlandini then handed a letter from General Kray, dated from Castellucchio, 26 July 1799 (8 Thermidor, Year VII), which was a final summons, which provided official proof of the retreat of the two French armies, beyond the Apennines, which gave him no hope of being rescued.

After reading this letter, the General-in-Chief replied to the parliamentarian that he did not believe that circumstances were as extreme for the fortress of Mantua as the Austrian general said; that besides, finding himself at the moment of entering the council of war, he would inform it of General Kray's letter, and keep him informed of the decision.

Lieutenant-Colonel Orlandini remarked that he was enjoined to wait for an answer and begged the General-in-Chief to allow him to remain until the end of the council; that if he refused this request, he was ordered, on his return, to resume the Allied bombardment, and that it was better for both parties that the effect be suspended. General Foissac-Latour surrendered to this reason; all his batteries being ruined. He therefore asked the parliamentarians to retire to a separate room, where they would remain with the officers of his staff, until his answer was sent; he commanded us to take advantage of the moment to advance, as far as possible, the most urgent repairs, and to show everywhere much activity and resolution. On all sides the workers answered these orders and the grenadiers asked for tools to assist the work at Pradella.

The commandant of Mantua then returned to the council of war, which was composed of forty-five superior officers: they were Obert, Commander of the 2nd Battalion of the 29th Légère; Girard, Commander of the 1st Cisalpine Demi-brigade; F. Pagès, Lieutenant, Commander of the Navy; Jovéroni, Captain, commanding the Cisalpine

Sappers; Chapuis, Captain, Commander of the pontoniers; America, Chef de bataillon of the artillery; Mosiecki, Major, commander of the 2nd Polish Battalion; Wolinski, Commander of the 3rd Polish Battalion; Baron, Chef de bataillon of the 31st Demi-brigade; Cappi, Chef de bataillon of the 1st Cisalpine Brigade; Marguel, Chef de bataillon of the 93rd Demi-brigade; Lelmi, Chef de bataillon of the 5th Brigade; Turrel, Chef de bataillon of the 31st Demi-brigade; P. Varennes, Chef de brigade; L. Fédon, Commander of the 31st Demi-brigade; Delisle, Chef d'escadron of the 7th Dragoons Regiment; Lacroix, Commander of the 15th Demi-brigade; Sicard, Chef de bataillon, 15th Demi-brigade; Malbrun, Chef de bataillon, 15th Demi-brigade; Jayet, Commander of the 2nd Helvetic Legion; Mesmer, Chef de bataillon of the 1st Helvetic Legion; Ott, Chef de bataillon, 1st Helvetic Legion; Pyre, Chef de bataillon, 1st Helvetic Legion; Armand-Gros, Chef d'escadron of the Piedmontese Carabiniers; Abyberg, Commander of the 1st Helvetic Legion; Eugene, Commander of the 1st Cisalpine Demi-brigade; Dembowski, Commander of the 2nd Polish Legion; Cerutti, Chef de brigade of the Cisalpine artillery; Kosinski, Adjutant-general, commanding the 2nd Polish Legion; Barthes, Chef de brigade of the 1st Helvetic Legion, Jonquière, Chef de bataillon of the Helvetic Legion, Girard, Chef de brigade, Borthon, Chef de brigade, commanding the artillery, Wielhorski, Général de brigade, Balleydier, Chef de brigade of the 29th Légère; Meyer, Général de brigade, Perigord, Chef de bataillon of engineers, Fontanieu, Général de brigade, Commander 2nd Piedmontese Infantry Brigade, Labadie, Chef de bataillon of the 6th Artillery Regiment, Gastine, Adjutant-general, Chief of the General Staff of the Division, Girardelet, Chef de bataillon of the 26th, Monnet, Général de brigade, Morel, Chef de brigade of the 56th Demi-brigade, Soulier, temporary commander of the Fortress of Mantua, General Foissac-Latour, President of the Council, and the Commissary of War Leclerc acted as authorizing officer and secretary of the council.

He asked them whether, with the remaining forces, we could hope to defend ourselves against a future assault. After the discussions exchanged between the members of this council, the general invited all the members to give all the instructions they would be able to give. The state of the garrison was recorded on the desk, noting as number of men per corps, and that of the soldiers in each corps, who could serve the infantry. As a result, the infantry capable of serving, with the deduction of men killed or wounded since the blockade, sick, soldiers employed as nurses in the hospital, patients in the corps, seamen, officers, sappers, musicians, drummers, miners, workers, gunners, etc., there were three thousand six hundred sixty one men being distributed as follows: one thousand five hundred men for the defense of the Migliaretto and Tea Gates; one thousand men for the service of the fortress and for the police, and nine hundred men in reserve, there remained only two hundred sixty one soldiers bearing bayonets, to defend the passage of the breach. These three thousand six hundred sixty one men were distributed as follows in the various units:

26th Demi-Brigade	221 men
31st Demi-Brigade, not incl. the garrison of citadel, which had	161
29th Demi-Brigade	517
45th Demi-Brigade	70
93rd Demi-Brigade	226
1st Helvetic Legion	190
2nd Helvetic Legion	156
1st Cisalpine Demi-brigade	411
2nd Polish Legion	580
56th Demi-Brigade	509
Total in the fortress	3,341 men
At Migliaretto	600
Total	3,941
To be deducted for auxiliaries to the gunners, requested by Chef de brigade Borthon	280
Effective force to defend the fortress	3,661 men

Two members of the council maintained that the fortress could be defended for two or three days at the most. The general having put this question to the vote, six people declared themselves for the affirmative. They were Monnet, Borthon, Labadie, Soulier, Pagès, Chapuis. All the others, thirty-eight, said no. When the second question was put to the vote, if the defense of the fortress were to be continued for two or three days, there were only four members for the affirmative: Borthon, Labadie, Pagès, Chapuis; and the others, forty in number, for the negative.

However, the parliamentarian Orlandini was there waiting impatiently for a definitive answer. Time was pressing, and General Foissac-Latour, with the majority of the opinions of the members of the council, proposed to General Kray to take as a basis for capitulation the conditions which General Bonaparte had granted in 1797 to the Marshal Würmser, in a nearly similar position. He demanded that the garrison be sent back by the shortest way and by military marches to the French army, to Genoa. General Monnet, who was the bearer of this project, returned from the headquarters at Castellucchio with the news that General Kray, less generous than Bonaparte had been to the old Austrian marshal, refused Foissac-Latour's proposals.

Consequently, on the same day, 10 Thermidor, a new council of war was immediately summoned; and, though it was necessary to yield to the imperious necessity, however, all the members unanimously opposed the garrison being taken prisoner of war to the Hereditary States of the Emperor, to be exchanged at the first opportunity. The council being consulted to know whether it accepted this condition, all its members declared that it was better to perish on the breach than to submit to the yoke of servitude.

Then the general proposed a draft letter from him to General Kray, by which he offered to surrender himself and all the officers as prisoners of war in place of their soldiers, and that the officers would thus serve as hostages to guarantee their non-activity in the French army for a limited time.

The council unanimously adopted this proposal, being firmly resolved, if it were refused, to bury itself rather under the walls of Mantua, to leave posterity a memorable example of its patriotic devotion, beside the shameful act of an enemy who defiled his loyalty by abusing the superiority of his weapons.

This noble and energetic protest was signed by the following officers: Obert, commander of the 2nd Battalion of the 29th Légère; Girardelet, Chef de bataillon of the 26th; Krolikiewicz, commander of the 1st Polish Battalion; Mosiecki, commander of the 2nd Polish Battalion; Labadie, Chef de bataillon of the 6th Artillery Regiment; Perigord, Chef de bataillon of engineers; Sicard, Chef de bataillon of the 45th Battalion; Meric, Chef de bataillon of artillery; Jonquière, Chef de bataillon;

Fédon, Chef de bataillon, commanding the 31st Demi-brigade; Marguel, Chef de bataillon of the 93rd Demi-brigade; Abaffour, Chef de bataillon, commander of the citadel; Eugene, commander of the 1st Cisalpine; Demi-brigade Tourel, Marguel, Chef de bataillon of the 31st Demi-brigade; Girard, Chef de brigade; Girard, Chef de bataillon; Jayet, Chef de bataillon of the Helvetic Legion; Verlato, Chief of the Cisalpine Artillery Battalion; Pyre, Chef de bataillon of the Helvetic 1st Legion; Mesmer, Chef de bataillon, 1st Legion; Armand Gros, Chef d'escadron, commanding the Piedmontese carabineers; Kosinski, Adjutant-general, commander of the 2nd Polish Legion; Varennes, chef de brigade; Malbrun, Chef de bataillon; Morel, commander of the 56th Demi-brigade; Cerutti, commander of Cisalpine artillery brigade; Ott, Chef de bataillon of the 1st Helvetic Legion; Joveroni, Captain, commanding the Cisalpine Sappers; Deslisle, Chef d'escadron 7th Dragoon Regiment; Baron, Chef de bataillon of the 1st Battalion of the 31st Demi-brigade; Foissac-Latour, Général de division; Cappi, Chef de bataillon; Lacroix, Chef de bataillon; Lelmi, Chef de bataillon of the 31st Demi-brigade; Fontanieu, General, commanding the 2nd Piedmontese Demi-brigade; Meyer, Général de brigade; Gastine, Adjutant-general; Soulier, commander; Leclerc, secretary of the council.

Finally, the articles of the capitulation were concluded on 10 Thermidor, Year VII (28 July 1799), in Castellucchio, between the two generals, and it was agreed that the garrison would be considered as prisoners of war until a perfect exchange was arranged and returned to France under Austrian escort; but that the officers would not go there, on their word, not to bear arms against the Allies, after having spent three months in the Hereditary States as hostages. On the 11 Thermidor (29 July), at the break of day, Lieutenant Colonel Orlandini arrived at Mantua with the capitulation signed, and on the 12 Thermidor (30 July), the garrison left the citadel with the honors of the war and deposited their weapons on the glacis.

CAPITULATION OF MANTUA

Headquarters at Mantua
Thermidor 10, Year VIII (July 28, 1799)

Foissac-Latour, Général de division, commandant of the Fortress and Citadel of Mantua, proposes:

To Baron de Kray, General of Artillery, commander of the troops of H.M. the Emperor, under Mantua, to surrender to him this fortress under the following conditions, deliberated by the defending council of war.

Art 1. The garrison of Mantua shall leave the fortress, passing through the citadel, on 12 Thermidor (July 30th), with all the honors of war, six field pieces leading. It shall surrender as prisoners of war. So that it avoid the shame and miseries of detention, the general who commands it, the other generals under his orders, the officers of the staff, and all the others of the garrison, consent to surrender themselves prisoners in Germany, in the closest of the Hereditary Lands, where they shall remain hostages for the non-commissioned officers and soldiers who shall be returned to France by the shortest route and shall not take up arms against the Emperor's and his allies' troops, until they have been exchanged. A a result, the garrison shall lay down its arms on the glacis of the fortress. The officers shall retain their swords, their baggage, and the number of horses that they have the right to maintain, according to their respective ranks. The army's employees shall equally be returned to France. The generals shall retain their secretaries, and all the domestic officers. We will accord one flag to General Froissac-Latour, in consideration of the rigorous defense that he has made.

Response. — Accorded in all its extent, adding, in consideration of the frank, brave and loyal manner with which the garrison of Mantua has conducted itself, the commander shall be free, as well as his staff and officers of the garrison, after having remained in the hereditary states, to return to their respective lands, on their word of honor, to not carry arms against His Imperial and Royal Majesty, until they have been exchanged. The three months shall start from the day the capitulation is signed.

Art. 2. The Cisalpine, Swiss, Polish, and Piedmontese troops shall be considered and treated, under all reports, as the troops of the French Republic. — Granted.

Art. 3. There shall be accorded to the general commanding the fortress, three covered caissons for the transport of his equipage, papers, and other objects that belong to him personally; these caissons shall not be visited, and he may dispose of the as he wishes. — Granted.

Art. 4. The Chief of Staff and the other superior officers shall have the facility to take away the papers relative to their administration and shall take caissons destined for this purpose and for the transport of their personal belongings. The commissioners shall be responsible for the returning of objects which, by their nature, belong to the fortress. — Granted.

Art. 5. We recommend to the loyalty and generosity of the Austrian government the tranquility of the inhabitants who were employed in the Cisalpine government, formally recognized by the Emperor in the Treaty of Campo-Formio, as well as all those who have manifested republican opinions; the Imperial commissioners and the bourgeois gunners having been treated in the same manner in the capitulation concluded between Bonaparte and General Würmser. — Granted.

Art. 6. There shall be named commissioner officers of the engineers and artillery, to whom shall be handed over all the objects belonging to this arm. — Consented.

Art. 7. There shall also be named commissioners of war and of provisions to whom shall be surrendered the magazines that are in the fortress. — Consented.

Art. 8. The sick and wounded, who cannot be transported, shall continue to receive the necessary care until the return of their health. At this time, the French surgeon who actually treated them shall remain with them. The commanding general shall name an officer who shall serve as their guard and to the measure that they are in a state to be transported, they shall be furnished all the means necessary to rejoin the army if they have been exchanged, or sent to France or Germany, under the conditions accorded to the others, with regards to their respective ranks. — Consented.

Art. 9. There shall be provided by the Austrians an appropriate and sufficient escort to guarantee all the individuals included in the present capitulation against any insult or popular riot, and the commanders of the escort shall be personally responsible. — Granted.

Art. 10. All that which, in the present capitulation, may be in doubt or produce difficulties shall be interpreted in favor of the garrison and according to the laws of equity. — Consented.

Art. 11. After the signing of the capitulation each shall reciprocally surrender hostages, who shall be, on the side of the French, a chef de brigade and a captain; on the side of the Austrians, a colonel and a captain. — Consented.

Art. 12. In awaiting the signing of the capitulation and the exchange of hostages, there shall be a suspension of hostilities on both sides. — Consented.

Art. 13. Migliaretto shall be occupied by an Austrian battalion, which shall detach 50 men to occupy the exterior part of the Cérèse Gate. The two-army corps shall have no communication, with the exception of the chiefs and those that have received the permission of their respective generals. — Consented.

Art. 14. The commissioner with executive power and the inspector general of the police of the Cisalpine Republic at Mantua shall be permitted to leave the fortress and go where they wish. — Consented.

Art. 15. There shall be two wagons accorded for the men in the general's suite, and whatever others who shall receive from him the order to follow the fate of the garrison. — Granted.

Art. 16. One will equally accord the wagons necessary for the transport of the effects of the officers and chiefs of the French army forming part of the garrison, and the same for those who are no longer able to leave this fortress. — Granted.

Art. 17. The generals and officers who wish to send to France part of their baggage may have it follow the march of the soldiers. If, however, General Kray, who knows true glory, does not think that his orders allow him to send the generals and officers to the destination of their troops, based on their word of honor [not to serve against Austria]. — Regulated by Article 1.

Additional Article

The Austrian deserters shall be returned to their respective regiments and battalions.

The commanding general of His Imperial Majesty shall permit them to live.

Done at the headquarters at Castellucchio, July 28, 1799.

Baron von Kray, General of Artillery
Maubert, Chef de brigade,
Commander-in-Chief of Engineers
Foissac-Latour, Général de division

Chef de brigade Borthon, Commander of the Artillery, did not sign the capitulation for personal reasons.

General Froissac-Latour

The 2nd Polish Legion shared the fate of its brothers-in-arms. Of the four thousand men who were part of at the beginning of the campaign it was reduced, at this time, to eight hundred men, both because of sickness and by military action.

An most unfortunate situation awaited these noble victims of their patriotic devotion however. Although the Legion was included in the capitulation as we have seen, nonetheless, an additional article was added to the treaty, which was held secret for the moment. It guaranteed to the Austrians the deserters, on the condition that their lives be spared. As the Legion consisted of, for the most part, men who were natives of Poland, which had become Austrian subjects by the odious partitions of 1772 and 1795, were regimented within the framework of their oppressors, the Austrian general made use of this secret condition in their regard, torturing it with a Machiavellian interpretation. Thus, when the garrison left the fortress, the Polish Legion was ordered to close the column, and at the moment when it was marching thus, and when the head and the center of the French were outside the city, the Austrians threw themselves on the Poles, tore the soldiers from their platoons, insulted even their officers, and, overwhelming them with insults, they forced them into their ranks or into the houses of the neighborhood. All the remonstrances of General Wielhorski and the senior officers were unsuccessful: this criminal act of injustice was pushed to such an extent that the Commander of Artillery Axamitowski, charged with twelve officers to bring our soldiers back to France, notwithstanding all his care, could only take about one hundred fifty men to Lyon.

General Wielhorski, Adjutant-General Kosinski, and all the rest of the officers were taken to Leoben, Austria, as prisoners of war.

Thus, ended this campaign, which had opened under such favorable auspices. Never had the Poles glimpsed the future in more brilliant colors than at the beginning of this new war, and their hopes had never been more cruelly disappointed. They were in the presence of their most cruel enemies, fighting the front turned towards their country, being able again to conquer it by dint of success, and the inevitability that attached to their footsteps wanted that this fight, which gave them so direct hopes, became for them a new source of reverses. It was wished that, at the moment when they hoped to shake their chains, they would be glued more closely than ever.

CHAPTER ELEVEN

France Regains the Initiative. — Its Preparations for War. — Position of the Armies. — The Battle of Novi. — Movement of the Polish Legion. — New Action Near Novi. — General Mack Takes Command of the Austrian Army. — Destitution of the Polish Soldiers at this Time. — Demarches of General Dąbrowski to Stop It. — Kosciuszko in Paris. — Polish Legions on the Danube. — Kniaziewicz. — Movement of the Army of Italy. — The Polish Legion Occupies San-Pietro-d'Arena. — Engagement of the Legion. — General Action. — Gopzon, Piawecki, Gryglinski, Szczubielski, Billing, Laskowski, Koszucki, Kozakiewiez, Storski, Kolodynski, Luicwiez, Wasilewski, Serwacki, Dzremer, Galecki, Truszkowski. — Jablonowski. — Dąbrowski is Struck by a Bullet. — New Battle of Novi. — Movement of the Legions. — The Army Retires Towards the Mountains. — Delapidatoin of the Polish Corps. — General Misery of the French Army. — Kasimir de la Roche. — General Dąbrowski Goes to Paris. — Letter to Him from Bonaparte. — Advantageous Conditions that Dąbrowski Obtained for His Legions. — Recruitment in France. — Reorganization of the Polish Corps.

Although the French Republic had proved in recent years that it alone could sustainably support the struggle against the coalition of European powers, although at various times it had made its enemies tremble, even for their own homes, its enemies were not repelled, and remained convinced that, sooner or later, valor would yield to numbers. At that time especially, when Austria, Russia and England, united together, had set in motion three hundred forty thousand men who threatened France from Genoa to Holland, it was thought impossible that it could withstand such a display of strength, and it was presumed that it was a final campaign for France. However, in this solemn circumstance in which the fate of the nation was to be decided by arms, the Executive Directory showed courage and firmness. Far from being appalled by the preparations of its enemies and standing on a timid defensive, it resolved to resume the offensive: this generous boldness, well in keeping with the national character, raised the confidence of the citizens in the interior, and filled the soldiers who fought outside of their homeland with enthusiasm.

To this end, General Brune was charged with presiding over the organization of a new army to be distributed on the coasts of the Channel, in Belgium and Holland.

Another army, whose headquarters were to be at Mainz, and whose line extended from Düsseldorf to Huningue, was to pass under the command of General Moreau, who knew so well this part of the theater of war. But until he was able return from the Army of Italy, where he was still, to his new destination, Major-General Muller was charged with presiding over the organization of this army.

The Army of the Danube, moving to the most interesting point of the frontiers of the Republic, obeyed General Masséna.

In order to defend Dauphiné and Savoy, and to strengthen, according to the circumstances, the Armies of Italy and the Danube, the Directory also organized a reserve under the name of the Army of the Alps; General Championnet was ordered to go and preside over its training at Grenoble.

Such was the position of the two parties at the moment when General Joubert took command of the Army of Italy. Marshal Suvorov, with his main body, composed of the Muscovite troops under his command, and the Austrian troops commanded by General Melas, covered the sieges of Tortona and Cuneo; General Kray was on his way to join Suvorov, with the troops who had served in the siege of Mantua, or supported this operation. The French army was still confined to the borders of Genoa and Piedmont.

General Joubert arrived at Genoa towards the end of July, and Moreau wished to give him the command; but Joubert begged him to delay his departure, and to give him some more of his advice.

According to the opinion of the French generals, it was necessary to wait, before acting, the arrival of General Championnet, who would come out of the Alps with his new army. But the orders of the Directory were to attack the Austro-Russians at once, and to make every effort to break the blockade of Tortona.

Such was the situation of the respective forces at the moment, of the battle of Novi, one of the bloodiest of the revolution.[1]

Without wishing to enter into the details of this battle, which will be found in the official report of General Moreau, we will only say that, on 21 Thermidor (11 August), General Dąbrowski was ordered to go to Ronco with the French and Cisalpine troops under his orders and leave the Legion in its position. Consequently, the Legion alone occupied all the posts that had hitherto held by the whole division.

The 27th (11th), a new order was issued by which the Polish Legion must go immediately to Arquata. Indeed, it was relieved of its position, and it arrived on the 28th (15th), afternoon, to its destination, at the time of the battle of Novi. General Dąbrowski moved it on the spot to protect the retreat of the army at the orders of General Moreau, Joubert having already been killed, and the French troops of the division moved to blockade Serravalle. The Cisalpine troops and the 55th Demi-brigade were all sent to reinforce the right wing commanded by General Watrin, in the battle of Novi. The Polish Legion advanced to Monterotondo and Ralestrina. This movement prevented the enemy, who was pursuing the army, from falling on the right flank, and forced them to move to the left. It then moved up to the heights of Gavi, where some discharges prevented it from penetrating further. Night having come, Dąbrowski received an order from General Saint Cyr, who already commanded the right wing of the army, to go and occupy the outlet of Arquata and Rigoroso, and to keep it to the last extremity. The 25th Chasseur à cheval Regiment joined the division, and the Legion set in motion at night. It reached this position on the morning of the 29th, and there found the enemy firmly resolved to dispute it. Meanwhile the Legion impetuously attacked it head-on; the 8th Demi-brigade leaving Burlasco, and the 17th Demi-brigade of Pratolungo (the 56th Demi-brigade and the cavalry had remained to support the attack on the reserve), and charged it so well, that it is obliged to flee to Serra-

[1]The total forces of the French in action, including 8,160 men detached, came to 43,090. Among these, there was a detachment of Poles in Colli's brigade, and the Dąbrowski Division, composed of the French 17th and 55th Demi-brigades, the Polish Legion, the 1st Cisalpine Legion and the Polish Cavalry, forming in all six battalions, that is to say 2,070 infantrymen and 50 horsemen. These troops were then part of the center and the right wing at the orders of General Saint-Cyr. The totality of Allied forces, ready to come into action, amounted to 63,000 men, 12,000 of whom were cavalry.

valle and to abandon its crews and its provisions. The fight lasted very late into the night, began again the next day, and continued throughout 1 Fructidor (18 August). Watrin's division having formed on the 2nd, behind the Legion at Ronco, came to raise it, and it was then able to go to the left in the Campofreddo defiles, leaving behind the 25th Chasseur à cheval Regiment. It arrived on the 3rd (20th) at its destination. The Polish cavalry remained at Voltri and Masone. The headquarters, the grenadiers and the 1st Battalion went to Campofreddo, the 2nd to Roneiglione, the 3rd to Cabane and Marcharolo, and the chasseurs to Montebello. The French troops of the division advanced forward, pressing their right wing to the left of Watrin's division, near Carosino; the center extended on Montebanno and Costa, and the left joined the one on the right of General St. Cyr, near San Lucca and Montebello.

The 1st Polish Battalion left for Genoa on the 7th (24 August), and the 2nd went to the headquarters at Campofreddo. The 106th Demi-brigade arrived in the division and occupied the positions of Montebello, Cabane, and Marcharolo; the chasseurs and the 3rd Polish Battalion moved to the left and occupied Ceretto-di-Sopra and San-Lucca, and the center Ronciglione and Rossiglionalto.

While these countermarches were being made to reach the positions mentioned above, some skirmishes took place between the outposts. The enemy was then in a position on the plain in front of the Legion.

On 21 Fructidor (7 September), the division, arrayed in this manner, attacked the enemy in his position. The French, near Casla, and the 2nd Battalion with the grenadiers formed the reserve. Watrin's division advanced to Novi, and that of St. Cyr to Acqui.

In this state, the enemy was attacked during the evening, surprised and overthrown at all points. The whole division pursued and occupied, at noon on the 22nd (8th), the position at Bisio on the Lemme, Castel-Adorno, Silvana as far as Trisobbio, where the Polish chasseurs were placed, and the 2nd Battalion was at Roceagrimaldi. The general staff of the division, the grenadiers and the 3rd Battalion went to Ovada, and the cavalry regiment to Molare and Cremolino. The enemy withdrew to Alessandria, and the Legion pushed its outposts to Spinola, Castel Vero, and Monte Alto. Some prisoners of war and a large quantity of food and fodder were the result of this expedition.

General Watrin, however, was compelled to withdraw from Novi, and resume his former position; consequently, the Legion also returned to its old position on the 24th (10 September) in the evening, without the enemy pursuing it. Saint-Cyr's division then made the same retrograde movement.

On the 26th (12 September), the enemy made a great movement towards Molare, seeming to wish to advance to Ponzone. The post of Oosla was reinforced on this ground, and the 2nd Polish Battalion moved into the position of San Lucca and Murbello. The enemy, seeing that they were ready to receive them on all points, resolved to retire to their old positions, and to leave the French troops in theirs.

Nevertheless, these motions announced a new direction in the operations of the allied cabinets of St. Petersburg and Vienna. Field Marshal Suvorov had been ordered to march with the Russian troops under his command to strengthen the allied Army of Switzerland, which the reckless march of the Archduke into Swabia had weakened and compromised.

On 7 September, Suvorov handed the command of the Austrian Army of Italy to General Melas and continued his march towards Switzerland in a single column. On 12 September, his troops arrived at Mortara, the 13th at Turbigo on the Tessin; on the 15th they entered the territory of Switzerland and encamped at Taverne. On the 17th Suvorov's headquarters were taken to Belliuzona, on the road to St. Gothard, by which he was to meet with the other troops under the orders of Generals Hotze and Rimsky-Korsakoff, in the heart of Switzerland. We know the results of the Battle of Zurich, 3 and 4 Vendémiaire, Year VIII (25 and 26 September 1799.) It was there that, in the words of the historian Thiers "the brutal energy of the Russians was going to meet learned and calculated energy, and break in front of it. "

Meanwhile, General Dąbrowski learned, by encouraging reports, that depots were beginning to increase in Nice and Villefranche, that a large number of officers and soldiers were cured of their wounds, although a part remained unable to serve; and that the troop, although absolutely devoid of clothing, was in continual activity, and constantly engaging the Montagnards and the Barbets.[2] For their part, the pris-

[2]Translator: The Barbets were Protestant rebels in the mountainous border region along the French-Sardinian border. They had fought the Royal Army in the Seven Years War and now fought the Revolutionary government.

oners of war officers used several occasions to write that they were treated by the Austrians like the other French officers, and that they had been transported to Hungary.

However, the Polish soldier was without pay, without shoes, without shirts and without uniforms, posted on dreadful mountains and arid rocks, obliged to cross them constantly in the rain, the snow and the frost, lacking food, sometimes for three or four days, and then forced to live from roots, never having a moment of rest, and always in the presence of the enemy. This was indeed the dreadful situation in which the Polish troops and the whole Army of Italy were at that time. In the midst of all these privations, however, the Poles suffered with admirable resignation; and, marching on the icy peaks of the Apennines, their glances still hovered in the distance, turned towards their native land, and their moral energy, stronger than all of their physical pains, made them see in the future that country, for which they fought so far from, powerful and regenerated.

It was in the meantime that Generalissimo Kosciuszko, General Kniaziewicz, and Major Kasimir Konopka, and Biernacki, informed General Dąbrowski that the French government had resolved to create a new legion on the Rhine under the orders of General Kniaziewicz, and that it had begun training. But it was written at the same time that there was no thought of the fate of the Legion in Italy, while it endured the cruelest privations on its side.

Chef de brigade of artillery Axamitowski and Major Moscicki announced to General Dąbrowski their arrival at Lyon with several officers and two hundred and eighty five men, trained both from the remains of the Mantua garrison and from other Poles who had concentrated in that city.

Such was the state of the Legions, when General Championnet, having learned of the changes that had taken place in the Allies' army, redoubled his efforts to affect his junction with the Army of Italy, of which Moreau still retained provisional command.

General Championnet, after entrusting the direction of the troops of the Army of the Alps to General Duhèsme, arrived, on 30 Fructidor (16 September) at Genoa, to take the post of Command-in-Chief. Moreau, pressed by the Directory, went to Paris, where he was to arrange with Minister of War Bernadotte, before going on the Rhine to receive from General Muller the command of the Army of Observation which had begun the organization.

As for the Polish Legion, it was then in the right wing of the Army of Italy, under General Saint-Cyr, whose Poles formed the 2nd Division.

Nothing new happened until the last complementary day of the Year VII.[3]

General Melas having succeeded Field Marshal Suvorov in the command of the Allied armies in Italy, it was reserved for the Austrian troops to complete, alone, the conquest of that country. For this purpose, the levies organized in the Hereditary States, in the provinces wrested from Poland, and in the states of Venice, were directed successively and with much activity on the points where the two generals, Melas and Kray, were at the point of that all the imperial forces formed an army of more than sixty thousand men, to which the Republicans could then oppose only thirty thousand more combatants.

On 2 Vendemiaire, Year VIII (21 September 1799), the Gallo-Polish division turned to the left to occupy the Sassello, Ponzone and Squanello defiles, and arrived on the 3rd (25th) at this position, having its headquarters and the grenadiers at Sassello, the 3rd Battalion at Voltri and Arenzano, on the seashore, the chasseurs at Cartasio and Malvicino, and the 2nd Battalion at Ponzone. The cavalry was in Moglia. French troops occupied Spargnetto, Monteacuto and Murbello. On the right wing, the left wing of Watrin's division at Ponte-Molara, and on the left the right wing of General Laboissière at Ponti, and the outposts along the Erro, close to Acqui. In this position, skirmishes took place with the enemy outposts, especially at Cartasio and Cavatora, as they fought for provisions; and these two points were occupied sometimes by the French, sometimes by the enemy.

On the 11th (3 October), the division received orders to go quickly to San Pietro d'Arena, near Genoa. A forced march was accordingly made and it arrived on the 12th (4th), having passed through Voltri. The Legion and the cavalry occupied Conegliano; the headquarters and French troops were at San-Pietro d'Arena.

On the 19th (11 October), the division received orders to cross Genoa, and to await new ones near Albaro; in the evening it was or-

[3]Translator: Complimentary days were days added to the Republican Calendar to make the year come to 365 days.

dered to march all night to Sori. It covered, by this march, an expedition that General Saint-Cyr had planned for Miollis' division, posted at Sori, and on the shores of the sea. The Legion arrived there on the 20th (12th) in the morning, and it was obliged to return the same evening take up its former position of San Pietro d'Arena, where it arrived on the 21st (13 October).[4]

As a result of new arrangements, General Dąbrowski received an order, on the 28th (20th), to send the 55th and the 17th Demi-brigades, which had hitherto been in his division, at Genoa, and he was given the 3rd and 106th, and the 1st Polish Battalion. This division assembled on the 29th (21 October) at Campo-Marone and arrived on the 30th (22nd) at Voltaggio, where General Saint-Cyr established his headquarters, and the division advanced, the same day, towards Novi. Having met the enemy, General Dąbrowski immediately reinforced the vanguard with his grenadiers and his chasseurs, and immediately attacked the enemy and drove them from Novi.

The 1st Battalion of the 3rd Demi-brigade, the grenadiers and chasseurs of the Legion, as well as a squadron of the Polish cavalry,

[4]According to the situation report of the Army of Italy, dated 17 October 1799, after the meeting of the Army of the Alps, when General Championnet took command, the total strength of the active army was 54,053 men, excluding Pouget's detachment, guarding the Col de Tende and the Maritime Alps, and the Grenoble and Briançon Military Divisions, under the orders of General Pallaprat, about 1,500 Italian or Polish, and 6,000 French conscripts. The foreigners guarded the passages of the Alps to stop desertions; the others formed the garrisons of the posts.

As for the Dąbrowski division, it was in the following state:

Dąbrowski, Général de division
Jablonowski, Général de brigade

Regiments	Emplacements	
3rd Légère	540	Campo Marone, Voltaggio
17th Légère	193	San-Pietro d'Arena
55th Line	442	San Pietro d'Arena
106th Line	697	Sori
106th Line	1,494	Campo Marone, Voltaggio
Grenadiers & Chasseurs	550	Soria, San-Pietro d'Arena
1st Polish Legion	608	Campo Marone, Voltaggio
Polish Cavalry	128	Campo Marone, Voltaggio
Total	4,652	

When the army took the offensive, it appears that General Miollis had Dąbrowski's troops relieved, and that part of them followed St. Cyr's column, and others that of Victor, for the 3rd Légère was found at the battle of Fossano.

all under the orders Chef de brigade Mouton, of the 3rd Demi-brigade, crossed the city, and occupied the gardens of the suburb towards Pozzolo. The 3rd Polish Battalion remained in the city itself.

General Laboissière's division advanced towards Pasturana, and that of Watrin passed through Novi in the night and took up position between the Polish division and that of Laboissière, so that the former formed the right wing.

In the morning General Dąbrowski received orders to go to the plain with his division, and to attack the enemy wherever he might be. The division having joined its vanguard, set out for Pozzolo-Formigara. General Laboissière began the attack, then came Watrin, and then Dąbrowski. The enemy was expelled from Pozzolo, and he withdrew gradually from one position to another. The more he retired, the more he strengthened his front until he arrived at Bosco. A howitzer was then given to the division.

The enemy formed in battle formation in front of this village and General Saint-Cyr ordered this movement to be imitated. The Polish Legion formed a column on the left wing, having the 1st Battalion in the lead. General Dąbrowski threw the chasseurs to his left, and the grenadiers, in mass, were posted a little ahead and to the right of this column. The 3rd Demi-brigade also followed in column. A battalion of the 106th Demi-brigade formed the right column, its 2nd Battalion formed the reserve, and the howitzer was placed between the 3rd and the 106th Demi-brigades. There was no cavalry to place in the line.

The enemy had twelve cannon and four batteries, a sufficient force of infantry and a lot of cavalry. These forces were in front of the Polish division, separated from it by a plain and by Bosco, on its rear. The divisions of Laboissière and Watrin at the same time drove back all the enemy units, which they found before them, and pushed them as far as Bosco: they took position there, pressing their right wing to the swamps that were there, and joining their left to the right of the line which was before the Legion, thus crowning the village, and covering the high road from Novi to Alexandria. General Karaczay, commanding the Austrian troops, having thus secured his right, charged Laboissière's division with such impetuosity, that at first it was obliged to retreat. At the same moment, General Saint-Cyr ordered Generals Watrin and Dąbrowski to attack the enemy, who had already begun to fire his batteries, and who, seeing little cavalry, advanced on his own. He also noticed that he was being answered with only one cannon. Watrin's left wing had followed the movement of Laboissière's division; but his right, covered with bushes and ditches, held firm in its position. General Dąbrowski made his preparations for the attack in the following manner: the 2nd Battalion remained in its position, and the 1st moved to the right to fill the gap between the Legion and the 3rd Demi-brigade; the grenadiers fell back a little to cover the chasseurs on the right of the 2nd Battalion. The division formed, in this way, four columns; two Polish, having its two intervals covered by grenadiers and chasseurs, and the two others, of the 3rd Demi-brigade, having its intervals covered by some cavalry and the howitzer. General Saint-Cyr left the 106th Demi-brigade in reserve and to observe the enemy's left. General Wladislas Jablonowski commanded the left-wing Polish column, and Strzalkowski the right-wing.

The attack began at the *pas de charge*[5], presenting the bayonet: the 2nd Polish Battalion charged the enemy's cavalry, posted opposite it, and overwhelmed it.[6] This cavalry overthrown, the grenadiers followed behind this battalion on the left, and rushed on a battery of four cannon vomiting canister and doing much harm to its center. They seized the guns, left them behind, and prepared themselves immediately to throw themselves on the infantry they saw before them. The enemy, at this moment, renewed a terrible fire, which staggered the Poles for a moment; they moved to the left, and this movement broke the column. The enemy cavalry, perceiving it, immediately charged the battalion and the grenadiers; and notwithstanding the fire with which the grenadiers and the chasseurs opposed it, they began to slash them. The 1st Battalion, by its side, had overthrown the enemy infantry before it, and forced the artillery to flee to the village. At this moment, General Dąbrowski, seeing what was happening on his left wing, and the flight of the enemy, repulsed by the 1st Battalion, immediately ordered this battalion to execute a half turn to the left, ordered a general discharge, and to fall, with the bayonets, on the enemy cavalry, which had already almost defeated the 2nd Battalion. The grenadiers also stopped and

---

[5]Translator: The pas de charge is a high speed marching cadence of one hundred twenty paces per minute.

[6]Translator: Infantry attacking cavalry was extremely rare. The only other successful such attack was by the Ismailovski Guard at Borodino, in 1812.

put themselves in position. He made the 1st Battalion, 3rd Demi-brigade move to the left, and all this battalion shouted: "Come on! It is necessary to support these brave Poles!" and they attacked the enemy cavalry with bayonets. General Saint-Cyr arrived with the reserve; the right of General Watrin was moving forward. With fixed bayonets they rushed on the enemy; the enemy was tumbled and overthrown on Bosco. The enemy cavalry, which had cut down our 2nd Battalion, had neither the time nor the ground to escape, and almost all of it was taken prisoners of war. The right wing of the enemy, who had attacked Laboissière's division, seeing what the rest of his body had become, began to flee; but it was obliged to run away along the Orba, because Bosco was already occupied by the Polish troops. Our whole corps advanced, pursuing, at every point, the enemy fleeing Bosco. The Legion went forward by Frugarolo; the 3rd Demi-brigade was sent by General Saint-Cyr to Quatro Cassini. The night came in the meantime, and Watrin was ordered to take a position to the right on the Scrivia, near Livalla; Dąbrowski, near Pozzolo and Quatro-Cassini, and Laboissière in Bosco and Fruirarolo, near the Orba.

The Polish Legion took four cannons in this victorious day of 2 Brumaire, Year VIII (24 October 1799), and made six hundred prisoners of war. On the other hand, it lost about three hundred men, who died on the spot or as a result of their wounds. The lieutenants of the 2nd Battalion —Gozon, Piawecki, Gryglinski, and Szczubielski – found the death of the brave, and, with the exception of only two, all the officers of this intrepid battalion were wounded; among others Captains Billing, Laskowski, Koszucki and Kozakiewicz; Lieutenants Storski, Kolodynski, Lukiewicz, and Sous Lieutenants Wasilewski, Serwacki, Szremer, Galccki, and Truszkowski.

The wounded of the 1st Battalion were Captains Melfort, Winnert, Ilinski; and in the grenadiers, Lieutenant Bogdanowicz.

General Jablonowski was slightly wounded and twice taken prisoner by the enemy cavalry but was subsequently freed by the Poles at Bosco.

General Dąbrowski himself only miraculously escaped this melee: at the very moment when, with a sword cut, he cut the fuse of an Austrian gunner who was about to fire his cannon, a bullet struck him, piercing a copy of Schiller's *Histoire de la guerre de trente ans,* which he had on him that day, and thus lost the strength to hurt him seriously.

That night the division resumed its position at Pozzolo, where everybody bivouacked; the chasseurs occupied Castel Gazo; so that during the morning of 3 Brumaire (25 October), everyone had returned to their destinations.

The Quatro-Cassini post was reinforced by the grenadiers and part of the Polish cavalry. The 2nd Battalion marched to Pasturana, to recover a little. The 3rd, under the orders of Chef de bataillon Swiderski, remained with the other part of the cavalry at Novi, where General Saint-Cyr had his headquarters.

The detachment of Quatro-Cassini continually pushed its outposts to San Giuliano, near Marengo, between Tortona and Alessandria, often having little skirmishes with the enemy.

General Championnet, difficulty seeing that his army corps, was consumed in partial combats, most often without result, resolved to attempt the chances of a decisive battle. To achieve this, and having disposed of the other troops, General Dąbrowski received, on the 10th (1 November), the order to detach General Yablonowski with the chasseurs and the 2nd Battalion, to block Serravalle. He had some French infantry and artillery with him.

On the 12th (3 November), the Polish division, with the exception of Jablonowski corps, went to Fresonara, on the Orba, to protect La Boissière's division, which the enemy, by some motions, proposed to attack.

During the morning of the 13th (4th), the Austrian army marched in two columns; one came by the main road from Alessandria to Tortona and proceeded from San Giuliano to Quatro Cassini; the other attacked Laboissière's division at Frugarolo. The Polish division advanced first; but the enemy column from San Giuliano sought to take it on the flank, and to this end moved into the plain between Pozzolo and Bosco, while a strong enemy column went directly to Pozzolo and Rivalta, where Watrin's division was stationed. His attack could not be expected, and he formed his flank to the right towards the enemy column. At the same time, as much cavalry as possible were sent to cover this movement. Laboissière left Frugarolo and Bosco and joined Dąbrowski near Fresonara. Dąbrowski advanced four cannons to protect the position of two divisions, which were in battle formation. Laboissière extended his left to Fresonara, and Dąbrowski formed his right in echelons, refusing a little to avoid being caught in the flank. We were being fired on from both sides, without undertaking anything of considerable importance. The Austrian army was still firing on Scrivia, masking its movement on the sides with its cavalry, of which it was abundantly provided.

General Dąbrowski sent a battalion of the 106th to occupy the heights between Basaluzzo and Pasturana, and to make the enemy believe that we were in force at this point. During these different movements and maneuvers, night came. Laboissière received an order from General Saint-Cyr to occupy Pasturana, and Dąbrowski the order to place himself on the heights that dominated that place and Novi.

During the morning of 14th (5 November), we were in position. Watrin's division, having been dislodged by the enemy from Pozzolo and Rivalta, was in front of the Polish division, covering Novi, which was still in our hands. The division formed the reserve, having on its right the 3rd Demi-brigade with two cannon and a howitzer, very close to the road which leads from Gavi to Novi; in the center was the Polish Legion and the valorous 106th Demi-brigade, covering the road from Novi to Francavilla, and the Polish cavalry was in position between the division and that of Laboissière. In a word, this position was the same as that occupied by the French army during the battle of Novi, where the brave Joubert was killed and the bloody battle where the French armies were to gain their revenge on the very places where he had given himself, by covering a defeat with a victory.

General Yablonowski was still bombarding Serravalle, where the enemy was showing good resistance.

During the morning of the 15th (6 November 1799), Dąbrowski received two more cannon. He placed them on an eminence between the Legion and the 106th Demi-brigade. The corps arrayed in this manner, General Saint-Cyr awaited the enemy.

General Kray, commander of the Austrian army who opposed the Polish division, began the attack at ten o'clock in the morning, the fog having prevented him from doing so sooner. He directed it on Novi, and on the Pasturana Heights. These positions were feebly manned, but they were so well defended that they made the enemy believe that

General Saint-Cyr had a large force there. The troops were ordered to withdraw and defend themselves from position to position, so that the enemy employed all his forces. Watrin's division placed itself to the right of the Legion, and that of Laboissière was to its left.

The enemy, obliged to pass by the defile between the position of the French army and Novi, pursued them, rushed in disorder behind them with its artillery, cavalry and infantry, and let itself be caught in the trap that the General Saint-Cyr had prepared for them. Then this general ordered that their front be attacked immediately, and the whole legion charged the enemy with their bayonets. The harried enemy tried to rally and take a stand but were overthrown on all points. The French took all the Austrian cannon and pursued them. The Polish Legion took two of them, and hotly pursued them with bayonets at their backs as far as Pozzolo. Laboissière's division fell on their right flank and pushed them back to Bosco. The advantage was decidedly on the side of the French and the fight won.

The enemy left many people on the battlefield, and a large number of prisoners remained in the hands of Gallo-Poles. The Polish Legion, which distinguished itself as usual, lost about 60 men killed and as many wounded. Among the latter was the leader of the Legion, the brave Strzalkowski, wounded so dangerously in both hands by canister, that he had to be removed from the field of battle. This deserving officer had already had the misfortune of being wounded in all the affairs where he had been in Poland, defending his country against foreign aggression. Lieutenant Zakrzewski was also injured.

Towards the evening the Gallo-Polish troops occupied Novi and Basaluzzo, and General Dąbrowski returned to his initial position.

On the 19th (10 November), the division was ordered to take Ovada's position on the left; General Jablonowski to lift the blockade of Serravalle and join us. The enemy being opposite, we were obliged to make this movement during the night of the 19th to the 20th. Accordingly the Legion passed to the left, passing through Tassarolo and Bisio, and on the 20th taking the following position: the artillery was returned to Gavi, considering the impossibility of putting it in position; the 3rd Demi-brigade, with the 1st Polish Battalion, at Silvana and Castelletto, and its outposts at Capriata; the demi-brigade, that inseparable companion of the labors and glory of the Polish division, went to Carponetto and Racca-Grimalda, pushing its outposts to Padagiera; the chasseurs were between these two demi-brigades; the headquarters was at Ovada, the grenadiers and the 3rd Battalion at Cremolino, the 3rd at Taglioto[7], and finally the cavalry at Molara; on the right of the division was that of General Watrin, and on the left that of General Miollis, which Laboissiere had just left.

On the 24th (15th), the 3rd Demi-brigade left for Genoa; the 1st Polish Battalion occupied Castelletto; the 2nd and 3rd Silvano.

Some movements were made, as much for the convenience of the troop as for that of the inhabitants, during which a few slight skirmishes took place between the outposts.

The entire right wing, under the orders of General Saint-Cyr, remained in this position until 5 Frimaire (26 November).

General Dąbrowski tried, in the meanwhile, to procure as much food as possible, since he was soon to be obliged to leave the plain, because of the great snow that usually falls in that season, and not to entirely lose communication between Genoa and the mountains; he managed to make small magazines for fifteen days in Campo-Freddo and Masone.

General Miollis retired the Frimaire 5th into the mountains, and, accordingly, our left wing made a retrograde movement, facing towards Acqui.

The enemy attacked the outposts of this wing, but these having been reinforced, they had to withdraw without having been able to succeed in the project which they had to make it leave this position. General Saint-Cyr allowed General Dąbrowski to remain in the plain as long as he would find it good, and the latter guarded all the outlets so well that the enemy could never break it, and he had his troops subsist. at the expense of the Piedmontese.

On the 10th and 11th (1/2 December 1799), so much snow fell that it was difficult to find the roads to the mountains, so it was necessary to withdraw.

Headquarters moved to Masone with the grenadiers, and the 106th Demi-brigade moved to Montebello, Cabane and Poggio. The Pol-

---

[7]Translator: It would appear that there is a typesetting error here, as two 3rd Battalions are identified. It is reasonable to suspect that the first reference is properly the 2nd Battalion.

ish Legion was at Ronciglione and Campo-Freddo and the cavalry was at Voltri. All other communications, on the right and on the left, had become so impassable because of the snows that it was as impossible for the enemy to attack the Legion as it was for Dąbrowski to move against them.

All these different battles and skirmishes, however, had cost the Poles a lot of men and horses. The soldiers, without being paid or dressed, but continually on the march or on duty, were often ill; besides, the bad season contributed to doubling the mortality rate, and the impossibility of treating them well in the hospitals meant that few recovered, and the number consequently diminished considerably. The cavalry was already reduced to one hundred horses, few of which were in a condition to serve and were exhausted by continual fatigues and exhausted by hunger. The depots in Nice and Villefranche were in the most terrible state and could only provide a half ration of bread to officers and soldiers alike, when at the same time the daily fight with the Barbets continued.

The artillery and the 2nd Legion were absolutely in the same condition, and they were obliged to march to Fort Barraux, between Grenoble and Chambéry.

General Dąbrowski spared no efforts with General-in-Chef Championnet to improve the situation of his unfortunate compatriots, and when he could not go personally before him, as his presence was always necessary in the camp, he sent his aide-de-camp to explain to Championnet the extreme misery in which the Legion found itself. But these efforts were fruitless, because the whole army was in the same state. The English pirates cut all communications by sea with France such that no ship could enter the ports of Liguria and as the land route from Nice to Genoa was still not usable in this season by wagons, the French were reduced to using pack mules to transport food. With the bad roads and lack of fodder, the army could never be sufficiently provided. General Championnet, however, consented that the artillery and the 2nd Legion could assemble at Marseilles.

In the midst of such a desperate situation for the Poles in Italy, their fate in France was no less painful. Biernacki, as we have seen above, sent by General Dąbrowski to Paris, returned at this period of his mission, and he brought the news that it was true that General

Kniaziewicz had obtained from the French government the order of to form a new Polish Legion on the Rhine, but that the state of affairs did not allow for money or any other means of organizing it could be furnished immediately, and, that consequently, the Polish Legion of Italy could not hope for any relief.

In such an overwhelming situation, all the Polish Corps appealed to General Dąbrowski, and wrote him a letter, begging him to go to Paris himself, and to find a means of putting an end to their misfortune. What increased their hopes at that time, and what supported General Dąbrowski in this difficult mission, was the arrival of General Bonaparte at Paris, returning from his expedition from Egypt.

Officers of the Polish Corps to
Général de division Dąbrowski, commander of said corps

Ovada, Frimaire 11, Year VI (December 2, 1799).

According to the order of the French government, you were sent to form the Polish legions in Italy under the eyes of Bonaparte; you gave them a distinguished existence, which later on by the Generals Berthier, Brun, and Moreau, was confirmed by the justice that was rendered them. The Legions are diminished by the war in half. Watch, General, their augmentation, this is the time. Who can be a better organ to Bonaparte, who is consul, than Berthier, who is now Minister of War, if it is not you? For the happiness of your country, for us, leave, General, for Paris.

Imitating your example by the way you share what you have, we offer you for the cost of this trip a month of our salary.

(Signature follows.)

Dąbrowski obtained permission to make this journey, and he left Genoa on the 17th (8 December), after having handed the command of the Polish troops to General Jablonowski.

It was again in this difficult circumstance that Citizen de la Roche rendered a service to the Legions, by facilitating this important mission of General Dąbrowski. He was then back from the trip he made from Rome to Naples, being attached to the corps of General Sarrazin, who chased off the English who had landed at Castelamare, and it was he who, together with Commandant Sibile and Captain Seneguier, managed to save the artillery of the army embarked at Porto-Lerici and disembarked in the presence of the English at the Gulf of Spezia. De la Roche arrived at Genoa at the moment when the shortage was about to produce disorder, and, touched by the abandonment in which the troops of the Polish legions were left, took all the necessary steps with the staff, the army's Intendant and the Genoa paymasters, and obtained the liquidation as well as the payment of their arrears. Such active co-operation altered the precarious position of the Polish troops; instead of misery, abundance and joy were spread throughout the corps. It was then that this corps made so noble an application to General-in-Chief Dąbrowski of the pecuniary sacrifices he had imposed upon himself; these sacrifices subdued the expenses of his mission to Consul Bonaparte, a mission that brought about a new reorganization of the Polish legions.

On his way, Dąbrowski met the artillery and the 2nd Polish Legion, who were already on the march to meet in Marseilles, and he ordered that all the individuals of these two corps who were at the depots at Nice and Villefranche go to Marseille to join them. Arriving at Paris and preceded by a reputation which his talents and devotion had earned so many titles, General Dąbrowski was received in the most distinguished manner. The Consul of the Republic, Bonaparte, hastened on every occasion to render justice to the illustrious leader of those Polish legions he had seen rise under his auspices and conquer with him. He gave the general a fresh proof of his satisfaction in the letter which he addressed to him immediately after his arrival at Paris.

Paris, this Nivôse 5, Year VIII (December 26, 1799).

Back in Europe, Citizen General, I learned with interest of the conduct that you and your brave Poles held in Italy during the last campaign.

Setbacks have obscured for a moment the glory of our arms, but everything promises us that it will soon shine with new bril-

liance. Tell your brave men that they are always present in my thoughts, that I rely on them, that I appreciate their devotion to the cause we defend, and that I will always be their friend and comrade.

Be assured, Citizen General, of my distinguished consideration and my attachment.

BONAPARTE.

Taking advantage of such a flattering welcome, General Dąbrowski presented his ideas and requests in detailed notes, and he obtained:

1.) An order for all the Polish Corps to gather in Marseilles;

2.) That this corps should be received in the pay of the French Republic, and that it should be composed of seven battalions of infantry, and one battalion of artillery, under the name of 1st Polish Legion, in the pay of the French Republic, and consequently the Polish cavalry regiment would go to the Army of the Rhine to join the so-called Danube Legion, commanded by General Kniaziewicz;

3.) That Polish officers, with orders from the government, should go to the depots of prisoners of war to enlist the Poles who were there;

4.) Finally, an order by which the Poles enjoyed the same rights to the benefits of the French government as the French themselves, all the officers and soldiers of the Legions could enter the Hôtel des Invalides.[8]

As a result of this determination, Colonel Grabinski, returning from Egypt to Paris, was placed in the Legion as a général de brigade, and sent to Dijon for purposes of recruitment; Major Kasimir Konopka and Captain Komorowski went to Lille for the same purpose, because in the bosom of all the Russian or Austrian armies there were Polish subjects who sighed after the favorable moment when, deserting the standards that had guided the foreign hordes to the enslavement of their country, they could serve it again by passing under the flags which alone would one day give them their freedom!

[8]Translator: When old soldiers retired from service, they lived in the Hôtel des Invalides.

Marseilles was the place assigned for the armament and the clothing of the Legion. The infantry received crimson cuffs and collars, the national colors of Poland, and the artillery kept its old uniform in its entirety. Polish marks of distinction did not undergo any change among the officers.

Chef de bataillion of Artillery Axamitowski received command of the Polish infantry and artillery troops in the Departments of the Rhône, Bouches-du-Rhône and Var, with orders to send to Toulon, Besançon, etc., officers to recruit among the prisoners of war.

General Dąbrowski, having finally finished the affairs of the Polish Corps, left Paris to go to Marseilles, where he arrived at 4 Prairial, Year VIII (21 May 1800). He nevertheless left Chief Dembowski, his aide-de-camp at Paris, to receive from the Minister of War what had not yet been delivered, and consequently he charged him with his correspondence with him.

The cavalry regiment had already left under the command of Chef d'escadron Alexander Rozniecki. The depots of Nice and Villefranche arrived in Marseilles. General Karwowski, not having left with the cavalry, was placed as chef de brigade in the Legion, and received the command of the Polish infantry distributed in the departments mentioned above.

The infantry and artillery, divided into different detachments, were continually at war with the Barbets in the interior of the country, and with the English on the coasts. These men often threatened to land and raid and even they sometimes succeeded at some points, but they were immediately forced to flee faster than they had come. The Austrians, having penetrated as far as the Var, the French troops were obliged to march on Antibes, and then to proceed to Nice. Recruits arrived from all sides, and in a very short space of time the 7th Battalion, whose Major Biernacki had obtained the provisional command, was organized and brought to completion. It occupied the cities of Avignon, Manosque, Arles, Mount Dragon, Tarascon, etc., and appeased the troubles which often broke out in these places.

The 4th, 5th, and 6th Battalions, the same ones which composed the former 2nd Polish Legion, which had been part of the Mantuan garrison at the time of the capitulation of that fortress, were then augmented; and as soon as they were halfway to full strength, they were sent to Aubagne, Toulon, etc., and at the same time recruiting depots were formed for the first three battalions still in the army. These three battalions could never reach Marseilles, for they were always marching and continually fighting with the army, where their services were necessary.

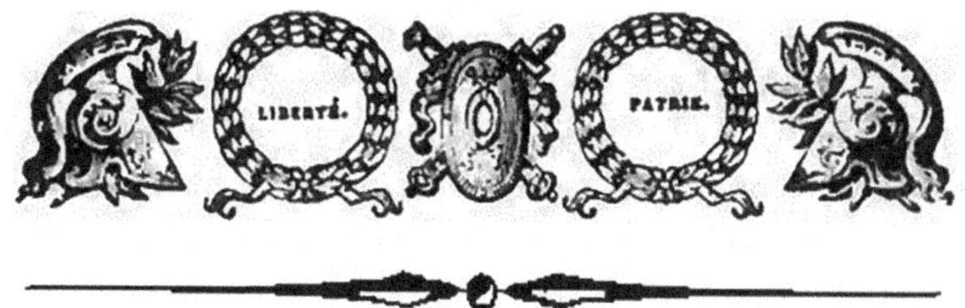

CHAPTER TWELVE

New Battles. — Engagement with the Barbets. — Death of Championnet. — Masséna Takes Superior Command. — Movement of General Melas. — Blockade of Genoa. — The Legion Withdraws to the Var. — Jablonowski. — The Austrians Pursue the Army. — Skirmishes and Actions on the Line. — Jablonowski. — The Legion Goes to Oneille. — General Bonaparte Crosses the St. Bernard. — Thirty Day Campaign. — Battle of Marengo. — Kasimir de la Roche. — Masséna Returns to Genoa 20 Days After Its Capitulation. — Bonaparte at Milan. — His Return to Paris. — New Efforts by Dąbrowski for the Regeneration of Poland. — General Dąbrowski goes to Milan. — New Hostilities. — The Polish Legion Enters the Field. — It Receives orders to Invest Peschiera and Sermione. — Siege of These two Fortresses. — Flotilla on Lake Garda. — Detail of Various Engagements Under the Walls of Peschiera. — General Chasseloup-Laubat Takes Command of the Siege. — Activity of the Besiegers. — Devotion of the Polish Troops. — Parlimentarian Sent to the Austrian Command. — Its Refusal. — Vigorous Attack. — Battle of Pozzolo; Wollodkowicz. — Armistice of Treviso. — Suspension of Hostilities. — Peschiera and Sermoine Are Evacuated. — Occupation of Mantua. — Movement of the Legions During the Suspension of Hostilities. — Peace of Luneville. — Junction of the Polish Legions of Italy with those of the Danube in Milan. — Their Dispersion and Destruction. — Conclusion.

While General Dąbrowski took action in Paris to improve the condition of his legions, the Polish troops occupied their old positions and were constantly in combat with the Austrians. These latter had moved on Cabane, Marcharolo, and Ronciglione, and forced the 3rd Battalion, under the orders of Chef de bataillon Swiderski to leave its position after a strong resistance and retire on Camp-Freddo. On 30 Frimaire, Year VIII (21 December 1799), General Jablonowski ordered Major Konopka (the Younger) to attack the enemy at Ronciglione with four companies of the 1st Battalion and to clear the position. Konopka executed this order, fell with impetuosity on the Imperial troops, threw them into the mountains behind the position, pursued them as far as

Ovada, and took many prisoners from them. He then occupied the designated position.

On 5 Nivôse (26 December), the Legion concentrated in Voltri to cover the coast against the English cruising the sea that bathes these shores, and to contain the Barbets in the interior of the mountains. Then on 27 Nivôse (17 January 1800), it moved to Oneilla (Oneglia); on the 29th. It was obliged to retrace its steps, and to march to Albenga, where it occupied on 1 Pluviôse (21 January) the passage of Zuccarello and Castel Bianco, and from there at last it went towards Garessio.

In the meantime, the Polish cavalry regiment left for Marseilles.

In this position, the Legion was obliged to fight daily against the regular troops, or against the Barbets, only to procure some food. There was absolutely nothing to live on, but that which could be snatched from the enemy; the shops of Genoa and others were empty. When the soldier were reduced to the last extremity, and unable to resist such dreadful misery, French troops came to relieve the Legion, and the Republican officers and soldiers shared with them the food they had brought. On 10 Pluviôse (30 January) the Legion moved to Oneille, and on the 17th (6 February) to Ponte d'Assio, to occupy the mountains bordering Piedmont.

Such was the state of affairs in Liguria, where the army was exposed to the cruellest privations, when General Masséna was appointed to the command of the Army of Italy. Indeed, he entered office on 21 Pluviôse (10 February 1800), the day of his arrival in Genoa. As for General Championnet, suffering from an epidemic that daily carried off officers and soldiers, he died on 10 January 1800, in Antibes. This illustrious general, whose thoughts were for his soldiers and for the country, who so gloriously led the Polish legions into Naples, and to whom he gave so much evidence of interest in the present campaign, carried off in his grave universal regrets and esteem.

Championnet's successor, Masséna, "the spoiled child of victory," by receiving from the 1st Consul Bonaparte all the powers necessary to remedy the distressing situation of the troops whose direction was entrusted to him, despite his incredible activity, gathered under his orders only about twenty-five thousand fighters, misery and disease having taken as many men as desertion. The efforts of this general could not procure for his troops a momentary relief!

Meanwhile, Masséna had reduced the cadres of the army in proportion to the number of combatants; several demi-brigades were merged into one. Changes had taken place among the general officers, Gouvion Saint-Cyr had been recalled to the Army of the Rhine, Victor and Lemoine were destined to be part of the Army of Reserve: Soult, Suchet and Gazan replaced them. On 5 April, the Army of Italy, divided into two corps or two great divisions, occupied the following positions: The right corps, under the orders of General Soult, was distributed in Roses, Monte Cornua, Toriglio, Bochetta, Campo-Freddo, Stella, Monte-Legino and Cadibone. He also furnished garrisons to Genoa, Savona, and Gavi; he was to provide for the safety of the coast, and to facilitate the arrival of foodstuffs at Genoa. The left corps, commanded by General Suchet, of which the Polish Legion was a part, had his right on Noli and its left at Var; the headquarters were at Pietra.

Such a considerable development, however, could not be restrained, since it was important to hold the passes of Tuscany, Plaisantain, Lombardy, and Piedmont; to defend the entrance of the Alps, and consequently the frontiers of the Republic; General Melas was preparing to break this line and isolate the two corps that defended it. On 5 April, the Austrian Headquarters came to Cairo. The intention of the Austrian general was to simultaneously attack the main outlets of the Apennine chain, but he wanted above all to occupy the French line as near as possible to Genoa, in order to force Masséna to withdraw his troops to that city, to starve it by the cooperation of the English squadron, and therefore hasten surrender.

These maneuvers, however, found constant opposition on the part of the republican army; it defended its positions with its ordinary valor. General Jablonowski, in partial engagements, gave fresh proofs of his personal bravery; he completely defeated the enemy division which debouched by the Tanaro, and took five hundred prisoners.

In the meantime, and during the day of the 10 Germinal (31 March), the Polish Legion went to San Remo, and thence to Nice on the 13th (3 April), to reorganize itself at Marseilles; but the Austrians having already formed the blockade of Genoa as early as 21 April and pushed back to the Var the corps of General Suchet, which included the Legion, it received the order to remain in Nice until a new disposition was ordered.

As for the city of Genoa, whose siege has since become so famous, General Masséna then had under his command to defend it force of barely twelve thousand men, a part of which was composed of Italian refugees then at Genoa, and which were voluntarily joined by a few hundred Poles taken prisoner from the ranks enemies during the last actions. Chef de bataillon Rossignol was appointed to command them.

All Suchet's army corps took, a position behind the Yar on 15 Floreal (5 May 1800); the Legion, which was on the left wing, occupied Gillette and the heights in the neighborhood. Chef de bataillon Bialowieyski took command of the Legion; General Jablonowski had obtained a French brigade belonging to Poujet's division.

The Austrians were always firing to their right and threatened to pass the Var opposite the left wing. On the 25th (15th), the Legion occupied Malaussene. It arrived there at the very moment that the enemy was in full march and had just crossed the river. Bialowieyski immediately attacked them, and obliged them, after a lively and obstinate resistance, to return to the Yar, which he even occupied on the left bank, after pursuing them.

Continuous skirmishes took place against Malaussene with the enemy outposts, on which the Legion always gained the advantage until finally the Chef de bataillon Bialowieyski passed the Var, on 1 Prairial (21 May). Major Konopka turned the enemy's position on the left with the 1st Battalion, while Bialowieyski attacked them directly with the rest of the Legion. After a very obstinate fight, the Austrians were forced to leave their position and retire to Utelle, where they were pursued. In this affair thirty men were killed and as many wounded including Polish Captain Parys.

On the 4th (24 May) Bialowieyski renewed the attack and drove the enemy from Utelle; he captured a great deal of food and ammunition. On the 6th and 7th (26th and 27th), Melas wanted to attack the Legion, but the Chef de bataillon Bialowieyski went forward on the River Vesubia and missed his company. The general, however, always maneuvered to the left, and the Polish Legion moved along this side and arrived near Lantosque, where the Austrians, seeing that they could not manage to turn this wing, withdrew to the where they were pursued, and finding themselves overwhelmed by this maneuver, threw themselves upon the Col de Tende, where they were still pursued and obliged to retreat.

In this defense of the line on the Var, rested on the French army, consisting of the thirteen thousand four hundred sixty-six men, Général de brigade Jablonowski, part of Rochambeau's division in the center, had one thousand three hundred five combatants under his command.

Then the Legion was ordered to blockade Ventimiglia, which surrendered on the 22nd (11 June), and it was there that it learned that, according to a convention between the two belligerent armies, General Masséna had evacuated Genoa on 16 Prairial (5 June 1800), taking with him the glory of a resistance that was fabulous.

The Polish Legion set out for Nice and returned to Oneille, on the 28th, to occupy the valley of that name, and contain the insurgents who had cut off all communication. It was in the midst of these events that the Army of the Reserve, under the immediate orders of General Alexandre Berthier and under the supreme direction of 1st Consul Bonaparte, opened the memorable thirty-day campaign.

Indeed, the 24 Floréal, Year VIII (14 May 1800), Napoleon began to make the wonderful passage of the Great St. Bernard. The 25th and 26th (15/16 May), after a partial commitment to Etroubles, the bridge of the Cluse is forced and the city of Aosta occupied. On the 28th (18 May), after the affair and the taking of Chatillon, the city of Bard shared the same fate on 1 Prairial (21 May). The 5th (25 May), the First Consul arrived at Verrez. The 6th, 7th, and 8th (26 -28 May), the fight of the Chiusella, the capture of Varallo and Vercelli were carried out with the same rapidity. On the 9th (29 May), the Sesia was crossed. The 11th (31 May), the passage of Tesin and the fight at Turbigo opened to the French the plains of Lombardy. On the 12th (1 June), Pavia surrendered unconditionally. On the 13th (2 June), the French entered Milan. The 17th (6 June), they passed the Po by Belgiojoso, and fought at San-Cipriano. On the 18th (7 June), they seized Cremona and Piacenza, after a battle in which one thousand six hundred men were takcn prisoner, and one hundred French delivered. The 20th (9 June), the battle of Montebello serves as a precursor to that of Marengo, and the 25 Prairial, Year VIII (14 June 1800) its plains were witnesses of a decisive affair, whose result was the restitution of Piedmont, Liguria,

Lombardy, the cession of twelve strongholds to the French, and the evacuation by the Austrian troops from all Italy to the Mincio, for the guarantee of the convention concluded at Alessandria, on 26 Prairial, Year VIII (15 June 1800), between the generals Alexandre Berthier and Melas.[1]

[1]A work much better known abroad than in France, made with luxury and at great expense, was published immediately afterwards and on the events in question. In its introduction, as in the explanations accompanying its beautiful maps and plans, it perfectly characterizes this memorable campaign. This is the broad and energetic manner in which it is described in the *Fastes militaires; Campagne de l'armée de la réserve*: "There is no place in the Universe,": it is said, "that recounts so many glorious exploits, which speaks so powerfully to thought and imagination, than this vast plain that closes the majestic Alps and the beautiful Apennines. Each century presents it to us as the theater of the most brilliant military feats, actions that have decided the fate of empires, terrible, melancholy scenes, which have cost tears to humanity, and deserved statues to heroes. There, the traveler discovers at every moment campaigns consecrated by the most imposing memories; at each step he stirs up the ashes of a warrior: all the demi-gods of modern times come to claim its admiration. The Alps, the Tésin, Marignan, Marengo, are proud of the names of Hannibal, Caesar and Francis I, Charles V, Catinat, Bonaparte: nature and men came together to make these countries famous."

We find in the expressions of this author a faithful picture of the sensations experienced by our compatriots, when, hastening to these beautiful countries, full of memories of their ancestors, they came to seal with their blood the last homage paid to their memory and to announce to the astonished Universe that the military glory of the Poles still existed.

Here is the concise manner in which the same work has outlined in a few lines the vast picture of this campaign: "The principal Austrian army, under the orders of General Elsnitz, was on the banks of the Var; another, under the Generals Hohenzollern and Ott, besieged Genoa; considerable corps were distributed on different points; General Melas, no longer listening to an imprudent security, rejoined his divided forces; a formidable army and a large artillery were gathered under the walls of Alessandria. There remained to the French a new triumph to obtain, a triumph which completed all their victories, and the day of Marengo annihilated all the hopes of our enemies and hastened the happy moment of peace. To destroy the dispositions of the enemy most skillfully combined, to divide their forces, to paralyze their principal measures, to cut off their communications and retreat, to change the theater of action, to harass and beat the isolated bodies, to cut off the armies at various points, and concentrate them to attack and defeat them in their totality; such were the important operations of the Army of the Reserve, rexecuting a masterpiece of maneuvers, which offers in the space of 30 days all the prodigies of the military art, prodigies which do not need the distance of time to enlarge them to command the admiration of the Universe."

Finally, the author, in concluding his narrative, makes the following considerations: "A comparison of the exploits which illustrated these countries two hundred twenty years before the Christian era, at the beginning of the sixteenth century and at the end of the eighteenth, and the historical comparison of their respective results will indicate sufficiently which of the three

As for the Polish Legion, after so much marching and fighting, after the misery and fatigue it had endured in the Alps and Apennines, the Legion was reduced to only eight hundred men under arms. The bad season, the mountains that had to be crossed without rest, the hunger and the almost total nudity, had caused many diseases. The soldiers succeeded each other in the hospitals, and seldom did they come back from their convalescence. However, the results of this Marengo campaign, a campaign never to be forgotten, were not long in influencing the fate of the Polish legions, and new laurels awaited the patriots in the fields of Lombardy.

The remains of the old Army of Italy, meanwhile, came to take possession of Genoa, and General Suchet entered it 22 June, at the head of his troops. Masséna went there himself on the 24th, twenty days after having left it in such an honorable manner.

Consul Bonaparte, on the other hand, went to Milan almost immediately after having ratified the Alessandria Convention. He was received with inexpressible enthusiasm. Although his stay was short,

---

epochs deserves the most attention. After having pierced the Alps, Hannibal conquered Turin, defeated the Roman armies; he mastered fortune by daring and talent. Enormous spaces were crossed, terrible difficulties overcome, formidable legions conquered, Rome was going to recognize a foreign domination: gave birth to heroes, the country is saved; it opposes the valor, the genius of Hannibal, the patience of Fabius and the brilliant heroism of Scipio.

Francis I asserted, in Lombardy, vain titles that had already caused blood flow under his predecessors; he forced the Col d'Argentiere, triumphed at Marignan, covered his laureled head four times. A generous prince, an intrepid warrior, he knew how to deserve applause for his happiness, and to share his reverses; but, attaching more importance to military glory than to its results, he could not be a statesman or a politician; with less brilliant qualities, less frankness, Charles V was happier and had a greater share in the destinies of Europe.

Emulating the most celebrated warriors, and endeavoring to surpass them all, knowing how to conceive cautiously, to execute with audacity, to reap the fruits of victory, Bonaparte changed the face of the states, the system of Europe, fixed upon himself all eyes, disconcerted the most skillful politicians: as hero and statesman, his life will offer one of the most interesting periods of modern history."

Such is the spirit and plan of this work, little known at present, whose success at the moment of its appearance has been prodigious. It is pleasant for us to say today that the initials K. D. L. R. under which this book appeared are those of Kasimir de la Roche. He had conceived and composed it during his spare time in peacetime, and not being able to be a member of the Polish legions in 1802 to be useful to his country, he wished to honor it at least as a publicist and historian.

he had time to reorganize the Cisalpine Republic, of which he had been the founder; he decided that the troops of the Army of the Reserve and those of the old Army of Italy should be united into one corps, under the name of the Army of Italy, of which General Masséna would take the command.

On 28 June, the First Consul, accompanied by Lieutenant-General Murat, Chef de brigade Duroc, and several other generals and superior officers left Milan to go to Turin, where General Berthier had already gone to organize the Provisional government of Piedmont. On the 30th, he arrived in Lyon, where the Prefect Verninac and the Lyonnais celebrated the presence of the hero. On 1 July, he took the road to Paris, and this road, adorned with cradles of flowers and lined by huge crowds, was from one end to the other a long triumphant arc.

In the meantime, General Dąbrowski was working at Marseilles on the execution of the new organization, the complement and the clothing of the Polish Legion, and the means of gathering it in one place.

Not doubting, on the other hand, that Bonaparte would not take advantage of his triumph at Marengo to crush Austrian power, or at least to restore Poland, the persevering and indefatigable Dąbrowski wrote the following letter to the First Consul, adding to it the summary of his plans for liberation:

Marseille, Messidor 18, Year VIII (7 July 1800)

Deign, Citizen First Consul, to take a moment's notice of the attached state; it contains materials for one of your finest trophies and prepares for you a glory so much purer as it will not cost a single drop of blood to the French people.

The Poles ask you, Citizen 1st Consul, the honor of making a last effort in favor of their unfortunate country; their brothers wait for them and call them. So please allow them the glory of going to break their irons, or to die for such a beautiful cause. The same ardor ignites the hearts of all our compatriots; and I, in drawing this plan, am only the interpreter of their unanimous devotion. If you wish for its development, Citizen 1st Consul, order it to be done, and will fly to surrender myself to your orders.

There are other details in support of this project that Citizens Wybicki and Zaïonczek will have the honor to report to you.

Dąbrowski

In the event that the war continues with the House of Austria, or that negotiations drag on at length, would it not be practicable to assemble on the left wing of the Army of the Rhine all the Polish Corps, which at this moment are partly in Italy, to bring them to twenty thousand to thirty thousand and to put them in a condition to enter the field as soon as possible? This corps thus assembled, organized and commanded by an enterprising general, zealous for his country, and provided with all the talents that a daring undertaking requires, should direct his march, for example, from Mainz directly on Eger, avoid as much as possible battles and sieges, and seek only to penetrate into Galicia, advancing through Bohemia and Moravia. The Emperor of Germany, not being able in such a short time to send an army against the Poles, will not be able to stop their progress; he will be able to oppose them only with recruits from Bohemia and Galicia, people tired of slavery, always dreaming of freedom and revolution, and who, at the sight of an army penetrated with the same spirit, will soon join in with it.

This army, led by a disinterested and firm man, with regard to order and discipline, has no reason to fear that towns and villages will close their doors, but will see them on the contrary lend themselves to all its needs.

The advantage which would result from this expedition for the French army is all too evident, for the march of the Poles will oblige the Imperial wing to retreat into Bohemia, while the left wing of the French army, still holding it in check, will prevent it from using all its forces against the Poles.

As for these, it's the only way to achieve the goal of their constant vows, the regeneration of their country. Their army running no risk, always seeing in front of its line of operation, without anxiety on its flanks and rear, will have only to march forward, to gather laurels and to reconquer Poland.

The efforts of the Poles will not fail to receive the army of their brothers, and help it to drive out the usurper, it would be easy for anyone to guess who does not ignore how impatiently this people is waiting for the right moment to shake off the yoke that oppressed him, accustomed to sacrificing everything to preserve their independence. Besides, the virtuous Kosciuszko is still there; his name will be a rallying cry for all good citizens; the esteem with which he enjoys, the confidence which his moral life inspires, will revive hope in all hearts, and the army under his auspices has the right to hope for achieving the most brilliant successes.

As for the political operations to be taken as soon as the army sets foot in Poland, we must abandon its direction to the advice and wishes of the French government, whose intentions would be fulfilled by those of the Poles who showed their patriotism and enlightenment, all the more ardently for the good of the Polish nation.

But what will the King of Prussia say then? Nothing, for the French government, not declaring itself openly for the Poles, can disavow a demarche, which is supposed to have been undertaken without its knowledge.

The King of Prussia will gather an army in Silesia? All the better, for the Emperor will be obliged to do the same, and he will thus weaken his armies on the Rhine and in Italy.

The King of Prussia will attack the Poles? No, it must be believed, on the contrary, that he will not put any obstacle to their entry into the Austrian possessions.

But what will Paul I[2] say? He will be delighted that Austria has one more enemy to confront, which will seem to fall like clouds. It is possible that he also gathers an army on the frontiers of Galicia; but this very measure will force the Emperor to oppose him with proportionate forces.

At the opening of negotiations for peace, the Poles being in possession of a third of the territory of their country, and constituted as a nation, will have legal titles to claim the assistance of the French Republic and its allies, and the French government

[2]Translator: Paul 1, Czar of Russia. (1754 - 1801)

will then have a justified right to rescue an oppressed people, to support their interests, and to negotiate for them. Such powerful protection will facilitate the consent of Prussia and Russia to divest themselves of the invaded provinces, with compensation in Germany for the first, and in Turkey for the second.

What will the Poles finally say? They will profess a religious veneration for the French nation, as their protective deity. They will raise monuments to the great Bonaparte, which will attest to future generations and the grandeur of their recognition and that of this hero, to whose genius they will have to conquer their ancient independence.

Dąbrowski.

Having thus fulfilled the wish of his heart, and not wanting to let any circumstance escape, General Dąbrowski, to obtain, in the meantime, with more certainty the permission to organize his legion again, directed Chef de brigade Grabinski and the Chef de Bataillon Axamitowski to go to General Masséna in Milan, to inform him of the urgency of his consent, and to make the necessary observations on this subject: the first (Grabinsky) was to remain at Milan, to form a depot for Polish recruitment, arming and dressing it with the help of the Austrian stores which had fallen into the power of the Republican Army.

During this time, a large number of recruits arrived in Marseilles. General Wielhorski, having returned from the prisons of Austria, and the other officers included in the capitulation of Mantua, went with them to that city. They returned at once to their old units, which they found half complete.

General-in-Chief Masséna received very well the two superior officers Grabinski and Axamitowski and gave orders to the three battalions scattered in Liguria and Piedmont to go to Milan, and to execute this order promptly, he charged Captain Hauke, who was later an aide-de-camp of General Dąbrowski, to reunite the whole Legion at Milan. Accordingly, he entrusted the command of the Polish troops stationed in and around Marseilles to General Wielhorski, charged him with presiding over the Legion's general board of directors, bringing together all his people, and then marching to Milan, and these instructions given, he himself set out to get ahead of the corps.

With new expectations presented to the Poles upon the opening of the winter campaign (1800 and 1801), General Dąbrowski went to the theater of war, and arrived at Milan on 11 Vendemiaire, Year IX (3 October 1800). There he already found the 1st and the 2nd Battalions together; the other battalions arrived there successively, and the depot at Marseilles, with the General Wielhorski, went there the 10 Brumaire (1 November).

The whole Legion was then organized. The Cisalpine government spared neither trouble nor money to dress it; the French funds provided its pay, and the Italian arsenals its arms.

On the 17th (8 November), General Dąbrowski passed the whole Legion in review; more than five thousand men were already in uniform and under the flag at that time, and several officers who had been made prisoners of war in previous campaigns were returning from Austria. It was through their channel that the Polish Legion learned of the death of the worthy and brave leader of the Legion, Forestier, who had succumbed to serious wounds in Hungary, where he had been held as a prisoner of war.

The resumption of hostilities having experienced some delays in Italy, both sides thought to come to blows. The Cabinet of Vienna had ordered General-in-Chief Bellegarde to avoid, as much as he could, to reopen the campaign before the army corps which occupied the Tyrol was able to enter into line with the Army of Italy to support its operations, although the latter was then sixty thousand strong.

The French army remained inactive by the same motives which kept the Austrian army in its positions. General Brune, appointed to the post of Command-in-Chief after the departure of Masséna, would not engage seriously with his adversary Bellegarde, before General Macdonald was advanced far enough in the Tyrol to cover his left flank and prevent the enemy troops from turning Lake Garda.

Be that as it may, as a result of the general provisions given to other corps, General Dąbrowski received, as early as 29 Brumaire (20 November), the order to enter the field as early as possible, with the Polish Legion, to form the 2nd Reserve Division. He therefore left Milan on the 30th (21st) with the 1st, 2nd, 3rd and 7th Battalions, four thousand four hundred men strong, and an artillery company.

General Wielhorski, Adjutant-Commander Kosinski, Chief of the General Staff, and all the other officers, POWs, who had just returned on parole, could not be employed during this campaign. They accordingly remained at Milan, as well as the 4th, 5th, and 6th Battalions, and three companies of artillery, to complete their organization.

Captain Royer then served as Chief-of-Staff to General Dąbrowski; Battalion Commanders Konopka and Regulski, aide-de-camp, and Captains Komorowski and Szmauch, the deputy commanders. This corps arrived at Brescia 4 Frimaire (25 November 1800).

The General-in-Chief Brune was not without anxiety on his right flank; this flank was commanded by General Dupont, who had returned to the line after his Tuscan expedition; and as he had left in this duchy only a small body under the orders of General Miollis, it was to be feared that this troop could not resist the efforts of the Neapolitan Army, which had already reached the frontiers of Tuscany, while General Sommariva, on his side, approached the Po with the Austrians and the insurgents, and a strong detachment of the Mantuan garrison attacked Marcaria, on the Oglio, on the extreme right of General Dupont.

In this expedition General Jablonowski commanded a French brigade. His bravery did not fail on this occasion, as in all actions where he found himself present. Also, to neutralize this attack, on 22 Frimaire (13 December), two companies of the 7th Battalion of the Polish Legion were sent to Guastalla, under the orders of the Chef de bataillon Biernacki, to occupy this position and to hold the Austrian troops from Ferrara in respect. This detachment sometimes had little business with the enemy, and always came out of it with advantage.

The center corps of the Army of Italy was then under the orders of General Suchet, and the left wing to those of General Moncey.

When the army began to act offensively, its reserve, and especially the Polish Corps reinforced by a battery of light artillery, followed the headquarters, and, accordingly, left Brescia on 28 Frimaire (19 December), reaching Rezzato same day, 29th (20th) at Lonato, 1 Nivôse, Year IX (22 December 1800) at Castiglione, on 3rd (24th) at Cavriano, where General Dąbrowski was ordered to march to the left for to invest

Peschiera, while the body of the army would pass the Mincio.[3]

While General-in-Chief Brune fought the battle of Pozzolo, the results of which were fatal to the Austrian army, General Dąbrowski set off on 4 Nivôse (25 December) from Rivoltella to invest the fortress of Peschiera, advantageously situated on the banks of Lake Garda, at the mouth of the Mincio, a very important point, which had always been disputed in all the wars waged for the conquest of Italy.

On retiring, during 4-6 Nivôse, Year IX (25 – 27 December 1800), the Austrian army, as soon as it was forced into the line of the Alincio, threw two thousand five hundred men into Peschiera; at the same time, it established a detachment of five hundred men in the town of Sermione, which, because of the ease of communications by water, formed part of the garrison of Peschiera, which were four or five Italian miles apart.

Sermione is located in a peninsula that extends towards the middle of the lake, over a length of nearly two miles, and forms a narrow strip of land, where nature seems to offer an easy defense. It is towards the end of this peninsula covered with olive trees, that one still finds ancient ruins and underground roads, called in the country the "Caves of Catullus." Indeed, they are the remains of a great palace belonging to the illustrious family of the Catullus, a Roman noble, where the singer of Lesbia found inspirations. It was then on these fields, illustrated by so remote an antiquity, that the soldiers of the Polish Legion, under General Dąbrowski's orders, were covered with modern glory.

To preserve Peschiera from any surprise, the Austrians had, for some time, maintained a well-equipped flotilla there, which dominat-

---

[3]The situation of the total Army of Italy, at the time of the month of December 1800, under the command of General-in-Chief Brune, was ninety-five thousand two hundred men, and three hundred fifty four cannons, but to this number it is necessary to add twenty-seven thousand men in hospitals.

As for the leaders and the Polish army, it was composed of: General Dąbrowski, part of the reserve of the corps under the orders of General Michaud, who commanded four Polish battalions of three thousand men.

While General Wielhorski, part of Lapoype' division, stationed in Lombardy, he commanded a Polish Legion of two thousand one hundred twenty men. Total Polish troops five thousand one hundred twenty.

Général de brigade Jablonowski, at the same time part of Petitot's division, stationed at Bologna, commanded the Provisional 4th Demi-brigade of the East, and the 4th Demi-brigade of the line, forming a total of two thousand two hundred forty men.

ed the lake and intercepted French communications. Blumenstein, a naval captain in the service of Austria, was its chief; he had organized it himself in 1798, by order of the Viennese Court. Most of the ships, which composed it, had been built at Riva, situated at the extremity of the lake, opposite Peschiera; but all the principal parts of these same ships had been prepared and numbered in the arsenal of Venice, then transported by water, as well as the artillery and all the apparatuses, to Vicenza, and from there, over land, to Riva. This flotilla, by Nivôse year IX, consisted of twelve to fifteen armed ships, and about six hundred fifty crewmen.

These ships were stationed in Peschiera, Sermione, Torri, etc.; from there they made incursions on the banks of the lake and in the surrounding villages, where they obtained provisions, which they continually supplied to the city of Peschiera and the entrances of Sermione.

The French naval forces on Lake Garda were, at that time, practically nil. There were only nine boats and six guns, two of which were iron 8pdrs and four 3pdrs, without ammunition, with only sixty men. These boats anchored at Salo, from which they rarely dared to depart, given the extreme disproportion of their strength.

Chef de division Sibille was then in Salo. His reports of 1, 16 and 17 Nivôse, Year 9 (22 December 1800, 6/7 January 1801), informed the army of the weakness of his means, and he said that he had not yet received the artillery which had been promised to him on 4 Frimaire (25 November 1800), adding that it was impossible for him to second the siege operations by water, but the boats he commanded were not useless, since they served to transport from Riva, towards the top of the lake, a convoy of munitions of war destined for the Army of Grisons. Citizen Sibille himself directed this expedition, which was dangerous, in which he lost a boat, which the Austrians seized.

However, the brave Lieutenant-General Delmas, commanding the Vanguard Lieutenancy, had already closely blockaded Peschiera as early as 30 Frimaire (21 December 1800). On arriving there with Général de brigade Cassagne, he had carried off, on the very glacis of this fortress, a rather considerable post commanded by an Austrian officer. This general left this position only to advance on Verona with the whole army. The 2nd Reserve Lieutenancy Division, on 3 Nivôse, was sent to replace it (24 December). This division, commanded by General Dąbrowski, was composed of the 1st Polish Legion, two squadrons of the 21st Chasseur à cheval Regiment, one of the one hundred seventy one men of the 1st Cisalpine Chasseur à cheval Regiment, and the 1st Temporary Provisional Légère Regiment, called "d'Orient.".

The 1st Battalion of the Polish Legion, along with the chasseurs of the 3rd Battalion of the same Legion, took post across the Sermione Peninsula, facing enemy entrenchments, leaning their left at Lake Garda. Two light cannons were placed to sweep the path and to repel the approaches of the enemy flotilla.

The 2nd, 3rd, and 7th Battalions of the Legion marched towards Ponti, and they placed themselves in front of this town to invest Peschiera on the right bank. As for the French demi-brigades, they marched as far as the Mincio.

The artillery was placed on the high road, which leads from Desenzano to Peschiera, and the cavalry was in reserve near Ponti. A Cisalpine cavalry regiment joined the Gallo-Polish division. It was placed at Lonato to support the left wing and maintain communication with Salo where the Rochambeau division was assembling.

Particular fights took place 5 and 6 Nivôse (26/27 December). The Austrians on this last day made a sortie on the side of the road to Brescia, and there they attacked the Polish outposts. An enemy gunboat attempted to drive the 1st Battalion from the Sermione Peninsula, but it was in vain; neither the cannoneers of the boats, nor a sortie made by the garrison of Sermione Peninsula, but neither the sortie by the garrison nor this could chase them from this post. The Austrians were even repulsed with vigor, after having killed six men and taken twenty prisoners.

On 7 Nivôse (28 December), Loison's and Gazan's divisions, forming part of the center's lieutenancy, were placed at Castel-Novo and Cavalcacello. They closed up the enemy in Peschiera on the left bank of Lake Garda. Several companies of scouts[4] from Gazan's division, having precipitately driving back the Austrian troops into the fortress and took post at a very small distance from the glacis, to better observe the movements of the enemy.

[4]Translator: The text says "compagnies d'éclaireurs," or "scout companies," but no such thing existed. These are probably voltigeurs.

Combining all their movements in their entirety, the Polish Legion gave prodigies of valor in the same day of the 7 Nivôse and showed a sustained intrepidity. General Dąbrowski, posted on the right bank of the Mincio, attacked the Austrian outposts all along the line, in the positions they occupied in front of the city as far as Ponti. He managed to tighten them around Peschiera in a ground about four hundred toises deep, where the enemy remained for some time covered by three houses called "Casa-Campustri"," Casa-Monteferro" and "Casa-Bianca." The Austrians lodged considerable posts there protected by the fire of the ramparts and that of the lunettes situated near the city, towards the road from Brescia. In the course of this day, the Polish Legion fought on several occasions with that fiery courage of its own, and always against superior forces. Chef de brigade Grabinski, adding new laurels to those he had picked up on the banks of the Nile, was able to double the energy of the brave men whom he led into battle; always at their head, he animated them by his example. The brave Chef de bataillon Chlopicki and the other Polish officers did not deny themselves any less; the impetuosity with which they attacked an enemy superior in number, wiped away the inferiority of their numbers and they had the glory of coming out of this unequal combat with victory. The enemy defended themselves valiantly; but they were compelled to retire to the fortress, which had since been completely surrounded, while the Polish Chef de bataillon Bialowieyski, on his side, was pressing closer to Sermione. On that day the Austrians lost sixty men of whom sixteen remained on the battlefield. General de brigade Grabinski was very dangerously wounded with a gunshot to the head, and the Legion had about fifty wounded men and about twenty dead.

The Polish artillery, advancing forward, prevented the communication of the enemy between Peschiera and Sermione. The 3rd Polish Battalion and a French demi-brigade were sent to the right bank of the Mincio, to encircle the fortress on that side. A bridge of boats had been established near Paradiso, to maintain the communication between the two banks, and the headquarters of the Gallo-Polish division was established at Ponti.

On 8 Nivôse (29 December), the enemy, seeking to harass the besiegers again, brought up six armed vessels, which appeared at ten o'clock on the right bank of the lake, between Peschiera and Sermione. They attacked these posts with sustained fire from their floating batteries. The Gallo-Polish troops came to shore with a piece of light artillery. This piece, which fired towards the entrance of the port, did not allow the enemy boats to return to Peschiera; they were therefore forced to go to sea and take refuge in the fort at the city of Sermione.

On the same day, towards eight o'clock in the evening, the garrison of Peschiera executed a vigorous sortie on the left of Dąbrowski's division, with the intention of recovering the former positions which it had lost the day before in front of the city. The Poles, guided by their intrepid Chef de bataillon Chlopicki, disputed the ground stubbornly. They were perfectly seconded by fifty men of the 21st Chasseurs à cheval, who had to suffer the very strong fire of the batteries of the ramparts. After a strong resistance, the enemy was obliged to yield. He hastily withdrew to his entrenchments, leaving the Poles masters of Monteferro. Six men were killed and twenty-five wounded in this skirmish. Captain Linkiewicz of the 7th Battalion of the Legion, who distinguished himself in this action, was one of them.

The 9th Nivôse (30 December) passed without any combat. General Dąbrowski employed that day to place two companies of the 7th Battalion on the right bank of the lake, and to put in battery two pieces of light artillery, which he had pointed at the entrance to the port of Peschiera. These two Polish companies were commanded and conducted with bravery and intelligence by Captain Laskowski.

In spite of the vivacity with which the Gallo-Polish troops commanded by General Dąbrowski attacked Peschiera, which contained a garrison of two thousand five hundred men, the force of the besieging corps, not exceeding four thousand combatants, was consequently far below the proportion required by the rules of attack and defense of fortresses. To give the siege all the proper activity, General-in-Chief Brune wrote to Général de division Chasseloup-Laubat, Commander-in-Chief of Engineers of the Army of Italy, a letter dated 6 Nivôse, Year IX (2 December 1800), by which he charged him with two great operations, the siege of Mantua and that of Peschiera. After having given him detailed testimony of the confidence which his military talents inspired in him, he ordered him to begin with the siege of the latter city, promising him all the help he might need to take the fortress.

All the troops and artillery required for this operation had not yet arrived under Peschiera. It was not until the 10 Nivôse (31 December 1800) that General Chasseloup received the formal order to take the direction of the siege and the superior command of the troops that were destined for it, which according to the order of the day of 10 Nivôse's (31 December), issued from the headquarters at Villafranca by the Général de division Oudinot, chief of the General Staff of the Army of Italy, were to consist of the 1st Polish Legion, the Italic Division, the 1st Provisional Demi-brigade, known as "d'Orient", the 1st Cisalpine Chasseur à cheval Regiment, a detachment of the French 21st Chasseur à cheval Regiment, and of a battalion of the volunteers from the reserve. General Dąbrowski was second in command of all the siege troops, and Chef d'escadron F. Hénin was appointed Chief of Staff of the Headquarters.[5]

Upon arrival of General Chasseloup, Dąbrowski's division, whose headquarters were still at Ponti, was still entirely placed on the right bank of the Mincio; the left bank had been guarded until then by the 19th Provisional Demi-brigade, the 21st Chasseurs à cheval Regiment, and the 99th Demi-brigade, which had been ordered to leave on the night of 10/11 Nivôse (from 31 December 1800 to 1 January 1801), to meet at the Center Lieutenancy of which it was a part. This demi-brigade was to delay its departure by a few hours, as prescribed by its movement order, and to wait for the 1st Provisional Légère Demi-brigade, which was on the right bank, to pass on the left bank to replace it; but it could not return to its post until the 11th, at daybreak. Petit, who commanded the 99th, continually urged General Chasseloup to let him go. The General, on the contrary, made him feel how much the presence of his demi-brigade was necessary for a few hours longer, until the arrival of the 19th. Petit then asked for an order in writing, which could relieve him of any responsibility. General Chasseloup sent it to him immediately, during the night of the 10th/11th. However, by an inconsistency which could become fatal to the besiegers, Citizen Petit departed with his demi-brigade without informing the general, and al-

[5]It is this distinguished officer who is author of the *Journal historique du Siège de Peschiera* which was printed in the year IX (1801) at Genoa, and from which we borrow several details concerning the feats of arms of the Polish Legion, to which the honorable Mr. F. Hénin (subsequently a maréchal de camp) pays it the tribute it deserves.

though at the very moment that he had asked for this authorization, it would have been given to him. He had no regard.

The conduct of this commander compromised the blockade of the fortress on the left bank. It was then completely devoid of troops, and the enemy could have made a sortie with impunity, destroyed the depots, and destroyed all the French resources around.

Such a critical position induced General Chasseloup to spend most of the night on horseback and bivouac on the ground with his staff and orderlies. He posted himself in such a manner as to be able to observe the movements of the enemy's garrison, and if necessary to arrange for a retreat on Ponti by the boat bridge, which we had already seen was thrown over the Mincio by General Dąbrowski, about two miles distant, below the fortress.

The troops forming then, on 11 Nivôse, Year IX (1 January 1801), the blockade on the right bank of Mincio contained only to three thousand fifty men.

1st Polish Legion	2,125
1st Provisional Légère Demi-Brigade "d'Orient"..	417
21st Chasseur à cheval Regiment	47
1st Italian Chasseur à cheval Regiment	171
1st Light Artillery Regiment (detachment)	24
3rd Miner Company	66
Sappers of different companies	130
Pontoniers	45
Artillery Train	25
	3,050

Besides this, the siege army received reinforcements of about one thousand men, who arrived successively during the course of the siege, namely, the 86th Demi-brigade on 19 Nivôse (9 January 1801); a detachment of the 55th Foot Artillery Regiment; a company of Polish gunners on the 29th (19 January); and about three hundred sappers from different companies.

The Italian Division and the Volunteer Battalion of the Reserve, which had been announced in the order of Nivôse 10th, did not appear at the headquarters.

Thus, the whole Gallo-Polish Army had only four thousand eighty-three combatants, of which the Poles formed the majority. So, they went to the Sermione Peninsula to contain the Austrian entrenchments. The rest was used to tighten the blockade of Peschiera and to supply men with the work of the siege. This troop was placed in a quite extensive circuit, divided by the Mincio, whose deep waters did not allow one to cross the ford. We could only communicate from one bank to another by a boat bridge, the swamps and the fire of the ramparts making this detour necessary to find a passable way.

This position was dangerous. The Gallo-Poles had to fight against a garrison of about three thousand, supported by more than six hundred armed sailors, who formed the crew of a fleet bristling with guns. The besieging corps was to be considered too weak to resist the sorties of an enemy entrenched in a fortress. He could come in unexpectedly and direct all his strength to one point. By attacking with more boldness, he would have infallibly destroyed the works of the besiegers and pushed their troops into their quarters; but fortunately, the Austrians confined themselves to a few engagements without results. The vivacity with which they were received from the first sorties discouraged them. They seemed to dread the ascendancy of the Republicans, who, already familiar with victory and accustomed to unequal combat, were burning to measure themselves against an enemy whose defeat they foresaw.

According to General Chasseloup's provisions, Chief of Staff Hénin dispatched the necessary orders for the location of the troops. The 1st Provisional Demi-brigade, containing four hundred seventeen men, passed 11 Nivôse (1 January 1801), very early morning, on the left bank of the Mincio, with the 3rd Polish Battalion, six hundred men strong, and the detachment of forty-seven men of the 21st Chasseur à cheval Regiment.

The temporary Provisional 1st Demi-brigade took position from the edge of the Mincio, and as close as possible to the fortress, to Casa-Massei, tightening its posts towards the lake, and straddling the road from Cavalcacello to Peschiera and on the way to this last town at Lacize.

The 3rd Battalion of the Polish Legion had its different posts from the mill, on the Mincio, to Val-Paradiso and below Monte-Piano.

The detachment of the 21st Chasseur à cheval Regiment was confined to Paradiso.

In this way, the enemy on the left bank of the Mincio was entirely constricted in the place, while on the side of the right bank it had remained around the walls of the city in a piece of ground of about 400 toises deep, and would have housed posts, protected by the fire from the walls and lunettes.

General Chasseloup had transferred, on 11 Nivôse (1 January 1801), his headquarters to Paradiso. He placed it definitively on the 1st, at Monte Piano, one mile from Peschiera. It was at this moment that he ordered the establishment of a flying bridge over the Mincio, below Paradiso, in order to facilitate and shorten communications with the right bank; but, given the difficulty of the ground, this bridge could only provide a path little suitable for military movements.

The commanding general, after having regularized the requisitions of food and fodder, which were forced to be made in the country by provisional agents, on 14 Nivôse (4 January), ordered a reconnaissance on the left bank of the lake as far as Garda. The Captain of Engineers Huart displayed, in this mission, all the activity and means of a distinguished officer. He succeeded, by his good intentions, in containing the enemy flotilla, preventing it from making requisitions, and finally pushing it to the upper lake.

General Dąbrowski, on the other hand, observed the same surveillance on the right bank of the Mincio and the lake, and on the Austrian entrenchments on the Sermione Peninsula, which the Chef de bataillon Bialowieyski attacked, and tightened still more, taking from the enemy several prisoners of war.

On 11 Nivôse, General Dąbrowski, having been informed of the movement that the Austrians were making out of their lines at Sermione, ordered the 1st Polish Battalion to go to meet them. These brave men dashed to meet the enemy and drove them back into their entrenchments; twenty-eight men were taken prisoner and five remained in the fortress. On the same day, at ten o'clock in the evening, six boats were seen on the lake, which presented themselves at the entrance of the port to supply the town; Captain Marchand, commanding the artillery of the division, soon obliged them to leave by pointing a 6pdr cannon at them.

The next day, 12 Nivôse (2 January), the enemy seemed to want to take revenge on the Sermione Peninsula. He appeared about six o'clock in the evening, supported by several infantry-filled boats, destined to reinforce the garrison of Sermione. Everything announced a plan of attack all the more to be feared, as the corps of besieging troops, on the right bank of the Mincio, was diminished by the 3rd Polish Battalion which had passed on the side of the left bank. The enemy, no doubt, was informed of it; but General Dąbrowski, by his activity and the precision of his actions, thwarted this project. He was able to use the little light artillery that was at his disposal so opportunely that, after a few discharges, the armed ships took off, and Sermione's garrison was again repulsed back to its entrenchments. The Gallo-Polish troops then ranged themselves in battle formation on the shore, and the Austrian flotilla, apparently thinking to avenge itself, directed against it, for more than three quarters of an hour, a fire sustained by its batteries.

On the 13 - 15 Nivôse (3-5 January) the enemy continued to harass the troops on the right bank; but the vigilance of General Dąbrowski always rendered vain the Austrians' efforts. In these last three engagements, the Austrians lost forty prisoners, and fifteen to twenty men remained in the fortress, without counting the wounded.

On the 16th (6 January), the garrison of Peschiera made a new sortie at two o'clock in the morning through the Brescia Gate, but was pushed back to the glacis of the city. The next day the Sermione garrison did the same, but the valor of the besiegers outweighed numbers. The Poles, who distinguished themselves again, had on their side the Captains Iurkowski and Parys wounded.

While these different actions succeeded one another without interruption, and the Gallo-Polish troops always came out victorious, General Chasseloup was engaged, without respite, in all the preparations for the siege. On 16 - 18 Nivôse (6 – 8 January), he traversed, in broad daylight, and not without danger, the whole line which could offer him points for attack. The officers of the engineers were always eager to accompany him; also exposed, they showed the same ardor and the same courage. The sappers also worked in the various depots assigned to them.

The great attack was commanded by Citizen Dabadic, and the small attack by Citizen Breuille, both chiefs of the engineer's battalion, and of distinguished merit.

General Lacombe-Saint-Michel, commander of the siege artillery of the Army of Italy, who was, on the 13 Nivôse (3 January), at the headquarters, made a reconnaissance of the blockade on both banks of the Mincio. He then proceeded to headquarters, near Major-General Marmont, Commander-in-Chief of the artillery of the army. On the 15th he was back under Peschiera.

The siege artillery was readied and the first parallels laid out (the workers being covered by the Polish skirmishers), the trench was opened on 22 Nivôse (12 January) at six o'clock on both sides of the Mincio. From that day until 28 Nivôse (18 January), the besieging army rivaled itself with zeal, talent, and courage; Chef de brigade of artillery Taviel, the Captains of Artillery Pellegrin, Devaux, Pauly, and Lieutenant Pion, particularly distinguished themselves. The naval officer Eugène Lacombe-Saint-Michel Jr., Captain Marchand, commander of the artillery of Dąbrowski's division, the pontoniers of the 8th Company of the 1st Pontonier Battalion, and Lieutenant Helek, who commanded them, were also distinguished by their activity and their intelligence. We owe praise to the Chef de bataillon Melliny, aide-de-camp of General Lacombe-Saint-Michel.

Finally, according to the general situation of the Gallo-Polish troops, at the time of 28 Nivôse (18 January), there were thirty guns of different calibers and nearly four hundred artillerymen, and in all four thousand eighty nine men of all arms.

However, before attempting a general attack on the enemy, General Chasseloup sent Captain Victor Martin, acting as an aide-de-camp for the Commanding General, as a parliamentarian, to the commander of Sermione, the Lieutenant Colonel Schnech, to engage him to surrender by capitulation; The latter referred to General Rogolsky, commander at Peschiera. On the other hand, the same General Chasseloup sent as a parliamentarian, the Chief of Staff Hénin, to the Austrian Naval Captain Blumenstein, to surrender the flotilla under his command by capitulation.

These steps having had no effect, we prepared for new fights. The moment to capture the enemy post in the Campustri House had arrived. The attack took place at four o'clock in the afternoon of 21 Nivôse (11 January). General Dąbrowski had made all the arrangements. He wanted to direct this dangerous expedition in person. Encouraging his soldiers, he showed them an example and exposed himself to the continual fire of the artillery, and thus added one of his finest jewels to his military crown.

Captain Marchand, commanding the artillery of Dąbrowski's division, had pointed a cannon and a 6-inch howitzer at the house. But as this post was protected by the batteries of the city and those of the lunettes, the enemy was not slow to respond to these two cannons by firing howitzer shells and the balls fell from all sides, and many far exceeded the place of the attack. One hundred thirty Poles, led by ten French engineers of the 2nd Company of the 2nd Battalion, commanded by Sergeant Rottanger, presented themselves fearlessly to capture the post. They advanced at the *pas de charge* under the fire of the fortress and directed their steps towards the house. Hardly within reach of a musket, the Gallo-Poles were greeted by a well-sustained fusillade. They endured it without answering. However, the enemy, entrenched in the house, kept shooting at them through the windows and the holes they had made in the wall. The Poles rivaled the French sappers with daring. All, without hesitation, advanced at the *pas de course.*[6] By a spontaneous movement they divided themselves into two columns, and, springing up with the rapidity of lightning, they melted on two sides on the house, and soon they broke the doors with axes. Such soldiers are so many heroes. The Sapper Brouillard, of the 8th Company of the 2nd Battalion, deserved to be distinguished among these brave men. It was he who was constantly at the head of this detachment arrived first at the main gate, forced it with an iron pike, entered the house with its bayonets, killed, and overthrew all of the batteries on the rampart. The bombs opposed its passage. His comrades followed him, and the post was carried by force. The enemy made an obstinate resistance until the last moment; twenty-two perished with weapons in hand, forty-five were taken prisoner. Others escaped through different holes under cover of darkness.

At the same time the garrison of Peschiera launched a sortie from the fortress with a detachment of two hundred men, no doubt to

[6]Translator: The pas de course is a cadenced march of two hundred fifty paces per minute, i.e. running in step.

help the post at Campustri; but in an instant they were put to flight and forced to speedily regain their entrenchments, leaving the animated soldiers the regret of not being able to join them.

The small attack trench was finally to be opened on the right bank of the Mincio. On 22 Nivôse (12 January) was the appointed day for this operation. According to the orders which had been sent out the day before, fifty French and Polish gunners were destined for the work on the trench. Two hundred Poles were sent forward to cover the workers. One hundred men of the 86th Demi-brigade, and four hundred Poles with two 3pdr cannon, formed the reserve. A hundred chasseurs à cheval from the 1st Italian Regiment were placed at the tail of the trench.

At six o'clock in the afternoon, all the troops were at their posts. Chief of the Staff Hénin himself adjusted the positions, and the opening of the trench was made in silence at eight o'clock in the evening.

The work was continued all night long with such activity that the next day the trench was wide enough and deep enough to sufficiently cover the workers. The enemy did not perceive our operations until about seven o'clock in the morning of 23 Nivôse (13 January), which it announced by heavy discharges of artillery, which continued all day, to which no reply was given. The garrison's cannon killed two men, and bursts of bombs wounded seven or eight.

On the following days, 24 - 26 Nivôse (14 – 16 January), the work was actively pushed forward. On the 27th, the company of miners, joined to one hundred Poles, were employed to finish the banquettes and to give the parallel and all the communications the proper width; so that on 28 Nivôse (18 January) all the works of the small attack were perfected, except the last battery, which was to be finished by the morning of the 29th. General Chasseloup, without wasting time, ordered that during the evening of the 24th (14th) the great attack trench should be opened, on the left bank of the Mincio. All his dispositions being ordered, the Chief of the Staff immediately dispatched the orders. Two hundred sappers, two hundred men of the 1st Provisional Demi-brigade and two hundred Poles, all equipped with siege tools, but also carrying their weapons to defend themselves in the event of a sortie by the garrison, went into the field at the indicated time. A guard of one hundred men was placed forward to cover the workers. The company of grenadiers of the 86th Demi-brigade, and thirty chasseurs à cheval of the 21st Chasseur à cheval Regiment, formed the reserve. These two detachments were posted at the engineer depot near the Mondella house, on the main road between Peschiera and Cavalcacello. The éclaireur company of the 3rd Polish Battalion, with fifteen chasseurs à cheval of the 21st Chasseur à cheval Regiment, was also placed in reserve towards the artillery depot, near the house known as Val-Paradiso, on the banks of the Mincio.

The work advanced without interruption. General Chasseloup, accompanied by all his staff, was among the workers, whom he animated with his presence. A deep darkness veiled the works. We were so close to the besieged that we heard in the silence of the night the Austrian soldiers talking in the city of Peschiera. It was nearly midnight when suddenly a fusillade was heard; it was accompanied by a few cannon shots and bullets. Three men were wounded. This event, which could be fatal to us, fortunately had no follow-up. It had been caused by the imprudence of a patrol of the 86th Demi-brigade, which had advanced too close to the walls of the place. The enemy, for the rest of the night, no longer showed distrust; he did not even throw fire pots, which could have betrayed the work of the besieged. This accident, far from being harmful, served only to excite the workers to sink into the trench; so that night was entirely stolen from the enemy, and in the morning the trench was deep enough to hide the soldiers.

Sunrise made the Austrians witnesses to the speed and extent of the night's work. They showed their spite in a way even more sensitive than they had during the small attack. It could be judged by the rolling fire that all their batteries kept vomiting on 23 Nivôse and the following days. They were content at night with hours of vigorous artillery fire, and then they threw mainly hollow carcasses. The surroundings of the fortresses seemed to be glowing. Cannister rained down on the advanced works, and balls and bombs were falling at distances very far from the town: they sometimes reached Monte-Piano and Paradiso, where Generals Chasseloup and Lacorahe Saint-Michel had established their headquarters.

There still remained a post to be removed, to expel the enemy entirely from the ground he occupied in front of the fortress, on the right bank of the Mincio. This post was in the house called Casa Bianca. The fire from Peschiera's ramparts and that of the four lunettes protected it. General Dąbrowski began the attack on the 25 Nivôse (15 January). The resistance of the Austrians was so stubborn that they stayed in the house until the next day, the 20th (16th). On that day, Chef de bataillon Chlopicki, of the Legion, that bravest among the brave, whose name is attached to all the glorious exploits of the Italian campaigns, was commanded to conduct a second attack. At the head of the Poles, he made a daring movement; his soldiers, animated by the example of their leader, redoubled their efforts and courage, and the post was carried at the points of their bayonets.

The following days, the works were continued with the same ardor and without interruption until the 28 Nivôse (18 January). The cannons were already in position, the embrasures unmasked, and the fire was going to open on all sides at once, when the news of the armistice concluded at Treviso on the 26th of the same month (16 January 1801) reached them during the afternoon of 28 Nivôse. On the same day, the Général de division Oudinot, Chief of the General Staff, passed through Peschiera as he carried the conditions of the armistice to Paris. All the work of the siege was suspended, the hostilities ceased, and the troops returned to their camps.

On the 20 Nivôse (19 January) General Rogolsky, commander at Peschiera, received an official copy of the armistice brought to him by De Bolza, an officer of the Austrian General Staff. The day for the evacuation of the place was fixed.

On 2 Pluviôse (22 January 1801), at seven o'clock in the morning, General Chasseloup, at the head of the Gallo-Polish troops, placed himself on the Verona highway near the glacis of Peschiera. There he paraded before him the strong German garrison of two thousand five hundred fifty eight men, not to mention the baggage train, consisting of sixty-five wagons, which evacuated immediately afterwards. We then entered the city, including the 1st Provisional Légère Demi-brigade, and the detachment of the 21st Chasseur à cheval Regiment, which formed the garrison. The other corps, which formed part of the siege troops, set out on the same day, in accordance with the orders they had received, to go to their respective destinations.

The Chef de brigade Sémélée, named commander of the Peschiera Fortress, arrived the same day, 2 Pluviôse (22 January), and immediately took possession of his command. It was he who supervised the execution of the articles of the armistice concerning the artillery, ammunition, the stores of the place and the surrender of the flotilla.[7] Before the conclusion of the armistice eight hundred men of the Polish battalions, who had remained at Milan, were sent to blockade the citadel at Ferrara, under the orders of Chef de brigade Karwowski. Once this fortress had surrendered to the French troops, conforming to the clauses of the armistice, Karwowski rejoined the Polish Legion below Mantua, with the detachment under his orders.

By virtue of the 12th article of the Treviso Convention between Generals Brune and Bellegarde, Mantua was, it is true, to remain in the power of the Austrians, but the French troops reserved to hold this place blocked at the distance of eight hundred toises from its glacis. General Dąbrowski was charged with the superior command of this blockade; and the whole Legion, with seven thousand armed and dressed men, assembled there and formed part of the blockade on the left bank of the Mincio. A French demi-brigade and a cavalry regiment joined it again. The blockade on the right bank was formed by Cisalpine troops under the orders of Général de division Lecchi, under whose command Dąbrowski sent Chef de brigade Karwowski with the

---

[7]In order to follow all the military operations of the French army from 18 December 1800 to 16 January 1801, readers will find among the supporting documents, No. 80, a historical journal of the Army of Italy, and in which the most honorable mentions of the bravery of Polish soldiers are so energetically expressed that we have thought it proper to present this official piece in its entirety.

It is in this same document that is designated under the simple title of General Henry, commander of one of the brigades of cavalry of the corps of Lieutenant General Moncey, the Polish General Henry Wollodkowicz. Coming from an illustrious family of Lithuania, and impatient to report himself, he voluntarily served under the French flag, and distinguished himself during several campaigns under the name of General Henry, not to compromise his family, which appeared to suffer from this generous resolution of Wollodkowicz.

This general, having distinguished himself on 25 December at the passage of Mincio, on the heights of the Volta mill, in front of Pozzolo, Captain Kasimir de la Roche, attached to Wollodkowicz's staff, accompanied by an artist named Muller, was engaged in tracing and unraveling this terrible struggle of a portion of the Army of Italy against the whole Austrian army, to follow up their work published on the Army of the Reserve, of which we have already spoken. General Wollodkowiez has since had the same Muller paint a picture of this passage, which they intended to represent the Army of Italy in their new work on this campaign; and we have reason to believe that this work will soon be shown to the public.

4th and 6th Battalions, to put him in a position to surround the fortress on this side, starting from Goito.

The headquarters of Dąbrowski, with the Legion's grenadiers, and a battery of light artillery, were assembled at Roverbella; the siege artillery, and the 6th Battalion were at Goito; the artillery at Pozzolo; 1st Battalion was at Marmirolo; the 2nd Battalion was at Due-Castelli; the 3rd Battalion was at Bancola.

The 2nd Battalion joined the infantry, and the French cavalry at Motella. The 7th was stationed at Formigoro and Barbaro.

On the other side of the Mincio were the 4th and 5th Battalions at Monlanara and Cortalone. They were united with the Cisalpine troops, who supported their right wing at the Mincio, near Pietola, and communicated with the 1st Battalion by a boat bridge.

After conferences between General Dąbrowski and the Austrian general commanding the fortress, the latter withdrew his outposts, and took position at eight hundred toises from the glacis. On 4 Pluviose (24 January), everyone was at his post.

In the meantime, the Chef de bataillon Dembowski, an aide-de-camp of General Dąbrowski, arrived from Paris on the 10th (30 January), and brought the flags for the Legion, as well as the two following letters, written on the subject by the War Minister Berthier:

Paris, Frimaire 3, Year IX (24 November 1800)

I announce to you, Citizen General, that I am taking the most effective measures to ensure that the eight flags, which you claim from me, are sent to you very promptly.

I am sure that these rallying signs cannot be entrusted to braver warriors.

The French nation will always appreciate the valor of the Poles, whom the same cause makes honorably to fight under its flag.

BERTHIER.

Paris, Frimaire 4, Year IX (25 November 1800).

I advise you, general, that the Chef de bataillon Dembowski will receive the eight flags for the 1st Polish Legion you command.

They will wear the inscription and will be decorated with an embroidery according to your wish and that of the Poles which make up the body.

BERTHIER.

The 25 Pluviôse (14 February 1801), the army was informed of the peace concluded in Lunéville the 6 Pluviôse, Year IX (26 January 1801), according to which the Austrians were to evacuate Mantua, and we set the 28th (17th) for the day of its execution.

The entire Legion was in order of battle on the main road from Mantua to Verona. The right wing, composed of a French demi-brigade, was supported by the citadel, the Polish artillery came next, then the battalion of grenadiers, composed of seven companies, and after them the seven battalions of infantry. In two ranks, on the left wing, was placed the French cavalry, and the general had distributed that same morning the flags with the ordinary ceremonies.

The whole troop was thus formed on parade, superbly dressed and armed. The Austrian garrison defiled before it with all the honors of war. A part of French and Cisalpine troops, and the 2nd and 7th Polish Battalions took possession of the fortress.

General Dąbrowski went with the other battalions to Milan, passing through Brescia. He received orders, on the way, to send two battalions to Florence and Livorno. The 1st and 3rd Battalions, under the command of Chef de brigade Grabinski were destined for this expedition and departed 6 Ventôse (25 February). The artillery headquarters, the grenadier battalion, and the 4th, 5th, and 6th Battalions arrived at 7 Ventôse (26 February) at Milan.

Towards the end of this month all the officers who had been made prisoners of war returned from Hungary.

On the 29th and 30th (20 -21 March 1801), General Dąbrowski passed a rigorous review, and sent a state of the Legion to the Minister of War, and another to General-in-Chief Brune, dated 1 Germinal, Year

IX (22 March 1801).

Meanwhile the Polish Legion of the Danube, which, under the command of the illustrious General Kniaziewicz, had just gathered a harvest of glory, was also entering Italy, and towards the end of the same month it reached Milan. This legion, about six thousand strong, and formed, when united to its brothers in arms, a Polish army of fifteen thousand men!

The Danube Legion having raised the two battalions from those of Italy in Tuscany, went to Reggio. In the month of Messidor (July 1801), General-in-Chief Moncey entrusted General Dąbrowski with the command of the Departments of Panoro and Crostolo.

Shortly after General-in-Chief Murat took the command of the army, and in the month of Fructidor, Year IX (end of August and beginning of September), the Legion was reunited in the two departments mentioned above.

A considerable body of Polish troops selected from those in Italy, commanded by Wladislas Jablonowski, embarked at Leghorn and Genoa for the unfortunate expedition to Santo Domingo. There, victim of a burning sky, it was almost entirely destroyed by becoming prey to a plague , which also reaped many French troops.

Lastly, some Polish detachments were sent to the south of Italy, where they were enrolled in the guard of the new King of Naples. It was in this corps and alongside several brave soldiers that one noticed a very distinguished officer, Adam Huppé, who earned his ranks on the battlefields in Poland, at Mantua, during the siege in 1799, and on the Danube, under General Kniaziewicz.

Thus ended, after five whole years of struggles and labors, the Polish legions of Italy, so faithful to their adoptive cause, and so badly rewarded for their fidelity. Delivered as a holocaust to the Machiavellianism of the three neighboring powers, these exiled patriots served the cause of a republic threatened in its independence, and while they poured out their blood to make their arms triumph, they could not obtain support from them for the conquest of their homeland and their freedom. But when we see with what pious constancy these proscribed children were occupied with the fate of the common mother, when we see them relating their combats in foreign countries to this patriotic intention, we cannot defend ourselves from the emotion, which history, in its impartial justice, must reserve beautiful pages for a sublime devotion, even though it remains without result.

SUPPORTING AND OFFICIAL DOCUMENTATION TO SERVE THE HISTORY OF THE POLISH LEGIONS IN ITALY

No. 1

Polish Constitution of 3 May 1791

In the name of God, etc.

Stanislaus Augustus, by the grace of God and the will of the nation, King of Poland, Grand Duke of Lithuania, Russia, Prussia, Mazowia, Samogitia, Kiev, Volhynia, Podolia, Podlaquia, Livonia, Smolensk, Seria, and Czerniechovia, etc.

Together with the Confederate states in double number representing the Polish nation.

Convinced that the perfection and stability of a new national constitution alone can assure our fate to all; enlightened by a long and fatal experience of the inveterate vices of our government; wanting to make the most of the conjuncture in which Europe is today, and especially the last moments of that happy age, which has restored us to ourselves; raised from the withering yoke imposed on us by a foreign preponderance; putting beyond our individual bliss, even above life, political existence, liberty within, and independence beyond the nation whose destiny is entrusted to us; wanting to make us worthy of the vows and the gratitude of our contemporaries, as well as posterity; armed with the firmest determination, and raising us above all the obstacles that might arouse the passions; having in view only the public good, and wishing to assure forever the liberty of the nation and the integrity of all its domains, we decree the present constitution, and declare it in its sacred and immutable entirety, until the end that it prescribes itself, the public will has expressly recognized the need to make some changes. We wish that all the later regulations of the present diet conform in all to this constitution.

Art. I. Religion of the government.

The Roman Catholic Apostolic Religion is and will remain forever the national religion, and its laws will retain all their vigor. Whoever abandons this worship for any other will incur the penalties of apostasy. However, love of neighbor being one of the most sacred precepts of this religion, we owe to all men, whatever their profession of faith, an entire freedom of belief under the protection of the government; consequently, in all the spheres of Poland, we assure a free exercise of all religions and sects, in accordance with the laws laid down in this respect.

Art. II. Noble Landowners.

Full of veneration for the memory of our ancestors, honoring in them the creators of a free government, we guarantee in the most solemn way to the corps of the nobility all its immunities, liberties and prerogatives, as well as the preeminence that it supplements in private life as in public life, and especially the rights and privileges conceded to this state by Vladimir the Great, Louis of Hungary, Vladislas Jagiellon, and his cousin Vilold, Grand Duke of Lithuania; as well as by Vladislas and Kazimirz, both Jagiellons; by Jean Albert, Alexander, and Sigismund; lastly, Sigismund Augustus, the last of the Jagiellonian family; which privileges we endorse, confirm, and acknowledge to be forever irrevocable. We declare the noble state of Poland equal to that of all other countries; let us establish the most perfect equality among all the members of this body, not only as to the right to possess in the Republic all kinds of offices, and to perform all honorable and lucrative functions, but also as to the freedom to enjoy, in an uniform manner, all of the immunities and prerogatives attributed to the Equestrian Order. Above all, let us wish that individual liberty and security, the property of all goods, movable, immovable, be at all times and in the most religious manner, respected in every citizen, and protected from any attack, as they have been since time immemorial. Let us solemnly guarantee that, in the laws to be decided, we will not introduce any change or restriction, which may bring the slightest prejudice to the property of anyone, and that neither the supreme authority of the nation, nor the agents of the government established by it, may not, under the pretext of royal rights, or such other whatsoever, form any claim to the charge of these properties, taken in their entirety or in their parts. This is why, respecting the personal safety and the legal property of every citizen, as the first bond of society and the foundation of civil liberty, we confirm, assure, guarantee and want that, respected over the centuries, they shall remain forever intact.

Let us recognize the members of the Equestrian Order as the first defenders of liberty and of the present constitution, and entrust to the virtue, the patriotism, the honor of each gentleman, the care to make them respect each other, as he must respect them himself, and especially to watch over the maintenance of this constitution, which alone can become the boulevard of the country, and the guarantor of our common rights.

Art. III. Cities and Bourgeois.

We wish that the law decreed by the present diet under the title of "Our Royal Cities Declared Free in the Whole Extent of the Domains of the Republic," has a full and complete vigor; that this law, which gives a truly new, real and effective basis, to the freedom of the Equestrian Order, as well as to the integrity of our common country, be regarded as part of the present constitution.

Art. IV. Settlers and Other Inhabitants of the Countryside.

As it is from the laborious hand of the farmers that the most fertile source of national wealth flows; as their bodies form the greater part of the population of the state, and that, by a necessary consequence, it is them who constitutes the principal force of the Republic; justice, humanity, and our own self-interest, of course, are all powerful reasons for us to receive this precious class of men under the immediate protection of law and government. To these causes, we now declare that all agreements entered into by the proprietors and their settlers, stipulating, in favor of the latter, some franchises or concessions under such and such clauses, either that the said agreements were concluded with the whole community, or separately with each inhabitant of the village, will become, for the two contracting parties, a common and reciprocal obligation, and this according to the express enunciation of said clauses, and the content of the contract guarantor of this agreement under the protection of the government. These particular agreements and the obligations they will impose, once they are accepted by a landowner, will be so binding on him, his heirs, or the purchasers of such lands, that they will not have the right to make, alone and by themselves, any kind of change. Respectively, the settlers may not derogate from these conventions, nor release themselves from the obligations to which they voluntarily submit themselves, whatever the nature of their possessions, than in the manner and according to the clauses stipulated in the mentioned contract; which clauses will be obligatory for them, and for always or for a time, according to the wording of said contract.

Having thereby secured to the owners of the lands all the emoluments and advantages that they are entitled to exact from their colonists, and wishing to encourage, in the most effective manner, the population in the domains of the Republic, we assure the most complete liberty to individuals of all classes, both to foreigners who come to settle in Poland, and to nationals who, after having left their country, would like to return to its bosom. Thus every man, whether foreigner or national, from the moment he sets foot on the lands of Poland, will be able freely and without any difficulty to assert his industry, in the manner and in such a place as he sees fit; he may, at his option and for whatever period of time, decide upon such agreements as he may deem appropriate, with respect to the establishment he wishes to form, under the payment of money or a labor clause; he can still fix himself, at his choice, to the city or the country; finally he can or will remain in Poland, or leave it, if he deems it appropriate, having previously satisfied all the obligations which he has voluntarily contracted.

Art. V. Government, or Character of the Public Authorities.

In society, all power comes essentially from the will of the nation. So that the integrity of the domains of the Republic, the liberty of the citizens, and the civil administration remain forever in perfect equilibrium, the government of Poland will have to bring together, under the present constitution, brings together three kinds of separate powers: the legislative authority, which will reside in the assembled states; the supreme executive power, in the person of the King and in the supervisory council; and the judiciary, in the magistracy already established, or who will be to that effect.

Art. VI. Diet, or Legislative Power.

The Diet, or assembly of states, will be divided into two rooms; that of the nuncios, and that of the senators, which will be presided over by the King.

The Chamber of the Nuncios is the image and the repository of the supreme power of the nation and will be the true sanctuary of the laws. It is in this chamber that all projects relating to (1) the general laws, that is to say, the constitutional, civil and criminal laws, as well as the permanent taxes, will be decided in the first place. For the decision of all these objects, the proposals emanating from the Throne, which will have been submitted to the discussion of palatinals, lands, and districts, and then brought into the chamber by virtue of the instructions given to the nuncios, must be taken first in deliberation. (2) To all other orders of the Diet, such as temporary taxes, value of currencies, public loans, ennoblement and other accidental rewards, statements of public, ordinary and extraordinary expenses; declarations of war, conclusions of peace, definitive ratification of treaties of alliance and commerce, all diplomatic acts and conventions relating to the law of nations; receipts and testimonies to be rendered to the magistrates in charge of the Executive Power, and all other public objects of prime importance. In all these matters preference will be given to proposals emanating from the Throne, which should be brought directly into the Chamber of Nuncios.

The chamber of senators, presided over by the King, will be composed of bishops, palatines, castellans and ministers. The King will have the double right, and give his voice, and resolve the parity when it will take place; what he will do, or in person, or by mission when he will not sit.

The right of this chamber shall be: 1.) to accept or suspend until a new deliberation of the nation, and this to the plurality of votes, as it will be determined by this constitution, any law which, after having passed according to the legal forms, in the Chamber of the Nuncios, will have to be returned immediately to that of the senators. This acceptance will give the proposed law the sanction which alone can bring it into force. The suspension will only stop the execution until the first regular diet, and then, if the Legislative Chamber agrees to renew the same law, the Senate will no longer be able to refuse to sanction it. 2.) In the orders of the diets relative to the objects specified above, the Chamber of the Nuncios shall forthwith communicate its decrees in this respect to that of the senators, so that the decisions on these forms are brought to the plurality of voice of both chambers; which plurality, legally stated, will become the interpreter of the supreme will of the states. Let us say that senators and ministers, in all cases where they will have to justify their operations both in the Supervisory Council and in any commission, will not have a decisive vote in the Diet, it will then sit in the Senate only to give the explanations and clarifications that the Assembly of Estates may require from them.

The diet will be considered permanent; the representatives of the nation, appointed for two years, must always be ready to assemble.

The ordinary Legislative Diet will be held every two years and will last the time fixed in the separate article on the organization of diets. National assemblies, which will be convened under urgent and extraordinary circumstances, may only decide on the objects for which they have been summoned, or on those which have arisen since its convocation.

No law enacted in an ordinary diet can be repealed in the same diet.

The assembly of states, to be complete, must be composed of the number of members to be determined in the article mentioned above, both for the Chamber of Nuncios and for that of the senators.

As to the rules to be observed in the keeping of the dietines, we confirm, in the most solemn manner, the law decreed in this respect by the present Diet; considering this law as the first foundation of civil liberty.

Since the legislative power cannot be exercised by the whole body of citizens, and the nation substitutes itself by its freely elected representatives or nuncios, let us rule that the nuncios appointed in the dietines, uniting in their persons the sacred repository of public confidence shall, under this constitution, be regarded as the representatives of the whole nation, both in law and in relation to the needs of the state in general.

In all cases, without exception, the orders of the Diet shall be brought to the plurality of votes; that is why we abrogate forever the liberum veto, the confederations of all kinds, as well as the confederate diets, as contrary to the spirit of the present constitution, tending to destroy the springs of government and to disturb public tranquility.

Wanting, on the one hand, to prevent the early and too frequent changes that could be introduced into our national constitution; on the other hand, feeling the need to give it, in the view of increasing public felicity, that degree of perfection, which can only be determined by experience based on the effects which will result from it, let us fix at every 25 years the term to which the nation may work on the revision and reform of the said constitution; wanting it to be summoned a diet of extraordinary legislation, according to the forms, which will be prescribed separately for its holding.

Art. VII. The King, the Executive Power.

No government, even the most perfect, can subsist, if the Executive Power is not endowed with the highest energy. Just laws make the happiness of the nations, and the execution of these laws depends on their effect. Experience has proved to us that it is to the little activity that has been given to this part of the government, that Poland owes all the evils it has experienced. A free Polish nation, and dependent on it alone, the right to create laws, to supervise all the parts of the Executive Authority, to choose for itself all the public officers employed in its various magistracies; we entrust the supreme execution of the laws to the King and his council, which will be designated by the name of the Supervisory Council.

The Executive Power will be strictly bound to supervise the execution of the laws, and to be the first conform to them. It will be active by itself, in all the cases where the law allows it; these are the ones where it needs supervision, execution, and even co-active force.
All the magistrates owe it an entire obedience; so we give it the right to take action, if need be, against that of those magistrates who neglect their duties, or who are resistant to its orders.

The Executive Power can neither write laws nor even interpret them; nor establish taxes or other contributions, under any name whatsoever; nor contract public debts; nor allow any change in the distribution of the revenue of the Treasury, determined by the Assembly of Estates; nor make declarations of war; nor finally to finalize treaties of peace, or such other treaties or diplomatic acts of any kind. It will only be able to maintain temporary negotiations with the foreign courts, and will supply what might be required, in ordinary or momentary cases, for the safety and tranquility of the state; operations to be reported to the next meeting of the states.

We declare the Throne of Poland elective, but by families only. All the removals, which were the consequences of the upheaval, which are periodically experienced in the Constitution at each interregnum; the essential obligation for us to secure the fate of every inhabitant of Poland, and to oppose the strongest protection against the influence of foreign powers; the memory of the glory and prosperity, which crowned our country under the uninterrupted reign of hereditary kings; the pressing necessity of diverting foreigners and powerful nationals from the ambition to reign over us, and, on the contrary, to excite the desire to cement national liberty together; all these reasons together have indicated to our prudence the establishment, once and for all, of the succession to the Throne, as the only means of securing our political existence. Accordingly, let it be decreed that, after the death of the King, who is now happily ruling, the scepter of Poland will pass to the present Elector of Saxony, and that the dynasty of future kings will begin in the person of Frederick Augustus; wanting the crown to belong to his male heirs, the eldest son of the reigning king will always succeed his father; and in the event that the Elector of Saxony does not leave a male child, the prince whom this elector will give to his daughter as a husband, the individual by the assembled states, and shall begin, in Poland, the order of succession in the male line. For these purposes we declare Marie-Auguste Népomucène, daughter of the Elector of Saxony, Infanta of Poland; retaining, moreover, to the nation the imperceptible right of choosing, to govern it, a second family after the extinction of the first.

By ascending the throne, every king will be bound to take an oath to God and the nation to conform in all things to the present constitution, to satisfy all the conditions of the pact which will be settled with the reigning Elector of Saxony, as with him to whom the throne is destined; a pact that will become obligatory for him, as were the old pacts with our kings.

The King's person will be forever sacred and out of reach. Doing nothing by himself, he cannot be responsible for anything to the nation. Far from ever being able to set himself up as an absolute monarch, he will only have to look upon himself as the chief and father of the nation; such is the title given to him, such is the character which the law and this constitution recognize in him.

The revenues that will be allotted to the King by the pacta conventa, as well as the prerogatives attributed to the throne, and guaranteed by the present constitution in favor of the future elect, will be forever protected from any attack.

Courts, magistrates, and arbitrary jurisdictions will draw up all public documents in the name of the King: coins and stamps will bear his imprint. The King having the widest power to do good, we reserve him the right to do grace to the guilty persons sentenced to death, whenever it is not a question of state crimes. The King shall serve as the Commander-in-Chief of the troops in time of war, and the appointment of all commanders, except for the right of the nation to request a change. He shall be authorized to appoint all military officers, as to appoint the civil officers, in the manner prescribed in this respect in detail separated from the various articles of the present constitution. It will be to him that the appointment of the bishops, the senators, the ministers, and the first agents of the Executive Power will be made, and that in accordance with the above-mentioned details.

The council charged with supervising, in concert with the King, the execution of the laws and their integrity, shall be composed, 1.) of the Primate, as head of the clergy and President of the Commission of Education, which may be supplanted by that of the bishops who will be the first in rank (these will not be able to sign any judgment); 2.) Five ministers, namely: the Minister of Police, the Minister of the Seal, the Minister of War, the Minister of the Treasury, and the Chancellor, Minister for Foreign Affairs; 3.) two secretaries, one of whom will keep the register of the council, and the other one for foreign affairs, both without a decisive vote.

The heir to the throne, as soon as he has reached the age of reason, and has taken the oath on the National Constitution, may attend all the sittings of the Council; but there he will have no voice.

The Marshal of the Diet, appointed for two years, will also sit in the Supervisory Council, but without being able to enter into any of its determinations, and only in order to summon the diet, which is supposed to be always assembled, in cases where he sees an absolute necessity. To make this summons; and if the King refuses to do so, the said Marshal will be obliged to send to all the nuncios and senators a circular letter, in which he will engage them to assemble as a diet, and will detail to them all the reasons which require this meeting. The cases which will absolutely require the convocation of the Diet will be only the following ones:

1.) All urgent cases concerning the law of nations, especially that of a war bordering on the frontiers;
2.) Domestic disturbances which would produce the fear of a revolution in the state, or some collision between the magistracy;
3.) The danger of a general famine;
4) When the nation would be deprived of its king, or by death, or by a dangerous disease.

All Council by-laws will be discussed by the various members of the Council. After having all the opinions, the King will give his, which must always prevail, so that uniformity will reign in the execution of the laws. Consequently, every decree of the Council shall be decreed in the name of the King, and signed by his hand; however, it must also be countersigned by one of the ministers sitting on the council; and, provided with this double signature, it will become obligatory and must be put into execution, either by the commissions or by any other executive magistracy; but only for objects that are not expressly excepted by the present constitution. If it happened that none of the ministers sitting on the Council wanted to sign the decree in question, the King must abandon it; and in case he persists in demanding its acceptance, the Marshal must demand the convocation of the permanent Diet, and convoke it himself, if the King seeks to drive him away.

The right to appoint the ministers will belong to the King, as well as the right to choose among his ministers that of each department, which he will please admit to his council. This admission will take place for two years, except the right of confirmation (this term expired) devolved to the King. The ministers who sit on the Council will not be able to sit on committees. If, in the Diet, two-thirds of the secret votes of the two chambers together require the change of a minister in the Council, or in such other magistracy, the King must forthwith appoint another to his place.

Wanting the board to be required to respond strictly to any offense that might occur in the execution of the laws, the supervision of which is entrusted to it, we declare that the ministers who will be charged with an offense of this kind by the committee charged with reviewing their operations will be responsible for their people and their property. Whenever such complaints take place, the assembled states will dismiss the ministers accused in the judgment of the Diet, and this to the simple plurality of votes of both houses, to be sentenced as they deserved, which will be proportionate to their prevarication; or to be dismissed absolved, if their innocence is obviously recognized.

To further order and accuracy in the exercise of the Executive Power, establish special commissions that will be linked with the Council, and required to fulfill its orders.

The commissioners who will have to sit there will be elected by the assembled estates, and will fill, until the end fixed by the law, the functions attached to their offices.

Commissions are those, 1st of Education, 2nd of Police, 3rd of War, 4th of Treasury.

The commissions of the good order, which the present diet has established in the palatinates, will likewise be subject to the supervision of the Council, and will have to satisfy the orders, which they will receive from the intermediary commissions mentioned above, and that respectively to the objects relating to the authority and obligations of each of them.

Art. VIII. Judicial authority.

Judicial power cannot be exercised by the legislative authority or by the King, but by magistrates chosen and appointed for that purpose.

These magistracies will be fixed and distributed in such a way that there is no one who does not find within his reach the justice he wishes to obtain, and that the culprit sees everywhere the sword of the supreme power ready to weigh on him. As a result, we establish:

1.) In each palatinate, land, and district, courts in the first instance, composed of judges elected to the dietines; these jurisdictions, whose first duty will be uninterrupted vigilance, must always be ready to render justice to those who claim it. The appeal of the sentences to be rendered will be carried to the supreme tribunals, which shall be established in each province, and composed of members appointed to the dietines. These tribunals, in the first instance as in the last instance, will be deemed to be territorial jurisdictions, and will judge all cases of law and fact, between the nobles or other landowners, and such other persons as may be.
2.) We confirm the municipal jurisdictions established in all the cities, according to the contents of the law carried by this diet in favor of the free royal cities.
3.) Each province shall separately have a tribunal called the referendorial, where the causes of free settlers will be judged, which, under the old constitutions, must emerge to these magistratures.
4.) We preserve in our former state our royal courts and assessorales, those of relations, as well as that which is established for the lawsuits of the inhabitants of the Duchy of Courland.
5.) The executive commissions will render separate judgments for all cases relating to their administration.

In addition to the courts for civil and criminal cases, established in favor of all classes of citizens, there shall be a supreme tribunal, referred to as the "Judgment of the Diet." At the opening of each state assembly, the members who sit on it will be appointed by election. This tribunal will deal with all crimes against the nation and the King, that is to say, crimes of state. We want a new civil and criminal code to be drafted by people designated for this purpose.

Art. IX. Regency.

The Supervisory Council, having at its head the Queen, and in her absence the Primate, will be at the same time the Council of Regency: the Regency will be able to take place only in the three following cases: 1.) during the minority of the King; 2.) if a constant alienation of mind puts the King out of the state to fulfill his functions; 3.) if he were made prisoner of war the minority of the King will finish at the age of 18 years; and his insanity can only be regarded as constant, when it is declared such by the permanent diet, by the plurality of three quarters of the votes of the two assembled chambers. In these three cases, the Primate of the Crown will at once summon the estates of the dictate, and if he differs from fulfilling this duty, it will be the Marshal who binds the diet, who will be bound to address, for this purpose, letters of convocation to the nuncios and senators. The permanent diet will determine the order in which the ministers shall sit on the Council of Regency and authorize the Queen to perform the functions of the King. When, in the first case, the King leaves his minority; that in the second he will have recovered the enjoyment of his intellectual faculties, and that in the third he will be restored to his states, the Regency Council will be accountable to him for all its operations, and responsible to the nation, on the person and property of each of its members, for the entire time of its administration, and this according to the content of the constitution, in the article of the Supervisory Board.

Art. X. Education of Royal Princes.

The sons of kings, whom the present constitution is destined to succeed to the Throne, must be regarded as the first of the children of the country. Thus, it is to the nation that the right to supervise their education belongs, without, however, prejudicing the right of paternity.

During the lifetime of the King, and as long as he governs himself, he will take care of the education of his sons, in concert with the Supervisory Council, and the governor that the estates will have assigned to the education of the princes. During the Regency, it is to this same council and to this governor that their education will be entrusted. In both cases, the governor will be required to report to each ordinary diet, and how the young princes will be raised, and the progress they have made. Finally, it will be the duty of the Education Commission to draft for them, under the approval of the estates, a plan of instruction, so that, directed on the basis of constant and uniform principles, the future heirs of the Throne early in the day, experience feelings of religion, virtue, patriotism, the love of freedom, and respect for the National Constitution.

Art. XI. National Army.

The nation owes to itself to defend itself against any attack, which might undermine its integrity; thus, all citizens are the defenders born of the rights and freedom of the nation. An army is nothing, but a part detached from the public force, subject to a more regular order, and always in a state of defense. The nation owes to its troops and its esteem, and rewards proportionate to their devotion to the defense of the state. The troops owe it to the nation to watch over the safety of its frontiers, as well as the maintenance of public tranquility; in a word, they must be the strongest shield of the Republic. But in order that they may never deviate from the object of their destination, they must be constantly subordinated to the Executive Power, in accordance with the regulations which will be made in this respect; consequently, they will be bound to make the nation and the King an oath to remain faithful to them, and to be the first defenders of the national constitution. According to this, the troops can be employed in the defense of the state in general, and that of the borders and fortresses, or to assist the executive force in the cases of refraction to the laws, on the part of anybody.

No. 2

Preparations for the Public Defense. – Decree Issued in the Séance of the Constituent Diet Of 16 April 1792.

Considering that a nation never found a more effective means of defending its prerogatives than when it sought them in its valor and in its own strength; having placed our greatest confidence in these means, and united in defense of the integrity of our prerogatives and our independence, we declare in the most solemn manner, and take God and all the peoples of the earth to witness that we do not think of declaring war on any power; that we make the greatest case of the friendship and the good understanding that has subsisted so far (and that we make vows to see it subsist forever) between us and our neighbors, and that we are solely engaged in the care of preserving the territory of the Republic, our freedom and our independence, in all their integrity, as well as to maintain our civil constitution, sanctioned by the votes of the whole nation, and in defense of which all the citizens will devote their lives and their goods.

Considering, furthermore, that we find ourselves in a time, and in a political position, where negotiations between the courts, concerning the present circumstances, require us, that for the guarantee of the territory of the Republic, for that of the nation and of our happy constitution, we have added, as much as we have in ourselves, to the weight and importance of these negotiations, and that we have, in an unforeseen case, the means of defense at our disposal, we decree what follows:

1.) The King, to whom our civil constitution entrusted the executive power, will use this power in all its extent, with the greatest activity and efficiency, to see to the defense of the nation, by directing the defensive forces of the Republic.

2.) We authorize the King to engage one, two or three foreign generals, known for their experience in the art of war, and to place them in the Army of the Republic, with the rank of Commander-in-Chief, in providing them in a manner that corresponds to their rank and granting them salaries and awards that are proportionate. We confide also in the King the care of engaging and appointing skillful foreign officers, who are experienced in the art of war, for the corps of artillery and engineering.

3.) We instruct the Treasury Commission of the two nations to negotiate without delay, then the declaration of urgency made by the King in the Supervisory Council (Straz), and at the requisition of His Majesty, a loan, either in the country, or abroad, of a sum of 30 million zlotys, on the cheapest possible conditions, by mortgaging the amount of this loan, for the security and surety of which we pledge our guarantee by the present decree, on the product of the sale to make starosties.

4.) We authorize the King in the Supervisory Board to dispose of both the money in the fund and the proceeds of the loan to the extent of the competition of 9 million zlotys for the preparation of national defense necessary; under the responsibility of the Minister, who will have countersigned on the Supervisory Board, and of persons to whom these funds have been entrusted, in the event that any part of this sum has been used for other purposes than for the preparations for national defense. And, in the event of anybody going to war against the Republic, either by a declaration or otherwise, we allow the King in the Supervisory Board to dispose of the remainder of the proceeds of the loan for the armed defense, also under the responsibility of both the minister who has countersigned on the Supervisory Board, and of persons to whom these funds have been entrusted, in the event that part of this sum is devoted to other objects to meet the needs of the war.

5.) At two months from the date, the ministers in the Supervisory Council shall report to the assembled estates in a diet, at the requisition even of a single nuncio, the employment that has been made of this money, in accordance with the provisions of the present decree; and the account of all the money employed will be returned to the estates constituted in dictation, to the nearest denier.

No. 3

Russian Declaration of War Against Poland of May 18, 1792

The freedom and independence of the Serene Republic of Poland has at all times excited the attention and interest of all its neighbors. Her Majesty, the Empress of all the Russias, who, as such, attached to that of her formal and positive engagements with the Republic, has been particularly committed to ensuring the preservation intact of these two precious attributes of the political existence of this kingdom. This constant and magnanimous care of Her Majesty, the effects of her love of justice and order, as much as of her affection and kindness for a nation that the original identity, language and so many other relationships with the one it governs, made it interesting in her eyes, no doubt embarrassed the ambition and the spirit of domination of those who, not satisfied with the portion of authority which the laws of the state assigned to them, sought extension at the expense of these same laws. In this view they have neglected nothing, on one side to weary the active vigilance of the Empress over the integrity of the rights and prerogatives of the illustrious Polish nation; and on the other to slander the purity and benevolence of her intentions by presenting them, on all occasions, in a way which is absolutely foreign to them.

Thus they had the perfidious address of interpreting the act by which Russia guarantees the legitimate constitutions of this nation, as an expensive and degrading yoke; while the greatest empires, and among others that of Germany, far from rejecting these sorts of guarantees, have considered them, sought and received them as the most solid foundation of their properties and their independence. Moreover, the recent event proves, better than any argument that might be employed, how much such a guarantee may be necessary and efficacious, and that without it the Republic, having succumbed under the blows of its domestic enemies, has only recovered from it, by the intervention of the Empress, any other title to her than only her friendship and her generosity.

However, emboldened by the ease with which a part of the nation embraced their erroneous opinions, those who had long meditated on its servitude and the ruin of its former liberty, awaited only the favorable moment for the execution of their destructive purpose; they thought they seized it when Russia was attacked by two powers at once. At that time, the Diet was assembled in Warsaw; the instructions of the palatinates bore that it was free and ordinary; however, it was suddenly converted into a confederate diet without any known or even apparent reason. The act of confederation, made public, announced the works that it was going to deal with; the principal objects were to be: "The maintenance of free republican government, that of the magistracy in their functions and common bounds, and the preservation of the property of the citizens. It was up to the Polish nation itself to judge, afterwards, and the result of the operations of this diet, how much it deviated from those objects that it had presented to the public confidence, to replace them with others who were diametrically opposed to them.

Without entering into the enumeration of all the illegalities and all the infringements of the laws and immunities of the Republic, that this confederated diet, or rather the faction that dominates there, is allowed, it suffices to say that after having usurped, confused, and united in it all the powers, whose meeting on one hand is incompatible with republican principles, it abused each of these powers in the most tyrannical way, prolonged its duration beyond three and a half years a term of which the annals of Poland do not present a single example, and finally consummated all its fatal enterprises, by completely overthrowing, on May 3, 1791, the edifice of the government in the shadow of which the Republic has flourished and prospered for so many centuries. That day saw it disappear, and on its ruins arose a monarchy, which, in the new laws by which it has been claimed to limit, offered only contradictions between themselves, incoherence with the old, complete insufficiency in all respects and does not even leave to the Poles the vain simulacrum of the liberty and prerogatives of which they have always been so jealous. The throne, elective as it was, is declared hereditary; and this law, which the wisdom of their ancestors dictated, and which forbids, during the lifetime of a king, to take care of the choice of a successor, has been violated as boldly as all those which guaranteed the permanent consistence of the Republic. The means which were used to consume all these acts of violence were well made to characterize them the day of the revolution, when the castle and the hall of the diet were filled with all the populace of Warsaw. Armed men were brought in, and the cannon were taken out of the arsenal; they were held ready to strike down those who tried to prevent the success of the plot. The Artillery Regiment and the Lithuanian Guard were assembled to support the populace; its fury was excited against those whose opposition was feared. Several nuncios who persevered in their patriotic sentiments were threatened with losing their lives. That of Kalisz (M. Suchorzewski), crawling on his knees to the throne, to humbly recall to the King the sanctity of the oath he had taken on the Pacta conventa, that sacred and indissoluble bond which united him to the nation, was mercilessly trampled underfoot, in spite of his inviolable character as a representative of this nation, and to the great scandal of all those of the Poles who have not yet entirely lost the feeling of their honor and their liberty; and it is a revolution carried out in this way, that its promoters try to pass for the free and spontaneous wish of the nation!

But these enterprising citizens did not limit themselves to the evils they caused to their unhappy homeland in its own bosom, they still sought to attract it from the outside, by precipitating it into disputes capable of degenerating into an open war with Russia, the former ally of the Republic and the Polish nation. It took nothing less than all the magnanimity of the Empress, and especially that fairness, this correctness of light with which she knows how to distinguish the intention of the party spirit from the general intention, to prevent the last extremities to which she has been incessantly provoked. A succinct statement of the facts will bring out the truth of that assertion. At the declaration of war that the Ottoman Porte was going to issue against Russia, the Empress' ambassador gave a note to the minister of the Republic without a diet then, to warn him about the passage of Russian troops into the states of Poland, and to propose to him to appoint, in the palatinates nearest to the quarters of his troops, commissioners with whom they could agree on the deliveries and the payment of food and fodder.

Everything was regulated and established in a friendly manner, and at the reciprocal convenience, in spite of the fermentations of malevolence, which were already beginning to break through. But as soon as the diet was formed, and the long-meditated project of destroying the Republic had prevailed over all the considerations relating to the maintenance of its internal and external repose, not only was it emphasized that the Russian troops, without exception even the small number of those who were in charge of the stores, which had been formed, were constantly withdrawn from Polish territory; but all sorts of hindrances to their supply were put in place, by opposing the formation of new stores for their subsistence, and by demanding that the troops that had been there should be transported beyond the frontiers of the Republic. On this occasion, the Treasury Committee put forward the unreasonable claim of the rights of exit to collect payment upon the passage of the Dniester, for these same stores amassed at great expense, and the great advantage of the Polish owners. Such processes in no way correspond to the respect due to neighboring states, united, moreover, by bonds of friendship and alliance.

The vexations of all kinds exercised against the subjects of the Empress were pushed to the point that some of them were on the lands of the Republic for trading businesses to which they indulged on the basis of treaties and the rights of men, they were maliciously accused of exciting the inhabitants of the place to revolt, and, on this pretext, seized and thrown into dungeons. The judges charged with investigating their trial and finding no trace of the crime, which was imputed to them, resorted to torment to extort confessions from them; and having obtained it in this manner, these pitiless judges condemned them to execution, and had them executed inhumanly. This first attempt at injustice, inhumanity, and cruelty, opened a vast field for inquisitions of all sorts, which dwelt chiefly on the inhabitants of the provinces, where the Orthodox Greek Religion is professed. The Bishop of Pereslavia and Abbot of Sluck, although a subject of the Empress, became one of the victims of this persecution, in spite of the high rank which he occupied in the church, and of the purity of his manners and the rigidity of his principles. He was suspected of crimes which were important to the malignant and the desire to maintain the fermentation which they had excited, to forge at all times; and this prelate was arrested and dragged to Warsaw, where he is still bound in a harsh captivity. The law of the people was no more respected towards the ministers of the Empress; for their chapel, which is supposed to be one of the very hotels which they inhabit, and which, by the escutcheon of the Imperial Arms of Russia, attached externally, clearly indicating a privileged place, was forced, and Polish soldiers came to snatch an incumbent, to drag him, without any reason, before a court that had no jurisdiction. The satisfaction which the Russian Minister has demanded has been evaded under the most frivolous pretexts. In a word, not only were all the solemn treaties binding Russia and Poland violated and transgressed in their most important points, but animosity was pushed to the point of sending an extraordinary embassy to Turkey, then in open warfare. With Russia, to offer it an offensive league directed against this latter power; that is what the ministerial correspondence of the Warsaw Cabinet will offer the clearest proof. The respect even due to the person and august rank of the Empress was not observed in the speeches held in a full session of the diet; and these insolences, far from being repressed as they deserved, were encouraged and applauded by the leaders of the faction that overthrew the laws and the government of the Republic. The number of these grievances, not to mention those which are suppressed to shorten the enumeration, is made to justify before God and the powers the part which Her Imperial Majesty would have taken to obtain a brilliant satisfaction. But it is not with this intention that she has just exposed them. Her natural equity does not allow her to confuse the entire Polish nation with one of its parts, which had surprised and betrayed her confidence. She is, to the contrary, intimately convinced that the greater number had no part in all that was done in Warsaw against her and against the Republic, her former friend; Her Majesty, therefore, is ready to sacrifice the just resentment which she must feel, to hope, more in conformity with her generous and peaceful sentiments, to have all grievances repaired by the assembly of a new diet more faithful to the mandates of its constituents, and to the cardinal and immutable laws of the state, which is not the one of the present, which, having violated them all in the most obvious manner, marked the seal of its own illegality with all those its operations that it executed in defiance of these laws. But if Her Imperial Majesty does not wish to listen to the voice of her own resentment, she cannot wax indifferent to that of the complaints addressed to her by a large number of

Poles, among whom there are several equally illustrious by their birth and the rank, which they hold in the Republic, only by their patriotic virtues and their capacity for the service of the state. Driven by a pure and laudable zeal for the salvation of their country and the recovery of their former freedom and independence, they joined together to form a legitimate confederation, as the only effective remedy to the evils that the illegal confederation, usurpers of Warsaw, has caused the nation. To this end, they requested the support and assistance of the Empress, who did not hesitate to assure them of both, being guided on her side by her feelings of friendship and benevolence for the Republic, and strictly fulfilling the duty imposed upon her by her treaties.

It is to fulfill her promises that Her Majesty has ordered some of her troops to enter the lands of the Republic. They present themselves as friends, and to cooperate with its reintegration in its rights and prerogatives. All who welcome them under these titles will feel, besides the perfect forgetfulness of the past, every assistance and safety for their persons and their properties. Her Imperial Majesty flatters herself that any good Pole, truly loving his country, will appreciate her intentions, and will feel that it is to serve his own cause to join with his heart and arms to the generous efforts which she will deploy, in concert with the true patriots, to restore to the Republic the liberty and the laws which the claimed Constitution of May 3rd has taken from it. If there were some who swayed because of the oath that the illusion causes them to speak or that force tears from them, let them be convinced that the only sacred and true oath is the one by which they swore to maintain and to defend to death the free and republican government under which they were born, and that to take up this old oath is the only way to repair the perjury they have committed by taking the new one. But if there are any who, by reason of their obstinacy in the perverse principles into which they have allowed themselves to be drawn, wish to oppose the beneficent views of the Empress and the patriotic wishes of their fellow-citizens, those will not take from them the rigors and evils to which they will be exposed, all the more justly because it was up to them to avoid them by a prompt and sincere abjuration of their errors. The undersigned, Envoy Extraordinary and Minister Plenipotentiary, who was to announce the intentions of His Imperial Majesty, and the just motives which determined them, is also to invite the illustrious Polish nation to put the greatest confidence in the generosity and disinterestedness that presides over the steps of Her Majesty, and which make her very anxious to see soon the Republic strengthen on its basis by a right balance of powers; which is the surest means of perpetuating its inner tranquility, as well as its relations of good neighborliness and good harmony with all its neighbors.

Done at Warsaw, the 7th (May 18, 1792 n.s.)
J. Boulghakoff.

No. 4

Discourses of Stanislas Soltyk, Nonce from Krakow, Given in the Last Séance of the Constituent Diet, 29 May 1792

"The moment has arrived, Sire, when, on leaving this place destined for the making of the laws, every Pole, who still has the feeling of honor, will, under your auspices, be put under the banner of liberty, and defend this land which saw him born; this darling land where he lives happily, because he is free. Yes, all Poles are willing to expose themselves to the greatest perils, because it is for the defense of their property, their children, their glory, their freedom, their king finally that they go there.

"As it is the last time that I ask for the floor, allow me. Sire, to address my speech to you, with the flattering boldness of a free Pole. I draw a veil on the first 20 years of your reign, I pass over them in silence; but please. Sire, in the career of the labors awaiting you, remove this frightening veil, and remember what you were, what was this nation, which, in good faith, abandons to you its destinies; and this aspect, I hope, will be the guide of your steps. Deign, Sire, to approach the second epoch of your reign; it is the time of the present diet: the nation has regained its liberty, you have gained the confidence of the Poles; they were really starting to love you. In this memorable dictum, the limits between the nation and the king were laid forever; the sovereignty remained with the nation, the Executive Power with the king; the nation was free, and its king is esteemed. I move on to the third epoch of your reign, which awaits you. Sire, deign to lend me an attentive ear; you are getting closer to the most critical moments of your life; they will prove whether you deserve to be ranked among the most famous monarchs, or whether, with your days, the memory of your reign must perish. Sire, you undertake the defense of your country, the generous nation has entrusted you with everything for this holy enterprise: you are the master of our goods, of our lives; the Poles, brave and valiant, will follow you everywhere to fight the common enemy of the country. Any way of negotiation with the neighboring powers is open to you; our ally, the King of Prussia, so much vaunted by his virtues and his loyalty, will no doubt come to our defense. If, on the contrary, our hopes were to vanish, if in this crisis, so fatal to us, we are abandoned to ourselves by the effect of an unfair conduct on the part of the Prussian ministry, then. Sire, the Pole, driven to despair, not by the fear of arms, but seeing that he lacks the faith of a solemn treaty, will be ready to ally himself with whomever your prudence will advise him. Sire, the entire nation entrusts its destiny; it gave you everything you asked for; and what you will still ask, it is ready to give it to you. But be careful not to give us just cause for mistrust; you have the hearts of all the Poles together, but all their eyes are also fixed on you; think that the public is making a harsh judgment on the actions of kings; follow the example of Frederick the Great, when he went to war; keep away from any appearance of luxury; in a word, that virtue and courage surround you, and may fortune accompany you. "

No. 5

Act of Accession of Stanislas Augustus to the so-called Confederation General of Targowica, in 1792

United of mind and heart with a free nation and a republican, who, from the rank of a simple citizen, raised me to the throne; willing, in concert with it, to cooperate in this salutary work, which must give a new and more durable basis for freedom, independence, the integrity of the Republic, and which tends to organize with more wisdom its political and civil administration, I give in to the impulse of the sentiment, which animates me: yes, it is the vow, it is the passion of the public good (which I must put above all other interests); it is the desire to assure your happiness, a generous and free nation, who dictates to me these new testimonies of paternal love which I offer you today. Sincerely attached to my country, knowing no other penalties, or other enjoyments than this, all my efforts have always been for its safety, its happiness, and its glory. But the particular views of my collaborators, the taste for reform and novelty have not always allowed me to follow the movements of a heart that is all yours.

The operations of the last diet show this. Seduced by new, bold maxims, which only tended to disturb the tranquility of nations, our legislators dared to break the respectable empire of the laws which, from the first centuries of the Republic, had served as its foundation; they tried to enslave Poland under the yoke of a monarchical and democratic government at the same time. A single diet has given rise to so many different laws, that, when it was necessary to write them and to enforce them, the difficulty of the enterprise made them give up. Moreover, the foundations that had been given to this new constitutional system, too weak to support them, were moreover directly contrary to the legislative system, which alone can ensure the existence of Poland. But today that every true Pole recognizes the mistakes of those who have misled him, after having lost their own way by ambition, I declare, as a king, who must be the leader of this generous republic, and as Poles who cherish their compatriots, that only the republican government, as our ancestors established, alone can perpetuate the duration and glory of Poland. In fact, whenever a nation, instead of correcting what its former government may have in it that is defective, tries to overthrow it from top to bottom, it draws on it all the terrible scourges that must necessarily to determine a sudden shock and forced of the body politic.

After having recognized, in the face of a republican nation, the wisdom and the truth of these maxims, I abandon the confederation formed in 1788, and the diet convened afterwards in Warsaw, under the presidency of Mr. Stanislas Nalencz Malachowski, the great referendum of the crown; dictates, which, in order to operate and strengthen more surely an impolitic and dangerous revolution, pronounced prolonged till the end of four years, against the constant use of the republic, and in defiance of the most express laws. I freely join with heart and soul the new confederation formed the vow of the whole nation, in Targowica on May 14 of this year, by the care and all the auspices of Mr. Stanislas Felix Potocki, Grand Master of the Artillery of the Crown; a confederation which has just been united with that of the Grand Duchy of Lithuania by a solemn and public act. I regard the operations it confesses as the only legal ones, I promise to comply with all the laws it proclaims, and swear to second it in all its views, which are only for the public good, in concert with a republican and free nation for centuries. I am all the more ready to take this step, that the plan of the reforms projected by this confederation offers to the impartial eye of good citizens nothing but what is just and salutary, and especially because the generous and selfless protection of Her Majesty, the Empress of all the Russias, brings tranquility back to the Republic, becomes for it a new source of prosperity, and more effectively guarantees its rights and its integrity. I therefore require that the present Act of Accession be registered in the chancelleries of the general confederations of the two nations, as well as in those of the territorial jurisdictions of the States of the Republic.

Done at Warsaw this 23rd day of July 1792.
Signed: Stanislaus-Augustus, King.

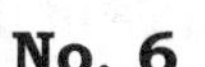

No. 6

Protest of Targowicans Assembled in Grodno, February 3, 1793, Against the Entrance of the Prussian Troops Into Greater Poland

Favorable events or great reverses had in turn brought Poland to an eminent degree of splendor or had precipitated it into a state of weakness and despair; but, in this alternative of opposing chances, an unshakable constancy had always noted the elevation of the national character. The short interval of the last four years obscures this honorable aspect for the nation. The Diet of 1788 collected at a time which, by a happy combination of circumstances, offered Poland the hope and the means of strengthening the foundations of its republican government, became for it a source of ills, aggravated by the contrast of vanished hopes. Seduction wiped out confident patriotism and distorted its pure and beneficent views.

The revolution of May 3, 1791 conceived and carried out without the attachment of the national will, without the help of neighbors, by transforming a republic into a monarchy, created despotism within, with the fear of external storms provoked by discontent. Neighboring courts. A constitution, which violated the ancient prerogatives of the citizen, cemented with the blood of his ancestors, equally incompatible with the political propriety of the powers that surround us, lacked the necessary foundations to assure its solidity. Faithful to her engagements, Her Majesty the Empress of all the Russia's, this august ally of Poland, and guardian of its government, deigned to offer to the nation, in the generous assistance of her power, a flattering prospect of the reestablishment of its freedom, independence, sovereignty and integrity. Virtuous citizens, determined to prefer death to slavery, did not hesitate to adhere to views so consoling for their country; while others who had retired to their homes, and yielding to circumstances, were only waiting for a favorable moment, that all foreshadowed them. The declaration of the Court of Petersburg assured the Poles their republic, a free government, national independence, and the integrity of their estates. Peace and freedom preceded the banners of the Russian troops, who entered the territory of the Republic, as friends and auxiliaries. However, the abusive use of the national forces, by opposing an unthinking resistance, soon caused every virtuous citizen to groan at the sight of the indiscreetly lavished blood of his brothers.

But at last the reign of terror and disorder vanished. The King, the Army, the whole nation, adhered to an inclination towards the confederacy, formed at Targowica, on May 14, 1792. Then confusion and consternation gave place to the blossoming of hope and joy. Calm was restored in the interior, with the assistance of external support, a reasoned confidence in the justice of the cause, and with the goodwill of the neighbors; everything combined to ward off anxiety: the national character forbade any idea of persecution. Thus, the person and the property of the individuals, the best known by their opposition to the views of the confederacy, were respected. The Russian troops, quartered in the various provinces, observed an exact discipline everywhere; and if at times some citizens had to undergo vexations, these isolated insults, of which, even in peace, one is not entirely safe from the part of the national soldier, were only the work of a few subordinate commanders, and were immediately repressed as known. The confederation was already thinking of reaching its goal; its labors, tending towards the regeneration of the republican government, were going to assure the liberty of the citizen, and to strengthen the friendship and the good harmony with the neighboring states; the Republic was already touching the moment when it was enjoying, in the midst of peace, the fruits of the active zeal of the citizens who had the courage to seize the tiller of affairs in a difficult crisis: the purity of their intentions unveiled made the clouds of their prevention disappear; and the nation looked forward with confidence to the result of the work undertaken for the public happiness. Such was the state of things in Poland when the declaration of the King of Prussia came to chill all hearts with fright and surprise. The motives of the entrance of the Prussian troops into the territory of the Republic could not fail to give rise to disturbing suspicions in the mind of the Pole, as loyal in his character as he was open in his conduct. Frightened of the so-called progress of democratism in Poland, and even more of the birth of the clubs intended to propagate it, the King of Prussia, on the eve of opening a second campaign, did not believe it desirable, it is said in this declaration, to leave an enemy in his rear that he had to fear. It is accordingly considered it an indispensable precaution to bring part of its troops into the territory of the Republic. A constant correspondence between the military commanders, the palatinal confederations, the civil magistrates and the general confederation, having enabled it to ensure that a perfect calm reigned from one end of the kingdom to the other, all measures and extraordinary precautions had seemed to them superfluous until that day. At the sight of the declaration of His Prussian Majesty, although astonished only at the assertions set forth therein, and in no way convinced of the reality of their object, the general confederation had satisfied in every respect that which it believed was due to its neighbor, to a friend, to an ally. Prussia declared in its reply that no species of trouble was manifested in the country, that all the revolutionary clubs were proscribed there; "That, besides, the public force, supported by the presence of the Russian troops, was more than sufficient to repress all the movements." It accordingly asked His Prussian Majesty "to revoke the orders given for the entry of a corps of his troops on the territory of the Republic." After this reply, the general confederation, rather than relying on the anxiety manifested by His Majesty, the King of Prussia, to the reality of the need, sent precise orders to all the corps of troops to keep themselves always ready to go, wherever the slightest indication of fermentation might require their presence.

These steps carried out left no doubt to the general confederation, to the whole nation, that His Prussian Majesty, reassured by so many motives, would stop the march of his troops. This deference was also analogous to the laws of good neighborliness and the dignity of a free nation. However, notwithstanding all these solemn assurances, notwithstanding the evidence of the facts alleged to support them, the Prussian army advanced, and one of its detachments appeared under the walls of Thorn; its inhabitants, faithful to their duty, having refused it entry, suffered an open attack; the guns were pointed, the gate was broken, the municipal guard was dislodged from its posts; and a defenseless city offered the spectacle of a place carried by assault; the Prussian regiments entered it, filling the air with shouts of joy. No soldier of the Republic was there to present any resistance: the city rested its safety on the public faith, and this was violated. At the same time, various Polish detachments in Greater Poland were besieged and dislodged from their posts by superior forces.

Full of confidence in solemn engagements, in the religion of treaties, could we ever believe to have to fear surprises, or an open violence, where everything should guarantee us to find only friendship and help? So, the few troops stationed on this frontier, having no other purpose than to watch the interior tranquilly, far from being sufficiently armed for war, were even devoid of cannons.

The high idea that we have formed of the justice and magnanimity of the King of Prussia always nourishes our expectation that this prince, enlightened by our answer, will stop the consequences of his first resolution; that, far from wanting to give support to the violation already effected on Polish territory, he will rather have at heart to convince the Polish nation of his constant benevolence, by evacuating his troops from the domains of the Republic.

Resting on the goodness of our cause, we have nothing to fear from any kind of pretensions to the charge of some parts of the states of the Republic guaranteed by so many treaties, and particularly by that of 1775, which binds His Prussian Majesty, as the other two neighboring courts. Faithful in consequence to our oaths, faithful to our attachment to the ancient prerogatives of our ancestors, faithful to our vocation, we protest in the most solemn way, in the face of the universe, against any usurpation of the least part of the states of the Republic. We declare loudly that we do not enter for anything, or in any way, in any concert whatsoever, tending to the detriment of some portion of Polish domains; that, on the contrary, we are ready to sacrifice the last drop of our blood for the defense of our liberty and our integrity.

We hope, moreover, that the two imperial courts bound by their guarantees, that even all the powers, by a succession of a community of national interest, will not see with indifference the manifest violation of the law of nations, the serious attacks on the tranquility of a neighboring and friendly state, as well as the open invasion of its domains. We expect, above all, that the august sovereign in whom we have placed all our confidence, and who in the face of Europe has devoted his benevolence to us, will not allow the weakening of the glory of his fame, and will find it rather analogous to his great soul to add to this crowd of memorable facts which have immortalized him, that it is no less glorious to lend, at critical moments, a helping hand to a free nation, worthy to every consideration to excite the general interest.

In thus manifesting all the purity of our intentions, we finally declare that no other view animates our efforts than that of transmitting to our nephews a republic well organized, free, and independent, and that this republic, which we will have regenerated, or we will keep it intact or none of us will survive its disaster.

Done at Grodno, at the Seance of the
General Confederation of the Two Nations, February 3, 1793.

Stanislas Felix Potocki,
Grand Master of Artillery and
Marshal of the General Confederation of the Crown.

Alexander Prince Sapieha,
Grand Chancellor of Lithuania and
Marshal of the Confederation of the Duchy of Lithuania.

No. 7

Declaration of Russia, Dated April 9, 1793, Relative to the Invasion of the States of the Polish Republic

The sentiments of the Empress in the declaration which her ministers issued at Warsaw on May 7-18th of last year, on the occasion of the march of her troops into Poland, undoubtedly had no other object than to obtain approval, by voluntary consent, and can add to it the gratitude of the Polish nation. All of Europe has seen how its statements have been received, and what has happened. To pave the way for the Confederacy of Targowica, that it might be in a position to exercise its rights and to deploy a legitimate authority, it was necessary to resort to arms; and the promoters of the Revolution of May 3, 1791, as well as their adherents, abandoned the field of battle and the struggle to which they had provoked the Russian troops, only after having been defeated.

But if open warfare ends, it escapes only to make way for secret intrigues, whose subtle springs are all the more dangerous, that they escape the most attentive observation, and even the activity of the lights.

The spirit of faction and revolt has grown such deep roots, that those who are perverse enough to make it an occupation to light and spread fire after having failed in their cabals near foreign courts, where they tried to make suspicious the views of the Russian Court, then worked to mislead the people, that it is always easy to lead, and have reached the point of inspiring in them the same hatred and dislike they bring to this court, which overthrew their hopes and their criminal designs. Without stopping on generally known facts, which are proved by the hostile sentiments of most of the inhabitants of Poland, it will suffice to say that they have abused even the principles of humanity and moderation that the generals and other officers of the Her Majesty's army observed, according to the express orders they had received, to the point of having them escape the insults and acts of hostility of all kinds, and that the most daring were carried away to the point of threatening to renew on them the Sicilian Vespers. This was the reward that the enemies of repose and order which Her Imperial Majesty sought to re-establish and strengthen were preparing for her magnanimous intentions! Let us judge by the sincerity with which most of them adhered to the Confederation, which subsists today, as well as the solidity and the duration of the peace which would have reigned in the Republic.

But the Empress, who has been accustomed for the last 30 years to fight the ever-changing dissensions in this state, and who puts her trust in the means Providence has given her to contain these factions, would have continued to employ her disinterested measures without respite, to silence her grievances and the just claims they allow, had it not been for unpleasant circumstances which announced dangers of greater importance. The inconceivable distraction of a nation formerly so flourishing, now dishonored, torn, on the edge of the precipice which will engulf it; this misguidance, which should have been a subject of horror for these anxious minds, appeared on the contrary a model worthy of imitation; they seek to introduce into the interior of the republic those infernal lessons which an impious sect, sacrilegious and senseless, has imagined for the destruction of all religious, civil and political principles. They have already formed in the capital, as well as in several provinces of Poland, clubs which fraternize with the Jacobins of Paris; they secretly spread their poison, blow it into the spirits, and let it ferment there.

The establishment of a home so dangerous for all the powers whose states reach the frontiers of the Republic ought naturally to arouse their attention; they have conferred by mutual agreement on the means of stifling the evil at its birth, and of removing from their frontiers that dangerous venom. Her Majesty the Empress of all the Russia's, and His Majesty the King of Prussia, by the consent of His Majesty the Emperor of the Romans, have found no more efficacious expedient than to enclose Poland into narrower bounds, to give it such an existence and such a proportion of extent as to give it the rank of a middle power, and to facilitate to it the means of procuring and maintaining, without loss of its former liberty, a wise and well-ordered government, which at the same time has enough activity to repress the disorders and factions that have so often disturbed its repose and that of its neighbors. Gathered in this design by the same principles and views, Her Majesty the Empress of Russia and the King of Prussia intimately convinced themselves that there was no other way to prevent the entire ruin of which the Republic was threatened, both by its intestine dissensions, and by the extravagant and monstrous opinions that have begun to be popular there, than to incorporate in their respective states those provinces of Poland that are now frontiers, and to take possession of them for the moment to protect against the destructive effects of the extravagant systems that they seek to introduce. At the same time as Their Majesties make known to the Polish nation this firm and irrevocable resolution which they have formed, they invite Poland to convene a diet to proceed, amicably, and make the necessary arrangements and measures, in order to procure for the Republic, and to assure it a firm, lasting, and unalterable peace.

Given at Grodno on April 9, 1793.

Jacques de Sieters,
Ambassador Extraordinary and Plenipotentiary of
Her Majesty the Empress of all the Russias.

No. 8

Protest of Vice-Grand-General of the Crown of Poland, Severin Rzewuski, of April 17, 1793

United by the bonds of a free confederacy, under the support of Her Majesty, the Empress of Russia, I had no other feeling than the freedom of my country and the gratitude for this sovereign. I regard the safety of the Republic assured against all acts, by the aegis of its friendship. I blessed her name and thought I would make vows for my country by forming them for this great sovereign. Such was my way of thinking, and that of all Poles; but the day of the 9th of April, when the declaration of the Courts of St. Petersburg and Prussia appeared, which threatened the usurpation of the territory of Poland on both sides, disturbed the public tranquility and mine; it poisoned that sweet time which I already enjoyed with the return of liberty. The new blow, so fatal to the country, is despairing, and coincides with the epoch of confederation, which, formed with the purest intentions, the most salutary views for the country, must, however, be terminated by the greater misfortunes, without being able to remedy them.

As for me, I know all that is in my power. And having invoked for my judge the Supreme Being as a witness of my intentions, I declare before the universe and my country, and I invoke the Empress even that I have constantly ignored the partition of Poland, that I have not contributed to it; that on the contrary, having always had in mind only its integrity and its freedom, it is I who wrote the article of the oath of confederation, by which each member swore never to vote any diminution of the territory of the Republic and its dependencies.

Soaking my pen in tears, I want to leave a memory of the misfortunes of my homeland and my own. I protest in writing against all the usurpations of Polish territory; I declare that I will never sign my signature to such an act, and that I will never consent to anything contrary to the oath I have given to God and to my country. My protest will not prevent the common misfortune; but I owe it to my oaths and my country. I will not try to avoid personal evils; whatever fate provides me, I will wait for it with resignation; and if I am unfortunate, at least I will never be guilty. I sign this protest, I deposit it in the acts of the general confederation, reserving the right to renew it with the Confederate nation and its public.

Given at Grodno, this 17th of April 1793.

Sevenin Rzewusk

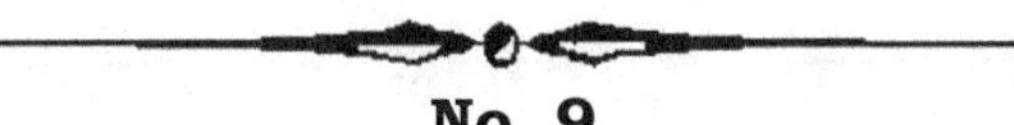

No. 9

Discourse of Joseph Kimbar, Nonce of the District of Upita (in Lithuania) to the Séance of July 17, 1793, of the Grodno Diet

My opinion is, he says, that we must not give in to the Russian ambassador; that we must put ourselves above his threats. Suffering is nothing for virtue; it knows that it is its essence to despise them, and, if necessary, to endure them all. Why scare so much, sire? All those who dare to defend their country, all those who refuse to put the seal on its annihilation, are threatened with exile to Siberia. Let's go to Siberia! It will not be without charms for us; its deserts will become for us an Elisha; for everything, down to our shadows, everything will tell us about our virtue, our devotion to our country. You, Sire, whose reign is marked by a continual chain of misfortunes, if, in the midst of these disasters, you have been a thousand times given the opportunity to make your name immortal and to acquire rights to the recognition of your nation and if, nevertheless, it has not gained any advantage from it, seize with more success that which presents itself today. Erase the mistakes of your first years, and if then the lack of experience could give reason to say that you would have wanted a more active, more determined, response to these reproaches by showing us under these white hairs more courage and more force.

Forgive, Sire, that I become your censor here! But whoever, like me, professes to be attached to you and to love his nation; whoever knows how to appreciate the words you have just pronounced yourself, the nation with the king, the king with the nation; whoever remembers the sacred word that you have just given us. If ever you should lend your hand to subscribe to a partition, what is it? That this one, I say, do justice to my feelings and my words. He will have to agree that it is pure truth that speaks through my mouth.

Sire, we love you; you can count on my whole affection; the nation loves you; the country which has served you as a cradle still supports you. Could you then never consent to deliver our fellow-citizens, our parents, our brothers, and this land, which nourished you in your childhood? "All that you possess as king, you have received from the Poles. It is you that our compatriots have been pleased to fulfill the benefits of the country; and would you have the heart to sign on their behalf their own slavery? What sweetness can finally be attached to a crown which cost you such sacrifices? You will not wish it any more at this price.

The general opinion is that, to carry it, you had obligations to Catherine. Show the whole world that it was God who had made you king. Show that you know how to reign with glory and to be faithful to your engagements, even when the force majeure submits everything to its will, and that a foreign power threatens to engulf everything. What affair can a crown have when it is necessary to wear it as a slave? You, Sire, who are our King and our father, yes, I dare to give you this name, and I am not only sure to be confessed by the greater part of the chamber, but in Siberia even these two titles will never fade from our hearts, drive us, if it is necessary, to Siberia. Come, since we are threatened, let's go to these sad deserts. Here again our virtue and yours will make those who have conspired our loss grow pale. (Here several voices were raised, "Yes, let's go to Siberia." Many nuncios shouted together and at the same time.) We, Sire, who are your children, we will follow you with all the enthusiasm of gratitude. And, the more you will bear the trouble of your devotion to the country, the more you will be dear to us, the more we will venerate you.

No. 10

Discourse by Ignace Goslawski, Nonce of Sandomir, In the Séance of September 6, 1793, At the Grodno Diet, Concerning the Three Chiefs of the Targowica Plot

He alone is entitled to rewards, who fills all his duties with fidelity. According to this principle, I ask you, gentlemen, can our generals and artillery generals require a pension, who have abandoned their country at this critical moment, when it is asking for their advice and help? I will doubtless perish with this unfortunate country; but the last breath I will exhale will be a reproach against these degenerate citizens, who, after having been an unnecessary burden on the soil of Poland, have finally delivered it to ravage and devastation. Dissatisfied with the new constitutional regime, which forced their haughty heads to bend under the rule of law, these so-called grandees had the baseness to creep indiscriminately at the feet of Russia, to obtain mercenary help from them. Whose help they could erect on the ruins of the government altars to their proud ambition, a throne to their oligarchy. It was at the foot of these altars, on the steps of this throne, that the Pole, degraded by their vile calumnies, weakened by their guilty efforts, was to bend his knee before these divinities of the day, whose boundless despotism would have ensured the empire. This mourning country still sheds tears of despair over the ingratitude of these unnatural sons, who paid for its attention by the most infamous betrayal. The inhabitant of these unfortunate countries can not contemplate, without a pain mingled with terror, the fatal consequences of his blind confidence, the result of the succor, equivocal at first, and soon dangerous, which he did not claim. Yes, it is the Branacki, the Rzewuski, the Potocki, these leaders, these supporters of the oligarchic league, who overthrew the Republic. Proud of vain titles, whose source they did not know, they dared to rise above the law. What did I say? They forced it to bend to their caprices; and always struggling with this throne, the object of their ambition, they tread the weak with a superb foot, who dared to assert their rights. They needed a king without power, laws without energy, a government without coherence and without force. It was to consolidate in Poland those odious principles that had been created by their hostile pride in every kind of yoke, and which their despotism supported; it was to propagate them and to enslave us, that they begged Petersburg for this disastrous succor, which, after having precipitated us into an abyss of misfortunes, finally engulfed them too. Oh baseness! Source of all our disaster! You have precipitated the fall of the Republic, and you are still surviving it! .... You do a lot more! Hast thou lavished your vile incense on the murderers of the country? Is it because blind chance has filled them with its gifts, that your brow has humbled itself before these impotent idols, whose worship is at last destroyed? Oh unhappy fatherland! These denatured children, whom you have nourished in your bosom, it is they who tear it apart! Deaf to your complaints, insensitive to your just regrets, they still insult your pain, filling with praise those who delivered to you the death-blow.

I do not claim to oppose the project of the Grand Treasurer. On the contrary, I will support it with vigor when it is time for it; but why not take into consideration the one who has been asking for our decision for more than a month? Is it because it shocks the pride of our aristocrats? I therefore ask the assembly to rule first on Mr. Ciemniewski's draft."

No. 11

Organization of the National Supreme Council, by Kosciuszko, of May 10, 1794

The will of most of the nation being known by the unanimous adherence of the Palatinates to the act of independence, accordingly, and by fulfilling the will of the citizens and the obligation imposed upon me in the Second Article of this same act, I appoint the National Supreme Council, and I give it the organization contained in the following regulation, divided into four titles. The first is relative to its composition; the second to its functions in general; the third to the distribution of work among its members, and the fourth to the form of its deliberations.

Art. I. Composition of the National Supreme Council.

1.) The National Supreme Council shall be composed of eight councilors and the Chief General of the Armed Forces.

2.) There will be 32 alternates, who, in the cases detailed below, will replace the advisers. The Supreme Chief will have no substitute.

3.) I appoint as advisers Ignace Zakrzewski, President of the City of Warsaw; Thomas Wawrzecki, Wielowieyski, Major General; François Myszkowski, President of the city of Krakow; Alolse Sulistrowski Ignacy Potocki, Jean Laskicwicz and Hugues Kollontaj. For alternates I appoint Jean Kilinski, Michel Kochanowski, Elias Aloe, Joseph Weyssenhoff, Nicolas Tomaszewski, Guillaume-Jean Horalik, Alexandre Linowski, François Wasilewski, Joseph Sierakowski, Ignace Zatonczek, Jan Buchowiecki, Jan Malachowski, Jan Horain, Francois Dmochowski, Daniel Ruczynski , André Kapostas, Pierre Biling, François Fribes, Thomas Umiastowski, Antoine Dzieduszycki, Christophe Medecki, President of the city of Luck; Augustin Deboli, Thadée Mostowski, Francois Gauthier, Charles Prozor, Joseph Dziarkowski, Antoine Tykiel, Joseph Wybicki, Joseph Szymanowski, Thadeus Matuszewic, Clement Wengierski, Sabath Palraowski, President of the Presbytery of the Greco-Eastern Church in Poland;

4.) If anyone of the councilors or deputies is suspected by the Supreme Commander of the Armed Force, or by the National Council, not to act faithfully towards the goal that the citizens proposed themselves in the act of the insurrection, or if he is accused of having contravened the regulation of this act, the council is authorized to remove him from his corps by a majority of the votes; but if the nature of the offense is more serious, it will be referred, by a plurality of votes, to the Supreme Criminal Court to be tried. One of the deputies will be called to replace this adviser;

5.) If any of the councilors cannot fulfill his duties, either because of illness, absence from the place of the council sittings, or by another public office of which he would be entrusted, one of the deputies will be called to temporarily replace him.

Art. II. General Foundations of the Council.

1.) The general functions of the members of the Supreme Council are expressed in the Act of Insurrection, Articles V, VI, VII, VIII, XII, XIII, XIV. The council in all its operations, must regard these articles as inviolable rules.

2.) The council shall organize without delay the commissions of good order, the criminal courts, and the central deputation in the province of Lithuania, which is absolutely necessary to supervise more closely the execution in that part of the republic. This deputation, to be appointed by the Supreme Council, will be under the immediate dependence of the Supreme Commander of the Armed Forces as well as the National Council; and, likewise, the other intermediate powers, according to the content of the Act of Independence;

3.) The Supreme Council shall refrain from the acts which are prohibited to it by Article XI of the Insurrectional Act. It will ensure that it has not violated by any of the executive powers;

4.) When the purpose of the insurrection has been successfully fulfilled, the council, together with the Supreme Chief of the Armed Forces, will summon the nation into palatinal assemblies. He will provisionally prescribe at these assemblies the mode of election of the representatives for the Grand Diet, which will receive a report from the Supreme Commander of the Armed Forces, the Council, and all the provisional powers, which will give him their operations; it is further entrusted with giving a constitution to the people, as is stated in Article XII of the Insurrectional Act;

5.) The National Council shall establish a regular correspondence with the commissions of good order, and the criminal courts in all the palatinates and districts to which it shall send its resolutions, and from which it shall receive reports;

6.) The Council shall provide for the preservation and safety of the National Archives and shall have them under its immediate supervision;

7.) It will send weekly, and if necessary, more often, to the Supreme Commander of the Armed Forces, an exact report of all its deliberations and resolutions.

Art. III. Sharing of Work Among Board Members, and Functions of Each

1.) The work of the Supreme Council will be divided into eight departments; namely, 1st that of order, 2nd of safety, 3rd of justice, 4th of finance, 5th of subsistence, 6th of supply of armies, 7th of foreign affairs, and the 8th of public instruction;

2.) The Citizen Sulistrowski will head the Department of the Order; Citizen Wawrzecki, that of safety; the Citizen François Myszkowski, that of justice; Citizen Kollontay, that of finance; the Citizen Zakrzewski, that of the subsistence; Citizen Wielowieyski, that of the needs of the army; Citizen Ignacy Potocki, the Foreign Minister; Citizen Jean Laskiewicz, that of public education;

3.) Each of the advisers shall administer the department entrusted to him;

4.) For each department, the Supreme Council shall call the above-named alternates, who shall work under the immediate supervision of the councilors in the departments to which they shall be attached. The other deputies will be sent to the palatinates and districts to hasten the execution of what will be ordered by the Supreme Commander of the Armed Forces or by the Council, and will be furnished with the necessary instructions;

5.) Within the competence of the Department of Order, are, the rolls, the post office, the couriers, the transports by land and by water, the publication and the sending of all the regulations and all the resolutions that the Supreme Chief of the Armed Forces and council will have taken;

6.) From the purview of the Security Department, are, examination of suspicious papers, police suspicious houses, passports, watch and examination of dangerous men, arrests, sending the accused to the criminal courts, public prisons, and the subsistence of prisoners;

7. Within the purview of the Department of Justice, are the oversight of the criminal courts and the execution of their judgments;

8.) The Department of Finance is responsible for the supervision, preservation and use of patriotic gifts, the sequestration of property of traitors to the country that has been legally condemned, and the supervision of the administration of such property; the administration of national property and all public revenues; the administration of paper money, when the national Council deems it necessary to establish it; loans for public purposes, whether in the interior or in foreign countries; pay interest on national debts; the administration of the national debt, both in terms of income and expenditure; the administration of the currency factory;

9.) In the Department of Subsistence is responsible for the surveillance of the cultivation of the lands, the quantity and quality of the subsistence; restoration of stores and their preservation; the supervision of mills, bakeries, breweries; public relief for citizens who lack food; the domestic and foreign trade of the country's productions;

10.) The Procurement Department of the Army will take care of the execution of the requisition of the men whom the General-in-Chief has requested; the supervision of military exercises, according to the regulations of the General-in-Chief; the supervision of the arming and the exercise of all the citizens of Poland, in villages, towns and cities, according to the regulations of the same chief; the supervision of factories and manufactures relating to the clothing and the equipment of the soldier; the manufacture of weapons and munitions of war, as well as the purchase of the same objects; military depots and arsenals, supply of horses; in a word, all that the Army will need, and what the General-in-Chief will require;

11.) The Department of Foreign Affairs oversees foreign correspondence, the dispatch of ambassadors and diplomatic agents, negotiations with foreign powers, the conclusion of provisional agreements;

12.) The Department of Public Education will be in charge of all matters relating to the propagation of enlightenment, that is to say, the supervision of universities, palatinal and parish schools, as well as establishments, both secular and ecclesiastical, relating to education; the propagation of the public mind by gazettes and other writings, by the instructions given to the people in churches and other public assemblies; by the entertainments and exercises which the council, in this view, must establish; finally it will have the administration and supervision of the funds devoted to education.

13.) Each of the counselors chosen for one of these eight departments shall have supervision over the persons who will be employed in his department, and he shall be responsible for their misdeeds and misconduct, if it were proved that after having been instructed, he did not denounce the culprits to the Council. This responsibility extends to the substitutes, when one of them will replace a councilor in his functions;

14.) Each of the councilors shall inform the Council of the state of affairs in the department entrusted to him; it will bring projects on which the Council must deliberate;

15.) Each of them, in his department, will maintain and supervise the correspondence to which the Council is bound by the article of this organization.

Art. IV. Mode of Deliberations of the Council.

1.) The Council cannot take any deliberation, if it does not contain at least five people;

2.) The councilors will preside in the sittings according to the age of each. The presidency will last one week;

3.) All matters will be decided in the Council by majority vote. In case of a tie vote, that of the president will decide the majority;

4.) When the Council deliberates on matters that require secrecy for some time, it will recommend it to its members by a particular decision, and the one of them who is not faithful to secrecy, will be removed from the Council as a traitor, and sent to the Supreme Criminal

Court;

5.) The Council will have as many specific registers, as there are departments, to register its dispositions and its resolutions. In addition, there will be a general directory, in which the substance of all the provisions and resolutions will be recorded, with a note of the counselors present at each sitting, and their individual opinion in each case;

6.) The councilors and substitutes will take the following oath: "I (state your name) swear, in the presence of God, to all the Polish people, that I will employ the power entrusted to me, not to oppress anyone, but to defend the integrity of the domains of the Republic, the recovery of national sovereignty, and the strengthening of the general liberty in my country";

7.) The Council shall make such special regulations for itself and for its departments and office as it thinks fit;

8.) I reserve the right to extend and detail this organization, as well as to increase the number of members of the Council, when, either according to the will of the citizens, or according to the decision of the Council, or according to my own conviction, I believe I must do it for the good of the nation.

Made at the camp near Polaniec,
May 10, 1794.
Tadeusz Kosciuszko.

No. 12

Letter from the King of Poland, Stanislas-Augustus to the Elector Frederich-Augustus

"Monsieur, my brother and cousin, I owe thanks to Your Electoral Highness for allowing Sir Dąbrowski to pass from your service to that of his country three years ago. I acquit myself all the more willingly, as this officer has filled and passed even all our expectations by his distinguished services which have earned him the esteem, not only of his compatriots, but even of those whom he fought with so much value and skill that it was offered to the same Prussian ranks as it had here, and the Russian generals testified for the same reason to make him a very special case, and makes the most favorable welcome.

"Now that the unfortunate destiny of Poland leaves General Dąbrowski unemployed, and which the sad uncertainty of our fate does not present to this worthy officer, he wishes to find for some time an asylum in the states of Your Serene Highness, under your gracious protection.

"This is what I am praying for in gratitude to this good man who has truly proved that he loved and knew how to serve his country, and consequently his king.

"The beneficent and generous sentiments of your well-known Electoral Highness do not leave me doubtful of the success of my prayer.

"I ask you at the same time to receive as kindly as I give you, the assurances of the high esteem and true friendship with which I am.

"Your brother and cousin,
"Stanislas Augustus, King."

No. 13
Letter from Citizen Barss, to the Poles United in Venice, August 20, 1795

"I have announced to you, citizens, by my last letter, dated the 11th of the present [month], that according to your intentions, which we have found in agreement with ours, I have presented to the government two notes. In the first, I have asked for the protection of the French ministers residing near the allied courts, for the secret agents in Poland that we have there, or that we may have, while at the same time exposing the mutual advantage which might result of an ongoing communication, which the French ministers, or those who have relations with them, would maintain by the way of our agents with our compatriots who are abroad. In the second note, I informed [them] that Citizen Oginski determined to depart for Constantinople. Here is the content of the answer that was made to me:

"The ministers of the Republic who are assigned to the foreign courts are obliged, citizen, by the nature of their employment, to collect the necessary information wherever they find it. As for the information concerning your country, the fate of which has never ceased to interest the Republic, it will be very agreeable for the said ministers to receive them by the means of those of your fellow-citizens who will be distinguished by their talents, by their love of liberty, and by the confidence that those of their confreres, who have escaped the pursuit of the enemies of their country, will give them. As a result, we do not need to give specific instructions to our agents about this. Those that have been given to them, relative to the general affairs of your country, conform to the maxims and interests of the free government, which deserves the confidence of all those who are oppressed.

"This is the answer that I was given in writing, and in particular I was informed that there were already letters sent to Constantinople for Verninac, relative to Citizen Oginski."

"Citizen Oginski will also receive a letter from Citizen Lallement, in which we express our feelings and our opinion concerning his journey. This open letter was handed over to the government, which promised to send it to Venice. There is nothing, therefore, to stop this citizen from undertaking a journey which promises us so much good, knowing the activity, the zeal, and the talents of him who sacrifices himself for the interests of his country. It is only a matter of regulating the correspondence by the way of Venice, of giving the Citizen Oginski the code for the correspondence with us and the other Polish agents, and all the papers necessary for his mission, which you will receive in a few days by the Minister of the French Republic in Venice.

"Barss."

No. 14

Letter from the Patriots United in Paris, to Citizen Michel Oginski, of August 20, 1795

"Citizen, it is very consoling for us to learn that, in the situation in which our homeland is at present, the citizens who have sacrificed as much as you, to save it are constantly putting into practice all the means which appear proper to them to raise it again.

"After announcing to you, in concert with our compatriots living in Venice, that you determined to go to Constantinople to follow the affairs of Poland, but that you wish to assure yourself, before you go there, of the protection of the Ambassador of the French Republic to the Ottoman Porte, Citizen Barss hastened to expose to the government these intentions, which are also those of all your compatriots.

"The opinion of the Committee of Public Safety is that the ministers of the Republic will like to receive useful information concerning Poland, whose fate has never ceased to interest the French Republic, those of our compatriots who have distinguished themselves by their valor, by their love for freedom, and by the trust that their brother refugees will give them.

"According to this statement, you cannot avoid persuading yourself that the Ambassador of the Republic at Constantinople does not welcome you with the same interest as his constituents wish to bring to us. We do not doubt that, when, through your cautious and active conduct, you penetrate the usefulness of your stay at Constantinople, he does not tell you according to the exigency of circumstances, and perhaps even confession of his government, some measures that meet the purpose of the trip you propose to undertake.

"In addition to the historical instructions on the relations of our country with Turkey that we have sent you, we still have some advice to give you.

1.) When you have arrived at Constantinople, take care not to declare the object of your mission to any other than to the Ambassador of the French Republic and to the persons whom he has indicated to you. It is necessary that you put all your skill into deceiving the agents of our enemies of our dealings with those who are interested in us.

2.) In those times when the Polish government is disorganized, or where the nation, oppressed by its enemies, can neither freely issue its wishes nor be governed as it wished, we cannot have other guides, so with these earnest demarches to restore to it its freedom and independence as our honor, our conscience, and the interest we all have in seeing it, as a result of a solid system rendered to all its rights. Consequently, the signatures of your fellow citizens, formerly members of the National Council, as well as those of several others chosen for this purpose by our brother refugees in Paris, can only serve you as indubitable proofs of the confidence that we do not hesitate not to agree unanimously.

"Besides, your patriotism, your zeal, your enlightenment, the services you have rendered to our common country, and especially during the last revolution, assure us of a conduct that will increase the respect of your compatriots and the recognition of our unhappy nation.

"Eager to cooperate in your work, we will help you with all the means that depend on us, and those of our fellow citizens whose thoughts are in line with ours, and who have in mind only the freedom and independence of our country.

"Signed Gabriel Taszycki, François Dmochowski, D. Mniewski,
P. Niemoiowski, Thomas Maroszewski, François Wyszkowski,
Joseph Kociell, Clement Liberadzki, Kasimir De la Roche,
Joseph Wybicki, Jan Dembowski, Charles Prozor,
Adam Bronic, Komuald Giedroyc, Xavier Dąbrowski,
Joseph Wielhorski, E. Zablocki, Ignace Iasinski, Francois Barss,
Jan Meyer."

Paris, this 20th of August, 1795.

This letter was handed by the patriots from Venice to Citizen Oginski, with the following note:

"By joining our wishes and our votes to those of our fellow citizens, who are in Paris, whose names are specified above, we certify the authenticity of this letter, which was issued to us from the Chancellery of Citizen Lallement, Minister of France, and the deposition of the original letter, by our compatriots assembled in Paris, to the

Committee of Public Safety.

"Signed Prusihski, F. S. Lazninski, G. Nagurski, T. Wvssogierd, X. Jezierski, J. Wemglenski, K. Kolysko.

"Venice, September 23, 1795."

No. 15

Information for Citizen Michel Oginski, Called by the Wish of His Compatriots to the Mission to Constantinople, Signed by the Poles Remaining in Paris, Approved by the Committee of Public Safety, on 29 Thermidore, Year III (August 16, 1795) and Sent to Venice by the French Ambassador Lallement, to be Given to Citizen Oginski

The Polish patriots, assembled in Paris with the intention of working for the salvation oftheir country, and animated by the same spirit as all their compatriots, who profess the principles of liberty and independence, having been convinced of the necessity of seeing as soon as possible at the Ottoman Porte, one of their fellow citizens, distinguished by his reputation, his talents and his prudence, unanimously cast his eyes on the Citizen Michel Oginski. The latter, on his way to the important post where the good of the country, the wishes of his compatriots, and the national honor call him, will receive the following instructions. These are not orders given to him, nor duties imposed on him; because his civic virtues and his feelings do not need it: they are data and results of observations, dictated by the love of the motherland, which ignites all our hearts, based on calculations that do not appear doubtful, because they rest on the unequivocal dispositions of the powers friendly to Poland on the present state of affairs in Europe, and on the measures already taken by the French Republic to work effectively for the safety of our country.

These instructions will be classified according to the three positions in which the person in charge can be found, namely: public, secret and specific.

Public Instructions

1.) Given the circumstances of the moment, all the steps, operations, insinuations and relations with the Divan, will be done confidentially as long as they will be preliminary measures, and will take an official character as soon as the results of these operations will have the expected effect.

2.) All these steps will always be made jointly with the French agents, in the name of the Republic of Poland, represented by the national authority, and recognized by the Polish nation in its state of independence.

3.) The bases upon which they will be supported, and the purpose to which they will be directed, are set forth in the following articles:

I. The Ottoman Porte recognizes in the Polish nation a friendly and allied nation.

II. The Poles, in fighting their enemies, fight against those of the Ottoman Porte, and thus cooperate in the safety and the consolidation of this empire.

III. The two states will remain armed against the common enemies until they are reduced to the impossibility of disturbing their tranquility, and of attacking their integrity and independence.

IV. During the war, the contracting parties will also be united in peace negotiations, which cannot be dealt with separately; and the Divan on the one hand, and the national authority recognized by the Poles on the other, undertake to take all the necessary measures respectively to determine the French Republic, Sweden, and Denmark, to support the steps of the contracting parties, and to obtain the favorable results that must be hoped for.

4.) These various communications will be accompanied by the political developments, notes according to the attached data, taken from the general plans taken into consideration by the French government, and even a part is in full execution at the present moment. Particular attention will be paid in these pieces to the present and future advantages that Poland's independence will bring to the interests of the Ottoman Porte. We shall endeavor to draw a picture of the power of the French Republic, of that common ally of the two parties, in whose hands lies the political balance of Europe. The means and efforts that the French people have employed to achieve this will be indicated; we will develop those which the Polish people have made in the last days to obtain their independence; we will endeavor to show that the last revolution of Poland has failed only by the abandonment in which the powers which were to be most interested in supporting it left it; the resulting dangers for Turkey will be described; it will be added that it will be for the wisdom of the present Divan, enlightened by the experience of the past, to support the efforts of the Poles, which the courage and love of the country have made them undertake; we will end by declaring that the principal object of the present mission is to strengthen the links formed by nature between the two parties, whose interests are common, and who have the same enemy to fight.

5.) All care will be employed in deciding the Ottoman Porte to declare beforehand to the Cabinets of Europe that it wishes, as soon as possible, to see Poland returned to her liberty, her integrity and her independence, for the good of the tranquility of Europe; that it invites the three co-dividing powers to take this statement into consideration; and that, while awaiting a satisfactory reply in this respect, it thinks it is necessary to double its armaments on land and sea, to guarantee its own safety.

6.) The contracting parties shall deal with each other, and enter into reciprocal relations, only provisionally, in order to speed up the period when the Polish nation is freed from its position, so that it may consolidate by treaties of alliance and commerce, the good harmony that we reciprocally seek to establish.

Secret Instructions

1.) A secret negotiation with the Divan will be opened to obtain an asylum in favor of the national authority, in some cantons of Moldavia. The most suitable place for this object seems to be Raya in Chocim, or Cadilie in Botossanie, which form the corner between Bukovina and Podolia. In this way, this gathering of Poles would be under the dual jurisdiction of the Prince of Moldavia and the Pasha of Chocim. "Thus, during the primitive organization, and in the event that the Porte does not deem it expedient to declare itself forthwith against Russia, this assembly may successively be transferred from one to the other district as the requisitions of the Russian commander of Kamienioc would appeal to Jassy or Chocim, protesting against this gathering.

2.) The Chargé de la mission at Constantinople will endeavor to demonstrate the advantages which would accrue to the Ottoman Porte as soon as it had granted this asylum. The first consequence would be an influx of Polish soldiers, who, according to the plan attached, would be easily organized, and would soon form a body of troops of considerable size, and in advance would be stipulated, in favor of these refugee servicemen, for asylum and food aid.

3.) If the two previous articles are accepted:

I. The Porte will be invited to declare to the French agents that it agrees to transport to its destination a field of artillery, guns and ammunition, which the French Republic proposes to deliver to the Poles.

II. The same declaration must be made for the artillery officers, who must go to the banks of the Dniester.

4.) The citizen M.O. shall come to an agreement with Alexander Turski, sent by the French Republic as a general-officer of the Turkish cavalry, on the means of militarily influencing the Ottoman Ministry, to obtain a speedy decision in relation to the following articles. a particular instruction, issued to the aforesaid compatriot are:

I. To insist on the necessity of giving orders to the Princes of Moldavia and Walachia to receive the Polish refugee servicemen, to allow them not only a free stay, but even to not prevent them in their organization.

II. To ask, in order to fix the center of this organization, the place closest to the Fortress of Chocim, that of Kamieniec to be the first object of the offensive enterprises.

III. Advise them to bring the main forces of the Turks to Oczakow, also to pass by Georgia, to recapture the Crimea from the rear, while this peninsula will be blocked by the fleet. This plan, the only one that can restore to the Ottoman Porte the last usurpations made on its territory by the Russians, will be executed all the more easily, that by favoring and seconding the efforts of the Poles against the Russian armies, on the banks of the Dniester, it will not need to employ so many of its own troops on this point.

5.) As soon as the above-mentioned dispositions and measures are taken, the action of the provisional reports shall be such as to the military operations and reciprocal negotiations of the two states with the other Powers their allies, if they were based on treaties that have been already concluded; that is to say, Poland, on the one hand, and Turkey on the other, will multiply and combine all their military operations against common enemies, to reduce them by force of arms, while they will use all their political means to consolidate and make triumphant the five-fold meeting of France, Turkey, Sweden, Denmark and Poland.

6.) The results of the above articles will form the preliminaries of the offensive, defensive and commercial alliance treaties, and will be provisionally secured by simple secret agreements between the two governments and communicated to the other allies as necessary.

7.) One will operate in all his relations with the Divan and according to ....

8.) The impulse to give to the Ottoman Porte must be the offensive against Russia and the defensive against Austria, in the event that it wished to desist from supplying the Russians with quotas according to the existing treaties, and that it did not interfere in any way with the military operations of the Poles. In an opposite case, one would act with hostility against this power, directing the main forces of Turkey (without prejudice however of those that one would use against the Russians) towards the fortresses of Navi, Gradiska and the Temeswar Banat, to make by there a diversion against the Austrian forces in Bukovina and Galicia, against which the Poles on their side would act.

9.) The Chargé de la mission Constantinople will transmit his reports to the national authority sitting in Moldavia and will send duplicates to the Polish agency in Paris, in charge of the general direction of political operations. He will maintain an active correspondence with the other Polish agents in Copenhagen, Stockholm, etc., as his instructions will be in contact with those which will be issued to them.

Special Instructions.

1.) Crutta, sent by the Polish government to Constantinople, will be immediately attached to the Polish Legation as a dragoman.

2.) Citizen Oginski will weigh in his wisdom if he can take advantage of Marion, formerly employed at the Foreign Office in Warsaw, and currently in Constantinople, where information can be taken from his account to the French Legation.

3.) We will not recognize as Poles, and we will only grant protection to those who have taken an honorable part in the last two revolutions. It may even be necessary, in case of need, to request, in the name of common interests, the local police to deal with those who seek to obstruct existing relations and to establish between the two states. Mr. Aksak, because of his connections with the Russian legation, could serve in the latter case.

4.) We shall endeavor to maintain among the Polish refugee's fraternal communication of principles and good harmony, which is appropriate to the dignity of good republicans.

5.) We will take all possible measures to ensure the correspondence, not only with the national authority through the couriers of the Princes of Moldavia and Walachia, or even emissaries particular, but also with Paris, by our compatriots residing in Venice, as well as with Stockholm and Copenhagen, by the agents of these two powers.

If there were any circumstance omitted from these presents, it is to the patriotism, the enlightenment, the talents, and the experience of the person in whom we confide to make up for it, in accordance with the bases we have adopted.

Our confidence in this regard, as well as in all that in which Citizen Oginski will operate, is as frank as it is unlimited."

Note: "The present instructions were written while Prussia was negotiating partial peace with the French Republic; they were stopped and ended when this peace was concluded and published. It is essential here to add that this circumstance does not change or modify any point of the above provisions, and that it should be regarded only as a more powerful means of deciding the Porte, Sweden, and Denmark to a meeting of forces against Russia.

We believe that it is necessary to enclose here several authentic printed forms which can serve to fix the political opinion in Europe based on the latest news received in Poland.

No. 16

Extract from Elie Temo's Memoires

So many intrigues, so many cabals, disgusted me so much during my stay in the capital city, that I made the resolution to leave it, and even to give up all civil functions. I left immediately for Blonir, a small town four leagues from Warsaw, where therewas a Polish corps of 6,000 to 7,000 men commanded by General Lieutenant Mokronowski, who was to observe all the movements of a Prussian corps of between 8,000 and 9,000 men and on a plain half a league from the city, under General Elsner's orders. I entered a cavalry regiment as soon as I arrived, and our camp kept its position for ten days in a row. On the 11th day, the Prussians attacked us and forced us, for the moment, to abandon the city, but the next day General Mokronowski, after having spread the rumor of our retreat towards the capital, attacked them during the night with so much vigor that he not only took back the city, but pursued them for a league beyond it. The enemy had many wounded in this affair, and lost a great quantity of baggage and ammunition, which his precipitate flight did not leave him time to remove; at the very moment of our victory a courier came from our General-in-Chief Kosciuszko, with the order to proceed without delay to Warsaw, which was immediately executed. The enemy was abandoned to his fright, the army made a forced march, and arrived at 10 o'clock in the morning at Marimont, a village situated an hour away from Warsaw, where it established its camp. They were still working there when the advance guards of the enemy army, commanded by the King of Prussia in person, appeared. But finding, against their expectation, an army ready to receive them, they made a retrograde movement to retreat to their army corps; the enemy set up camp half a league from ours, and a few days passed without any other engagement than frequent skirmishes on both sides. One night the Prussians, under the cover of darkness, attacked us with surprising impetuosity; our regiment stationed near the enemy, and awaiting orders, I was sent forward with 20 cavalrymen. Scarcely had we made 100 steps that we were surrounded by a force majeure, and despite a long resistance, having lost eight men killed and wounded, we were forced to surrender. (I learned later that the Poles were successful in repelling the enemy.) We were kept for two days at headquarters and were asked a thousand questions; but being unable to draw any enlightenment from us, we were destined, ten in number, to be transported to the fortress of Glogau in Silesia; among us was a Polish gentleman named Skwarski, whose possessions were a league from the enemy's camp. He had a wife and a child, had only concerned himself with his domestic affairs, and had not left his habitation, imagining that the asylum of a quiet and unarmed man would be respected. But as soon as the Prussians heard of it, deaf to the voice of humanity and nature, they tore him from his house, and under his very eyes delivered it to pillage. After 12 days' march we arrived at Glogau. We were led to the commander who was named Ritz. He received us with kindness and consideration which astonished us all. After having questioned us, he repeated to us that he would try, as far as possible, to soften the rigor of our situation, and then he distributed us to different parts of the city. This unexpected reception and the pleasure I had in finding among the other prisoners of war before us, several officers who were my friends, made me almost insensible to my misfortune. The first moments of our joy passed to communicate to one another the state of affairs of our country; they then hastened \to describe to me the gentleness and affability with which the captain had treated them till then.

I went to him the next day to pay him my respects and to express my deep gratitude to him. "Sir," said he, "when you were taken prisoner of war, you are no longer an enemy, but a man entitled to the hospitality of men." Such a language emboldened me to speak to him with confidence, and in the course of our conversation I recognized in him a sound judgment, a great deal of wit and knowledge; he spoke perfectly the French language, handled the pencil and the brush rather as an artist than an amateur, and finally united all the qualities of an amiable man with those of a true philosopher. He often brought us to his home, especially those who knew German or French. He conversed amicably with us and lent us books from his library; it was considerable, and each of us found there, according to his taste, something to amuse himself with or to learn from.

The inhabitants of the city also filled us with attentions and friendships. We had thus spent three months in the most profound tranquility, when the news spread that the inhabitants of Greater Poland, encouraged by the example of the valiant Kosciuszko, had risen against the King of Prussia, to recover their liberty, and their national independence. This news, which was still a confused rumor, was noted by the arrival and the fright of the Bishop of Posnania, Raczynski. This man having risen to this place by high treason and deceit had just escaped the just revenge of the patriots. It was very little to him to have betrayed his country; he had again sought to attract the benevolence of the King of Prussia by all sorts of calumnious instigations. This monster, furious with the respect and humanity with which we treated the commander, declared to him that his devotion to the interests of the King of Prussia forced him to observe that the fortress of Glogau being situated on the border of the possessions of the King of Prussia and from the territory of greater Poland, which was now in insurrection, it was exposed to the enemy's attacks, and the danger was all the greater in that it contained a large number of Polish prisoners, among whom were several skillful officers; that he had even reason to suspect that these officers maintained a secret correspondence with the insurgents; that, consequently, it was prudent not only to treat them with more care, but even to take all the measures of rigor required by the circumstances.

The commander, indignant at such a proposition, replied that no one had more his master's interests at heart, but that he could reconcile the interests with the honor of His Majesty, without the need of a Pole to slander his compatriots. Confused at having failed so badly, the treacherous defector wrote directly to the King of Prussia and told him with more darkness all that he had advanced to the commandant. The latter did not speak to us of what had happened, and always continuing to act towards us with the same goodness, we were very far from suspecting anything; until, having received an order from the King, he summoned us to declare to us that his will was that at that very moment we should be transported to Neisse, a very strong place 20 leagues from Glogau. He added that he was sorry that this order deprived him of the pleasure of easing our lot, and of enjoying our society until the day of our deliverance. He assured us, however, that no distance would upset the feelings of friendship and esteem which we had inspired in him, and that he congratulated himself on being able to render us a last service. "I have the order," he continued, "to have you transported separately; but on the strength of your characters and your word sof honor, I leave you the consolation of traveling together, and you will have for a guard only one captain."

This last favor, added to the memory of his good treatment, touched us so sensibly, he was so penetrated himself, that our goodbyes resembled those of a good father and his children.

The third day after our departure, we arrived at Neisse. In surrendering ourselves to General Hamff, commandant of the fort, the captain, who had escorted us, praised our conduct, both during our stay at Glogau and during the journey. But the general, without seeming to pay attention, asked if any of us spoke German. The captain, who in the trip had spoken with me, appointed me to the captain. " Who are you? said he, in a sudden, rough voice. "I am an officer." — "How! Are you an officer? And who raised you to this grace?" — "The one who had the power, Kosciuszko, our generalissimo." — "What! This wanderer, this wretch who has the audacity to declare war on crowned heads? But this rash man and all his adherents will soon receive the price of their crimes." He stopped only after vomiting torrents of insults. To all this I replied that he had good luck to insult us, since we were prisoners; that, moreover, we waited calmly for our fate, and that we had nothing to answer here to his questions or his outrages. "You will be taught soon," he resumed in a rage, "as you treat your kind. At the same time, he ordered an officer to conduct us to the bottom of a casemate, where 40 of us were huddled together, without distinction, although there were among us six to seven staff officers. The casemate was so damp that we felt the water that was condensing from the vault fall on our heads; scarcely had we been given to sleep a few arms full of wet and dirty straw. In this sad situation we had plenty of time to reflect on the striking contrast of the character of the two generals, to whose care we were successively entrusted; one full of spirit and humanity, the other steeped in grossness and insolence. At the end of a fortnight we were dragged out of our dreadful subterranean dungeon; we did not know what to attribute this sudden change; but we soon learned that, on our return to Glogau, our escort had reported to General Ritz about our reception and the treatment with which we had been threatened. General Ritz had immediately written to Lieutenant-General Wendessen, who was in charge of all of the fortresses in Silesia, and had revealed to him the means which had been used to denegrate us, and had given the best proof of the manner in which we had behaved during our stay at Glogau; finally he had answered on his head for our loyalty and our good conduct. This letter produced its effect: Wendessen did not hesitate to send the commander of Neisse the order to soften our captivity as much as possible, and to treat us with all the respect which the law of nations demands in favor of prisoners of war; adding, moreover, that he was vouching for our good conduct on his own responsibility. It was thus that we again owed the softening of our misfortune to the humanity and good offices of General Ritz. From that moment nothing extraordinary happened until the arrival of the order of the King who directed that we be set free. According to the content of this order, a passport was issued to each of us, by means of which we could go to safety to the place we had chosen. Colonel Krynicki and I, especially related, asked for a passport to Warsaw, where I had my family and friends and business called him. We had proposed to leave our homeland to seek refuge in a free country, safe from the incursion of our enemies. According to this plan, we left Neisse, and continued on our way to Posen, the capital of Greater Poland; I had a sister there; I proposed to my friend to rest, and to spend a few days there. On arriving, we went down to a furnished hotel where the first person we met was a Pole detained by the Prussians in that same house. As he approached us, he told us that, having learned that we were Poles coming out of captivity, he could not resist the desire to see us. "I am a prisoner here," he added, "and though I have not the advantage of knowing you, I take the sincerest joy in your deliverance." We were infinitely touched by that sensitivity and candor. The colonel replied that we could not give him our gratitude better than by seeking to know him more closely, and that we hoped that he would not refuse to tell us the story of his misfortunes.

"I was," said he, "one of the inhabitants of Great Poland, my name is Dąbrowski: inflamed by the noble example of Generalissimo Thaddeus Kosciuszko, I had knelt with many of the patriots of that great province, all of them set on fire with the desire to wrest our country from the odious yoke which oppresses us. We agreed one day to raise the standard of liberty, and of the order which was to be observed in that undertaking as great as it was dangerous, the leaders of the insurrection, the palatine, the land or the district in which we were to stir up an uprising, and the march we had to follow. The day arrived, I made the revolution in the palatinate of Kalisz and the land of Kutno; the act was drawn up, and in a unanimous voice I was elected chief of the armed force."

"Despite the vigilance of the Prussians, I succeeded in removing some small scattered garrisons. The electric spark spread everywhere, and soon all Greater Poland was in insurrection. The King of Prussia, occupied at the siege of Warsaw, was then caught between two fires; he began to run out of ammunition, a considerable convoy that his army was waiting for by the Vistula had just been sunk thoroughly by the insurgents, who had at their head Major General Mniewski, a Polish senator, one of those who had contributed the most to the revolution of Greater Poland.

"He was forced to raise the siege and retreat to defend his own states. At this news the insurgents all assembled in a designated place, and Kosciuszko gave orders to General Dąbrowski, who commanded part of the army before Warsaw, to take 4,000 men, to pursue the King of Prussia, and to join the insurrection of Great Poland, which was executed. After this junction, our progress became faster; the province was almost entirely purged of Prussians; they did more, and took different towns, such as Labiszyn, Bydgoszcz, etc. But in the midst of these victories the pearl of the battle of Maciejowice, and the taking of Kosciuszko, slowed the course of our successes. The order of the general who succeeded Kosciuszko was to abandon facing the enemy, and to retire promptly to the capital with all the forces, leaving only a few weak divisions in the province to maintain the fire of the revolution. I was among those who remained and having attracted to me several small bodies of troops, I gathered up to 3,000 men: with these forces much inferior to those of the enemy, who had returned from all parts of our province I managed to keep him in check until I heard the terrible news of the capture of Praga, and the general rout of our troops. Seeing then the impossibility, and the uselessness of holding on longer, I resolved to surrender. For this purpose, I marched towards Kolo, where there was a Prussian commander, under Colonel Burgsdorff; I informed him of my intention by a trumpet. He came to meet me, gave me a warm welcome, and showed me the powers he had to capitulate with all those who would come forward, protesting to me in the most positive way that everything he promised me would be so religiously observed as if the orders emanated from the King himself. Reassured by his word, and especially by the King's signatures, I submitted to a capitulation, the main articles of which were: 1.) That neither I nor any of my people would be sought out, under any pretext whatsoever because of the insurrection. 2.) That no one of them should be forced into service with the King of Prussia; but that they could accept his goodwill. 3.) That with the certificate that I would give them to have served under my orders, they could return home peacefully. 4.) Finally, both me and my people in their homes would be safe from insults and search.

"After he had consented and signed this capitulation in the King's name, I gave each of us the agreed certificate, and went quietly to my house. I had been there for two days, when on the third, early in the morning, Prussians came to surround my house with soldiers, and to assure my person. Nothing was more painful to me than to see myself arrested in the very name of him who had signed our capitulation; I showed it and asked what right or violation of such a solemn convention I had committed. I was told that the King had ordered everything to be promised; but that as soon as the capitulation was signed, the chiefs should be arrested and treated as rebels. How is it that armed citizens repelling a foreigner from their homeland could ever be called rebels? They took me away from my home to take me to these places, where I waited every moment for the result of the cruel fate reserved for me."

Strongly touched by his story, we felt better than ever that great truth that nothing in the world brings men closer than adversity. From that moment we devoted to him a boundless friendship. The particular interest that his misfortunes had inspired in me would attract me constantly to him; all my spare time was used to console him or to distract him. I was not long in discovering in him a character and sentiments worthy of a better destiny, and I endeavored to justify the unreserved confidence with which he honored me. I instructed my sister about the friendship I had conceived for him. She showed the desire to know him, we repaired to her home, she approved my new affair, and made her more intimate as a result.

It is, I think, necessary to report here that, a few days after my arrival, I met a woman whom I had known at Warsaw; I was delighted to see her again and asked her by what chance she was in this place. She told me that in the troubles that had followed the revolution, she had determined to leave the capital, and to follow, in Great Poland, a starost of this province. "We were not there any sooner," she added, “than the starost learned that his wife had discovered me. He planned a trip to Saxony, and we left for Dresden. It is from this last city that we return to righteousness." I asked her if he was at Posen. "No," she said, "he's just gone." I report this as a fact that has served me much later.

Back home I found a note from my friend, he was waiting for me, and conjured me to go to his home as soon as possible. I ran there and was not a little astonished to find him in the most frightful consternation; as soon as he saw me, he threw himself into my arms and exclaimed: "I am lost! Dear friend, read this letter." It was an anonymous letter announcing that he did not have a moment to lose, that a judgment had just been delivered condemning him to eight years of detention in a fortress and that he had to be transported there at the latest in two days. He had no other resource than the quickest escape. Penetrated with grief, I exclaimed in my turn: "Well! let's run away, my friend. He interrupts me with warmth. "No, I will not abuse your good heart, I will not suffer you to rick your life to save me." — "How!" I said to him, "is that how you now answer my friendship? You reject my offers? Do you believe, knowing your misfortune, that I will suffer less because I am far from you? Let us not anticipate the miseries of the future; let us rather confide in destiny; yes, my friend, let's hope she will not be as cruel as men." After some resistance he finally yielded to my prayers; he consented to admit me to the sharing of perils where his escape would expose him. It was no longer a question of taking the necessary measures for the execution of our project. We decided to take refuge in Saxony. As we could not take the post, I undertook to keep two horses ready with a carriage which belonged to my friend, and to furnish him with a coat of livery by means of which he was to follow me disguised as a servant.

Finally, to better conceal our design, I even went to the commandant to inform him that I was planning to leave for Warsaw. He received me amicably, advised me to remain, and promised to place me in the Prussian military, where I could obtain a favorable rank, because I spoke German. I politely replied that I was sensitive to his offers, but that the desire to see my parents prevailed over all other ambitions. During this conversation he was congratulated on the regiment, which His Prussian Majesty had just granted him. I took advantage of this moment to go out, and to take care of the arrangements, which remained for us to take. I had the satisfaction of getting everything we needed.

I went to my sister's house, where I found the colonel, my friend. I prepared them by a few deftly arranged detours to the confidence I wanted to make to them, and I ended by declaring to them our project. Their friendship for me was at first very alarmed; but soon they confirmed themselves in my resolution and wished to know the course which we proposed to follow in order to execute it. I told them that I already had the horses and the clothes of a servant, that the next day at 5 o'clock in the evening (it was winter), I would leave with a servant whom we had brought into our secret, who would serve me as a postillion, and would take me in the carriage out of the city at an agreed distance, and there my friend would come to join me in his livery.

This plan was approved by my sister, and for greater safety she offered to take him herself to the appointed place. To do this, it was decided that he would follow her as if he had been her servant. All that remained for my friend then was to intoxicate the soldier who was guarding him, who did not give him much trouble. The next day, at the appointed hour, I left the city, and arrived at the rendezvous, where my sister soon joined me accompanied by my friend. We were stung by our emotions, and made seven leagues at a trot, so the horses were greatly fatigued; we stopped at the post office; it was past midnight, the postmaster was in bed. He shouted, "Who is there? "I answered," It's me. "He immediately opened the door. "Ah! Is it you, my lord? He said. "Yes, it's me; give me horses quickly." So, taking advantage of her misunderstanding and the peculiarities I had of the woman I had met at Posen, I asked her, "How many days has the starost been here?" — "Three days; he even slept at my house." — "And how do you find the women who accompanied him." — "She was very beautiful; her countenance was of an angelic sweetness, and the starost seemed very much in love with her. Yes, you are right; I spent a whole day with them."

We were there with our conversation when I was told that the horses were ready, and I was delighted that chance would have helped us as well. On my way I resolved, if my name was asked at the next post, to say that my name was Raynauld, and that I was going to Leipzig for business; which was all the better for us when we were on the eve of the fair that was being held in this city in the New Year. I took care to recommend to my friend not to speak a word of Polish. We made three posts in succession without any accident. Arrived at the fourth, we found a Prussian landrath (tax judge). This meeting was not too pleasant; I made a sign to my friend that he understood very well, he went out at once. For me I went to the window as if to look out, but all my attention was in my ears, and I listened to the speeches that were held in the room. I heard the landrath say to the postmaster: "These people seem to me suspicious." This remark frightened me all the more because we had no other passport than the one that had been issued to me after my enlargement, which bore my real name, and which I could use only to go straight to Warsaw. The only fruit that I had removed from my captivity was to appreciate the Prussian character; it was also from this knowledge that I regulated all my steps. So I approached the landrath, and said to him in a Prussian tone: "Monsieur landrath, I have good news to share with you; our brave Ditter (commander of the city of Posen) has received an award for his loyal services; the King has just given him a regiment of dragons." — "Is it really true? how happy I am! He is a very good man." — "Yes, sir, nothing is truer." I found myself at his house the same day he got the announcement. "Well, then, you can also give me news of the partition of Poland, and tell me whether our king will keep the city of Warsaw or not?" — "He will keep it, do not doubt it. Russia wanted to play at the end as usual; but our king categorically announced that there was no detour to be made, and that it was necessary to declare oneself." — The Prussian, radiant with joy, regaled me with brandy; and the horses being ready, he escorted me to the carriage.

Escaped from this danger, we had no other to run, except the city on the border between Prussia and Saxony. It was 1 o'clock after midnight when we went down to the post office; We were asked if we had our passports. I answered no. "I am very sorry for it," said the one who questioned us; but you are stopped until you have explained yourself on this point. I replied that I was ready to give all the necessary explanations, but that I asked in pardon that I should be sent as soon as possible, since, traveling on business, I had no time to lose. He went to give my answer to the director who was in bed and left me a few minutes to think of an expedient that could help me out. He returned to tell me that I had to come with him to the director. I told him: "Tell the director that it is very cold, that I am very well with my fire, that he can come to my room if he wants to interrogate me himself, or he can send in his place whoever he thinks fit; that I was no more surprised to endure such quibbles, that at last I told him that I was from the Court of Prince Suikowski, of the city of Leszno, and that it was for his own business that I was going to Leipzig. He went. I had every reason to hope that this ruse would dispel any distrust, for the prince was one of the King of Saxony's favorites, and known for such in the country: that was also what happened. Our man returned to excuse him in the name of the director, and to make sure that if I had said at first that I was in the prince's court, I would not have had the slightest difficulty. We blessed Providence, and at last we breathed a freer air on entering the territory of Saxony.

No. 17

Letter from Citizen Parandier to Citizen De la Roche

My dear friend, the tie of sweet illusions is past for us. The misfortune of Poland presents only an image of carnage, devastation, and death. The Polish people will now live only in history unless some strange effort, tried on several points on the north, breaks the chains that weigh them down. Terror is used to press their souls. In Lithuania and Great Poland scaffolds are erected and all who have showed any greatness of spirit, of generosity, or patriotism are to be immolated.

Catherine has made a joke of her promises. She has declared that there will be no amnesty. Potocki, Mostowski, and Wawrzecki have already been taken to Petersburg, suffering the fate of Kosciuszko. The peasants are disarmed, their houses burned, and their lands ravaged. Everything announces the misfortune of a pending famine. I attempt to take this trip against the advice of all my friends here. If I do not succeed and we are left free, I shall go to Hamburg, from where I shall make my report to the Committee (of Public Safety); there I will serve myself with my codes.

An accident occurred with our carriage which holds us here. Twice its axle has broken. The wheels are in the mist pitiful state. Great repairs have become necessary and we thought it better to make them here than elsewhere. I cannot paint for you a picture of our sufferings; my body, which has suffered the fatigues of the trip, has suffered greatly for a long time. Every night I have a fever, which weakens me greatly; but as tomorrow I leave without stopping, I look for some relief from the shocks of the trip. Bronic is no better than me. We both suffer. Address your letters to Hamburg; it is there where something will happen, as it is there that I count on establishing my reports, once I have arrived. I have written to Constantin (Stammaty). Address all my letters to him. Advise Rheinhart that it is impossible for me, before having arrived, to make use of my codes. I must feel it.

I wish to write to Barss, but really I do not have the strength; this letter should be common to both of you. Adieu. A thousand wishes to all our friends; we are to them dead and alive.

Second Letter.

Berlin September 15, 1795

I address to you, my dear friend, Citizen Royer, of whom I have spoken to you so many times, and who deserves your esteem and all your friendship. He will give you a lot of details that many letters could not contain. I spent a week with him at Rhinsberg, and I saw there how we would like some good for our business: but we fear Russia, and we still want to handle it carefully. I expect that I will have a lot to work on; nothing will be decided for the affairs of Poland before a peace with France, and it is in the interest that this great power will take in the affairs of the North, on which the fate of Poland depends. Royer will share with you my ideas for its regeneration and the maintenance of its independence. You will give him the welcome he deserves, either by his knowledge or by his patriotism, as pure as it is enlightened and energetic. I have been in Berlin for a few hours, I will stay here for a few weeks, anticipating that this time will not be entirely lost for our interests. I would have liked to see Gaillard here; I do not know who can retain him again. All that was missing was a man here to do excellent things. You will make Royer acquainted with information that is useful for us and for him, and I will always send my letters by Hamburg to Lagau, who will hold them for me.

Farewell, dear friend, in a few days I will write to you with some details.

Parasdier

No. 18

Report of General Dąbrowski, Presented to the Berlin Cabinet, of March 1796

If one wanted to start a revolution in Poland, it would be in the party that came to power in Austria. It should break out the same day in Leopol, Jaroslav, Lublin, Sandomierz and Krakow. This country being stripped of Austrian troops, it is sure that the Russian troops of Podolia and Ukraine will hasten to enter Galicia to crush the revolution. Russian commanders already have the order. At the moment when Muscovite troops wish to enter Galicia, it is necessary that the King of Prussia publish a manifesto, by which he declares that, as the Emperor has no troops in this part of his states, he will admit a part of his to maintain order and tranquility. This corps must hasten to seize the Palatinates of Krakow, Lublin, and Belz, as far as the Carpathian Mountains, to master the whole left bank of the Bug. As this maneuver can be done even before the Russians can foresee it, it cannot fail to succeed. Then the King of Prussia, in this position, should declare himself, or one of his house, the constitutional king of the Poles, under the guarantee of the French Republic, and summon to Posen the Constituent Diet of 1791 (which is only postponed), where the ministers of the guaranteeing and allied powers should also gather, and where the French minister, as representing the nation in which the Poles have the most confidence, would take over the management of political affairs. The appeal will at the same time call upon the whole nation to defend the country. This appeal would produce the greatest effect, and would insult all the palatinates, so that in the first moment the Russians would not know whether they ought to fear the Prussians, or the Polish insurgents. To give more authority, harmony, and confidence to that general insurrection, it would be necessary for the diet to give the general command of the army to a French general. He would have to be a man who had gained reputation in this war, a firm man endowed with a creative genius.

In the early days, this Polish armed force can be composed only of light troops, so many people on horseback as chasseurs; which would supply the void which is in the army of the King of Prussia. It can be used with great success, both in the outposts and in the reconnaissance of the country, to gather the stores, capture baggage, and harass the enemy.

Great Poland, where the insurrection must not take place, can raise and maintain at least 30,000 infantrymen, who must be armed and equipped by the King of Prussia, and commanded by Polish officers. At the same time, one could, under the auspices of the French army, raise Polish corps among the nationals. These corps would be sent little by little to Poland to increase the number of its defenders. It is certain that a large part of the Austrian troops will desert; which would weaken the enemy, and completely disorganize his army. The King of Prussia, as the protector and defender of the Poles, may be reassured against any insurrection in his states, and even in the invaded provinces of Poland; thus he will be able to employ all his troops from the interior against the frontiers of Russia. Moreover, his army being constantly covered by the Polish light troops, will have no fatigue to bear, and will always be provided with the necessities

I believe that if the King of Prussia sends to Memel a corps of 20,000 men, which would stand on the defensive against the Russians on the side of Courland and Samogilia, he will have nothing to fear from it. The line of operations of this corps is to begin in Königsberg. Another corps of 30,000 Prussians, commanded by an active and enterprising officer, should act offensively from Warsaw towards the Bug, and from there to Pripyat. He will begin his line of operations at Lenczyca on the Warta, where a corps of Poles, formed in Greater Poland, will serve as a reserve to provide the Prussian armies with the necessary assistance. The 3rd Corps of 30,000 Prussians should support his right wing on the Carpathian Mountains, and advance offensively towards the Pruth and Dniester.

The Polish troops would hold the outposts and the communications between the Prussian corps. The line of operations of this corps would begin at Czenstochowa and Kosel and would have the advantage of the great road that leads from Krakow to Leopol. Food cannot be lacking in a country as fertile as Poland, and if a body of Polish insurgents can be in the rear of the Muscovite army, it can easily remove stores, capture convoys, and to put them in a state where it is impossible for them to act offensively. An invasion of the insurgent Poles into the Austrian Bukovina, where there is a large number of horses, can become of an essential utility to the common interest. I believe that in seeking to aid Poland in this way, and that if the Ottoman Porte sees the King of Prussia acting in Poland as an ally of France; I believe, I say, that it will not hesitate for a moment to declare herself against Russia and Austria. The role that Sweden would play in this case is not easy to foresee; but Denmark, with its fleet, could declare the Baltic Sea neutral, and shelter Prussian and Polish shores from a Russian descent, which would provide the Prussian left wing with a sure support. The King of Prussia should persuade the Elector of Saxony to bring an observation force of 20,000 men into Lusatia, and to gather the rest around Dresden.

The troops on the line of demarcation or neutrality should advance towards Franconia and cover it against an invasion on the part of Austria, while the French Army of the Rhine and Moselle would push the Austrians into Bohemia. The corps in question would precede the French army, along the borders of Saxony, and pass, if necessary, into

Silesia, to cover this country, as well as Saxony, against the invasion of the Austrians. As long as the war against France continues, Austria will have very few means to prevent the success of this project and the loss of Galicia. When the Emperor would even draw troops from the Rhine and the Danube, as it would take them several months to reach their destination, they would find that country already lost to Austria. By this diminution of forces on the Rhine and the Danube, France would have more facility to act successfully in Bohemia and on the banks of the Danube.

If the Prussian troops, as well as the Polish insurgent patriots, respect the borders of Hungary and Transylvania, we can be assured that these two nations will not do anything against the Poles, with whom they have lived in good understanding for many centuries. In the very event that Austrian troops were arriving from the Rhine and the Danube, the King of Prussia could send a flying camp to Plesse, Zator, and Biela to prevent the Austrian corps from acting on the Vistula. If this corps wanted to be carried along the Carpathians, by Hungary, on the road that leads from Eperies to Dukla, in Galicia, the Prussian flying camp can rub shoulders and take a position in Dukla.

The question arises here: whether the Emperor would not willingly sacrifice Galicia, consenting to the existence of Poland, provided the Russians moved away from its frontiers; for it is evident from the policy and greed of Russia, that if the Emperor is not separated from this power by Poland, he can expect in a short time to lose Transylvania, Wallachia, and part of Hungary, since all these countries profess the Greek Religion.

The greatest and most essential enemy of Poland and Prussia is, therefore, Russia, to which, however, it is difficult to oppose sufficient force to the three Prussian armies in the positions I have just proposed, for it must have an army in Finland, another in the Crimea, a third towards Otschakof, and one on the Dniester facing Turkey, since it is impossible for it to trust these two powers. As it is evident that the Russian army will be constantly surrounded by the patriotic insurgents who will destroy its stores, cut off its communications, and capture its baggage, without which it cannot march, it will be forced to stand on the defensive. Besides that, having to deal with regular troops, the Russians will have to act on a very wide line, on which it is very difficult for them to supply all the needs of its army. The Russians will have for the line of operations Riga, against the Prussian army, which would act on Memel; Smolensk, against that of Bug, and Kiev, against that of the Carpathians. They cannot count on Kamieniec-Podolski, because this place has neither stores, nor arsenal, and that it would go of its own will to the Poles. It is easy to see the obstacles the enemy will encounter in forming such an extensive line of operations, especially in a country which is in insurrection, where every peasant is a declared enemy of the Muscovites.

All over Poland there is not a single fortress that is tenable. It is true that the surroundings of Brzesc-Lilewski and Pinsk, situated in the middle of Poland, surrounded by marshes and rivers, might furnish the Russians with a rallying point, from where they can move on the Baltic and the Carpathians, where they would have some means of rescuing these two points; but besides that the Russians do not know the advantage of this position, it will always be easy to advance a corps on Dubienka, which would flank it. Besides, the general insurrection of Poland will prevent the arrival of provisions, of which the country absolutely lacks, and which it can only draw from the Ukraine and White Russia. The Russians will, therefore, be compelled to return to their usual maneuvers, which they employed in the last wars against the Poles, who attacked them and sought to expel them from Poland; they retreated as quickly as possible, abandoning their stores, their baggage, and even their artillery; they stopped only at their old frontiers, where they rallied, strengthened, and afterwards advanced in order into Poland; for the Poles, who were little used to maneuvers, could not stand up to them, and were obliged, on retiring, to abandon the whole country, as far as the Vistula; but the campaign would turn out very differently, if the Poles were supported by the Prussian troops, whose tactics are much superior to those of the Russians.

Polish troops, with the help of Galicia, could, in a short time, rise to 100,000 men. I am therefore convinced that if the King of Prussia, together with the Poles, attacks the Russians, they will be obliged in the first campaign to retreat on the one hand to Livonia, and on the other to the Dniester. But I repeat again that it would be necessary for France, by her minister to the Republic of Poland, to employ every means possible to preserve the Poles' confidence in the King of Prussia, and to convince him that they are fighting for their country and their freedom.

I do not consider the public and economic advantages that the King of Prussia would derive from the restoration of Poland, but merely observe these advantages from the purely military point of view: first, the King of Prussia, by the restoration of Poland, removes from its frontiers an enemy as powerful and as dangerous as Russia. In the second place, in the present state of things, the Emperor wishing to attack the King of Prussia, does not need to pass the Bohemian Mountains, but being master of Krakow, he will fall on the back of Silesia, towards the Oder. Thirdly, the Russians, in concert with the Austrians, can in a campaign advance from the position of Brzesc-Litewski up to the Oder. Finally, in case of war, if the King of Prussia does nothing for Poland, the Poles will always be more against him than his party.

Dąbrowski

No. 19

Letter from General Dąbrowski to Citizen Parandier

Dresden, June 24, 1796

L ......, who assured me of your good memory, also told me that I may go to Berlin in person, since I have nothing to fear as a result of the arrest of my compatriots. I think it is my duty to represent to you that the Prussian government's approach deserves to be appreciated more than it seemed to me to be according to the observations of the aforesaid L .... I even opine very strongly that it is not the mere intrigue of the Russians, who have awakened the vigilance of the Prussian government, but probably the imprudence of my compatriots, for the proof of which I transmit here to you what I have learned from the source itself. Forestier, both without your knowledge and mine, maintained a correspondence with the patriots of Warsaw, who include among them many very exalted heads: immediately he passed to them not only the ideas that the R .... had traced touching the existence of Poland, but still told them that they were already in full activity; he even passed the note that I had submitted to ...., preparing him in advance for a sure and satisfactory answer. All this heated the spirits to such an extent that he sent from Warsaw courier after courier with letters to myself. One of them was ordered to look for me. It was then that Forestier told him that I was far from here. Of all these letters I received none, since the 16 letters, which arrived from Warsaw, by a single post addressed to a certain Mardonius, which did not fail to shake the Prussian government; and it is said that the answers of the above-mentioned letters were intercepted and read, and that they occasioned the arrest of Mardonius and Forestier.
"At Thorn we found a way to communicate with the prisoners, but then we were told they were taken to Spandau. I fear that Forestier's papers have fallen into the hands of the government; if that is so, I find myself compromised, like so many other honest people. As far as my actions are concerned, I can boldly show myself in Berlin; but who can assure me not to be dragged by the aforesaid citizens into some labyrinth, who would not leave me embarrassed, especially in the states of the King of Prussia?

L......... also told me that my note presented to ...... was taken into consideration by the French government; but that the present circumstances did not permit him to act definitively. As Holland begins to seriously organize a formidable army, would it not be possible, and at the same time useful, to form against the Imperial Army a Polish corps, composed of Austrian deserters, for the service of Holland? A trustworthy Polish citizen, who comes straight from the Austrian Army, assures me that no other language is spoken [by them] than Polish, and that the soldiers are burning with the desire to desert to the French, provided they see their legions composed of their citizens; which, in my opinion, is very easy to conceive and do, since such an enterprise can only produce a great disorganization in the enemy army, diminish its strength, and thereby weaken it.

This will be of great advantage to the French, and the Dutch will gain as well, for they will acquire a brave and republican corps, on which they can rest quietly. Moreover, they will not be recruits newly raised, but soldiers accustomed to fire and bayonet, and who, fighting against the enemy, will feast on the sweet consolation of avenging themselves on the oppressors of their country. And if at last France, together with its allies, wants and recognizes the necessity of a political existence of Poland, it will be able to use these corps, to which all the others, raised or trained in due course, will join with eagerness. Nothing will be easier while compensating Holland for the costs and expenses made by means of the commerce, which it has always maintained with Poland.

Here, dear friend, is my desire to see my country born again; I hope it will be possible to form Polish corps in all the republics and all the states of Europe, allied with France, where they will learn to persuade themselves that it is not bravery alone, but order and tactics that triumph over the enemy; for it is not with the Germans that the Russians will be driven out of their old frontiers; but these Polish cohorts, disciplined and returning to their homeland, will be better able than any German to fight in the north, since to all the knowledge acquired, they will add the advantage of being born under a climate that makes them robust and bold, and enables them to endure all sorts of fatigues, and the most severe cold. Feeling completely restored now, it's almost impossible for me to stay idle longer, and I'm talking to you, dear friend, to find out if I could not find a way to be a volunteer with armies of the French Republic. I do not claim service, rank, or money; my only object is to fight for the Republic, and to instruct myself; to see, and to make myself better able to serve my homeland and humanity.'

Dąbrowski.

No. 20

Letter from General Dąbrowski, to Citizen Kasimir De la Roche

Leipzig, August 30, 1796

Citizen,

Being on the point of leaving, I make it a real duty to reiterate my warmest thanks for all the friendships with which you have filled me since the moment of our meeting, and especially for the interest you have shown in this matter that regards me, and of which I have just had new proofs by the way of my friend Tremo. Be convinced that you did not oblige an ungrateful man, and that I will have a real pleasure to prove to you constantly how much I desire to deserve the continuation of your friendship. It is especially by a good use of advice that I believe to convince you of the price I attach to it.

No doubt the union, concord, and prudence of the Polish patriots are the only means that can promise us and deserve the attention of those nations which are interested in helping us; and that, given the current state of affairs, it would be disadvantageous for us to want to do something without the help of the House of Prussia. I can assure you, therefore, that every patriotic Pole, who wishes to restore his country, knows very well how to appreciate your counsels, in accordance with the great interests of our country; and this number is not small. For me, wherever I find myself, my actions will be regulated according to these principles. It is only to be hoped that the Prussian government would take steps to maintain good order and harmony between the Polish citizens and the officials of the present government, and to desire not to be angered by ill-advised spirits. who, by their physical and moral misfortunes, can easily be brought to a useless great feat for them, but no less unpleasant to Prussia, especially if it is decided and maintained by the way of the Russians. (Warsaw is currently home to a large number of soldiers, especially those who suffer the most inconvenience, and you say that in the time of the Russians, despite their disorderly behavior, this class has been respected and managed.) Whoever knows the stirring ardor of this court, its spirit of intrigue, coupled with the situation of the affairs of the North, will soon find the key to this evil. Nothing will be easier for him than to win one or two Prussian individuals, and at the same time excite the Poles who, without knowing it, will lend themselves to the wickedness of their wiles. These fears, which give rise to the news I have just received, prescribe the necessity of communicating them to me immediately, as I have every reason to hope that they will be taken into consideration, and that you will make your possible to try to prevent this harm.

I have asked you, in my last, to send me the 300 ducats that were to be handed to you on my behalf, by Wyganowski; but as he is slow in sending them to me, and I find myself in a hurry, you will have the complaisance to make him pass the attached enclosed, and add, please, a few lines from you to make this consignment . There is also a paper from me, good for 400 ducats, and from which I have drawn 100 ducats; as soon as the sum reaches you, you will be so kind as to send it to me at headquarters. I also dare to flatter myself that you will not refuse me the honor of your news and will continue your advice and counsel. And I will be proud to testify to you in all places the feelings of esteem and friendship that I have devoted to you for life.

Dąbrowski.

No. 21

Letter from Citizen Eli Tremo to Citizen Kasimierz De la Roche

Leipzig, August 27, 1796

.... We were all delighted to hear that your trip was not without fruit. The general has charged me to send his respects to you, he commends himself to your friendship and good memory, and begs you to be persuaded of the reciprocal. He would very much like to hear from you at headquarters, through Mr. P ....

Dear friend, as I do not hope to see you soon (because even the shortest absence is unbearable for friends), I beg you to receive my farewells and continue your friendship, which is for me an indispensable price; you know my feelings too well to doubt one moment. I entreat you therefore in faith for our friendship to continue your news, and especially to write to me before your departure for the place of my destination. I cannot refrain from confessing to you that I am burning with impatience to go there. Yes, dear friend, all my imagination is carried there; I already taste the pleasure of seeing these heroes, those defenders of liberty, receive us with fraternity, extend to us the hand of friendship, to pity us! What are the reasons for raising a courage, which, besides the misfortune of groaning under the cruel yoke which oppresses us, is still tired of seeing and hearing only individual baseness and calumny, while union and concord should be the greatest point of our rally. Farewell, dear friend; I embrace you with all my heart and beg you to be persuaded of all the feelings of esteem and friendship I have devoted to you for life.

Your friend and servant,
Elie Tremo

No. 22
Act of Confederation Prepared at Krakow, January 6, 1796

We, the undersigned, citizens of the Republic of Poland, have full confidence in the loyalty of the French nation, a nation to whom alone belongs the glory of supporting with all its might all people who, knowing the price of freedom, will make efforts to recover it.

We flatter ourselves that the French nation has recognized in our last efforts, on the one hand, the interest and the unanimous desire to make a diversion, which would oblige the enemies of France to share their forces; on the other, the energy that has made us not to be afraid of the coalition of neighboring powers, leagued for our annihilation.

Convinced that, although success has not responded to our enterprises, we have made ourselves worthy, by our attempts, to count on the support of the French nation; assured, moreover, that France could not find a more natural ally than a people animated by the same feeling of liberty, and jealous of having to recover it, declare in the name of the Polish nation, on behalf of all our compatriots whose voices, suffocated by oppression cannot speak, but whose sentiments are with our good cause, on the confidence which our courage gives us, the generosity of the French nation, in the name of our compatriots, whose voice is stifled by the oppression from which it cannot escape, whose sentiments are well known to us:

1.) That the hope of our liberty is founded on our good cause, on the confidence which our courage gives us, the generosity of the French nation, and the equity of the powers that have not had direct part in the attacks made against our existance.

2.) That we look at each other from this moment, each one in particular, and all in general hereinafter undersigned, united by an indissoluble bond. That at the first call of this generous nation, we are ready to sacrifice everything, goods, existence, and all that is in our power; promising to carry us en masse, or separately, wherever, according to a combined system, our presence will be necessary and decided by plurality.

3.) Declare further that we recognize our deputation established in Paris, and the agents who depend upon it, as legally constituted.

4.) As the circumstances in which we find ourselves, and the precautions that we are obliged to take, do not allow us to give to this writing, by a greater number of signatures, and by its publicity, all the authenticity which could mark it at the seal of the general will of the nation, we answer for all the authorizations which these same circumstances prevent us from making public at present, and which will appear as soon as we can give to this act all the necessary publicity.

5.) In addition, we reserve for ourselves to give another declaration, and to expose to the eyes of the whole of Europe all the kinds of oppression which we have suffered from our enemies, and the perfidy they put in the offense and the violation of their treaties.

6.) We propose at the same time to demand the support of all the nations which, in the annihilation of ours, are threatened by the same fate by the disproportionate ambition of these powers, whose policy is to play the most sacred treaties.

In faith of which we sign this manifesto, one copy of which will be preserved in our protocol, and the other sent and communicated wherever necessary.

No. 23

Letter from Citizen Oginski to Citizen Verninac

Constantinople, May 21, 1796

Citizen Minister, the news of which all have been kind enough to share with me about an insurrection in Poland, in the neighborhood of Kamieniec, made me think seriously. After discussing this object with Citizen Turski, we found many reasons to believe that it was possible, though perhaps imprudent and hasty. The despair that animates the unfortunate, the inhuman conduct of Russian employees, the horror of slavery, the hope of support from defenders of freedom, and of those who cannot be indifferent to the unfortunate fate of Poland; everything, in a word, must lead the Poles to want to shake off their yoke.

In a country devastated and covered with ruins, on a land still smoking with the blood of so many brave citizens, who sacrificed themselves for their country, the Poles who survived the disaster of their country, and who could not leave their native home not only suffer personally, they shed tears over the fate of so many thousands of their compatriots who groan in the prisons of Petersburg, or who are reduced to populating the icy regions of Siberia; they do not lose sight of so many unfortunate victims who experience a painful existence in foreign countries, deprived of their country, their property, and all relations with their families and friends. These painful feelings remind them of the noble efforts of the authors of the last insurrection. They awaken their energy, revive their courage, and revive in them hatred, animosity and vengeance, against the oppressors of Poland.

The moments of suffering are very long and painful, citizen minister, and one would never believe to be able to get rid of it quickly enough! It would not be surprising, therefore, that, without waiting for a change in the political system of Europe, the Poles would have entrusted to the uncertain fate of a new insurrection their deplorable destiny! After all, what remains to them, but to transmit to their descendant's misery and slavery, or to wash in their blood the reproach of the ignominious shackles with which they have been loaded.

I think that the insurrection of which you have been given details is very possible; and if it has not yet taken place, its explosion can only be postponed. That being the case, it would be very painful for me, if, animated by sentiments which made my compatriots act, I did not share their efforts, and if I did not employ the most eager care to assist their projects, by the execution of the orders which have been entrusted to me by the organ of their representatives.

You have read, citizen minister, the letter addressed to me by the Polish deputation in Paris; I also informed you of the negotiations that I had made in later letters, referring to separate instructions entrusted to me at Venice. You have been informed by this communication of the object of my journey to Constantinople, and of the duties which had been imposed on me.

It is for the sake of my acquaintance that I have the honor to represent you today, Citizen Minister, how urgent it is for the Poles to know whether the steps they will undertake will be supported by the Turkish government; if they can count on its support and financial assistance.

You know that deceptive hopes based on erroneous ideas lead to reckless enterprises, and that lack of hope extinguishes the patriotism of those who have the best intentions. I would not like to see my compatriots in either of these positions; but I would like accurate information on the current state of political affairs, and the intentions of the Polish friendly powers, as the rule of their conduct.

In the event that the insurrection has begun or should take place later, it is essential for the Poles to be informed of the way in which the Turks will consider this approach ... Would you not consider it convenient, citizen minister, to probe the Turkish government on this subject, taking as a pretext the news that has come to you? Do you not think it necessary to take steps to obtain that I be admitted under your auspices, to the Reis-Effendi, to make myself known to him, and to procure for me in the future the facility of making representations to him on the affairs of Poland, if the circumstances required it?

My request will not seem to you indiscreet, when you will observe that the object of my solicitude is a country dear to me; that the prayers that I address to you are the result of the intimations of my fellow-citizens, of which I pride myself to be the organ; that all our confidence rests on the part that France will take in [determining] our fate, and that mine in particular is very strongly supported by your zeal, a citizen minister, to serve the cause of liberty; on your dexterity to conduct business; on your love for humanity, and on the lively interest which you have seemed to take on every occasion in the misfortunes which have overwhelmed Poland.

Michel Oginski

No. 24
Letter from Citizen Verninac

Constantinople, July 1796

Citizen Minister, a great number of Polish officers, who, in the last insurrection of their country, escaped death and slavery, and have since then escaped in pursuit of the enemy; and, finding an asylum abroad, they expected the effects of fate, the protection of the French government, and the support of the powers that they regard as natural allies of Poland, a change to the sad situation of their country, and an end to their misfortunes.

Some of them, tempted by Russia and Prussia to enter the service of the armies of these powers, have rejected offers the acceptance of which would have cost too many sacrifices to their hearts. They refused to serve the oppressors of their homeland; and, equally insensitive to the largesse that was promised to them as to the severity of the fate with which they were threatened, they founded their wealth, their consolation, and their hope in perseverance and patriotism.

In general, these sentiments of admiration and enthusiasm, which they cannot fail to inspire to all the friends of liberty, were borne by the French nation, and each of them waiting for the restoration of the country only by France aspired to fight as a simple soldier in the ranks of those brave republicans, whose victories belittled their enemies, covered the French nation with glory, and facilitated the means of protecting the weak and the oppressed.

Such are, Citizen Minister, the sentiments of the Polish officers, for whom I wish I could interest you, and inspire you with the respect they deserve. I will not speak to you of those who have had the good fortune of being placed in the French armies, nor of those who have the hope of entering it, and still less of those who have means of subsistence without having need for foreign help. I would like to fix your attention on those Polish soldiers who, unable to penetrate to the borders of France, groan in indigence and misery, on the borders of Turkey, without finding a safe haven, without enjoying protection, and without meeting a helping hand who wants to relieve their ills.

They flattered themselves with finding in the provinces of Turkey a refuge where they would be safe from danger.

They thought they deserved the kind of hospitality that the Poles never refused to the Turks, and that they showed themselves principally to those who were in Warsaw after the last campaign, showering them with consideration and generosity.

They had no doubt of the benevolence of a government, which should make common cause with the Poles in order to prevent the dangers that threaten it, and which seem inevitable, according to the rapid progress and the increase of the power of a common enemy.

They are even persuaded that this government would not be indifferent to their fate and deaf to their demands; but the difficulty is finding a voice to be heard.

It is to you, citizen minister, a representative of this generous and magnanimous nation, who overthrows the oppressors of innocence, and who protects the oppressed; it is to you, whose sensitive soul knows how to sympathize with suffering humanity, that it is proper to be the organ and support of so many brave soldiers who come to claim your assistance.

Please, Citizen Minister, represent to the Turkish government how honorable and useful it would be for it to open its frontiers, and to offer help to unfortunate officers who might one day defend it at the cost of their blood. Let it know how advantageous it would be to determine a point where these soldiers could come together to be ready to act at the first call. Tell it about the political considerations and the reasons for its own interest that should make it aware of this.

It is in vain that the fear of exciting suspicions and provoking the vengeance of a neighboring power would present obstacles to the execution of this project. Such a formidable enemy does not need pretexts to declare war and invade states.

I firmly believe that the fate of Poland must not be indifferent to the Ottoman government; I beseech, therefore, that the misfortune of the Polish officers who come to ask for asylum and support cannot fail to inspire it with a keen interest.

France has always been a friend of the Polish nation, and ostensibly protected all my compatriots who, in their emigration, have asked for their support. Among all the friendly nations, and even among the neutral powers who have not taken part in the last events of Poland, the Poles found, after their last revolution, a refuge and the protection of the governments. Why, then, would they not flatter themselves to see the Turks disposed to offer an asylum and help to individuals of a nation whom they have always regarded as a friend and natural ally?

It is for the second time that I take the liberty of addressing you, citizen minister, with regard to this object. I do not hesitate to bother you by speaking on behalf of those officers who implore your interposition, as well as on behalf of all my compatriots who have authorized me to do so.

Please, by a word of answer, put me in the case to prove to my constituents' eagerness that I put my instructions to completion, and that I can bring some consolation to these brave soldiers who expect all of your generous care, and of the influence you have with the Ottoman Porte.

Michel Oginski

No. 25

Letter from Citizen Oginski to Citizen Aubert-du-Bayet

Constantinople, October 26, 1796

Citizen ambassador, the Polish refugees gathered in Paris, unwilling to neglect any step that might contribute to the re-establishment of their unfortunate country, thought it expedient to have an agent at Constantinople, who was the organ of the feelings of the true patriots, and who by the information that he would communicate to the Ministry of France on the dispositions of the inhabitants in the interior of Poland, as well as by the reports which he would transmit to his compatriots on the intentions of the Turkish government, could establish a useful relation between Poland, Constantinople, and Paris. Honored by the confidence of my fellow citizens, I gladly took charge of this commission.

Seven months of residence in this capital have made me aware of the always friendly intentions of the French government for the affairs of Poland, the zeal of its ministry to assist them, and the little effect which resulted from a government too much blinded to its true interests, or too weak to seek to prevent the dangers that threaten it. I dared flatter myself four months ago, according to the assurances I received from Citizen Verninac, that war could break out, and this idea revived my hopes. The good dispositions of Sweden; the energy of the

Poles, encouraged by the protection of France; the gathering of Turkish armies on their frontiers promised me very favorable results; but since then things have changed very much.

After the time of the defection of the Swedes, the Turks had less than ever the will or the possibility to make war. They told Citizen Verninac; they did not hesitate to declare it to you, citizen ambassador; they have frankly explained themselves on their state of weakness and helplessness, on the feelings of friendship which they bring to the Poles, and on the impossibility in which they find themselves to help them; on their hatred for the Russians, and on the fear they have of manifesting it.

It is only up to you, citizen ambassador, to combine the qualities of a negotiator with those of a warrior, to change the nature of the political and military spirit of the Turkish government, and to force it, so to speak, to know the true interests of the Ottoman Empire. It will not fail to happen by your influence and your representations, or it will never happen.

On the supposition of success, it would undoubtedly be of great benefit to the Poles, who, by abandoning themselves up to now the illusory promises of the allies, have lost sight of the paths which energy and patriotism would suggest to them; but while waiting for this salutary change in the system of the Turkish government, which will probably be wrought by the zeal and activity, which you deploy in your negotiations, I think it is necessary to submit to your knowledge and your decision some ideas which are the result of several conferences we had together on the affairs of Poland:

1.) It seems to me that for the next six months my presence is completely useless in Constantinople; for, without doubt, there will be no question of commencing hostilities against Russia in this advanced season. And, moreover, the Poles can do without a representative where they will find a friend and a protector like you, citizen general;

2.) It seems to me indispensable for the French government, for you, who represent it, and for my fellow refugees, to know exactly, and with all possible details, what is the present state of the disposition of Polish minds, and what are the forces and means of the Poles in the interior of the country, in order to establish a system for subsequent operations;

3.) It would be necessary to agree verbally with the members of the Polish deputation established in Paris, in order to arrange with them a plan of military operations which, according to your observations, is the only one which may be suitable in Poland, in the present circumstances;

4.) After having examined exactly the present situation of Poland, and having probed the minds of the inhabitants, it might result in the necessity of speeding up steps, reckless to the truth, and perhaps too hasty, but which, according to your opinion, they alone are capable of saving Poland, and of awakening the Turks to make common cause with us.

According to these considerations, I determined to go in person to the parts of Poland, that are under the domination of Austria and the King of Prussia.

In case I find Polish minds prepared, well-disposed, and ready to burst without the need of further delay and other help, I will come back to the border to inform you, and to await the indications that you will judge about sending me. If not, I will send you an exact and detailed account of the internal situation in Poland, and I will continue my journey to Paris to consult with the Polish deputation.

I will establish a communication between Galicia and Bucharest, and you will receive, as a citizen ambassador, detailed information on Poland from one of my compatriots, who will gladly undertake to keep up with you a regular correspondence.

In addition, I have the honor to inform you that I leave in my place at Constantinople General Rymkiewicz, a brave soldier, and a well-deserved citizen of the country, who enjoys the esteem and confidence of all good people, and who will not fail to communicate to you the news he will receive, either from the Polish deputation in Paris or directly from Poland.

I submit, citizen ambassador, this project to your decision. Your answer will be the rule of my conduct.

Michel Oginski

No. 26

Letter from the Minister of War Petiet to General Dąbrowski.

Paris, Brumaire 5, Year V (October 26, 1796)

I received, General, with your letter, dated Véndémiaire 19th, the observations which you have addressed to me concerning the advantages which would result, for France and Poland, from the formation of some legions of a French-Polish corps, with the Armies of the Rhine and of Italy. I hastened to forward them to the Directory. I will send you its decision.

Petiet

No. 27

Letter from General Dąbrowski to the French Ambassador to Berlin, Caillard

Paris, Brumaire 5, Year V (October 26, 1796)

I hasten, citizen minister, to give you my news, or rather to give you an exact account of my work, it is for this reason that I think I must classify it in three parts:

1.) My arrival to the French army;
2.) The reasons for my departure for Paris;
3.) The use that I thought I should make of your wise counsel.

1.) I must, above all, reiterate my warmest thanks for the letter to General Jourdan, who not only deserved the most favorable reception from him, but also facilitated me and procured the knowledge of a large part of French generals, who have all shown me much friendship, and the most peculiar solicitude for the ills of our country. On the desire that I made them known to be placed as a volunteer in the wake of the Republican armies, before my plan to train the Polish legions was accepted by the government, they unanimously advised me to go without delay to Paris, and to seek permission from the Executive Directory; some even offered to support my request to the government; among these was General Klêber, who had already shown a keen interest in me, and he was kind enough to give me letters of recommendation to speed up the fulfillment of my wishes that I went to Paris.

2.) Arriving in Paris on the Véndémiaire 9th (September 30, 1790), I first handed over my letters of recommendation, then I presented to the Minister of Foreign Affairs the note and the attached plan; but so far I am waiting for an answer. So much for me.

3.) I afterwards hastened to fulfill the task that you have kindly imposed on me in your letter of the Thermidor 26, Year IV, from Berlin, with the keen interest inspired by the love of my country. and the desire to meet your expectations. Well! In spite of all this, and the goodwill of some of my compatriots, it has for the moment been impossible for me to provide for it. The only fruit I have gathered is that I have learned that the spirit of the same system animates all Poles, and that they are convinced that without the help of France and Prussia, there is no existence for Poland. All the disputes that reign among them come from the fact that there were individuals who knew how to guess the current system before the time, even dared to announce and support it; that the others not only fought it, but also treated them as persons subordinated to the House of Prussia. Now that the force of circumstances and conviction bring them back to the same end, they do not want to admit the wrongs they have done to others; on the contrary, they prefer to give rise to new ruses, and being unable to say that they are Prussian partisans, they maintain that they are agents of King Stanislas Augustus. This is also how we represent the newcomer Stanislas Woyczynski, and perhaps myself; and it is thus some well-known persons, besides the citizen Parandier himself, who endeavored to make his mission suspect, and extend suspicions to others. But whatever it is, nothing will discourage me. I will always seek my consolation in my own feelings and in the esteem of a man as respectable as you. This, citizen minister, is about the situation of my fellow refugees in France. I am delighted, however, to be able to announce to you that calm and serenity are beginning to be reborn among the Polish patriots, and that there are a number of them who, far from having the ridiculous claim of representing the nation, not only complies with circumstances, but presents a mode which, according to me, is the only one capable of accommodating all parties, and in agreement with the great interests of Poland. That's what it consists of:

As soon as the favorable moment has arrived to decide upon the restoration of Poland, we should, without communicating this plan to the Poles, directly address the marshals of the Constituent Diet, that is to say, Messrs. Malachowski and Sapieha, in which rests the power of the limited diet, and who, possessing in all its latitude the confidence of the Polish nation, will be able to best meet the expectations of the French government, and will still have the precious advantage of bringing together the suffrages of the King of Prussia, since they had that of treating in time with him. This is what we try to make known to the French government, and that I hasten, on my side, to communicate to you, and submit to your prudence and your wisdom.

Polish Lieutenant General,
Dąbrowski

No. 28

General de Division Berthier,
Chief of Staff of the Army of Italy,
to Citizen Tremo,
Aide-de-Camp to General Dąbrowski

Milan, Nivôse 15, Year V (January 4, 1797)

Polish Lieutenant General Dąbrowski, a Polish patriot, recommended by the Minister of War to General-in-Chief Bonaparte, was authorized by the Congress of the State of Lombardy to employ all means that are in his power to form a Polish Legion, which shall be in the service of Lombardy, and the General-in-Chief having authorized the Congress of State of said land to send Aide-de-Camp Tremo to France, he is authorized to leave from Milan to move initially to Chembéry, he shall take the orders of General-in-Chief Kellerman, to from there move to the depots of the prisoners of war taken by the Army of Italy where he shall designate all the Polish prisoners of war who, voluntarily, wish to enter into this new Polish corps, formed in Lombardy. In addition, Citizen Tremo shall conform to the attached instructions.

Alexandre Berthier

Certified to conform to the original.

Général de division Kilmaine

No. 29

Letter of Citizen Elie Tremo to Citizen Kasimir De la Roche

Liberty *Equality*

Dijon, Nivôse 30 (January 9, 1797)

Aide-de-Camp of Lieutenant-General Dąbrowski to Citizen Kasimierz de la Roche.

A century ago, dear friend, you have heard nothing from me; do not charge me with negligence; occupations and trips without number are the only reason. I hasten to tell you that my mission is going well. Everywhere I find Poles who love their country, and who are all ready to attest to that with their blood. Oh! What pleasures this mission has already furnished me; what brave people it has introduced to me in France; how many friends of liberty who are interested in our lot and who show me the greatest interest! Oh! May this example ignite all the hearts of the Poles; can they sacrifice, forget everything for the good of the public! It's up to you, my dear friend, it's up to any good Polish man who loves his country to work there. Let us do all we can, and we will find the reward in our actions, and happiness in our homeland. Goodbye, fraternity and friendship until death.

Elie Tremo.

P.S. Write to me under the address of General Pille, Commander of the 18th Military Division, and give me news of all that may interest me.

No. 32
Project Presented to the General-in-Chief of the Army of Italy, BONAPARTE.

Mantua, 5 Germinal, Year V (25 March 1797)

If the French government wants to revive Poland with the Poles themselves, and at the same time produce a strong diversion against the Emperor, it must act today, as in the American War, when men and money were sent directly to and from Washington. This project has the advantage of not compromising France in case of failure, and its execution will infallibly awake the Turks from their lethargic sleep, or they are buried; here it is:

Two thousand French infantry, 500 horses, and an artillery service for 60 cannon, will be attached to the Polish Corps.

The Polish Legion of Italy, with a strength of 6,000 men, can, by acting quickly, be returned in 20 days to Palma-Nuova, armed and dressed, and join the requested French corps. These troops must receive two months' pay; 300,000 francs must be paid into their military fund to undertake the following operation:

The column will march immediately on Fiume, and from there it will take the road to Carlstadt to worry the enemy who, too weak to defend themselves, will fall back on the Calpa and the Corona, to dispute, with the republicans, the passage of these two rivers; but after having deceived him by this stratagem, they will throw themselves into Turkish territory.

The Polish patriots will at once convince the negotiators at Constantinople to justify their demands to the Sublime Porte. The Turks, friends of the Poles, the inhabitants of Dalmatia and Serbia, those of Wallachia and Turkish Moldavia, all-natural enemies of the House of Austria, will not oppose the Poles, and these, after having crossed these provinces, will enter Bukovina and Galicia, making part of Poland, and swarming with men attached to their country, and ready to fight to restore its independence and freedom.

The Emperor, surprised by such an unexpected and prompt invasion, will finally have to oppose this column with force, and he will be obliged to detach a corps from the left wing of his army in Italy to defend his states, but the Polish column will soon become an imposing and formidable army corps. Thousands of languishing patriots in Wallachia and Dalmatia will meet with their brothers in arms; an insurrection will at the same time break out in the part of Poland subjected by the Austrians, and the Imperialist corps, which will cross Hungary and Transylvania to rub shoulders with the Polish column (because the Emperor will not risk entering the Turkish territory, for fear of attracting a new enemy), stopping it in its march, and preventing it from invading Bukovina, will fall between two fires, and will not be difficult to overthrow.

The Great Lord [Sultan] is too much interested in the regeneration of Poland not to help the Poles in their marches, and he will be forced to form an army of observation on the borders near the theater of war.

As the Emperor of Russia is not today, by his principles, far from improving the lot of Poland, the patriots will be able to negotiate with him, and flatter themselves that they will succeed. The King of Prussia, delighted to see the full weight of a new war in the North fall on the eternal enemy of his crown, will get along with Russia, and perhaps together with Paul I will put Poland on a good standing.

In case this project will not succeed, but nobody will lose anything; here is the proof:

1. The Poles who now form the Legion will never return to their country, as long as it is deprived of its independence and its freedom, and, in the case where their plan does not succeed, they will return to the point where they were left before undertaking it and will seek again a foreign asylum.

2. The French soldiers who will share with the Poles the glory and dangers of this enterprise will be, in any event, always protected by the Turkish government and may be returned to France.

3. Finally, the French government, under the protection of which the Polish Legion finds itself, having only indirectly been involved in this expedition, can in no way compromise itself,

and will be left for some money.

But it will perhaps be objected that the Turks will oppose the march of the Poles and will not let them pass on their lands. I answer that it is extremely difficult to meet this obstacle, and that, if it takes place, the Poles will at least have the satisfaction of having shown that there is no danger that they be ready to run in the hope of returning to their dear country, and to break the shameful shackles which keep it enslaved.

Dąbrowski

No. 33

Plan Projected by the Polish Patriots Gathered in Pairs for the Regeneration of their Republic

Paris, 26 Germinal, Year V (15 April 1797)

Poland, without political existence and without national representation, can calculate the possibility of its regeneration only on the interest of its allies. Its hope is based only on events which change the face of Europe, and it is here that it must fix its system of operation.

It is on these principles that any plan prepared by the Polish patriots must be based, it is also on these principles that the following reflections are based:

The French Republic, which triumphs everywhere over its enemies, every day finds fresh motives to convince itself of the hatred of the House of Austria. This power, despite the continual failures it experiences, stubbornly persists in the system of continuing the war. It restricts its union with the natural enemies of France; it seeks to fan the fire of discord between this nation and its natural friends; it maintains fermentation in the minds of neighbors; it gives birth and nourishes internal dissensions.

There is no doubt, from this observation, that France, taking advantage of the favorable circumstances that arise and the superiority of its forces, would not wish to reduce the House of Austria to the impossibility of harming it, inn the future by either political or military operations.

The continual triumphs of the French Republic have not yet put it into effect, in the case of having nothing more to fear for its government and for the integrity of its possessions. The loss of the Netherlands by the House of Austria is not only counterbalanced by the new acquisitions in Poland, but even these new conquests, by rounding up its states, considerably reinforce its power in the North. The natural allies of France are not in a position to sway the combined forces of Austria with those of Russia, and consequently they cannot maintain the influence of the Republic in this part of Europe.

The French government, which conceives the full force of this truth, wanting to secure the first rank among the powers of Europe, to maintain the balance of political forces, cannot deviate from its allies in their political and commercial relations. and, finally, to consolidate its existence and ensure the integrity of its possessions, will undoubtedly find it indispensable to put the House of Austria in the impossibility of being prejudicial to it. It is on the basis of these principles that it will be necessary to reduce the House of Austria to confine itself to its possessions in Germany, and to restore independence to all possessions, starting from Italy to Galicia. This is the true means of weakening the real forces of Austria, and of increasing those of France and its allies. Already political plans are beginning to be realized, either directly or indirectly. The marked protection that France gives to the nascent republics of Italy makes it presumable that, if the Carinthians, Croats, Slavonians, Hungarians and Galicians follow the example of the Lombards by shaking off the yoke of the House of Austria, their insurrections could only suit the system of the French government from several points of view.

In the first place, because all these neighboring peoples, united by the identity of interests and opinions, would form a federal line powerful enough to resist the efforts of the House of Austria, and to assure their political existence at home like the Swiss.

In the second place, because all the newly insurgent nations under the auspices of France would much weaken the forces of their natural enemy, as they would increase those of the French Republic, to face either the House of Austria or some other enemy power.

Thirdly, because the Ottoman Porte, France's oldest ally, threatened with ruin on the side of Russia, could find a more effective barrier to take cover from this danger, than in separating itself from the House of Austria, which is a friend and ally of Russia, by the states of new republics, peaceful and tranquil and according to the principles of their constitutions enemies of Austria, by the interest of their own conservation, and conforming by impulse to the Frenchsystem.

Finally, we will add, that, the Mediterranean and Austria being freed by this means from the domination of England, the commerce of the Levant, the most lucrative for France, could resume this superiority which it has enjoyed for so many centuries.

This is the foundation of our plan, which the state of the present circumstances suggests to us. This plan, the execution of which can only take place in so far as it answers the views of the French government, must be presented to it first and foremost, with the object of making it known to it, and the motives of our hopes, and the means which our own forces offer for the destruction of its natural enemy and to increase the number of its allies.

Let us now see what we should do to carry it out with as much activity as energy.

1. It is essential that three of our fellow citizens, enjoying our confidence and that of the whole nation, incessantly go to Italy to try to get General Bonaparte's and the government's permission that the Polish Legions that are in the pay of Lombardy advance through Trieste, towards Hungary, and, on the other hand, the scattered Poles in Wallachia and Moldova who are close to the Danube, and are also trying to penetrate into the interior of Transylvania from Hungary.

2. To make the march of the Polish legions more effective, and to facilitate the insurrection in Hungary, it would be necessary that those citizens who undertake to go to Italy choose two of their compatriots to enter Hungary, to inquire about public opinion, to consult with the Hungarian patriots, to inform them of the march of the Polish legions, and to communicate to them the whole plan, according to the subsequent circumstances; they will be given an exact note, which we have in our hands, touching the good dispositions of the Hungarian patriots, as well as information on the local of Hungary.

3. With a view to facilitate and accelerate an explosion in Hungary, we will, at the same time, send an emissary to our patriots in Galicia, insinuating them not to compromise themselves by overly hasty steps, but without sending many of them, known by their intelligence and patriotism, to Hungary, with orders to communicate to those Hungarian patriots who deserve their confidence, our plan, by assuring them of the patriotic spirit which animates the Galicians, and telling them about the march of the Polish legions to form a nucleus of military forces in Hungary.

As for the act of insurrection by the Galicians, it should be conceived in Hungary, taking for reason that Gaillicians and Hungarians, having been formerly under the rule of the Russian princes and then under that of the Jagellons, and having not ceased to be brought together by the principles of liberty, and by the bonds of friendship and good-neighborliness, presently unite their common and inseparable efforts to shake off the yoke of the Germans. This cautious step, by manifesting the intentions of the Gailicians, would place them under cover from Russian hostilities, in case they were determined to embrace the cause of the House of Austria, and at least it would not openly shock the powers concerned with the partition of Poland.

According to the patriotic sentiments and the love of liberty that characterize the Hungarian nation, we must not doubt the energy they will put into their explosion when they are informed of the intentions of the French Republic towards them. It must be observed, moreover, that the absence of Prince Joseph Palatinus of Hungary, and the departure of all the principal magnates of the country for Vienna, will contribute to removing the obstacles that the insurrection might experience.

4. The Polish citizens who are going to Italy will maintain an exact communication with the emissaries from Galicia who will be in Hungary, to arrange, according to events, the moment when the Gaillicians can act on their own without compromising the common cause.

5. They will also address the respective governments of these new nascent republics in Italy, to make them aware of the interest which should lead them to divert the forces of the House of Austria by supporting our plan. And to facilitate the formation of the federal legion, they should engage them to make addresses to Croats, Slavonians, Dalmatians, Hungarians and Galicians; it is not to be doubted that all the nations dependent on the House of Austria will hasten to shake off the yoke that oppresses them, and the Dalmatians, offended by the Venetians and unaccustomed to suffer slavery, will embrace the plan of the federation as soon as it reaches their knowledge.

No. 34

In Consideration of the Particular Interest That Attaches Itself to Events in Question, Where the Poles took a Very Active Part, And Where Many of these Brave Men Sealed with their Blood the End of the Insurrections that Austria Ceaselessly Foments, It will not be Useless to Report Here the Table of the Uprisings In Verona, the States of Venice on the Mainland, And the End of this Aristocratic Republic

While General-in-Chief Bonaparte used every means to paralyze the hostile intentions of the Venetian government at the opening of the campaign of 1796, Adjutant-General Landrieu was charged with corresponding with the secret societies organized in the cities on the Terraferma [mainland][1], to foment and maintain the spirit of insurrection against the aristocratic government, in order to make a powerful

[1]Translator: At this time Venice included a large poart of the mainland of Italy adjacent to the city. They were called the "Domini di Terraferma."

diversion to the plans of the senate, which was determined to second the Austrian efforts in this new campaign. An insurrectional movement was to break out when the French army crossed the Tagliamento; the senate was informed of plots against it and hastened to direct a body of Slavons against the main soruce of the revolt, Bergamo. These troops were about to enter the city, when, on the morning of March 15th, the conspirators and their numerous partisans took arms, and seized the gates of the city to block the entrance of the Slavons.[2] The French garrison, under the pretext of riot, assembled under arms; the officers encouraged the malcontents and promised them support. The people of Bergamo left the city with resolution, attacked the Senate's troops, threw them back, and pursued them down the road to Brescia. This first success emboldened the insurgents; they proclaimed their liberty, established a municipal government, and at once appointed deputies to go to Milan to ask the Cispadane Republic for help. Milan sent them clothes, weapons, and ammunition. In a few days several battalions were organized; Italians from different countries, Poles, and a few Frenchmen met with these troops and marched on Brescia, where the Lecchi and Gambara families had already prepared the insurrection. This improvised army arrived on the 27th at the gates of Brescia, which were opened to it by the inhabitants. The latter joined the people of Bergamo and attacked the barracks where 500 Slavons arrived a few days before. Attacked unannounced, these soldiers were disarmed and taken prisoner. We made sure of the person of the Proveditor Battaglia; and, in the intoxication of their enthusiasm, the inhabitants of Brescia imitated those of Bergamo, proclaimed their liberty, and established a municipality.

At the news of these two events, the Venice Senate, seeing force was insufficient to stop the progress of such a well-calculated uprising, resorted to the means used by governments without energy: it sent many emissaries to the Terraferma, responsible for lavishing gold to change minds, and affect a counter-revolution. Priests and monks, who are powerful auxiliaries in such cases, spread themselves into the mountains, seeking to fanaticize the gullible inhabitants of the cottages, and, by their insidious speeches, to persuade them that it was a meritorious and proper work to open the doors of celestial bliss to them, then to arm themselves against the French, wo were servants of the devil. These means succeeded at the whim of those who employed them. Soon the entire population of the western shore of Lake Garda and the Sablia Valley, reunited with the troops of the Senate, came to form a camp at Santa Eufemia, near Brescia. But the Venetian nobles, less blinded by their personal interests, ought to have remembered that the fanaticism of liberty is at least as powerful as that of religion; they should not have forgotten that the handful of inhabitants of Padua from which they derived their origin, refugees in the lagoons of the

[2]Translator: Slavons are speakers of Serbian and Croatian.

Adriatic, to avoid the oppressive yoke of the Goths, had been able to keep the forces of these barbarians in check.

The inhabitants of Brescia did not allow themselves to be intimidated by this collection of bribed fanatics and soldiers; they had put the city in a state of defense. Attacked on April 4, 1797, they supported with vigor a prolonged cannonade; and the next day, although informed that their adversaries had received reinforcements during the night, especially in cavalry, from Verona, they did not hesitate to attempt a sortie against the camp at Santa Eufemia. They forced their entrenchments, dispersed the troops who defended them, and pursued them to the neighborhood of Lonato. After this first advantage, it was not difficult for them to disperse a large and numerous force of insurgents on the plain, who had also approached Brescia.

The Venice Senate had made the city of Salo the fulcrum of its operations against the insurgents; it was resolved that they should march on that city. A corps of 1,200 men commanded by Lecchi, and four cannon, came out of Brescia for this purpose: the insurgents having no gunners, some French gunners disguised themselves for the service of the cannon. Terraini, which dominates Salo, was promptly captured; and the inhabitants of the city, to avoid the misfortunes of an assault, made their submission and delivered hostages. But at the moment when the Brescians entered Salo, the Slavic troops, beaten on April 5th, before Brescia and reunited with the insurgent peasants from the mountains, suddenly fell upon Lecchi's column, and drove it back into Salo. In the disorder caused by this surprise, some French and Polish soldiers who were part of the Bresciane troop met and bravely cut their way through the enemy. The Brescians and the Bergamasques took refuge in the houses and barricaded themselves; but the Venetian soldiers and peasants manage to take them prisoners despite their desperate resistance.

This failure caused consternation in Brescia and Bergamo; these two cities demanded prompt succors from Milan. General Lahoz gathered some French and Poles who were in the depots, and some Lombard battalions, and set out to Salo. On the other hand, the French commander of Peschiera and the chief of the navy, won by the seductions of the conspirators, decided, on April 10th, to send the French flotilla on Lake Garda to Salo. The commander of the boats, who had some infantry on board, summoned the Proveditor Cicognaelle General Fioravanti, who commanded the Slavons, to take the fortress, whose occupation, he said, was necessary for French operations against the Austrian army. General Fioravanti replied that the Venetian Republic had an even more urgent need for this place, to make it a bulwark against the insurgent Brescians, and consequently refused to comply with the request. The French commander then fired at the town, and the frightened inhabitants and garrison then sought shelter in the mountains.

Although the intervention of the French in the quarrel of the Terraferma insurgents against the Venetian government was no longer a mystery, the officer who commanded the flotilla wanted to save appearances, saying that the inhabitants of Brescia were ready to lay down their arms, if those of Salo and the Venetians who were in this city wanted to do the same; and he offered himself as a hostage to guarantee the promise of the Brescians. These proposals were rejected by General Fioravanti. Then the Milanese column, commanded by General Lahoz, after meeting with the debris of that of Lecchi, marched on Sarezzo, which he seized. The Venetian troops lost, in this action, 200 to 300 men, three cannon, and a large quantity of muskets abandoned by the peasants in their flight.

On the 11th, General Lahoz marched on Salo, abandoned by its inhabitants, but some Slavons defended the approaches. They were promptly dispersed; and an act of treason was, it is said, the cause of the sack of the city. A Venetian detachment, having been cut off by Lecchi's troops, fired on the Brescians after having surrendered themselves prisoner: they rushed furiously into Salo, which they pillaged and ravaged.

In this situation, Bonaparte had attained the end that he had proposed to himself, by paralyzing the aid which the Venice Senate might have provided to the Austrians in the Carthinian campaign. But while the Republic of Venice sought to retain, under its aristocratic yoke, a part of the people of Terraferma, the faithful Tyrolese, no doubt satisfied with the paternal government of Austria, had risen en masse to defend its cause, previously at the time in question; and this incident seemed to favor for some time the hatred and the plans of revenge of the Venetian Senate against the French.

When General Joubert, who had vainly sought General Laudon to disturb the march, left the Tyrol to join, by the Drava Valley, the main body of the Army of Italy at Villach, the Austrian general returned from Prunecken to Botzen, and from that last city to Trent, where he arrived on April 10th, after having sent to the right bank of the Adige a column to attack the detachments that the French had left at Arco, Uiva, and Torbole, north of Lake Garda. Too weak to withstand superior forces, these detachments retreated after a fairly vigorous resistance. Those who could not reach Peschiera by the way of Garda, Bardolino and Lacize, threw themselves on Castel-Nuovo, were armed and made prisoners: those of Arco and Riva gained the road to Trento on the left bank of the Adige, left a garrison at Chiusa, and arrived at Verona.

The inhabitants of this city had not participated in the revolt of Bergamo and Brescia; the event of Salo finished exasperating the spirits against the French, who were regarded as the first sources of the troubles of the country. A general fermentation manifested itself; and General Balland, who commanded in Verona, not believing himself safe in the midst of a riotous populace, shut himself up, with the few troops and the French he had with him, in Fort Saint-Felix and the two other castles that defended the fortress; but, forgetful or unable to do this operation, the hospitals, filled with wounded and sick, were not evacuated.

The moment seemed favorable for the Venice Senate to carry out its plans for revenge. Bonaparte was sunk in Carinthia; General Laudon, chasing before him all the French posts, advanced on the Lower Adige; all the measures had already been taken; all the magistrates and other agents of the government had received their instructions, with the precautions and the secrecy which is put into a conspiracy. The tocsin sounded the signal of a general insurrection in the provinces of Terrafirma; it rang the same day at Vicenza and Padua; and it was only with the greatest difficulty that the French managed to escape being massacred in these two cities. They were less happy in Verona. On Easter Monday, after vespers, all the isolated soldiers were stabbed, the sick and wounded were slaughtered in the hospitals. The city was soon filled with a multitude of fanatical peasants, led by priests and monks, who advanced simultaneously against the three forts or castles, in which General Bailand and 3,000 French were shut up.

Informed of the result of the conspiracy, the Venice Senate at once ordered General Fioravanti to march with the corps of Slavons he commanded to assist the insurgents; and at the same time the advance guard of General Laudon advanced by the reverse slopes of Monte Baldo, at some distance from Verona. The garrison of the fort of Chiusa capitulated for want of food; the insurgents, in the delirium of the success they had just received, massacred these French soldiers in the most barbarous manner.

However General Lahoas, after the Salo expedition, had descended to Lonato. Informed of the events of Verona and the other towns of Terraferma, he marched towards the Lower Adige. On the other hand, General Laudon was informed of the armistice concluded between Bonaparte and Archduke Charles; and the latter, retiring on the Rivalta, on April 18th, with all his Tyrolese, abandoned the insurgents and the Slavons to their own forces.

The siege of the three forts at Verona was none the less continued. The Senate had sent reinforcements of men, artillery, and ammunition to General Fioravanti, and the insurgents were not unaware that General Lahoz's corps was too weak to undertake anything against them. This general had in fact stopped at Somma Campagna, where he had taken up his position to await General Kilmaine, who was hastily rushing with about 5,000 men from the garrisons of Lombardy and Mantuan. The junction of the two corps took place on April 21st.

General Fioravanti, informed of Kilmaine's march, wished to prevent the French attack, by ordering a general sortie for the 22nd.

Kilmaine had precisely the same intention as his adversary; so that the two parties met at 6 o'clock in the morning, at the Croc-Mianka. The French threw themselves impetuously on their enemy and overwhelmed them with the first shock. General Fioravanti tried to rally the Slavons on a large farm, hoping to stay there; but a shell set fire to the Venetian caissons and the explosion drove all those who were assembled from the farm; a great part were buried under the ruins of the building, the rest dispersed into the country; a very small number returned to Verona.

In advancing to meet the Venetians, Kilmaine had ordered General Lahoz to march on Pescantina, occupied by the insurgents, for the purpose of passing the Adige to turn Verona. The insurgents defended themselves with vigor; but the French artillery having set fire to the village, it was abandoned. The Gallo-Lombard column came to crown the heights which dominate Fort St. Felix, and General Lahoz was able to communicate with General Balland. Thus, on the evening of the 22nd, Verona was invested on both banks of the Adige.

General Fioravanti had been so frightened by his defeat, that instead of retiring to Venice by the road to Vicenza, which was still free, he preferred to rely on the generosity of the victors. He came, with the 3,000 Slavons he commanded, to lay down his arms at Croce-Bianca, and surrender himself as a prisoner of war. On the same day, April 23rd, the French took possession of Verona.

General Victor, whose division was confined to part of the new Cispadan Republic and the march of Ancona, had, at the first news of the disturbances, which we have just described, assembled all the troops available to march on the principal theater of the insurrection. He came to meet General Kilmaine, at Verona; and their combined forces presented a total of about 15,000 men. The assemblies were promptly dispelled, and calm was restored. General Victor then went to Vicenza; and, on April 28th, his troops were in front of Treviso and Padua. General Kilmaine divided his troops into the submissive country. The terror which the Venice Senate had spread over the land then reigned in the capital of that republic; and these foolish nobles, who had flattered themselves for a moment that they could overwhelm the French, now awaited in silent stupor the result of the terrible events which had just happened.

Bonaparte, occupied with the preliminaries of peace which were being negotiated at Leoben, had had to suspend the effects of the vengeance which provoked the conduct of the Venetian government. However, the Doge had received, as early as April 9th, a letter from the French general, in which he demanded satisfaction for the attacks on the French. The Senate had made an evasive answer, which decided the destruction of the Venetian Republic.

The articles of Treaty of Leoben had scarcely been signed, when columns of the French army marched in the direction of Venice, preceded by a manifesto in which Bonaparte set forth the grievances of France against that state. The army was assembled in the mainland provinces towards the end of April. Masséna's division occupied Padua; Joubert's corps settled in Vicenza and Bassano; General Serrurier was at Sacile, Augereau at Verona, and Victor's division withdrew to the Adige, and took position along this river.

This gathering of the French army, at a moment when peace had just been concluded with Austria, inspired the greatst alarm in the Senate. Powerless to defend themselves, these haughty noblemen resorted to negotiations, and implored the clemency of an irritated enemy. A conference was held on May 3rd, in the lagoons of Marghera, between Bonaparte and a deputation of senators; and the result was a suspension of arms, pending the conclusion of a peace treaty, which the patricians Moccnigo, Giustiniani, and Dona, were charged with negotiating on behalf of the regency.

Bonaparte imposed the precondition for the conclusion of peace that the three inquisitors of state and ten of the most influential members of the senate, regarded as the instigators of the insurrection, should be delivered to the French government. But the senate, not believing that it had to give up such cowardly men whose operations it had sanctioned, tried to drag out the negotiations, in order to give the chosen individuals time to escape.

Austria, however, saw quietly, and even with secret joy, what was happening in the states of Venice. It appears that one of the secret articles of the preliminaries, which was never made completely public, already promised the Emperor compensation on this side, for the cession of Belgium and the abandonment of Lombardy. Soon also the Venetian government, once so prudent, so measured in its determinations, was going to learn at its expense the results of its secret alliance or treacherous connivance with one of the three powers which, two years before, had annihilated and shared the unhappy Kingdom of Poland.

A general and extraordinary fermentation agitated all minds, and the precursory signs of a great political upheaval had already preceded, as we have seen, the return of Bonaparte to the mainland. Cries of liberty and the manifestation of the strongest hatred against Venetian despotism were pronounced by all the inhabitants of the intermediate classes between the patricians and the populace; they desired the destruction of a government which had kept them and their ancestors in the most humiliating oppression. The insurrection had spread as far as the fleet, where the malcontents spoke of displaying the tricolor flag. The Senate had to fear seeing the ships delivered to the French; the olygarchy was expiring.

On May 11th, the Grand Council resigned from office, and handed authority into the hands of 30 senators, who solemnly declared in their first assembly that the old democratic form would be reestablished as it existed before the Revolution of 1209. This late determination, which two months earlier would have saved the state, was now powerless to prevent its destruction. But Bonaparte, who might not see himself without repugnance as the instrument of the dissolution of this ancient republic, seemed disposed to protect the operations of its new government, when the delirium of some patricians precipitated the catastrophe of which Venice was threatened and weakened the remnant of pity that the French general had for it. The day after the installation of the new government committee, a gathering of Slavons and bribed seamen carrying the standard of Saint-Mark roamed the streets, causing everyone in their path to join them, and looted the houses of the 30 senators and members of the government. Venice, having no armed force capable of reestablishing order by dissipating these mutineers, was exposed for 16 hours to all the horrors of a civil war, and found itself on the point of being buried, by the fury of the rebels, under the ruins of its government. The insurgents, however, in their greatest excesses, respected the rights of the nations, and the embassy of the minister of France (Lallement) was spared.

In this extremity, there remained no other course to take than to call in the French troops. The merchants, the principal artisans, and even the members of the former government, judged it expedient to hasten the end of this terrible crisis, by inviting the French to hasten their arrival. On the 16th, they landed on St. Mark's Square, numbering from 2,000 to 3,000 men, and took possession of Fort St. Mark, the arsenal, and the Rialto Bridge. Terror soon succeeded the first movement of fury among the populace, which was abandoned by those who had excited it to this uprising.

A municipality chosen in the name of the people was installed by the commander of the French troops. It took steps to restore, as far as possible, some of what had been looted on the 12th. In order to calm the public mind, it issued a proclamation in which it spoke in moderation, and even in honorable terms to the former government; it undertook to maintain the bank, the mint, and other public establishments; it recognized the public debt and promised to pay it. It could therefore be expected that the new order of things would be maintained. However, Bonaparte, who knew better than any one how much the hope of the Venetian patriots was chimerical, had the modesty not to strengthen it by his presence, and refrained from entering Venice.

(*Victoires et Conquêtes des Français de 1792 à 1815*, Vol. VII, p. 144-156. Paris 1818; C. L. F. Panckoucke, éditeur.)

No. 35

Stanislas Malachowski, Marshal of the Consituant Diet Of Poland, to Citizen Bonenau, Chargé d'affairs of the French Republic to the Polish Republic

It has been very consoling for me to learn of the advice you give to your good and old friends, concerning the means which might bring us back to our former political existence. Whatever the mode that current events will indicate to affect the re-establishment of our unhappy country, it is our duty to seize all the legitimate means that can lead us to this end. What you have given us coincides exactly with our intentions, and it is obvious that it is your devotion to cooperate as much as it is in you to our restoration that has made you anticipate the effects. Yes, citizen, the resumption of the functions of our national representation of the year 1791 is the only means that, in the present circumstances, it suits us to follow. Who is it that, in these moments of general arrangement among the European powers, can more legitimately, and, I dare say, more effectively, provoke in favor of our nation, the interests of the guarantor powers of the integrity of our country, if not us, that this same nation had made itself custodians of its imprescriptible rights?

All those who, like you, are aware of our laws, cannot ignore, citizen, that the exercise of acts of national sovereignty belongs only to our legally convened diets. Our enemies respected this principle; they recognized its legitimacy at the very time they were indulging in the usurpation of our territory. Their conduct, at the time of the partition of 1772, furnishes an irrefutable proof of it.

It is as universally known that the diet, freely convened in 1788 and continued until May 29, 1792, was only postponed, it is not dissolved, and that existing by law, its members have only to meet to make it as legitimate as it was before being postponed.

It is according to these incontestable principles, Citizen, that I thought it my duty to summon the nuncios of our dietines, and the representatives of our towns. It is not, I told them, by partial insurrections, which are fruitless, that we can still save our country; but by raising a common voice to invoke the guarantee of the most solemn treaties, the interest of nations and governments, as well as the principles of universal justice.

This diet has just been summoned, as you desired, Citizen; but as the exercise of its functions cannot be accomplished in a land inundated by foreign troops, I propose to transport it, in accordance with the Act of Limitation of May 29, 1792, to a country where it is not disturbed in its quiet operations.

The Cisalpine Republic, whose legions are composed in part of our compatriots who have devoted themselves to the maintenance of its independence and freedom, will doubtless not refuse an asylum to our representatives.

I have recommended to our fellow-citizen and sent Barss to make representations to the Cisalpine Directory, in order to induce him to designate for us a place for the meeting in question, the purpose of which may not reasonably disturb the divided powers of Poland. In the course of our operations, we propose nothing more than to invoke, I repeat, the commitments of the treaties, the recognized principles of the law of nations and justice, considered as the basis of any political society.

On your side, dear and respectable Citizen, in concert with our envoy Barss, as well as with the Citizens Kochanowski and Woyczynski, nuncios of this Diet of 1791, which I engaged to go to inform you of its convocation; please, I say, support their solicitations by all means. I thought it essential to address you on this occasion, as an agent of your republic to us, and I hope that your experience in such affairs, the zeal that you have always put to the interests of our country during your stay of 25 years among us, the knowledge of our laws and our interests, the general esteem that you have rendered to it, a captivity of four years suffered for the cause of freedom, you will use your credentials to fix the attention of the French government to the wisdom of the advice you have given us, and to our just request for power to facilitate its execution as soon as possible.

I salute you, respectable friend, with all the cordiality and esteem you have inspired in us. Please give notice of this letter and make use of it that you deem most useful to our interests. It is only the expression of my firm will to seize a legitimate way of making our last efforts for the re-establishment of our unfortunate country.

Malachowski

No. 36

Letter from Citizen Oginski to Citizen Bonneau

Paris Floréal 9, Year V (28 April 1797)

Citizen, a 25-year stay in Poland has made you very particularly knowegable of our country, as well as the character of the Polish nation. Your wise conduct has reconciled you with the general esteem; and the persecution which the love of liberty has made you feel has set the seal to all the credentials that make you commendable to your country, interesting to the eyes of the friends of humanity, and worthy of the esteem of all good people. It is in all these respects that we have experienced indescribable pleasure in learning of your arrival in Paris. You could not fail to speak to the French government about Poland; you owe it to France as its agent, as a good citizen, and as holding to the cause of liberty and independence ....

It is not up to us to deepen the intentions of the French government on the means of restoring Poland; but we would like to guess and advise everything it wants us to do on our side to respond to its views ....

You know, citizen, our zeal and our devotion to the country; you are not unaware of the connections and reports we have kept with our countrymen in Poland; you will not be surprised at the solicitude with which we beg you to give us some clarification on this subject. It is especially important for us to know whether the project of a Polish diet, in Milan, has been proposed by the opinion and according to the insinuations of the French government. We would be charmed to learn it by the organ of the one who, like you, is a citizen, our esteem and our trust.

Michel Oginski.

No. 37

Liberty *Equality*

Bonneau, Consul General, Chargé d'affairs of the French Republic in Poland to Lieutenant General Dąbrowski, Commander of the Auxiliary Polish Legions of the Cisalpine Republic, And to the Brave Citizens Forming those Legions

Worthy General, brave Poles, who, forced to seek asylum and being avengers against the tyranny which oppresses your country, will precede the recovery of its liberty, by triumphing along side of our invincible legions and under the orders of the hero who guided them, the freedom of Italy; receive the lively expression of the gratitude with which the letter which you have addressed to me has penetrated me. You have undoubtedly attached too much value to what little I have been able to tempt you for the zeal and devotion which attach me to your cause. What sensitive heart, what appreciator of an illustrious and valorous nation, worthy of a happier destiny, does not share the same sentiments with me? Long living among you, I enjoyed the advantage of being able to appreciate you more particularly, because I could more particularly know you. You are too honored when you fall, your reexistence becomes too necessary for Europe, to fear that it will be forgotten. Receive my wishes in this regard, share the hopes that animate me. The moment when they are fulfilled will fill you with a sweeter joy than that which you will make me feel. In the meantime, enjoy the glory which your nation displays in the splendid valor you show, as well as your wisdom, and your patriotism. It is the sacred fire that you have carried with you, which will not be extinguished in your hands, and which you will bring back to your country of birth. May I then enjoy the touching spectacle that you will offer, and, placed in your midst, give me the happy testimony of having contributed to it otherwise than by my vows.

Bonneau.

No. 38

Explanation Submitted by Citizen Bonneau To Citizen Tallelyrand-Périgord, Minister of Foreign Relations, on the Content of the Dispatch Dated 27 Themidor, Year V (14 August 1797) By Citizen Parandier

Citizen Minister, the note that I had the honor to give you yesterday, the 17th of the current month (September 3rd), dissipates in advance the cloud that could rise on my account for the report contained in the letter dated Thermidor 27th (14 August 1797), written by Citizen Parandier.

I have never had the bold audacity or the mad recklessness to do anything that could compromise the government, by putting forward in the council what I gave to the Poles. What they are doing at the moment, they are doing entirely on their behalf, without any promise, without authorization, solely for the reason of attempting a last effort to raise in any way the existence of their unhappy homeland, taking advantage, if possible, of the interest that they can inspire in Europe in the next pacification.

This is not to be doubted, by reading the letter addressed to me by Marshal Malachowski, that I have not failed, Citizen Minister, to put in original in your hands.

The advice I gave to the Poles is therefore a piece of advice that I have announced to them to give them only from myself, and that, moreover, I have been careful not to allow myself, even in this way, without first having expressly been advised, as everything made it a duty.

This is what I did a few days after my arrival here, first in the report by myself presented to the Minister of Foreign Relations, A report put by him under the eyes of the executive power; This is what I have since repeated several times to the same Minister, by announcing to him on several occasions the resolution which the Poles were about to take, of reopening their constitutional diet in Lombardy, and informing it of the purpose of this determination for which I represented to it that they did not need any authorization from anybody, and that in case of prejudiced utility on our part, it was enough not to seek to trouble them.

I hope that this explanation, according to the most exact truth, by making known the real state of this affair, will not leave any subject of reproach towards me. I gave simple advice to the Poles: I gave it as being solely mine; it is of themselves that they have determined to follow it. I will not, however, hazard this same advice until having advised them several times and beingn assured against all disapprobation, since a word would have sufficed to arrest me, if it had been judged proper.

Moreover, Citizen Parandier's report on speeches may have been interpreted on his part beyond the meaning that was intended to be given by them, perhaps also produced by those who are said to have kept them by exaggerated hopes, falls in the most complete manner by the explanations that Bonneau did not fail to give, on their arrival, to the two nuncios that Citizen Parandier quotes, and which the marshal has indeed sent here to come to terms with me. I had the honor of presenting them to you, Citizen Minister; thus, referring again to Marshal Malachowski's letter, as to dispel any subject of reproach, I invoke your testimony even on the hopes they have shown you, and on the speeches that they have given you.

Bonneau, Consul General,
and responsible for Polish affairs.

No. 39

Alexandre Berthier, Général de division,
Chief of the General Staff of the Army of Italy,
To Général de division Dąbrowski,
Commander of the Polish Legions.

At the Headquarters in Milan
25 Brumaire, Year VI (15 November 1797)

General Dąbrowski, commanding the Polish legions, was ordered to assemble, in Rimini, the three Polish battalions that are united in Emilia (formerly Romagna). He is advised that the battalion that is in Milan must also go to Rimini, and that it will be replaced by the one in Mantua. He will also have under his command a Venetian battalion, which is at Mantua, three battalions of Brescians, the 4th Cisalpine Legion, and all the Brescian hussars, and 12 pieces of artillery that are with General Lahoz. Generals Lahoz and Lecchi, employed in this army corps, will be under his command. Citizen Bianchi d'Adda, an engineer officer, will also be attached, as well as a senior artillery officer. Adjutant General Trivulzi will be Chief of Staff. General Dąbrowski will go to Rimini to gather and establish these different corps of troops.

No. 40

Address to the Inhabitants of the Duchy of Urbino, Presented by the Deputies of the Same Duchy

To General of the Army of Italy,
Alexandre Berthier, in Milan.

After the horrible attack by which the Court of Rome overcame its crimes, we expected, day by day, to have a devastating army set off on the soil of fanaticism and treason. We expected France, just and generous to the innocent people, but as terrible and inexorable towards the guilty, to point out, by the most memorable vengeance, its just resentment; and, reducing to powder the usurped throne of the king-priests, would at once destroy the seat of infamous imposture that has caused so much evil to Europe. We were deceived in our waiting. Here is this army which, even from afar, terrifies the capitol: terrible in its vengeance, which it banishes forever from the country of the Scipios and the Camilles the holy fraud and the hypocratic mitrer; yes, let it come, the wish of all peoples solicits its presence.

You, accustomed to guide it to victory, show it the way to Rome, and we will call you the second liberator of Italy. We ourselves will unite our weak arms to your terrible arms; and although we can not flatter ourselves with contributing to your victories, we will at least prove to you that the crimes of the perfidious Rome have filled us with indignation, and that we wish to have somewhere at the most just and most holy national revenge.

Remember, however, oh Citizen General, that all the peoples to whom your army passes will not deserve your anger; that blind fanaticism has not inspired them all, against you, with an implacable hatred; that almost all have strongly disapproved of the violence and perfidy of the capital. Remember that if, by a fatal necessity, the people must be the innocent victims of the crimes of kings, those deserve to be respected and protected, who at all times have indicated their attachment to republican principles; those who, at the time of the Roman cruelties, had shaken off the yoke of the sacred tyrants, and demanded union with the Cisalpine Republic.

France could not confuse its fate with that of the Romans without failing in the principles of justice, without renouncing the rights of man, on whom it raised its republic, without covering itself with an eternal ignominy in the eyes of Europe, without dishonoring its name to the terrible tribunal of fair posterity.

The province of Urbino, last year, sent by its deputies to Gorice, to the General-in-Chief, its unanimous vow for liberty and for its incorporation into the Cisalpine. The minutes and authentic documents of our solemn declaration exist with the hero Bonaparte. If our request was not successful, it at least received applause and promises. Surrendered by the fatal combinations of politics under the yoke of our tyrants, we showed how impatiently we waited for the favorable opportunity to deliver them and seized the first moment that fate presented to us.

Pesaro, Fano, Urbino, Fossombrone, were freed on the Nivôse 2nd; from that time, they had sent deputies to Milan to ask for a meeting at the Cisalpine, when on the 9th of the same month an execrable attempt was made in Rome against the law of nations and of humanity. Whatever may be the sinister sounds that envy and slander spread against the revolution of these cities, their wish was well-pronounced; they have themselves contributed to their enfranchisement; they felt their rights, and the Cisalpine arms were only called to maintain tranquility and good order. Justice, reason, and the sacred rights of man, therefore, require you to distinguish this province from others, and to be equally exposed to the scourge of a vengeful army. The slight advantage which would result to your magnanimous nation could not serve as a compensation for the glory it would lose.

The Province of Urbino, Citizen General, sends you the Deputies Mosca-Barzi and Galanlara to make you such fair representations; they will tell you that these peoples, by recovering their rights, have so much felt the dignity of man, that they are ready to die under iron rather than suffer the humiliation of being confounded with the guilty; they will tell you that these peoples will share with their brothers-in-arms their homes, their crops, the fruits of their industry, but that they intend to receive them as grateful hosts, and not as enemies and avengers of the crimes of Rome; they will finally tell you that the whole province is full of confidence in your enlightened patriotism, and that it expects from the generous heart of Berthier what had been granted, in part, by the liberating hero of Italy. Finish such a beautiful work; do not deceive our hopes and let us raise before Europe a monument of gratitude to your heroic justice and beneficence.

No. 41

The Consuls, in the Name of the Roman Republic, to the Executive Directory of the French Republic

Governing Citizens, Rome, which was the seat of liberty and the example of virtues, and which, by the vicissitude of ages and fortune, was reduced to the most shameful slavery, has at last been restored to its former dignity; the invincible and generous French army which, by avenging the nations, protects the rights of man, has affected this memorable prodigy.

The Roman eagle, like the phoenix, is raised from its own ashes, and the tree of liberty is planted on those of Brutus, Fabricius, Pompey and Tullius. The magnanimous shadows of our heroes, evoked by the hero Berthier, will all gather on the capitol, rejoicing to see the triumphal way of the Roman Republic charged with the triumphs of the French Republic.

The Roman people ran from the seven hills to this sublime spectacle, and compared this great epoch of its new destiny to that in which our ancestors regulated the destiny of the world; all hearts being filled with horror for slavery, and transported by the enthusiasm of independence, the people demanded unanimously their sovereignty, and acknowledged to have the benefit and the assurance of the worthy General Berthier, acting in the name of the great nation; and he is impatiently awaiting Citizens Monge, Daunou and Florent for the great charter of the social contract. But the government of the Roman Republic had scarcely been confided to us by the sovereign people, and confirmed by the General-in-Chief, that we had the pain of seeing the cradle of the Republic threatened by the hydra of fanaticism. We have been amply compensated for this anxiety, passing by the joy we felt at seeing, at the same moment, the heads of this hydra, shot down by the French army, united to the national militia, so that an indissoluble bond of fraternity has been formed between us, your brave soldiers and their valiant officers showing themselves at the same time as being our defenders and liberators.

Doubtless, the tree of liberty has already cast deep roots, and will produce the most vigorous germs, since it has been sprinkled with the blood and sweat of French and Roman patriots. Full of admiration for the energy of the sovereign people, it is with the expression of the greatest sensibility, that we hasten, guiding citizens, to assure you of the most earnest gratitude, which we will transmit to our future generations. The most glorious labors of the French Republic, which will overshadow the fame and splendor of ancient and modern governments, will have the advantage that they have for the first time extended the eternal principles of morality to the rights of nations; and the bonds which will now unite, thanks to you, nations to nations, will be the same as those which unite man to man.

Greetings and respect

Rongati, President, Constantini, Angelucci, Bonnelli, Pessuti, Russi, Consuls, Bassal, Secretary General.

No. 42

Note on the Negotiations Held with the Austrian Courtfor the Re-establishment of Poland, Sent to General Bernadotte, Minister of the French Republic, to the Court of Vienna

Rimini, 6 Ventôse, Year VI (24 February 1798).

As the reestablishment of Poland cannot take place without the concurrence of some of the powers of the north, we must consider which of these powers is most capable of co-operating, and the easiest to determine. The presumption falls on the Emperor of Germany, and here are the motives on which it is based. Of the three powers which divided Poland, the Emperor had the least interest in its dismemberment, he did not have the same need to enlarge [his territories] as the King of Prussia, to whom the usurpation of Polish territory has acquired the advantage of improving the geographical position of his former domains. The House of Austria could not conceive the same views of ambition and conquest as Russia, which has not made its way easily to Constantinople except by annihilating by this part a formidable power, which has so often successfully opposed its efforts against the Ottoman Porte.

The restitution of the provinces acquired from Poland will therefore cost less to the Emperor than to these co-partitioners, because he will lose less. Let us add: That the Emperor is the only one who will derive real benefits from the reestablishment of Poland, for Poland restored to its original state will serve as a barrier against two powers, whose respective interests render very dangerous to the House of Austria when they confine its states. The Emperor, stronger than each of these two powers taken separately, would have less to fear of a coalition of his two adversaries by declaring himself in favor of the Poles, because, his quality of protector conciliating to him the universal confidence of the latter they would second it powerfully, they would join together to fight the common enemies; animated by feelings of gratitude which are dear to them, they would have all the more deference for his insinuations and his opinions, that they would believe them dictated by the love of the general good. Neither Russia nor Prussia can in any way captivate the minds of the Poles; one is hated by the persecutions with which it has overwhelmed them for half a century; the other is hated for the betrayals and perfidies of which this people, so often seduced, was the sad victim in 1793. Of all the wrongs reproached by Poland to its usurpers, the Emperor is the one who always less allowed; even the public opinion of the Poles is by this very fact less contrary; he will consequently have less difficulty in gaining their confidence, especially when they know that France would have preferred it to help them recover their freedom and their rights. It follows from these considerations and these reasons that it is upon the Emperor that the choice of the French Republic must fall to make it the instrument of the reestablishment of Poland; but what is the means of engaging him? The treaty of alliance made with France, the guarantee of its assistance by placing on the constitutional throne of Poland Prince Charles of Austria, married with the Princess of Saxony, is incontestably the surest and the most efficacious to determine it.

Let us see if France can do it without compromising itself vis-à-vis the other powers of the North, and without running the risk of a war with some of them. There are only two to whom the union of France with the Emperor would be shady: Russia and Prussia, as long as Poland serves as a bulwark to them, are interested in its restoration, that England must desire by the interest of its commercial relations, and that the Emperor must see at least with indifference, because the guarantee of its constitution by France, and the treaty which will be the continuation, will reassure it against the vain phantoms of enlargement of the House of Austria, which the King of Prussia might make it dread. Only Russia and Prussia could be alarmed by the Emperor's union with France; but Russia, by its local position and by its political position, cannot undertake anything against France, but as Prussia cannot confide in its own strength, and too weak to support two wars at once, it would not dare to commit any hostility against France. France. These two powers would attack only the Emperor and it is probable that they would do it for several reasons:

1.) By the fear of a too great enlargement of the House of Austria, an enlargement however imaginary, because the elevation of a prince of the family of the Emperor to the throne of Poland could never procure for it the advantage of dominating the minds, as the national character of the Poles would oppose it with the greatest obstacle; Constantly attached to their rights, accustomed to struggling incessantly with their king, they would be still more warned against the pretensions of him whom the power of his house would make in their eyes an object of mistrust and continual surveillance; besides, the confidence they would have in the protection of the French Republic would encourage the good patriots to always keep their eyes open to the king's demarches, and experience, and the recent memory of the past, would preserve them from blindness, and avoid the pitfalls in which one would like to lead them;

2.) By the interest of possession. It is indeed important for Russia and Prussia to retain those they have acquired over Poland, at least until a certain time;

3.) On the one hand, by the foresight of the obstacles facing it, Poland increases its forces to oppose Russia's plans of conquest, which is very eager for it, and which has the constant intention of increasing its territory at the expense of the Ottoman Porte, on the other hand spoke of the fear of the King of Prussia, that the Poles would one day be tempted to recapture the provinces that had been taken from them by his predecessors, and which, being indebted to the Emperor, would not help him to to take back his.[3]

It is still more probable, however, that the reasons which might lead these two powers to oppose the Emperor's provisions in favor of the Poles, would yield to their reflections on the difficulties they would have to overcome.

They cannot conceal from themselves that by entering into war with the Emperor, as an ally of France and protector of the Poles, they might come into conflict with him, with the Poles, with Turkey, with Sweden, the Elector of Saxony, and even with France. Besides, the peculiar circumstances do not permit them to gather forces sufficiently large to be able to face their adversaries. The Tsar, only recently seated on the throne, is not strong enough to not always hold a part of his troops ready against the efforts of the discontented, who worry him incessantly by plotting, in various parts of his states, conspiracies against him. The King of Prussia's troops being, to a greater extent, composed of Poles who were forcibly engaged into his service, they would be seen deserting at the first news of a war undertaken for Poland; evidence as frequent as it is recent cannot give him any doubt about it. Russia and Prussia would not fail to recognize these obstacles and would have the prudence not to attempt vain efforts; and, in order to avoid the dangers of too hazardous enterprises, they would submit to what they would like to grant them by general pacification. The role that France would play in pacification is appropriate to its dignity, generosity, character and principles. It is up to the first nation of Europe to repress injustice and oppression. Posterity, like the present generation, will see it, with equal admiration, founding a republic in

[3]Translator: This is a reference to Silesia, which Frederick the Great took from Austria in the Seven Years' War.

the south, and at the same time bringing out another of its ruins in the north. This double triumph will be the height of its glory. In order to achieve the reestablishment of Poland, in the views and terms above, the French Republic could, after having made a treaty of alliance with the Emperor, recognize jointly with it and the Cisalpine Republic, a national representation of Poland in the persons of the Marshal of the Constitutional Diet and of the deputies to the same diet, who would assemble on the territory of the Cisalpine Republic. This diet is recognized throughout Europe; not being ended, but only suspended, it could be legally reassembled. This national representation, after having placed itself at the head of the remaining Polish troops in Italy, would endeavor, in concert with the friendly powers, to instruct the whole nation as soon as possible of its recovery, in the forms that would have been agreed upon for the place of its sessions. If Russia and Prussia, foreseeing the consequences of this political event, decided at first to take the proper course to accede to the general pacification, then the Polish national representation should be seconded by France, to the effect of intervening in the negotiations for general peace. If, on the contrary, these two powers, blinded by their peculiar interests, wished to defend themselves and oppose the progress of the dictates, this diet would proceed to the operations which would suit the circumstances and which would be indicated to it by the powers co-operating in the happiness of its nation.

Dąbrowski.

No. 43

Bonneau, Consul-General and Chargé d'Affairs of the French Republic In Poland to Citizen Bernadotte, General of the Armies of the Republic And Its Ambassador to Vienna

Paris, Ventôse, Year VI (February-March 1798)

Citizen Ambassador, only my zeal makes me undertake to address this letter to you without having the advantage of being known to you, you will kindly, I hope, excuse me because of the motive what could have a little chance on my part without such a step.

My goal, citizen ambassador, is to offer you the product of my dim insight on an object that I have particularly meditated.

I have imagined, in fact, that among the interests, which are at this moment in your care, includes that of unfortunate Poland, so important in itself and relative to the general system, so precious to the friends of liberty, to the enemies of the the most odious oppression, which cannot have been forgotten. I have gone farther, and I have persuaded myself that, having restored the return of my long captivity, on the possible restoration of this interesting nation, a project the views of which have not been disapproved, we might have decided to make use of it in the instructions which one would have thought necessary to bring to you, in which case, more extensive developments on this project, on the ways to bring about the execution and to make it complete when and in what way it will be suitable to the Poles who surround me at this moment with their confidence, might be agreeable to you, and seem to you of some use.

On the basis of this supposition, Citizen Ambassador, receive the offer of all that could depend on me, and please dispose of my zeal. To raise Poland by means of negotiation, whose present circumstances, as well as the very real interest of two co-sharing courts, seem to offer the means; and to restore with it the equilibrium entirely lost in the north; to raise it only partially so as not to excite irresistible oppositions on the part of the oppressors who partitioned it, and yet to make it, henceforth, a solid power in the general system to be created in Europe; to glorify, by this reexistence, the power of our republic and the sacred cause of liberty; support the Empire and our most threatened allies; to even facilitate peace with the first, by maintaining its integrity and more, and rendering it on the north side more than would be lost by our Rhenish our conquests; this is in the midst of various other effects of eminent importance for Europe and for us, which I shall not dwell here upon detailing, the result of the ideas which I have taken the liberty of expounding, by offering a plan for the Polish restoration.

This plan is reduced in substance to reintegrate Poland with what the last partition had taken from it, by means of retrocessions obtained from the three courts; to reunite this country, thus partially raised in Saxony, to strengthen it; and, in order to complete everything, to incorporate both into the Empire.

I think I have been informed, citizen ambassador, that you yourself have not refused any consent to this project, when the Polish patriots who had evidently adopted it had the honor of speaking to you in Paris, and at the same time spoke of the plan to provoke it by reopening [the diet] outside [of Poland] and making their diet act. I desire that the personal dispositions in which they had the good fortune to find you have since been seconded by the determinations which the government has made and will have determined to confide in you.

In any case, I flatter myself at least that you will want to do justice to the feelings that have animated me by addressing this letter; let me end it with the homage that a martyr of liberty, who has suffered four years for it and the nation in the shackles of Russian tyranny, thinks itself particularly entitled to render to one of the heroes who have so gloriously triumphed.

Bonneau.
Dominique Street, near Barq, No. 167.

No. 44

In the Name of the Cisalpine Republic, One and Indivisible, The Executive Director to General Dąbrowski, Commander of the Polish Legion

Milan, Prairial 16, Year VI (4 June 1798)

The Directory expanded the provisions that you expressed in your letter brought by Colonel Chamand saved you the necessity of establishing the best available information, demands the same Directory must update us on the discussion and the deliberations on the object of the convention between the Polish Legions of the Cisalpine government used in the south per your letter until the return of the Legions to the Cisalpine Republic.

The president of the Executive Directory.
Costabili
For the Executive Directory.
The General Secretary Pagani

No. 45

Letter from General-in-Chief Macdonald To Citizen Florent, French Commissioner

Rome, Thermidor 23, Year VI (10 August 1798).

Terracina is in the power of the French; this guilty city has experienced the fate of Ferentino and Frosinonc.

Yesterday, at 6 o'clock in the morning, Adjutant-General Maurice Mathieu gathered the columns about a league from Terracina, on the road that leads to it. There he was attacked on all points by about 1,000 well-armed brigands, dragging with them eight cannons. Some of these rebels had scattered into the marshes and reeds. After six hours of terrible combat, French valor, seconded and rivaled by Polish bravery, has conquered. The insurgents' cannon was captured, and the city taken at the point of the bayonet. In vain some handfuls of rebels took refuge there and sought to defend themselves; they were cut to pieces or fled to the mountains; another part has reached the seashore and embarked.

We have to regret the brave, among whom the Polish Major Podoski, who was killed. Captain Lacroix, my aide-de-camp, had his thigh pierced by a bullet; some Polish officers and two French were wounded. The total loss in killed and wounded amounts to about 40 men, including officers.

Adjutant General Maurice Mathieu, commanding the attack, directed it with rare intelligence, and made the best arrangements. He had a horse and a servant killed.

All the officers, whether French or Polish, and all the troops displayed a distinguished bravery. The chiefs perfectly assisted the general. Captain Lebrun, aide-de-camp, entered the city first, which was absolutely deserted.

P. S. I have just received a new report from Adjutant-General Mathieu; he advises me that the city of Terracina has been completely pillaged, in spite of the efforts of the general and the chiefs. It was impossible, he said, to obviate this disaster. A rebel city, where one of our commanders was assassinated, where our troops were received with gunshots, could it find favor in front of soldiers drunk with revenge?

A boat mounted by rebels who fled was sunk by our artillery.

The flag of rebels bearing a Madonna was taken.

Macdonald

No. 46

Championnet, General-in-Chief to the Executive Directory

At the Headquartes at Terni
15 Frimaire, Year VII (5 December 1798)

Citizen Directors, since the battles of Terni and Porto Fermo, I expected every day new attacks by the Neapolitans, and I was very surprised at their inactivity; but they used this time to reunite their scattered troops, and to carry them to my right. In fact, General Macdonald was attacked yesterday in his camp at Civita-Castellana by five columns coming from Baccano. The strength of the enemy was 40,000 men. General Macdonald, surrounded on all sides, showed great talent; he received the attack with that courage which distinguishes the man of character, and by his skilful dispositions he has disconcerted the projects of the enemy.

General Kellermann, commanding his advance guard ahead of Nepi, was attacked by the first column, coming from Monterosi, which was pushing vigorously ahead. This general had with him only three squadrons of the 19th Chasseurs à cheval Regiment, two pieces of light artillery, and the 1st [Battalion] of the 11th Demi-brigade; this handful of brave men routed the enemy's 8,000-strong column, killed or wounded 400 men, took 15 cannon of all calibers, 30 ammunition caissons, 2,000 prisoners, including 50 officers, and several of higher ranks, flags, standards, 800 to 900 horses or mules, the military chest, 3,000 muskets, ndall the baggage and effects of encampment; he then pursued them to Monterosi, where the soldiers took a huge booty. The talents and bravery of General Kellermann are too well known to receive an useless eulogy here.

I appointed on the field of battle the Chef d'escadron Bru, [acting] commander of the 19th Chasseurs à cheval, who by his activity and his dedication perfectly assisted General Kellermann. I ask you, Citizen Directors, to confirm this appointment, Citizen Humbert commanding this regiment having died in Rome on the day of our departure.

Brigadier Lahur, commander of the 15th Légère, prevented the second column from entering through Rignano, whence, following the old road to Rome, by which it wished to debouch: the enemy lost 30 horses on this point.

The third column was overthrown by the Polish General Kniaziewicz, at the moment when it debouched by Fabrica on Santa Maria di Falari. This brave officer, at the head of his legion, of the Roman Legion, the 2nd and 3rd Battalions of the 30th Demi-brigade, two squadrons of the 16th Dragoon Regiments, a company of the 19th Chasseurs à cheval, and three pieces of light artillery by the rapidity of his attack, he took from the enemy 8 cannon, 15 ammunition caissons, and took 50 prisoners, including two senior officers.

The night ended the fight, and it seems that the Neapolitans left a lot of people on the battlefield. The Roman Legion, which was for the first time under fire, fought perfectly. The result of this day is 23 cannon, all of French caliber, 45 caissons, 8 to 900 horses and mules, standards and flags, the military chest, 52 officers, 2,000 prisoners, luggage, etc., etc.

On our side, the loss was 30 men killed and twice as many wounded.

All the units that fought yesterday did wonders. I hastily collected the names of those who have distinguished themselves.

Bru, commander of the 19th Chasseurs à cheval Regiment; Villeneuve, chef de bataillon; the Citizens Iclsch, Esse, captains; Espoulier, Delfortain, Faile, Ser, lieutenants; Coquet, Lemaire, sub-lieutenants, all of the 15th Légère Demi-brigade; the citizens Lelein, captain; Callandre, Estafor, lieutenants; DeLouche, captain of grenadiers; Fermot, captain, who, though wounded, rushed upon the cannon and took them, all from the battlefield.

Citizens Laforge, sous-lieutenant, Doucerin, maréchal-des-logis; Segnier and Siber, brigadiers [corporals] of the 19th Chasseurs à cheval, behaved perfectly; Citizen Laforge, yesterday, in the surprise of Monterosi, took and wounded seven Neapolitan horsemen.

Greetings and respect,
Championnet.

No. 47

Championnet, General-in-Chief
To the Executive Directory

At the Headquarers at Rietti
21 Frimaire, Year VII (7 December 1798)

Citizen Directors, the enemy column, beaten on the 16th in Otricoli, retired to the heights of Calvi, where it entrenched itself. I was informed, on the 18th, that General Mack himself had passed the Tiber on a boat bridge, near Civita-Castellana, with a corps of 8,000 to 10,000 men, and that he had taken up position at Cantalupo, to strengthen the corps at Calvi, and still try to cut off our communications by returning to Otricoli or Terni by Aspra and Collisepoli. I immediately ordered Macdonald to move General Mathieu's brigade to Calvi by Otricoli, and that of the Polish General Kniaziewicz to the same point, moving by Magliano, while Lemoine debouched from Rieti carrying a corps on Calvi by Contigliano, and took possession of Civita Ducale, a Neapolitan territory, and threatened Aquila. The movement went perfectly well. In the night of the 18th to the 19th, all the columns started under a horrible rain and dreadful paths. Macdonald's troops arrived at daybreak, on the 19th, in front of Calvi; they attacked the enemy on the heights, and after a fierce battle the 11th Demi-brigade, climbing a very rough mountain, threw the enemy into the city, where they were followed and surrounded. They were summoned to surrender, but they made ridiculous proposals. Macdonald came, and passed him his ultimatum thus conceived: "The column will surrender unconditionally as prisoners or be killed without mercy.[4] " They immediately surrendered;

[4]Translator: The phrase used was "passée au fil de l'epée" or "passed over the sword," which does not translate well, but means they would be cut down. In

5,000 prisoners, including Marshal Mocsk, 20 senior officers and 100 subordinate officers, 5,000 good muskets with cartridges, 300 horses, 15 flags or banners, 8 of which were burned by an explosion of bullet pouches near a bivouac, and 8 cannons fell in our power as the fruit of this attack. I will not speak of the bravery of the troops; the action speaks for them. Special praise is due to Generals Mathieu and Kniaziewicz, to aide-de-camp Trinqualli, to Citizen Calvin, Chef de brigade of the 11th Brigade, to the three Chefs de bataillon, and to Citizen Borghese, the former Roman prince, adjutant-general of the National Guard of Rome.

I have just received the news that the left corps of the army has seized the fort of Civitella; I have no detailed report, it is only announced that it was filled with much artillery.

Greetings and respect,
Championnet.

No. 48

Report of Adjutant General Bonnamy, Chief of General Staff, to theMinister of War

At the Headquarters at Rieti,
21 Frimaire, Year VIII (7 December 1798).

Citizen Minister, I told you about the fight and the victory of Otricoli.

To restore perfectly the communications of the right in the center of the army, it was necessary to drive the enemy from Mount Calvi, and to make itself master of the road that leads from Terni to Rome by Cantalupo.

General-in-Chief Championnet ordered General Macdonald to move two columns on Calvi. General Mathieu was detached, on the night of the 18th to the 19th, with the 11th Demi-brigade, and two squadrons of the 16th Dragoon Regiment, and marched on Calvi, while General Kniaziewicz turned the position, leading the 1st and 2nd Battalions of his legion, the 2nd Battalion of the 30th Demi-brigade, and a squadron of the 19th Chasseurs à cheval Regiment. Terni was covered by some infantry companies, the only ones that could be assembled there, and during this time General Lemoine was at Rieti, where he had orders to take a position in front of this city, to seize Civita-Ducale, which he did, and to push parties by Introdozo on Aquila. General Duhem, encamped at Ascoli, received notice of this movement, and

this case, it means the city would be attacked and no mercy would be shown.

was ordered to harass the enemy, to maintain him on his side with skirmishes.

General Mathieu and the Polish general attacked Calvi, overthrew all that was present, blockaded this city, and summoned the Neapolitans to surrender. They spoke, they sought to procrastinate so as to receive the reinforcements that they expected; but General Macdonald summoned them, and delivered to the victorious column two generals, 20 senior officers, 100 subordinate officials, 4,000 to 5,000 men, 300 horses, 5,000 muskets, as many cartridges, 15 flags or standards, and 8 cannons: this is the result of this day.

General Mathieu took a position, and he soon learned that General Mack was marching in person at the head of a considerable corps, to assist at this point; but the news that he learned slowed down his progress, and all the reports that were made told the General-in-Chief that Mr. Mack was encamped at Canlalupo, straddling the road which leads from Terni to Rome, by the left bank of the Tiber, which he passed on a boat bridge to the left of Civita-Castellana.

The days of the 20th and 21st were used to push different reconnaissances to confirm the enemy's movement. For this purpose, General Lemoine scouted the road to Introdozo and Reiti to Rome, had searched the banks of the Tanaro and those of Satto. The patrols did not learn anything; communications were established, however, from the right to the center by Contigliano.

The enemy having been reported only on the point of Cantalupo, the General-in-Chief conjectured that, beaten every time he had detached columns, Mashal Mack had gathered his forces so as to penetrate [the French forces] with all his forces.

As far as his position permitted, General Championnet unite [his forces] on his side, and tomorrow he will be in the presence of the enemy, heading from Terni, Calvi, by the Vacone inn, on Cantalupo, and holding Rieti. The already victorious troops are perfectly disposed, and I hope, Citizen Minister, to have nothing but success to report to you.

Greetings and respect,
Bonnamy.

P.S. General Duhesm seized the citadel of Civitella. By the occupation of this place, he supports the left of the army, and will be free to execute any movements he is ordered to make.

No. 49

Championnet, General-in-Chief To the Executive Directory

At the Headquarters at Calvi,
Nivôse 15, Year VII (4 January 1799)

Citizen Directors, I have waited, with extreme impatience, for a result of my operations to give you news of the army. Many obstacles had to be overcome to reach it; the continual rains, the snow, the flooding of torrents, the insurrections of the peasants who harassed our flanks, cut off our bridges, intercepted our communications, often gave me great anxiety; but the courage of the army, the energy of the general officers, have surmounted everything, and I have today to announce to you that the French Republic is mistress of the two Abruzzes, by the taking of Pescara; that his troops occupy the fortress of Gaete, and that the right of the army of Rome is encamped before Capua.

I will only indicate the points of passage of the army; I charge my chief of staff to enter into this in greater detail.

The first division, under the orders of General Macdonald, after the most painful marches, passed the Carigliano at two points, Ceprano and Isola; the roads were dreadful, the entrenched positions in front of this river were formidable: the enemy left 80 cannons.

While this division was in motion, I had detached General Rey on Terracina, with the 7th and 25th Chasseur à Cheval Regiments, the Polish Legion, and some light artillery; he had orders to capture the batteries placed in the Fondi defiles at Itri, armed with seven cannons, which he did; to seize Gaete, to pass the Garigliano, and to arrive before Capua: an order that could not be executed better than General Rey did.

In the meanwhile, General Kellermann, whom the remains of the Damas column and the resistance at Viterbo held far from the army, announced to me, finally, that after having defeated General Damas, subduing Viterbo, and delivering the French prisoners, this rebellious city held hostage by him he marched to join the army; his cavalry was ordered to join the first division at Ceprano; his person, with the 15th Légère and his artillery, met at Fondi with General Rey.
The first division, after having crossed the Garigliano, moved, in three marches, in front of Capua, and summoned this fortress to surrender. General Mack, who commanded in person, replied that, covered by the Volturno, having a stronghold and an entrenched camp, he wished to defend himself. At this reply General Macdonald ordered the attack; two redoubts were carried by the grenadiers of the 3rd Demi-brigade;

we lost some men, and the brave General Mathieu had his arm broken by canister shot. All who know him are greatly affected, and the Republic has lost a distinguished soldier for some time. I will let you know by my next post the bravery of several soldiers.

General Rey, faithful to his instructions, joined by the troops under the orders of General Kellermann, presented himself before Gaete; this fortress defended by 4,000 men, 70 pieces of cannon, 22 mortars, with provisions and ammunition for a year, holding in its port seven feluccas armed for war, many transport ships, a bridging train, several boats laden with wheat, announced that it would defend itself. General Rey had a howitzer emplaced and had several shells thrown into the fortress; the garrison fell into disorder; the enemy general demanded a capitulation and was told to surrender or there would be no quarter; he obeyed. It garrison became prisoners of war, except for the general, and 63 officers, who were sent back to their homes with a promise not to serve against the French Republic. We found in the place a 100 milliers powder, 20,000 muskets, etc.

General Rey, who had especially employed the Polish Legion in this attack, gave the greatest eulogy. He greatly praised Chef de brigade Kniaziewicz, who commands this brave legion. I appointed him général de brigade, although he is in the pay of the Cisalpine Republic. I ask you for a letter expressing satisfaction with his actions. General Rey also speaks very favorably of Captains Hinski and Laskowski, and Lieutenant Linkiewicz; he asked me, which I granted immediately, the rank of sous lieutenant for the Citizen Mangourit, son; that of chef d'escadron for Citizen Gourdel, my aide-de-camp. By confirming these different appointments, Citizen Directors, you will reward dedication, talent and bravery.

General Rey, having left a garrison in Gaete, bridged the Garigliano, joined the first division before Capua; he is in line today.

The preparations for defense made by Mack give the hope for a pitched battle which I will give when the column of General Lemoine, who has marched from Acquila on Sulmona, has joined me, as well as part of Duhesme's division.

The left wing of the army, under the orders of General Duhesme, after the most wise and painful marches, has arrived in front of the fortress of Pescara, which General Monnier has seized. It was defended by 3,000 men, 44 cannons, several mortars; the garrison came out with the honors of war, leaving its weapons on the glacis. We found huge stores in the fortress and in the harbor, 12 milliers of powder and 2 million cartridges.

General Monuier conducted this attack with the boldness and talents for which he is known; he was perfectly assisted by his aide-de-camp Girard, and Boyer, aide-de-camp of General Duhesme; I have appointed these two officers, captains a long time ago.

Such is, Citizen Directors, the position of the Army of Rome, which I soon hope to proclaim the Army of Naples.

It is rightly that I speak to you here of the Chef de bataillon Chabrier, an engineer officer, who has rendered me great service by the local knowledge he has acquired in the field. This officer prepared a precious map.

All the reports confirm the flight of the King of Naples. Mr. Pignatelli was appointed Viceroy.

The day before yesterday, at Saint-Germain[5], Captain General Mack asked me for an armistice.

Greetings and respect,
Championnet.

No. 50

The Minister of War to General Kniaziewicz, Commander of the Polish Legion in the Army of Rome

Paris, Nivôse 10, Year VII (30 December 1798)

In reporting to the Executive Directory on the advantages won over the Neapolitan Army by the troops of the Republic, General Championnet made it known, Citizen General, with what bravery you led to victory the Polish and Roman Legions, and especially at the defense of Civita-Castellana. By associating yourself with the exploits of the French soldiers, the Executive Directory had already given proof of its confidence in a brave defender of Polish liberty, and it now enjoys giving an adopted son of the great nation a testimony of its satisfaction by awarding you one of the prizes for the courage of the leaders of its warriors. It offers to your valor a reward worthy of it, by donating armor from its national factory. The Directory has sent me to send it to you. I am happy to inform you and to announce that it will be sent to you shortly. Receive, Citizen General, the assurance of the particular esteem which I bear to your military virtues.

Debois Crancé

---

[5]Translator: "Saint-Germain" is how it reads in the text, but this is French for the Italian "San Germano." No San Germano was found in the vicinity of Naples.

No. 51

The Executive Directory to Citizen Kniaziewicz, Chef de la Légion

Paris, 1 Pluviôse, Year VII (20 January 1799).

The Executive Directory has read with satisfaction, Citizen, the story of the courage which you and your gallant legion have shown to the attack of Gaete, which the French army has just taken from the King of Naples. You have shown yourself worthy of the cause you have embraced, you have merited such from free men. The Directory has applauded the justice that General Championnet has restored to you by appointing you général de brigade; it will be pleased to learn that the Directory of the Cisalpine Republic has confirmed this promotion; the conduct of Captains Ilinski and Laskowski, and Lieutenant Linkicwicz on the same occasion, also deserves praise. The Directory invites you to testify its satisfaction.

The Chairman of the Executive Board,
Reveillière-Lepaux.

By the Executive Directory,
Secretary General Lagarde

No. 52

Expedition Plan to Retake the Debouches of Pontremoli and Cento-Croci, Occupied by the Enemy

Sarfana, Prairial 4, Year VII (23 May 1799)

The left column commanded by Chef de brigade Brun will leave Borghetto, and he will move near Varese to attack Cento-Croci, whence he will drive out the enemy. He will push as far as possible, nevertheless throwing on his right a good part of his troop to prevent the enemy from moving on Pontremoli. If, beyond Cento-Croci, there is no good position to occupy, and, on the contrary, it offers the enemy the means of making considerable progress and resuming the offensive after reinforcement, then Chef de brigade Brun will only throw a few skirmishers to his right, in front of Cento-Croci, to harass him and force him to retreat to the left. He will leave 400 well-placed men at Cento-Croci, and with the rest of his column he will carry himself by the shortest and most practicable way, descending to his right to join the column of Citizen Graziani, who is also at his orders, and who must attack the enemy at Zeri, and drive him beyond Pontremoli.

The column of the Citizen Graziani, who is under the orders of Citizen Brun, will leave Piana, and by the road to Borghetto will move by Brugnato, Suvero, Pietra-Tospiano, and then will attack and will remove the enemy at Zeri. This position occupied, he will immediately inform Citizen Brun, so that he can adjust his movement accordingly, to force the enemy to retire and abandon Pontremoli. In the case that he would hold firm, the column will move quickly on the heights of Monte-Sungo to cut their retreat, while the corps that Chef de brigade Brown detached will fall on Pontremoli and will seek to identify the enemy. Citizens Graziani and Brun will arrange, in advance, this movement together, in the way that they will believe the most suitable; they will fix the hour of departure of their respective columns, and will assure the means of communication between them, as well as precautions necessary to help each other.

Before leaving the positions of Verano and Folia, the Citizen Brun will form an elite detachment of 300 men, including 100 from the demi-brigade and 200 Ligurians, including the grenadiers. This corps will pass the Varra to Bocca-di-Batagna, coming by Caperano and Bolano, and will go to Podenzano against the enemy; it will make movements throughout the day without worrying the locals. This small column will be held in the heights of Bolano. This same elite detachment will have on its right the Polish chasseurs who are in San Stefano and Fosdinovo, will have orders to reconnoitre as far as Ribola in front of Aulla, and take up position behind the Ullella. They will pretend to want to cross the river to attack Aulla, and to favor the simulated attack of the elite detachments, which must take up a position at Podenzatio.

The reserve will go to San Stefano, leaving 100 men to Sarzanella, including 80 Ligurians and 20 Poles. From there the reserve, the detachment of elite and the Polish chasseurs will attack Aulla.

The center column of Citizen Ledru, leaving Fivizzano, will attack Sassalbo abruptly, observing his left. He will make his maneuver so as to be able to make as quickly as possible his junction with the columns of Brun and Graziani, who must have already gained the heights of Pontremoli Island and Monte-Sungo. Before leaving Fivizzano, he will leave 200 men commanded by a firm officer in this place. If it is true that the enemy has a camp at Sant Anastasio, which Citizen Ledru will secure in advance, the battalion of the 3rd Demi-brigade, which is at Piazza, will be ordered to make a move forward, after the successful capture of Sassalbo; however, so that, at the moment when the battalion of the 3rd Demi-brigade attacks the enemy, a detachment from Sassalbo may fall on the rear and cut off its retreat.

Finally, the right-hand column, commanded by the Chef de brigade de Partes, having left 100 men at San Pellegrino and 100 men at Cusielnovo, will attack the enemy on all points. Citizen De Partes will maneuver in such a way as to present him with forces on all points, and if he succeeds in seizing some tenable position, he will remain there, otherwise he will remain in his position during the night. He will advise the commander of the San Marcello column, part of Montrichard's division, of his operation, so that the latter should push forward a strong reconnaissance on his side so as to attract the attention of the enemy on that side.

The headquarters, with the reserve, will be at San Stefano, and will move forward by Aulla. It is there that the leaders of the columns will give the necessary information to the general commanding the division.

The troops of Brown's brigade chief will set off; they will go to Borghetto, on the 6th, as close as possible to Varese, and on the 7th, will attack Cento-Croci.

Graziani's column will leave its current position on the 6th, will bivouac in Borghetto, the same day outside the village, and will attack Zeri on the 7th.

The detachment of 300 men, destined to move on Podenzano, will pass the Varz on the 6th and at daybreak on the 7th, will be in in Podenzano. The Polish chasseurs [shall be] at Fosdinovo and San Stefano, as well as the reserve with the headquarters, will go on the 7th, at the break of day, to the position indicated, to attack Aulla, Villa Franca and Pontremoli.

Chief Ledru will attack Sassalbo on the 6th, and if he succeeds in his enterprise, he will make his movement on Pontremoli.

Chef de brigade De Partes will attack and worry the enemy during 7th and 8th and will invite the commander of San Marcello to do the same.

The commanders of the Ledru, Brun, and Graziani columns will have three days worth of bread for their troops. At the same time, they will leave orders in their respective quarters to prepare food for two meals for two days, and that the day after departure they will send for each column a first convoy of bread for two days, and then on.

The general commanding the division recommends to the commanders of the columns the strictest discipline, to march their troops united and militarily, and to make them bivouack during their marches in military positions capable of defense. They will scrupulously respect the inhabitants and their property. As much as possible, we should avoid engaging in affairs with the insurgents, as this would entail the necessity of burning and looting their homes, and that would stop the march of our troops. We must march forward, and if we find, on the way, armed peasants on the road, we must disarm them, and in case of resistance shoot them, but always following with the mass its march towards the designated point. The good conduct of the soldiers, the gentleness and prudence of the chiefs, will earn the confidence of the inhabitants, will assure us the communication between our columns and our rear, and will facilitate the means of sending them relief supplies and ammunition. The general reiterates his orders in this respect and recommends this object very much to all the chiefs; do and ordered as above.

The général dedivision,
commanding the Apennine Passes,

Dąbrowski

No. 53

Movements and Actoins of the Division Commanded by General Victor

From 23 Prairial to 3 Messidor Year VII (11 – 21 June 1799)

The division set off, the Prairial 24th, from the positions of Cento-Croci and Monte-Sungo to debouch into the Parmesan by Fornovo, where it arrived on the 20th. This post had been evacuated by the enemy on the 25th. On the 27th, it went to Borgo San Donino, chasing before it the Austrian parties whose object was to observe its movement. On the 28th, it continued on its way to Placentia, where the same parties were assembled; they made only a slight resistance and withdrew behind the Trebbia, after leaving a garrison in the castle.

The same day it took a position at Borgo San Antonio. A demi-brigade entered Plaisance to serve in this fortress. On the 29th, it passed the Trebbia, having orders to drive out enemy outposts to settle behind the Tidone, and to not engage in anything that could become serious. The généraux de brigade had entirely conformed to this order, and the division was established when skirmishers crossed the bridge to provoke the enemy, and a general, commanding a division too weak to claim to form an attack, passed the bridge, in turn, and engaged in an affair which nearly caused the army a misfortune, which chance alone could repair. All the troops that were then on the Tidone were forced to fight to support their predecessors. Bravery has made up for the number, and the enemy had only weakly pushed them back. Losses were nearly equal on both sides.

On the same day, at 10 o'clock in the evening, the combined divisions of Victor, Rusca, and Dąbrowski, and Salm's brigade, retreated behind the Trebbia. The Salm brigade, forming the vanguard, was established in San Niccolo.

On the 30th, the enemy made a movement on its right with the intention of seizing the Tuna heights and establishing its line on the left bank of the Trebbia in front of Grignano, opposite Gossolungo. The united divisions have gone to this last village, with the exception of Salm's brigade, which withdrew to San Niccolo. Victor's division, having its left towards the center of Gossolungo, extended by its right to the way of Campre-Moldo. Rusca's division, with its right to the left of the first, extended to its left, up the Trebbia to the Favernasco heights. Dąbrowski's was ordered to seize Tuna, and to establish fairly strong posts at Cassaliggio and Monte Calzone. The cavalry was to sweep the whole country as far as Tidone. The enemy had, as has just been said, prevented this movement, and were in a position to attack Dąbrowski. It attacked him with impetuosity, and the Polish troops, surprised by a fight they had not expected, poorly informed, hastily redeployed on Rusca's division, after having lost some men. All the troops then put themselves in battle order. The 4,000-strong enemy attempted to cross the Trebbia River, but two demi-brigades, with 400 horse, forced them to back down in disorder after a stubborn struggle of about two hours. The enemy have lost a lot of men, our loss was not considerable. The divisions, after this fight, formed on a single line along the Trebbia, from Gossolungo to the Carata heights, and thus passed the night of the 30th to Messidor 1st.

On the 1st, at 9 o'clock in the morning, 2,000 men under the command of General Dąbrowski crossed the Trebbia to reach the Tuna heights and attack the enemy's right flank, while Rusca's division, then reduced to 2,000 men, and that of the General Victor with 4,500, threatened the front and the left flank of the Russian camp, to attack together at the moment when General Dąbrowski would be heard. The reserves were arranged to rescue the attackers on all points of the line. The attack was, therefore, begun by General Dąbrowski, and successively by Rusca's and Victor's divisions. It was lively and very well supported. The enemy strongly resisted and victory uncertain during the eight hours of the battle. It was necessary to make difficult efforts to drive them out of their camp, which we did not reach until night, when it was no longer possible to pursue our successes. It was decided that the troops would resume their first position, which was executed with the greatest order. The enemy had lost an infinity of soldiers in this bloody battle. Our loss is about 1,000 men both killed and wounded or prisoners.

Generals Rusca, Dąbrowski, and Grandjean, were wounded.

The troops displayed a courage worthy of the best days of this war. It was necessary, because these united divisions together had only 8,000 men, who had before them all the Russian army, whose valor is not to be doubted. This army was not only superior in numbers but was supported by formidable artillery.

The Messidor 2nd, the combined divisions have made their retreat, in consequence of the orders which were given to them, on San-Giorgio, and from there to Castel-Arquato.

On the 3rd, Rusca's and Dąbrowski's divisions moved to the Taro, and that of Victor to Formoso, from where it left, on the 4th, to take back its positions at Pontremoli and Cento-Croci.

Victor

No. 54

Movements of the 2nd Division, under the Orders of Général de brigade, Provisional Commander, During the Retreat of Messidor 2, Year VII (20 June 1799)

According to the order of march, Rusca's division, commanded by General Calvin, set out, Messidor 2nd, from Gossolungo at 5 o'clock in the morning; it took the head of the column, went to San Giorgio, passing through Settimo and Podenzano. It arrived at San Giorgio about 9 o'clock in the morning, followed by Dąbrowski's division. Victor's division closed the march. When these two divisions had crossed the Nura, General Victor, who commanded the column, had them established on the banks of this river, to the right of San Giorgio, the left leaning against said village, acting as an intermediary of the line; on this central point and in the direction of the ford it established two pieces of artillery. It was about 10 o'clock when this movement was affected (here this division passed under the command of General Dąbrowski); the enemy, who had always followed us and constantly harassed the column, appeared on the opposite side. The skirmishes began; at the same time some columns having appeared, our artillery fired on them. Then the enemy sought to establish batteries to oppose ours, but they were dismounted immediately. From that moment the fire ceased entirely. It was then noon. It was in a security similar to that of a troop which, traveling in stages, stops to refresh itself. Some of the soldiers were drunk, the gunners were not at their posts, the cavalry had almost completely unchained its horses, and the village was finally full of soldiers. During this time the enemy made his movement on the right and on the left, in order to cut off our retreat. The execution of his design was very weak; for, while he was trying to turn our wings, a column cutting the river went to the center and seized a cannon and a howitzer that were in position on the direction of our ford.

The retreat was ordered for an hour after noon, the right and the left [columns] made their movements at the same time. The Poles scarcely passed the San Giorgio heights, when the rumor spread through the village that the enemy had already entered it and appeared on all the advances; the alarm was equal to the surprise, and the disorder surpassed all the rest: The Poles contributed a great deal to it. At last all was tumultuously on the road; artillery, cavalry, infantry, everything was confounded. The park having gone on Cadeo and Fiorenzuola, one tried to delay the march of the column to give it the time to evacuate; then the rumor spread that it was attacked and even taken. Adjutant General Gauthrin passed all the cavalry they met on the right and left of the road, in order to flank the column and to scout the enemy's movements; the road became freer, and Adjutant General Gauthrin pressed the evacuation of the artillery. General Calvin remained with the 55th [Demi-brigade] retiring in echelons, and Adjutant General Gauthrin moved to the 17th [Demi-brigade]. Arriving near a village, four to five miles from San Giorgio, he found the enemy who had entirely enveloped this village, and who was firing on every point. As he went forward to see if he could not penetrate into the village, he saw the aide-de-camp of General Victor who was retreating, and who told him that the road was entirely cut off. Then Adjutant-general Gauthrin returned to the 17th [Demi-brigade], and in order to order it to assemble, and to follow the side-road taken by General Victor's aide-de-camp, who was on Firenzuola, he found it surrounded by the enemy, and it was no longer possible for it to succeed. He rallied about a battalion of fugitives of all kinds and made his way to the road taken by this aide-de-camp. He was followed about a quarter of a mile by the enemy, who afterwards left him alone.

Arrived at a junction of roads, this adjutant-general saw Victor's column, which was defiling on the right. He went over to it with the debris he had gathered, unaware of how far the retreat was going.

General Victor made a position on this column on a mountain and proceeded the next day to Borgo San Domino.

Gauthrin, Adjutant-General,
Chief of Staff 2nd Division

No. 55

State of the Garrison of Manuta
On Messidor 5, Year VII (23 June 1799)

Fortress of Mantua	Men	
26th Légère Demi-brigade	566	
29th Légère Demi-brigade	832	
31st Demi-Brigade	2,024	
45th Demi-Brigade	657	
93rd Demi-Brigade	487	7,681 men
1st Helvetic Legion	434	
2nd Helvetic Legion	460	
1st Cisalpine Légère Demi-brigade	785	
2nd Polish Legion	837	
7th Dragoon Regiment	454	
Piedmontese Carabiniers	145	
Citadel		
5th Foot Artillery Regiment	15	
6th Foot Artillery Regiment	53	952 men
1st Battalion/31st Demi-Brigade	884	
Fort St. George		
56th Demi-Brigade	774	
26th Légère Demi-Brigade	310	
93rd Demi-brigade	88	1,372 men
Gunners	175	
7th Dragoon Regiment	25	
Migliaretto Front		
2nd Bn, 31st Demi-Brigade	674	
2nd Bn, 2nd Polish Legion	357	1,272 men
Foot Artillery	241	
Pradella Advanced Post		
Foot Artillery	103	
2nd Bn, 29th Demi-Brigade	392	535 men
7th Dragoon Regiment	40	
Total		11,812 men

No. 56

Letter From General Foissac-Latour to Austrian General Kray Relative to the Polish Officers of the 2nd Legion

Mantua, Germinal 24, Year VII (13 April 1799)

It has been reported to me that the Polish officers who serve in the French army, and who have been made prisoners, are forced to serve in the Austrian Army as simple soldiers. If that were the case, I should have to say to you that no good can be obtained for the service of His Majesty, the Emperor, and that this procedure would seem to announce the contempt of a military rank recognized by the French Republic, and of which these officers justify possession by courage and honorable conduct in our armies. If they could be considered guilty, should we punish them in a manner which seems likely to be shared by our other troops, which no one will ever surpass in glory, the resentment for such behavior? I am convinced that I am badly informed, or that, if this is the case, you would not refuse, in the future, to act more respectfully towards brave allies of France, whom the chances of war have placed in your hands.

Foissac-Latour

No. 57

Citizen Foissac-Latour, Général de division, Commander-in-Chief of the Fortress of Mantua, to Citizen Joseph Wielhorski, Général de brigade, In the Service of the Cisalpine Republic, Commander of the 2nd Polish Legion

Mantua, Germinal 28, Year VII (17 April 1799)

The requests that you make of me, Citizen General, are legitimate in the eyes of justice, and supported by the admiration excited in our army by the distinguished and courageous conduct of your nation, in the battles which it has already fought with us against the enemies of freedom. It is, therefore, with pleasure that I announce to you that they will be solemnly granted to you by tomorrow's order of the day,

and that the officers under your orders will enjoy it from Floreal 1st, of the next month; that is to say, from the day after tomorrow, they will be understood, for the next day, on the role of distributions according to their rank; they will be under the police of the French commissioner of war, and will receive, all without distinction, the appointments of the rank of second lieutenant.
When your forces permit you the activity, I designate you as the commander-in-chief of the advanced posts of Migliaretto, which the enemy has attacked today; and I believe it to be a useful deed to the defense of this place and to our common glory.

You will take the nearest possible accommodation in town to this interesting position.

Foissac-Latour

No. 58
Order of the Day of Germinal 29th (18 April)

Général de brigade Wielhorski is appointed Commander-in-Chief of all the posts at Migliaretto and Thé, and advanced posts on the ground before these entrenchments to the enemy's positions, land bounded on the left by the lower lake and on the right by the marsh, which leans on the demi-bastion, side 6, of the works of Thé Island. He will take this command as soon as his health permits; meanwhile, this important command is entrusted to the Chef de bataillon Girard, of the 31st Demi-brigade; he will be referred to as Commander-in-Chief of the Migliaretto front.

The Chef de brigade Balleydier, of the 29th Légère Demi-Brigade, is appointed commander of the Pradella Front, and outposts situated in front of this work, between the marshes mentioned above, and the upper lake to the enemy positions.

These commanders will take the dwellings as near as possible to the points entrusted to their courage, their intelligence, and their republican patriotism.

Independently of the ordinary guards previously fixed for these two posts, there will daily be a reserve battalion shared between them, in the proportion of a third for Pradella, and two-thirds of its strength for Migliaretto. These reserves will begin their service at night, and will retire on the next day, after they have received the permission of the respective commanders. They will stay at the bivouac near the Migliaretto and Pradella Gates, to go outside in case of a night attack.

From now on, the total strength of the garrisons will be divided into three equal parts: one will provide guards and workers; the second will always be ready to march and will provide for reserves and detachments; the third will be fully at rest. Unemployed reserve troops will be consigned to their barracks; the officers will wear a high collar and will be within arm's reach.

The Polish Corps having been put under the police of the French commissioners of wars will remain under the police of these same commissioners at Mantua.

Polish officers à la suite or supernumerary, present, doing the service, will enjoy the rations of their respective ranks; and all, without distinction of their rank, with a second lieutenant's salary.

Consequently, the commissioner of war will will include them in his distribution records and in his journals, in accordance with this provision. He will ask General Wielhorski for his state.

(*What follows is the special provisions relating to food and forage, artillery and engineering.)*

No. 59

General Instruction for the Defense of the Outlying Post of Migliaretto, Under the Commander-in-Chief General Wielhorski

Mantua, Germinal 30, Year VII (19 April 1799)

The first object to be proposed by the enemy in the attack he may organize between the villages of Pietro andCérèse, is to advance near the fortress to open a trench. To reach this goal, he has only two paths, one on his right, the other on his left. They are dikes that start from the dry ground that we occupy in front of the Migliaretto works, which will end at the foot of the Ceresus curtain wall that the enemy can occupy initially. On its front, the enemy is separated from the Migliaretto plain by a flood or marsh almost at all times impassable. At the moment, it is certainly impassable.

For the same reason, we have only these two paths to reach it on this side; but it can be attacked on its left by a sortie made by the Pradella Gate. Its right is covered by the lower lake and could only be faintly disturbed by the gunboats at this point on the lake.

Nevertheless, if he had not the attention to defend it by cannon, these boats could execute a landing on his rear, if one learned that they were not well supported. Otherwise, the maneuver would be bad and expose the sortie to being captured.

The essential object is therefore first to prevent the enemy from crossing the Pietole and Ceresus Dikes: they are commanded by the heights which the enemy occupies and have for them only the advantage of two long defiles placed between two marshes, and that we can enfilade with our cannon, which also can fire on them obliquely: both are cut by bridges. I had not given the order to break that of Pietro, which was of two bays; however, this was done, and it deprived us of an offensive means at a time when it was not yet time to reduce ourselves only to the defensive. It is difficult to restore, because the middle approach being demolished, spars cannot reach from one abutment to another.

The Cérèse bridge is defended by a square, masonry tower, under which there is a post which must be only for infantry; on the left of this tower is a former Austsrian entrenchment, behind which is placed another post destined to support that of the tower; finally, there is a platform on which I have mounted a cannon with six rampart guns; their object is to cover the ground and to worry the enemy from farther away. If the enemy beat the top of this tower with cannon, or if he manages to throw a single bomb into it, this defense would fall. On the occasion of the little affair of the 28th, the bridge was very bravely disputed, and the enemy withdrew with some loss; but this bridge was destroyed to prevent a surprise, then restored the next day by the pontonniers. I'll see if we can put a bridge there that can be removed at will; but, in any case, this point must be disputed with determination, without, however, exposing ourselves to losing too many men, by the danger of communicating it, when the dyke is beaten on both sides by the enemy, and can no longer cover those who can follow the setbacks. The two dikes in question are interconnected by a transverse dyke about 700 toises long. This last dike, which faces the enemy, is furnished with artillery; two main batteries are placed at its junction points with the previous ones, which are thus enfiladed by these batteries. The object of the other cannon spread over its length is to produce a cross fire; and the whole of this defense must balance the enemy placed on the curtain wall, which is parallel to it, at a distance of 375 toises.

At the Piétole dike, there is a post near the bridge, and another further back.

If the enemy had forced the Cérèse post and passed the cut at Piétole, it would be necessary to divide all the fires on these two dikes. Then it would be necessary to protect this artillery with two battalions of infantry, and to hold back, out of the range of cannon, near the fortress' glacis, a reserve of 150 mounted men, to charge the enemy on both sides, in case he should have entered the plain. The two batteries on the dyke should defend themselves in their position to the end, at the risk of being taken, because we could hope to retake them again later, because of the difficulty of taking the cannon away by the dyke during the heat of the fight; but it would be necessary to withdraw the gunners at once so as not to lose them, and also to save the caissons, which one would hold for this purpose hitched at a fair distance.

By thus defending the batteries of the dykes, which the cavalry can approach at the gallop, it would be necessary to remove the pieces of the transverse dike in a position closer to the fortress, towards the middle of the plain, and place them in front and on the flanks of a reserve battalion to be held in line, so as not to obstruct the fire from the fortress, which could beat the ground in front of it; but this position should be taken only when the enemy has a success which threatens them with being taken.

The enemy, becoming master of the junction of the Ceresus Dike, would probably seek, if they were in force, to extend to their left. Some grenadier companies on our right might prevent it; but it would require some cannon placed in the battery occupied by the Austrians on the way ahead of the Ceresus works, and the grenadiers must be supported by two cannons placed in the middle of the path on the right, that this battery also defends. In this way, there would be a double crossfire, directed over the entire terrain from the lower lake to the marsh on the right. It will be necessary, in this disposition, to take such positions, that one leaves with the cannon from the fortress as much play as possible, either in front of the troops moving onto the plain, or by the gaps left between the infantry units. The commanders of the batteries of the place, in particular that of the new Bastion No. 1, in which I have placed 24pdr cannons, will have to be warned, and put the greatest circumspection in the direction of their fires, so as not to shoot our people.

If the enemy was thrown back, the cavalry should then charge them with the greatest vivacity. At the right of the junction point of the Cérèse Dike, extends the dike that faces the extension of the curtain wall that forms the crescent from left to right: it is good to hold a few cannons and a little of infantry, to quarrel with the enemy by fire directed on the height. This dike needs to be relieved: the engineer has the order. However, if the enemy builds batteries on the height, it would become imprudent to hold in this position, which would always be dominated.

In general, if it were possible to only engage in this plain in an equal combat, it would be against all principles and prudence to attempt it, because the losses which the besieged may take are such, that a man lost for it always counts for three attackers, and that it would deprive itself of the advantages of the fortifications.

Thus, in the case of an only equal enemy force found to have forced the dikes, it would be necessary to only then engage and attract the enemy, by means of a retreat, until they are within a good range of the fortress' artillery. Then the infantry troop would retire in the covered ways, under the protection of this fire, and the cavalry would return to the city, and would remain close enough to come out again.

It is important, 1.) to recognize the paths and barriers that lead to it; 2.) to exercise the troops in the planned retreats, combined so as to win the gates and barriers successively, with order, and each troop which has been appointed to it; 3.) not to be joined by the enemy who, profiting from the fray and the disorder, could throw himself into the fortress with the troops who would be withdrawing in confusion. To advance when the enemy yields, to yield when the enemy advances, to lure him into the fire from the fortress; to attack him with vigor if he staggers, and to remember that he has but two passes behind him, and that it is possible to throw him into the marsh, are still principles which must not be forgotten.

This is, in general, the best way, in my opinion, to fight outside without being too exposed. General Wielhorski, who is in command of this post, would not have needed these details, and his experience and his military talents are so sure that he will grasp any ideas that may be lacking.

He will send me a report every morning. Whenever he thinks he needs any reinforcements or help, he will advise me of it, and I will personally support his efforts in the great circumstances in which other points would not require my presence for even more decisive reasons.

I will give new developments to my ideas, if the enemy besieges us and manages to open the trench in this part, despite the obstacles with which we opposed him.

Works will still be constructed, if circumstances permit.

The commander of the engineers will give General Wielhorski an idea about the land he is charged with defending.

Foissac-Latour

No. 60

Report of Citizen Wielhorski on the Sortie on the Migliaretto Front on Floréal.

Mantua, Floréal 19, Year VII (8 May 1799)

Accorging to the general order given to make a sortie, I left the city's gate 2 o'clock in the morning; at 3 o'clock, I was at the head of my column, which was under the advancedCérèse Tower. I immediately passed a company by the right and left of the village to capture the little enemy posts and to turn the village ofCérèse, while the rest of the column advanced directly by the main road. After a quarter of an hour we were masters of the village ofCérèse. Then I directed a column of 400 infantry, 50 dragoons, and two cannons down the road to San Benedetto, with orders to move on San Giabio, and from there, to turn by the left to take Virgiliana in the rear. The reserve, with about 200 men, took position before the village ofCérèse, on the road to Borgo-Forte. While the column marched on San Biagio, a small body of infantry, supported by some dragoons, was detached directly against the village of Pietole, which they captured with the assistance of some gunboats, which fired on the village. The column directed on San Giabio found an enemy battalion before the village, supported by two canon and a squadron of hussars. The enemy battalion, formed en masse, advanced on our column after having fired a few cannon shots on it. Our column, weakened by the scouts and several small posts that it was obliged to leave on the various roads, received the enemy with canister fire; but it could not resist his superior forces, which forced it to fall back. The retreat that I made was protected by a company drawn from my reserve and some dragoons, was executed in the greatest order. It took nearly an hour and a half to reach the main route; during this time, an enemy battalion came en masse to present itself within cannon shot, on the road to Borgo-Fote, probably to cover the retreat of all the posts that the column from Pradella had forced back, because it made no movement. I prohibited disturbing this column counting that the column in Pradella would take it in the rear. Seeing, however, that my San Baigio colulmn and the detachment from Pietole had been obliged to retreat, and fearing that my reserve would be cut off, I issued the order to retire as well, and all returned to the lines. Only one infantry caisson was left on the road to prevent the enemy cavalry from falling on our rearguard. We would have been able to save the caisson had not the mules become resistant. Once I was back in the lines, I attempted to draw on me as many enemy as possible; to this end I fired my cannon and volleys of musketry; but only 400 Tyrolian jagers advanced and they were scattered in the ditches and behind the trees, which covered the landscape. We remained in this state for about an hour; then I saw on my right some skirmishers from the Pradella column. I sent some men from my side to support them, when I received a reinforcement of 200 men, and the order to still capture the village ofCérèse, and to resume my position forward to protect the Pradella column. This was executed. We held the position until the return of the Pradella column.

My loss consisted of an infantry caisson and a 3pdr artillery caisson.

Six soldiers killed, both non-commissioned officers and soldiers.

The wounded consisted of 10 officers, and 59 non-commissioned officers and soldiers, all Polish.

And we lost as prisoners, 19 Polish non-commissioned officers and soldiers.

A French gunner, Cisalpine gunner, and a Polish gunner were wounded. One had a concussion, and a wagon driver was wounded. Not having received a report from the detachment of the 31st Demi-brigade or the dragoon regiment, I am unaware of their losses. I know positively that one officer of the 31st Demi-brigade was wounded. The chef de brigade of the Poles had a horse killed under him. The enemy lost about 60 dead and 80 prisoners, including two wounded. The number of their wounded is unknown. I have only praise for the detachment of the 31st Demi-brigade. Its conscripts are only conscripts in name. In fact, they are brave soldiers who conducted themselves as if they had made many campaigns. The dragoons also were perfectly led.

Général de brigade, Commander-in-Chief of said front,

Wielhorski

No. 61

Report of Chef de brigade Dembowski, Commander-in-Second of the Column Sortieing by the Crese Gate, to General Foissac-Latour, Commander-in-Chief, on the Sortie of Floréal; 19th.

Mantua, Floréal 22, Year VII (11 May 1799)

Conforming to the orders that I have received, I departed on the 19th, at 3:15 a.m. by theCérèse Gate, with a column confided to my command, which contained 400 Polish infantry, 50 dragoons, two cannons, 30 sappers, and five miners, to attack the village ofCérèse and to surprise that post.

The night before the attack, I brought my officers together and gave each their destination, by showing it to them on a map. I gave them the order that as soon as that the village was taken, to rally, except the company of chasseurs that I had designated to serve as my flankers on the right and left. I had advised the officers that we would not remain an instant inCérèse; that we would be relieved there by the first battalion, to march then on the rear of Virgiliana.

I then moved toCérèse in the following manner: I detached the two companies, which moved along the road that was to surround this location, and to prevent the retreat of the enemy on Borgo-Forte. This task was completed. Officier Kisielnicki, who commanded 30 men, arrived at the point indicated behindCérèse, but only with five men, the rest of his detachment not having followed him.

While these two companies attacked Cérèse by the flanks, I attacked it frontally with my column, when a light fusillade by the enemy scattered my infantry. I had great difficulty rallying and putting them in order. Once reorganized I attacked again and I captured the village. Despite the precise orders that I had given and repeated to rally atCérèse after it was taken, I could only assemble 400 men, which I rallied, with difficulty, with the assistance of my adjudant and some dragoons.

The first battalion arrived and having taken my positions, I marched out, and followed the road to San Benedetto, sending on my right and left some dragoons to rally to me the rest of my column (which was dispersed and without order), in order to move, as my orders directed, behind Virgiliana, and present a front to the enemy.

I formed 180 men by pelotons, and I took every means to be gentle towards my officers, so that they would march their troops in the greatest order. I could not reach it, and in spite of all my entreaties, before arriving even before the enemy, the officers allowed the soldiers to leave their ranks, so there remained only seven to eight men per company. I had to leave a post of 50 men on the way to Pietro; I could not do it, given the few people I had left; I left only four dragoons there, to be able to warn me if the enemy was trying to cut off my retreat, since Pietro was not yet in our power. I continued my way to the houses of Parma, where, according to the order of General Wielhorski, I had to leave another detachment of 50 men commanded by an intelligent officer, who was to observe the enemy at San Biagio, where he could send help; I could not do it, for I had only 50 men left; I would have been obliged to march alone with the two cannons.

While I made my arrangements to march through the fields with these 50 men, and to carry me below Virgiliana, I noticed the enemy coming from San Biagio in force, formed in column, having skirmishers on their left and right. I had the cannon put in battery and fired 18 to 20 shot and canister; but given the few men I had to support both cannon, and that the roads where I had to leave detachments were not guarded, I ordered the cannon withdrawn and supported them with the infantry, as well as possible.

I observe that approaching the path to Pietole, where I had left four dragoons, I sent by my adjutant, General Wielhorski, a report to inform him of the few people who remained, inviting him to send me the rest of the dragoons, who were behind, and also to send two platoons of infantry from the reserve to guard these roads and rescue me when necessary, which the general did; and the adjutant of the Legion placed in the position that I had indicated to him the two platoons with the cavalry, which he had also brought me. I then retreated; the cavalry did its duty well; but the infantry disbanded and did not wish to retire in order. I took every gentle means first to stop the soldiers and prevent them from fleeing; I placed skirmishers on the flanks, who also fled; but I had at last arrived where the adjutant had placed the two platoons sent to me by General Wielhorski. The country and the position were very advantageous, and I thought I could momentarily defend myself and do great harm to the enemy's cavalry; but I was no more surprised to find the two platoons were not there, and I do not know by what order they retired. It was therefore necessary for me to employ all the means again, and even to strike the soldiers, to make them march more slowly, and to arrive, in order, atCérèse. I render all possible justice to the cavalry, especially to the officers, who have distinguished themselves very well.

I had not yet collected my column on the dike at theCérèse Gate, when General Wielhorski gave me the order to go, with the Poles and a detachment of the 31st, commanded by a chef de bataillon, to take Cérèse back by force as the enemy had occupied it. It was in this last attack that I saw many Poles hiding in ditches, and behind the gate, and who, instead of marching forward, had retreated. I was so desperate that I gave the cowards who fled saber-strokes; and as soon as I had assembled 100 Poles, I put myself at the head of the detachment of the 31st to acquit myself of the orders I had received, and to facilitate the retreat of the column, which had left by the Pradella Gate. I did it perfectly and stayed there until I received the order to withdraw. This is the true report of what happened in the column whose command was entrusted to me, and which I am able to prove by those who were under fire with me.

The denunciation that has been brought against me for striking soldiers (which the very officers have approved) is real. I hit cowards who were fleeing; I have done only my duty: the law orders me to do it.

I said, I admit, that I would prefer to command a platoon of the 1st Battalion rather than the 2nd. The officers to whom I made these remarks deserved them; for, instead of remaining in column by platoon on the road, they dispersed with their companies into skirmishers without having received the order [to do so], and we were no longer able to rally them.

I observe that it is not everything to go to the fire and to fight well; besides this, it is necessary to execute the orders that one receives and to be able to maintain one's troops in the ranks. I observe again to those who have formalized these remarks, that if I had the column in order when I met the enemy at San Biagio, I would not have been obliged to retire; that I could have beaten the enemy, take his posts behind Virgiliana, as my ordes directed.

I have always been at the head of the column; none of those who inculpate me can claim to ignore the orders I have so many times repeated.

Greetings and respect,
Dembowski.

No. 62

Letter from General Foissac-Latour to General Wielhorski

Mantua (Floréal 22, Year VII (11 May 1799)

I address you, my dear general, concerning the letters that I wrote respectively to the officers of the 2nd Polish Legion and to Chef de brigade Dembowski. This officer, who has probably been guilty of grave wrongdoing, is too commendable for his zeal and his courage, so as not to deserve for this time the forgetting of his outbursts, on the part of those who know how to appreciate his qualities and who are animated by the desire for the good of the service. I would not count on the effect of my writings to put this affair to bed, if I did not support you; it will be agreeable to me to owe success to the effects of your wisdom, and to the credit so well deserved which you enjoy with the Polish nation, and of all those who, like myself, have been able to appreciate you.

Foissac-Latour.

No. 63

Letter from General Foissac-Latour to the Corps of Officer of the 2nd Polish Legion, Relative to the Affair of Chef de brigade Dembowski

Mantua, Prairial 2, Year VII (21 May 1799)

I am surprised, citizens, that after the letter I wrote to you concerning your dispute with Chef de Brigade Dembowski, you have returned to your complaints. In telling you that my intention was not to deny justice, but only to give no further action to this matter at the present, you must not conceive the hope of changing a resolution, which essentially deals with the good of the service, and to the position in which we find ourselves. I observe, besides, that if Chef de brigade Dembowski has really struck some Poles, it is probably on them that the accusation of this commander is made, and which is the subject of your complaints. Facts of this kind are difficult to clear up; and the wrong in question being the most serious of all, is also that of which one defends oneself with the greatest heat; the leader, in such a case, deserves some belief, and no one would undertake to take upon himself the danger of the command, if he were to be accompanied by one who will slander him every time he accuses a subordinate, if he does not support his accusation with evidence established by a formal procedure. Doubtless, at another time, Citizen Dembowski will justify his actions, and I do not claim to rob you of the right to judge between him and those who believe themselves unjustly attacked. For the rest, I declare that he has appointed no one to me, and that I do justice, in general, to the courage and the good spirit which animates you.

Foissac-Latour.

No. 64

Letter from General Foissac-Latour, in Response to that of Adjutant-General of the Polish Legion Kosinski, Dated Floréal 28

Mantua, Prairial 9, Year VII (28 May 1799)

I have received, citizen, your letter of the 28th of the last month, by which you complain against the provisions of my agenda of the same date, which gives you the command of the Polish Legion. It is very extraordinary that you regard this mark of confidence and honor as a kind of degradation, while it was the object of the ambition of many French généraux de brigade, who solicited, as a grace, to be put at the head of a body to serve in a more active way. Not wishing and not having to place Citizen Dembowski in it, for reasons familiar to you, none other than you could be invested with these functions. Take, then, Citizen, more just idcas, and give me the opportunity to put yourself in the position to deploy the zeal and courage you have already given proof, and which must be animated by a new vehicle to the head of the brave Legion of which you are the commander.

Foissac-Latour.

No. 65

Letter from Citizen Borthon, Artillery Commander of the Fortress to Citizen Axamitowski, Commander of the Artillery of the Polish Legion.

Isle of The, Messidor 19, Year VII (7 July 1799)

I am going to send you, citizen, two 8inch and one 6-inch howitzers, so that, with those that you have, you can shoot against the redoubts raised by the enemy.

You will shoot them from 5 o'clock in the evening until nightfall. During the night a few shells will be fired from time to time, having identified, during the day, the places to be repaired.

You will prepare the ground for receiving these pieces, while waiting for their platforms to be made.

You will work on the construction of batteries and platforms, without stopping until they are completed.

You will ask General Wielhorski to provide you with the workers and the services you will need.

Greetings and fraternity,
Rorthon.

No. 66

Letter from Citizen Rorthon to Citizen Axamitowski

I received, my dear commander, your letter of this morning. I approve of the arrangements you have made for the construction of the batteries, but I differ essentially with you in two respects: 1.) You will allow me to remark to you that it is not from 5 o'clock in the evening until the night at the enemy work, nor at periodical intervals during darkness, but all the time, day or night, that the enemy shall be seen or heard in their works; because it may occur from 5 o'clock to nightfall that they will not expose anyone and then our shots will be lost. In addition, you will lose then in the darkness when you do not sieze the opportunity where workers are heard, frequently in a continuous manner. It will result from this disposition that they can work in great peace between the periods you have indicated. You will therefore kindly ask the commander of the artillery of Migliaretto to follow, as to the time of the action, all that will be prescribed by General Wielhorski, with whom it would have been convenient for you to concert your measures, as well as a previous order he has issued.

The generals, being responsible for the posts, cannot be deprived of the faculty of defending them in their own way, subordinate to my orders. The artillery has to give on this point only advice according to his art, that is to say those which tend to determine the more or less advantageous effect of a battery whose location has been ordered by the general. This principle is too much for the good of the thing and for what has been practiced at all times in the war, for you to be able to oppose its application. 2.) You are telling me that you have asked General Wielhorski for the servants necessary for these batteries; I observe that it would not be up to him to provide them, but to the chief of staff. But you do not need it; of the 209 gunners attached to the Migliaretto front, there are only 59 in service; the surplus therefore gives you a large enough margin that you can avoide fatiguing the infantry with the artillery's discharge, even supposing that it is occupied with the construction of the epaulements. Make, therefore, my dear commander, all the proper arrangements for moving you away from this foreign aid.

Borthon

No. 67

Reports from General Wielhorski to General Foissac-Latour

Messidor 18, Year VII (6 July 1799)

The enemy started two redoubts in front of the Pajolo Canal, between Ceresa and Pradella. That of the left can easily beat the scarp before our battery on the road; the other beats Pajolo's battery, and the The Island Battery No. 6. I fired a few cannon shots at the workers this morning; some were killed, I saw one carried away.

It seems that the enemy puts a lot of activity and importance in these works. As he makes peasants work there, at the first cannon shot all the workers have fled; I saw them brought back to the work by an infantry detachment with blows of sticks. This is what has engaged me to place a howitzer in front of the work, to our right, which throws shells right into the work, while a 12pdr cannon enflides one of its faces. To beat the work to our left, I had a 5pdr and a 6pdr cannon, which cross their fires. At 11 o'clock, the workers left the work, probably to go to dinner, and I gave the order to the artillery officer who commanded these cannons to start firing again as soon as the workers would renew their work.

The number of the workers employed by the enemy, his perseverance, and the promptness with which he has constructed these works, prove that it was not mere cuts that he wished to make; the engineer officer, whom the citizen Maubert sent me, judged likewise on the spot.

Yesterday in the day we heard a cannonade, however feeble, on the side of Bozzolo, as well as the fire of musketry, but which seemed rather a fire of skirmishers.

The distance of the cannonade was estimated to be about four or five leagues away.

Wielhorski

Messidor 18, Year VII (6 July 1799).

The work of the enemy has increased considerably during the night; he continues to put the greatest activity into it. As the batteries for our cannon were not completed, and are not yet finished, I have not been able, by my fire, to delay the work. Near the village of Piétole, the enemy cut a lot of wood. Yesterday in the day we heard a cannonade and musketry on the side of Borgo-Forte.

Wielhorski

Messidor 20, Year VII (8 July 1799).

All night long, 11 guns have not ceased to play on the enemy's works; this fire did the best job. The enemy has abandoned his works; but he has begun a new one on his left, between the last battery and the tile works; all our fire is directed now on this new work, which proves that it is a countervallation they have undertaken. As the cannon intended to fire on these works will probably have to run all the way, I think it is useless to have embrasures done at this moment; besides because of the thickness of the dike, these embrasures require a lot of earth and work, it seems to me that we will always be in time to do them when the enemy has established his batteries. I am waiting for your orders in this respect, Citizen General. The water washed away this morning the lands which supported the bridge in front of the battery on the road, so that the bridge collapsed; I sent for a boat from the navy, to maintain communication with the tower ofCérèse.

Wielhorski.

Messidor 22, Year VII (10 July 1799).

Our artillery did not stop playing all night, with all the success we could wish for. The enemy's work has hardly advanced; and this morning, at half-past five, I saw eight to ten men come out of the trench, both killed and wounded; unfortunately, they will surely be almost all peasants.

The fire took yesterday evening at a little house behind the entrenchment; this greatly favored the throwing of shells during the night; judging by the way the artillery has been served, it is likely that the enemy has lost a lot of people.

To spare the gunners, I, in concert with the commander-in-chief of the artillery, ordered that only orderlies and an officer should be left all along the line of the works during the great heat of the day. The gunners will remain at Thé Island, always ready to go to their posts as soon as the officer sees the workers in train. At night we heard wagons coming from Pietro and heading towards Cérèse; they were fired at, but we could not tell what it was.

Wielhorski.

Messidor 22, Year VII (10 July 1799).

At 3 o'clock in the morning, the enemy attacked the Cérèse tower with six shots fired at almost the same time. This fire dismounted a 3pdr and shook the tower to the point that the rubble began to fall. At the same time the infantry, which had come from the back of the dike, broke the mill; the post was forced to retreat to the battery on the road, protected by the guard which was marching to get to the tower. We had a man killed, and two drowned in the battery ditch on the road; following this, the enemy began a very fierce cannonade on the whole front of my posts, starting with his boats, located at the entrance of the Mincio. He had only nine cannon, not counting two boats; but he walked them along the whole length of the line. We responded with a lively and well-fed fire, both of the battery on the road, and four cannons placed at the corner of the old line, as well as batteries at Pietole and those of the lunettes of Battery No. 6 and Battery No. 1 of Migliaretto. Our fire was so lively and so well-directed that it soon extinguished that of the enemy; in fact, towards 10 o'clock, the enemy did not shoot at all. During this cannonade happened several notable events. A 6pdr struck was in its mouth by a ball, without any gunner being hurt; another shot struck the wheel of a cannon and dismounted it, without touching any other gunner; finally, a ball struck a 12pdr caisson full of cartridges,

The firmness and zeal of the officers and gunners in general, deserve the highest praise. Among other things, Chef de bataillon Axamitowski, commanding the artillery at the Migliaretto front, showed a lot of zeal and activity, passing from one battery to another under enemy fire. Citizen Viereck, Deputy Commander-in-Chief of Artillery, personally pointed and directed, for a long time, the fire of Migliaretio Battery No. 1; after that he went ahead several times to watch his people and reconnoiter the enemy. The Polish artillery captain displayed rare activity and zeal. Citizen Bourotte, sergeant-major of French artillery, showed much calmness by making use of the 24pdr (which he directed after the Citizen Viereck had left it), as in a school exercise, by commanding all the maneuvers; he then went to the battery on the road. The Citizen Foubert, a gunner of the 7th Company, 2nd Regiment, and Citizen François, a Polish gunner, both orderlies of Migliaretto Battery No. 6, helped only by the infantry post, fired their battery very successfully. Citizen Krawczynski, a Polish artillery corporal, of the lunette guard, seeing that Battery No. 6 was more effective, went there to help the two orderlies. The artillery commander also praised Citizen Bobiliet, Sergeant in the 5th Regiment, who, in charge of the details of the service, did not cease to be very useful and to assist it even in many things that did not regard it; under the fire of the enemy, he had some guns changed and put back; he placed among them three very advantageously, and worked tirelessly for the good of the service.

Our loss, in spite of the terrible enemy fire, which was crossing the battery of the road, is reduced to one man, besides the three mentioned above. We were obliged to abandon to the enemy the howitzer and the 4pdr, which were in the tower, as well as all the rampart guns. At present, only a few guns can be fired from time to time, to prevent the enemy from returning to the tower, which he evacuated to the south, after having begun a work in front of the tower, and one between the tower and the village. He is now working on a battery on the right of the tower.

The loss of the enemy could not be assessed, but the ground in front of the tower was full of dead.

Wielhorski.

Messidor 23, Year VII (1 July 1799)

The enemy left us very quiet that night. Towards 4 o'clock in the morning they sent us nine shots at different times, but all of small caliber and not a shell. According to their fire, I judged that it was three or four pieces that they brought from Pietole to Pradella, and that on the road they stopped from time to time to fire. They did not work at all in the tower, nor in the work in front of it. As for the one I thought existed between the tower and the village, I recognized today that there was none. The smoke they were making yesterday, the men who came and went in these places, had deceived me, as well as those who thought they saw me.

During the night, many wagons have been heard moving from Pietro to Pradella, and many rockets were fired on the whole circumference of the fortress by the enemy. The tower seems to still be abandoned; there is only one sentry forward; it is probable, however, that there is a post at the mill. The 3pdr and rampart guns were removed that night, which proves, I believe, that they do not really intend to keep it.

Our works have not advanced much this night; however, Citizen Mauberta drew up a little plan, which I commissioned the artillery commander of the Migliaretto front to execute; this will greatly strengthen the position. I could not get the pikes to the battery on the road, since there is no banquette in the merlons, which are nearly six feet high. I wanted to place it on the communication between the road and the cannon on the left: but the parapet, degraded by the water, is not yet repaired, so that it is impossible to place anyone there. To speed up the necessary works, it would require the workers, the sappers and gunners being fatigued from the work be sent reinforcements. My garrison, which is on duty, can not supply them. Please, Citizen General, give me your orders in this respect.

Wielhorski.

Messidor 24, Year VII (12 July 1799).

The enemy has quietly allowed us to continue our work during the night, and even during the day; as he also worked, we sent him a few cannon shots, to which he did not reply, which might lead one to believe that he had withdrawn his artillery.

This opinion is again based on what we have heard at night, and seen yesterday evening, the enemy boats passing from the troop and moving effects or baggage from one bank to the other of the Mincio, that is from Pietro to Saint-Georges. At that distance we could not distinguish objects; but we presume the noise and the trouble they had in loading and unloading the boats, that it was artillery. Our work on the battery on the road has advanced well last night. I enclose here a copy of the report from my artillery commander, so if you would have the kindness, Citizen General, to give orders accordingly, if you consider them necessary. I have just ordered this commander, after having agreed with Citizen Borthon, to spare the shells as much as possible, and to fire them only when the enemy has fired them.

I thought he was below us to fight unevenly at this moment, and that we should only send him shot, when he sends us only shot.

Wielhorski

No. 68

Report of Artillery Chef de Bataillon Axamitowski to General Wielhorski

Messidor 24, Year VII (12 July 1799).

In spite of many obstacles and very little help given to me by the engineers, I took care myself in the construction and repair of the battery on the road. You have seen, Citizen General, the work I had done that night; it was, however, done by the gunners of my garrison, whom I had to have awaken three times since yesterday, 5 o'clock in the morning, till 8 o'clock today. The engineers have sent me an officer and nearly 40 sappers yesterday evening, who did nothing at all, remained only three hours, and retired at night.

At 11 o'clock they sent me 60 infantry volunteers; these helped me a lot. Today there are still about 40 sappers with a sergeant; but they work only on what is most essential, namely, the bases on which the epaulments and the crossbeams were to be placed.

It is indispensable, Citizen General, that you induce Citizen Maubert to take a part in this urgent work ordered by the General-in-Chief, to send someone to execute the plan to build the bases, and to raise the epaulements on which it is my duty to have the remainder done by my gunners, overwhelmed with the work they have had up to this moment, and the great part is done by the engineers, as tonight, on the base and the thickness of the parapet, on the left, where the howitzer was; this is to continue for all the front, the way to widen to the right of the 12pdr, which is on the right, where I need a crossbeam, which I will do. There are epaulements to raise; It is necessary for all this that today at 5 o'clock in the evening he should bring at least 200 workers, two engineers and some overseers, and they must be ordered to work six hours in a row; that is, from 6 o'clock until midnight, under the full moon. We must bring in two thousand sacks, another 2,000 pegs, and we must work hard.

As for the work of the gunners, provided they do not give me different orders from more than one side, I will take care of it as my duty.

Citizen Borthon just sent me an order to remove the howitzer that was isn the battery on the road, without order to replace it. Please give me your orders in this regard. Our work at Pietole continues, but it is also essential that the engineer do his job. I have crossbeams to install, which I cannot do without repairing the bases and the ground. The enemy is very quiet today; he, however, from time to time work on his works; we fired at them. I communicated the order concerning the conservation of ammunition, especially that of shells.

Axamatowski

No. 69

General Wielhorski to General Foissac-Latour

Messidor 25, Year VII (13 July 1799)

You have been informed, Citizen General, by daily reports how many men the Legion has lost from sickness. A similar situation state is sent daily to the commander of the fortress; but without having regard either to our strength, nor to many requests, he continues to charge us with the same service.

The strength of the 1st Battalion, such as it is today, comes to 212 fusiliers, 51 are on guard and 90 are at work, in total 141 men. There remain only 71 fusiliers free for service. Tomorrow it is necessary, as a result, as today, to add 70 men to those who have been in service, and who are not relieved.

The strength of the 2nd Battalion today is 264 fusiliers. It furnished 72 men for the guard and 90 workers, a total of 162 men. There remain free from service 102 men. As a result, tomorrow 60 men shall be newly employed in the service.

The healthiest are not in a state to sustain such fatigues, above all in the bad air of Mantua, and it is necessary to expect a wasting away of the corps if you do not find means to soften their service; but the General-in-Chief, who knows the strength of everything, shall confront them together and shall assure himself that there is no partiality in the distribution of the work. Then, I am sure, that the most just distribution of the work will occur, or at least everyone will be convinced that it cannot be otherwise, and the discontent that currently exists, because one supposes that we are given more of this work than others, shall cease.

Your zeal for the good of your subordinants, Citizen General, is too well known to me, for me not to expect a prompt response.

Wielhorski

Messidor 27, Year VII (15 July 1799)

At 5 o'clock in the morning the enemy unmasked four embrasures in a battery on the right of the Pajolo angle; he fird several shots and a stray shot killed two horses hitched to a caisson, on the dike which leads to the road to Pajolo.

Another battery, with three embrasures, was also unmasked, but it did not fire. This evening we heard some cannon and musketry fire on the side of Peschiera.

Wielhorski

Messidor 28, Year VII (16 July 1799)

At 6 o'clock in the morning, the enemy began to fire on our works on the battery on the road with seven small caliber cannon, which grealty disturbed them. This had engaged me, in concert with the artillery and engineer commanders, to issue orders to withdraw from this work, and to only work at night.

The battery at the Pajolo angle has been very happily evacuated this evening. Citizens Périgord, Borthon, and I, spent the morning reconnoitering and executing the orders that you gave us yesterday. There still remains to me in the first line nine small caliber cannon, not including the lunettes. This is all that exists to stop the enemy from advancing.

As in this moment it is impossible to put the artillery of the garrison in the city, because from one moment to another the gunners may be necessary; that The Island is uninhabitable, I believe it would be advantageous to encamp this garrison. There is, in the interior of the entrenched garrison, a spot appropriate for this. All that is missing is to have wood to construct some boats. I believe, as well, that it would be useful every night to encamp an infantry reserve. It would be close enough to support any point that the enemy might attack, as otherwise it takes two hours for the reserve to come during the night from the city. If you judged this appropriate, I pray you only, Citizen General, to issue orders that I be furnished the wood necessary for the construction of some boats.

Wielhorski

Messidor 29, Year VII (17 July 1799)

FIRST REPORT

The enemy constantly leaves to work peacefully; but he puts an astonishing effort into perfecting his own works. During this evening we heard wagons and many trains. Our works advance as well, but it is necessary that we draw many soldiers for this work, this evening at 7 o'clock.

We fired a few cannon shots, and we continued to fire a few now and then against the enemy's workers when they are heard. They have not responded since yesterday evening.

SECOND REPORT

The same day.

The enemy has fired a few cannon shots and fired a few bombs on the battery on the road, but without the least effect; all the shots fell in the water. I have established, this morning, a chain of little posts, running from the Pietole Battery to the angle of the Pajolo Dike, such that all my front is guarded. This evening we displaced two 12pdrs from the Pietole Battery, which were enfiladed and taken obliquely by four cannon and a howitzer. For two days now, we have no longer heard Russians songs, which they have the habit of singing at retreat. I presume they have left my posts.

THIRD REPORT

The same day.

The enemy has put in a great amount of work in a new battery, facing the battery on The Island. We fired an 8-inch bomb, full chamber and at 45 degrees of elevation, and it fell in the middle of the workers, where it detonated, and, as a result, had a great effect. However, as I know your intentions, I will not continue this firing without your authorization. I await your orders.

Wielhorski

Messidor 30, Year VII (18 July 1799)

The enemy has put much work into his batteries on the right and left of the village of Cérèse, and he is constructing a new one facing my battery on the road. I believe his plan is to heavily bombard on that side, to prevent us from sending assistance to Pradella, when they attack it. They fired about 20 howitzer shells at me during the day yesterday and this morning, but they had no effect. The battery that they began yesterday facing Battery No. 6 on The Island, has not advanced. They did not work on it this evening. My mortar battery has continued to fire during the night, from half hour to half hour with the same success, although the bombs for the 8-inch mortars are not the proper caliber.

I owe the accuracy of our fire to Citizen Bourotte, sergeant major, of whom I have spoken in my report of the 22nd. It is only due to the strength of the wedges and the ground that he was able to accurately fix the bombs in the mortar. He did the same with the 8-inch mortar, which could only with difficulty be served, because he lashed the bomb against the walls of the case; it is probable that the chamber was not accurately drilled in the center. There are very few people vis-à-vis my front; the tower still appears to be abandoned and we do not see any troop, nor even isolated soldiers pass and recross as before.

Wielhorski

Thermidor 1, Year VII (19 July 1799)

The enemy has left us in peace this morning; he has only fired two cannon shits from his battery at the Pajolo Angle.

Conforming to your order, I had a ricochet shot fired from Battery No. 6 on Thé Island, against the enemy works. It perfectly succeeded with a 12pdr, which was placed to enfilade the trench.

I also placed on the side of this cannon an 8-inch howitzer, which, I hope, will have a great effect; but as it is necessary to change the embrasure, the howitzer will not be in battery until this afternoon. The mortars of the battery on The Island continued to have the best effect. The parapet, of this same battery, necessary to place cannon, has been begun; but it appears that the engineering officer who directs this work ha never known that this is only a parapet; he did nothing more than straighten it; thickening the bottom, in such a manner that one loses a great part of the platform (which is already too narrow) where it is necessary to place a stopper. It will be necessary, I believe, for the commander of engineers to have the work inspected by someone else so that the workers are not fatigued by unnecessary work that will have to be undone later. In general, the works do not advance. The battery on the road, which requires only two crossbeams to be put under cover, is still not complete, even though we have worked on it for three nights. The artillery and the engineers are equally at fault. It is not for me to judge the fault or reason; but what is certain is that the work does not advance and it is essential, in order to hold this post when the enemy bombards it, that these crossbeams are in position. I have seen this morning two fishing books between the battery on The Island and the enemy's works. Nothing prevents these people from landing on the other side and carrying news to the enemy. It seems to me that from this point on it is necessary to prohibit any fishing. For that it is necessary, I believe, to gather all the fishing boats and have the Navy guard them; without this measure, it is impossible for us to prevent the enemy from receiving news of our daily condition.

Wielhorski

No. 70

Letter from General Foissac-Latour to Adjutant-General Kosinski

Mantua, Thermidor 2, Year VII (20 July 1799)

I applaud, my dear comrade, the seal and military knowledge you have shown in the observations you made in the letter you addressed to me dated the 1st of the month. I think, however, that your views are not applicable to the circumstances in which we find ourselves. The artillery and engineering commanders, with whom I consulted this morning, the plan in hand, are of the same opinion as me. I would be very much at ease if you could come yourself to confer in a little discussion. For this purpose come and dine with me this evening at 6 o'clock; I will tell you that which I have agreed to substitute for the means that you have proposed.

Froissac-Latour

No. 71

General Wielhorski to General Froissac-Latour

Thermidor 2, Year VII (20 July 1799)

Yesterday evening, at 8 o'clock, the enemy fired three batteries against that of the road, at the moment when the workers arrived.

The success of his fire is always the same. Today he only shoots when he sees a few people together.

In accordance with your orders, we have reconnoitered the Batteries Nos. 4 and 5 on Thé Island. They see perfectly the works of the enemy, and the location of the guns has been determined. We threw a few bombs that night, they all succeeded.

The work on the battery on the road does not advance, the sappers being occupied elsewhere with more essential tasks.

I believe that infantry workers, led by an artillery officer destined for that purpose, would easily complete the work, provided that they were provided with sandbags

It would be essential that this work be completed, both to put the battery under cover and no longer give the enemy the reasons to shoot.

Wielhorski

Thermidor 3, Year VII (21 July 1799).

The enemy is still shooting at our battery on the road; we answer them with the Pietro battery. It was observed yesterday that a cannon shot which when directly into the enemy battery, caused a lot of noise and screams; the battery was silenced immediately. Throughout the night we heard a lot of movement in the village of Pietole, including Russian songs; this language has been frequently heard. We also heard on the mountain side a very lively cannonade. Work was quite advanced tonight, especially at the battery on the road. Bombs have been thrown into the enemy works, all of which have been very successful.

Wielhorski

Thermidor 4 Year VII (22 July 1799).

The enemy continues to shoot against me; they fired in the direction of Thé Island Battery No. 6; yesterday and today they fired some 17pdr balls; two of these fell in the city. We heard that night a lot of artillery trains on the side of Pajolo.

Wielhorski

Thermidor 5, Year VII (23 July 1799)

Yesterday, about 8 o'clock in the evening, 20 to 30 enemy light infantry passed the Pajolo Canal at the salient angle of the dike, and, having hidden themselves in the reeds, fired a few shots at the post which is established there. This shootout had neither results nor success. This morning, an equal number came unarmed, to the edge of the marsh in the reeds; it seems to be for work; however, neither mallets nor noise were heard which could indicate the type of work. Our works had advanced well that night on the road battery; next night, I hope everything will be complete. A few cannon shots were fired and some bombs were thrown into the enemy's works, always with the greatest success. The enemy, as usual, fired his batteries, two of them on the battery on the road, and one against the Bastion No. 6 on Thé Island. Yesterday evening a 17pdr ball broke a few spokes on the wheels of the two cannons in our Pajolo Battery, but they are not out of service.

Wielhorski.

Thermidor 6, Year VII (July 24, 1799).

At 3 o'clock, the enemy began to fire on my whole front with 15 cannons, besides the two boats, which also sent me some shot. All their blows were directed at the battery on the road, on Thé Island and on the Migliaretto Bastion No. 1. So far I have only one man wounded at the post of the entrenched camp, by a stray ball. Two women, in the artillery district of The Island, had one arm and one leg carried away. The enemy is still firing, but he has slowed it down a lot.

We answered him with all the cannons that could play; the artillery was perfectly well conducted, as much for the accuracy of the shots as for the coolness and the activity put into the effort.
Wielhorski

During the night of Thermidor 6th /7th, Year VII (24/25 July 1799)

Commander Girard tells me that the first battery on the road is carried away, that the enemy is in front of the entrenched camp. I'm so unhappy that I can not get out of bed.

Wielhorski

No. 72

Letter from General Foissac-Latour to General Wielhorski

Thermidor 7, Year VII, at 2 o'clock (25 July 1799).

I need to learn, General, what effective arrangements are being made to take back the battery from the dike. I am informed that the enemy has arrived equipped with tools to entrench, and if we leave him the time and the faculty, he will make a bridgehead at this point, will settle on the dike, and will envelop us in this part of a circular row of batteries. I beg you to tell me what you think of it, to confer with General Fontanieu and the brave Girard, and to send me a reply. On the other hand, the workers are at the foot of the Pradella Glacis, buried in ditches. At 2 o'clock we will have a meeting.

Foissac-Latour.

REPLY.

I believe, general, that it is indeed very essential to flush the enemy out of the battery on the road; I am even sorry that it could not have been done yet; by settling down along the old dyke, it will be very inconvenient for us; and we do not have a work that sees this dike in the rear, so that we will be unable to harm him. A very important consideration is that the new lunette on the road is not in a state of defense, being very little advanced, which weakens my center a great deal. I am going to ask General Fontanieu and Girard to come to my position; I will confer with them, and I will not fail, general, to send you our plans and our observations. I will be carried on a stretcher, General, to go to the meeting, if it is impossible for me to go there on foot.

Wielhorski.

No. 73

Report of Chef de bataillon Axamitowski,
of the Polish Artillery,
Commandant of this Arm on the Front of Thé and Migliaretto,
To General Fontanieu.

Thermidor 7, Year VII (25 July 1799)

I send you, Citizen General, the detailed state of the cannons, which are in position at the different batteries of our post, with the state and quantity of the men necessary to serve them. We have 17 cannons at the Thé Island Battery: I have designated only 50 men to serve them, and I think this is a great economy. To the Migliaretto Bastions Nos. 1 and 2, there are seven pieces; I have assigned 80 men to them.

At the lunette, on the road, eight men for two cannons.

At the entrenched camp, 18 men for 10 cannons.

At the New Lunette, 20 men for 10 cannons.

At the battery on the Pajolo Dike, four men.

The quantity of men needed for the batteries would be 124; now the cannons that have to be served by these men are in the case of being fired all at once. If I do not have this number of men, I am not in a position to answer for my post; and it is not enough to be able to supply 180 men for the batteries, it is still necessary to raise them. We would then need 250 gunners, and then we will have no more reproaches to make, because my batteries would beare devoid of gunners; I beg you to take into consideration my painful situation. I have only 100 gunners available in my garrison: I ask you how I can supply such extensive needs. I observe you that out of these 100 men, four or six patients die every day.

Axamitowski.

No. 74

Report of Général de brigade Meyer, Commander of the Defense of Migliaretto and Thé Island And the Replacement for General Wielhorski, to General Foissac-Latour.

Thermidor 8, Year VII (26 July 1799)

According to the opinion of the defense council and your orders, Fort Saint-Georges is evacuated. We worked on it immediately. All the munitions that could be carried away were thrown into the ditches of Saint-Georges or into the lake. All the howitzers and bronze artillery were brought back to the city, with the exception of one piece that remained in the cemetery and could not be retrieved. The iron cannons have been left; and, according to your instruction, they were spiked, and the wheels of the carriages were cut to pieces. The commander of the artillery Iakubowski and Lieutenant Meunier were again of the greatest use to me and contributed greatly in accelerating this important work; we were supported by the zeal of all our troops.

On the same evening, I was eager to send you, from the depot of the 45th, what is indispensable to strengthen the Migliaretto camp, where there was reason to fear a repeated attack.

It was nearly midnight when the first rocket I had sent up in the air warned the outside guards to abandon their posts in silence and to withdraw under the cannon of the fort.

The internal troops still retained their place; a second rocket announced to the troops of all arms that they had to meet in the great place d'arms.

The third gave the signal to depart. The whole column set out to return to town, and the grenadiers of 56th, to protect the retreat, mounted immediately on the parapet of the St. George bridgehead.

These brave men, as commendable by their disinterestedness, their discipline, and their delicacy, as by a foolhardy courage, perceived, at the moment when I ordered their retreat. There were small pieces of artillery, which had been placed on the flank of the bridgehead, and that for lack of sufficient horses it had not been possible to tow them back into the city, and many of them immediately began to bring them down; they brought them back with them.

Nothing equaled their pain when they learned of the order to evacuate Fort Saint-Georges; they called it their favorite colony, because they had seen its establishments born and formed under their eyes; they had so many times cemented its maintenance with their blood! You remember, general, that the various camps I had established seemed like so many separate villages: the men who had gathered there had built, each at his pleasure, vast and convenient huts on the ruins of a city once opulent and flourishing by its industry and its arts. Each cabin had its shelters against the sun, domestic animals, its garden formed with taste and intelligence, its household established in form. It was there, under a burning and murderous climate, that they kept talking about their dear country, their families in mourning, the splendor of their ancient exploits; it was there, in the midst of the sweetest harmony, that they had so often consoled themselves with all the privations imposed on them by the present moment, and that they were constantly drawing new strengths in the love of their country. and in that noble emulation, which had been established among them. As soon as the troops had all passed the double drawbridge of St. George's, I had it immediately broken up and destroyed, according to your instructions. This operation finished, I went to town to give you a temporary verbal account; it was then 2 o'clock in the morning.

Meyer

From the Same to the Same.

The same day.

I have taken this morning, my general, in conformace with your orders, the command of the Migliaretto front, in the place of General Wielhorski, whose illness has obliged him to cede to me his post. The enemy's fire is always the most sustained. They particularly fire against the Saint-Alexis Bastion and the right branch of The Island, where they directed their principal shots to batter a breach.

We only weakly responded to them; we did not have sufficient gunners; they are on edge; they lack the manpower to make the most urgent repairs on the platforms, which are falling into pieces. I have had fired, in my presence, at the right branch of the Thé, several bombs in the enemy works, which were opposite it and I have had the opportunity to be very content with the skill of those who had fired them.

The enemy works hard to bombard the reverse of the entrenched camp at Migliaretto; he has established batteries at Saint-Georges, perfectioned those at Casa-Zanetti, and established a third at Zippata.

Meyer

No. 75

Letter from General Meyer, Commander of the Defense of Migliaretto and The Island, to Chef de brigade Maubert.

Thermidor 9, Year VII (29 July 1799)

I forward to you, citizen commandant, the report which has just been made to me, and whihch informs us that the dike, which joins the Saint-Nicholas Bastion to Migliaretto Bastion No. 2 has been broken. The waters flow with astonishing rapidity. I think that we must work on it immediately, and with activity, otherwise our ditches will soon be exhausted.

Meyer

No. 76

Report from General Meyer to General Foissac-Latour.

Thermidor 9, Year VII (27 July 1799)

The enemy has not stopped all night firing bombs and howitzer shells. Their fire resumed their ordinarly activity at daybreak. A shot struck the dike that links the entrenched camp with the Saint-Charles Battery of the city, the waters of the ditch of the body of the fortress flew into the lower lake. The breach became from moment to moment more considerable, such that if it had not been repaired immediately, the ditches of the body of the fortress would be dry in an hour.

Meyer

No. 77

Report of General Moreau to the Minister of War, On the Battle of Novi, given on Fructidor 28, Year VII (15 August 1799)

It appears, Citizen Minister, that the battle of Novi was an affair of paraties, that everyone tells it in his own way, and that one wishes to attribute to his friends or his enemies the successes and the setbacks that have been experienced there. It is important that we know in the Republic the most exact truth about this unfortunate event, but which will always honor the courage of the brave Army of Italy.

The army under the orders of General Joubert was divided into two corps: the one on the right commanded by the General Saint-Cyr, having two divisions under the orders of Generals Watrin and Laboissière, and occupying debouches from Genoa to Novi, had from 15,000 to 16,000 men; the one on the left at the orders of General Perignon, also composed of two divisions, commanded by Generals Grouchy and Lemoine, guarded the Bormida and Tanaro Valleys. The rest of the army guarded the Levant and Ponent Rivers, the Col de Tende and the city of Genoa.

The General-in-Chief, whose plan was to liberate Tortona, decided to attempt the meeting of the army at Novi. He repaired to the corps on the left, went from Savona by the valley of the Bormida to Acqui and Capriata, where he left about 2,000 men, to ensure his subsistence, and arrived, during the night of Fructidor 27th, on the heights of Novi, and he placed his left at Pasturana, the right hand resting on the left of General Saint-Cyr, who had arrived there the same day, at 7 o'clock in the morning. His right was supported on the Scrivia; a small corps of troops, under the orders of General Dąbrowski, invested the fort of Serravalle.

The same day the enemy army received the troops from the siege of Mantua; it had no more detachments, and was entirely united; its right was on Bosco, its center at Pozzolo, its left on Tortona, and its reserve to Rivalta. It came to 48,000 infantry and 10,000 horse. Its right, under the orders of Generals Kray and Bellegarde, had about 22,000 Austrian infantry, and came to be placed on the evening of the 27th in front of General Perignon's corps, overflowing it a little to the left, which was to cover the Pasturana in Capriata.

The left of the enemy, about 18,000 Austrian infantry, stretched from Pozzolo to Scrivia, facing our right. Its reserve, with 8 battalions of grenadiers, 3 or 4 infantry batalions, and 6 squadrons of cavalry, remained at Rivalta. The enemy cavalry was in the second line of these attacks, and divided nearly equally between them.

The Commander-in-Chief had plans to attack the enemy and could not take up a defensive position. The appearance of the considerable forces, which he found against him, caused him to assemble, on the evening of the 27th, at Novi, his généraux de division, and all agreed that, especially with our inferiority of cavalry, it would be more than imprudent to descend into an immense plain, where the slightest setback would lead to the complete defeat of the army.

Although the General-in-Chief did not share with me all his plans, I thought I saw that he was determined not to attack the enemy, but to take his former positions to wait for the movement of the Army of the Alps to rid him of some of the forces opposed to him. He ended the meeting by sending everyone back to their posts, saying that the reconaissances of the morrow would determine him.

At 5 o'clock in the morning of the 28th, we were about to mount our horses to ride along the line, when an orderly came to announce that our left had been attacked. We immediately went before the front on the right. The enemy was in battle formation about two cannon shots distance from our position and had not yet made any movement. Upon arriving at the point where they were fighting, I remarked to the General-in-Chief that I fond some troops badly placed. He invited me to rectify the positions of part of them and he charged himself with correcting the other. I moved to his left about 500 or 600 toises.

About a half hour after I had left the General-in-Chief (it was then nearly 7 o'clock in the morning), I saw that the enemy was making shocking progress on my right. I saw our troops retiring in disorder and the enemy'ssuccess was more dangerous as it separated the corps of Generals Saint-Cyr and Pérignon. I immediately sent the order to General Colli, who held the extreme left of our right, to send two battalions to re-establish the battle. I had march on my side some of the troops that I had placed, and who had the enemy behind them, and in whose rear they found themselves. Teir attack was resolute and stopped the corps that was making progress. General Serras also rallied his troops which I had seen recoiling. He pushed them into the battle with much courage and the success of this first attack remained completely with us. I learned at this tiem of the death of the brave General Joubert; and although I was without character with the army, having taken no command, each having sent me to ask for orders, I thought that the good of the army required that I take command of it. The enemy had attacked at the same time the other troops of the left; their efforts were repulsed everywhere. Generals Pérignon, Grouchy, Lemoine, Grandjean, Charpentier, Partouncau, and Gareau, commanded these troops; Generals Richepanse and Clausel commanded their reserve; the Russians then began to attack Novi, defended by Général de brigade Gardanne, who was part of General Laboissière's division. The other two brigades, under the orders of Generals Quesncl and Colli, filled the plateaux from Novi to the right of General Pérignon. Divisional general Watrin, having under his orders the Généraux de brigade Darnaud, Petitot, and Calvin, descended into the plain, attacked the Russian left flank, cleared Novi, na d completely defeated them. The ardor of the troops pushed them further than their general officers wished.

I went to this attack of which I had been warned; but, approaching Novi, I saw our determined success, and I returned to the left, where the enemy had just recommenced their attack. General Perignon told me that he supported himself, and to watch on his right. I ordered General Colli to march again, and his troops helped those of General

Lemoine to repulse the enemy. Hardly had our affairs been re-established on this point, than the Russians, with fresh troops, attempted to again attack Quesnel's and Colli's brigades, forming to the left of General Laboissière. Our artillery had been placed on the plateaux by General Debelle, supported by the troops next to them. The enemy's attack, though impetuous and executed by considerable forces, was repulsed by canister and musketry fire directed with a coolness and a precision that is hardly found in the maneuvers of the best trained troops.

The attacks on the left succeeded each other for two hours, at two hour inervals; on the right the enemy was alternately at both extremities, but everywhere he experienced the most obstinate resistance.

About 3 o'clock in the afternoon, Novi and Quesnel's and Colli's brigades were still under attack. General Watrin had descended into the plain to support them, and this movement had been completely successful; but the reserve from Rivalta arrived along the Scrivia, and quickly gained the plateaus behind our right. Another corps, coming from the blockade of Torlone, also went to Serravalle, and forced General Dąbrowski to leave the blockade of this fort. General Watrin's troops went as fast as possible to stop this movement; but the soldiers, exhausted by nearly 12 hours of marching and fighting, did not arrive in time. Many collapsed from fatigue; the enemy was marchiung with extraordinary speed to seize the road from Novi to Gavi, and if this movement had been entirely successful, the the army was done.

Fortunately General Saint-Cyr had kept three reserve battalions at his center, and a small body of cavalry under the orders of General Guerin. He had the enemy attacked just as he was about to settle on this road. The 106th, by a most brilliant charge, stopped the enemy's efforts, took General Lusignan, and gave us time to evacuate Novi and withdraw all the troops still engaged in the plain.

The position of the left and the rest of Laboissière's division was extremely dangerous; the artillery could no longer retreat by Novi, and there was only one way left by Pasturana; I ordered it to take it, and I sent the order to General Perignou to follow the same movement, ordering that all his troops resume their old positions. The retreat of this part of the army began at about 5 o'clock.

All the double caissons and the least necessary pieces went to Pasturana, and we began to leave the plateau half an hour later, continually harassed by the enemy; unfortunately, his numerous forces had enabled him to throw quite a large number of parties on all the roads, which stopped the march of the convoy near Pasturana. In this village there was an encumbrance of guns and caissons, which had the double inconvenience of stopping our march and rendering the soldier uneasy about his retreat: some troops were hastily sent forward, which cleared the way: the convoy resumed its march, but we had lost an hour, and we had the enemy on our hands. Some of our troops were sent by the paths to the right and left of the village; some shaken, even in disorder, in spite of their chiefs.

Generals Perignon, Grouchy, and Colli stood at the head of the village, and performed prodigies of valor with a battalion of the 68th, one of the 64th, the 6th Hussar Regiment, and the 16th Dragoon Regiment; but overwhelmed by numbers and embarrassed by the convoy, they fell into the hands of the enemy, covered with wounds. Placed in the village of Pasturana, I saw the impossibility of saving all the artillery, and I had sent order by order to these generals to abandon it; but either they could not execute them, or that they would not execute them, for we were already surrounded by enemies, and, in the darkness, I was obliged to retire to Gavi without hearing from them; I was still hoping that they could have reached the road to Capriata and Acqui, where we had some troops.

The army was almost all gathered around Gavi; I directed each corps to its former position.

Our exact loss was about 5,000 wounded, 300 to 400 killed, 800 to 900 prisoners; we left 40 artillery wagons in Pasturana, two-thirds of which were caissons. If many wagon drivers had not cut the traces of their horses, we would have lost only a half of this. We took from the enemy 2,000 prisoners and two guns while fighting.

Many motives have determined the loss of this battle; first, the disproportion of enemy forces, which exceeded ours by a third in infantry and three-fourths in cavalry. We occupied a battlefield from which we had to march to the enemy, and where we should not have accepted battle. It was an immense expanse, which gave us only two passes to withdraw and from its support on the right, which was the fort of Serravalle, was occupied by the enemy; the General-in-Chief was well aware of all these inconveniences, and I have no doubt that he would have reoccupied the old positions again by the same evening, if the enemy had given him time. We still had a significant disadvantage when fighting, which was not being able to take advantage of our successes. The repulsed enemy could not be broken; he ran to reform himself in the plain, where we could not pursue him, as he was under the shelter of his cavalry, and recommenced his attacks as soon as he was reformed.

It took our troops more than human courage to sustain in this position more than 12 hours of fighting, without having had time to eat. I am convinced that if fatigue had not prevented them from going behind our right with the speed, which the march of the enemy required, we could have stopped their progress; but the soldiers and officers were weary. We moved all our wounded to Genoa, although without means of transport. The prisoners were very useful for this purpose.

The enemy admits in all his reports the loss of 10,000 men, while the local inhabitans claim it was 15,000, and you must believe that if it had not been immense, it would not be limited to probing our positions, since the Army of the Alps, whose strength it knew perfectly could not threaten him until the 11th of the next month.

There, Citizen Minister, are the exact details of the battle of Novi, the bloodiest of this war, and which, though disadvantageous for us, has brought terror into the ranks of our enemies. The spirit of division will throw disfavor on such or such corps of our troops, on such or such generals: I dare assure you that we have done our duty as devoted republicans. We surely made mistakes, but infinitely less than the enemy, who did not know how to profit from his immense superiority, and the advantage of his terrain to destroy the entire army.

The chief-of-staff sends you the names of the corps and generals who have fought. This is the truest eulogy that can be made of them.

Moreau.

No. 78

Report of the Chief of Staff of the Right Wing of the Army of Général de division Massol, Commandant of Ligura, the City of Genoa and its Forts in a State of Siege

Headquarters at Novi
Brumaire 2, Year VIII (24 October 1799)

General, this morning the enemy, by order of the General Saint-Cyr, was attacked at Pasturana, Bezaluzzo and Bosco; he was completely beaten, according to the wise and excellent dispositions of the general, who had his horse killed during the affair. Three cannons, 1,000 prisoners, and all the points attacked were carried; among others, that of Bosco, where the enemy had his camp, and received the fight.

More than the ordinary intrepidity of the French allowed them to obtain such great successes on an immense plain; without cavalry and without artillery, where 4,000 French attacked 5,000 Austrians in an excellent position; they overthrew them and routed them, despite seven cannons and about 1,200 Austrian cavalry horses, against which the French column had none.

I will give you, General, further details; I cannot, at this moment, name to you the units that have greatly distinguished themselves; but you know those who make up the right wing; the 106th. the 3rd, and the 62nd Demi-brigades, and the Poles among others, were particularly well-illustrious.

This affair was directed and executed by Generals Watrin, Dąbrowski, Jablonowski, and Darnaud, under General Saint-Cyr. The enemy is now behind Bormida, and I hope he will not pass it again.

Greetings and consideration.

Guyot.

No. 79

The Minister of War to Général de division Dąbrowski, Commander of the 1st Polish Legion

Paris, Floreal 7, Year VIII (17 April 1800).

By your letter of Germinal 15th, last (April 5, 1800), you invite me, Citizen General, to take into consideration the fate of those officers and soldiers of the Legion whom you command, who, by the consequences of wounds received in the service of the Republic, are unable to continue their activity.

These brave soldiers are entitled to the benefits of the government, as well as the officers and soldiers of the national troops; they are eligible in the same cases as the latter, either in the demi-brigades of national veterans, when they are still in the possibility of serving in the interior or in other places, or at the national Hôtel des Invalides, or finally, to the enjoyment of their retirement pay, according to the law of the Fructidor 28th, Year VII, when they will be recognized as being absolutely incapable of doing any service.

In order for me to be able to grant one of these three kinds of retirement to those whom you consider to be elegible, it is necessary that you send me for each individual:

1.) A memoir which establishes the duration of his service in the armies of the Republic;
2.) The campaigns he has made;
3.) The circumstances and the time when he was injured, and which further indicate the reward for which he will be offered. The presentation of this report will be certified by the Legion's Board of Directors.
4.) A certificate of health officer of the corps or hospitals of the

army, which notes the seriousness of the wounds and the privations which result from it.

These two documents will be referred by a commissioner of war, and approved by the General Inspector of the Army, either by you or, in your absence, by the general who commands the division of which the 1st Polish Legion is a part.

I beg you to observe, moreover, that each report requesting, a pension, must mention the place where the member concerned wishes to retire.

Carnot.

No. 80
Historical Journal of the Army of Italy, by General-in-Chief Brune, of Frimaire 27 to Nivôse 26, Year IX of the French Republic (December 18, 1800, to January 16, 1801), Made and addressed to the Minister of War by Général de division Oudinot, Chief of the General Staff.

At headquarters in Treviso,
Nivôse 27, Year IX (17 January 1801).

Citizen Minister,

During the course of the glorious campaign which the Army of Italy opened and ended in the space of 30 days, I had the honor to send to you the reports of its marches and the actions which have illustrated them; but these reports having sometimes had to feel effects of the precipitation and the continuity of the movements, I make a point of presenting to you today all the operations of the campaign, jealous to make known to the government the name of the brave men who are distinguished, and assign to them the tribute of glory to which they have so much a right.

I will not neglect any facts, any details, knowledge, or reports that have come to me.

The Brumaire 30th (November 11, 1800), the army was set in motion for the resumption of hostilities, fixed for Frimaire 1st, according to the denunciation made by General-in-Chief Brune to the Count de Bellegarde, General-in-Chief of the Austrian army.

Our situation in Italy forced us to defend the Genoese coast against the incursions of the English, who, since the occupation of Tuscany by our troops, had given credibility to the rumors of a pending descent to seize Livorno. Major General Dulaulois, commander in Liguria, had to pay particular attention to guaranteeing the Gulf of La Spezia from any maritime enterprise, while General Miollis, having under his orders a brigade, a regiment of French cavalry, and the Cisalpine Legion of Major General Pino, opposed the enterprises of the Neapolitan Army, commanded by de Damas, who combined his operations with General Sominariva, commanding a corps of 7,000 Austrians at Ancona, and with de Millius, who commanded another of 4,000 men at Ferrara. Their goal was to invade Romagna, the Ferrarois, and subsequently invade Tuscany, or force us to a powerful diversion on the right bank of the Po.

General Miollis, therefore, had sufficient strength for a short-lived defense; because it was beyond the Mincio that we had to consolidate our power in Italy, and we must not make the mistake of weakening the army too much to preserve the establishments which a victory should give us.

The General-in-Chief contented himself, after putting Fort Urbain in a state of defense, to leave on the right bank of the Po, under the orders of General Petitot, an observation corps of about 3,000 men, French and Cisalpine, for observe from Bologna the movements of Generals Sommariva and Millius.

General Petitot had orders to keep himself as near as possible to the enemy, to oblige him by his demonstrations not to make detachments on the left bank of the Po, by depriving him of the knowledge of the troops opposing him, to which was joined, however, the brave Bologna National Guard, 4,000 strong. This disposition had its full effect: the efforts of De Damas, who penetrated and was beaten in Tuscany by the brave Miollis, Sommariva's marches towards Ferrara, and Millius' attacks, produced no considerable event. to divert the General-in-Chief from the plan he had adopted.

Lieutenant-General Soult commanded in Piedmont: his experience, and his perfect knowledge of the country, were necessary to destroy the influence of the enemy, who did not despair of forming a general insurrection behind us at the first news of a setback. The available forces consisted of four Piedmontese battalions, all the depots of the army, a regiment of French cavalry, and two of Piedmontese cavalry regiments.

The interior of Cisalpine showed no appearance of trouble; General Lapoype commanded there.

The active army, with 55,000 combatants, including 8,000 cavalry, was placed behind the Chiesc and Oglio, the right supported by the Po, and the left on the Caffaro River, above Lake Idro, where it had to communicate with that of the Grisons. General Rochambeau commanded the second division of the left wing, then occupied Ponte di Legno, the Val, Camonica, and the outlets of the Tonal where the troops of the Army of Grisons were to relieve ours. General Delmas commanded the vanguard, General Dupont the right, General Suchet the center, General Moncey the left, and General Michaud the reserve; it was composed of a French division, commanded by the brave General Gardanne, who had just been exchanged, and a division of Poles, commanded by General Dąbrowski.

General Davout was at the head of the cavalry reserve. General Kellermann commanded the division of cavalry, and General Rivaud the division of dragoons: 160 guns, 100 of which were attached to the divisions and 60 to the reserve under the command of General Laclos, formed the army's artillery; it was of similar caliber, well stocked, and organized so as to procure a good and easy service. This creation was due to the constant care of General Marmont, who developed the greatest talents during the course of the campaign. Brigadier Alix, who distinguished himself in all circumstances, was the Director General of the Parks.

The enemy army, with 80,000 men entrenched behind the Mincio, on a ground bristling with redoubts and island forts, under the protection of 100 cannon and three fortresses, had its army corps, properly speaking, on the line of the Mincio, supporting his flanks at Montebaldo and Po. Lake Garda, on his right, was covered with a flotilla of 27 ships, three of which were armed with 12 cannon each; and, to ensure their cruisers Sermione Island had been fortified. This position had the advantage of intercepting the great communications of Desenzano at Peschiera and causing fears of descent on the right of the lake.

General Wukassowich's corps, deployed from Trento as far as the outlets of the Tonal, had the double object, according to the circumstances, to prevent us from turning Lake Garda, to penetrate to Trent, to defend the Tonal against the Army of Grisons, or to envelop our left in descending through the valleys in the Bergamasque and the Brescian.

The vanguard, commanded by Baron von Hohenzollern, with a strength of 20,000 men, was entrenched on the right of the Mincio; his outposts extended from Desenzano to Borgo-Forte.

The Convention of Castiglione prohibited the Austrians from havnig either entrenchments or fixed positions on the right of the Mincio.

The same conditions were to be observed by the French army from Chiese and the Lower Oglio; but as the enemy, by cutting off Sermione Island and fortifying the Volta, had broken the treaty, the General-in-Chief resolved to seize Lonato, and Salo Cove on Lake Garda; he thus made himself master of an excellent position, and deprived the Austrians of a safe harbor where he could have a flotilla built to oppose theirs.

General Moncey occupied Salo, and General Delmas established his vanguard on the superb heights of Lonato. Such was the situation of the Army of Italy on Frimaire 1st (22 November), that it could even take the offensive that day; but the Army of Grisons had to co-ordinate its movements with ours and become an intermediary between us and the Army of the Rhine. Only Baraguay d'Hillier's division had been able to reach Valtelline; the abundance of the snow and the rigor of the season retarded the progress of the other divisions; so we were obliged to hold ours in position, and to observe the enemy; they were anxious about our plans, and fearing that we might concentrate on Trent, they then sent a large part of their forces there, while General Damas entered Tuscany, and General Sominariva approached the Po, where the Austrians and insurgents united. At the same time the plan was immediately formed to take the important post of Marcaria on the Oglio. The Austrians hoped at least that this attack, by which they seemed to want to cut our communications with the Po, would force us to weaken ourselves in our beautiful mountain positions. The General-in-Chief, having received the notice in time, made known to the generals of the right and center the plans of the enemy on the position of the line where their troops were established, General Calvin, of Monnier's division was immediately ordered to settle at San Martino, to see to the preservation of Marcaria. Despite the continual rain, the troop showed the greatest patience and the greatest resolution, there was never more security and activity.

Frimaire 14th (December 5th), General Calvin was on a reconnaissance towards Torre-d'Oglio where the enemy pretended to want to erect a boat bridge, when a large body of infantry, supported by cavalry and artillery presented itself at Campitello and San Michele, with the intention of surprising Marcaria. Our posts were forced to retreat; Général de brigade Ferey, at the head of the 24th Légère, made vigorous measures of defense. At the head of 200 men, and a platoon of the 11th Hussars, commanded by Sous-Lieutenant Duvergés, Captain Chollet, seeing his retreat cut, resolved to make use of his bayonets, overwhelmed the infantry, and repelled a detachment of cavalry that supported it. Meanwhile, General Calvin arrived at the sound of musketry and cannon; it had two battalions of the 24th Légère and a squadron of the 11th Hussars commanded by Captain Sainte-Marie. This help arrived in time; courage was about to give way to numbers: the fight resumed.

The enemy was shaken; the 11th Hussars attacked with advantage the Erdody Hussars; Captain Chollet so intelligently turned the 6th Austrian Jäger Battalion, that it laid down its arms and was taken prisoner. The success of this affair was complete and praises the talent and the courage of General Calvin, the resolution of Chef de brigade Ferey, and advantageously designates Captain Chollet; Maréchal de logis Radhuillet earned praise, as did Sous-Lieutenant Laforest of the 2nd Cisalpine Regiment. The 24th Demi-brigade and the 11th Hussars proved themselves worthy of their reputations.

However, the Austrians, under the orders of de Millius, supported by Sommariva's corps, which had marched on Imola, advanced ahead of Ferrara, made themselves masters of Bondeno, captured a Cisalpine battalion, and pushed parties as far as Guastalla. General Petitot, in these circumstances, made the arrangements that were required, and, not believing himself strong enough, concentrated his troops at Modena. The National Guard of Bologna was not shaken and had a good countenance; its conduct deserves the highest praise. Fortunately, Sommariva lost time and missed the opportunity offered by his superiority of numbers. Quickly informed of these movements, the General-in-Chief had sent a reinforcement of two battalions of line infantry, and a regiment of cavalry under the orders of General Jablonowski. This officer, accustomed to partisan warfare, made Sommariva believe that he had managed to make a strong diversion to us. Tuscany caused great anxiety, but General Miollis reassured us by his resolution and his vigorous dispositions; with a handful of men he imposed on the entire Neapolitan army. The troops of the Army of the Grisons, however, arrived successively, and, according to the letters received from the headquarters at Chiavenna, they were to be in position on the 25th. The army had heard the happy news of the victory at Hohenlinden. The army erupted with joy and expressed its impatience to fight. Nothing, indeed, delayed our offensive operations: the detachments from Rochambeau's division had just been relieved at Tonal, and the Splughen had been passed. The enemy, foreseeing that we should not delay in finding him, thought it expedient to come, on the 25th, to reconnoitre our line with artillery. His main forces were deployed before Lonato; a few sharpshooters executed a fairly sharp fire; but there was no important action. The General-in-Chief, accurately informed of the intention of the enemy to concentrate their forces for a near attack, and, according to the last letters, not yet able to count on coordinating actions with the Army of the Grisons, whose troops were detained by the difficulty of the marches in mountains surrounded by precipices, and covered with snow, left the Italian Legion, commanded by General Lecchi to unite the movement of the two armies, and decided to march forward. On the 27th, the reserve division, the artillery and the cavalry, encamped in the Montechiaro plain; the headquarters were transferred to Castelnedolo. A great reconnaissance was ordered for the next day; its aim was to check the position of the Austrians on the right of the Mincio, and to know the importance they attached to the different points of their line. This reconnaissance perfectly fulfilled the views of the General-in-Chief and gave him the opportunity of judging for himself the ardor and good will of the troops. Everywhere the enemy posts were overthrown; the enemy lost 150 prisoners and had many more dead and wounded. Our loss was very slight; the aide-de-camp of General Cassagne, employed at the vanguard, was wounded dangerously; the army corps of the center occupied the ground destined for it; Citizen Bouquet, commander of the 13th Chasseur à cheval Regiment, executed at the head of his regiment several brilliant and perfectly directed charges; a brigadier of this corps, wounded and dismounted, seized an enemy horse, and returned to the charge.

On the 29th (20 December 1800) the army established itself on the positions from which it had driven the enemy the day before.

On the right wing, Major-General Watrin ordered General Musnier to march at daybreak at the head of the 6th Légère and 22nd Demi-brigade to reconnoiter Rodigo and Santa Maria, who met the enemy a mile from Gazoldo, he overtook it and pursued it until near Santa Maria, then returned to Gazoldo, and left a battalion of the 6th Légère under the orders of Chef de bataillon Sarret, in position at 1,000 before, while Chef de bataillon Jumelle, of the 22nd Légère cleared the enemy from Rodigo and took from them the flour and grain they had gathered there.

Soon the enemy, seeing that he had only one battalion before him thought he could impose on it with demonstrations of his numerous cavalry, and even capture it; but this attack, although carried out with much superior forces, and supported by an impetuous charge of cavalry, could not intimidate the brave Chef de bataillon Sarret; a moment was enough for him to rally his outposts, to put his battalion in order, and to use his carabineers to oppose the first shock of the Austrians under the protection of their fire; his battalion took a more advantageous position, defended itself with bravery, and gave General Musnier time to come to his aid. The other two battalions of the 6th Légère and the 22nd Légère arrived from Gazoldo with a squadron of the 11th Hussars; then the enemy was in turn forced to withdraw, retiring on Santa Maria. The fall of night ended the pursuit.

In the center of the army, General Clauzel's brigade, to return to Guidizolo, was forced to drive out the enemy a second time.

General Colli's brigade of Loison's division, was attacked by several regiments in front of Cerezola and received them at half-range without firing; the enemy, astonished by this good countenance, retreated in disorder, and lost 300 prisoners.

On the left wing, two battalions of the 102nd met the enemy at Solferino, and drove them away; the 3rd, directed on Cavriana, experienced a long resistance; but led by General Roudet, there in person, the enemy was dislodged, lost 30 prisoners and more killed and wounded.

The General-in-Chief, after having himself reconnoitered the positions at Cavriana, returned at night to Montechiaro, where he established his headquarters and ordered the movements for the next day.

Lieutenant-General Delmas, commanding the vanguard, was ordered to attack Ponti and observe Peschiera.

Lieutenant General Moncey received the order to seize the heights of Monzambano; the center, under the orders of Lieutenant-General Suchet, was destined to capture the entrenchments on the Volta, and to take up a position there. Lieutenant-General Dupont was charged with favoring these operations by making with one of the divisions of the right wing strong demonstrations on Goito, and by employing the other to threaten Castellucchio, and to face what might come from Mantua.

Rochambeau's division, part of the left wing, had to stand on the defensive, and observe the enemy's movement towards Salo.

The reserve divisions, commanded by Lieutenant-General Michaud, composed of the cavalry, the artillery, and the pontoons, were ordered to proceed to Castiglione, as well as the reserve brigade of headquarters commanded by Général de brigade Seras.

On the 30th, at daybreak, the General-in-Chief went by Castiglione on the line; both sides were already firing at each other, and the action was taking place at the vanguard and the left wing.

The Mermet, Bisson, and Beaumont brigades, of the vanguard corps, advanced on Pozzolengo; They met the enemy there. This post was immediately attacked by Mermet's brigade, which turned the village, and forced the enemy to retreat to the Monzambano heights.

Mermet's and Beaumont's brigades promptly captured the positions at Ponti.

Cassagne's brigade, coming from Rivoltella, arrived there at the same time; this brigade, which had been charged with observing Peschiera, did it so closely that it carried off on the glacis an enemy post commanded by an officer.

The whole vanguard took a stand in front of Ponti, after having taken 100 prisoners.

The left wing had to overcome great obstacles to reach the point that had been designated to it; the enemy occupied Cavriana with forces far superior to those that had been there the day before; so he took advantage of the goodness of his position.

General Merle's brigade, composed of the 3rd Battalion of the 12th Légère and the 102nd Demi-brigade, was charged with attacking it. The village, turned by the battalion of the 12th Légère, was captured with the assistance of the 102nd Demi-brigade.

Lieutenant-General Moncey immediately marched on Monzambano through Castellaro; he gathered, behind Boudet's division, his artillery, and his cavalry brigade.

The enemy was present and occupied on the right a sort of camp cut off by nature, and of very difficult access. If the Generals Moncey and Boudet continued their march on Monzambano, they evidently left their right flank and their rear compromised; learning, moreover, that Monzambano was not occupied, they did not hesitate to attack the enemy in their positions.

General Schitt's brigade, composed of the 1st and 2nd Battalions of the 12th Légère and the 91st Demi-brigade, with that of General Merle, began to turn the enemy's right, while the Seriziat brigade, composed of the 60th, formed in closed columns, attacked him in front.

Forced into this position, the enemy took a second back, under the protection of several pieces of artillery that beat the front of the 102nd Deni-brigade.

The nature of the ground and the imposing forces rendered the second attack the most vivid; it took nothing less than the intrepidity of our troops to climb these mountains under heavy fire, and carry off a success as complete as it was rapid.

A battalion of grenadiers commanded by Adjudant-commandant Foy, a very distinguished officer, formed the reserve of this division and supported its movements.

The difficulties of the roads slowed the march of the cavalry brigade, commanded by General Henry (Wollodkowicz), and deprived it of taking part in the action.

The enemy, repulsed with violence, would inevitably have lost all means of retreat, if night had not stopped our pursuit. It retreated on Borghetto with loss of at least 300 prisoners and 1,000 dead or wounded.

After having given all the troops under his command the most deserved praise, the general Boudet makes a particular mention of the value and the talents of the Citizens Captaine and Prévost, chefs de bataillons of the 102nd.

The Lieutenant-General Moncey established his army corps on the positions he had just taken from the enemy. A column led by Lieutenant-General Delmas to the rear of Castellaro, greatly facilitated the occupation of this village by General Moncey's troops, where he felt resistance.

The attack of the Volta by the army corps of the center experienced some delays, its troops having been able, because of the bad roads, to complete their meeting on Guidizolo only at 2 o'clock in the afternoon.

General Suchet, on their arrival, made his arrangements to capture the redoubts; they obtained a complete success. Général de division Gazan marched to the entrenchments which defended the position and made himself master of them; Loison's division, moving at the same level, cleverly maneuvered to turn the village and attacked it head-on.

The enemy was met at the village of Fousta in front of the Volta and was overthrown. They support themselves on their right; but General Compans, at the head of the 13th Légère, executed, at this point, such a vigorous charge that it determined the flight of the enemy: then the center took position two miles forward, on the right of the Volta.

To assist the operations of the center, Lieutenant-General Dupont marched with Watrin's division and its reserve towards Goito.

The enemy, forced in front of Santa Maria by the Général de brigade Musnier, having received at the moment powerful reinforcements from Goito, and presented in the plain a line of about 8,000 men, commanded by the General Major von Aspre.

Général de division Watrin immediately made arrangements to attack: the 6th Légère marched first; it had on its left a battalion of the 22nd Demi-brigade; the 28th held its right, the 40th was in reserve.

The combat was engaged with the greatest vivacity; our troops were distinguished by the order of their march and the precision of their fire, under a hail of bullets and canister.

Already the enemy was staggering on all points; a charge made on the highway by a squadron of the 11th Hussar Regiment, supported by our infantry, determined the enemy's flight; they were pursued to the gates of Goito.

Our skirmishers reached the banks of the Mincio and did a great deal of harm to the enemy while they crossed the Goito Bridge where they lost at least 300 men killed or wounded. Lieutenant-General Dupont praised the brilliant valor and known talents of General Watrin; he gives the same justice to Général de brigade Musnier; also the brave Mason, commander of the 6th Légère, Chef de bataillon Sarret of the same corps, the Adjutant-Commandant Jacquelin, the Captain of Engineers Bernard, who had a horse wounded under him, and Lieutenant Liezmann, attached to the staff.

Général de division Monnier attacked Castellucchio with equal success; he ejected the enemy as far as Curtalogne; he restrained them with a battalion which he established at Santa Maria delle Grazie. A brigade protected Marcaria. Charged by the General-in-Chief to follow the movements of the left wing and the advance guard of the army to inform him of the result of the attacks on Monzambano and La Voila, I was within reach, Citizen Minister, to render justice to the learned dispositions of the general officers, and to admire the brilliant courage of our soldiers; the ardor, the air of assurance of the 60th and 102nd Demi-brigades of Boudet's division, climbing the mountains and overthrowing the enemy in spite of the strongest and most sustained fire, are above all praise; Lieutenant-General Moncey had, during that day, a horse killed under him; the Général de division Boudet, had two; Captain Bausch, deputy to the general staff, was also dismounted.

We took about 900 prisoners from the enemy; he also had at least 2,000 hors de combat.

This success without clouds, complete on the whole line, caused us to conceive what could be undertaken with such troops. They had forgotten the sufferings of a long and painful bivouac during continual and cold rains and demanded by singing songs to be led against the enemy.

The Pluviôse 1st (January 21, 1801) was used in reconnaissance. On the 2nd, the General-in-Command ordered Lieutenant-General Dupont to make Watrin's division move to the left to link up with the troops of Lieutenant-General Suchet.

In the necessity of tightening the blockade of Goito at the same time on the right bank of the Mincio, and presenting to the enemy imposing forces on this point, Monnier's division, recalled from Marearia and Castellucchio, came to establish itself on the right of Watrin's division.

Général de brigade Jablonowski, detached on the right of the Po with a corps of about 3,000 men to fight the incursions of the enemy parties joined with hordes of insurgents, after reestablishing communications with Tuscany, pacified the country, and keeping the enemy in check, he was ordered to rally his troops and move by forced marches to Marcaria, and from there to Castiglione, leaving Cisalpine troops to guard Bologna whose inhabitants were all armed in our favor, at the orders of the Général de brigade Julhion; Guastalla was defended by 200 men of the Polish Legion, and Fort Urbain by 300 Frenchmen.

On the 3rd, the Polish Legion, commanded by General Dąbrowski, was detached before Peschiera to conceal our movement on the Mincio; two battalions, two squadrons of French troops, and 200 chasseurs of the Italian Legion, were joined to the Poles.

The General-in-Chief, having fixed the passage of the Mincio the next morning, ordered Lieutenant-General Dupont to leave his positions in front of Goito, as early as the evening of the 3rd, and to carry his army corps to La Voila, leaving only one cavalry post to observe Goito. He had to order General Monnier to join him, leaving a strong cavalry observation posts at Marcaria and Castellucchio. Orders were at the same time sent to the lieutenants-general to regulate their march, and to make known to each the point, the rank, and the hour of the passage of his army corps. The actual attack was to take place under Monzambano, the vanguard at the orders of Lieutenant-General Delmas was directed to attack first.

Lieutenant-General Moncey, with Boudet's division and the reserve of the left wing, was destined to support the movement of the vanguard.

Lieutenant-General Suchet, commanding the center, was ordered to leave it at the disposal of the Lieutenant-General Dupont, charged with the false attack at Molino de la Volta near Pozzolo, using the bidging train, which he had at his disposal, and to move up the Mincio to cross at Monzambano, after General Boudel.

In operating these movements General Suchet was charged with deploying his artillery in front of Borghetto, to reject the enemy, and continue to observe it with Loison's division, in concert with General Dupont's left wing.

Two regiments of chasseurs à cheval, under the command of General Quesnel, were detached from the center corps with two pieces of light artillery, to observe the movements of the Goito garrison. Lieutenant-General Michaud, commander of the reserve, was ordered to carry himself from Cavriana to Monzambano, to pass immediately after the center which was to be followed by the cavalry and artillery reserves, as well as the reserve brigade of the general headquarters, commanded by Général de brigade Seras.

By the care of General of Artillery Marmont, and under the protection of 40 guns, two bridges were to be thrown in front of Monzambano at daybreak. The General-in-Chief established his headquarters at Monzambano.

At the same time, Lieutenant-General Dupont was ordered to execute his passage by force at the reentrant angle formed by the Mincio in front of the Volta.

The passage executed, he was to be established militarily and with precaution under the protection of his artillery, placed on the right bank, and await the result of the operations of the army at Monzambano.

Whatever was the precision brought in the expedition of the orders and the activity of the general officers to execute them, the obstacles which the columns encountered in extremely difficult roads, in the height of winter, especially for the artillery and pontoons slowed down their progress, and made it impossible for many to meet at the right time.

This mishap determined the General-in-Chief to postpone the passage to the next day, without giving any order to restore the bridge at Molino de la Voila, near Pozzolo. He saw this operation as producing a diversion that was more useful and stronger than if it had taken place at the same time as the real attack by Monzambano, where we had all the advantages of a good establishment before and after the passage of the Mincio, besides the indispensable necessity in which we put the enemy, forcing him to deprive himself of 12,000 men to establish garrisons, which could have been cut off by our right.

For several days a thick fog protected our movements, and forced the uncertain enemy to guard the heights of Valeggio, keys of all the positions of his line, and from which he could, from the camp which he had established there, send his strength to any threatened point.

The Mincio is never sufficiently fordable for an army, when the Salliouze Canal is closed: the fords, in the lowest waters, are in small numbers, and always to the advantage of the left bank, which dominates almost everywhere the right, except at the reentrant angles of Mozambano and Molino, near Pozzolo, which had on the left a very decided commanding position. The General-in-Chief, who had reconnoitered them himself, regarded these points as very favorable, and the enemy knew their advantage; he had flanked it with enormous redoubts studded with numerous artillery, the little plain in front of Monzambano, which is naturally closed to the right and to the left by Valeggio and Sallionze; it offered to our troops the favorable access to the mountains, which are connected with the entrenched camp of Castelnovo, which was the center of all operations.

The point of Molino, situated between Valeggio and Goito, whose troops could take our columns in the flank and reverse, facing the plains of Villafranca, where the whole enemy army could deploy and enjoy the advantage of his numerous cavalry, did not inspire him with such lively fears; the ground in front of the reentrant angle, where it was necessary to arrive was low, difficult for the artillery, and little suited to the development of an army.

The proximity of Mantua also allowed Bellegarde to have 12,000 more men: there was no doubt that he did not wish to be attacked there.

It was probable that, to oppose our enterprises, the enemy would maneuver to force us to make diversions and to divide our forces; he could have General Rochambeau attacked at Caffaro by Wukassowich, moving into our rear, under the protection of his flotilla, or debouch from Peschiera on the right of the Mincio when our passage was being affected.

The General-in-Chief, persuaded that such is the advantage of a vigorous attack, that the whole of a good defense is difficult to seize, persisted in his resolution to march against the enemy, and to prevent the execution of his plans by attacking himself; he thought that the best way to secure the rear of the army, and to cover Italy, was to carry the theater of war beyond the Adige.

Lieutenant-General Dupont, who had taken up a position near the Volta from the 3rd at 10 o'clock in the evening, and who had scarcely three miles to go in a country without the slightest obstacle, was at the edge of the Mincio opposite Pozzolo at the break of day.

Chef de brigade of Artillery Bardenet, strongly assisted by the Chef de bataillon of Engineers Rouziez, launched several boats under the protection of eight cannons, and the fire of musketry of Watrin's division. Immediately the excellent Chef de brigade, Mason, of the 6th Légère, at the head of the skirmishers of this corps, and of those of the 28th and 40th Demi-brigades, threw himself into these boats and set foot on the right bank. Already the enemy posts on the banks of the river had been flushed out and several were captured.

Général de brigade Maçon had been able to take cover in an advantageous position to protect the bridge, which Général de brigade Bardenet had the talent to build in less than two hours despite the constant fire of enemy artillery.

Already the 6th Légère, led by Brigadier General Musnier, had crossed the bridge, and followed the offensive movement of the sharpshooters; an enemy corps of about 1,200 men could not prevent the establishment of our troops, and would take turns on Pozzolo, disputing the ground foot-by-foot.

The 28th and 40th Demi-brigades began to pass, while the 22nd Demi-brigade was observing Borghetto on the left bank.

General Watrin pursued this first advantage, and continued to drive his troops, when the General-in-Chief sent orders to engage no major action on the left of the Mincio, and to confine himself to protecting, by the fire of the batteries, the bridge that had just been thrown at Molino.

The troops who had passed the Mincio were then engaged in advantageous combat: General Dupont asked to pursue his first successes; and General Suchet, who felt that the right wing would be too weak in the number it would have to fight, sent an officer to headquarters to obtain permission to support with his troops those of General Dupont.

The General-in-Chief was well-informed that the enemy had 40,000 men under Villafranca, including the garrison of Mantua, whose proximity allowed him to employ: his cavalry and 13 battalions of reserve grenadiers. We must have wished that Bellegarde, seduced by the appearance of a great affair at Pozzolo, neglected the important positions of Monzambano, by which we were to attack him the following day at daybreak, and that the main forces of his army were removed from it. It was to be feared, however, that the enemy, by offering slight successes to the first columns which would have passed, would excite their ardor into pursuing him into his positions, in order to be able, with an enormous advantage of strength, to overthrow them into the Mincio. It was necessary to prevent this danger without preventing the diversion which the false attack on our right had to make.

There was only a boat bridge at Molino; a second trestle, which was built there, could not be finished until later. The center had scarcely been able to pass before dark, because of the brevity of the days which have only eight hours in this season; and if prudence did not preside over the operations of the right, supported by the center, whatever might have been the speed of the march, the army, to take part in the action, abandoning its strong positions on the Upper Mincio exposing its flanks and rear to inevitable reverses, could only happen to witness a defeat. The General-in-Chief, therefore, persisted in the plan he had adopted; but, not wishing to destroy the enthusiasm inspired by the first successes in an operation as difficult as the passage of a river covered with strongholds and redoubts, he ordered General Boudet, who knew the ground perfectly, to invest Borghetto, relieving General Suchet's troops there, which he authorized to support the attack of General Dupont, leaving to the prudence of the latter to profit from its advantages without compromising his brigades, far from the natural entrenchments of Molino, where the superior fire of the artillery on the plateau offered him shelter and certain successes.

Meanwhile the enemy was getting stronger; General Watrin passed the Mincio with the rest of his division and two pieces of light artillery.

The 10th, sustained by the fire of our artillery, we managed to seize the village of Pozzolo. So the general Watrin placed his troops along the dike, from Pozzolo to the Volta mills, and stood on the defensive, presenting to the enemy the figure of a bridgehead that was difficult to strike.

Every moment saw the enemy's forces grow. It was noon when Monnier's division, after a painful march, arrived from his camp at Santa Maria, and took his battle position on the left bank.

This division, composed only at this time of the 24th Légère and 58th Demi-brigade occupied Pozzolo and gave Watrin's division the facility to tighten his line by a movement on the left.

Lieutenant General Suchet returned with his army corps to his former positions on the Volta. He was in a position to appreciate the advantages that fortune offered to the army and felt that the help of his troops was indispensable for the right wing to emerge gloriously from its enterprise.

All the artillery of the center was united on the plateau overlooking the left bank. Gazan's division, the right wing of General Suchet's lieutenancy, formed in battle, as much to impose on the enemy as to encourage our troops.

The Austrian columns swelled incessantly, and while General Watrin was operating on the left, the enemy, supported by the fire of a large force of artillery, fell furiously upon the 6th, 28th, and 40th of the line: nothing can to express the bravery and coolness with which these three demi-brigades alone sustained this terrible shock for nearly two hours.

Impatient to see that his infantry could not abandon to Watrin's division the natural entrenchments, which covered it, Bellegarde, astonished at the impotence of his best troops against a single division, directed on it, by its right flank, a impetuous charge of cavalry.

This terrible effort was itself without effect. Two squadrons of the 11th Hussar Regiment, commanded by Chef d'escadron Martigues, made daring prodigies on this occasion; 20 cannon, placed on the circular height of the right bank of the Mincio, did indeed support Watrin's division, and carried the most frightful ravage in the Austrian ranks. The murderous effect of these batteries, the unshakable nerve of the 6th Légère, 28th, and 40th Demi-brigades, the skill of General Watrin's dispositions, obliged the enemy to change his plan; they carried their main forces to our right, and directed all their attacks on Pozzolo.

Major-General Mounier, who maintained himself with advantage in this imposing position, suddenly had to combat such a superiority of numbers that, in spite of the bravery of the 24th Légère commanded by the brave Ferey, and the vigor of the 58th he could not keep his establishment at Pozzolo, where a column of Hungarian grenadiers went. This village was destined to undergo all the vicissitudes of the fate of the arms, it was lost and taken again three times.

Lieutenant-General Suchet, witness of the truly heroic efforts of the right wing, judging at the same time how his position could become critical by the physical impossibility of making head with 7,000 men against an entire army, which had the faculty to renew at each instance its attacks with fresh troops, hastened to bring Clauzel's brigade, of Gazan's division, over the Mincio to form a reserve for General Dupont.

Hardly had this brigade been formed a few toises from the banks of the river, than Lieutenant-General Dupont was obliged to move it into the line, to resist the terrible shock of the enemy; it was overthrown; the impetuosity of the charge was such that the position of the right wing and Clauzel's brigade seemed entirely desperate. Our troops retreated with frightening precipitation, the enemy thought himself certain of victory, when the corps of the center was on the right bank within reach of taking part in the action on the left bank; the fire of this infantry, that of 20 guns that vomited canister, suddenly arrested the enemy. The earth was strewn with their dead, and our generals seized this moment to rally our troops. General Watrin, which nothing could have forced him from his position, knew how to profit by the hesitation of the enemy; at the sound of his voice, the intrepid 6th Légère, 28th, and 40th Demi-brigade, came out of their entrenchments and in turn charged the enemy with the last vigor.

Lieutenant-General Dupont ordered the same charge all along the line; it was strongly supported by the artillery of the right wing, under the orders of Chef d'escadron Sezille; the brave 1st Hussar Regiment and part of the 3rd Chasseur à cheval Regiment took the most active part; everywhere the enemy was pushed back; their rout became complete, they lost in an instant all the ground they has just gained; Watrin's division took 1,000 prisoners, a flag, five cannons and their caissons. The enemy abandoned the battlefield covered with his dead, his wounded and his weapons. General Monnier returned to Pozzolo. The ardor of our troops had carried them away in the pursuit of the fugitives, such that there was no longer a reserve to cover the bridge. Lieutenant-General Suchet felt the consequence and sent the rest of Gazan's division over the Mincio.

No sooner had General Gazan united his division on the left bank than the enemy, who had assembled their forces, undertook a fresh attack on Pozzolo, and succeeded in obtaining the advantage over the brave 24th Légère, and 58th Demi-brigade of Monnier's division, who were exhausted with fatigue by a long and bloody resistance, and by the repeated attacks they had had to sustain.

Watrin's division was then more than three miles into the plain pursuing its advantages. This general, perceiving the success of the right, which was beginning to lose ground, for fear of being turned himself, resolved to fall back in good order, and to come under the protection of our batteries from the right wing.

A battalion of the 8th Légère, under the orders of Chef de bataillon Marguerit, of Gazan's division, in concert with the 24th Légère, led by his commander, Citizen Ferey, returned to the village; the enemy could not resist their impetuosity, and our troops were once more masters of Pozzolo.

Half an hour later, the Austrians with a reserve of six battalions advanced in two columns, one directed on the left and the other on the village, which they still managed to seize, in spite of the most obstinate resistance. Our troops retreated, General Gazan led a vigorous charge; he ordered General Lesuire to re-attack the village with the 72nd Demi-brigade and a battalion of the 99th; another battalion of the 96th was moved on the left.

The ensemble and vigor of these movements obtained the greatest success. On the right, General Lesuire and Chef de brigade Ficatier, of the brave 72nd, took the village; the Austrians, routed, abandoned two cannons to the power of Chef de bataillon Jeannin, which were those which the division of the right was forced to abandon by the loss of its draft horses.

Captain Mathieu, of the 8th Légère, had locked himself up with 30 chasseurs in a house in the village of Pozzolo, and held out until the 72nd returned there.

The 24th Légère also constantly maintained skirmishers there.

Chef de bataillon Jeannin and Berthezin of the 72nd were wounded in this attack; the first also had his horse killed under him. Chef de brigade Fatiatier, of the same corps, who was not confirmed in his rank, merited by his bravery the justice of being promoted.

The battalion of the 96th, which had marched on the left of the village, headed by Captain Tripoul, General Gazan's aide-de-camp, pushed the enemy into the plain, and brought back 300 prisoners, including a major.

Général de division Loison, having arrived from Borghetto, had replaced General Gazan on the right bank. Upon his arrival, this general, to strengthen a battalion of the 99th, placed by order of Lieutenant-General Suchet, in a little wood on the right bank, had established a battalion of the 43rd there. This battalion had such a great effect, that it contributed powerfully to stopping the enemy; but in less than an hour it suffered a loss of more than 80 men.

But the shocks succeeded each other on the left bank with an incredible liveliness. Bellegarde, who shuddered to see the honor of his army compromised by the unexpected resistance of a corps so inferior in number, renewed his efforts, and still managed to seize the village, whose occupation was to decide the fate of the battle; but Lieutenant-General Suchet sent Colli's brigade, of Loison's division, across the bridge. In opening his attack, General Colli formed the 13th in colonne d'attaque and sent the 2nd Battalion, under the orders of Chef de brigade Sémélé, to take the village by the right, while he advanced in front with the 3rd Battalion, supported by another of the 106th. The drums sounded the charge and the whole line followed the impetus given by Colli's brigade. Général de division Davout, commanding the cavalry of the army, had just arrived with some regiments of dragoons on the right bank. Perceiving the necessity of reinforcing our cavalry on the opposite bank, he ordered Général de brigade Rivaud take a brigade of dragoons over the Mincio, to support the center of the line, and, followed by a detachment, he went to his person, with Adjutant-Commandant Lavalette and several senior cavalry officers; but scarcely had the chef de brigade of the 6th Dragoon Regiment, Citizen Lebaron, crossed the bridge at the head of the sappers and some 40 dragoons of his regiment, that the danger became urgent.

A column of 2,000 Hungarian grenadiers successfully resisted the efforts of our troops with on the right. General Davout, without considering the inequality of his forces, ordered Général de brigade Lebaron to execute a vigorous charge: this officer executed this order with the greatest bravery. General Davout, Général de brigade Rivaud, Adjudant-Commandant Lava, and Chefs de brigade Rigaud and Beckler, with some of the officers of the staff, dashed forward with the handful of brave men.

The assault, as vigorous as it was well-directed, of Colli's brigade, the generous devotion of the weak detachment of the 6th Dragoons and the officers who followed it, the impetuous charges of the 11th Hussar Regiment, the 3rd and 4th Chasseur à cheval Regiments, the general élan of the whole line, all combine to fix a victory so long uncertain; the broken enemy was overthrown on all points, the 6th Dragoons advanced to the village, and took 300 prisoners; General Colli, with his brigade, closely followed them; the 28th Légère and 68th Demi-brigade marched to the same level; the fugitives were pursued far and wide; the night itself did not put an end to this struggle, as long as it was bloody, that we were masters of the battlefield, and the retreat of the enemy decided the victory in our favor.

It was 6 o'clock; General Watrin had just returned his troops behind the natural entrenchments of the mills of the Volta, to avoid any surprise during the night. Hardly had they entered this line, when the enemy, perceiving the darkness, attacked them with their grenadier reserve, which had just arrived from Valeggio.

At the moment when it least expected it, a hail of bullets, shells and shot was directed at Watrin's division. The moon, which appeared at intervals, revealed masses of grenadiers, marching fearlessly on our entrenchments, from which they were no more than 25 paces away:

the troops felt that it was necessary, on such a difficult occasion, to be victorious or thrown into the river.

Under the orders of Generals Musnier and Petitot, the Adjutant-Commandant Sacqueluc, the intrepid Chefs de brigade Macon, Valhubert, and Legendre, and the brave Chefs de bataillon Taupin, Michel, Boys, and Guilardet, fought well and hard. They killed a large number of Hungarian grenadiers and compelled them to retire in disorder. The darkness was so great that it would not have been prudent to pursue them.

It was by this last effort that the troops of Watrin's division crowned the successes they had obtained all day long over an enemy ten times greater in number: the 6th Légère, 28th and 40th Demi-brigades reaffirmed their former reputation for bravery and coolness.

The enemy, pushed back by the left of the line, turned his efforts against the village of Pozzolo. About 8 o'clock he directed his artillery fire against it; but the 43rd Demi-brigade, of Loison's division, with the 24th and 5th of Monnier's division, succeeded in rendering his enterprises unsuccessful; firing finally ceased after 9 o'clock in the evening.

This day, brilliant for the troops of the republic, was very deadly for the enemy, and had a great influence on the morale of his troops during the rest of the campaign. His loss was at least 4,000 men, dead or wounded, and more than 2,000 prisoners, including several senior officers; he lost nine cannons and their caissons; a flag was captured by Citizen Joseph Pierron, maréchal-de-logis of the 11th Hussars, who, despite the serious wound he had received, had not withdrawn from the fight. Our loss amounted to about 900 men killed or wounded; we had to regret that of several brave officers. Among the wounded was Général de brigade Calvin (he died as a result of his wound); Citizens Valhubert, commanding officer of the 28th Demi-brigade, a distinguished officer; Lusignan, chef de brigade of the 58th, had in the course of the day two horses killed under him; Chef de bataillon Kenn, of the 24th Légère, Chef de bataillon Vivenol, of the 28th Demi-brigade; the two captains aide-de-camp of General Watrin, Chauconin and Laborde; Boyer, Chefs de bataillon of the 43rd; Maquart, of the 106th, and the brave Brossier. The too brave Chef de bataillon Sarrel, of the 6th Légère, was killed; his loss was very painful to his corps.

In order to render to each one the portion of glory which he acquired by day, it would be necessary to mention all the individuals who fought that day: generals, officers, and soldiers, all competing with bravery, and performed prodigies of valor.

Lieutenants-General Dupont and Suchet met to pay tribute to the conduct and talents of Generals Watrin, Monnier, Gazan, Loison, Davout, Musnier, Carra-Saint-Cyr, Petitot, Gobert, Salva, Lesuire, Clauzel and Colli, and the Adjutant-Commanders Sacqueluc and Girard.

The corps which fought, and which for the same reason distinguished themselves, were, on the right wing, the 6th Légère, 28th and 40th Demi-brigades of Watrin's division; the 24th Légère and 58th Demi-brigade of Monnier's division; the 11th Hussar Regiment: almost all the officers of this intrepid regiment or their horses were wounded; the 4th Chasseur à cheval Regiment and the light artillery, commanded by Chef d'escadron Sezille.

In the center, the 8th, 72nd, and 99th of Gazan's division; the 43rd and 106th of Loison's division; the 3rd Chasseur à cheval Regiment,: the three brigades of the center took at least 900 prisoners and four cannons.

All the generals gave a brilliant testimony of the zeal and talent of Chef de brigade of artillery Bardenet: this brave officer rendered the most essential services in the morning, presiding over the establishment of the bridge; he added to it throughout the course of the battle, by his activity and the advantage he was able to draw from our batteries established on the right bank: he was effectively assisted by the Citizens Vaudre and Berthier, distinguished officers; more than once the artillery, directed by them, preserved our brave men from an inevitable loss.

A host of brilliant actions illuminated this day, but not all of them have yet been collected.

Besides Citizen Pierron, maréchal-de-logis in the 11th Hussars, who, although wounded, did not leave the battlefield and took a flag from the enemy, I cite with interest Citizen Moreau, also a maréchal-des-logis in the 11th Hussars, who, at the head of a small number of brave men, took 2 cannons and 400 prisoners.

Citizen Nicolle, maréchal-des-logis in the 16th Dragoon Regiment had his horse disabled, while rallying the troops in a moment when, pressed by the enemy's cavalry, they experienced some disorder.

Captain Godefroy, of the 6th Légère, swam the Mincio to tie the first boat to the left bank.

Brigadier Lagrenade, of the 11th Hussars, seized a cannon with Maréchal-des-logis Moreau.

Chef de bataillon de Courtois of the 43rd Demi-brigade, and Adjutant Major Garnier of the same demi-brigade, each seized a flag and thus marched at the head of their corps to lead them to victory.

The brave Lieutenant Brossier did prodigies of valor and was wounded.

Brigadier Sémélé, still at that time at the head of the 43rd, justified the confidence of his chiefs, and acquired a new right to the benevolence of the government.

Chef d'escadron Martigne of the 11th Hussars was covered with fame as well as all his regiment.

The brave 72nd had five flag bearers killed on this day.

The aide-de-camp of General Colli, Citizen Coqueron, had a horse killed under him.

Captain of Engineers Bernard rendered the greatest services to Watrin's division, both in his arm and as a staff officer

Captain of Engineers Bois-Chevalier had a horse killed under him.

Chef de bataillon of Engineers Rouziez, commanding this arm at the lieutenancy of the center, showed talent and a great activity in the establishment of the bridge, to which he worked with Chef de brigade Bardenel. It was to the care of the Citizen Rouziez that we owed the bridging train in the center.

It was he who built a second bridge in the evening.

There are few battles, Citizen Minister, whose gain has been disputed with so much fury and so great an inequality of number: the valor of the troops of the Republic never manifested itself more brilliantly.

The operations of that day brought no change to the plan of the General-in-Chief for the passage of the army on Monzambano; he occupied himself only with making for the right wing the new dispositions which his establishment on the left bank necessitated.

Lieutenant-General Suchet was ordered to bring back across the Mincio the three brigades of the center which he had detached in order to support the corps of Lieutenant-General Dupont, to place one of his brigades in observation before Borghetto, and to march with the rest of his troops to take place in the column that was to pass the Mincio at Monzambano.

Lieutenant-General Dupont was instructed to stand in position under his batteries, and remain on the defense on the left bank until the next morning at 10 o'clock, at which time he would not fail to hear the engagement of the army, and might attempt what his prudence and circumstances would suggest to him to approach by his left from Valeggio.

On the 5th, according to the wishes of the General-in-Chief, as early as 5 o'clock in the morning, 40 guns were put in battery on the right bank at Monzambano to protect the establishment of the bridges. It is to the talent and indefatigable activity of Général de division Marmont, commander-in-chief of this arm in Italy, that the army is indebted for its superb artillery.

At 7 o'clock in the morning, six carabinier companies, commanded by Citizen Devilliers, Chef de bataillon of the 25th Légère, passed the Mincio by boat, and covered the making of the bridges.

At 9 o'clock, when one of the bridges was completed, the whole vanguard passed the river, and formed in the plain in four columns.

A general charge was ordered by Lieutenant-General Delmas; the columns moved and marched in the most imposing order without firing a single shot of gun or cannon, suffering across their front a considerable fire of musketry and canister, and on the flank a lively cannonade from the redoubts that crowned the summits of Salionzo.

The enemy soon yielded to such an impetuous attack and fled precipitately; all who resisted was killed or taken prisoner. The brigades of Cassagne and Bisson pursued them more than three miles to the heights of Valeggio.

General Lapisse's brigade, and that of the dragoons, commanded by General Beaumont, went to the left to contain the forces which the enemy had collected by the redoubts.

The 1st and 9th Dragoon Regiments performed a charge as succcessful as it was bold to reach their position.

To divert the fire which greatly inconvenienced the two brigades of the left, four pieces of light artillery were put into battery within canister range of the first redoubt. This battery, constantly directed by the Chef de bataillon of Artillery Aubry, maneuvered for more than an hour in this position with the greatest valor; 22 gunners or train soldiers and 20 horses were wounded or killed.

The 9th Dragoon Regiment, placed behind this battery, was covered by a small wood barely 60 toises from the redoubts. This regiment, experiencing a very violent fire from an enemy corps in this wood, Chef de brigade Sebastiani, without waiting for the arrival of the infantry, had a squadron of his regiment dismounted , and this squadron, serving on foot, withstood the efforts of the enemy with a great deal of order and assembly, repulsed him from the heights, and facilitated the rest of the regiment the means of furnishing a vigorous charge which compelled the enemy to regain their entrenchments with a considerable loss.

General Lapisse's brigade successively attacked and bayoneted three fiercely defended positions. Twice that brave infantry, unmoved by cavalry charges, waited for them within reach of a pistol, and was able to force the enemy into a precipitous flight.

Meanwhile, Generals Cassagne and Bisson had taken up positions on the Valeggio heights; Soon they were besieged by the enemy's reserve, all composed of Hungarian grenadiers, numbering 12,000 men.

It took nothing less than the bravery of our troops to sustain for more than two hours the repeated shocks of such superior forces; the outcome of this unequal struggle could have put us at a disadvantage. Already our troops were beginning to bend, when Boudet's division, forming part of Lieutenant-General Moncey's corps, near which he was in person, reached the heights. The drums sounded the pas de charge all along the line and our columns surged forward; everywhere the enemy was pushed back; his rout became complete. He lost four cannons, a caisson, and about 2,000 prisoners.

This movement carried part of the vanguard to Valeggio; the general-in-chief had sent, to assist it, the reserve brigade of the general headquarters, commanded by Général de brigade Séras. On this point a most obstinate resistance was encountered; three times Valeggio was taken and lost.

The converged grenadiers of Boudet's division, led by the Adjutants Dalton and Devaux, came efficiently to assist the efforts of the 52nd Demi-bigade; they occupied Valeggio for good, and took two cannons. The castle still held. Adjutant Dalton was shot in the chest, fighting at the grenadiers' head. (This estimable officer, with the most promising future, died as a result of his wound.)

Lieutenant-General Suchet had left General Lesuire's brigade on the right bank, in front of Borghetto.

At the first cannon fired on Valeggio by the troops of the vanguard, General Lesuire, according to the orders received, marched at the head of the brave 72nd, against the palisaded redoubts at Borghetto: the courage of these brave men could not, at first, overcome such obstacles; many fell at the foot of the entrenchments; the others were, for a moment, repulsed; soon rallied, they flew to launch another attack, when the Austrian commander asked to capitulate; 2,000 prisoners, including 29 officers, 5 cannons, 2 howitzers and 80 horses were the result of this surrender.

Thanks to all these memorable actions, the rest of the army made its way and took a stand. General Bisson, in the night, occupied the castle of Valeggio.

The day of the 5th was decisive for the campaign. The troops marched in admirable order and showed the same bravery as the day before at Pozzolo. The defeat of the enemy was complete: they lost 14 cannons, and about 4,000 prisoners.

Skillfully led by Lieutenant General Delmas, the vanguard performed prodigies of valor. It consisted of the 19th, 20th, 25th, and 28th Légère Demi-brigades; the 1st Provisional Légère Demi-brigade; the 1st, 2nd, 26th, 52nd, 62nd, and 78th Line Demi-brigades, the 10th Hussar Regiment, and the 1st and 9th Dragoon Regiments. General Delmas was powerfully seconded by Generals Lapisse, Cassagne, Charpentier, Chief of staff of the vanguard, Beaumont, Bisson, and Mermet. This brave general was previously wounded by a ball while commanding at the head of his troops on the road to Valeggio.

General Boudet, of Moncey's lieutenancy, rendered, as well as his division, singularly services on this day.

The artillery supported its old reputation for bravery, accuracy, and celerity.

Staff officers and line officers who figured deserve the highest praise; all fought with distinction; the Chef de brigade Alix, Director General of the artillery parks, gave proof of talent and activity in the construction of the bridges of which he was charged; he was perfectly seconded by the Chefs de bataillon of Pontoniers, Ponge and Dardenne.

Among the wounded superior officers were the Chef de brigade Gaspard, commanding the 1st Provisional Légère (he had an arm carried off by a cannonball, and this brave man rejoined his unit a month later); Godinot, of the 25th Légère, the Chefs de bataillon Devilliers, of the 25th Légère, and Debesque, of the 52nd Line Demi-brigade, all officers of the highest distinction.

Général de brigade Beaumont, at the head of the 1st and 9th Dragoon Regiments, had a wounded horse; General Lapisse hada horse killed under him; the brave Chef de brigade Balthazard of the 7th Légère had a wounded horse; the Citizen Beyermann, of the 7th Légère, had a horse killed and another wounded; Citizen Martin, deputy, had his horse wounded.

We must not ignore the valor that spread in this day, on the front of the line of the vanguard, by the Citizens Andrieu and Hervo, adjutant-commandants, Demangeot, Chef d'escadron, and Gustave Knorring, aide-de-camp of General Oudinot, Chief of the General Staff; Soubeyran-Thiery, Chef d'escadron; Flour, Chef de bataillon; Lamothe, Bausch-Delmas, Captains; Lutailly, lieutenant-deputy to the general staff: all these officers, accompanied only by four chasseurs, of the 14th and 21st Chasseur à cheval Regiments, contributed not a little, by this sudden and honorable impulse, to repel, in concert with Cassagne's and Bisson's brigades, the enemy who sounded the charge and marched in far superior forces against these two brigades. Led by a general hors de ligne, where the resistance was the most obstinate, they overthrew all that was in their path, succeeded in capturing a cannon, and gave, by this devotion, time for Boudet's division to arrive. In this charge, the general who was at their head had a wounded horse under him; Adjutant-Commandant Andrieu had his horse killed under him and captured two Hungarian grenadiers; he had his horse shot under him a few hours earlier.

Chef d'escadron Thiery was knocked down with a rifle butt. Citizen Chapelle, aide-de-camp to Général de brigade Vignolle, was killed beside his general, who was present at this affair.

On the 6th, Lieutenant-General Delmas, after having completely surrounded the Salionzo Redoubts, prepared to take them by force when the enemy surrendered. Fourteen cannons, 1,000 prisoners, and two flags fell into our hands.

Scouts from Clauzel's brigade, of Gazan's division, in pushing a reconnaissance on Salionzo, entered the last redoubt at the moment when the Austrians abandoned it, seized five cannons, and took 23 prisoners from the rearguard of this column.

Forty-two cannons, two howitzers, approximately 11,000 prisoners, including 120 officers and three flags, are the fruit of the days of Nivôse 4th, 5th, and 6th.

The enemy, forced to retreat behind the line of the Adige, afterwards made his garrisons at Peschiera, Mantua, and Legnago, and evacuated Goito, which he could no longer defend. Général de brigade Quesnel seized it and covered it with two regiments of chasseurs à cheval in the valley.

Considering Borghetto and Goito on the Mincio as two good bridgeheads that secured his line of operation, the General-in-Chief gave his orders to move the army on the line of the Adige. A detachment of 150 cavalry of the 22nd Cavalry Regiment, under the command of Chef d'escadron Delort, was charged with repelling a reconnaissance towards Mantua.

This detachment drove the enemy from Marmirnolo, and Raucheli, and sent out small parties which advanced to a mile and a half of the place; the enemy was dislodged from the positions from Castelli, Villa Imputa and Castellaro.

Chef d'escadron Delort, and Sub-Lieutenant Boure, carried out their missions with as much bravery as intelligence.

On the 7th, the vanguard at the orders of Lieutenant-General Delmas took position at Pastrengo, and on the heights of Pallazuolo; on the left bank of the Adige it only met a few small posts detached from Bussolengo. A corps of 4,000 Austrians was detached under the orders of Major-General Rousseau, to occupy Rivoli and the Corona. General Delmas observed him with a corps of 2,000 men; the rest of the army took position on the ground between Verona and Legnago, in front of Bossobuono, the line extending to the left by Costora, Castel-Nuovo, and terminating at Cavalcacello.

Loison's and Gazan's divisions were in the second line that day, the first in Castel-Nuovo, the second in Cavalcacello. Lieutenant-General Suchet, who commanded them, was obliged to use his left to restrain the enemy in Peschiera by the left bank of the lake, while Major-General Dąbrowski, at the head of the Polish Legion, invested it from the right bank.

Six companies of scouts from Gazan's division, drove the troops in front of them into the fortress, and took up a post 150 toises from the glacis.

On the same day, the outposts of the garrison of Peschiera, which extended on the right bank of the Mincio to within a musket shot of Ponti, were attacked on all points by the Polish troops under the orders of General Dąbrowski.

In spite of the strongest resistance, the enemy was forced to cede before the impetuosity of the 2nd and 7th Polish Battalions, who, led by Chef de bataillon Chlopicki, charged them three times with bayonets, and pushed them up to the glacis of the fortress.

Chcf de brigade Grabinski, wounded in this action, showed the greatest activity and bravery. Chef de bataillon Chlopicki, distinguished in his military career by several brilliant actions, gave on this occasion proofs of the greatest courage joined to the rarest coolness.

The 1st Légère and the 1st of the Orient, also employed at the siege, at the same time dislodged the enemy from all the houses they occupied throughout the whole line. The loss of the enemy was, on this day, in front of Peschiera, 100 prisoners and a greater number of dead and wounded.

The fortress of Mantua was observed by a strong detachment. Général de brigade Jablonowski, recalled for this purpose from Marcaria, came to establish himself at Goito and Marmirnolo.

Major General Chasseloup, Inspector-General of Engineering and Commander of Engineers in Italy, was charged with the direction and command of the siege of Peschiera.

On the 8th, the enemy who had advanced the greater part of his positions and sent across the Adige the bulk of his army, made, to unmask his movement, some demonstrations in front of the village of Santa-Lucia, deployed some troops, and lined an entrenched camp with artillery that he had formed in front of the camp at the fortress of Verona, guarding the main road from that city to Mantua.

Monnier's division, which was part of the right wing, had orders to move on Santa-Lucia; a battalion of the 24th Légère turned the village, marched on the enemy which flanked it, and threw them back.

During this time, the rest of the 24th Légère and the 58th Demi-brigade advanced on the center of the village, to the right of the main road. The enemy returned to Verona.

Gardanne's division, skillfully led on the left in colonnes serrées and marching by echelons, had turned Santa-Lucia, and had established itself on the plateau that dominated the Verona Basin.

The divisions of Loison and Gazan took positions between Sona and Palazzuolo.

Boudet's division, by a forced march, moved from Costora to a position near Gardanne's division, supporting its left on the Adige.

The cavalry reserve was placed behind the army's right and observed Legnago and Mantua.

The General-in-Chief ordered that a reconnaissance be executed all along the line on the 9th.

The enemy showed themselves on all points in sufficient force to cause us to presume that they intended to defend the passage of the Adige.

The skirmishers from Monnier's division, supported by a battalion of the 24th Légère Demi-brigade and two squadrons of the 11th Hussar Regiment, pushed back to the glacis of Verona those of the enemy who had advanced on the village of Tomba.

Some howitzer batteries had been constructed during the night of the 8th/9th, under the direction of Captain of Engineers Bernard, with the protection of a battalion of the 22nd Demi-brigade. Fire began at 5 o'clock in the morning; many bombs fell into the city; several started fires, but we made no progress.

Strong demonstrations were made at the same time by the right wing on the banks of the Adige, between Verona and Porto-Legnago, in order to draw the enemy's forces in that direction.

The same day the garrison of Peschiera executed a vigorous sortie on the right wing of Dąbrowski's division, with the plan of retaking the positions he had taken from them on the day of the 7th. But all these efforts were in vain and after two hours of stubborn combat, they were driven back into the body of the fortress.

The Polish troops, led by Chef de bataillon Chopicki, gave on this occasion new proofs of their bravery and their devotion; they were perfectly seconded by a picket of 50 men from the 20th Chasseur à cheval Regiment.

Orders were given to advance the bridging train which had served on the Mincio; the lack of transports and the bad state of the roads had made their march extremely slow and difficult. Finally, on the 10th, they were united at Bussolengo. The General-in-Chief also transported his headquarters there.

The crossing of the Adige was ordered for the break of day on the 11th. It was to be executed at two points. The first, which was the principal crossing, was to be about a mile above Bussolengo, at the re-entrant angle formed by the Adige; the second, which was only a feint, was to be executed as a bridge of rafts before the Chievo.

All the dispositions were taken during the night and the troops began moving before daybreak.

At 9 o'clock in the morning on the 11th, the converged carabineers of the vanguard crossed the Adige in boats to cover the establishment of the bridge above the Bussolengo. The bridge was erected with the greatest celerity under the protection of the fire of 60 cannon which lined the right bank. The crossing was affected without opposition on the part of the enemy, who expected to be attacked below Verona.

The vanguard crossed first, two brigades of Boudet's division crossed after them, and the third, under the orders of General Schitt, moved up the right bank to move on Rivoli. The two divisions of Suchet's lieutenancy crossed after Boudet's division.

The vanguard, soon formed on the left bank debouched with the greatest celerity, marched rapidly on Pescantina, which it captured, and then moved on Castel-Rotto, where it took up positions.

During its advance, the vanguard took a large number of prisoners.

The troops of Lieutenant General Moncey moved up the Adige and took a position at Volargne. They surprised an enemy grand'garde, which they took prisoner at the gates of Chiusa.

To support these operations and cross over the rest of the army, the corps under the orders of General Dupont had maintained its positions before Verona; supported by the cavalry reserve, it executed a demonstration before this fortress. The enemy locked themselves up in it after losing a few men. At the same time, Gardanne's division simulated its passage before Chievo.

If the rapidity of the river and the lack of necessary materials prevented Lieutenant-General Michaud from establishing his raft bridge, the reserve corps still completed its goal, established by the General-in-Chief, of stopping it with artillery fire and musketry, and forcing the retreat of an enemy column of about 4,000 men which attempted to move up the river to support the corps that was on the upper Adige. This corps was soon forced to retire.

The march of Lieutenant-General Moncey towards the sources of the Adige had as its goal to oppose the enemy forces that had gathered on the side of Roveredo.

To the same end, the General-in-Chief expedited, on the 10th, the order to Général de division Rochambeau, who remained at Salo, on the right bank of Lake Garda, to assemble his troops and march on Riva, from there on Torbole, then to the vicinity of Roveredo on the right bank of the Adige, and to concentrate his forces on Mory. He was, after having captured the forts of Riva and Torbole, to send a detachment on Corona to take in the rear the enemy corps of 2,000 men, which held that position and to then affect his junction with Lieutenant-General Moncey.

General Rochambeau was to give word of his movements to the General-in-Chief of the Army of Grisons so that he could profit from this diversion. Lecchi's division, which was then detached under his orders, was to march on the Sarca and then on Trento.

All these dispositions were successfully executed with perfect harmony.

During the morning of the 12th, Lieutenant-General Moncey received orders to continue his march on Roveredo, where he was to join and unite to him Rochambeau's division.

The divisions on the left, forming the Lieutenancy of General Moncey, momentarily finding themselves detached, I shall, Citizen Minister, for more clarity in my account, abstain for an instant of following their movement, so as not lose sight of the army marching on Verona.

During the night of 11th/12th, Lieutenant-General Michaud, who was unable to, for reasons I will soon relate, affect his passage before Chievo, rapidly moved to cross, with the reserve, over the bridge below Bussolengo.

Lieutenant-General Dupont equally had orders to leave his position before Verona and to march on Bussolengo, to cover this post and the bridge.

The movements of the reserve, in moving up the Adige, had left the village of San Massimo uncovered. A party of Austrian hussars, coming out of Verona, pushed to this point and captured a few wagons and prisoners.

The 1st Cavalry Regiment was from the night before in a position on the plain, a great distance from the right of the village so that its movement was not seen by the enemy.

Informed of what had happened on his left by the arrival of many fugitives, Citizen Margaron, commander of the 1st Cavalry, set out and personally reconnoitered San-Massimo, resolved to capture the village and hold it. It became very important for him to place and serve with advantage the six cannons from the cavalry reserve, that had been left at his disposition.

A charge executed on the village by a division of the 1st Cavalry, at the moment when a squadron of the 8th Dragoon Regiment, sent from Bussolengo favored the movement on the left, stopped the enemy and obliged them to fall back on the large body of cavalry that they had on the plain.

The enemy had deployed a line of about 1,200 horse. Having acquired confidence in the small number of our troops, they did not delay in marching against them with the greatest vivacity.

Its vanguard, consisting of about 500 horse, moved out at a gallop, while the rest of the unit, formed into two lines, supported by the fire of several cannon, advanced at the trot.

During this time, Chef de brigade Margaron had deployed his regiment to vigorously receive the shock; he had placed three cannons at the head of the village, two on the left, and one in the rear.

In an instant, the enemy vanguard arrived with impetuosity. It divided by squadrons and surrounded the village, while the bulk of them followed closely. The gunners anticipating that some cannon would be captured executed the most rapid fire. The enemy stopped. The 1st Cavalry Regiment broke by divisions and platoons to face all the points, charging everywhere with great impetuosity, and obtaining the most complete success. The enemy was in full flight abandoning about 100 prisoners.

Unfortunately, the weakness of each detachment did not permit us to push the advantage, which though decisive, would have allowed us to capture the 500 horse that formed the vanguard of the enemy corps. But what could at most 200 braves do, who, beyond the disadvantage of having to disperse into small units, had to guard a position and six cannons?

Chef de brigade Margaron, in reporting of this action, praised the bravery of his regiment; officers and horsemen all fought with the greatest valor; each officer had acted with his detachment and the success was equal everywhere. The regiment suffered only two men wounded and one killed.

The artillery rendered the greatest services; also, Chef de brigade Margaron praised it in the most particular manner.

The large corps of cavalry continued to observe the enemy before Verona; 500 horse were detached before Mantua and Porto-Legnago.

The army, united in force on the left bank, continued its march on Verona.

The vanguard, obliged to gain the heights to turn the fortress, which still held out, suffered the greatest difficulties in moving by Piedmont towards Masso, the principal summit and the watershed on the Val-Penthena. This route, which is practicable in some seasons of the year for the local wagons, offered obstacles that appeared insurmountable. They were forced to manhandle the cannons and their caissons over the snow and ice and open a route heretofore unknown to the armies over the steep rocks, which was a work executed by the grenadiers, sappers, and gunners. All these men gave new proofs of their zeal and intrepidity.

The corps of Lieutenant-General Suchet advanced on Parona; Loison's division, marching in the first line was supported by Bazan's division.

A squadron of the 13th Chasseur à cheval Regiment, commanded by Chef d'escadron Prince, and seconded by a battalion of the 8th Légère, executed a vigorous charge towards Parona, and captured about 100 men and 80 horses from the Austrian 7th Hussar Regiment, with the commander of this detachment and two other officers.

The aides-de-camp to the General-in-Chief at the head of his guards, charged at the same time with the greatest impetuosity, powerfully adding to the success of this coup de main. Brigadier Mouton wounded five hussars with his own hand and captured two of their horses.

The enemy was repelled by Loison's and Gazan's divisions and driven under the cannon of Verona.

A battalion of the 13th Légère (Compans' brigade) stood firm before the charge of some enemy cavalry and obliged it to retreat precipitously.

General Colli, at the head of his brigade, attacked, at 8 o'clock in the evening, the heights of San Leonardo and Tagliaferro, and made himself master of them after a strong resistance on the part of the enemy. The division took 22 prisoners, including 2 officers.

The results of this was the occupation of all the posts attacked, 250 prisoners, several officers, and 100 horses.

During the night, the enemy army, after taken its garrison out of Verona, left Verona and took a position on the Caldiero heights.

The next day, the 13th, at 9 o'clock, according to the orders of the General-in-Chief, the Adjutant General Campanna presented himself at the gates of Saint-Georges with a detachments of chasseurs à cheval, and summoned General Rieze, the commander of the place, who withdrew with the garrison into the forts, and opened the gates. At noon our troops made their entrance.

The vanguard blockaded the forts and obliged the advance posts to retire with losses.

In descending on San Michele, it overthrew all the enemy forces that sought to oppose their march, and took position, its right on the Adige, and its left on Proviano.

The enemy army, in retreating on Vicenza, left in the forts of Verona, Saint Feliz and Saint Pierre, about 1,000 men. They abandoned to us 1,100 of their sick in hospitals.

In Verona we discovered two depots each with 1,000 muskets, 2,00 sacks of Turkish wheat, 300 sacks of rice, and another magazine of canteens, cooking pots, etc.

The divisions that passed through the city did so in the greatest order. A part of Loison's division was established in Verona and the rest took up positions behind Saint Martin.

Gazan's division established itself at San Michele.

On the 14th, Watrin's division moved on Santa Lucia and Monnier's division was charged with investing the forts.

The vanguard marched on Saint Martin; the enemy presented a strong resistance there but were soon obliged to cede tovalor and the impetuosity of our troops.

Général de division Lapoype was charged with blockading Mantua.

The blockade of of Ferrare was confided to Général de brigade Vignolle. To recognize the services that Bologna had rendered on the right of the Po, before the passage of the Mincio, the General-in-Chief granted to the national guard of this city the honor of marching on Verrare, and to form the investment of the citadel. As a result, 2,000 men were ready to depart, and, in their expedition, they comported themselves like veteran troops.

I will not resume, citizen Minister, the account of the movements of Lieutenant-General Moncey, which I have left at his passage of the Adige, on the 11th, and moved up the left bank of this river with the brigades of Generals Merlhe and Sériziat, of Boudet's division, the grenadier reserves of the left wing, commanded by Adjutant-Commandant Fay, the 12th Hussar Regiment, and the 9th and 21st Chasseur à cheval Regiments; General Schitt, with his brigade, marched to the same level on the right bank towards Rivoli and Corona.

General Moncey, arriving at Volargne, as I have had the honor of telling you earlier, sent out a reconnaissance by the 12th Hussars to the gates of Chiusa, where it surprised and captured a grand'garde; General Boudet attempted to capture the castle as well, but the enemy, under the cover of its walls, made such a fire that the general limited himself to blockading thc fort (it was night) and resumed studying it and captured it.

During the early morning of the 12th, Lieutenant-General Moncey had Chiuse turned by the reserve, after great fatigues, in climbing the difficult and steep rocks.

During this time, Général de division Boudet, who had reconnoitered the position, advanced an 8pdr cannon, placing it before the castle's gate. He gave the signal to attack. Although the gate was walled up, it soon offered a practicable passage. The enemy, shaken by the vigor of the attackers, shocked at the same time to see plunging fire striking them from the heights that our braves had climbed and which they had judged unclimbable, quickly retired, leaving in the power of the 102nd Demi-brigade a large number of wounded and about 100 prisoners.

Two large ditches, cut across the highway, assured the retreat in preventing our cavalry from pursuing them.

General Moncey now moved on Dolce.

Général de division Boudet marched in the valley, while the grenadier reserves, with two battalions of the brigade of General Sériziat moved along the heights to cut off the enemy's retreat.

Général de brigade Schitt, who had marched on the 11th to observe the position of Rivoli, saw that he could attack it with advantage. The enemy had maintained themselves for some time, but they were obliged to retire and General Schitt took 144 prisoners.

Part of the enemy column moved along the right bank of the Adige; the rest rejoined the troops that defended Corona.

The column, which had retired along the right bank, took position and established three cannons on an elevation that commanded the road from Chiusa to Dolce, and formed by this means a line with the troops posted in front of this latter village.

The enemy profited from this to make his retreat and our troops entered Dolce without impediment.

General Schitt, on the right bank, had pursued the enemy as far as Corona, but having found them in large numbers and in a very strong position, he resolved to surprise them.

At 10 o'clock in the evening, he marched again and expressly prohibited the firing of a single musket shot.

The enemy were carried at bayonet point. They lost 30 men killed or wounded and a further 500 prisoners, including a major and seven other officers. General Schitt's forces suffered only a very light loss.

The 94th Demi-brigade conducted itself, in this operation, with the greatest bravery. On the 13th, Lieutenant-General Moncey left Dolce before daybreak, looking to arrive at Ala during the day.

Fifty-five hussars, commanded by an officer, cut off by the march of our troops, surrendered.

The enemy's advanced posts, established before Borghetto, were overthrown by our skirmishers.

A detachment of 20 men of the 12th Hussar Regiment charged with such vigor against a force of 30 enemy hussars, that all of them were taken prisoner. The 12th Hussars suffered four men and seven horses hors de combat.

During its march, the brigade of General Merlhe had repeatedly squabbled with the enemy. Upon his arrival before Ala, this general found in position, more than 3,000 men supported by five cannons.

A part of the 102nd Demi-brigade penetrated into the city at the pas de charge, while the rest of the corps moved along the mountains to turn the enemy. The engaged in an extremely sharp exchange of musketry in the streets and everywhere else.

Four cannons, put in battery on a strong position selected by Chef de bataillon Lecapitaine, fired canister with such success that it disconcerted all the enemy's dispositions. It fired on them relentlessly for two hours.

General Boudet, seeing that his left was about to be turned, sent the 60th Demi-brigade there with two cannons. Their fire soon stopped that of the enemy, who from this moment executed their retreat on all points, abandoning their wounded and 680 prisoners.

Our loss was no more than 50 wounded.

General Boudet, in rendering homage to the known valor of the 102nd Demi-brigade, particularly cited its conduct during this day.

The artillery, by its activity, equally rendered great support. The troops took up a position that evening before Ala.

Général de brigade Schitt had received orders to move, on the 13th, to Avio. He executed this very difficult march and recrossed the Adige, on the morning of the 14th, with the 91st Demi-brigade.

The 12th Légère had orders to move up the right bank towards Mori, and to follow the movement of the corps of the left bank on the Marco.

Lieutenant-General Moncey marched, on the 14th, on Marco. The enemy had assembled 6,000 men at that point. General Laudon commanded there in person and proposed to make a strong resistance. The vanguard of Boudet's division quickly encountered the enemy in force at Seraval; their line extended from the Adige to the crest of the mountains. He resisted the approach of our troops and greeted them with the most sustained fire. However, the 102nd marched at the pas de charge and threw them back, taking 180 prisoners and wounding many others.

The enemy, forced at Seraval, retired the troops that lined the peaks of the mountains. These troops followed, during their retreat, a path which, from the heights, moved behind Marco and came to place themselves on the rocks that were in front of the village. They established themselves in this part under the protection of a strong force of infantry that they found there and five cannons.

A frontal attack against their front would have been very uncertain, so General Boudet occupied himself with turning their position.

The 3rd Battalion of the 60th Demi-brigade was charged with this operation and followed, for this purpose, the same path that the enemy had used in their retreat from Seraval. The march of this battalion, which the nature of the ground to cross rendered most difficult, was slowed by the fire of eight enemy companies and a large number of Tyrolian jägers armed with two shot carbines.

The enemy added further to his means of defense by throwing against this brave battalion masses of rocks, but nothing disconcerted them. Skillfully led by their leader, Citizen Larue, they crossed all obstacles, reached the heights, and took 278 prisoners.

This intrepid battalion suffered only about 20 men killed or wounded.

Night prevented the enterprise against the enemy. When the moon rose, General Boudet made several efforts to throw them back, but finding this impossible, he determined to await daylight and the end of the movements of the corps charged with returning to the position.

The enemy, well understanding that their position had become critical, thought only of retreat, but they executed it too late, as General Boudet's vanguard, which attacked before daybreak, caught its rearguard and took about 200 prisoners.

The city of Roveredo was evacuated. A deputation came to bring the news to Lieutenant-General Moncey. Our troops occupied it on the 15th.

There we found a hospital in the city containing 300 sick Austrians.

Général de division Boudet praised in the most flattering manner the general officers of his staff and the troops of his division.

The 102nd, 91st, and 60th Demi-brigades and the 12th Légère received the greatest praise; the 3rd Battalion of the 60th Demi-brigade, commanded by Citizen Larue, had in particular distinguished himself. All the arms seconding this attack, the infantry, cavalry, and artillery, did their duty.

The enemy's loss on the Upper Adige, from the 11th, the day of the crossing, to the 15th, rose to about 1,200 men killed, wounded, and prisoners. Our losses did not exceed 200.

Citizen Richaud, a soldier of the 102nd, quite distinguished himself by his intrepidity. In the head of the action, at Ala, he threw himself into the middle of an enemy platoon, put four men hors de combat, and took six prisoners.

All the vanguard crossed, but the enemy opposed it with the greatest resistance beyond the bridge on the Chiampo and the Agua. Our skirmishers were repulsed. The picket of dragoons commanded by Captain Letord, after having twice charged and sabered the enemy hussars, were obliged to withdraw.

Général de brigade Beaumont moved rapidly forward at the head of the 1st Dragoon Regiment to stop the progress of the Austrian cavalry. Several deep ditches prevented them from reaching the enemy, and even from deploying. The excellent Chef de brigade Viallanes reconnoitered a defile that was as narrow as it was difficult. He consulted only his bravery to cross under the enemy's fire and in an instant his regiment was formed on the far side. The enemy, shocked by this audacious movement, stopped, and precipitously moved to cover itself with another ditch to avoid a charge of the 1st Dragoon Regiment. Night approached. The General-in-Chief, having resolved to take, during the night, a position beyond the Agua, ordered a general charge along all the line. The grenadier battalion of the Lapisse brigade, with the 1st, 2nd, 78th, and 26th Demi-brigades, under the orders of the same general, threw themselves forward and chased the enemy away. The dragoon brigade, rivaled the audacity of the infantry. Chef de brigade Sébastiani, of the 9th Dragoons, rode down everything he found before him, but he was stopped in the middle of his charge by the Agua Ravine. He was struck in the helmet by a musket ball.

General Beaumont and Chef de brigade Viallanes charged along the highway with the 1st Regiment, throwing over several pelotons of cavalry, and drove back some skirmishers. Soon they were greeted by the most violent fire of two battalions placed on their flanks and beyond the road. Three times they returned to the charge and three times they were received with the same fire.

Only night ended the battle. The enemy profited from the night to retire. They lost during this day about 600 prisoners, including 150 wounded, which they abandoned at Montebello, where the headquarters was established.

The vanguard took up a position beyond the Agua.

Captains Letord, of the 3rd Dragoon Regiment, and Watrin, of the 1st Dragoons, distinguished themselves. The first defended in hand-to-hand combat the defile against an Austrian hussar colonel and forced him to retire. The second was dismounted twice.

Captain Cotillon, commander of the converged grenadier battalion on the left showed himself again to be worthy of leading grenadiers and was wounded in the arm.

Citizen Jusseraud, Adjutant-Major, had his leg broken in the first battle.

Captains Lessec and Chauvin, Lieutenant Prévost, Sous-lieutenant d'Amau, of the grenadier battalion, gave the greatest proofs of great courage in the pursuit of the enemy.

Citizen Jean-Baptist Varange, a fusilier of the 26th Demi-brigade demonstrated his bravery and took several prisoners.

At 7 o'clock in the morning on the 18th, the vanguard left its positions before Montebello and moved directly on Vicenza.

The divisions of the center moved a mile in front of Vicenza on the road from Padua.

The reserve stopped a mile to the rear.

We found in the hospitals of Vicenza 723 wounded Austrians.

On the 19th, the General-in-Chief ordered Lieutenant-General Demas to move on Armiola.

The vanguard faced during its march, principally before Armiola, the efforts of the major part of the Austrian army.

The enemy employed all his means to stop its movement, defending with the greatest stubbornness all the positions that the land offered at each stop, breaking bridges or blocking the approaches with cuts or abatis. In vain these obstacles multiplied under the steps of the brigade of General Cassagne. His courage surmounted everything.

Near Armiola, the enemy divided their forces, one part moving on the road to Bassano and the other to Cittadella.

Lieutenant-General Delmas pursued them down the road to Bassano for some time, leaving a brigade in observation, and then marched with those of Generals Cassagne and Compans on Cittadella.

The 20th and the 25th Légère consolidated their brilliant reputation. These two demi-brigades withstood for the entire day the efforts of the enemy and constantly maintained the most wonderful order, under a hail of canister and musketry, receiving with calm several cavalry charges, and always pushing them back with loss.

The 19th and 28th Légère showed no less valor at the end of the day. On the left they launched an attack which determined the enemy's retreat, who was reinforced by troop coming from the Tyrol.

We took from them, in several actions, about 300 prisoners. Their loss in dead and wounded was no less significant. Ours did not exceed 100 men hors de combat.

On the 20th, the General-in-Chief made his dispositions for the crossing of the Brenta. He ordered Lieutenant-General Michaud to momentarily take command of the vanguard, in the place of Lieutenant-General Delmas, who had become very ill.

Loison's division received the order to move to Camisano and to push a reconnaissance on Curtarolo.

Gazan's division moved before Vicenza on the road to Marostica.

Two squadrons from the 11th Hussar Regiment, led by Chef d'escadron Martigues, entered Padua, which had been evacuated by a corps of 3,000 Austrians.

Lieutenant-General Michaud was charged with executing, at daybreak on the 21st, the demonstrations necessary to cross the Brenta in front of Cittadella. He had, at the same time, the order to capture this city and to take up a position forward, towards Castel-Franco.

To second this operation and to facilitate it, the General-in-Chief ordered the divisions of Loison and Watrin, and that of the reserve dragoons, then to move, at the same time, on the left bank of the Brenta, by the road to Ponte-et-Tor, Rampazzo, Camisano, and Curtarolo, cutting the road from Padua to Cittadella, and then to march on the latter city as soon as their passage was completed.

Twelve light cannons were destined to protect the march of these divisions.

In order to deceive the enemy, and to oblige them to divide their forces, the General-in-Chief had Gazan's division, with six cannon and a regiment of cavalry, at Bassano, by the road to Marostica.

The infantry and cavalry reserves, supported by three companies of light artillery, received orders to take up a position before Lisiera.

All these dispositions made, the vanguard moved on Brenta, and threw back without great efforts from the other side all the posts that the enemy still had on the right bank of this river. The General-in-Chief ordered the river be crossed immediately.

Twenty-five cannons, carefully deployed by General Marmont, Commander-in-Chief of Artillery, quickly suppressed the enemy fire opposing us from the left bank. Under the protection of our batteries, the 10th Hussar Regiment crossed at Gui, and pursued the enemy so aggressively, that it captured a cannon and took 200 prisoners.

All the vanguard followed this movement and established themselves on the left bank of the Brenta, in front of Fontaniva.

Lieutenant-General Moncey, commander of the left wing, who found himself on the 18th at Levico with all his corps, had to continue his march on Bassano. The General-in-Chief awaited news with the greatest impatience, but his orders had been punctually executed and General Moncey entered Bassano at 8'oclock in the morning of the 21st. The left wing, by a march that was as skillfully as it was promptly executed, had crossed, in the space of eight days, 130 miles of difficult and frequently disputed roads. It had chased the enemy from several strong posts and took 2,000 prisoners.

Upon arriving at Bassano, General Moncey had the roads to Citadella and Castel-Franco scouted by the 12th Hussar Regiment. The commander of this corps, Citizen Fournier, conducted himself with as much bravery as wisdom. All day he was at grips with the enemy and he took more than 100 prisoners and 21 horses.

On the 22nd, the vanguard was directed by Cittadella on Castel-Franco. General Cassagne's brigade marched by the left of the road to turn Castel-Franco, while the brigade of General Lapisse, following that of General Compans and the dragoons, moved to the front.

The enemy occupied Saint Martin and wished to defend the position. General Lapisse had the village attacked by the 1st and 2nd Demi-brigades, while his two demi-brigades on the left and his artillery continued their march down the highway.

The enemy united his forces between San Andrea and Tre Ville, and developed a considerable line of cavalry, which appeared to extend beyond our right wing; but our artillery, directed by Chef de bataillon Aubry, obliged them to pull away, after inflicting much damage on them.

The enemy drew advantage from the covered roads, and before Castel Franco, they put their infantry in ambush and executed a long resistance.

Lieutenant-General Michaud, fatigued by the enemy's' tenacity, ordered that Castel-Franco be taken by assault.

General Lapisse, at the head of a detachment of the 9th Dragoon Regiment, and a battalion of grenadiers, charged the enemy with his known intrepidity, threw back all those that opposed his passage, and reached the center of the city, but forces infinitely superior prevented him from passing further. He had his artillery advance. Effectively seconded by it, he ordered a second charge of his grenadiers. The enemy ceded to their effort and abandoned the fortress. General Lapisse pursued them more than three miles and took more than 300 prisoners.

The grenadier battalion and the 9th Dragoon Regiment did themselves great honor on this day. Captains Letord and Tanalus, of the 9th Dragoons had their horses killed under them.

Captains Lessec and Chauvin, Lieutenant Prévost, and a sous-lieutenant in the grenadier battalion, continued to give proofs of their bravery.

Général de brigade Cassagne, who arrived on the enemy's right flank at the moment when they began their retreat, attacked them at Salvarosa, and put them to rout. The Austrians were pursued beyond Vedelago where night forced them to stop and take up a position.

The 10th Hussar Regiment again earned being cited by General Cassagne; Captain Debar and Lieutenants Kamps and Teron were particularly distinguished. The two latter charged an infantry column and pushed into their ranks. Citizen Teron had his horse killed under him.

General Compans' brigade seconded alternatively, and always with success, those of Generals Lapisse and Cassagne.

The vanguard inflicted a considerable loss this day on the enemy, taking about 600 prisoners. Captain-adjoint to the staff, had his left hand was carried off by a shot before Castel-Franco.

Gazan's division, coming from Bassano, found the enemy at Godego, chased them out, and moved to second the operations of the vanguard under Castel Franco.

While the enemy marked, thus, each day with new successes, the garrison of Mantua, which to this time was constantly held hidden behind its entrenchments, made a large sortie, but without success, against the corps that held it blockaded.

At 6 o'clock in the morning on the 22nd, strong enemy detachments presented themselves before our posts, while two columns of 2,000 men each , advanced with great intrepidity, one against Marmirolo and the other against Rivalta.

The enemy used gunboats on Lake Mantua to protect the march of his column on Rivalta.

Our troops, though inferior in number, were strong in their courage and disputed the ground foot-by-foot with the enemy, ceding nothing until they were threatened with being turned.

The troops from Marmirolo retired on Marengo and those in Rivolta on Sacca, where they awaited the enemy, but seeing that they did not dare to follow them, they took the offensive and soon forced them to abandon the villages that they had ceded earlier.

Chef d'escadron Remi, of the 6th Dragoon Regiment, at the head of his troop, assaulted Marmirolo.

Chef d'escadron Barillier, of the 4th Chasseurs, succeeded at Rivalta, and pursued the enemy as far as Curtalone. One hundred infantry, which had gathered on the banks of the lake, owed their salvation to boats, into which they barely had time to climb.

The enemy, in this affair, lost about 60 dead and wounded. Our loss was four dead and about 20 wounded.

Général de brigade Jablonowski, commander of the advance posts of the blockade, knew how to get the most out of his troops. All gave proof of their firmness and bravery. The 4th Provisional Demi-brigade, the 6th Dragoon Regiment, and the 4th Chasseurs particularly distinguished themselves at this time.

It is to remark that the troops who defended Marmirolo numbered only about 300 men, as much infantry as cavalry; that Rivalta was only occupied by 250 men, and that these detachments were engaged by columns of about 2,000 men each.

This attack by the garrison of Mantua forced me, Citizen Minister, to a digression which furnishes me one more proof of the superiority of our soldiers, but I hasten to report on a very vast field, and where the major events appear to await us.

The divisions of Boudet and Rochambeau, of the Moncey's lieutenancy, occupied Bassano and Asolo, and scouted the left of Castel Franco. On the 22nd, General Moncey had received orders to march with all the troops of his lieutenancy, along the Bosco del Mantello, in order to move by the right of the river on Ponte-di-Piane, and to cut off, by this maneuver, the Austrian rearguard from the battle corps. The movement of the rest of the French army was, therefore, that of the left and was to be executed on the 23rd; but the reports of all our generals in line and the reconnaissance's of the staff officers gave credence to the rumor that the enemy had spread since that, under the conduct of Generals Davidovich, Wukassovich, and Laudon, the three Tyrolian divisions had united, and wished to attempt some sort of battle in the

Trevisau plains. The General-in-Chief issued orders accordingly.

In ffect, on the 22nd, towards the end of the day, the demonstrations and the forces that the enemy had moved onto the heights of Vedelago, Saint Florian, and Albarado (a superb battlefield), caused us to believe there would be a great action the next day.

At daybreak on the 23rd, the General-in-Chief made his dispositions. His lines were established. The same formed columns only awaited the order to march out.

A reconnaissance by the vanguard was directed on Vedelago, an advanced post of the enemy. It was captured and 200 prisoners were taken.

Not far from there, favored by covered ground, the enemy appeared to have formed his lines, supporting his right on Boxco-del-Montello, and extending his left to the highway to Treviso, by way of Fossalonga.

On the end of a long low ridge he had posted numerous vedettes and platoons of infantry and cavalry were very close to them.

At noon, the General-in-Chief moved in person on the line of our advanced posts. After having moved along them, he issued the orders to attack, but the strong parties of cavalry, sent on the line, sufficed to drive back every enemy that appeared. They were pursued vigorously. We took 300 prisoners. Our reconnaissances pushed beyond the village of Sola. The fall of night obliged a suspension of their march and the army took up its position.

On the 24th, all the lieutenant generals and generals of artillery and cavalry went, at 4 o'clock in the morning, to the general rendezvous at Fossalonga. The General-in-Chief explained his plan to them, which consisted of cutting off from Pavia all the Austrian rearguard units that remained on that side of the river.

He ordered General Delmas, who had resumed command of the vanguard, to march on Ovadina, passing by Postuma.

Lieutenant-General Moncey was to establish an observation post at Rivasecca, to the left of Bosco-del-Montello, and to move Rochambeau's division on Ponte-di-Pavia. Moncey had been established the night before at Falze and he was to march Boudet's division on Sala, following the movement of General Rochambeau.

Lieutenant-General Suchet was to march in the direction of the vanguard, placing all his cavalry to the right rear of his lieutenancy with the light artillery, and to take Villa Orba for his right-hand line of advance.

Lieutenant-General Dupont was to send Watrin's division to the right of Suchet's lieutenancy, having Fontone as his line of march and was to move to the level of the highway from Treviso to Ponte-di-Pavia. General Gardanne was to march on Piava-di-Cusignana.

General Davout was to follow, with his reserve cavalry, the movement of the vanguard, to leave a regiment at Camalo to cover the artillery park there.

All the army was to march out at 10 o'clock in the morning to execute these orders.

The vanguard did not encounter any Austrians until they reached Visnadello, where they had deployed considerable forces, especially cavalry. The 10th Hussar Regiment, led by the intrepid Lasalle, charged several times with audacity and success. The brave Teron, who did not stop to give proofs of his personal bravery throughout the course of the campaign, was wounded by a saber cut in this action.

Cassagne's brigade, after a sharp resistance by the enemy, dislodged them from Lovadina even though they were supported by 10 cannons.

At the same time, General Compans' brigade received orders to move on Spresiano, clearing out the enemy there and taking some prisoners.

The rest of the army marched without encountering any obstacles, and that evening occupied their assigned positions.

During the course of the day, the vanguard pushed a reconnaissance on the right, towards Treviso, of the 9th Dragoon Regiment, commanded by Chef de brigade Sébastiani. Upon arriving at the gates of the city, this reconnaissance encountered a squadron of the Ferdinand Hussars. Sébastiani convinced them to suspend their entry into Treviso, alleging that Bellegarde's (Commander-in-Chief of the Austrian Army) plenipotentiaries were enroute to the negotiate an armistice. General-in-Chief Brune was now at Villa Orba, following the movement of the army's center, which was moving to establish itself at the level of the highway from Treviso, towards Ponte-di-Piave. The exterior of Villa Orba was guarded by two pelotons of the 15th Chasseur à cheval Regiment. They saw some enemy hussars on the right of the city of Marengo. The General-in-Chief ordered two pelotons of the 15th and a battalion of grenadiers, commanded by General Brune, of Suchet's lieutenancy, to move forward. The Chef de brigade of Artillery Mossel, followed by some horse gunners, rushed at the hussars and sought to turn them. He was accompanied by Citizen Petiet, aide-de-camp to the General-in-Chief. They encountered a line of skirmishers , who greeted them with pistol shots and then fled at a gallop towards Ponte-di-Piave. The chasseurs of the 15th Regiment pursued them. Chef de brigade Mossell and the aide-de-camp Petiet pushed to the side of Treviso and there they suddenly found themselves facing an enemy cavalry squadron of 250 horse. Concealing his surprise, Chef de brigade Mossel knew how to supplement his strength with a ruse. Speaking in German to the Austrian squadron commander, he called on them to surrender, assuring them that they were being turned by very superior forces and there remained no means for him to escape. He declared that he would be responsible for the least hostile act by any member of his troop.

Général de brigade Seras arrived quickly with Citizens Guillemet, Sordis, and Laharpe, aides-de-camp to the General-in-Chief, and Citizens Camas and Devaux, aides-de-camp to General Marmont. They confirmed the assurances given by Chef de brigade Moselle, that they would not use any rigor towards this squadron, if they accepted the propositions that had been made to them. During this conference, aide-de-camp Sordis went to the 15th Chasseur à cheval Regiment, which was a great distance away. Already two pelotons of this regiment, mentioned earlier, were on a height. The Austrian major no longer doubted the impossibility of his retreat. He surrendered as the entire 15th Chasseur à cheval Regiment arrived, as well as a battalion of grenadiers, under the orders of General Brune.

By this ruse de guerre, due to the presence of mind of Chef de brigade Mossel, and the wisdom of the aides-de-camp of the General-in-Chief, 50 hussars, a major and eight company officers were dismounted and were taken prisoners of war without a shot being fired. We captured 250 horses. That same day aide-de-camp Laharpe, sent on a reconnaissance by the General-in-Chief on Istrana, at the head of 5 gardes à cheval, took another 30 prisoners.

The officers kept their horses and the hussars their portmanteaus.

Night prevented any further harassment of the enemy. The army took up positions on the points which it had been ordered to occupy. The General-in-Chief established his headquarters at Treviso.

From Frimaire 27th, the army had moved from the banks of the Chiese to the edge of the Pavia. It had crossed three rivers regarded as the strongest barriers in Italy and rejected all the Austrian army beyond the fourth. It the Italian Tyrol and all the continental Venetian states from the right bank of the Pavia. The Austrians lost 15,000 prisoners, 100 dead or wounded, 45 cannon, 20,000 muskets, 3 flags, and significant magazines that had fallen into its victories.

Such was its brilliant position when envoys from the enemy presented themselves. They carried words of peace. The asked for a suspension of arms in order to treat for an armistice.

The General-in-Chief granted a suspension of hostilities of 24 hours.

There was no doubt that the enemy, after the reverses it had suffered, would not be forced to retire behind the Isonzo without giving battle. It could only weakly oppose the crossing of the Piave, and risk some fighting to cover its retreat. But it opened for us an exhausted land where hunger had chased away the inhabitants.

The French army was threatened by a lack of food. It had no magazines established in Lombardy from which it could draw grain; those that could be established with the greatest celerity could not, for some time, have an assured system of transportation.

The enemy had left 20,000 men in our rear, in the fortresses along the Mincio and the Adige. The blockade of these fortresses, indispensable for our communications with the Cisalpine Republic, held before them a considerable corps that weakened the active army. The Veronese people, who we had given during the campaign of the Year VI a terrible example of revolt, inspired distrust in us.

The enemy had need of a long armistice and an armistice of a few days was useful for the French army. That which was concluded united all the advantages; it only lasted 23 days and included a 15-day warning, far too short to permit anything other than the movement of their baggage, while it surrendered to us the fortresses of Peschiera, Legnago, Ferrara, Ancona, and the castles of Verona, it assured our communications with the Cisalpine Republic. It also gave the French the time necessary to bring up provisions into a region that was absolutely exhausted and to bring up before the enemy all of its forces.

The General-in-Chief invested with full powers Général de division of Artillery Marmont, and Citizen Sébastiani, Chef de brigade of the 9th Dragoon Regiment. The armistice was concluded on the 26th. The enemy abandoned to us six fortresses and retired behind the Tagliamento.

In such a state of things, nothing could have stopped the victorious march of our army and the resumption of hostilities would give us Mantua or move us to the gates of Vienna.

While the armistice was signed at Treviso, Monnier's division, employed in the siege of the castles in Verona, gathered up the last laurels of this memorable campaign. The siege works were pushed with great vigor by Chef de brigade of artillery Allix, charged with the attack under the orders of General Monnier. Their trench was within 10 toises of the ditch when the enemy capitulated. The garrison, 1,700 men, was taken prisoner o war.

The General-in-Chief, the ceaseless witness of the fatigues and devotion of his army, paid the tribute to the army it justly deserved. To appreciate their true valor of the constancy and calm of the French soldier in the middle of such privations, it was necessary to compare this to their bravery. All the arms revitalized their courage and glory.

The General-in-Chief expressed his satisfaction to the general officers, who had perfectly seconded him and the staff officers who had served him with so much distinction.

A multitude of brilliant actions occurred. I regret, Citizen Minister, for not being able, until this moment, to gather them all. I will hurry to present your efforts before the government.

Oudinot

Leonard Chodzko

Supplement to the Journal of the Operations of the Army of Italy
TUSCAN DIVISION

At the moment where the army, by its victories, came to compel the enemy to demand a suspension of hostilities, Général de division Miollis, commander in Tuscany, for a long time recommendable in the career of arms by his talents, his bravery, and the severity of his principals, after having long fought against the enterprises of the insurgents, supported by the Austrians, had obtained constant successes, and maintained himself in a land with a handful of brave men, was now threatened with a new attack.

A considerable corps of Neapolitans, commanded by General Damas, had entered Tuscany in three columns.

Already the principal corps, with 5,000 men, of which 1,000 were cavalry, led by General Damas in person, had captured Sienna, and moved to attack General Miollis in Florence, but this general thought he should avoid the fatigues of this march.

Obliged to maintain a respectable garrison in Livorno and guard his communications as much as circumstances and the small number of men at his disposal allowed, he had barely 2,000 men available. He hastened to lead this weak corps, consisting of French and Cisalpine troops, by forced marches, and arrived on Nivôse 24th before Sienna.

The enemy had taken a position in front of the city but attacking it and throwing it back was the effect of the impetuous shock of four troops.

The Cisalpine troops, skillfully led by General Pino, who had under his orders General Palombini, charged with a rare impetuosity and obtained complete success.

Chef d'escadron Langlois, of the 2nd Chasseur à cheval Regiment, at the head of some sappers and a detachment of this regiment, fell on the enemy as they retreated, and captured a cannon.

This Neapolitan column would have been completely destroyed if the ardor of our troops had not been held back for nearly a half hour, while they were engaged in beating down the gates of the city with cannon shots and blows of axes. The enemy was, nonetheless, pursued for six miles beyond Sienna, and abandoned in their flight three cannon and their caissons, 400 dead or wounded, and about 300 prisoners.

Citizen Gombert, adjudant-sous-lieutenant in the 2nd Chasseur à cheval Regiment, distinguished himself on this occasion. This officer, charging with Chef d'escadron Langlois, received a musket shot in the arm at the moment when the detachment captured a cannon. Despite his wound, he refused to leave the battlefield and it took a second shot to force him to leave the battlefield.

Chef de brigade Montserras, of the 29th Demi-brigade; Chef d'escadron Lavillette, aide-de-camp to General Miollis, and Sous-Lieutenant Martin, of the 2nd Chasseur à cheval Regiment, distinguished themselves equally on this day.

General Miollis had this corps of fugitives pursued for three days without catching them. This victory completed the delivery of Tuscany from the Neapolitans and insurgents and assured the tranquility of the region.

Lieutenant-General Soult had contained and calmed the uprisings in Piedmont, which, without the vigor of such an experienced general, would have had the most serious results.

Oudinot

ARMISTICE

Concluded on Nivôse 26, Year IX (16 January 1801) Between General-in-Chief Brun, Commander of the French Army of Italy and General Bellegarde, Commander-in-Chief of the Austrian Army.

The generals-in-chiefs of the French and the Imperial and Royal Armies in Italy, wishing to stop the effusion of blood, at the moment when the two governments are occupying themselves with concluding a peace have named and equipped with full powers the Citizens Marmont, Général de division and advisor of state, and Sébastiani, chef de brigade of dragoons, and the Count von Hohenzollern, lieutenant-general, and Baron von Zach, major general, to treat on an armistice which was ordered on the following conditions:

Art. 1.) There shall be an armistice between the armies of the French Republic and those of His Majesty the Emperor and King of Italy, until Pluviôse 4th (January 25th), the date of the expiration of that of the armies of Germany.
The hostilities cannot resume until 15 days after notification has been given to the respective generals-in-chief in Italy.

Art. 2.) In this armistice shall be included all the corps forming part of the French armies of Italy and Grisons, and those of the Imperial armies and of the Tyrol.

Art. 3.) The French armies shall march out after tomorrow, Nivôse 28th (January 18th) to occupy their new line; that line shall follow the left bank of the Livenza, from the sea to its source, near Solunigo; from there it shall move on the high crest of the mountains that separate the Piava from the Zelina, passing over Mounts Maur, Crompitz, Randthal, and Spitz, descending from there int the Luckang Valley, near Aigga, moving up the mountain to re-descend into the Drauthal, to Mitterland, on the Crawe, to Lientz, where it shall encounter the line of demarcation fixed by the convention in Germany.

Art. 4.) The Imperial and Royal Army shall take for its line of demarcation the right bank of the Tagliamento, from the sea to its source, near Mount Maur; this line shall move from this point and follow that designated by the preceding article, which finds itself common for the two armies.

Art. 5.) The land between these two lines of demarcation is declared neutral. One cannot permit troops to canton there. The only thing that shall be there are posts or pickets to guard the roads; the post cannot be further from the rivers than a half mile.

Art.6.) One shall draw a line that shall divide the neutral line between the two parties, for the gathering of food; this line shall be marked by the Zelina Stream as far as the Barca Stream, passing by Villalta, Porto Genaro, and follow the Limene to the sea.

Art. 7.) The fortresses of Peschiera and Sermione and the castles of Verona and Legnano, the city and citadel of Ferrara, the city and fort of Ancona, shall surrender under the following conditions:

1.) The garrisons shall freely leave with the honors of war; they may take with them their arms, equipment, and property to rejoin the Imperial army.

2.) All the cannon bearing the Imperial crest, with their ammunition, and all other Imperial property, which shall be designated in the following articles, shall freely depart, and will be given, for the execution of this evacuation the Imperial Army six weeks.

3.) All the artillery, bearing other crests than the Imperial crest, shall be handed over to the French army along with its ammunition.

As for transportation, the French army charges itself with furnishing boats for the evacuations of the fortresses of Verona, Legnago, and Ferrara to the sea.

The French army shall furnish the means necessary to take to Verona the effects from the fortresses of Sermione and Peschiera, which shall be embarked on the Adige.

The part of the flotilla actually existing on Lake Garda, which was captured by the French before the reduction of Peschiera, shall alone remain in their possession, and that remaining as the property of the Austrian army, can only be evacuated by the Mincio and the Po and by the means available to the Austrian army. In the case where, in the term of six weeks agreed upon for the total evacuation of the effects belonging to the Austrian Army, if part of this flotilla cannot be evacuated, it shall leave it undamaged to the possession of the French army.

4.) The provisioning of the fortresses shall be divided into equal parts; the garrisons shall take only half and the other half shall remain to the French army. The cattle shall follow the garrisons in its totality.

5.) The fortresses shall be placed in depot until the peace under the control of the French army, which takes the engagement to conserve them in their actual state.

Art. 8.) Orders shall be immediately sent to the fortresses to surrender and the commanders shall come out of them as soon as possible, and in no more than three days after the receipt of the orders that shall be sent to them by extraordinary Austrian couriers.

The commissioners named for the evacuation of the fortresses shall remain there until the end of this operation, with the Austrian guard necessary to police the magazines.

Art. 9.) The commissioners destined to receive the arsenals and magazines may alone enter the places before the exit of the Austrian garrisons; the French garrisons shall occupy only one of the gates, 12 hours before their entrance into the fortress.

Art. 10.) The sick who shall remain in the fortresses shall not be made prisoners of war; the French army shall always take care of them and return them to the Imperial Army, which shall be responsible for the expenses that may be occasioned.

Art. 11.) In the case where one or several of these fortresses find themselves having surrendered by the time of the arrival of the couriers, who shall be expedited by General-in-Chief Bellegarde, there shall be no change in the capitulation, which has been executed in its entirety.

Art. 12.) The fortress of Mantua shall remain blockaded by the French posts placed 800 toises from the glacis, but we shall permit the delivery of 10 days of provisions every 10 days for the garrison. They shall be fixed at 15,000 rations of flour and 1,500 rations of forage; with other provisions in proportion.

The bourgeois shall from time to time have the liberty to bring in the provisions that they believe appropriate, but not exceeding the daily consumption, which shall be calculated on the basis of the population. The movement of food for Mantua shall be established by the Po River to the Governolo, and then by the Mincio.

Art. 13.) The French shall respect the individuals attached to the Austrian government, as well as the property and no one shall be punished for their political opinions.

Art. 14.) The map by Albe shall serve to regulate in the discussions that may arise on the line of demarcation laid out above.

Art. 15.) There shall be given the necessary passports for the expedition of couriers.

Prepared in duplicate at Treviso, Nivôse 26, Year IX (January 16, 1801)

Signed: Count Hohenzollern-Hechingue
Lieutenant-General of His Majesty the Emperor and King;
Zach, General-Major, Quartermaster

General; Marmont Général de division, Counsellor of State ;
Horace Sébastiani, Chef de brigade.

Identical Copy :

Chief of Staff, F. Hénin
Minister of War, A. Berthier

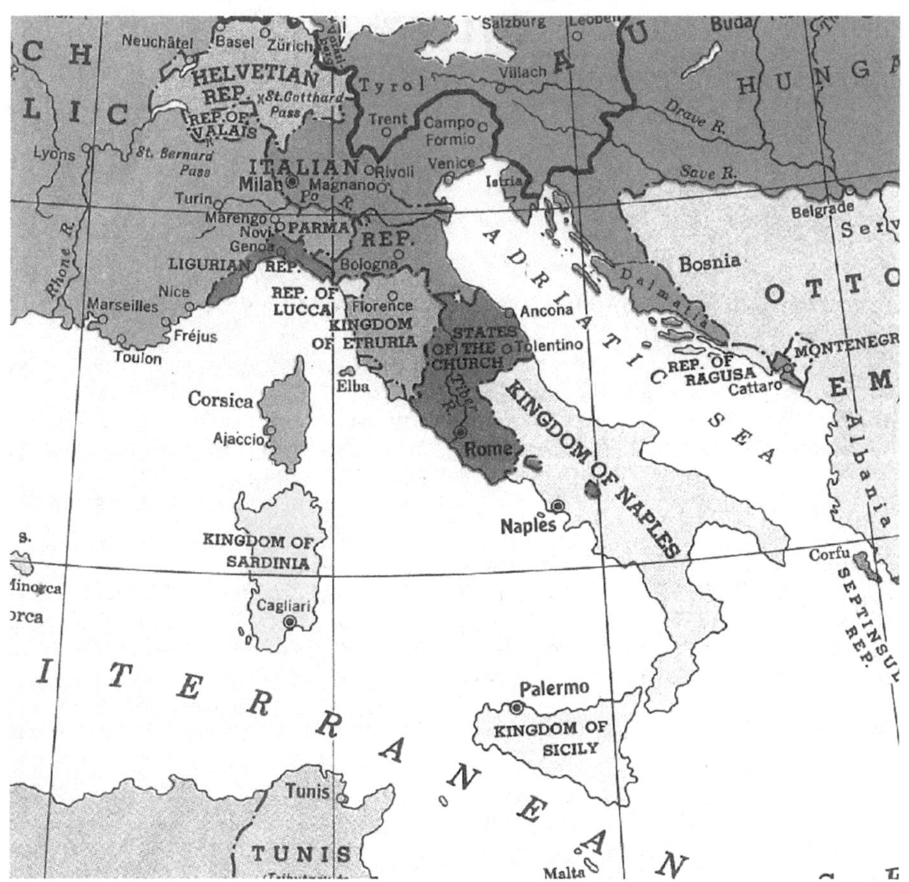

Italy in 1805

INDEX

Look for more books from Winged Hussar Publishing, LLC – E-books, paperbacks and Limited Edition hardcovers. The best in history, science fiction and fantasy at:

https://www.wingedhussarpublishing.com
or follow us on Facebook at:
Winged Hussar Publishing LLC
Or on twitter at:
WingHusPubLLC
For information and upcoming publications